Lake Ontario

1813

Burlington
Heights

Newark   Fort Niagara

Fort George

Stoney
Creek   1813   Queenston   Lewiston

Beaver Dams

UPPER   Lundy's Lane   NEW
CANADA   Chippawa   *Niagara R.*   YORK

1814   *Grand
Island*

Chippawa R.   1814   Black Rock

Fort Erie   Buffalo

0   20 Miles

Lake Erie

LOWER
CANADA

Montreal

Ottawa River   Lacolle
Mill

Châteauguay

Crysler's Farm   Plattsburgh
French
Mills

St. Lawrence River

Burlington

U   VT

CA

York
oronto

over

MA

*esqu
Erie)*   *ecticut
River*

Hartford
CT

973.5 WAR

The War of 1812

Pittsburgh   NJ

Carlisle   York

RGINIA   Washington

THE WAR OF 1812

THE WAR OF 1812

WRITINGS FROM AMERICA'S
SECOND WAR OF INDEPENDENCE

Donald R. Hickey, *editor*

THE LIBRARY OF AMERICA

Volume compilation, introduction, notes, and chronology copyright © 2013 by
Literary Classics of the United States, Inc., New York, N.Y.

Some of the material in this volume is reprinted
by permission of the holders of copyright and publication rights.
See Note on the Texts on page 802 for acknowledgments.

Dartmoor Prison engraving on page 703 courtesy
The Granger Collection.

Endpaper maps copyright © 2013 by
Lucidity Information Design, LLC.

The paper used in this publication meets the
minimum requirements of the American National Standard for
Information Sciences–Permanence of Paper for Printed
Library Materials, ANSI Z39.48—1984.

Distributed to the trade in the United States
by Penguin Group (USA) Inc.
and in Canada by Penguin Books Canada Ltd.

Library of Congress Control Number: 2011943154
973.5   ISBN 978-1-59853-195-4
———

First Printing
The Library of America—232

Manufactured in the United States of America

The War of 1812:
Writings from America's Second War of Independence
is published with support from

THE ANDREW W. MELLON FOUNDATION

and

THE BODMAN FOUNDATION

Contents

Introduction.   xxi

James Madison: War Message to Congress
"A solemn question": Washington, D.C., June 1812.   I

U.S. House of Representatives, Committee on Foreign
   Relations: Report on the Causes and Reasons for War
"An immediate appeal to Arms": Washington, D.C.,
June 1812   10

Thomas Jefferson to James Madison
"A solecism worthy of Don Quixot": Virginia, May 1812 . . .   23

Andrew Jackson to Willie Blount
"The spirit of the whole people is on fire": Tennessee,
June 1812   25

Tecumseh: Message from the Confederate Nations to
   Their British Allies and Huron Brothers
"All this Island will rise as one man": Northwestern Frontier,
June 1812   27

James Monroe to John Taylor
"Trade & fight, & fight & trade": Washington, D.C.,
June 1812   30

James Madison: Proclamation of War
"The last resort of injured Nations": Washington, D.C.,
June 1812   36

Hezekiah Niles: "War against England"
"Long live America": Baltimore, June 1812   38

Thomas Jefferson to James Madison
Canada, Commerce, and War: Virginia, June 1812   44

Thirty-four Members of the U.S. House of Representatives:
   from "An Address of the Minority to Their Constituents"
"What are the United States to gain by this war?":
Washington, D.C., June 1812   46

Maryland House of Delegates, Committee of Grievances
   and Courts of Justice: Report on the Baltimore Riots
Silencing the Anti-War Press: Baltimore, Summer 1812   54

Israel Pickens: Circular Letter to His Constituents in North
    Carolina
"Your country calls": Washington, D.C., July 1812.   69

William Ellery Channing: *A Sermon, Preached in Boston,
    July 23, 1812, the Day of the Publick Fast*
"It is a war fraught with ruin": Boston, July 1812.   72

William Hull: Proclamation
*"I come to find enemies not to make them": Upper Canada,
    July 1812*   85

Isaac Brock: Proclamation
"Repel the invader": Upper Canada, July 1812   88

Thomas Verchères de Boucherville: Journal
*With Tecumseh and the British: Northwestern Frontier,
    July–August 1812*.   92

Nathan Heald to Thomas H. Cushing
*The Fort Dearborn Massacre: Northwestern Frontier,
    August 1812*.   102

Caleb Strong to William Eustis
Massachusetts Defiant: Boston, August 1812   105

James Madison to Thomas Jefferson
"The wheels of war": Washington, D.C., August 1812   110

Robert Lucas: Journal
Hull's Capitulation: Michigan Territory, August 1812   113

Cornelius Flummerfelt: "The Bold Canadian"
A Ballad of Detroit: Upper Canada, August 1812   118

Moses Smith: from *Naval Scenes in the Last War*
*"Old Ironsides" Captures HMS Guerrière: North Atlantic,
    August 1812*   121

New-York City Committee of Correspondence: from
    *Address . . . in Support of the Nomination of The Hon.
    De Witt Clinton*
*De Witt Clinton for President: New York City,
    August 1812*   130

James Madison: Address to the Delegations of Several Indian
    Nations
*Advice to America's Indian Friends: Washington, D.C.,
    August 1812*   139

Stephen Van Rensselaer to Daniel D. Tompkins
Alarm and Distrust in New York: Niagara Frontier,
   August 1812   143

Daniel Curtis to Jacob Kingsbury
Siege of Fort Wayne: Northwestern Frontier,
   September 1812   145

A. W. Cochran: from a letter to Rebecca Cochran
Circumstances and William Hull: Lower Canada,
   September 1812   152

John Strachan to John Richardson
Fifteen Reasons for War on America: Upper Canada,
   September 1812   154

George McFeely: Diary
Yankee Ingenuity: Pennsylvania, October 1812   158

Jared Willson to Alvan Stewart
Battle of Queenston Heights: Upper Canada, October 1812 . .   160

John Strachan to William Wilberforce
The British–Indian Alliance: Upper Canada,
   November 1812   164

Alexander Smyth: Proclamation
"The hour of renown": Niagara Frontier, November 1812 . . .   169

William Atherton: from *Narrative of the Suffering & Defeat*
   of the North-Western Army
A Chronicle of Wretchedness: Northwestern Frontier,
   September 1812–January 1813   171

William B. Northcutt: Diary
Battle of the Mississinewa River: Northwestern Frontier,
   December 1812   181

Elias Darnell: Journal
"Remember the Raisin!": Northwestern Frontier,
   January 1813   193

James Madison: Second Inaugural Address
War and the American Character: Washington, D.C.,
   March 1813   207

Henry, Earl Bathurst to Sir Thomas Sidney Beckwith
The Rules of Engagement: London, March 1813   211

Patrick Finan: from "Recollections of Canada"
Battle of York: Upper Canada, April 1813   214

John Richardson: from "A Canadian Campaign"
Siege of Fort Meigs: Ohio, May 1813   220

Thomas Jefferson to Madame de Staël
Tyrants of Land and Sea: Virginia, May 1813   228

George McFeely: Diary
"The flag from Fort George": Upper Canada, May 1813. . . .   235

John Le Couteur: Journal
Battle of Sackets Harbor: Upstate New York, May 1813   240

Joseph Penley Jr.: from *The Sanguinary and Cruel
War of 1812–14*
*Life Aboard a British Prison Ship: Lower Canada,
June–August 1813*   245

Philip B. V. Broke to John Borlase Warren
*HMS Shannon Defeats USS Chesapeake: Massachusetts Bay,
June 1813*   256

John C. Calhoun to James Macbride
"Party sperit": Washington, D.C., June 1813   260

Laura Ingersoll Secord: Incident at Beaver Dams
A Canadian Paul Revere: Upper Canada, June 1813   262

John Le Couteur: Journal
Battle of Beaver Dams: Upper Canada, June 1813   264

James Monroe to Thomas Jefferson
The President in Peril: Washington, D.C., June 1813   267

"P." (Richard E. Parker) to the *Richmond Enquirer*
British Atrocities at Hampton: Virginia, June 1813   270

Blackbird: Message from the Ottawa Nation to William
Claus
The Death of Joseph C. Eldridge: Upper Canada, July 1813 . .   276

William B. Northcutt: Diary
Skirmish on the Sandusky: Ohio, July 1813   278

George Croghan to William Henry Harrison
Battle of Fort Stephenson: Ohio, August 1813   281

Black Hawk: from *Life of Ma-ka-tai-me-she-kia-kiak or Black Hawk*
The White Man's Way of War: Northwestern Frontier,
Summer 1813 284

James Fenimore Cooper: from *Ned Myers; or, A Life Before*
the Mast
Storm and Shipwreck: Lake Ontario, August 1813 285

James Inderwick: Journal
The Wounded of USS Argus: Southwest Coast of Britain,
August 1813 294

Thomas Hart Benton: Broadside
A Brawl with Andrew Jackson: Nashville, September 1813 . . . 300

Philip Freneau: "The Battle of Lake Erie"
"We have met the enemy and they are ours": Lake Erie,
September 1813 303

Washington Irving: "Biographical Memoir of Commodore
Perry"
"The nerve of a hero": Lake Erie, September 1813 306

Tecumseh: Speech to Henry Procter
"We are determined to defend our lands": Upper Canada,
September 1813 323

John Richardson: from *War of 1812*
Battle of the Thames: Upper Canada, September–
October 1813 325

William Henry Harrison: Proclamation
An Armistice with the Indians: Northwestern Frontier,
October 1813 332

Red Jacket: Message to Erastus Granger
Indian Grievances: Niagara Frontier, October 1813 333

John Le Couteur to Philip Bouton
Terror, Delight, and Thoughts of Home: Upper Canada,
October 1813 335

Robert Purdy to James Wilkinson
Battle of Châteauguay: Lower Canada, October 1813 339

Charles Ball: from *Slavery in the United States: A Narrative*
Runaway Slaves in the Chesapeake: Maryland, Summer–
Fall 1813 345

James Scott: from *Recollections of a Naval Life*
American Characteristics: Maryland, Winter 1813–14   353

Francis Jeffrey: A Conversation with James Madison
A British Editor Interviews the President: Washington, D.C.,
November 1813   358

Henry Clay to Thomas Bodley
"If Canada is conquered": Washington, D.C.,
December 1813   363

Cyrenius Chapin to the *Buffalo Gazette*
The Case Against George McClure: Niagara Frontier,
December 1813   366

Eber D. Howe: from "Recollections of a Pioneer Printer"
Revenge by Fire: Niagara Frontier, December 1813   370

Amos Hall to Daniel D. Tompkins
The Burning of Black Rock and Buffalo: Niagara Frontier,
December 1813   374

George Prevost: Proclamation
"A full measure of retaliation": Upper Canada,
January 1814   381

Henry Kent: A Winter's March
Across the Northern Ice: Saint John, New Brunswick–
Kingston, Upper Canada, Winter 1814   387

Arthur Wellesley, Marquess of Wellington, to Henry,
   Earl Bathurst
Prosecuting War on America: Garris, France,
February 1814   393

The Crew of USS *Essex* to the Crew of HMS *Phoebe*
Fighting Words: Valparaiso Harbor, Chile, March 1814   396

A Midshipman of HMS *Phoebe* to the Crew of USS *Essex*
"Your vile infamy": Valparaiso Harbor, Chile,
March 1814   398

David G. Farragut: from *The Life of David Glasgow Farragut*
The Capture of USS Essex: Off Valparaiso, Chile,
March 1814   400

Andrew Jackson to John Wood
Words Before an Execution: Mississippi Territory,
March 1814   406

Andrew Jackson to Rachel Jackson
Battle of Horseshoe Bend: Mississippi Territory, March 1814 . .   409

Robert Young to Phineas Riall
British Unrest at Fort Niagara: Niagara Frontier,
   March 1814.   412

George McFeely: Diary
Second Battle of Lacolle Mill: Lower Canada, March 1814 . .   413

Benjamin F. Browne: from *"Papers of an old Dartmoor*
   Prisoner"
The Rough Allies of Dartmoor: Devon, England,
   Spring–Summer 1814.   417

Alexander Cochrane: Proclamation
A British Appeal to American Slaves: Bermuda,
   April 1814   424

Thomas Jefferson: from a letter to John Adams
"The Attila of the age dethroned": Virginia, April 1814. . . .   426

Henry, Earl Bathurst to George Prevost
British Aims in North America: London, June 1814.   429

Albert Gallatin to James Monroe
"Pride and vindictive passions": London, June 1814   432

Stephen Popham to James Yeo
Battle of Sandy Creek: Upstate New York, May 1814   435

N. W. Hibbard to Alvin Hunt
Carrying the Cable: Upstate New York, May–June 1814 . . .   438

Jarvis Hanks: Memoir
A Tale of Five Deserters: Niagara Frontier, June 1814   442

William E. Horner: from "Surgical Sketches"
The U.S. Wounded at Fort Erie: Niagara Frontier,
   July 1814   444

Winfield Scott: from *Memoirs of Lieutenant-General Scott*
Battle of Chippawa: Upper Canada, July 1814   448

Isaac Chauncey to Jacob Brown
"A higher destiny": Lake Ontario, August 1814   454

John Le Couteur: Journal
Battle of Lundy's Lane: Upper Canada, July 1814.   457

William Dunlop: from "Recollections"
A British Surgeon's Lot: Upper Canada, July 1814   461

Shadrach Byfield: from "Narrative of a Light Company
  Soldier's Service"
The Loss of an Arm: Upper Canada, August 1814   465

John Le Couteur: Journal
Battle of Fort Erie: Upper Canada, August 1814   469

Jarvis Hanks: Memoir
The Day After Fort Erie: Upper Canada, August 1814   474

Andrew Jackson: Address to the Cherokee and Creek Nations
*The Treaty of Fort Jackson: Mississippi Territory,
  August 1814*   476

Big Warrior to Benjamin Hawkins
*"Think for your red friends": Mississippi Territory,
  August 1814*   479

Alexander Cochrane to Commanding Officers of the North
  American Station
"Destroy & lay waste": Bermuda, July 1814   483

Robert Rowley to Owsley Rowley
*British Depredations in Chesapeake Bay: Maryland and
  Virginia, August 1814*   485

James Scott: from *Recollections of a Naval Life*
From Benedict to Bladensburg: Maryland, August 1814. . . .   490

Joshua Barney to William Jones
Battle of Bladensburg: Maryland, August 1814   502

Dolley Madison to Lucy Payne Washington Todd
*"Dear sister, I must leave this house": Washington, D.C.,
  August 1814*   506

Paul Jennings: from *A Colored Man's Reminiscences of James
  Madison*
*A Slave's View from the White House: Washington, D.C.,
  August 1814*   508

George R. Gleig: from *The Campaigns of the British Army
  at Washington and New Orleans, 1814–15*
Storming the Capital: Washington, D.C., August 1814   511

Mary Stockton Hunter to Susan Stockton Cuthbert
"The most suicidal act ever committed": Washington, D.C.,
   August 1814 522

George R. Gleig: from *The Campaigns of the British Army*
   at Washington and New Orleans, 1814–15
The British Retreat from the Capital: Washington, D.C.,
   August 1814 526

Thomas Boyle: Proclamation
A U.S. Blockade of the British Isles: London, August 1814 . . . 533

Philip Reed to Benjamin Chambers
Battle of Caulk's Field: Maryland, August 1814 535

George Gordon, Lord Byron: "Elegiac Stanzas on the Death
   of Sir Peter Parker, Bart."
Death of a Kinsman: London, August 1814 539

Isaac Monroe to a Friend in Boston
The Bombardment of Fort McHenry: Maryland,
   September 1814 541

Francis Scott Key: "Defence of Fort M'Henry"
"The Star-Spangled Banner": Maryland, September 1814 . . . 544

Roger B. Taney to Charles Howard
The Life and Legend of Francis Scott Key: Maryland,
   September 1814 547

William Dunlop: from "Recollections"
Thinning the Ranks at Fort Erie: Upper Canada,
   Summer 1814 555

Jarvis Hanks: Memoir
The New York Militia Redeemed: Niagara Frontier,
   September 1814 560

Thomas Macdonough to William Jones
Battle of Lake Champlain: Upstate New York, September 1814 . . 562

Thomas Jefferson to Samuel H. Smith
The Library of Congress: Virginia, September 1814 565

Samuel C. Reid to the *New-York Mercantile Advertiser*
A Naval Battle in a Neutral Harbor: Fayal, Azores,
   September 1814 568

Benjamin F. Browne: from "Papers of an old Dartmoor
     Prisoner"
Democracy and Royalty in Dartmoor: Devon, England,
     Fall 1814   574

Timothy Pickering to Caleb Strong
The British Terms for Peace: Washington, D.C.,
     October 1814   581

Thomas Jefferson to James Madison
Ways, Means, and Ends of an Ongoing War: Virginia,
     October 1814   587

Charles Willing Hare to Harrison Gray Otis
A Federalist Calls for a Convention: Philadelphia,
     October 1814   591

John C. Sherbrooke to Henry, Earl Bathurst
The "Federal States" of America: Halifax, November 1814 . .   594

The Duke of Wellington to the Earl of Liverpool
Wellington Weighs In: Paris, November 1814   602

Daniel Webster: "Speech on the Conscription Bill"
"Is this civil liberty?": Washington, D.C., December 1814 . . .   606

Treaty of Peace and Amity between His Britannic Majesty
     and the United States of America
The Peace of Christmas Eve: Ghent, December 1814   621

Albert Gallatin to James Monroe
"As favorable as could be expected": Ghent, December 1814 . .   631

The Earl of Liverpool to George Canning
The Prime Minister on the Peace: London, December 1814 . .   635

George R. Gleig: from *The Campaigns of the British Army
     at Washington and New Orleans, 1814–15*
Target New Orleans: Louisiana, December 1814   639

Thomas ap Catesby Jones to Daniel T. Patterson
Battle of Lake Borgne: Louisiana, December 1814   644

Harrison Gray Otis and Fellow Delegates from New England:
     Report and Resolutions of the Hartford Convention
"If the Union be destined to dissolution": Connecticut,
     December 1814–January 1815.   648

Harry Smith: from *Autobiography*
"*A most murderous fire": Louisiana, January 1815*.   666

A Kentucky Soldier's Account of the Battle of New Orleans
"*Like a sea of blood": Louisiana, January 1815*.   670

Harry Smith: from *Autobiography*
Reckoning the Loss: Louisiana, January 1815.   676

Andrew Jackson to James Monroe
Report on the Battle of New Orleans: Louisiana,
January 1815   679

Thomas Jefferson to Marquis de Lafayette
The "*Robespierres of Massachusetts": Virginia,*
February 1815.   682

James Madison: Special Message to Congress
The War Ends: Washington, D.C., February 1815   689

National Aegis: "The Peace"
"*We have gloriously triumphed!": Massachusetts,*
February 1815.   692

George Prevost: General Order
A Commander's Farewell: Lower Canada, March 1815   696

Lewis Peter Clover: from "Reminiscences of a Dartmoor
  Prisoner"
The Dartmoor Massacre: Devon, England, April 1815   699

John Quincy Adams to William Eustis
An Uncertain Peace: Ealing, England, August 1815   706

James Madison: Seventh Annual Message to Congress
Mr. Madison's War: Washington, D.C., December 1815   709

Chronology.   719
Biographical Notes.   734
Note on the Texts.   802
Notes   817
Index   872

Introduction

For decades it had no name. Until the middle of the nineteenth century, when the Mexican-American War forced the issue, it was known simply as "the late war," an imprecise name for a complex and confounding conflict. Even now, two centuries on, the War of 1812 remains America's most obscure war, remembered, if at all, for "The Star-Spangled Banner," the burning of Washington, and the Battle of New Orleans. Though scores of books have been written on the subject, most Americans would have difficulty identifying the underlying causes of the war, and few are aware of how bitterly it polarized the young republic, indeed that it provoked talk of disunion. Fewer still recall that it involved the invasion of Canada, though north of the border the contest is largely remembered as a war of American aggression.

The War of 1812's status as a forgotten conflict is the more to be regretted when one considers the richness of the record left by its participants, American, British, Canadian, and Indian. This volume presents the best of this extraordinary literature: 140 letters, memoirs, poems, songs, speeches, sermons, editorials, journal entries, and proclamations by nearly a hundred men and women, both famous—Thomas Jefferson, Andrew Jackson, Tecumseh, James and Dolley Madison, and the Duke of Wellington, to name a few—and obscure. The more political of these writings reveal the then-novel dynamics of making war in a democratic state, showing in dramatic form the interplay of partisanship and propaganda as ideological certainties confront the uncertain experience of war. The more personal, especially the vivid and often moving accounts by soldiers and sailors like Shadrach Byfield and William Atherton, speak to the brutality of a war that tested not only courage and physical stamina but also the ability to find meaning in suffering. Told firsthand in the pages that follow, the War of 1812 is a story that still resonates today.

When, in the fall of 1811, President James Madison composed his Annual Message to Congress, his mind was preoccupied with war. Great Britain and France had been at war almost continuously since 1793, and, as the world's leading neutral power, the United States was caught in the middle, its maritime rights violated and its commerce looted. To Madison and other Jeffersonian Republicans, Great Britain posed the greater danger to America's sovereignty and interests. The British had issued a series of regulations—commonly referred to as the Orders-in-Council—that sharply curtailed U.S. trade with the European continent. They also routinely stopped American merchant vessels on the high seas and impressed or removed seamen to fill out the crews of their chronically un-dermanned warships. Although the Royal Navy professed to target only British subjects, some 6,000 American citizens were caught in the British dragnet between 1803 and 1812.

Between 1806 and 1811, the Republicans had tried to win greater respect for American rights by cutting off U.S. trade with the European belligerents. Jefferson's notorious embargo (1807–9) was only the most controversial of these measures, which were collectively known as "the restrictive system." The restrictive system boomeranged on the United States, destroy-ing American prosperity and cutting into government revenue without winning any concessions from the European powers. Although Madison himself had been the system's chief archi-tect, by the end of 1811 he had concluded that the nation needed to consider stronger measures to redress its grievances. In his opening address to Congress on November 5, the presi-dent spoke of Britain's "hostile inflexibility" and called for putting the nation "into an armor and an attitude demanded by the crisis."[1]

Guided by Speaker of the House Henry Clay of Kentucky and other "War Hawks," Congress over the next several months enacted a war program. On March 9 the President tried to stimulate the war spirit further by publicizing a series of letters purchased from John Henry, a British spy who had visited Federalist New England in 1808–9. Although the letters were supposed to show that British officials were interfering in the nation's domestic affairs and even fomenting disunion, they

---

[1]James Madison to Congress, November 5, 1811, in *Annals of Congress: De-bates and Proceedings in the Congress of the United States, 1789–1824*, 42 vols. (Washington, D.C., 1834–56), 12th Congress, 1st session, 13.

proved to be far tamer, suggesting that Henry was on little more than a routine intelligence-gathering mission. Federalists resented this attempt to impugn their patriotism, and when they discovered that the administration had paid the staggering sum of $50,000 for the documents, they were furious.

When the USS *Hornet* arrived from Europe in late May without news of any British concessions, the War Hawks urged President Madison to submit a war message to Congress, and he did not disappoint them. On June 1 the President sent a secret message to both houses calling on Congress to consider further action against Great Britain. To avoid public commotion, Congress took up a war bill in secret, the House passing it 79 to 49 and the Senate by a margin of 19 to 13. Every Federalist voted against the decision, and so, too, did about 20 percent of the Republicans. When President Madison signed the bill on June 18, the War of 1812 began. The United States had declared war for the first time, and by so narrow a margin that it is still the closest vote on any formal declaration of war in the nation's history.

Although the violations of U.S. rights had occurred on the high seas, the United States planned to target the British where they were most vulnerable: in the six North American provinces commonly referred to as Canada. Such was America's population advantage over Canada—7.7 million to 500,000—and so questionable was the loyalty of both the old French population and the new American immigrants who had flocked to Canada after 1792 that most Republicans expected an invasion to meet with little resistance. Thomas Jefferson thought that the conquest of Canada as far east as Montreal would be "a mere matter of marching" and that the rest would fall the following year.[2] Other Republicans agreed. According to Virginia congressman John Randolph of Roanoke, an outspoken critic of the war, they expected "a holiday campaign": with "no expense of blood, or treasure, on our part—Canada is to conquer herself—she is to be subdued by the principles of fraternity."[3]

---

[2] Jefferson to William Duane, August 4, 1812, in Jefferson Papers, Library of Congress, Washington, D.C., microfilm edition, reel 46.

[3] Speech of John Randolph, December 10, 1811, in *Annals of Congress*, 12th Cong., 1st sess., 447.

While Republicans across the nation welcomed the news of war with celebrations and illuminations, the departing British minister, Augustus J. Foster, reported that "the President was white as a sheet and very naturally felt all the responsibility he would incur."[4] Madison's foreboding was well founded. A decade of Republican economy had significantly weakened the nation's defense establishment, and the war preparations authorized the previous winter were far from mature. In the colorful words of Congressman Robert Wright, the Republicans were willing "to get married, & buy the furniture afterwards."[5]

The U.S. Army, about 12,000 strong in June 1812, was in a sad state, most of the men raw recruits and their officers without experience. The enemy, by contrast, was formidable. The British boasted some 10,000 disciplined regulars in Canada, and their officers were combat-tested. The British could also count on Indian allies, who were superb scouts, trackers, and skirmishers and whose reputation for ferocity could tip any battle by panicking the enemy. More daunting still for the young republic were the logistical challenges of waging offensive warfare on a distant and thinly populated frontier, where food was scarce, the roads crude, and the waterways undependable or controlled by the enemy. About the only thing the United States could count on in 1812 was a small navy that was in fighting trim and a fleet of privateers that could harass British trade around the world.

The United States launched multi-pronged incursions into Canada in 1812 and 1813, but they ended mostly in failure. The only success was in the Old Northwest, where Oliver Hazard Perry's victory over a British squadron on Lake Erie paved the way for William Henry Harrison's triumph over an Anglo-Indian force in the Battle of the Thames. This battle cost the great Shawnee leader Tecumseh his life and shattered the Indian confederacy that he had forged. Andrew Jackson enjoyed similar success in the Old Southwest, where in a series of engagements culminating in the Battle of Horseshoe Bend

---

[4]Richard Beale Davis, ed., *Jeffersonian America: Notes on the United States of America Collected in the Years 1805–6–7 and 11–12 by Sir Augustus John Foster, Bart.* (San Marino, CA, 1954), 100.

[5]Quoted in William A. Burwell to Wilson Cary Nicholas, May 23, 1812, in Nicholas Papers, University of Virginia, Charlottesville, VA.

he delivered blow after blow to hostile Creeks, known as Red Sticks because they carried red war clubs. But welcome as these victories in the West were for the Americans, Canada remained in British hands, and British leaders remained unbowed.

Although the United States took the offensive in the first two years of fighting, Napoleon's defeat and abdication in the spring of 1814 brought the war in Europe to an end, and this shifted the balance of power in the New World. Freed from their commitments in Europe, the British redeployed men, material, and warships to America, forcing the United States on the defensive. The British, however, faced the same difficulties waging offensive warfare that Americans had, and in the end they proved no more successful. Although the British burned many public buildings in the nation's capital and plundered exposed communities in the Chesapeake and on the Atlantic coast, the opposing forces fought to a bloody stalemate on the Niagara frontier, and the British were rebuffed at Plattsburgh and Baltimore. Moreover in the last great battle of the war in early 1815, the British sustained a costly and lopsided defeat at the hands of Andrew Jackson at New Orleans.

In the war at sea, the U.S. Navy enjoyed surprising success initially, winning a string of single-ship duels that boosted American morale and stunned the British. Especially noteworthy were the cruises of the USS *Constitution*, which won three separate duels and (because enemy round shot appeared to bounce off its twenty-two-inch hull) earned the nickname "Old Ironsides." But in the end the Royal Navy gave about as good as it got, and its blockade, which ultimately blanketed the entire Atlantic coast, had a punishing effect on American trade and deprived the Treasury of much-needed customs revenue.

Throughout the war the administration had trouble raising the men and money that it needed. To get army recruits, Congress repeatedly boosted the enlistment bounty until by the end of the war it was $124 and 320 acres of land. (The combined value of the cash and land was twice what the average unskilled worker made in a year, probably the equivalent of $30,000 today.) Congress was loath to increase taxes to keep pace with the soaring cost of the war, and by the fall of 1814 the government was insolvent. Unable to meet its obligations, it defaulted on the national debt in November.

The administration also had to contend with unrelenting Federalist defiance. Federalists everywhere opposed the war, and in Congress they presented a united front against war legislation. The only exceptions were bills to expand the navy and build coastal fortifications, which they considered sound long-term investments in national defense. In New England, Federalists went further, withholding their militia from federal service, obstructing the war effort in other ways, and even talking of secession. The climax of their defiance was the Hartford Convention, a regional conference that aired New England's grievances against the war and attacked Republicans for more than a decade of mismanagement.

The British had repealed the Orders-in-Council at about the same time that the United States declared war, but this news did not reach Washington until eight weeks later, and by then the die was cast. No common ground could be found on the impressment issue, and thus the war continued. The British spurned a Russian mediation proposal in 1813 but offered to hold direct talks with the United States. To represent the nation, the administration chose a distinguished delegation that was headed by John Quincy Adams and included former speaker of the house Henry Clay and former secretary of the treasury Albert Gallatin. The British, preoccupied with preparing for the Congress of Vienna, which would forge a general peace settlement in Europe, chose a less distinguished peace commission headed by Admiral James Gambier. The talks, held in Ghent (in present-day Belgium), did not get under way until August 1814, and they dragged on for more than four and a half months, much longer than anyone had anticipated.

By the time the negotiations had begun, the United States had dropped the impressment issue, but the British, eager to capitalize on their military ascendancy, laid down their own terms for peace. They demanded the establishment of an Indian barrier state in the Old Northwest, the surrender of U.S. territory in northern Maine and present-day Minnesota, the unilateral American demilitarization of the Great Lakes, and an end to U.S. fishing privileges in Canadian waters. No one thought this would be the last Anglo-American war, and Britain's principal objective was to provide better security for its subjects in Canada and its Indian allies in the West. But the terms stunned the U.S. delegation, and when they were published in the United States, Republicans and even some Federalists were outraged.

The U.S. delegation held firm against these demands, and the British, who were becoming increasingly war-weary after more than twenty years of conflict, gradually retreated. On December 24, 1814, the two delegations signed the Treaty of Ghent (also known as the Peace of Christmas Eve), which simply restored the status quo ante bellum—the state that had existed before the war. The British ratified the agreement on December 27, but slow communication delayed the arrival of the treaty in Washington until February 15. The U.S. Senate approved it unanimously the following day, and when President Madison added his signature later that day, the War of 1812 ended.

Although the United States suffered only 2,300 killed and 4,500 wounded in battle, U.S. deaths attributable to the war were around 20,000. Most of the victims were militiamen who had been called out for varying degrees of service, ranging from a few hours to a few months, and had succumbed to one of the contagious diseases common to military camps of the day. The British sustained around 10,000 deaths, the Indian population perhaps 7,500. The war cost the United States $158 million and Great Britain probably about the same amount.

Did the cost in blood and treasure justify the U.S. decision to go to war? Most Republicans thought it did. From the beginning they had called the contest a "second war of independence," and while Britain's maritime practices never truly threatened the Republic's independence, the war did in a broad sense vindicate U.S. sovereignty. But it ended in a draw on the battlefield, and the maritime issues that had led to hostilities were not even mentioned in the peace treaty.

For all concerned the war was fraught with consequences. The biggest winners were Great Britain and Canada. The British had surrendered none of their maritime rights, and Canada, instead of being swallowed up by the United States, remained in British hands. Although the war was quickly forgotten in Great Britain, the one lesson that British leaders learned was that they must accommodate the rising republic across the Atlantic, even if that occasionally meant sacrificing interests in the British Empire.

In Canada, the war cemented the bonds of loyalty to the mother country. But after Canada became independent in 1867, Canadians realized that the War of 1812 had been an important benchmark in their history. Those who had contributed to the preservation of Canada—Isaac Brock (the hero of Detroit who had perished at Queenston Heights), Tecumseh (the great Shawnee leader who had forged a native confederation before being slain at the Thames), and Laura Secord (who had warned the British of a pending U.S. attack at Beaver Dams)—were lauded as heroes, and the war itself was remembered as a kind of Canadian war of independence.

The big losers in the war were the Indians. As a proportion of their population, they had suffered the heaviest casualties. Worse, they were left without any reliable European allies in North America. The British no longer cultivated them, and this left the Indians without any way to counter the rising power of the United States. The crushing defeats at the Thames and Horseshoe Bend left them at the mercy of the Americans, hastening their confinement to reservations and the decline of their traditional way of life.

For the United States, the consequences of the war were also profound. The Jeffersonian Republicans, who before the war had been hostile to peacetime defense spending, after the conflict embraced a sizeable army and an ambitious program of naval expansion and coastal defense. Those who had shown a talent for command dominated the military and naval establishments in the postwar era, and both services emerged from the war with a new sense of professionalism. Politically, the Republicans came out ahead, claiming credit for the victories and blaming all the misfortunes of the war on Federalists. Four men who had played key roles during the war—James Monroe, John Quincy Adams, Andrew Jackson, and William Henry Harrison—were elected president, and three—Daniel D. Tompkins, John C. Calhoun, and Richard M. Johnson—were elevated to the vice presidency. If during the war opposition to administration policies enjoyed growing popular support, especially in New England, with the coming of peace it became a political liability, and the Federalists paid the price. Although the party was headed for extinction anyway, its wartime opposition carried the taint of treason and hastened its demise.

The nation emerged from the war with a host of symbols and sayings that shaped the cultural landscape in the years that followed. Among the new symbols were "Old Ironsides," "The Star-Spangled Banner" (written after the successful defense of Fort McHenry), Uncle Sam (a nickname that was first used during the war), and the Kentucky rifle (which won an inflated reputation as a war-winner). Among the enduring sayings were Perry's terse after-action report ("We have met the enemy and they are ours") and Captain James Lawrence's words upon being mortally wounded aboard the USS *Chesapeake* ("Don't give up the ship!"). These symbols and sayings helped Americans understand who they were and where their nation was headed.

Two additional symbols enjoyed an especially exalted status in the postwar world: Andrew Jackson and the Battle of New Orleans. Jackson emerged from the war as an outsized hero, and his commitment to democracy and slavery as well as to territorial expansion and Indian removal epitomized the jarring forces that would shape the nation in the postwar era.

The victory at New Orleans was no less important because it transformed how the war was remembered. Americans boasted how they had defeated "Wellington's *invincibles*" and "the conquerors of the conquerors of Europe."[6] They forgot the causes of the war and lost sight of how close the nation had come to military defeat and financial collapse. They remembered instead that they had beaten back an attempt to re-colonize the nation, that they had decisively defeated the conqueror of Napoleon and the Ruler of the Waves.

Much of the postwar literature reflected this buoyant mood. Official reports and eyewitness accounts that had been published during the war were joined by a growing number of histories and memoirs. And new material continues to surface, much of it from British and Canadian sources, broadening our understanding of the war and its often profound effect on the

---

[6] *Niles' Weekly Register* 8 (March 4, 1815), 1; Speech of George M. Troup, February 16, 1815, in *Annals of Congress*, 13th Cong., 3rd sess., 1156.

lives of those who were caught up in it. Reflecting the archival work of generations of scholars, this book is the first comprehensive collection to gather the best written and most illuminating of these documents in a single volume. By allowing us to experience the War of 1812 in the words of those who lived it, it makes a compelling case for the importance of remembering America's forgotten conflict.

Donald R. Hickey

James Madison: War Message to Congress

In his Annual Message to Congress of November 5, 1811, President Madison had expressed little hope that the British Orders in Council —wartime regulations restricting the trade of neutral nations with Napoleonic France and its allies—would be repealed through diplomacy. He observed that Great Britain persisted in hostile acts against American ships and seamen "which, under existing circumstances, have the character, as well as the effect, of war on our lawful commerce." Madison recommended that the nation be put "into an armor and an attitude demanded by the crisis," and Congress adopted war preparations. By the spring, with no concessions from Britain forthcoming, Speaker of the House Henry Clay and other Republican "War Hawks" of the Twelfth Congress urged the President to recommend war. On Monday the first of June 1812, Congress met specially in its separate chambers to hear an urgent and secret message from the President. Madison's personal secretary, Edward Coles, delivered copies from the White House to the Capitol, and the message was read to all assembled.

WASHINGTON June 1st. 1812

I communicate to Congress certain Documents, being a continuation of those heretofore laid before them, on the subject of our Affairs with Great Britain.

Without going back beyond the renewal in 1803, of the war in which Great Britain is engaged, and omitting unrepaired wrongs of inferior magnitude; the conduct of her Government presents a series of acts, hostile to the United States, as an Independent and neutral nation.

British cruisers have been in the continued practice of violating the American flag on the great high way of nations, and of seizing and carrying off persons sailing under it; not in the exercise of a Belligerent right founded on the Law of Nations against an Enemy; but of a municipal prerogative over British subjects. British jurisdiction is thus extended to neutral vessels, in a situation where no laws can operate but the law of nations, and the laws of the Country to which the vessels belong; and a self-redress is assumed, which, if British subjects were wrongfully detained and alone concerned, is that substitution of force, for a resort to the responsible sovereign, which falls within the definition of War. Could the seizure of British subjects, in such cases, be regarded as within the exercise of a Belligerent right, the acknowledged laws of war, which forbid an article of captured property to be adjudged, without a regular investigation before a competent Tribunal, would imperiously demand the fairest trial, where the sacred rights of persons were at issue. In place of such a trial, these rights are subjected to the will of every petty commander.

The practice, hence, is so far from affecting British subjects alone, that under the pretext of searching for these, thousands of American Citizens, under the safeguard of public law, and of their national flag, have been torn from their country, and from every thing dear to them; have been dragged on board ships of war of a foreign nation; and exposed, under the siverities of their discipline, to be exiled to the most distant and deadly climes, to risk their lives in the battles of their oppressors, and to be the melancholy instruments of taking away those of their own brethren.

Against this crying enormity, which Great Britain would be so prompt to avenge; if committed against herself, the United States have, in vain, exhausted remonstrances and expostulations: And that no proof might be wanting of their conciliatory dispositions, and no pretext left for a continuance of the practice, the British Government was formally assured of the readiness of the United States to enter into arrangements, such as could not be rejected, if the recovery of British subjects were the real and the sole object. The communication passed without effect.

British cruisers have been in the practice also, of violating the rights and the peace of our Coasts. They hover over and harrass our entering and departing Commerce. To the most insulting pretentions, they have added the most lawless proceedings in our very harbors; and have wantonly spilt American blood, within the sanctuary of our territorial jurisdiction. The principles and rules enforced by that nation when a neutral nation, against armed vessals of Belligerents hovering near her coasts, and disturbing her commerce, are well known. When called on, nevertheless, by the United States to punish the greater offences committed by her own vessels, her Government has bestowed on their commanders, additional marks of honor and confidence.

Under pretended blockades, without the presence of an adequate force, and sometimes without the practicability of applying one, our commerce has been plundered in every Sea; the great staples of our Country have been cut off, from their legitimate markets; and a distructive blow aimed at our agricultural and maritime interests. In aggravation of these predatory measures, they have been considered as in force, from the dates of their notification; a retrospective effect being thus added, as has been done in other important cases, to the unlawfulness of the course pursued. And to render the outrage the more signal, these mock blockades, have been reiterated and enforced, in the face of official communications from the British Government declaring, as the true definition of a legal Blockade "that particular ports must be actually invested, and previous warning given to vessels bound to them, not to enter."

Not content with these occasional expedients for laying waste our neutral trade, the Cabinet of Great Britain resorted, at length, to the sweeping system of Blockades, under the name of orders in Council; which has been moulded and managed, as might best suit its political views, its commercial jealousies, or the avidity of British cruisers.

To our remonstrances against the complicated and transcendent injustice of this innovation, the first reply was that the orders were reluctantly adopted by Great Britain, as a necessary retaliation on decrees of her Enemy proclaiming a general Blockade of the British Isles, at a time when the naval force of that Enemy dared not to issue from his own ports. She was reminded, without effect, that her own prior blockades, unsupported by an adequate naval force actually applied and continued, were a bar to this plea: that executed Edicts against millions of our property, could not be retaliation on Edicts, confessedly impossible to be executed: that retaliation to be just, should fall on the party setting the guilty example, not on an innocent party, which was not even chargeable with an acquiescence in it.

When deprived of this flimsy veil for a prohibition of our trade with her enemy, by the repeal of his prohibition of our trade with Great Britain; her Cabinet, instead of a corresponding repeal, or a practical discontinuance, of its orders, formally avowed a determination to persist in them against the United States, until the markets of her enemy should be laid open to British products: thus asserting an obligation on a neutral power to require one Belligerent to encourage, by its internal regulations, the trade of another Belligerent; contradicting her own practice towards all nations, in peace as well as in war; and betraying the insincerity of those professions, which inculcated a belief that having resorted to her orders with regret, she was anxious to find an occasion for putting an end to them.

Abandoning still more all respect for the neutral rights of the United States, and for its own consistency, the British Government now demands, as prerequisites to a repeal of its orders, as they relate to the United States, that a formality should be observed in the repeal of the French Decrees nowise necessary to their termination, nor exemplified by British usage; and that the French repeal, besides including that portion of the Decrees which operate within a territorial jurisdiction, as well as that which operates on the high seas against the commerce of the United States; should not be a single and special repeal in relation to the United States, but should be extended to whatever other neutral nations, unconnected with them, may be affected by those Decrees. And as an additional insult, they are called on for a formal disavowal of conditions and pretentions advanced by the French Government, for which the United States are so far from having made themselves responsible; that, in official explanations; which have been published to the world, and in a correspondence of the American Minister at London with the British Minister for foreign affairs, such a responsibility was explicitly and emphatically disclaimed.

It has become indeed sufficiently certain, that the commerce of the United States is to be sacrificed, not as interfering with the Belligerent rights of Great Britain; not as supplying the wants of her enemies, which she herself supplies; but as inter-

fering with the monopoly which she covets for her own commerce and navigation. She carries on a war against the lawful
commerce of a friend, that she may the better carry on a commerce with an enemy; a commerce polluted by the forgeries
and perjuries, which are, for the most part, the only passports
by which it can succeed.

Anxious to make every experiment, short of the last resort
of injured nations, the United States have withheld from Great
Britain, under successive modifications, the benifits of a free
intercourse with their market; the loss of which could not but
outweigh the profits accruing from her restrictions of our
commerce with other nations. And to entitle these experiments
to the more favorable consideration, they were so framed, as to
enable her to place her adversary under the exclusive operation
of them. To these appeals her Government has been equally
inflexible; as if willing to make sacrifices of every sort, rather
than yield to the claims of justice, or renounce the errors of a
false pride. Nay, so far were the attempts carried, to overcome
the attachment of the British Cabinet to its unjust Edicts, that
it received every encouragement, within the competency of
the Executive branch of our Government, to expect that a repeal of them, would be followed by a war between the United
States and France, unless the French Edicts should also be repealed. Even this communication, although silencing for ever
the plea of a disposition in the United States to acquiesce
in those Edicts, originally the sole plea for them, received no
attention.

If no other proof existed of a predetermination of the British Government against a repeal of its orders, it might be
found in the correspondence of the Minister Plenipotentiary
of the United States at London and the British Secretary for
Foreign Affairs; in 1810, on the question whether the Blockade
of May 1806 was considered as in force, or as not in force. It
had been ascertained that the French Government, which
urged this Blockade as the ground of its Berlin Decree, was
willing, in the event of its removal, to repeal that Decree;
which being followed by alternate repeals of the other offensive Edicts, might abolish the whole system on both sides. This
inviting opportunity for accomplishing an object so important
to the United States, and professed so often to be the desire of

both the Belligerents, was made known to the British Government. As that Government admits that an actual application of an adequate force is necessary to the existance of a legal Blockade, and it was notorious, that if such a force had ever been applied, its long discontinuance had annulled the Blockade in question, there could be no sufficient objection on the part of Great Britain to a formal revocation of it; and no imaginable objection to a declaration of the fact, that the Blockade did not exist. The declaration would have been consistent with her avowed principles of Blockade; and would have enabled the United States to demand from France the pledged repeal of her Decree; either with success, in which case the way would have been opened for a general repeal of the Belligerent Edicts; or without success, in which case the United States would have been justified in turning their measures exclusively against France. The British Government would, however, neither rescind the Blockade; nor declare its non-existence; nor permit its non-existence to be inferred and affirmed by the American Plenipotentiary. On the contrary by representing the Blockade to be comprehended in the orders in Council, the United States were compelled so to regard it, in their subsequent proceedings.

There was a period when a favorable change in the policy of the British Cabinet, was justly considered as established. The Minister Plenipotentiary of His Britanic Majesty here, proposed an adjustment of the differences more immediately endangering the harmony of the two Countries. The proposition was accepted with the promptitude and cordiality corresponding with the invariable professions of this Government. A foundation appeared to be laid for a sincere and lasting reconciliation. The prospect, however, quickly vanished. The whole proceeding was disavowed by the British Government, without any explanation which could, at that time, repress the belief, that the disavowal proceeded from a spirit of hostility to the commercial rights and prosperity of the United States. And it has since come into proof, that at the very moment, when the public Minister was holding the language of friendship, and inspiring confidence in the sincerity of the negociation with which he was charged, a secret agent of his Government was employed in intrigues, having for their object, a subversion of our Government, and a dismemberment of our happy union.

In reviewing the conduct of Great Britain towards the United States, our attention is necessarily drawn to the warfare just renewed by the Savages, on one of our extensive frontiers; a warfare which is known to spare neither age nor sex, and to be distinguished by features peculiarly shocking to humanity. It is difficult to account for the activity, and combinations, which have for some time been developing themselves among tribes in constant intercourse with British traders and garrisons, without connecting their hostility with that influence; and without recollecting the authenticated examples of such interpositions, heretofore furnished by the officers and agents of that Government.

Such is the spectacle of injuries and indignities which have been heaped on our Country: and such the crisis which its unexampled forbearance and conciliatory efforts have not been able to avert. It might at least have been expected, that an enlightened nation, if less urged by moral obligations, or invited by friendly dispositions on the part of the United States would have found, in its true interest alone, a sufficient motive to respect their rights and their tranquility on the high seas, that an enlarged policy would have favored that free and general circulation of Commerce, in which the British nation is at all times interested, and which in times of war, is the best alleviation of its calamities to herself, as well as to other Belligerents; and, more especially, that the British Cabinet, would not, for the sake of a precarious and surreptitious intercourse with hostile markets, have persevered in a course of measures, which necessarily put at hazard the invaluable market of a great and growing Country, disposed to cultivate the mutual advantages of an active commerce.

Other Councils have prevailed. Our moderation and conciliation, have had no other effect than to encourage perseverance, and to enlarge pretentions. We behold our seafaring Citizens still the daily victims of lawless violence committed on the great common and high way of nations, even within sight of the Country which owes them protection. We behold our vessels, freighted with the products of our soil and industry, or returning with the honest proceeds of them, wrested from their lawful destinations, confiscated by prize courts, no longer the organs of public law, but the instruments of arbitrary Edicts; and their unfortunate crews dispersed and lost, or forced, or inveigled in British ports, into British fleets: whilst arguments are employed, in support of these aggressions, which have no foundation but in a principle equally supporting a claim, to regulate our external commerce, in all cases whatsoever.

We behold, in fine, on the side of Great Britain a state of war against the United States; and on the side of the United States, a state of peace towards Great Britain.

Whether the United States shall continue passive under these progressive usurpations, and these accumulating wrongs; or, opposing force to force in defence of their national rights, shall commit a just cause into the hands of the Almighty disposer of events; avoiding all connections which might entangle it in the contests or views of other powers, and preserving a constant readiness to concur in an honorable re-establishment of peace and friendship, is a solemn question, which the Constitution wisely confides to the Legislative Department of the Government. In recommending it to their early deliberations, I am happy in the assurance, that the decision will be worthy the enlightened and patriotic Councils, of a virtuous, a free, and a powerful Nation.

Having presented this view of the relations of the United States with Great Britain, and of the solemn alternative growing out of them, I proceed to remark, that the communications last made to Congress, on the subject of our relations with France, will have shown, that since the revocation of her Decrees, as they violated the neutral rights, of the United States, her Government has authorized illegal captures, by its privateers and public ships: and that other outrages have been practiced, on our vessels and our Citizens. It will have been seen also, that no indemnity had been provided or satisfactorily pledged, for the extensive spoliations committed under the violent and retrospective orders of the French Government, against the property of our Citizens seized within the jurisdiction of France. I abstain, at this time, from recommending to the consideration of Congress, definitive measures with respect to

that nation, in the expectation, that the result of unclosed discussions between our Minister Plenipotentiary at Paris and the
French Government, will speedily enable Congress to decide,
with greater advantage, on the course due to the rights, the
interests, and the honor of our Country.

JAMES MADISON

U.S. House of Representatives, Committee on Foreign Relations: Report on the Causes and Reasons for War

After the President's war message was read before the House, it was referred to the Committee on Foreign Relations, whose acting chairman was John C. Calhoun, a thirty-year-old War Hawk from South Carolina. Two days later, the committee was ready with its report, which was principally if not entirely the work of Calhoun. A Republican colleague in the Thirteenth Congress, Representative Charles J. Ingersoll of Pennsylvania, later recalled the young Calhoun's persuasiveness as an orator: "[he was] slender, erect, and ardent . . . speaking with aggressive aspect, flashing eye, rapid action and enunciation . . . carrying home conviction beyond rhetorical illustration." On the day after Calhoun's speech, the House adopted a war bill, 79–49. The Senate would debate the bill until June 17.

June 3, 1812

The Committee on Foreign Relations to whom was referred the Message of the president of the United States of the 1st of June, 1812, Report,

That, After the experience which the United States have had of the great injustice of the British Government towards them, exemplified by so many acts of violence and oppression, it will be more difficult to justify to the impartial World their patient forbearance, than the measures to which it has become necessary to resort, to avenge the wrongs, & vindicate the rights and honor of the Nation. Your Committee are happy to observe, on a dispassionate review of the conduct of the United States, that they see in it no cause for censure.

If a long forbearance under injuries ought ever to be considered a virtue in any Nation, it is one which peculiarly becomes the United States. No People ever had stronger motives to cherish Peace: None have ever cherished it with greater sincerity and zeal.

But the period has now arrived, when the United States must support their character and station among the Nations of the Earth, or submit to the most shameful degradation. Forbearance has ceased to be a virtue. War on the one side, and peace on the other, is a situation as ruinous as it is disgraceful. The mad ambition, the lust of power, and commercial avarice of Great Britain, arrogating to herself the complete dominion of the Ocean, and exercising over it an unbounded and lawless tyranny, have left to Neutral Nations an alternative only, between the base surrender of their rights, and a manly vindication of them. Happily for the United States, their destiny, under the aid of Heaven, is in their own hands. The crisis is formidable only by their love of peace. As soon as it becomes a duty to relinquish that situation, danger disappears. They have suffered no wrongs, they have received no insults, however great, for which they cannot obtain redress.

More than seven years have elapsed since the commencement of this system of hostile aggression by the British Government, on the rights and interests of the United States. The manner of its commencement was not less hostile than the spirit with which it has been prosecuted. The United States have invariably done every thing in their power to preserve the relations of friendship with Great Britain: Of this disposition they gave a distinguished proof at the moment when they were made the victims of an opposite policy. The wrongs of the last War had not been forgotten at the commencement of the present one. They warned us of dangers, against which it was sought to provide. As early as the Year 1804 the Minister of the United States at London was instructed to invite the British Government to enter into a negotiation on all the points on which a collision might arise between the two Countries, in the course of the War, and to propose to it, an arrangement of their claims on fair and reasonable conditions. The invitation was accepted. A Negotiation had commenced and was depending, and nothing had occurr'd to excite a doubt that it would not terminate to the satisfaction of both the parties. It was at this time, and under these circumstances, that an attack was made, by surprise, on an important branch of the american Commerce, which affected every part of the United States, and involved many of their Citizens in ruin.

The Commerce on which this attack was so unexpectedly made, was that between the United States and the colonies of France, Spain, and other enemies of Great Britain. A Commerce just in itself; sanctioned by the example of Great Britain in regard to the trade with her own colonies: and sanctioned by a solemn act between the two Governments in the last War: and sanctioned by the practice of the british Government in the present War, more than two years having then elapsed, without any interference with it.

The injustice of this attack could only be equalled by the absurdity of the pretext alledged for it. It was pretended by the British Government that, in case of War, her enemy had no right to modify its colonial regulations, so as to mitigate the calamities of War to the inhabitants of its colonies. This pretension, peculiar to Great Britain, is utterly incompatible with the rights of sovereignty in every independent State. If we recur to the well established, and universally admitted law of Nations, we shall find no sanction to it, in that venerable code. The Sovereignty of every State is co-extensive with its dominions, and cannot be abrogated, or curtailed in its rights, as to any part except by conquest. Neutral Nations have a right to trade to every Port of either belligerent, which is not legally blockaded; and in all articles which are not contraband of War. Such is the absurdity of this pretension, that your committee are aware, especially after the able manner in which it has been heretofore refuted, and exposed, that they would offer an insult to the understanding of the House, if they enlarged on it; and if any thing could add to the high sense of the injustice of the British Government in this transaction, it would be the contrast which her conduct exhibits in regard to this trade, and in regard to a similar trade by Neutrals, with her own Colonies. It is known to the World, that Great Britain regulates her own trade, in War and in Peace, at home and in her colonies, as she finds for her interest: that in War she relaxes the restraints of her colonial system in favor of the colonies, and that it never was suggested that she had not a right to do it; or that a neutral in taking advantage of the relaxation violated a belligerent right of her enemy. But with Great Britain every thing is lawful. It is only in a trade with her enemies, that the United States can do wrong: with them all trade is unlawful.

In the Year 1793 an attack was made by the British Government on the same branch of our neutral Trade, which had nearly involved the two Countries in War. That difference however was amicably accommodated. The pretension was withdrawn, and reparation made to the United States for the losses which they had suffered by it. It was fair to infer from that arrangement, that the Commerce was deemed, by the British Government, lawful, and that it would not be again disturbed.

Had the British Government been resolved to contest this trade with Neutrals, it was due to the character of the British Nation, that the decision should be made known to the Government of the United States. The existence of a negotiation, which had been invited by our Government, for the purpose of preventing differences, by an amicable arrangement of their respective pretensions, gave a strong claim to the notification, while it afforded the fairest opportunity for it. But a very different policy animated the then cabinet of England. Generous sentiments were unknown to it. The liberal confidence and friendly overtures of the United States were taken advantage of to ensnare them. Steady to its purpose and inflexibly hostile to this Country, the British Government calmly looked forward to the moment when it might give the most deadly wound to our interests. A trade just in itself, which was secured by so many strong and sacred pledges, was considered safe. Our Citizens, with their usual industry and enterprise, had embarked in it, a vast proportion of their shipping, and of their capital, which were at sea under no other protection than the law of Nations, and the confidence which they resposed in the justice and friendship of the british Nation. At this period the unexpected blow was given. Many of our Vessels were seized, carried into port and condemned, by a Tribunal, which while it professes to respect the Law of Nations, obeys the mandate of its own Government in opposition to all Law. Hundreds of other Vessels were driven from the Ocean, and the trade itself in a great measure suppressed.

The effect produced by this attack on the lawful Commerce of the United States, was such as might have been expected from a virtuous, independant, and highly injured people. But one sentiment pervaded the whole american Nation. No local interests were regarded, no sordid motives felt. Without looking to the parts which suffered most, the invasion of our rights was considered a common cause, and from one extremity of our union to the other, was heard the voice of an united People, calling on their Government to avenge their wrongs, and vindicate the rights and honor of the Country.

From this period the British Government has gone on in a continued encroachment on the rights and interests of the United States, disregarding in its course, in many instances, obligations which have heretofore been held sacred by civilized Nations.

In May 1806, the whole Coast of the Continent from the Elbe to Brest inclusive was declared to be in a State of Blockade. By this Act, the well established principles of the Law of Nations, principles which have served for ages as guides, and fixed the boundary between the rights of Billigerants and Neutrals, were violated. By the law of Nations, as recognized by Great Britain herself, no Blockade is lawful, unless it be sustained by the application of an adequate force; and that an adequate force was applied to this blockade, in its full extent, ought not to be pretended. Whether Great Britain was able to maintain legally, so extensive a blockade, considering the War in which she is engaged, requiring such extensive naval operations, is a question which it is not necessary at this time to examine. It is sufficient to be known that such force was not applied, and this is evident from the terms of the Blockade itself, by which, comparatively, an inconsiderable portion of the Coast only was declared to be in a State of strict and rigorous blockade. The objection to the measure is not diminished by that circumstance. If the force was not applied, the blockade was unlawful, from whatever cause the failure might proceed. The Belligerant who institutes the blockade cannot absolve itself from the obligation to apply the force under any pretext whatever. For a Belligerant to relax a blockade, which it could not maintain, with a view to absolve itself from the obligation to maintain it, would be a refinement in injustice not less insulting to the Understanding than repugnant to the law of Nations. To claim merit for the mitigation of an evil, which the party either had not the power or found it inconvenient to inflict would be a new mode of encroaching on neutral rights. Your Committee think it just to remark that this act of the British Government, does not appear to have been adopted in the sense in which it has been since construed. On consideration of all the circumstances attending the measure, and particularly the character of the distinguished Statesman who announced it, we are persuaded that it was conceived in a spirit of conciliation and intended to lead to an accommodation of all differences between the United States and Great Britain. His death disappointed that hope, and the act has since become subservient to other purposes. It has been made by his successors a pretext for that vast system of usurpation, which has so long oppressed, and harassed our Commerce.

The next act of the British Government which claims our attention, is the Order of Council of Jany. 7th. 1807, by which neutral Powers are prohibited trading, from one Port to another of France, or her allies or any other Country with which Great Britain might not freely trade. By this order, the pretension of England, heretofore disclaimed by every other power, to prohibit neutrals, disposing of parts of their Cargoes at different Ports, of the same enemy, is revived and with vast accumulation of injury. Every enemy, however great the number, or distant from each other, is considered one, and the like trade even with powers, at peace with England, who from motives of policy had excluded, or restrained her commerce, was also prohibited. In this Act the British Government evidently disclaimed all regard for neutral rights. Aware that the measures authorized by it could find no pretext in any belligerant right, none was urged. To prohibit the sale of our produce, consisting of innocent articles at any port of a belligerant, not blockaded, to consider every belligerant as one, and subject neutrals to the same restraints with all, as if there was but one, were bold encroachments. But to restrain or in any manner interfere with our Commerce with neutral Nations, with whom Great Britain was at Peace, and against whom she had no justifiable cause of War for the sole reason that they restrained or excluded from their Ports, her commerce, was utterly incompatible with the pacifick relations subsisting between the two Countries.

We proceed to bring into view the British Order in Council of Novr. 11th. 1807. which superseded every other Order, and consummated that system of hostility on the commerce of the United States which has been since so steadily pursued. By this Order all France and her allies, and every other Country at War with Great Britain, or with which she was not at War, from which the british flag was excluded, and all the Colonies of her enemies, were subjected to the same restrictions, as if they were actually blockaded in the most strict and rigorous manner; and all trade in articles, the produce and manufacture of the said Countries and colonies, and the Vessels engaged in it, were subjected to capture and condemnation as lawful prize. To this order certain exceptions were made, which we forbear to notice, because they were not adopted from a regard to neutral rights, but were dictated by policy, to promote the Commerce of England, and, so far as they related to neutral powers, were said to emanate from the clemency of the British Government.

It would be superfluous in your Committee to state, that by this order, the British Government declared direct and positive War against the United States. The dominion of the Ocean was completely usurped by it, all Commerce forbidden, and every flag driven from it, or subjected to capture and condemnation, which did not subserve the policy of the British Government, by paying it a tribute and sailing under its sanction. From this period the United States have incurred the heaviest losses, and most mortifying humiliations. They have borne the calamities of War, without retorting them on its authors.

So far your Committee has presented to the view of the House, the aggressions, which have been committed under the authority of the British Government, on the Commerce of the United States. We will now proceed to other wrongs which have been still more severely felt. Among these is the impressment of our Seamen, a practice which has been unceasingly maintained by Great Britain in the wars to which she has been a party since our Revolution. Your committee cannot convey in adequate terms, the deep sense which they entertain of the injustice and oppression of this proceeding. Under the pretext of impressing British Seamen, our fellow Citizens are seized in British ports, on the high seas, and in every other quarter to which the british power extends, are taken on board british Men of War, and compelled to serve there as british subjects. In this mode our Citizens are wantonly snatched from their Country and their families; deprived of their liberty and doomed to an ignominious and slavish bondage; compelled to fight the battles of a foreign Country and often to perish in them; our flag has given them no protection; it has been unceasingly violated and our Vessels exposed to danger by the loss of the Men taken from them. Your Committee need not remark that while this practice is continued, it is impossible for the United States to consider themselves an independant Nation. Every new case, is a new proof of their degradation. Its continuance is the more unjustifiable, because the United States have repeatedly proposed to the British Government an arrangement which would secure to it the controul of its own people. An exemption of the Citizens of the United States from this degrading oppression, and their flag from violation, is all that they have sought.

This lawless waste of our Trade, and equally unlawful impressment of our Seamen, have been much aggravated by the insults and indignities attending them. Under the pretext of blockading the harbours of France and her allies, british squadrons have been stationed on our own Coast, to watch and annoy our own trade. To give effect to the blockade of European Ports, the ports and harbours of the United States, have been blockaded. In executing these Orders of the British Government, or in obeying the spirit which was known to animate it, the Commanders of these squadrons have encroached on our jurisdiction, seized our Vessels, and carried into effect impressments within our limits, and done other acts of great injustice, violence and oppression. The United States have seen with mingled indignation and surprize, that these acts instead of procuring to the perpetrators the punishment due to unauthorized crimes, have not failed to recommend them to the favor of their Government.

Whether the British Government has contributed by active measures to excite against us the hostility of the savage tribes on our frontiers, your Committee are not disposed to occupy much time in investigating. Certain indications of general notoriety may supply the place of authentic documents, tho' these have not been wanting to establish the fact in some instances. It is known that symptoms of British hostility towards the United States have never failed to produce corresponding symptoms among those tribes. It is also well known that on all such occasions abundant supplies of the ordinary munitions of War have been afforded by the agents of British Commercial Companies, and even from British Garrisons, wherewith they were enabled, to commence that system of savage warfare on our frontiers which has been at all times indiscriminate in its effect, on all ages, sexes, and conditions and so revolting to humanity.

Your Committee would be much gratified if they could close here the detail of British wrongs, but it is their duty to recite another act of still greater malignity than any of those which have been already brought to your view. The attempt to dismember our Union, and overthrow our excellent constitution by a secret mission the object of which was to foment discontents and excite insurrection, against the constituted authorities and laws of the Nation as lately disclosed by the Agent employed in it, affords full proof that there is no bound to the hostility of the British Government towards the United States, no act however unjustifiable which it would not commit to accomplish their ruin. This attempt excites the greatest horror, from the consideration that it was made while the United States and Great Britain were at Peace, and an amicable negotiation was depending between them for the accommodation of their differences, thro' public Ministers regularly authorized for the purpose.

The United States have beheld with unexampled forbearance, this continued series of hostile encroachments, on their rights and interests, in the hope, that yielding to the force of friendly remonstrances, often repeated, the British Government might adopt a more just policy towards them, but that hope no longer exists. They have also weighed impartially the reasons which have been urged by the British Government in vindication of these encroachments, and found in them neither justification nor apology.

The British Government has alledged in vindication of the Orders in Council that they were resorted to, as a retaliation on France, for similar aggressions committed by her, on our neutral Trade with the British dominions. But how has this plea been supported. The dates of British and french aggressions are well known to the World. Their origin and progress have been marked with too wide and destructive a waste of the property of our fellow Citizens to have been forgotten. The Decree of Berlin of Novr. 21st. 1806 was the first aggression of France in the present War. Eighteen Months had then elapsed, after the attack made by Great Britain on our neutral Trade with the colonies of France and her allies, and six Months from the date of the Proclamation of May 1806. Even on the 7th. of Jany. 1807, the date of the first British Order in Council, so short a term had elapsed, after the Berlin Decree, that it was hardly possible that the intelligence of it, should have reached the United States. A retaliation which is to produce its effect, by operating on a neutral power, ought not to be resorted to 'till the neutral had justified it by a culpable acquiescence in the unlawful act of the other belligerant. It ought to be delayed until after sufficient time had been allowed to the neutral, to remonstrate against the measure complained of, to receive an answer, and to act on it, which had not been done in the present instance. And when the Order of Novr. 11th. was issued, it is well known that a Minister of France had declared to the Minister Plenipotentiary of the United States at Paris, that it was not intended that the Decree of Berlin should apply to the United States. It is equally well known, that no american Vessel had then been condemned under it, or seizure been made, with which the British Government was acquainted. The facts prove incontestibly that the measures of France, however unjustifiable in themselves, were nothing more than a pretext for those of England. And of the insufficiency of that pretext, ample proof has already been afforded by the British Government itself, and in the most impressive form. Altho' it was declared that the Orders in Council were retaliatory on France for her Decrees, it was also declared, and in the Orders themselves, that owing to the superiority of the British Navy, by which the fleets of France, and her allies, were confined within their own Ports, the french Decrees were considered only as empty threats.

It is no justification of the wrongs of one Power, that the like were committed by another; nor ought the fact, if true, to have been urged by either, as it could afford no proof of its love of justice, of its magnanimity or even of its courage. It is more worthy the Government of a great Nation to relieve than to assail the injured. Nor can a repetition of the wrongs by another power repair the violated rights or wounded honour of the injured party. An utter inability alone to resist could justify a quiet surrender of our rights, and degrading submission to the will of others. To that condition the United States are not reduced nor do they fear it. That they ever consented to discuss with either power, the misconduct of the other, is a proof of their love of Peace, of their moderation, and of the hope which they still indulged, that friendly appeals to just and generous sentiments, would not be made to them in vain. But the motive was mistaken, if their forbearance was imputed, either to the want of a just sensibility to their wrongs, or a determination, if suitable redress was not obtained, to resent them. The time has now arrived when this system of reasoning must cease. It would be insulting to repeat it. It would be degrading to hear it. The United States must act as an independant Nation, and assert their rights, and avenge their wrongs, according to their own estimate of them, with the party who commits them, holding it responsible for its own misdeeds, unmitigated by those of another.

For the difference made between Great Britain and France, by the application of the non-importation act against England only, the motive has been already too often explained, and is too well known, to require further illustration. In the commercial restrictions to which the United States resorted, as an evidence of their sensibility, and a mild retaliation of their wrongs, they invariably placed both powers on the same footing, holding out to each in respect to itself, the same accommodation, in case it accepted the condition offered, and in respect to the other, the same restraint, if it refused. Had the British Government confirmed the arrangement, which was entered into with the British Minister in 1809, & France maintained her Decrees, with France would the United States have had to resist, with the firmness belonging to their character, the continued violation of their rights. The Committee do not hesitate to declare, that France has greatly injured the United States, and that satisfactory reparation has not yet been made for many of those injuries. But that is a concern which the United States will look to and settle for themselves. The high character of the american people is a sufficient pledge to the World that they will not fail to settle it, on conditions which they have a right to claim.

More recently the true policy of the British Government towards the United States, has been completely unfolded. It has been publicly declared by those in Power, that the Orders in Council should not be repealed, until the french Government had revoked all its internal restraints on the British Commerce; and that the Trade of the United States, with France and her allies, should be prohibited, until Great Britain was also allowed to Trade with them. By this declaration it appears, that to satisfy the pretensions of the British Government, the United States must join Great Britain in the War with France, and prosecute the War until France should be subdued; for without her subjugation, it were in vain to presume on such a concession. The hostility of the British Government to these States has been still further disclosed. It has been made manifest that the United States are considered by it as the Commercial Rival of Great Britain, and that their prosperity and growth are incompatible with her welfare. When all these Circumstances are taken into consideration, it is impossible for your Committee to doubt the Motives which have governed the British Ministry, in all its measures towards the United States since the year 1805. Equally is it impossible to doubt, longer, the course which the United States ought to pursue towards Great Britain.

From this review of the multiplied wrongs of the British Government since the commencement of the present War, it must be evident to the Impartial world, that the Contest which is now forced on the United States, is radically a Contest for their Sovereignty and Independence. Your Committee will not enlarge on any of the injuries, however great, which have had a transitory effect. They wish to call the attention of the House to those of a permanent Nature only, which intrench so deeply on our most important Rights, and wound so extensively and vitally our best Interests, as could not fail to deprive the United States of the principal advantages of their Revolution, if submitted to. The Controul of our Commerce by Great Britain in regulating at pleasure, and expelling it almost from the Ocean; the oppressive manner in which these Regulations have been carried into effect, by seizing and confiscating such of our vessels, with their Cargoes, as were said to have violated her Edicts, often without previous warning of their danger; the impressment of our Citizens from on board our own vessels, on the high Seas, and elsewhere, and holding them in bondage till it suited the convenience of their oppressors, to deliver them up, are encroachments of that high and dangerous tendency, which could not fail to produce, that pernicious effect. Nor would those be the only consequences that would result from it. The British Government might, for a while, be satisfied with the ascendancy thus gained over us, but its pretensions would soon increase. The proof which so complete and disgraceful a submission to its authority would afford of our degeneracy, could not fail to inspire confidence, that there was no limit to which its usurpations, and our degradation, might not be carried.

Your Committee, beleiving, that the freeborn sons of America are worthy to enjoy the liberty which their Fathers purchased at the price of so much blood and treasure, and seeing in the measures adopted by Great Britain, a course commenced and persisted in, which must lead to a loss of National character & Independence, feel no hesitation in advising resistance by force—In which the Americans of the present day will prove to the enemy and to the World, that we have not only inherited that liberty which our Fathers gave us, but also the will & power to maintain it. Relying on the patriotism of the Nation, and confidently trusting that the Lord of Hosts will go with us to Battle in a righteous cause, and crown our efforts with success, your Committee recommend an immediate appeal to Arms.

Thomas Jefferson to James Madison

On May 25, 1812, while composing his war message, the President wrote to his longtime ally Thomas Jefferson seeking counsel on a piece of what he called "puzzling" business: how to justify war against Great Britain only, when France, too, was hostile to neutral shipping. "To go to war with England and not with France," he wrote, "arms the Federalists with new matter, and divides the Republicans, some of whom with the Quids"—the dissident Republicans who did not follow Madison's lead—"make a display of impartiality. To go to war against both presents a thousand difficulties, above all that of shutting all the ports of the Continent of Europe against our Cruisers who can do little without the use of them. It is pretty certain also, that it would not gain over the Federalists, who would turn all those difficulties against the Administration. The only consideration of weight in favor of this triangular war as it is called, is that it might hasten through a peace with Great Britain or France: a termination, for a while at least, of the obstinate question now depending with both." Jefferson's reply was candid.

DEAR SIR   MONTICELLO May 30. 12.

Another *communication* is inclosed, and the letter of the applicant is the only information I have of his qualifications. I barely remember such a person as the Secretary of mr. Adams & messenger to the Senate while I was of that body. It enlarges the sphere of choice by adding to it a strong federalist. The triangular war must be the idea of the Anglomen, and malcontents, in other words the federalists and quids. Yet it would reconcile neither. It would only change the topic of abuse with the former, and not cure the mental disease of the latter. It would prevent our Eastern capitalists and seamen from employment in privateering, take away the only chance of conciliating them, & keep them at home idle to swell the discontents; it would compleatly disarm us of the most powerful weapon we can employ against Gr. Britain, by shutting every port to our prizes, & yet would not add a single vessel to their number; it would shut every market to our agricultural productions, and engender impatience & discontent with that class which in fact composes the nation, it would insulate us in general negociations for peace, making all the parties our opposers, and very indifferent about peace with us, if they have it with the rest of the world, and would exhibit a solecism worthy of Don Quixot only, that of a choice to fight two enemies at a time, rather than to take them by succession. And the only motive for all this is a sublimated impartiality at which the world will laugh, and our own people will turn upon us in mass as soon as it is explained to them, as it will be by the very persons who now are laying that snare. These are the hasty views of one who rarely thinks on these subjects. Your own will be better, and I pray to them every success & to yourself every felicity.

TH: JEFFERSON

Andrew Jackson to Willie Blount

Since 1810, the Shawnee warrior Tecumseh—"Crouching Panther" in the language of his people—had led a confederacy of Indian tribes on America's northwestern frontier whose aim was to defend Indian lands, ways, and interests against encroachment by the United States. In the fall of 1811 Tecumseh visited Tennessee, Georgia, and Mississippi Territory in hopes of expanding his campaign to the South. He found a ready ally in the Red Stick Creeks, a traditionalist faction of the larger, more moderate Creek Nation. In the spring of 1812, a band of Red Sticks attacked a new white settlement in Humphreys County, Tennessee, near the Duck River. On May 12, five tribe members invaded the home of settler Jesse Manley while he and his nearest neighbor, John Crawley, were absent. They scalped and murdered Manley's wife and five children, killed an adolescent boy hired to protect them, and kidnapped Mrs. Crawley. Andrew Jackson, a forty-five-year-old major general of the Tennessee militia, asked Governor Willie Blount for permission to retaliate. In his reply, Blount advised restraint while he sought approval, which was not forthcoming, from Madison's distracted War Department.

Hermitage June 5th. 1812

Dear sir,

I have this moment returned from the State of Georgia. My heart bleeds within me at hearing of the wanton massacre of our women and children by a party of Creeks since I left home.

With infinite regret I learned that Genl. Johnson at the head of 500 men was in the neighborhood of this massacre, at the time of its perpetration, and yet omitted to send a detachment against these marauders or to follow them himself, with his whole force. Thus far they have escaped with impunity carrying off an unfortunate woman along with them. But this cruel outrage must not go unrevengd. The assassins of Women and Children must be punishd.

Now Sir the object of *Tecumpsies* visit to the creek nation is unfolding to us. That incendiary, the emissary of the *Prophet*, who is himself the tool of England, has caused our frontier to be stained with blood, and our peacefull citizens to fly in terror from their once happy abodes.

The sooner we strike, the less resistance we shall have to overcome; and a terrible vengeance inflicted at once upon one tribe may have its effect upon all others.

Even the wretches upon the wabash might take some warning from such a lesson. We must therefore march to the heart of the Creek Nation: a competent force can be raised at the shortest notice; for the spirit of the whole people is on fire. They burn to carry fire and sword to the heart of the Creek Nation, and to learn these wretches in their own Towns and villages what it is to massacre Women and Children at a moment of profound peace. I wait therefore for your Orders! Give me permission to procure provisions and munitions of war, and I pledge myself for the ballance. Twenty five hundred brave men from the 2nd Division will be ready on the first signal to visit the Creek towns, and bring them to terms without the aid of presents and annuities.

In the mean time I have issued an order to prepare the Militia for this Event: and I only wait your orders or those of the general government to carry it into effect. Other orders shall be issued for placing an immediate force upon the frontier, under cover of which the citizens may resume the labours of their fields. I wait with impatience for your answer. I have the honour to be with great consideration yours Respectfully

Andrew Jackson

Tecumseh: Message from the Confederate Nations to Their British Allies and Huron Brothers

June 8, 1812

In September 1811, while Tecumseh was recruiting allies in the South, William Henry Harrison, governor of the Louisiana and Indiana Territories, marched a thousand American troops to Prophet's Town, the confederacy's largest settlement, near the confluence of the Wabash and Tippecanoe rivers. Harrison had hoped, through a massive show of force, to break the rebellious spirit of the settlement's founder, Tenskwatawa ("the Prophet"), who was Tecumseh's younger brother and the religious leader of the confederacy. But on the morning of November 7, the Prophet, responding to his people's anxiety, authorized a surprise attack on the American camp, and Harrison, after leading his men to a costly victory, burned Prophet's Town to the ground and destroyed its food supplies. Six months after the Battle of Tippecanoe, Tecumseh, accompanied by a delegation of Shawnees, Kickapoos, and Winnebagos, traveled from Prophet's Town to Machekethie, forty miles west of Fort Wayne. His purpose was to receive the Hurons into the confederacy—an offer brokered by the British. It was also to censure publicly the Potawatomi, who in the summer of 1811 instigated skirmishes with Americans ("Big Knives") in Illinois that prompted Harrison's fatal march. Tecumseh's words are rendered in the English of Esidore Chaine, a Huron speaker employed as an interpreter for the Huron Nation (Tecumseh's "Brothers") and the British (his "Father").

Father, & Brothers Hurons!
    Brother Hurons,
  You say you were employed by our Father and Your own Chiefs to come and have some conversation with us, and we are happy to see You and to hear Your and our Father's Speech. We heartily thank You both for having taken the condition of our poor Women and children to Your considerations: We

27

plainly see that You pity us by the concern You shew for our welfare; and we should deem ourselves much to blame if we did not listen to the Counsel of Our Father and our Brothers the Hurons.

Father and Brothers! We have not brought these misfortunes on ourselves; We have done nothing wrong, but we will now point out to You those who have occasioned all the mischief—

Our Younger Brothers the Putewatemies (pointing to them) in spite of our repeated counsel to them to remain quiet and live in peace with the Big Knives, would not listen to us— When I left home last Year to go to the Creek Nation, I passed at Post Vincennes and was stopped by the Big Knives, and did not immediately know the reason, but I was soon informed that the Putewatemies had killed some of their people; I told the Big Knives to remain quiet until my return, when I should make peace and quietness prevail—On my return I found my Village reduced to ashes by the Big Knives—You cannot blame Your Younger Brothers the Shawanoes for what has happened: the Putewatemies occasioned the misfortune. Had I been at home and heard of the advance of the American Troops towards our Village, I should have gone to meet them and shaking them by the hand, have asked them the reason of their appearance in such hostile guise—

Father & Brothers! You tell us to retreat or turn to one side should the Big Knives come against us; had I been at home in the late unfortunate affair I should have done so, but those I left at home were (I cannot call them men) a poor set of people, and their scuffle with the Big Knives I compare to a struggle between little children who only scratch each others faces— The Kikapoos and Winibiegoes have since been at Post Vincennes and settled that matter amicably.

Father & Brothers. The Putewatemies hearing that our Father and You were on the way here for peaceable purposes, grew very angry all at once and killed Twenty-seven of the Big Knives.

Brothers!—We Shawanoes, Kikapoos and Winibiegoes, hope You will not find fault with us for having detained You so long here; We were happy to see You and to hear Your and

Our Father's words; and it would surely be strange if we did not listen to our Father and our eldest Brother.

    Father & Brothers! We will now in a few words declare to You our whole hearts—If we hear of the Big Knives coming towards our villages to speak peace, we will receive them; but if We hear of any of our people being hurt by them, or if they unprovokedly advance against us in a hostile manner, be assured we will defend ourselves like men.—And if we hear of any of our people having been killed, We will immediately send to all the Nations on or towards the Mississippi, and all this Island will rise as one man—Then Father and Brothers it will be impossible for You or either of You to restore peace between us.

James Monroe to John Taylor

In April 1811, James Monroe, a Republican stalwart and the American minister to Great Britain from 1803 to 1807, left the governorship of Virginia to become Madison's secretary of state, replacing Robert Smith, a controversial figure ill-suited for the post. In this letter to a longtime political friend and supporter, Monroe reflects on his first year in office and voices his growing conviction that only war could break the deadlock with Britain and restore American trade with Europe. While Monroe's diplomacy and bellicose rhetoric were largely ineffectual with the British government, there was growing opposition to the Orders in Council among Britain's commercial class. Three days after Monroe wrote this letter, Lord Castlereagh, the foreign secretary, announced in Parliament that the Orders in Council would be suspended if America in turn abandoned the last of its trade restrictions, the non-importation act of 1811. Had the British better publicized their desire for conciliation—or had there been a transatlantic cable in 1812—war might well have been averted.

WASHINGTON, June 13, 1812.

DEAR SIR,—I have been afraid to write you for some time past because I knew that you expected better things from me than I have been able to perform. You thought that I might contribute to promote a compromise with Great Britain, and thereby prevent a war between that country and the United States: that we might also get rid of our restrictive system. I own to you that I had some hope, tho' less than some of my friends entertained, that I might aid in promoting that desirable result. This hope has been disappointed. It is most certain however that I did everything in my power to promote it, consistent with the rights and interests of this country. My communications were conciliatory; on the ground of blockade nearly of accord; and no other interest was pressed to increase the difficulty of adjusting that respecting the orders in Council. Everything too was said, in an informal way, which could be said, with propriety, to bring about an accommodation. Nothing would satisfy the present Ministry of England short of unconditional submission, which it was impossible to make. This fact being completely ascertained the only remaining alternative was to get ready for fighting, and to begin as soon as we were ready. This was the plan of the administration when Congress met in December last; the President's message announced it; and every step taken by the administration since has led to it. The delay, it was hoped, would give to Great Britain an opportunity to reflect further on the subject, and to change her policy. But the misfortune is that we have been so long dealing in the small way of embargoes, non-intercourse, and non-importation, with menaces of war, &c., that the British government has not believed us. Thus the argument of war, with its consequences, has not had its due weight with that government. We must actually get to war before the intention to make it will be credited either here or abroad. The habitual opponents of the government, and some who have lately become so by particular causes, more violent than the old federalists, expected when the Congress met, that the administration would recommend the bolstering up the non-importation act as the sure means of bringing the British government to reason: that it would propose some new and more efficient plan for preventing smuggling, and catching smugglers. They came here, as there is good cause to believe, prepared to treat with vast asperity and contempt such an inefficient expedient. When they found that they had misconceived the views of the administration they were rather at a loss how to proceed. To oppose war would be inconsistent with their past conduct, I mean the malcontents; to join in with the views of the administration very inconsistent with their present plan. It required time to digest a system of conduct suited to present emergencies. The committees of foreign relations in the two Houses, and of war, apparently united, and sincerely so, as most of the members were, in resisting the foreign aggressions, consulted the administration as to the force that would be necessary for the purpose. The object of the administration was not to starve the cause. In case of war it might be necessary to invade Canada, not as an object of the war but as a means to bring it to a satisfactory conclusion. The estimate of the force had relation to that measure. In raising a force equal to it, it was sought not to go beyond it for two reasons, that the standing army should not be greater than was absolutely necessary, and secondly that no taxes ought to be imposed which could be avoided. The administration thought that 20,000 men (regulars) with volunteers and militia would be adequate to every object. The old establishment was 10,000, which it was proposed to complete, to be enlisted for five years; the other 10,000 to be enlisted for a shorter term. As soon as this estimate was known the persons alluded to separated themselves immediately from the government, taking what was called strong ground, and introducing a bill for 25,000 additional troops, making in the whole 35,000, all for five years. By this they attempted to gain credit, as being great advocates for war, and to throw discredit on the administration by implying on account of the moderation of its views that it was not in earnest, and really did not contemplate war. By enlisting the whole for *five years*, a difficult thing in this country, the means of making war were put at a distance; and by the volunteer plan (which was not intended to be by the administration the revival of Mr. Adams measure, but a regular body, under a popular name, for short enlistment) by keeping the appointment of the officers out of the hands of the President, that force was rendered nugatory. And as it seemed to be substituted to the militia, on the idea that the latter could not be marched without the limit of the United States, the arms of the government were in fact tied up till the regular force for five years should be raised, or as many of it as would be necessary for efficient measures. The system of revenue by internal taxation, of course, as that on trade was impaired by the restrictive regulations, was to be adopted to this great establishment of 25,000 men. The latter seemed to be a necessary incident to the former, indeed grew out of it; and satisfied I am that the report of these taxes from the Treasury was forced on that Department to shew how the war was to be maintained, which it had proposed (on a very different scale however) rather as the means of defeating the measures of the government, and breaking it down, than to give effect to that war.

The government has gone on and made its preparations, in

which it has succeeded better than was expected; and finally, after proposing an embargo, which was prolonged to connect it in character with the former one, has brought distinctly the subject of war before the legislature as the only possible means of giving effect to the just claims of the country on foreign powers. This proposition passed rapidly through the House of Representatives, but has hung in the Senate.

Mark the conduct of certain individuals in the latter body where every pestilent scheme has been contrived and managed since the commencement of the session. It is here, and not so much by the federalists as by men heretofore the strong advocates of war, who promoted embargoes &c., that the plan of 25,000 men was set on foot. These men have unceasingly circulated the report that the Executive did not intend to make war, and thereby deceived the people, and deceived the British government, depriving our country of the effect which that argument might have had in the British Cabinet. These men being now brought to the issue, by the proposition for war, are those who create all the embarrassments in the way of it. They ask a statement of the military force, expecting that their dilatory measures would have had less success than has actually attended them, how many troops (regular) are in all our towns, and along our coast, our frontiers, &c., as a motive for delay. The government has met these calls by fair statements, and is willing to take great responsibility on itself in every thing that it recommends. I have no doubt that the measure will finally pass, and perhaps by the votes of those very men, who, finding that their inconsistency and improper views are seen thro', and perhaps that they cannot defeat it, will join in to mask their real conduct & views from the public eye.

In the commencement of this European war the United States had the alternative either to leave our commerce to itself, or to yield it all the protection in their power. I am convinced if the former plan had been adopted that the republican party would have been overset long since, if the Union itself had not been dissolved. The Eastern people would have complained that their rights and interests were sacrificed by those in power, who were planters & negro holders, who cared for the sale of their wheat, corn, and tobo. only. The other plan was preferred, of yielding to it what protection we could. In pursuing this plan I have always thought that a fair and reasonable arrangement with the great maritime power was the true interest of this country. On this principle I signed the treaty with England, which was rejected, & its rejection has been followed with the restrictive system of embargo, non-intercourse, &c., which failed in their object. In coming here I found my country in the same controversy with the same powers, & at issue particularly with G. Britain, & the question after the failure of the negotiation with Mr. Foster, if it may be so called, whether we shall submit, or maintain our rights against that power; on that point I could have no doubt. My letter from Richmond did not propose a surrender of those rights. It explained the treaty which had been rejected according to our understanding of it. It did not even say that it ought to have been adopted. It expressed a confidence in the patriotism and wisdom of the admn., & a wish to aid it in asserting our rights under the restrictive system, aided, no doubt, by other causes, particularly a desire in those out of power to get into power, a desire in many to change our system of govt., in others to separate the Union. A strange revolution has been produced, considering the interests of the different parts of the U States as to the supporters & opponents of present measures. It is strange to see Southern people supporting neutral & maritime rights, who have comparatively so small an interest in their support, against Eastern people, whose prosperity depends on the support of those rights. The truth is the restrictive system contributed much to produce this effect. The government had it in its power to make a compromise in this point with its opponents by retiring from the contest with G. Britain, repeating the non-importation act, & leaving our commerce to be regulated by her govt. The opponents of the govt., federalists & others, invited this course, & had it been taken their opposition must have ceased. But where would it have left the U States? & what effect would it have had on the character & destiny of our republican system of govt.? My idea was that such a step would have put it in great danger, if it had not subverted it eventually. The govt. thought it important to the best interests of our country to go forward, & push the controversy with decision, since it could not be avoided.

My candid opinion is that we shall succeed in obtaining

what it is important to obtain, and that we shall experience little annoyance or embarrassment in the effort. I have great hope that decision here will at an early day rid the British nation of its present ministry, and that an accommodation will soon follow the change. Should the war however be prolonged I do not apprehend either invasion, the desolation of our coast, the battering our towns, or even any greater injury to our commerce than has existed since 1807, the period of the first embargo. I am persuaded, on the contrary, that it would be more flourishing in war than it has been since 1807, taking the whole term of five years together. Spain & Portugal must have provisions; Britain herself wants, & must have them, as do her Islands. If war does not procure immediate accommodation her govt. will afford vast facilities to our trade. It will find its way to hungry mouths.

Nor do I apprehend any dismemberment of the Union, or opposition to the govt. These are idle fears. They serve to excite alarm, to aid the cause of opposition, but if we open our ports & *trade & fight, & fight & trade*, & let all the embarrassments proceed from the enemy, & none from our own govt., I think we shall soon have much internal quiet.

James Madison: Proclamation of War

June 19, 1812

For two weeks after it passed the war bill, the House held its breath as the Senate, meeting in secret session, debated the measure. (John Roberts of Philadelphia, a House Republican who had voted for war, wrote to a relative, "The suspense we are in is worse than hell—!!!") Some senators favored a limited maritime war against Great Britain, and others a maritime war with both Great Britain and France, but in the end the administration Republicans, under the leadership of Senate president pro tempore William H. Crawford, carried the day. On June 17, the Senate adopted the House bill unchanged, 19–13. The President signed the bill into law on Thursday, June 18, and the War of 1812 began. Madison informed the nation the following day.

By the President of the United States of America
A Proclamation

Whereas the Congress of the United States by virtue of the constitutional authority vested in them, have declared by their act bearing date the 18th day of the present month, that war exists between the United Kingdom of Great Britain and Ireland, and the dependences thereof, and the United States of America and their Territories; Now therefore, I James Madison, President of the United States of America, do hereby Proclaim the same to all whom it may concern: And I do especially enjoin on all persons holding Offices, Civil or Military, under the Authority of the United States, that they be vigilent and zealous in discharging the duties respectively incident thereto: And I do moreover exhort all the good people of the United States as they love their Country, as they value the precious heritage derived from the virtue and valour of their fathers, as they feel the Wrongs which have forced on them the last resort of injured Nations, and as they consult the best means, under the blessing of Divine Providence, of abridging its calamities, that they exert themselves in preserving order, in promoting Concord, in maintaining the authority and the efficacy of the Laws; and in supporting and invigorating all the Measures which may be adopted by the constituted authorities for obtaining a speedy, a just and honorable peace.

In Testimony whereof, I have caused the Seal of the United States to be hereunto affixed, and signed the same with my hand.

Done at the City of washington the nineteenth day of June A.D. 1812 and of the Independence of the United States of America the thirty Sixth.

JAMES MADISON
By the President
JAMES MONROE Secy of State.

Hezekiah Niles: "War against England"

June 27, 1812

On September 7, 1811, Hezekiah Niles, formerly the editor of the daily broadsheet the Baltimore *Evening Post* (1805–11), published the pilot issue of America's first newsweekly, *The Weekly Register*. The magazine's prospectus promised that its coverage of politics would be conducted "with justice and impartiality, so that the 'public reason' may fairly discern the merits of a case in controversy," and so it was, quickly establishing *Niles' Register* as the paper of record for its period. The opinion pages, however, were unabashedly partisan. "The publisher is, in the common language of the day, a 'democratic republican,'" Niles told his readers, "and, as a duty he owes his own creed, will enforce it as well as he can." The *Register*'s politics, he continued, "shall be *American*—not passive, not lukewarm, but active and vigilant—not to support individuals, but to subserve the *interests of the people*." The following editorial epitomizes the *Register*'s politics not only at the beginning of the war but throughout it.

Our ancient and inveterate foe, has at length been proclaimed by the constituted authorities of the United States of America. For many years we endured what no independent nation ought to have suffered for a moment, and pursued negotiation like an *ignus futuus*, becoming more and more involved by insults and injuries; submission to one wrong preparing the way for another. In the valley of humiliation, at the foot of the throne of her ideot monarch, at the threshold of the palaces of the knaves who administer the government in his name, we sought justice and begged for peace: not because we feared war, but from that moderation which distinguishes the people, as well as the government of the United States. While we thus entreated mercy, many thousand seamen, *our brethren*, *neighbors* and *friends*, were groaning out a weary life on board the vessels of her navy: whipped, spurned and kicked by every creature that pleased to abuse them, and some were *murdered*, basely and deliberately murdered, for nobly attempting to regain that "freedom which is their birth-right," for gallantly designing to seek their liberty through blood and slaughter. The indignity, abuse and destruction of our seamen, and through them, the violent assault on the sovereignty of the country itself, has long cried for revenge, as preventive of the practice in future: for rather than admit the principle for one solitary hour, or in a single instance, that an American seaman, or a seaman sailing under the American flag, may be kidnapped by these *Algerines*, there is not a *true man* among us that would not exclaim—"*war—a war of extermination against them*."* Great Britain herself would nobly sink into absolute ruin before she would suffer *her* vessels to be so searched or *her* seamen so carried away. How monstrous then is it for her to practise towards the United States what she would indignantly refuse to permit another to do to her people! It is traitorous, and shews a mean and pitiful spirit, to palliate or *in any manner* excuse, or justify, the impressment of our seamen by the *British*. It springs from a heart so base and sordid, that he who is guilty of it may well be suspected of a *disposition* to sell his father, mother, wife and children to the *Turks* for a handful of sequins; to till the soil, or gratify the lust of a master, as slaves. It is an idea that the *British*, as a nation, would spurn at, with the mind of one man; though some *shop keepers* might wish it tolerated, provided they made a few pence by the compromise between the sovereignty of their country, and, indeed, the freedom of their own persons, and the pitiful profits of trade.

On the various points now at deadly issue between *our country* and this *foreign* nation, after the able and masterly manner in which they have been pourtrayed in the message of the president, and in the report of the committee of foreign relations, it becomes us to be silent; simply recommending a frequent perusal of these papers to all who doubt the justice of the stand we have taken. All the world has witnessed our forbearance—our desire of peace has been attributed, even in our own country, to fear. Let the world behold with how great force and power the slumbering *Eagle* will redress her wrongs

---

*"War—a war of extermination against every man, woman and child of France." Speech in the senate of the United States, 1799.

when aroused from the nest where she nourished her young, harmless and unoffending. *Let her breast plate be* UNION.

It is the *law of the land* that we defend ourselves from British aggressions: it is the legal authority of the country that we shall retaliate our wrongs as the only means to end them. For six years we have contemplated the necessity of this resort, the idea has become familiar, and war has lost half its horrors from being in perspective so long. Our means to carry it on are simple: we are young and vigorous, in all the freshness of youth as to national resources. They require only to be called into action; and we should contemn and despise the creature that underrates them.

The whole population of G. Britain is 12,562,144 souls. The white population of the United States is about half as many. In Great Britain, at least three fifths of the laboring classes are *paupers*; in the United States there are none such but the halt, the lame, the blind and the infirm and insane. On this population, so miserably oppressed and worn out Great Britain levies war taxes to the amount of 70 millions of pounds sterling, or about $25 per annum for every man, woman and child on the island. Is any man prepared to say that *we*, a nation of freemen, with full bellies and fertile land, could not pay as much were it necessary? Is the slave more profitable than the free laborer? Compare *Ohio* with some of the other states and answer the question. Will the man who sees before him no other prospect than monotonous labor and poverty, work as cheerfully and do as much, as he who beholds, in his industry, the ease of old age, with independence for his children?

A one hundredth part of the people of Great Britain cannot point to a spot, and say,—that is mine, or it belongs to my father, or *uncle*, or COUSIN.—But a majority in these states can proudly place their foot on the soil and exclaim,—*this is mine*, or *it belongs to my father*. The road to competency is free to all, and the same perseverance, frugality and industry that a poor *Englishman* exercises merely to *exist* at home, would make a man *rich* in the United States, in a few years. Whence comes this horrible clamor about "*taxes and loans and the like*," but of *anti American* principles? In time of *peace*, every soul in England, on the average, pays a tax of 14 dollars *per annum*, to government. The United States, in time of WAR, require their people to exert themselves, and pay *two dollars* each to fight their own battles, or less than one twelfth part of what Englishmen pay to support their oppressors. God forbid that the time shall ever arrive when this people may be taxed like the people of England; but how contemptible it is, to be alarmed at the payment of so pitiful a sum from the full coffers of the nation at large, accumulated by many years of unparalleled ease and prosperity! As to the loans, there is a fund that will pay them a thousand times over. We have 650 millions of acres of land to dispose of, which, in due time, will bring us two dollars an acre. But independent of this, *it is ascertained* that the *usual revenues*, in time of peace, are sufficient to defray all the expenses of government, and reduce the loans, expected to be made, as fast as desirable.

It is the law of the land that we fight England—it is also the will of the people, goaded by insults and injuries. Hitherto we have been divided into two great political sections, but professed a common object of preserving our glorious constitution pure and inviolate, and of giving perpetuity to the present system of things. An honest difference of opinion existed as to the best means of accomplishing these matters, though some perhaps may have had sinister views. At a time like the present, every *honest* diversity of sentiment will be sacrificed, or, at least, suffered to rest in peace for a season, on the ALTAR OF UNION. All men admit (or at least every man but a *knave* or a *fool*, MUST admit) there is just cause for war against *England*, if war can be just, as quakers and some others deny. The injuries received from *France* do not lessen the enormity of those heaped upon us by *England*; nor can the crimes of one nation palliate the offences of the other. In this "straight betwixt two" we had an unquestionable right to select our enemy. We have given the preference to *Great Britain*, not only for our supposed capability to coerce justice from her, but also on account of her more flagrant wrongs. For, putting her on a par with France as to her violations of our commercial rights, what shall we say of IMPRESSMENT, of the murders by the *Indians*, of the mission of *Henry*? Besides, *France* is invulnerable to us; we might as well declare war against the people of the moon as against her; but Great Britain is tangible in her tenderest points. It is contended by some that if one of these powers does us justice, the other will follow the lead. Though we do not subscribe to this doctrine in its fullest extent, we cannot suffer from making an experiment of that which it was impossible to avoid—for war was inevitable, save by the interference of Him who moulds the hearts and dispositions of man.

It is not to be supposed that every man will approve a general measure; but the minority must submit to the majority. It is the first principle of our solemn compact with each other—it is the life of the republic; and of those even who disapprove of a law, the majority will support it while it has authority, though they may exert themselves to repeal it. Unfortunately, and to the lasting disgrace of those who are guilty of it, many endeavors are making to raise up an opposition having for its object the defeat of their own government and the triumph of a *foreign enemy*. It will not amount to much—the good sense of the people will prevail, as it did in 1776. At that time about one third of the inhabitants of these states were openly or covertly opposed to independence: many through prejudice, some through fear, and a great many from bribery, corruption and interest. The same causes may prevail to a certain extent at this day; and it is to be expected that all that were *tories* in heart, or in deed, in the war for establishing independence, will also be opposed to the war for preserving it. But the number of such is contemptible. We can watch them better than our fathers were able to do. In 1776, the vessel of state was launched into an unknown sea, to contend with a nation whose power it had been our pride to extol; with whom, and for whom, we had fought, bled and conquered; and we were as children, devoid of arms and the munitions of war, and destitute of every thing but patience and courage. In 1812, we have a stable and solid government, operating upon known and accepted principles to the remotest corners of our territory; we are abundantly supplied with weapons of defence; we are in a state of comparative manhood, and will meet the enemy with confidence over whom we triumphed in infancy.

Let every man, solemnly, in his "closet" put this question to himself:—"Would I send another ambassador to England to crawl on his hands and knees and beg, that my countrymen may not be stolen like *African* negroes, by the accursed traders in human flesh?"

The spirit of the people is up—the proposition must come from the other side of the water. We have *retreated* to the edge of the precipice—we have used every argument and exerted every means, to repel the adversary, without striking a blow. We can retire no further. We must strike or perish. The *United States* were compelled to "unbury the tomahawk," or become *colonies.* We have solemnly determined on the former, and may God speed the cause.

WAR IS DECLARED—GREAT BRITAIN IS THE ENEMY.—What American will excite divisions among the people, and give aid and comfort to the jealous and unprincipled foe? Who will admit an *intruder*?—I once saw a man and his wife contending for the *breeches*—a person interfered with a view to injure the man. The *pair* left their *private* quarrel to repel the *general* grievance —they mauled the *foreigner*, and then resumed the "management of their own affairs in their own way." So let it be with US.

To both parties (if two parties *will* exist) we humbly recommend forbearance and temper. It is not possible for any rational man to believe that the majority of one is under *French* influence, or of the other under *British* influence. There must be, and is, bad men in both sides—but nine tenths of either have a common object in repulsing the enemy. A little time and patience with prudence, will bring about a perfect union, when the war *really* begins. The exertion of all are wanting that its duration may be short; let us not fret each other by general censures which no gentleman would particularly apply to his neighbor who happens to differ in sentiment on some minor points. By such means, in the course of a few months, our jarring opinions will settle down in peace, and every man be prepared to say, *Long live America, the asylum of freedom—sovereign, independent and happy.*

Thomas Jefferson to James Madison

In a letter of April 27, 1809, former president Thomas Jefferson had written to his successor, James Madison, that the expansion of the American republic throughout the whole of North America would be possible in their time because the European powers would be too preoccupied warring against each other to hold on to their territories. If America could secure Florida and Cuba from Spain, he wrote, "we should then have only to include the North [Canada] in our confederacy, which would be of course in the first war, and we should have such an empire for liberty as she has never surveyed since the creation: & I am persuaded no constitution was ever before so well calculated as ours for extensive empire & self-government." Jefferson wasted little time returning to the theme of the conquest of Canada in this, his first letter to Madison after the declaration of war.

———————

DEAR SIR   MONTICELLO June 29. 12.

I duly recieved your favor of the 22d. covering the declaration of war. It is entirely popular here, the only opinion being that it should have been issued the moment the season admitted the militia to enter Canada. The federalists indeed are open mouthed against the declaration. But they are poor devils here, not worthy of notice. A barrel of tar to each state South of the Patomac will keep all in order, & that will be freely contributed without troubling government. To the North they will give you more trouble. You may there have to apply the rougher drastics of Govr. Wright, hemp and confiscation. To continue the war popular two things are necessary mainly. 1. to stop Indian barbarities. The conquest of Canada will do this. 2. to furnish markets for our produce, say indeed for our flour, for tobacco is already given up, & seemingly without reluctance. The great profits of the wheat crop have allured every one to it; and never was such a crop on the ground as that which we generally begin to cut this day. It would be mortifying to the farmer to see such an one rot in his barn. It would soon sicken him of war. Nor can this be a matter of wonder or of blame on him. Ours is the only country on earth where war is an instantaneous and total suspension of all the objects of his industry and support. For carrying our produce to foreign markets our own ships, neutral ships, & even enemy ships under neutral flags, which I would wink at, will probably suffice. But the coasting trade is of double importance, because both seller & buyer are disappointed, & both are our own citizens. You will remember that in this trade our greatest distress in the last war was produced by our own pilot boats taken by the British and kept as tenders to their larger vessels. These being the swiftest vessels on the ocean, they took them, & selected the swiftest from the whole mass. Filled with men, they scoured every thing along shore, & compleatly cut up that coasting business which might otherwise have been carried on within the range of vessels of force and draught. Why should not we then line our coast with vessels of pilot boat construction, filled with men, armed with canonnades, and only so much larger as to ensure the mastery of the pilot boat? The British cannot counter work us by building similar ones, because, the fact is, however unaccountable, that our builders alone understand that construction. It is on our own pilot boats the British will depend, which our larger vessels may thus retake. These however are the ideas of a landsman only. Mr Hamilton's judgment will test their soundness. Our militia are much afraid of being called to Norfolk at this season. They all declare a preference of a march to Canada. I trust however that Governor Barbour will attend to circumstances, and so apportion the service among the counties, that those acclimated by birth or residence may perform the summer tour, and the winter service be allotted to the upper counties.

I trouble you with a letter for General Kosciuzko. It covers a bill of exchange from mr Barnes for him, and is therefore of great importance to him. Hoping you will have the goodness so far to befriend the general as to give it your safest conveyance, I commit it to you, with the assurance of my sincere affections

TH: JEFFERSON

Thirty-four Members of the U.S. House of Representatives: from "An Address of the Minority to Their Constituents, on the Subject of War with Great-Britain"

Late June 1812

Even before the Senate voted for war, Federalists in the House of Representatives had enlisted their most articulate and impassioned spokesman, forty-year-old minority leader Josiah Quincy of Massachusetts, to draft a public letter of dissent. The fourteen-thousand-word letter, which incorporated contributions by Quincy's close friend Senator James A. Bayard of Delaware, was published in Washington as a pamphlet, reprinted in more than twenty far-flung editions, and then serialized, in full or in part, in nearly every newspaper in the country.

———————

The undersigned, Members of the House of Representatives, to their respective constituents:

A Republic has for its basis the capacity and right of the people to govern themselves. A main principle of a Representative Republic is the responsibility of the Representatives to their constituents. Freedom and publicity of debate are essential to the preservation of such forms of Government. Every arbitrary abridgment of the right of speech in Representatives, is a direct infringement of the liberty of the people. Every unnecessary concealment of their proceedings, an approximation towards tyranny. When, by systematic rules, a majority takes to itself the right, at its pleasure, of limiting speech, or denying it altogether; when secret sessions multiply; and in proportion to the importance of questions, is the studious concealment of debate, a people may be assured that, such practices continuing, their freedom is but short-lived.

Reflections, such as these, have been forced upon the

attention of the undersigned, Members of the House of Representatives of the United States, by the events of the present session of Congress. They have witnessed a principle adopted as the law of the House, by which, under a novel application of the previous question, a power is assumed by the majority to deny the privilege of speech, at any stage, and under any circumstances of debate. And recently, by an unprecedented assumption, the right to give reasons for an original motion has been made to depend upon the will of the majority.

Principles more hostile than these to the existence of Representative liberty, cannot easily be conceived. It is not, however, on these accounts, weighty as they are, that the undersigned have undertaken this address. A subject of higher and more immediate importance impels them to the present duty.

The momentous question of war with Great Britain, is decided. On this topic, so vital to your interests, the right of public debate in the face of the world, and especially of their constituents, has been denied to your Representatives. They have been called into secret session, on this most interesting of all your public relations, although the circumstances of the time, and of the nation, afforded no one reason for secrecy, unless it be found in the apprehension of the effect of public debate on public opinion; or of public opinion on the result of the vote.

Except the Message of the President of the United States, which is now before the public, nothing confidential was communicated. The Message contained no fact, not previously known. No one reason for war was intimated, but such as was of a nature public and notorious. The intention to wage war and invade Canada, had been long since openly avowed. The object of hostile menace had been ostentatiously announced. The inadequacy of both our Army and Navy, for successful invasion, and the insufficiency of the fortifications for the security of our seaboard, were everywhere known. Yet the doors of Congress were shut upon the people. They have been carefully kept in ignorance of the progress of measures, until the purposes of Administration were consummated, and the fate of the country sealed. In a situation so extraordinary, the undersigned have deemed it their duty by no act of theirs to sanction a proceeding so novel and arbitrary. On the contrary, they made every attempt in their power to attain publicity for their proceedings. All such attempts were vain. When this momentous subject was stated as for debate, they demanded that the doors should be opened. This being refused, they declined discussion; being perfectly convinced, from indications too plain to be misunderstood, that in the House all argument with closed doors was hopeless; and that any act, giving implied validity to so flagrant an abuse of power, would be little less than treachery to the essential rights of a free people. In the situation to which the undersigned have thus been reduced, they are compelled reluctantly to resort to this public declaration of such views of the state and relations of the country, as determined their judgment and vote upon the question of war. A measure of this kind has appeared to the undersigned to be more imperiously demanded, by the circumstance of a message and manifesto being prepared, and circulated at public expense, in which the causes for war were enumerated, and the motives for it concentrated, in a manner suited to agitate and influence the public mind. In executing this task, it will be the study of the undersigned to reconcile the duty they owe to the people, with that constitutional respect, which is due to the administrators of public concerns.

In commencing this view of our affairs, the undersigned would fail in duty to themselves, did they refrain from recurring to the course in relation to public measures, which they adopted and have undeviatingly pursued from the commencement of this long and eventful session; in which they deliberately sacrificed every minor consideration to what they deemed the best interests of the country.

For a succession of years, the undersigned have from principle disapproved a series of restrictions upon commerce, according to their estimation, inefficient as respected foreign nations, and injurious chiefly to ourselves. Success, in the system, had become identified with the pride, the character, and the hope of our Cabinet. As is natural with men, who have a great stake depending on the success of a favorite theory, pertinacity seemed to increase as its hopelessness became apparent. As the inefficiency of this system could not be admitted, by its advocates, without insuring its abandonment, ill success was carefully attributed to the influence of opposition.

To this cause the people were taught to charge its successive failures, and not to its intrinsic imbecility. In this state of things, the undersigned deemed it proper to take away all apology for adherence to this oppressive system. They were desirous, at a period so critical in public affairs, as far as was consistent with the independence of opinion, to contribute to the restoration of harmony in the public councils, and concord among the people. And if any advantage could be thus obtained in our foreign relations, the undersigned, being engaged in no purpose of personal or party advancement, would rejoice in such an occurrence.

The course of public measures also, at the opening of the session, gave hope that an enlarged and enlightened system of defence, with provision for security of our maritime rights, was about to be commenced; a purpose, which, wherever found, they deemed it their duty to foster by giving to any system of measures, thus comprehensive, as unobstructed a course as was consistent with their general sense of public duty. After a course of policy thus liberal and conciliatory, it was cause of regret that a communication should have been purchased by an unprecedented expenditure of secret service money, and used by the Chief Magistrate to disseminate suspicion and jealousy; and to excite resentment among the citizens, by suggesting imputations against a portion of them, as unmerited by their patriotism, as unwarranted by evidence.

It has always been the opinion of the undersigned, that a system of peace was the policy, which most comported with the character, condition, and interest of the United States; that their remoteness from the theatre of contest in Europe was their peculiar felicity, and that nothing but a necessity, absolutely imperious, should induce them to enter as parties into wars, in which every consideration of virtue and policy seems to be forgotten, under the overbearing sway of rapacity and ambition. There is a new era in human affairs. The European world is convulsed. The advantages of our own situation are peculiar. "Why quit our own to stand upon foreign ground? Why, by interweaving our destiny with that of any part of Europe, entangle our peace and prosperity in the toils of European ambition, rivalship, interest, humor, or caprice?"*

---

*Washington.

In addition to the many moral and prudential considerations, which should deter thoughtful men from hastening
into the perils of such a war, there were some peculiar to the
United States, resulting from the texture of the Government
and the political relations of the people. A form of government, in no small degree experimental, composed of powerful
and independent sovereignties, associated in relations, some of
which are critical, as well as novel, should not be hastily precipitated into situations, calculated to put to trial the strength
of the moral bond, by which they are united. Of all states, that
of war is most likely to call into activity the passions, which are
hostile and dangerous to such a form of government. Time is
yet important to our country to settle and mature its recent
institutions. Above all, it appeared to the undersigned, from
signs not to be mistaken, that if we entered upon this war, we
did it as a divided people; not only from a sense of the inadequacy of our means to success, but from moral and political
objections of great weight and very general influence.

It appears to the undersigned, that the wrongs, of which the
United States have to complain, although in some aspects very
grievous to our interests, and in many humiliating to our pride,
were yet of a nature which, in the present state of the world,
either would not justify war, or which war would not remedy.
Thus, for instance, the hovering of British vessels upon our
coasts, and the occasional insults to our ports, imperiously demanded such a systematic application of harbor and seacoast
defence, as would repel such aggressions, but, in no light can
they be considered as making a resort to war, at the present
time, on the part of the United States, either necessary or expedient. So, also, with respect to the Indian war, of the origin
of which but very imperfect information has yet been given to
the public. Without any express act of Congress, an expedition
was, last year, set on foot and prosecuted into the Indian territory, which had been relinquished by treaty, on the part of the
United States. And now we are told about agency of British
traders, as to Indian hostilities. It deserves consideration,
whether there has been such provident attention, as would
have been proper to remove any cause of complaint, either real
or imaginary, which the Indians might allege, and to secure

their friendship. With all the sympathy and anxiety excited by the state of that frontier, important as it may be, to apply adequate means of protection against the Indians, how is its safety insured by a declaration of war, which adds the British to the number of enemies?

A nation like the United States, happy in its local relations; removed from the bloody theatre of Europe; with a maritime border, opening a vast field for enterprise; with territorial possessions exceeding every real want; its firesides safe; its altars undefiled; from invasion nothing to fear; from acquisition nothing to hope; how shall such a nation look to Heaven for its smiles, while throwing away, as though they were worthless, all the blessings and joys which peace and such a distinguished lot include? With what prayers can it address the Most High, when it prepares to pour forth its youthful rage upon a neighboring people; from whose strength it has nothing to dread, from whose devastation it has nothing to gain?

If our ills were of a nature that war would remedy; if war would compensate any of our losses, or remove any of our complaints, there might be some alleviation of the suffering, in the charm of the prospect. But how will war upon the land protect commerce upon the ocean? What balm has Canada for wounded honor? How are our mariners benefitted by a war, which exposes those who are free, without promising release to those who are impressed?

But it is said that war is demanded by honor. Is national honor a principle, which thirsts after vengeance, and is appeased only by blood, which, trampling on the hopes of man, and spurning the law of God, untaught by what is past and careless of what is to come, precipitates itself into any folly of madness, to gratify a selfish vanity or to satiate some unhallowed rage? If honor demands a war with England, what opiate lulls that honor to sleep over the wrongs done us by France? On land, robberies, seizures, imprisonments, by French authority; at sea, pillage, sinkings, burnings, under French orders. These are notorious. Are they unfelt because they are French? Is any alleviation to be found in the correspondence and humiliations of the present Minister Plenipotentiary of the United

States at the French Court? In his communications to our Government, as before the public, where is the cause for now selecting France as the friend of our country, and England as the enemy?

If no illusion of personal feeling, and no solicitude for elevation of place, should be permitted to misguide the public councils; if it is indeed honorable for the true statesman to consult the public welfare, to provide in truth for the public defence, and to impose no yoke of bondage; with full knowledge of the wrongs inflicted by the French, ought the Government of this country to aid the French cause, by engaging in war against the enemy of France? To supply the waste of such a war, and to meet the appropriation of millions extraordinary for the war expenditures, must our fellow-citizens, throughout the Union, be doomed to sustain the burden of war-taxes, in various forms of direct and indirect imposition? For official information, respecting the millions deemed requisite for charges of the war; for like information, respecting the nature and amount of taxes deemed requisite for drawing those millions from the community, it is here sufficient to refer to the estimates and reports made by the Secretary of the Treasury and the Committee of Ways and Means, and to the body of resolutions, passed in March last, in the House of Representatives.

It would be some relief to our anxiety, if amends were likely to be made for the weakness and wildness of the project, by the prudence of the preparation. But in no aspect of this anomalous affair can we trace the great and distinctive properties of wisdom. There is seen a headlong rushing into difficulties, with little calculation about the means, and little concern about the consequences. With a navy comparatively nominal, we are about to enter into the lists against the greatest marine on the globe. With a commerce unprotected and spread over every ocean, we propose to make profit by privateering, and for this endanger the wealth of which we are honest proprietors. An invasion is threatened of the colonies of a Power which, without putting a new ship into commission, or taking another soldier into pay, can spread alarm or desolation along the extensive range of our seaboard. The resources of our country, in their natural state, great beyond our wants or our hopes, are impaired by the effect of artificial restraints. Before adequate fortifications are prepared for domestic defence; before men, or money, are provided for a war of attack, why hasten into the midst of that awful contest which is laying waste Europe? It cannot be concealed, that to engage in the present war against England is to place ourselves on the side of France, and exposes us to the vassalage of States serving under the banners of the French Emperor.

The undersigned cannot refrain from asking, what are the United States to gain by this war? Will the gratification of some privateersmen compensate the nation for that sweep of our legitimate commerce by the extended marine of our enemy, which this desperate act invites? Will Canada compensate the Middle States for New York; or the Western States for New Orleans? Let us not be deceived. A war of invasion may invite a retort of invasion. When we visit the peaceable, and as to us innocent, colonies of Great Britain with the horrors of war, can we be assured that our own coast will not be visited with like horrors? At a crisis of the world such as the present, and under impressions such as these, the undersigned could not consider the war, in which the United States have in secret been precipitated, as necessary, or required by any moral duty, or any political expediency.

George Sullivan,
A. Bigelow,
Wm. Ely,
Wm. Reed,
Laban Wheaton,
Richard Jackson, jr.,
Epaphroditus Champion,
Lyman Law,
Timothy Pitkin, jr.,
Benjamin Tallmadge,
James Emott,
Thomas R. Gold,
H. M. Ridgely,
P. B. Key,
John Baker,
Joseph Lewis, jr.,
A. McBryde.

Martin Chittenden,
Elijah Brigham,
Josiah Quincy,
Samuel Taggart,
Leonard White,
Elisha R. Potter,
John Davenport, jr.,
Jonathan O. Moseley,
Lewis B. Sturges,
H. Bleecker,
Asa Fitch,
James Milnor,
C. Goldsborough,
P. Stuart,
James Breckenridge,
Thomas Wilson,
Joseph Pearson.

Maryland House of Delegates, Committee of Grievances and Courts of Justice: Report on the Baltimore Riots

With 47,000 residents, Baltimore in 1812 was America's third largest city and the only major Atlantic port solidly in the Republican camp. Its diverse population—mainly of French, German, and Irish heritage —was loosely united by boomtown pride, strong trading ties to France, and enmity toward Great Britain. On June 20, Alexander Contee Hanson, editor of the *Federal Republican*, a twice-weekly broadsheet that was the strongest Federalist voice in the city, published an editorial condemning the "unnecessary" war and pledging to use "every constitutional argument and every legal means" to end it. Murmurs of violence against "the traitor Hanson" immediately filled Baltimore's dockyards, back rooms, and taverns, and on the evening of the 22nd a mob of several hundred men converged on the newspaper building to destroy it. Five months later, the Federalist-dominated Maryland House of Delegates began its inquiry into the ensuing riots, three separate but related attacks on the *Federal Republican* and its property, personnel, and sympathizers that left one dead and six others seriously injured.

THE COMMITTEE

OF GRIEVANCES AND COURTS OF JUSTICE,

To whom the following Order of the House of Delegates of November the eighteenth, eighteen hundred and twelve, was referred—

"ORDERED, That the Committee of Grievances and Courts of Justice be and they are hereby instructed, to inquire into the late Riots and Mobs in the City of Baltimore, and the causes thereof, with a view to ascertain whether there has been any culpable inertness or neglect of duty on the part of any of the Civil or Military Officers of the state, or whether the defect is in the Law, in order that the proper remedy in either case may be applied."—

BEG LEAVE TO REPORT, IN PART—

That in compliance with the Order of the House of Delegates, and under the exercise of a general power with which the Committee of Grievances are invested, they have inquired into the recent disturbances which have so agitated the city of Baltimore, and depressed the reputation of our state in the eyes of our sister Republics, "the causes thereof, and the conduct of the civil and military officers in relation thereto." They find, from the testimony collected by your committee, and which accompanies this Report, that the city of Baltimore has for a long time been considered as the ardent advocate of every measure of the general government leading to the War in which the Nation is now engaged.

That the Federal Republican, edited by Messieurs Hanson and Wagner, exercising a constitutional right of reviewing the measures of the national cabinet, arraigned, in glowing colours, the integrity and policy of the system which was to plunge the nation into hostilities: That the exercise of this right produced a general spirit of intolerance against that establishment; and that leading and distinguished advocates of the administration, were so far forgetful of the spirit of our constitution, of the sacred protection which the freedom of the press required from their hands, and of their obedience to the sovereignty of the law, as to indulge in denunciations against the establishment, and to circulate the horrible impression, that the same course of strictures upon the measures of the cabinet, would, after a declaration of war, merit and receive the summary application of popular vengeance. The fitness and correctness of this doctrine were inculcated by the instrumentality of the democratical presses, having an extensive circulation amongst that description of persons the most likely to be impelled to excesses, and the fit instruments of outrage— That under the influence of the feelings excited by the above improper expressions of distinguished characters, and publications in the democratic papers, committees were organized by men of daring character, (only one of whom has been named to your committee,) to obtain subscribers to a plan, having for its undisguised object, the demolition of the Office of the

Federal Republican. In this effervescence of the public feeling, and state of preparation, the Congress of the United States declared war on the eighteenth of June. The editorial remarks in the Federal Republican on the ensuing day, reprobated the motives and expediency of the measure: The ministerial papers replied to those remarks in a style of bitterness and acerbity, well calculated to direct and secure the consummation of the promised threat of revenge. On Sunday rumours were afloat, and a belief entertained, that public meetings at Pamphelion's Hotel, The Apollo, and Stewart's Gardens, had determined to silence the press. On Monday the paper appeared without remarks on the attitude which the Congress had assumed; but still, well grounded apprehensions were entertained by Mr. Wagner, that his establishment and person were both endangered, and he took the precautionary measure of removing his book of accounts from the office. In the evening the plan of lawless outrage was commenced by a parcel of boys and a few men. The assemblage quickly augmented, bringing with them fire-hooks, and every apparatus requisite for the destruction of the building. The operations of the Mob were conducted with a regularity and subordination inducing a belief that the whole was the result of a digested system of operations, and terminated in a loss to the proprietors of three or four thousand dollars.

In this work of destruction a Frenchman was the most conspicuous and vociferous against the establishment, upon account of the general tone of its politics. A portion of the rioters, under a belief that Mr. Wagner was concealed in the old office of discount and deposit, attempted to enter the same; from this they were diverted by the zeal of two democratic gentlemen, who gave them assurances that Mr. Wagner was not there. The destruction of the house cost much labour and time; during which many stood by, and contributed nothing to the protection of the rights guaranteed to the citizens by our form of government. From the force of this remark, your committee with pleasure except the names of Edward Johnson, the mayor of the city, and judge Scott, who used every persuasive suggestion to divert the mob from their outrages; but who omitted to attempt a resort to the protection created by the vigilance of the legislature, in procuring a requisition for a military force,

when they saw the civil authority inadequate to the security of
Mr. Wagner and his property. From the office of discount and
deposit a part of the mob proceeded to the house of Mrs.
Wagner's father; and a committee, appointed by themselves,
searched every apartment of the house; there an Irishman was
the most noted for his savage threats. They next visited Mr.
Wagner's own house, and used every stratagem which rage
suggested, to hunt out the contemplated victim of their revenge. No efficient measures being adopted the ensuing morning by the constituted authorities of the city, to arrest the
rioters, and to cause them to enter into the customary recog-
nizance to keep the peace, they were emboldened, and sought
for new victims; they collected in the evening, with a force almost incredible, at the house of one Hutchens, charged by
them with using expressions derogatory to the character of
General Washington. They demanded him, with expressions of
rage evidencing a determination to sacrifice him—The mayor
had prevailed on him to escape. To prevent any violence to his
house, and to cause the rioters to disperse, it was suggested
that the mayor and George E. Mitchell, Esquire, late a member
of the executive council, should enter the house and search it;
this they did amidst the cries of Hutchens's children, and reported to the mob that he was not to be found—They then
dispersed, with promises of future vengeance against him, and
those who either should rally for his protection or for the
preservation of the peace of the city. To the shipping, regularly
cleared out according to the laws of the United States to un-
prohibited ports, and bearing the products of our soil, they
turned their attention; and in their strength, by dismantling
the vessels, they prohibited to the merchant the pursuit of
wealth in the channels sanctioned by the government of his
country. In the wantonness of their cruelty the unfortunate
blacks attracted their attention; and Briscoe, a free negro,
charged with the expressions of affection for the British nation,
has to deplore the sacrifice of his houses, (amounting to about
eight hundred dollars,) by their unfeeling agency. An African
Church, erected by the piety of the well disposed for the improvement and amelioration of the blacks, became to them an
object of jealousy; and rumours of a combination for its destruction, at length aroused the municipality of the city from

its lethargy, and a patrol of horse, by overawing the turbulent, gave to this unhappy place the appearance of quiet.

Your committee have omitted to present to your consideration a variety of incidents, where private revenge sought its gratification under the imposing garb of zeal against the reputed enemies of their country; and where those citizens who have sought an asylum here from the oppressions of their own governments, attempted to gratify their embittered passions by proscriptions of each other, the alleged causes of which existed before their emigration. To this source may be traced those convulsions of the city, where the United Irishmen and Orange-Men were the most prominent. During this prostration of the civil authority, Mr. Wagner sought an establishment in the District of Columbia, where the Federal Republican was revived. Mr. Hanson, impelled by considerations of duty to his country, and believing that a decisive stand ought to be taken for the preservation of the freedom of the press, resolved on its re-establishment in the city of Baltimore. A right *secured to him by the first principle and express language of our compact.* Woful experience had taught him to believe, that the same spirit of intolerance which led to its first annihilation, would again manifest itself, by an attempt to prevent its re-establishment; and confidently expecting that a resistance on the first onset would lead either to the dispersion of the mob, or the interposition of the civil authority, and thus cause a recognition of his right to locate his establishment there; he organized, by the aid of his personal friends in Montgomery, a force for, and a plan of, defence, but not of aggression. In execution of this design he came to Baltimore on Sunday the twenty-sixth of July—his friends arrived on the same day; their arrival was known but to few. The means of defence and resistance, had been previously prepared and deposited in the house, with a secrecy and caution, defying a suspicion of the object; and on Monday morning the Federal Republican was circulated amongst the subscribers, purporting to be printed at No. 45, Charles-street. This paper contained spirited strictures upon the lawless temper of the city, and the indisposition of the civil or military officers to discharge the respective duties of their office; and upon the executive of Maryland. It does not appear to your committee, that the state of preparation in which Mr. Hanson and his friends were, was known to the citizens generally, or that any acts were done by them, either calculated to excite irritation or apprehension of aggression in the minds of the citizens—Their course of conduct during the whole day evidenced a determination to adhere to the original design, of avoiding all ostentation of preparation, and to act entirely on the defensive. During the day, information was communicated to those in the house, that an attack would be made; every precaution which prudence and humanity suggested was adopted, to prevent any occurrence which might attract the attention of the mob. About early candle light, the wicked and daring attempt to expel a citizen from his residence, or to involve in one common ruin himself and his property, was commenced, and continued, notwithstanding frequent and reiterated solicitations by the persons in the house to the mob, to desist and retire; and not until the windows were shattered, was even a fire of intimidation permitted from the house. At this, the mob dispersed; but shortly returned with a drum, and fire-arms, and with an increased violence attacking the house most furiously in the front and rear. But the same spirit of forbearance animated its defenders, till the door was burst open, when a discharge of musquetry wounded some of the assailants. Judge Scott hurried to this scene of uproar, and, with Mr. Abell, used every persuasive argument to induce the mob to desist, but with no success; his language and authority were alike treated with contempt. Every exertion which men divested of reason, and inflamed by passion could make, was made to destroy the defenders of the house—To execute this savage design, the door was again burst open, and a man by the name of Gales, the chief of the mob, shot dead as he entered. A field-piece was procured by the mob, and elevated at the house.

While this bloody scene was acting before the house of Mr. Hanson, many well-disposed citizens, alarmed for the peace of the city, and anxious for the preservation of the persons in the house, gathered at Brigadier-General Stricker's; who, irritated by Mr. Hanson's return to the city, which might be the innocent cause of a requisition being made upon him by the civil authority, which would necessarily be attended with a responsibility, received some of the applications which were made to him, for the interposition of a military force, in a style well adapted to excite irritation; but still consented to obey any call which the magistracy should deem it expedient to make on him. But such was the intolerant spirit of the magistracy against that establishment, or such was their anxiety to avoid any responsibility for their official duties, that great difficulty and much delay occurred in procuring two magistrates sufficiently devoted to the public good, and their oath of office, to sign the requisition. Major Barney, of the cavalry, before this, had received an order to repair to his general, which he obeyed with alacrity, and received from him a copy of the orders herewith submitted. Major Barney, with about thirty horsemen under his command, moved down between 1 and 3 o'clock to the house. The mob, apprehensive of an efficient resistance, were alarmed, and at his approach generally retired. But his conduct soon dispelled their fears, and gave rise to a belief among them that he was either unwilling, or incompetent, to enforce their dispersion. Thus all apprehensions of the military or civil interposition being banished, the timid were emboldened, and the daring unchecked by any suggestions of a future accountability.

The mayor, the attorney-general, general Stricker, and some citizens distinguished by their political consequence, became the negotiators between the gentlemen in the house and their vindictive assailants. This negotiation terminated in an arrangement, that Mr. Hanson, and his friends, should be conducted to the gaol as a place of security, under a solemn pledge, that every possible exertion should be made for their protection, and the security of their property.

A military escort was prepared, and a guard of unarmed citizens. A hollow square was formed, within which Mr. Hanson and his friends, accompanied by those who had promised them protection, and some other citizens of the greatest political weight, entered; and thus attended by hundreds crying for vengeance, and pressing on for their destruction, they reached the gaol. During this agonizing march, when the ferocity of the mob excited a general belief among those who had confided themselves to the civil power that their destruction would ensue before they should be put into the promised place of protection, frequent attempts were made to massacre them, by the throwing of stones, notwithstanding it endangered the lives of the political favourites of the mob.

Some of those who had been in the house at the commencement of the attack, attempted by various modes to insure a retreat—Some were arrested in their flight by the mob; and the savage temper of this "many headed monster" displayed itself in the cold and deliberate manner in which it planned the execution of its captives.

Revolutionary France furnished the lawless precedent of exhibiting upon the lamp post, by the irresponsible fiat of the populace, those who were supposed wanting in duty to the republic. A native of our country was seized on, and an attempt made to imitate the example set by the blood-thirsty Parisians.

From the completion of this sanguinary deed they were prevented by a stratagem suggested by democratic gentlemen, inducing a procrastination until an appointed hour, when they repaired to the place of confinement, to drag forth their victim, before then removed by the interposition and zeal of his friends.

After Mr. Hanson and his friends were placed in gaol, a general apprehension was entertained that the mob would, on the ensuing night, endeavour to force their prison, and glut their vengeance on the unarmed prisoners. The whole city was in a state of commotion; the criminal court was closed, and the anxious and inquiring countenances of the citizens denoted an apprehension of an approaching tragedy, in which all the barbarities which ferocious men, unchecked by the wholesome restraints of the law perform, would be exhibited. The prison was surrounded by groups of an infuriated mob, eternally demanding vengeance.

The weight of character, the necessary concomitant of wealth and political standing in society, was not generally brought into action to allay the excited feelings of the city; but, on the other hand, a belief was impressed that Mr. Hanson and his immediate political friends, were enemies to the country; that his visit to Baltimore was the consequence of an arrangement to insult and dragoon the citizens; that they were murderers; that they would avail themselves of a constitutional right to change the *venue* to an adjoining county, and thus escape the punishment due to their crimes—The Whig gave extensive circulation to these strictures. The general spirit of intolerance against the establishment, united with the occurrences of the day, and these excitements, produced an apathy among the well disposed, and gave an increased activity to the turbulent and vindictive.

The mayor and brigadier visited those confined in gaol, refused them arms for defence, and gave them solemn assurances that a guard would be stationed in and around the gaol, and that whatever power the civil or military could wield, should be given for their protection. Other citizens repaired to Judge Scott's, and required that the military should be ordered out; and after a considerable delay the requisition to brigadier-general Stricker was procured, who issued to col. Sterett, commanding the fifth regiment, to major Barney, of the cavalry, to colonel Harris, of the artillery, the respective orders accompanying this report. It appears to your committee that whatever may be the construction of the orders given to colonel Sterett, general Stricker verbally forbid him to deliver out to the men under his command ball cartridges. Of colonel Sterett's regiment thus ordered out, but thirty or forty obeyed the call of their commander; this defection, in the opinion of your committee, may be traced to the united causes of indisposition to protect the persons in the gaol, an apprehension of immediate danger, of future proscription, and to the inefficient preparation under which they were ordered to march—of the cavalry but a few attended.

During these operations in Gay-street, it was known to those ferocious monsters who panted at the gaol for the blood of their unarmed fellow-citizens, that the military were ordered out. The mayor used every persuasive argument to induce them to disperse, and to effect that, gave them a solemn pledge that neither Mr. Hanson nor his friends should be bailed. These assurances, united with apprehensions of a formidable resistance from the military, produced from some a reluctant promise that the gaol should not be attempted—Some of the most daring had left the gaol, and repaired to see the operations of the force convening to arrest the completion of their horrid designs. At this unfortunate moment, an interchange of opinion took place between general Stricker and others, which resulted in a belief that the interposition of the military would not be requisite, and that if any should be required, the force collected would be insufficient; orders were given to dismiss the military—it was the signal of destruction. The mob collected with a savage impetuosity, and heedless of the feeble opposition formed by the intreaties of the mayor, they attacked the sanctuary of the prisoners—The outer door was opened by treachery; the inner doors yielded to their rage and force; they entered the room of the gentlemen; there a scene of horror and murder ensued, which for its barbarity has no parallel in the history of the American people, and no equal but in the massacres of Paris. The good, the venerable, the gallant General Lingan, whose early life was distinguished by his active and manly exertions to rescue this country from the controul of a British parliament; who was honoured by the confidence of the immortal saviour of the nation, and who practised every christian virtue, was here overpowered by these sons of murder, and became the victim of their merciless ferocity. Seven or eight of the gentlemen were thrown in a heap, under an impression, entertained by these assassins, that they were dead. Some effected their escape by stratagem, or by the interposition of some protecting friend. One was detained as a subject for the trial of every refinement of torture which their fiend-like invention suggested. The humanity of certain medical gentlemen was exerted, and by their interposition, under Divine Providence, those supposed to be dead were restored to life and society. On the ensuing day a general terror prevailed throughout the city.

Your committee further find, that no attention was paid to the preservation of the house and property thus abandoned, but that a few men were suffered, during the day, to be actively engaged in doing every possible injury to the same. Federalists, deeming themselves insecure from a conviction, arising from past occurrences, that the civil power was too feeble for their protection, and that the military were unwilling to rally around the judiciary when the object was either the security of their persons or property, fled in every direction—No exertions were made to arrest the disturbers, and they assumed to themselves the sovereign power of controuling the government of the United States, by regulating the concerns of the post-office. They assembled with a view to the demolition of the office, in order to collect and destroy the papers of the Federal Republican, transmitted by mail to subscribers in the city. The activity of Mr. Burral, of the post-office, discovered the combination, and with promptitude communicated to the mayor and brigadier-general the grounds of his belief. They became at last convinced of the fact, which the experience of all countries had proved, that the mobs of populous cities can only be restrained and overawed by the application of an efficient force—And the general, without any written requisition, but upon assurances that any should be given thereafter which the result of his opposition might require, ordered out the whole of his brigade, at the head of which he appeared, as became a military chief. A distribution of ball took place, and every preparation was made, evidencing a determination to disperse the tumultuous. But even here, surrounded with the military, the civil power did not abandon the same wretched system of concession and conciliation; for it appears to your committee, that upon the manifestation of a spirit of insubordination among some of the military, the mayor proposed to the post master to deliver up the Federal Republican papers, to be carried to the dwelling of the mayor, with a solemn assurance to the mob, that they should be returned in the morning by the mail to Washington. The post-master stated the embarrassments arising from the nature of his official duties; and upon a consultation at the residence of Mr. Burral, the proposition was abandoned, and a resolution adopted to protect the establishment. Before which, the mayor avowed a determined resolution to protect the office, but at the same time to allay the irritation of a portion of the militia, who complained of their being called out for the protection of the Federal Republican, he stated, "You are not assembled to protect the paper; you are marched here to protect the property of the United States, and to support the laws. I, myself, would draw my sword, and head my fellow-citizens, to put down that establishment." An order from the colonel, and the voluntary charge by two of the horse, dispersed the rioters. For many successive nights a military guard was stationed; a determination was manifested that the peace of the city should be preserved, and it produced the effect—The grand jury, in its regular course, investigated the subject, and presented some of those engaged in the murder and riots. They were arrested and committed to prison; threats of rescue were made; a military force was stationed during the night at the prison, and artillery planted in the hall of the gaol. These operations were attended with an uniform result, establishing incontrovertibly, that the course of forbearance and concession selected by those charged with the preservation of the peace of the city, was productive of no other effect than to embolden the wicked. The trials took place—The first of them exhibited a temper in the jury, utterly inconsistent with the object of criminal jurisprudence, the punishment of the guilty; the attorney-general of Maryland frequently declared his belief that no conviction against the offenders could be had; and still omitted to enter a suggestion on the record that the state could not have a fair trial, and to pray that the records might be transmitted to another county. An universal acquittal of the most blood-thirsty ensued; and the melancholy apprehension is now entertained, that the wicked have nothing there to fear from the retributive justice of the state.

Your committee further find, that the ordinary power with which the magistrates are invested for the preservation of the peace of the city, was in no instance, except as stated by your committee, called into action; that the constables are corrupt, and exercise an undue influence over the magistracy, that the Court of Oyer and Terminer and General Gaol Delivery is conducted in a manner inconsistent with the dignity due to a tribunal invested with such extensive power.

Your committee find, that during the morning of the twenty-eighth of July, John Montgomery, Esquire, did, in order to prevent the firing of the cannon levelled at the house, make use of every exertion, and encountered great danger, and that during these agitations, frequent meetings of the most respectable citizens of both parties were convened by the mayor, in order to concert some plan of operations to insure the peace of the city, and which uniformly resulted only in recommendations to the turbulent to forbear, and recommending a proclamation, to be signed by the magistracy, calling on the peace officers to be vigilant in the preservation of order.

Your committee have presented to your consideration the

causes and extent of the late riots—They now will submit to you an expression of their opinion, formed upon a dispassionate examination of the testimony, "as to the conduct of the Civil and Military Officers in relation thereto." It is the opinion of your committee, that during all the agitations which have convulsed the city of Baltimore, Edward Johnson, Esquire, did every thing which could be required of him as a private citizen; but they have to regret, that, as Mayor, charged with the preservation of the quiet of the city, his forbearance, and indisposition to resort to the ordinary powers of coercion, with which he was invested, against the turbulent and wicked, was so distinguished as to encourage a belief that he connived at and approbated their excesses. That he was guilty of a most reprehensible indiscretion, when he used to the refractory militia intemperate language against the Federal Republican, the inevitable effect of which was to sanction and excite, by his weight of character, the popular excesses against the same. That when he, at the Post-Office, surrounded with the military and his political friends, submitted a proposition, the object of which was to ensure the triumph of the illegal combinations of the Mob, he evidenced a timidity, and a want of judgment, irresistably inducing a belief of his unfitness for the station which he filled. That his course of forbearance, united with the wicked inertness of the magistracy, and deplorable corruption of the constables, nurtured and gave maturity to that horrid spirit of licentiousness, which terminated in the tragical and lawless events detailed by your committee.

That General Stricker, aware of the ferocious and blood-thirsty temper of the Mob, who were eternally vociferating "blood for blood," and seeking to satiate their vengeance by the instrumentality of a field-piece levelled at the house, failed to gratify the spirit of the requisition made on him by the civil power, when he issued to Major Barney orders not calculated to ensure the return of order and peace, by enforcing the dispersal of those who were violating both.

That Major Barney erred, when (although tied down by his orders, and evidencing every disposition to prevent the effusion of blood and to allay the violence of the Mob,) he attempted, by conciliation and persuasion, to induce the Mob to disperse, which had the effect to banish that awe and apprehension which the presence of an armed cavalry naturally inspires. That his pledge to the Mob, that none of those in the house should escape, was calculated to give all that confirmation which would necessarily result from the expression of his opinion, that the gentlemen in the house were the aggressors, and that the Mob, of course, were justified in their horrid outrages. That General Stricker, knowing as he did, that a portion of his brigade manifested a spirit incompatible with the gratification of any military order, which the requisition on him demanded, and being present, when the sanguinary temper of the rioters evidenced itself, in a force incompatible with the safety of the persons marching to the gaol, and unchecked either by the interposition of the military force with which they were surrounded or by the presence of the political friends of the mob, failed to do his duty to his country when he omitted to order out a larger portion of his brigade on the 28th— That he was guilty of a manifest departure from every principle of prudence, when he, by a verbal, rendered unavailing a written, order, given to Colonel Sterett, to fire on any assailants. This restriction, in the opinion of your committee, merits the most decided reprobation, as being utterly inconsistent with, and having a direct tendency to render inoperative, any application of a military force; nor can the dismissal of the troops on the evening of the twenty-eighth day of July, when opposite opinions were entertained as to the designs of the turbulent, when the civil power was lulled into a fatal security by assurances of an efficient military co-operation, when the General and his advisers were vibrating between apprehensions of danger and belief of security, when no exertions were made to sound the temper of the different quarters of the city, be considered in any other aspect than as the act of a timid mind, seeking to avoid a responsibility for the awful consequences resulting from an efficient military resistance. If the military assembled as a portion of the fifth regiment, was inadequate for the purpose of defence, General Stricker owed it to the solemnity of the occasion, to his pledge to the gentlemen in the gaol, to his duty to his state, to appear in the most impressive manner, and to invite all, either attached by military pride, by political association, or by personal confidence, to rally under his banners. That such a course of military preparation would have been productive of a result favourable to humanity, and our pride of state, is apparent from the occurrences connected with the operations at the post-office. The public had a right to demand that those wretches who had thus trampled on the law, and outraged humanity, should, by a fair administration of justice, be brought to punishment; it had a right to expect that the law officer of the state would see, that at least an impartial trial should be had.—Your committee are therefore of opinion, that John Montgomery, Esquire, the Attorney-General, when he believed that the sovereignty of the law could not, either from corruption in the jurors, or the influence of public feeling, an event anticipated from the very genius of our government, be vindicated in the city of Baltimore, was bound, both by his duty and his oath of office, to enter a suggestion of his belief, and pray for the removal of the trials to an adjoining county. This omission, in the opinion of your committee, demands from this house a severe animadversion.

All which is submitted.

By Order.

LOUIS GASSAWAY, Cl'k.

1813

Israel Pickens: Circular Letter
to His Constituents in North Carolina

A staunch supporter of President Madison, Israel Pickens served North Carolina in the U.S. House of Representatives from 1811 to 1817. This letter to his constituents was privately printed, together with Madison's war message and proclamation of war, as a twelve-page pamphlet issued on Independence Day, 1812.

---

*To the Citizens of Burke, Rutherford, Lincoln,
Buncombe, and Haywood*

Washington City, July 4th, 1812.

Fellow Citizens,

After the most solemn deliberation which has consumed a difficult and tedious session of eight months, our country has at length appealed to arms, for defence of its insulted rights and its wounded honor. Having tried in vain every pacific expedient, we are now at open war with Great Britain. The land and naval forces are charged with its vigorous execution. And the most active preparations are making to meet it.

The causes which have led to this last alternative of nations, are but too well known and too seriously felt by every portion of our citizens, to require a recital. Nothing more need be said to a brave & generous people than, that YOUR COUNTRY CALLS. War has been waging on the part of our enemy during a long period of professed friendship, and has only been aggravated by our earnest endeavors to maintain peace. The indignities to our flag, within our own sovereignty—the seizure of our property, in the course of a lawful trade—the capture of our citizens, in pursuit of an honest livelihood—their separation from their friends and their country, against whom they are often compelled to turn their arms—the savage warfare against the peaceful inhabitants of our frontier, which is clearly proved to proceed from British arms and influence—the

insidious attempt lately discovered to sever our union, by secret agency, which has not only roused the indignation of
every real American, but has excited the abhorrence of every
honest Britton; and has well nigh shaken that corrupt ministry
from power—These acts so incompatible with the safety, the
peace, the honor and sovereignty of this nation imperiously
call us to arms.

The injuries we have sustained from France have raised in
every American's soul a just indignation which nothing can,
which nothing ought to allay but the most prompt and ample
amends. This has been required by our government as the only
condition on which any terms for future intercourse will be
admitted. If the encouragement held out by that nation, of
redress for the past and assurances for the future, should not
soon be realized, I trust we will use the best means in our
reach, to exact respect to our rights as well from France as
from England.

I have the satisfaction to inform you that a resort to internal
taxation is not necessary at this time, and it is to be hoped that
other sources of revenue may be found to avoid a system so
obnoxious in its best form, and which would have proved very
inconvenient to our citizens at this embarrassing moment.

The long forbearance of our government, which has been
imputed to a want of energy in our councils, it is hoped, will
now be attributed to its true cause, a love of justice, and a sincere desire to cultivate peace. A trial is now to be made how far
a free government is capable of its own preservation. On the
issue of this interesting experiment rests the fate of the only
free republic on earth.

On this day thirty-six years, our nation took its birth among
the empires of the world. Through every portion of this period
have we grown in resources, in population, and in national
character. All the improvements and arts which ornament civilized life are advancing with unexampled rapidity. Institutions
which contribute to national and individual prosperity are rising over our land. Industry has caused this wilderness to give
way to fields of plenty. Agriculture, our country's great ornament and support, is improving in a degree unknown to other
countries. The world has been wondering at this prodigy of
national grandeur. A momentous task is imposed on us—the

defence of the civil and religious liberties, the honor, the independence handed us from our brave ancestors. United we are
able for the important duty, tho' opposed by a world combined.

Honest difference of political sentiment has existed among
us, as has been the case in every free nation; and in ordinary
times this difference has proved a useful check against the
abuse of power; but now, having arrayed our country in arms,
we have but one cause to support. "He that is not for his
country is against it." Every patriot hand will be raised together
against the common enemy: One heart and one soul will
breathe the nation's spirit; and one united nerve will brace the
national arm.

Let us rise together—our cause is just—the God of our fathers, who has heretofore blessed our exertions, will again be
our guardian and our shield.

Israel Pickens.

William Ellery Channing: A Sermon, Preached in Boston, July 23, 1812, the Day of the Publick Fast, Appointed by the Executive of the Commonwealth of Massachusetts, in Consequence of the Declaration of War Against Great Britain

On June 26, 1812, exactly one week after Madison's proclamation of war, Governor Caleb Strong declared the coming 23rd of July a day of "fasting, humiliation, and prayer" for the people of Massachusetts. He implored the citizens of the commonwealth to assemble in their churches and beseech God "that He would give wisdom, integrity, and patriotism to our national and state governments," "inspire the President and Congress, and the Government of Great Britain, with just and pacific sentiments," and "humble the pride and subdue the lust and passions of men, from whence War proceed." On the day of public fast, William Ellery Channing, the thirty-two-year-old minister of Boston's Federal Street Church, preached a sermon to his Congregationalist-Unitarian audience that subsequently found national popularity as an anti-war tract.

LUKE XIX. 41, 42.

And when Jesus was come near, he beheld the city, and wept over it, saying, If thou hadst known, even thou, at least in this thy day, the things which belong unto thy peace! but now, they are hid from thine eyes.

THESE words were pronounced by Jesus Christ, just before his death, when approaching, for the last time, the guilty city of Jerusalem. From the Mount of Olives he surveyed this metropolis of his nation, its lofty towers, its splendid edifices, and above all, its holy and magnificent temple;—and as he looked, his benevolent heart was pierced with sorrow at the scenes, which opened on his prophetick eye. He saw this city, now so crowded, so opulent, so secure, surrounded by the armies of Rome. Instead of security, he saw terror and consternation. He saw the sword wasting without, and he saw famine within, more fatal than the sword, carrying death in the most horrid forms, into what were once the abodes of plenty and joy. He saw the invading army gradually approaching, and at length scaling the walls of Jerusalem, and weary with slaughter, calling in the aid of fire to complete the work of desolation. He saw the rapid flames levelling all the magnificence which was spread before him, and even seizing on the temple of God, ascending its lofty battlements, and leaving not a vestige of its consecrated altars. As he looked forward to the ruins of his country, he wept and exclaimed, Oh that thou hadst known the things which belong to thy peace!

The emotion, which Jesus now expressed, undoubtedly arose from the general benevolence of his character. He would have wept over any city, doomed to this awful destruction: but as Jesus always discovered the sensibilities of human nature, we are authorized in believing, that his grief on this occasion was rendered more poignant by the consideration, that Jerusalem was the metropolis of his country—that its ruin would be followed by the dispersion and misery of the nation to which he belonged. His tears were tears of patriotism, as well as benevolence. We here learn that it is a part of our character and duty, as christians, to be affected by the prospect of national suffering. The miseries of our country, as far as they are unfolded to us, should arrest our attention, should draw tears from our eyes, and lamentation from our lips; should increase our interest in our native land, and rouse every effort for its security.

On this day, there is a peculiar propriety in directing our minds to this subject. This is a day, set apart for national sorrow and humiliation. It is a day, when forsaking our common pursuits, and especially forsaking our pleasures, we are to penetrate our hearts with our national danger and sins, and to offer, in the temple of the Almighty, penitential acknowledgments and earnest prayers, that he will spare and protect our country. On this day, the calamities, which we feel or fear, should be brought home to us, that our prayers may be more earnest, our humiliation more deep, our purpose more sincere to renounce our sins, and to perform our duties as citizens and as christians.

I am sensible that on this subject—the calamities of our country—there is danger of indulging excessive apprehension. I know that the mind of man is querulous and discontented—that he is prone to turn from the bright part of his prospects, to forget his blessings in magnifying his dangers, and to say that all before him is darkness and sorrow. In speaking of our calamities as a nation, I desire not to forget that we have been a highly favoured people, and that we have still many benefits, which it becomes us to acknowledge with gratitude, and which distinguish us from other nations. When I speak of our calamities, I do not mean to say, that our state is as wretched as that of Spain and Portugal; nations overrun with armies, drenched with blood, thinned by famine;—we are not as wretched as France, sinking as she is under tyranny as galling as the world ever knew, yet forced to suppress her groans, forced to give up, without a murmur, her treasures, her children, to her merciless lord. A lot worse than ours can easily be conceived. Many fruits of our former prosperity are left us; and, with few exceptions, the inestimable blessings of liberty continue to be the honourable distinction of our country. But, whilst we acknowledge this with thankfulness, is it not true, and ought we not to feel it, that our prosperity is rapidly declining, and that dangers of tremendous aspect are opening before us? Why is it, my friends, that on this day you have suspended your common pursuits, and are now assembled in the house of God? It is because our country, which has been so long the abode, the asylum of peace, is at length given up by God to the calamities of a state of WAR. Have we not cause of lamentation and alarm?

In all circumstances, at all times, war is to be deprecated as one of the severest judgments of God. The evil passions it excites, its ravages, its bloody conflicts, the distress and terror it carries into domestick life, the tears it draws from the widow and the fatherless, all render war a tremendous scourge.

There are indeed conditions in which war is justifiable, is necessary. It may be the last and only method of repelling lawless ambition, and of defending invaded liberty and essential rights. It may be the method of preventing or repairing injury, which God's providence points out by furnishing the means of successful warfare, by opening the prospect of a happy termination. In these cases we must not shrink from war; though even in these we should lament the necessity of shedding human blood. In such wars our country claims and deserves our prayers, our cheerful services, the sacrifice of wealth and even of life. In such wars we are comforted when our friends fall on the field of battle; for we know that they have fallen in a just and honourable cause. Such conflicts, which our hearts and consciences approve, are suited to exalt the character, to call forth generous sentiments, splendid virtues, to give ardor to the patriot, resolution to the hero, and a calm, unyielding fortitude to all classes of the community. Could I view the war in which we are engaged in this light, with what different feelings, my friends, should I address you! We might then look up to God and commit to him our country with a holy confidence. We might then ask his blessing on all our efforts, without being rebuked by the fear, that this holy and beneficent being views us with displeasure. It would then be my duty to revive the spirits of the drooping, to reprove the fears of the trembling, to exhort you to gird on the sword, and not count your lives dear to you in asserting the cause of your country and mankind. But, in our present state, what can I say to you? I would, but I cannot address you in the language of encouragement. I can offer you no reflections to sustain you in your calamities—no bright prospects to animate hope and to lighten the pressure of immediate suffering. We are precipitated into a war, which, I think, cannot be justified—and a war, which promises not a benefit, that I can discover, to this country or to the world. We are suffering much, and are to suffer more—and not one compensation for suffering presents itself, whether we consider the influence of the war on ourselves or on foreign countries.

That we have received no injuries from the nation, which we have selected as our enemy, I do not say—I am not prepared to deny that the orders of England are infractions of our rights,*

---

*The author has wished to speak with diffidence on the subject of the Orders in Council, knowing that a diversity of sentiment on this point, exists among wise and good men in this country.

but when I consider the atrocious and unprovoked decrees of France, on which these orders were designed to retaliate; the unprecedented kind of war, which these orders were designed to repel—when I consider the situation of England, that she is contending for existence, whilst her enemy is avowedly contending for conquest—and when I consider the conduct of our own government in relation to the two belligerents, the partiality and timid submission they have expressed towards the one, the cause of suspicion they have given to the other, and the spirit in which they have sought reparation from England— I am unable to justify the war in which we have engaged. To render a war justifiable it is not enough that we have received injuries—we must ask ourselves, have *we* done our duty to the nation of which we complain?—have we taken and kept a strictly impartial position towards her and her enemy?—have we not submitted to outrages from her enemy by which he has acquired advantages in the war?—have we sought reparation of injuries in a truly pacifick spirit?—have we insisted only on undoubted rights?—have we demanded no unreasonable concessions? These questions must be answered before we decide on the character of the war, and I fear the answer must be against us. When I consider the restrictions formerly laid on our commerce for the purpose of pressing with severity on England, and on England alone—when I consider the demand we have made on that nation, that she shall revoke a blockade which at first we approved, and of which we did not for years make a complaint—when I consider another demand we have made on England, that she shall believe in the repeal of the decrees of France, although evidence of repeal has not been given her—when I consider our unwillingness to conclude an arrangement with her on that very difficult and irritating subject of impressment; notwithstanding she proffered such an one as our own minister at that court, and our present secretary of state declared "*was both honourable and advantageous to the United States*"—when I consider, what I blush to repeat, the accusation which we have brought against England without a shadow of proof, that she has stirred up the savages to murder our defenceless citizens on the frontiers—and when with all this I contrast the yielding, abject spirit with which we have borne the threats, insults, pillage, confiscations and atrocities of her enemy—I cannot say that we have done our duty, as a neutral nation, to England; that we have sought reparation in a friendly spirit; that we have tried with fairness every milder method before we made our appeal to arms—and if this be true, then the war is unjustifiable. If we have rushed into it, when we might have avoided it by an impartial and pacifick course, then we have wantonly and by our own fault drawn on ourselves its privations and calamities. Our enemy may indeed divide the guilt with us,—but on ourselves, as truly as on our enemy, falls the heavy guilt of spreading tumult, slaughter, and misery through the family of God.

If on the ground of right and justice this war cannot be defended, what shall we say when we come to consider its *expedience*, its effects on ourselves and the world. It is a war fraught with ruin to our property, our morals, our religion, our independence, our dearest rights—whilst its influence on other nations, on the common cause of humanity, is most unhappy.

Do any ask, what are the evils which this war has inflicted or threatens?—we may first mention the immense loss of property to which it exposes us.—I know that property is often overvalued—and in this country, the love of it is too strong, too exclusive a passion. I do not mean to encourage this passion by deploring the loss of property as the worst of evils—*still it has* its value—and one great object and duty of government is to secure and protect it.

By this war much of our property is placed beyond our reach—shut up in the ports of our enemy—not through the improvidence of our merchants—but in consequence of a severe law of our own government—a law which had no other foundation but the pretext that France had revoked her injurious decrees.

In addition to this, the war has exposed to capture all our wealth floating on the ocean. We have chosen for our enemy a nation which commands the seas, which can block up the mouths of our harbours—and we have invited her numerous cruisers to make a prey of our defenceless ships and unsuspecting seamen, who are now returning from every quarter of the globe.

But this is not all. Still more must be lost to us by the melancholy suspension of active pursuits, which this war must induce in the commercial states. This war is a death-blow to our commerce. The ocean, which nature has spread before us as the field of our enterprise and activity, and from which we have reaped the harvest of our prosperity, is, in effect, forbidden us. We see it laving all our shores—we hear the noise of its waves—but it is our element no longer. Our ships and superfluous produce are to perish on our hands—our capital to waste away in unproductive inactivity. Our intercourse with all foreign nations is broken off, and the nation, with which we sustained the most profitable intercourse, is our foe. Need I tell you the distress, which this war must spread through the commercial classes of society, and among all whose occupations are connected with commerce. How many are there from whom the hard earnings of years are to be wrested by this war, whose active pursuits and cheering prospects of future comfort are exchanged for discouragement, solicitude, and approaching want.

In addition to this, as our resources are decreasing, the publick burdens are growing heavier; and government, after paralyzing our industry and closing the channels of our wealth, are about to call on us for new contributions to support the war under which we are sinking. And to fill up the measure of injury, we are told, that this war, so fatal to commerce, so dreaded by the friends of commerce, is carried on for its protection. We are required to believe, that restriction and war, the measures which have drained away the life-blood of our prosperity, are designed to secure our rights on the ocean.

But loss of property is a small evil attending this war—its effect on our *character* cannot be calculated. I need not tell you the moral influence of a war, which is bringing to a gloomy pause the activity of the community—which is to fill our streets with labourers destitute of employment—which is to reduce our young men to idleness—which will compel a large portion of the community to esteem their own government their worst enemy. Regular industry is the parent of sobriety, and gives strength to all the virtues. A community must be corrupted, in proportion as idleness, discontent and want prevail. We have reason to fear, that these temptations will prove too strong for the virtue of common minds—that with the decline of commerce, the sense of honour and uprightness in pecuniary transactions will decline—that fair dealing will be succeeded by fraud—that civil laws will be treated with contempt—that habits of dissoluteness and intemperance, already too common, will be awfully multiplied—that our young men, thrown out of employment and having no field for their restless activity and ardent hopes, will give themselves up to lawless pleasure or immoral pursuits.

Let me here mention one pursuit, which this war will encourage, and which will operate very unhappily on our character. I have said that the ocean will be abandoned—I mistake —The merchant vessel will indeed forsake it; but the privateer will take her place. The ocean is no longer to be the field of useful and honest enterprise. We are no longer to traverse it, that we may scatter through the world the bounties of Providence. Henceforth plunder—plunder is our only object. We are to issue from our ports, not to meet the armed ship of our enemy—not to break her naval power—not to wage a war for publick purposes, a war which will reflect honour on our country, and give some elevation to our own minds—we shall go forth to meet the defenceless private merchant, and, with our sword at his breast, we are to demand his property, and to enrich ourselves with his spoils. This pursuit is indeed allowed by the law of nations; but Christians, and the friends to publick morals, must dread and abhor it as peculiarly calculated to stamp on a people the character of rapacity and hardness of heart. Yet this is the pursuit, this the character, in which Americans are henceforth to be found on the ocean.

But all the ruinous effects of this war are not yet unfolded. To see it in its true character, we must consider *against what nation it is waged,* and *with what nation it is connecting us.* We have selected for our enemy the nation from which we sprang, and which has long afforded and still offers us a friendly and profitable intercourse—a nation, which has been, for ages, the strong hold of Protestant Christianity—which every where exhibits temples of religion, institutions of benevolence, nurseries of science, the aids and means of human improvement—a nation, which, with all the corruptions of her government, still enjoys many of the best blessings of civil liberty, and which is now contending for her own independence, and for the independence of other nations, against the oppressor of mankind.

When I view my country taking part with the Oppressor against this nation, which has alone arrested his proud career of victory, which is now spreading her shield over desolated Portugal and Spain, which is the chief hope of the civilized world—I blush—I mourn. On this point, no language can be exaggerated. We are linking ourselves with the acknowledged enemy of mankind—with a government, which can be bound by no promise, no oath, no plighted faith—which prepares the way for its armies by perfidy, bribery, corruption—which pillages with equal rapacity its enemies and allies—which has left not a vestige of liberty where it has extended its blasting sway—which is, at this moment, ravaging nations that are chargeable with no crime but hatred of a foreign yoke. Into contact and communion with this bloody nation, we are brought by this war—and what can we gain by building up its power? what, but chains which we shall deserve to wear?

Will it be said, that France, while unjust to the world, has yet, by her special kindness and good offices and fidelity to this country, brought us under obligations to become her associate.—Have we then forgotten her insulting language to our government—have we forgotten our property, which she seized in her own ports without a colour of justice—have we forgotten our ships burnt on the ocean? This is the nation with whom we are called to interweave our destinies—whose conquests we are ready to aid!

On this subject too much plainness cannot be used. Let our government know, we deem alliance with France the worst of evils, threatening at once our morals, our liberty and our religion. The character of that nation authorizes us to demand, that we be kept from the pollution of her embrace—her proffered friendship we should spurn—from her arms, stained, drenched with the blood of the injured and betrayed, we should scorn and should fear to receive aid or protection.

I have thus pointed out some evils of the war, and the question now offers, what are we to gain by it? What compensation is offered us for losses and calamities so immense? What brilliant successes are placed within our reach? Is it on the ocean or on the land that we are to meet and spoil our foe? The *ocean* we resign to England; and, unless her policy or clemency prevent, we must resign to her our cities also. She can subject them to tribute, or reduce them to ashes. With what language shall I speak of a government, which plunges a country so defenceless into such a war? In better times, indeed, we had a growing navy, which, if fostered, might now have afforded us important aid. But, since we have made the mournful discovery, that commerce is to be protected by restriction, our navy has been suffered to dwindle into insignificance, and its poor remains, I fear, will only serve to expose our brave and hardy seamen to destruction. Is it said we can invade the enemy's provinces. But what can we gain by invasion? Of territory we have too much already. We are sinking under our unwieldy bulk. Plunder, I trust, is not to be our object; and if it be, will even the most oppressive exactions extort from these provinces as much as we must spend in conquering and retaining them? Let it be remembered too, that this conquest will cost us something more than wealth. It will cost us blood, and not the blood of men whose lives are of little worth—of men burdensome to society, such as often compose the armies of Europe. In this part of our country, at least, we have no mobs, no overflowing population, from which we wish to be relieved by war. We must send our sons, our brothers to the field—men who have property, homes, affectionate friends, and the prospect of useful and happy lives. That government will contract no ordinary guilt, which sheds such blood for provinces, which are our neighbours, which have never injured us, which are a charge to the parent country, and can give to us no aid in the present conflict. What then have we to gain? Was ever war waged so completely without object—without end—without means—with less prospect of a happy termination?

It only remains to consider the duties which belong to us in this unhappy state of our Country—what sentiments become us in relation to God, to our rulers, and to our country. Our duties in relation to God are obvious. It becomes us to approach this righteous Governour of nations and holy disposer of events with deep humility—to acknowledge his justice in our sufferings—to confess before him our sins, and sincerely to renounce them. Whilst our indignation is called forth towards the men who have exposed us to the calamities of war, let us look beyond them to God, who on this, as on other occasions, employs human agents to punish guilty people. Who of us, my friends, has a right to send up murmurs to God? Whose heart does not accuse him of many offences? Who can look round on his country, and not see many marks of ingratitude to God, and of contempt of his laws? Do I speak to any who, having received success and innumerable blessings from God, have yet forgotten the giver?—to any who have converted abundance into the instrument of excess and licentiousness—to any who, having been instructed by the gospel, have yet refused to employ in works of benevolence the bounty of heaven—to any who are living in habits of intemperance, impurity, impiety, fraud, or any known sin? To such I would say, it does not become *you* to complain of your rulers, or of the war. *You* have helped to bring on us this scourge, to call down the displeasure of God. *You* are among the enemies of your country, and the authors of her ruin. My friends, if God be a moral governour, no individual and no nation can continue to prosper in the violation of his holy commandments. Let then this day be something more than a day of empty forms. We owe to ourselves and our country deep sorrow for our sins, and a sincere purpose that we will labour by our reformation, by our prayers and exemplary lives, to bring down a blessing on our land.

Our duties to our rulers are not so easily prescribed. It is our duty towards them to avoid all language and conduct which will produce a spirit of insubordination—a contempt of laws and just authority. At the same time we must not see, without sensibility, without remonstrance, our rights violated, and our best blessings thrown away. Our elective form of government makes it our duty to expose bad rulers, to strip them of unmerited confidence, and of abused power.—This is never more clearly our duty than when our rulers have plunged us into an unjustifiable and ruinous war,—a war which is leading down to poverty, vice and slavery. To reduce such men to a private station, no fair and upright means should be spared; and, let me add, no other means should be employed. Nothing can justify falsehood, malignity, or wild, ungoverned passion. Be firm, but deliberate—in earnest, yet honest and just.

To those, who view the war in the light in which it has been now exhibited, one part of duty is very plain. They must give no encouragement, no unnecessary voluntary support to the war. They should leave the awful responsibility of this destructive measure entirely with our rulers, and yield no aid (except for defensive purposes) but what the laws require. Do any of you think, my friends, that even this degree of support is not due to a government which has wantonly sacrificed our interests, and denied to some members of the national confederacy almost all the benefits which induced them to accede to the Union? I answer, that a government may forfeit its right to obedience, and yet it may be the duty of citizens to submit. Resistance of established power is so great an evil,—civil commotion excites such destructive passions,—the result is so tremendously uncertain,—that every milder method of relief should first be tried, and fairly tried. The last dreadful resort is never justifiable, until the injured members of the community are brought to despair of other relief, and are so far united in views and purposes as to be authorized in the hope of success. —Civil commotion should be viewed as the worst of national evils, with the single exception of slavery. I know that this country has passed through one civil war without experiencing the calamitous consequences of which I have spoken. But let us not forget, that this was a civil war of a very peculiar character. The government which we shook off was not seated in the midst of us. Our struggle was that of nation with nation, rather than of fellow citizens with one another. Our manners and habits tended to give a considerateness and a stability to the publick mind, which can hardly be expected in a future struggle. And, in addition to these favourable circumstances, we were favoured by heaven with a leader of incorruptible integrity, of unstained purity—a patriot who asked no glory but that of delivering his country—who desired to reign only in the hearts of a free and happy people—whose disinterestedness awed and repressed the selfish and ambitious—who inspired universal confidence—and thus was a centre and bond of union to the minds of men in the most divided and distracted periods of our country. The name of WASHINGTON I may pronounce with reverence even in the temple of the Almighty; and it is a name which revives the sinking spirits in this day of our declining glory. From a revolution, conducted by such a man, under such circumstances, let no conclusions be hastily drawn on the subject of civil commotion.

I must now close with offering a few remarks on our duty to

our country. Let us cling to it, my friends, with filial love. Though dishonoured, though endangered, it is still our country —it gave us birth—it holds our dearest friends—and such are its resources and improvements, it may still be the first of nations. Let us not forsake it in this evil day. Let us hold fast the inheritance of our civil and religious liberties, which we have received from our fathers, sealed and hallowed by their blood. That these blessings may not be lost—that our country may yet be honoured and blest—let us labour to improve publick sentiment—to enlighten publick understanding—to exalt men of wisdom and virtue to power. Let it be our labour to improve the moral and religious character of our citizens. Let us remember that there is no foundation of publick liberty but public virtue—that there is no method of obtaining God's protection but adherence to his laws.

Finally, let us not despair of our country. I have in this discourse suggested many painful views—but the design is not to depress, but to rouse you to exertion. Despondence is unmanly, unchristian. If all that we wish cannot be done for our country, still something may be done. In the good principles, in the love of order and liberty, by which so many of our citizens are distinguished—in the tried virtue, the deliberate prudence, the unshaken firmness of the chief magistrate, whom God in his great goodness has given to this Commonwealth— in the uprightness of our cause—in the value of the blessings which are at stake—in the peculiar kindness which God has manifested towards our fathers and ourselves—we have motives, encouragements, and solemn obligations, to resolute, persevering exertion in our different spheres, and according to our different capacities, for the publick good. The times in which we are called to act are trying, but our duty is clear. Let us use with vigour every righteous method for promoting the peace, liberty and happiness of our nation—and having done this, let us leave the issue to the wise and holy providence of HIM who cannot err—and who, we are assured, will accept and reward every conscientious effort for his own glory and the good of mankind.

William Hull: Proclamation

July 13, 1812

William Hull, a distinguished veteran of the Revolutionary War and the governor of Michigan Territory since 1805, was nearly sixty years old and recovering from a stroke when, in February 1812, President Madison appointed him Brigadier General of the Army of the Northwest. In late spring of that year, the infirm Hull assembled in Ohio an army of regulars and militia, many of whom referred to him as "the Old Lady." Hull's marching orders, issued before the declaration of war, called for him to proceed to Fort Detroit, which he reached on July 5 with about two thousand troops. A week later he crossed the Detroit River into Upper Canada (present-day Ontario), seized the town of Sandwich (Windsor), and announced his intention to take Fort Amherstburg, which lay just to the south. Before attacking he issued the following proclamation, which, while prompting a few hundred Canadian militia to return to their homes or to seek protection within U.S. lines, also served to strengthen the resolve of Fort Amherstburg's defenders—325 regulars and 850 militia under the command of Lieutenant Colonel Thomas B. St. George, and about four hundred Indians under the leadership of Tecumseh.

By WILLIAM HULL, Brigadier General and Commander of the North Western Army of the United States

A PROCLAMATION

INHABITANTS OF CANADA! After thirty years of Peace and prosperity, the United States have been driven to Arms. The injuries and aggressions, the insults and indignities of Great Britain have *once more* left them no alternative but manly resistance or unconditional submission. The army under my Command has invaded your Country and the standard of the United States waves on the territory of Canada. To the peaceable unoffending inhabitant, It brings neither danger nor difficulty I come to *find* enemies not to *make* them, I come to *protect* not to *injure* you

Separated by an immense ocean and an extensive Wilderness from Great Britain you have no participation in her counsels, no interest in her conduct. You have felt her Tyranny, you have seen her injustice, but I do not ask *you* to avenge the one or to redress the other. The United States are sufficiently powerful to afford you every security consistent with their rights & your expectations. I tender you the invaluable blessings of Civil, Political, & Religious Liberty, and their necessary result, individual, and general, prosperity: That liberty which gave decision to our counsels and energy to our conduct in our struggle for INDEPENDENCE, and which conducted us safely and triumphantly thro' the stormy period of the Revolution. That Liberty which has raised us to an elevated rank among the Nations of the world and which has afforded us a greater measure of Peace & Security wealth and prosperity than ever fell to the Lot of any people.

In the name of my *Country* and by the authority of my Government I promise you protection to your *persons*, *property*, *and rights*. Remain at your homes, Pursue your customary and peaceful avocations. Raise not your hands against your bretheren, many of your fathers fought for the freedom & *Independence* we now enjoy Being children therefore of the same family with us, and heirs to the same Heritage, the arrival of an army of Friends must be hailed by you with a cordial welcome. You will be emancipated from Tyranny and oppression and restored to the dignified station of freemen. Had I any doubt of eventual success I might ask your assistance but I do not. I come prepared for every contingency. I have a force which will look down all opposition and that force is but the vanguard of a much greater. If contrary to your own interest & the just expectation of my country, you should take part in the approaching contest, you will be considered and treated as enemies and the horrors, and calamities of war will stalk before you.

If the barbarous and savage policy of Great Britain be pursued, and the savages are let loose to murder our citizens and butcher our women and children, this war, will be a war of extermination.

The first stroke with the Tomahawk the first attempt with

the scalping knife will be the signal for one indiscriminate scene of desolation. *No white man found fighting by the side of an Indian will be taken prisoner.* Instant destruction will be his Lot. If the dictates of reason, duty, justice, and humanity, cannot prevent the employment of a force, which respects no rights & knows no wrong, it will be prevented by a severe and relentless system of retaliation.

I doubt not your courage and firmness; I will not doubt your attachment to Liberty. If you tender your services voluntarily they will be accepted readily.

The United States offer you *Peace*, *Liberty*, and *Security* your choice lies between these, & *War, slavery, and destuction*. Choose then, but choose wisely; and may he who knows the justice of our cause, and who holds in his hand the fate of Nations, guide you to a result the most compatible, with your rights and interests, your peace and prosperity.

(signed)   Wm Hull

By the General
  A. F. Hull
    Captn. 13 U.S. Regt. of Infanty. & A.D.C
      Head Quarters at Sandwich
        13th July 1812

Isaac Brock: Proclamation

July 22, 1812

Hull dithered at Sandwich. He built carriages for cannons, tried to keep open his supply lines to Ohio, and squandered the element of surprise and the confidence of his men. Meanwhile Major General Isaac Brock, the president of Upper Canada and commander of the province's armed forces, moved quickly to answer Hull's "insidious proclamation," which he allowed "was having a considerable effect on the minds of the people." Brock, age forty-two, was everything Hull was not: youthful, prudent, inspiring, decisive. After issuing his counter-proclamation, Brock quickly amassed some three hundred troops and set sail from Long Point, on the north shore of Lake Erie, in a race to reinforce Fort Amherstburg before it was lost.

PROCLAMATION.

The unprovoked declaration of War, by the United States of America, against the United Kingdom, of Great Britain and Ireland, and its dependencies, has been followed by the actual invasion of this Province in a remote Frontier of the Western District by a detachment of the Armed Force of the United States. The Officer commanding that detachment has thought proper to invite his Majesty's Subjects not merely to a quiet and unresisting submission, but insults them with a call to seek voluntarily the protection of his Government. Without conde-scending to repeat the illiberal epithets bestowed in this appeal of the American Commander to the people of Upper Canada on the Administration of his Majesty, every Inhabitant of the Province is desired to seek the confutation of such indecent slander in the review of his own particular circumstances: Where is the Canadian Subject who can truly affirm to himself that he has been injured by the Government in his person, his liberty, or his property? Where is to be found in any part of the world, a growth so rapid in wealth and prosperity as this Colony exhibits,—Settled not 30 years by a band of Veterans exiled from their former possessions on account of their loyalty, not a descendant of these brave people is to be found, who under the fostering liberality of their Sovereign, has not acquired a property and means of enjoyment superior to what were possessed by their ancestors. This unequalled prosperity could not have been attained by the utmost liberality of the Government or the persevering industry of the people, had not the maritime power of the Mother Country secured to its Colonists a safe access to every market where the produce of their labor was in demand.

The unavoidable and immediate consequence of a seperation from Great Britain, must be the loss of this inestimable advantage, and what is offered you in exchange? to become a territory of the United States and share with them that exclusion from the Ocean, which the policy of their present Government enforces.—you are not even flattered with a participation of their boasted independence, and it is but too obvious that once exchanged from the powerful protection of the United Kingdom you must be reannexed to the dominion of France, from which the Provinces of Canada were wrested by the Arms of Great Britain, at a vast expense of blood and treasure, from no other motive than to *relieve* her ungrateful children from the oppression of a cruel neighbor: this restitution of Canada to the Empire of France was the stipulated reward for the aid afforded to the revolted Colonies, now the United States; the debt is still due, and there can be no doubt but the pledge has been renewed as a consideration for Commercial advantages, or rather for an expected relaxation in the Tyranny of France over the Commercial World.—Are you prepared Inhabitants of Upper Canada to become willing Subjects or rather Slaves, to the Despot who rules the Nations of Europe with a rod of Iron? If not, arise in a Body, exert your energies, co-operate cordially with the King's regular Forces to repel the invader, and do not give cause to your children when groaning under the oppression of a foreign Master to reproach you with having too easily parted with the richest Inheritance on Earth.—a participation in the name, character and freedom of Britons.

The same spirit of Justice, which will make every reasonable allowance for the unsuccessful efforts of Zeal and Loyalty, will

not fail to punish the defalcation of principle: every Canadian
Freeholder is by deliberate choice, bound by the most solemn
Oaths to defend the Monarchy as well as his own property; to
shrink from that engagement is a Treason not to be forgiven;
let no Man suppose that if in this unexpected struggle his
Majesties Arms should be compelled to yield to an overwhelming force, that the Province will be eventually abandoned; the
endeared relation of its first settlers, the intrinsic value of its
Commerce and the pretensions of its powerful rival to repossess the Canadas are pledges that no peace will be established
between the United States and Great Britain and Ireland, of
which the restoration of these Provinces does not make the
most prominent condition.

Be not dismayed at the unjustifiable threat of the Commander of the Enemies forces, to refuse quarter if an Indian
appear in the Ranks.—The brave bands of Natives which in-
habit this Colony, were, like his Majesty's Subjects, punished
for their zeal and fidelity by the loss of their possessions in the
late Colonies, and rewarded by his Majesty with lands of superior value in this Province: the Faith of the British Government
has never yet been violated, they feel that the soil they inherit
is to them and their posterity protected from the base Arts so
frequently devised to overreach their simplicity. By what new
principle are they to be prevented from defending their property? If their Warfare from being different from that of the
white people is more terrific to the Enemy, let him retrace his
steps—they seek him not—and cannot expect to find women
and children in an invading Army; but they are men, and have
equal rights with all other men to defend themselves and their
property when invaded, more especially when they find in
the enemies Camp a ferocious and mortal foe using the same
Warfare which the American Commander affects to reprobate.

This inconsistent and unjustifiable threat of refusing quarter
for such a cause as being found in Arms with a brother-sufferer
in defence of invaded rights, must be exercised with the certain
assurance of retaliation, not only in the limited operations of
War in this part of the King's Dominions but in every quarter
of the globe, for the National character of Britain is not less
distinguished for humanity than strict retributive justice, which
will consider the execution of this inhuman threat as deliberate

Murder, for which every subject of the offending power must make expiation.

Isaac Brock. Maj. Gen. and President.

God Save the King.

Head Quarters Fort George, 22nd July 1812.
By order of His Honor the President,
J.B. Glegg, Capt. A.D.C.

Thomas Verchères de Boucherville: Journal

July–August 1812

While Hull prepared for battle, the British and Indians plotted, together and separately, to deal strategic blows to American numbers and morale, especially along the supply lines in Michigan Territory. They found a game accomplice in Thomas Verchères de Boucherville, a young French Canadian fur trader and general merchant in the town of Amherstburg, who joined Tecumseh and Adam Muir, captain of the 41st Regiment of Foot, in guerrilla strikes at Brownstown and Maguaga (Monguagon). Boucherville vividly recorded his adventures in a journal, written in French, and first published in Montreal in 1901.

One day in July a band of Indians composed of Shawnees with Tecumseh at their head, besides some Ottawas and Potawatomi came to my store—I have always enjoyed the confidence of these children of the forest—and asked me if I would go with them to Petite Côte, three miles beyond our picket at River Canard, to deliver a blow at the enemy. I could not refuse, since in that case I would have sunk very low in their estimation, so I answered that I would gladly go with them. Accordingly, I made my preparations, not exactly those for a ball, but rather to try to exchange some English for American balls. I dressed lightly, the better to make my escape if necessary, for the moment the Indians believe themselves vanquished they take to their heels and run like rabbits; then with my musket, powder and balls, I joined the others and we all marched off. There were about a hundred and fifty warriors, with myself the only white man among them. On reaching Petite Côte we arranged ourselves according to the Indian fashion on either side of the road, hidden among high stalks of corn so as not to be seen, and waited thus in ambush for the American cavalry, which, the Indians said, usually came in the afternoon to drill just beyond reach of our fieldpieces which, as

I have mentioned, guarded the bridge. About three o'clock several fine squadrons approached. They were soon opposite the field where we were hidden, when suddenly from both sides came a furious discharge of musketry accompanied with arrow flights, which felled a large number of these men on their handsome mounts. Those who were not slain on the field begged for mercy but the Indians are absolutely deaf to all such entreaties, demanding nothing less than the death of their enemy. What a carnage followed! Those with the slightest chance to escape tried to do so, some successfully, others less fortunate. One poor horseman who had received only a slight wound which, however, prevented him from keeping his saddle, threw himself from a bridge into the river, hoping thus to elude his terrible adversaries. It was in vain; swift as winged steeds the warriors pursued, avid for blood. As the wounded horseman jumped into the water a young Shawnee brave leaped upon him and killed him with a single blow of his tomahawk. After a couple of hours the warriors returned from hunting the fugitives, having slain several of them. For the first time in my life I had taken part in a frightful carnage. I was filled with a horror of the war. Yet I must admit that the heart soon becomes hardened when these bloody scenes are repeated; this I learned when I engaged in similar excursions later on.

On Tuesday evening, August 7th, a vigorous alarm was sounded, the drummer who patrolled the streets beating the call to arms. I was at dinner with the gentlemen who were staying with me, and I hurried out to ask the drummer what he meant by his racket. His name was Molesworth, of the Forty-first Regiment. He replied that Major Muir was about to cross the river to Brownstown with several companies of soldiers and a large number of Indians to intercept the Americans coming from River Raisin to Detroit with provisions for their army; he needed all the loyal subjects of the King who would join him, and all were welcome. I deliberated a little and resolved to join the expedition. Hurrying back to the diningroom I informed my clerks of my decision, as also Messrs. Lacroix and Berthelet. Unknown to anyone I then went out to bury at the corner of my house two full gallons of coins, doubloons, guineas, and piasters. This I did without the knowledge of a single soul, indiscreet as it was should I receive a mortal wound. Without further hesitation, and forgetful of all else but the expedition, I set out for the Shipyard, the place fixed for its departure, and placed myself under the command of Major Muir as a volunteer. I met Tecumseh there, at the head of the Indian bands. Truly it was a beautiful spectacle to see so many boats and nearly three hundred canoes assembled together. The aborigines rent the air with their war whoops. Other volunteers joining Major Muir were Alexis Maisonville, Jean Baptiste Barthe, James Eberts, the two Cadotte brothers, and Alexis Bouthilier, a native of Longueuil; also Mr. Jean Baptiste Baby, accompanied by Richardson of Amherstburg of the regular army. The officers of the Forty-first Regiment whom I knew were Major Muir, Captain Tallan, Lieutenants Clemow, Bender, and Sutherland, and Dr. Faulkner. Undoubtedly there were others, but I do not remember any more.

Setting out about three o'clock in the afternoon, it was a little after four when we disembarked on the other side of the river at the place best suited for our operations. The first thing done was to construct a long cabin of branches to shelter us from bad weather. All the next day we lay expecting the enemy but they gave no sign of life for they had been warned by spies that a strong party of British and Indians were in waiting at Brownstown. I cannot conceive how these despicable beings had managed to come near enough to be able to report that we were there to dispute the way, seeing that we had immediately stationed Indians in the woods as a patrol.

We had strict orders not to light any fire during the night lest we attract the attention of the Americans. It was very damp, being in the neighborhood of the lake and surrounded by marshes, and we suffered from the cold, the more so as we had not yet received any blankets nor even provisions. The empty stomachs of the soldiers were crying aloud with hunger.

————

We had been preceded on the evening of our arrival at Brownstown by a band of Shawnees and Ottawas who had been sent by Superintendent Elliott to reconnoiter the American position at River Raisin. They told us that they had seen wagons loaded with provisions for Hull's army at Detroit, which was in need of stores of all kinds. Pressed by hunger, Hull that same day sent a body of cavalry to meet the reinforcement that was coming to him and of which he stood in such need, but it had been attacked by our Indians that afternoon between Brownstown and Monguagon. According to their custom they formed an ambush on each side of the road which Hull had opened for the passage of his army through the dense forest and the American troops fell into the trap. Arrows and musket balls rained upon them from every side, sowing death and creating a panic in the ranks easy to understand. All who had not already bitten the dust fled galloping away to escape being taken by their ferocious enemy. A young Shawnee named Blue Jacket, who was very agile and courageous, rushed upon one of the American cavalrymen, and leaping up behind him, with his right hand killed the American with his tomahawk in the very instant the latter was about to run him through with his sword. Another American who had witnessed this struggle between his friend and the young warrior turned back and attacked poor Blue Jacket, who, exhausted by his exertions, was overcome and slain. The carnage which the Indians perpetrated in this encounter was horrible. They scalped everyone they could overtake and placed these trophies of their bravery on long poles which they stuck up in the ground by the roadside. They also drove long stakes through the bodies of the slain which were left lying thus exposed. It was a hideous sight to see and little calculated to encourage the enemy when passing by it on the way to Detroit.

As soon as we reached Brownstown we saw that this band of savages had met the enemy. There, on the bare ground, lay stretched a poor young Virginian, the body covered with blood from two deep gashes with a knife. Needless to say, it, too, was scalped. A moment later another young man radiant with life was brought to us, who had been captured by the Potawatomi. The chief of the tribe, a perfect savage and avid for human blood, at once summoned several old squaws who were in the habit of following the warriors to take care of their camps, and ordered them to kill his captive in our presence. Major Muir was at hand with several companies of the Forty-first Regiment and they interposed, seeking by every possible means to redeem the unfortunate prisoner who awaited such a terrible fate. After a lengthy parley with this demon thirsting for human blood he finally consented not to slay the poor fellow on our promise that when we returned to English territory he would be given a barrel of rum and outfits of clothing for all his family.

While we were thus treating for the redemption of the prisoner, and even as the affair was being concluded in the interests of humanity, piercing shrieks resounded from the depths of the forest. It was the death cry of some of the savages who had defeated the American cavalry in the afternoon. A funeral convoy then appeared before our eyes. Four members of the tribe of Blue Jacket carried his body on their shoulders and the procession was now in our midst. I knew at once that all was over for our young American, and that nothing in the world could save him from a cruel death. They deposited the body of Blue Jacket at the feet of the prisoner. The blow of the cavalryman had almost severed the head, and as though for the first time the young man comprehended the sad fate that awaited him. He became pale as death, and looking round at us all in turn, in a low voice and with an expression torn by anxiety, asked if it were possible the English allowed such acts of barbarity. The shrieks of the savages drowned whatever response was made, though it seemed to be one of sympathy.

The chief had already raised the hatchet over his head, entirely oblivious of the arrangement for ransom consummated between Major Muir and himself, and with ferocious and bloodshot eyes regarded his prey. The old squaws drew near and at a signal from this tiger, for he was one really, one of them plunged her butcher knife into the neck of her victim, while another stabbed him in the side. The young soldier staggered and was about to fall when the chief laid him at his feet with a powerful blow of the tomahawk.

Spectators of this disgusting scene, we all stood around overcome by an acute sense of shame! We felt implicated in some way in this murder, for murder it was and of the most atrocious kind! And yet under the circumstances what could we do? The life of that man undoubtedly belonged to the inhuman chief. The government had desperate need of these Indian allies. Our garrison was weak and these warriors were numerous enough to impose their will upon us. If we were to rebuke them in this crisis and compel them to observe our manner of warfare, in place of leaving them to their own barbarous practices, they would withdraw from the conflict and retire to their own country on the Missouri whence they had come to join us.

———

Before we left Brownstown Major Muir had sent a canoe to notify Colonel Procter of the approaching engagement and to ask him to send over a company of soldiers without delay for our relief in case of need.

Arrived at Monguagon and stationed in the ravine awaiting the enemy, our men had a brief rest. I found that I had on my left my good friend, Mr. Jean Baptiste Baby, and I asked him for a pinch of snuff to keep me in countenance a little. An instant later and we could easily hear the American drummer who seemed to beat with less assurance as he approached the ravine where we lay flat on our bellies, as though he feared something of the kind. The enemy formed a square to receive us on all four sides. Still hidden, we awaited the signal to charge. Scarcely a moment elapsed when a brilliant officer mounted on a superb steed appeared on an eminence. His hat was crowned with plumes fully three feet in length. But his inspection was of brief duration for on the instant a bullet struck him and he fell dead at his horse's feet. Firing now began on our left, the Indians in the cornfield being nearest to the approaching enemy. They quickly advanced upon us, and the engagement became general. For fifty minutes the firing was terrible. Fortunately the balls and grapeshot of our adversaries lodged in the treetops, in place of striking our ranks. At the appointed moment, with the two ranks face to face, Major Muir ordered the bugler at his side to sound the bayonet charge. Just then the company of grenadiers of the 41st commanded by Captain Bullard, which General Procter had sent to reinforce us, came up. We were not at all sorry to see them for things were getting decidedly hot for us. At this moment an officer of the regiment stationed on my left, shouted to me, "Take care de Boucherville! The Kentuckians are aiming at you!" But he himself received the bullet in his head and fell over into my arms. "Well, old fellow!" I said to myself, "You came out of that all right!" I was not yet safe, however, for an instant later I was wounded in my turn.

The grenadiers, who had been sent by the General to reinforce us, were stationed in the center. The signal which Major Muir was to give for the charge had not been explained to them, and thinking it was an order to retreat, they turned to the rear without firing a single shot. The fusillade on both sides was very heavy. There was not the slightest breeze and the smoke became so dense we could not see twenty paces before us. Finally, we were obliged to draw back because of the unexpected and groundless retreat of the grenadiers and that, too, at the very moment of victory, for the enemy's center had broken. Only the two wings of their army were composed of regular soldiers, and these were wavering because of the great number of killed and wounded. Thus the grenadier company, in place of helping us, succeeded only in throwing our ranks into disorder and was the sole cause of our defeat. This is painful to say, yet it is the simple truth.

Our troops defiled at a quick step and as they retreated fired their guns behind them, thus exposing the wounded in the rear of the army to death. Among those exposed to this irregular fire were a Mr. Berthe, another soldier, and myself. There had been many others but they were on ahead. We dove into the woods to escape the shower of bullets which poured upon us from both sides, for the enemy were in close pursuit of our men. Out of sight at last, we hid under the trunk of a big tree which had fallen into the water of the surrounding cedar swamp.

Our soldiers returned to Brownstown and rushed into the boats for Amherstburg which were under the command of Lieutenant Bender. Tecumseh and his Indians crossed the river in their canoes. It is well to mention here that our forces in the moment of action did not exceed two hundred regulars, about fifteen Canadian volunteers, and two hundred Indians, while those of our adversary, commanded by Colonel Miller, were two thousand five hundred strong, according to their own report of the engagement.

The Americans spent the night on the field of battle, carrying off and burying their dead, that the number of casualties might not be known. I can speak truthfully of this for I passed the night with my companions only a few hundred feet from them. The Kentuckians, who seemed to be stationed as sentinels, were often almost upon us but fortunately we were not discovered. At last, in spite of the inky darkness, we ventured to leave this amphibian retreat, seeking, if possible, a more comfortable shelter. About ten in the evening the rain began to fall in torrents and we were soaked to the bone. The thunder growled incessantly over our heads but luckily the lightning served to guide us. We suffered cruelly from hunger and seemed to be getting weaker. At last we came upon a slight elevation in the cedar swamp, which, although almost surrounded by water, was relatively dry and at least out of sight of the enemy.

I treated my wound as well as I could, for it was bleeding some though quite painless, by applying a little earth after the manner of the Indians, then tied it up with a towel which I had taken the precaution to bring with me in case of accident. We passed the remainder of the night here in this sad plight, for the rain lasted until dawn, and it was followed by a gale so violent that the limbs of the trees fell all around us. We were in quite as much danger, if not more, than in the battle of the preceding afternoon, but a divine providence came to our aid and saved us alike from strife and storm, both equally murderous. All that awful night we were beset with mosquitoes, who made war upon us in their own fashion. The soldier with us, tired and hungry, had slept with his mouth open and wakened only when it was too full of these hateful insects for further sleep, to spit them all out.

At daybreak I told Mr. Berthe that we must leave our hiding place and try to reach the river, which could not be far away. After a prayer to God to lead us safely into harbor I struck out with my two companions. All three of us had muskets. About four in the afternoon we reached the bank of the Detroit River and decided to make our way to Brownstown, being careful not to fall into the hands of the enemy, who might easily have taken up their quarters in that place. Not a soul was in sight, but we were not yet out of our difficulties. To get to Amherstburg we must have a boat, and where could we find one here? Without boat or canoe, what could we do? Suddenly it occurred to me to search the ruins where we had taken refuge, the former habitation of an old Huron chief who had gone to Canada at the breaking out of hostilities, for some boards and strands of basswood which the Hurons usually kept on hand in these wigwams. Providence had indeed come to our aid for there was an abundance of both, as well as some dry planks.

We built a raft, then without waiting to consider the risk of our undertaking, we decided to cross the river as far as a certain island about two and a half miles distant. We reached it, though not without considerable danger. More and more we were yielding to fatigue, but we hastily crossed the island under cover of its deep verdure so as to get in sight of Amherstburg and if possible signal for help. On the shore lay a quantity of bark, left there in the spring by the Indians, and the soldier, overcome by fatigue and hunger, threw himself down on a pile to rest. Immediately several rattlesnakes crawled out from beneath it, scaring him so that he jumped into the water and would not come out but stood there waiting for someone to come to his rescue. Mr. Berthe and I wiped out our muskets and fired several shots to attract attention. We also made flags of our shirts on the ends of long poles and used these for a signal. Soon a boat manned by some Hurons came out in our direction but hesitated, as though fearing a ruse on the part of the Americans. In midstream it stopped as though uncertain what to do. We were anything but encouraged. A moment afterward a medium-sized canoe filled with Sauteau started out directly toward us. Never have I seen one man so glad to see another as the Indian in command of the boat was to see me. He said nothing to my companions, scarcely recognizing them, in fact, in accord with Indian etiquette.

Without loss of time we took our places in this light craft. There were seven of us and I really experienced more fear in that crossing than in that from the American side to Isle St. Laurence, which we had just left. Arrived at Amherstburg, from all sides came my friends, officers, civilians, and natives, to congratulate me on my safe return. They all thought they would never see me again, since some Indians had reported that they had seen me in the battle covered with blood and with a dead soldier at my side. In fact there had been one, the young officer who had so coolly called out "De Boucherville, take care. The Kentuckians are aiming at you!" After I had thanked all who had come down to the shore to greet me, we separated to go to our respective homes.

Entering mine, the first thing I did was to throw myself on a sofa to rest. At once I fell into a sleep as deep as though I had taken a strong dose of opium. In the meantime many visitors called to inquire after my health, among others Tecumseh and the officers of the 41st, who remained for my wakening to enter into conversation with me. It was five in the afternoon before I roused from my long sleep to find myself in a goodly company. How comforting were my sensations at this moment! In the first place I had joined the army of His Majesty my King as a volunteer from a sense of duty. I had played the part of a good soldier and had shed my blood as the loyal Canadian I was. In fact I can but admit that deep in my inmost soul there was a feeling of pride.

My wound was troubling me somewhat at this time. The earth I had applied naturally caused an inflammation. Next day the surgeon extracted the ball but he could not do the same for the shot scattered in my left thigh, which still bothers me, especially in damp weather. The good Tecumseh brought me an Indian doctor who was a recognized healer among the Shawnee and who used nothing but herbs. This man assured me that the wound would soon heal if I bathed it with what he would give me and nothing else, and that he would guarantee that in a few days I would again be fit to serve my King and Country. I consulted with Dr. Faulkner of the regiment and with Dr. Richardson, my regular physician, and both agreed that there was no harm in the treatment. My Indian doctor therefore returned the next day and started in with his herbs. Ten days later the wound was healed and I was able to resume my duties.

Nathan Heald to Thomas H. Cushing

By the summer of 1812, Captain Nathan Heald, age thirty-six, had commanded Fort Dearborn, on the Chicago River, for more than two years. On August 9 he received orders from General Hull to evacuate immediately and remove his garrison to Detroit, since Fort Mackinac, the island outpost where Lake Huron meets Lake Michigan, had fallen to the British on July 17, leaving Fort Dearborn exposed to attack. Heald detailed the disastrous consequences of executing Hull's orders in this, his official report to the adjutant general of the U.S. Army.

———————————

PITTSBURG, October 23d, 1812.

SIR: I embrace this opportunity to render you an account of the garrison of Chicago.

On the 9th of August last, I received orders from General Hull to evacuate the post and proceed with my command to Detroit, by land, leaving it at my discretion to dispose of the public property as I thought proper. The neighboring Indians got the information as early as I did, and came in from all quarters in order to receive the goods in the factory store, which they understood were to be given them. On the 13th, Captain Wells, of Fort Wayne, arrived with about 30 Miamies, for the purpose of escorting us in, by the request of General Hull. On the 14th, I delivered the Indians all the goods in the factory store, and a considerable quantity of provisions which we could not take away with us. The surplus arms and ammunition I thought proper to destroy, fearing they would make bad use of it if put in their possession. I also destroyed all the liquor on hand after they began to collect. The collection was unusually large for that place; but they conducted themselves with the strictest propriety till after I left the fort. On the 15th, at 9 o'clock in the morning, we commenced our march: a part of the Miamies were detached in front, and the remainder in our rear, as guards, under the direction of Captain Wells. The situation of the country rendered it necessary for us to take the beach, with the lake on our left, and a high sand bank on our right, at about 100 yards distance.

We had proceeded about a mile and a half, when it was discovered that the Indians were prepared to attack us from behind the bank. I immediately marched up with the company to the top of the bank, when the action commenced; after firing one round, we charged, and the Indians gave way in front and joined those on our flanks. In about fifteen minutes they got possession of all our horses, provisions, and baggage of every description, and finding the Miamies did not assist us, I drew off the few men I had left, and took possession of a small elevation in the open prarie, out of shot of the bank or any other cover. The Indians did not follow me, but assembled in a body on the top of the bank, and after some consultations among themselves, made signs for me to approach them. I advanced towards them alone, and was met by one of the Potawatamie chiefs, called the Black Bird, with an interpreter. After shaking hands, he requested me to surrender, promising to spare the lives of all the prisoners. On a few moments consideration, I concluded it would be most prudent to comply with his request, although I did not put entire confidence in his promise. After delivering up our arms, we were taken back to their encampment near the fort, and distributed among the different tribes. The next morning, they set fire to the fort and left the place, taking the prisoners with them. Their number of warriors was between four and five hundred, mostly of the Potawatamie nation, and their loss, from the best information I could get, was about fifteen. Our strength was fifty-four regulars and twelve militia, out of which, twenty-six regulars and all the militia were killed in the action, with two women and twelve children. Ensign George Ronan and doctor Isaac V Van Voorhis of my company, with Captain Wells, of Fort Wayne, are, to my great sorrow, numbered among the dead. Lieutenant Lina T. Helm, with twenty-five noncommissioned officers and privates, and eleven women and children, were prisoners when we were separated. Mrs. Heald and myself were taken to the mouth of the river St. Joseph, and being both badly wounded, were permitted to reside with Mr. Burnet, an Indian trader. In a few days after our arrival there, the Indians all went off to take Fort Wayne, and in their absence, I engaged a Frenchman to take us to Michilimackinac by water, where I gave myself up as a prisoner of war, with one of my sergeants. The commanding officer, Captain Roberts, offered me every assistance in his power to render our situation comfortable while we remained there, and to enable us to proceed on our journey. To him I gave my parole of Honour, and came on to Detroit and reported myself to Colonel Proctor, who gave us a passage to Buffaloe; from that place I came by way of Presque Isle, and arrived here yesterday.

I have the honor to be yours, &c.,

N. HEALD,
Captain U.S. Infantry.

THOMAS H. CUSHING, ESQR.,
Adjutant General.

Caleb Strong to William Eustis

On July 21, 1812, Secretary of War William Eustis wrote to Caleb Strong, the governor of Massachusetts, regarding the commonwealth's desultory war preparations. Eustis complained that "a detachment from the militia of Massachusetts for defence of the maritime frontier" —forces deemed necessary to the strategy of Major General Henry Dearborn, commander of the northeast sector of the U.S. Army— "have not been marched to the several stations assigned them." Eustis implied that Strong had ignored the President's order of the previous spring that each state prepare militia for service. He concluded by warning the governor that longer delay might be followed with "injurious consequences to our country. . . . The danger of invasion, which existed at the time of issuing the order of the president, increases, and I am specially directed by the president to urge this consideration to your excellency, as requiring the necessary order be given for the immediate march of the several detachments . . . to their respective posts." Strong's reply was civil yet firm.

BOSTON, *August 5*, 1812.

SIR:

I received your letter of the 21st July, when at Northampton, and the next day came to Boston. The people of this State appear to be under no apprehension of an invasion; several towns, indeed, on the sea coast, soon after the declaration of war, applied to the Governor and Council for arms and ammunition, similar to the articles of that kind which had been delivered to them by the State, in the course of the last war; and, in some instances, they were supplied accordingly. But they expressed no desire that any part of the militia should be called out for their defence, and, in some cases, we were assured such a measure would be disagreeable to them.

You observe, in your last letter, that the danger of invasion which existed at the time of issuing the order of the President, increases. It would be difficult to infer, from this expression, that, in your opinion, that danger is now very considerable, as the President's order must have been issued before war was declared, your former letter being dated the 12th of June, and General Dearborn's, who was then at Boston, on the 22d of that month; besides, it can hardly be supposed that, if this State had been in great danger of invasion, the troops would have been called from hence to carry on offensive operations in a distant Province. However, as it was understood that the Governor of Nova Scotia had, by proclamation, forbid any incursions or depredations upon our territories, and as an opinion generally prevailed that the Governor had no authority to call the militia into actual service, unless one of the exigencies contemplated by the constitution exists, I thought it expedient to call the Council together, and, having laid before them your letter, and those I had received from General Dearborn, I requested their advice on the subject of them.

The Council advised, "that they are unable, from a view of the constitution of the United States, and the letters aforesaid, to perceive that any exigency exists, which can render it advisable to comply with the said requisition. But as, upon important questions of law, and upon solemn occasions, the Governor and Council have authority to require the opinion of the Justices of the Supreme Judicial Court, it is advisable to request the opinion of the Supreme Court, upon the following questions:

1st. Whether the commanders in chief of the militia of the several States have a right to determine whether any of the exigencies contemplated by the constitution of the United States exist, so as to require them to place the militia, or any part of it, in the service of the United States, at the request of the President, to be commanded by him, pursuant to acts of Congress?

2d. Whether, when either of the exigencies exist, authorizing the employing of the militia in the service of the United States, the militia thus employed can be lawfully commanded by any officer but of the militia, except by the President of the United States?"

I enclose a copy of the answers given by the judges to these questions. Since the Council were called, a person deputed by the towns of Eastport and Robinston, on our Eastern boundary, at Passamaquoddy, applied to me, representing that they had no apprehensions of invasion by an authorized British force, but that there were many lawless people on the borders from whom they were in danger of predatory incursions, and requesting that they might be furnished with some arms and ammunition, and that three companies of militia might be called out for their protection. The Council advised that they should be supplied with such arms and ammunition as were necessary for their present defence, which has been ordered. They also advised me to call into the service of the United States three companies of the detached militia, for the purposes above mentioned. I have this day issued an order for calling out three companies of the detached militia, to be marched, forthwith, to Passamaquoddy, and to be commanded by a major. Two of the companies will be stationed at Eastport, and one company at Robinston, until the President shall otherwise direct.

I have no intention officiously to interfere in the measures of the General Government, but if the President was fully acquainted with the situation of this State, I think he would have no wish to call our militia into service in the manner proposed by General Dearborn.

It is well known that the enemy will find it difficult to spare troops sufficient for the defence of their own territory, and predatory incursions are not likely to take place in this State: for, at every point, except Passamaquoddy, which can present no object to those incursions, the people are too numerous to be attacked by such parties as generally engage in expeditions of that kind.

General Dearborn proposed that the detached militia should be stationed at only a few of the ports and places on the coast; from the rest, a part of their militia were to be called away. This circumstance would increase their danger; it would invite the aggressions of the enemy, and diminish their power of resistance.

The whole coast of Cape Cod is exposed, as much as any part of the State, to depredations; part of the militia must, according to this detaching order, be marched from their homes; and yet, no place in the old colony of Plymouth is assigned to be the rendezvous of any of the detached militia.

Every harbor or port within the State has a compact settlement, and, generally, the country around the harbors is populous. The places contemplated in General Dearborn's specification, as the rendezvous of the detached militia, excepting in one or two instances, contain more of the militia than the portion of the detached militia assigned to them. The militia are well organized, and would undoubtedly prefer to defend their firesides, in company with their friends, under their own officers, rather than to be marched to some distant place, while strangers might be introduced to take their places at home.

In Boston, the militia are well disciplined, and could be mustered in an hour upon any signal of an approaching enemy, and in six hours the neighboring towns would pour in a greater force than any invading enemy will bring against it.

The same remark applies to Salem, Marblehead, and Newburyport, places whose harbors render an invasion next to impossible. In all of them, there are, in addition to the common militia, independent corps of infantry and artillery, well disciplined and equipped, and ready, both in disposition and means, to repair to any place where invasion may be threatened, and able to repel it, except it should be made by a fleet of heavy ships, against which nothing perhaps but strong fortifications, garrisoned by regular troops, would prove any defence, until the enemy should land, when the entire militia would be prepared to meet them.

Kennebunk is unassailable by any thing but boats, which the numerous armed population is competent to resist. Portland has a militia, and independent corps, sufficiently numerous for its defence; and the same is the case with Wiscasset and Castine.

Against predatory incursions, the militia of each place would be able to defend their property, and, in a very short time, they would be aided, if necessary, by the militia of the surrounding country. In case of a more serious invasion, whole brigades or divisions could be collected, seasonably, for defence. Indeed, considering the state of the militia in this Commonwealth, I think there can be no doubt that, detaching a part of it, and distributing it into small portions, will tend to impair the defensive power.

I have thus freely expressed to you my own sentiments, and,

so far as I have heard, they are the sentiments of the best informed men. I am fully disposed to afford all the aid to the measures of the National Government which the constitution requires of me; but I presume it will not be expected, or desired, that I shall fail in the duty which I owe to the people of this State, who have confided their interests to my care.

I am, sir, with respect, your most obedient and humble servant,

CALEB STRONG.

Hon. W. EUSTIS, *Secretary of War.*

James Madison to Thomas Jefferson

In a letter to the President of August 5, 1812, Jefferson again stressed the necessity of America's conquering Canada and resuming free and unfettered trade with the world. "With Canada in hand," he wrote, "we can go to treaty with an off-set for spoliations before the war. Our farmers are cheerful in the expectation of a good price for wheat in autumn. Their pulse will be regulated by this, and not by the successes and disasters of the war. To keep open sufficient markets is the very first object towards maintaining the popularity of the war, which is as great at present as could be desired." Madison replied to this and to further letters from Jefferson with the following notes on the current campaign.

DEAR SIR   WASHINGTON Aug. 17. 1812

I have recd yours of the 10th. and return as you request, the letter of Mr. Higginbotham. He will probably have understood from Col: Monroe that the consulate of Lisbon is the object of numerous & respectable candidates.

The seditious opposition in Mass. & Cont. with the intrigues elsewhere insidiously co-operating with it, have so clogged the wheels of the war, that I fear the campaign will not accomplish the object of it. With the most united efforts, in stimulating volunteers, they would have probably fallen much short of the number required by the deficiency of regular enlistments. But under the discouragements substituted and the little attraction contained in the volunteer act, the two classes together, leave us dependent, for every primary operation, on militia, either as volunteers or draughts for six months. We are nevertheless doing as well as we can, in securing the maritime frontier, and in providing for an effective penetration into Upper Canada. It would probably have been best if it had been practicable in time, to have concentrated a force which could have seized on Montreal & then at one stroke, have secured the upper Province, and cut off the sap that nourished Indian hostilities. But

this could not be attempted, without sacrificing the western &
N. W. Frontier, threated with an inundation of savages under
the influence of the British establishment near Detroit. Another reason for the expedition of Hull was that the unanimity
and ardor of Kentucky & Ohio, provided the requisite force at
once for that service, whilst it was too distant from the other
points to be assailed. We just learn, but from what cause remains to be known, that the important fort at Machilimackinac
has fallen into the hands of the Enemy. If the re-inforcement
of about 2000 ordered from the Ohio, and on the way to
Hull, should not enable him to take Malden, and awe the Savages emboldened by the British success, his situation will be
very ineligible. It is hoped that he will either be strong eno', as
he has cannon & mortars, to reduce that Fort, or to have a
force that will justify him in passing on towards the other end
of Lake Erie, and place the British troops there, between him,
and those embodied under arrangements of Dearborn &
Tomkins at Niagara, for the purpose of occupying the central
part of Upper Canada. In the mean time the preparations agst.
Montreal are going on, and perhaps may furnish a feint towards it, that may conspire with the other plan. I find that
Kingston at the East End of L. Ontario is an object with Genl.
D. The multiplication of these offensive measures have grown
out of the defensive precautions for the Frontier of N. York.

We have no information from England since the war was
known there, or even, seriously suspected, by the public. I
think it not improbable that the sudden change in relation to
the orders in Council, first in yielding to a qualified suspension, & then a repeal, was the effect of apprehensions in the
Cabinet that the deliberations of Cong: would have that issue,
and that the Ministry could not stand agst. the popular torrent
agst. the orders in Council, swelled as it would be by the addition
of a war with the U. S. to the pressure of the non-importation
act. What course will be taken, when the declaration here shall
be known, is uncertain, both in reference to the American
shipments instituted under the repeal of the Orders, and to the
question between vindictive efforts for pushing the war agst.
us, and early advances for terminating it. A very informal, & as
it has turned out erronious communication of the intended
change in the Orders, was hurried over, evidently with a view

to prevent a declaration of war, if it should arrive in time. And the communication was accompanied by a proposal from the *local* authorities at Halifax sanctioned by Foster, to suspend hostilities both at sea & on land. The late message of Prevost to Dearborn, noticed in the newspapers has this for its object. The insuperable objections to a concurrence of the Executive in the project are obvious. Without alluding to others, drawn from a limited authority, & from the effect on patriotic ardor, the advantage over us in captures, wd. be past, before it could take effect. As we do not apprehend invasion by land, and preparations on each side were to be unrestrained, nothing could be gained by us, whilst arrangements & reinforcements adverse to Hull, might be decisive; and on every supposition, the Indians wd continue to be active agst. our frontiers, the more so in consequence of the fall of Machilimackinac. Nothing but triumphant operations on the Theatre which forms their connection with the Enemy, will controul their bloody inroads.

I have been indulging hopes of getting away from this place, in the course of this present week. It is quite possible however that my stay here may be indispensible. As yet I have less of bilious sensations than I could have expected.

Your two letters to Kosciuzco have been duly attended to. Affectionately yours

JAMES MADISON

Robert Lucas: Journal

The loss of Fort Mackinac, William Hull reported to the War Department, had "opened the Northern hive of Indians," which he imagined "swarming down in every direction." After several Indian raids on his supply lines left him dreading a similar ambush at Sandwich, he retreated to Fort Detroit, a decision that caused near-mutiny among his officers. On August 13, the commander of Upper Canada's forces, Isaac Brock, arrived at Fort Amherstburg and, upon conferring with Tecumseh, concluded that now was the moment to attack the enfeebled "Old Lady." On the 15th he sent Hull a summons to surrender: "It is far from my intention to join in a war of extermination," Brock wrote, "but you must be aware that the numerous body of Indians who have attached themselves to my troops will be beyond controul the moment the contest commences." Hull fretted but stood his ground, and Brock and Tecumseh readied their troops to attack at sunrise. Robert Lucas, a thirty-year-old volunteer from Ohio, was with Hull the morning the siege began.

16th This morning about daybrak the British renewed ther fire upon the fourt, and it was returned from our Battery. The roaring of the cannon was tremendious but there was but little injury done, one Shot axidentally killed a man, in the plain, and two by axident being nearly Spent fell within the garrison, one of which killed Ensign Sibly and a Soldier from Mackinaw and the other killed Lieut. Hanks Doctor Reynolds Surgeonmate to Colo Cass Rgt from Zanesville and Wounded Doctor Blood Surgeon mate in the 4th U S Rgt The ball took of intirely one of Doctr Reynolds legs, and the other partly of he Died in about a half an hour after, (he was Said to utter the following words about the time he expired) "fight on my brave comrade. I shall nevr see Zanesville I die in peace"—Peace be to his manes—but his comrades was prevented from fighting, by their commander—for the fort was Surrendered about 8 oclock, the Gnl Capitulatd—at the time the Gnl raised a flag of truce on the walls of the garrison, the 4th Regt and a small part of Colo McArthurs was in the fort, Colo Finleys Rgt was posted on the North of the plain back of the fort. And Major Denny with part of Colos. McArthurs and Casses Regts along Some Pickets South of the plain, a Part of the Michigan Militia in the upper part of the town and a part in the plain; 2–24 pounders loaded with grate shot and Musket balls placed on a Commanding eminence, below the town, and indeed our whole force was placed in a situation that the enemis flank and front must have been exposed let them make an attack upon what part they would,—Every man was waiting with anxiety the approach of the enemy and expected a proud day for his Countary, at the Same time Colos. Cass and McArthur was within a few miles and would have fell upon the enemies rear, (altho not known to us at that time) our army thus placed, I was on the back wall of the garrison viewing the movements of Some Indians that made their appearance in the plain and was catching som horses, and was just decending the wall with a view of joining colo Finleys flank to meet them when I was Called to by Some of my acquaintanc, and informed that a white flag had been raised upon the wall, I was struck with estonishmnt and returned to enquire the caus I was informed that Gnl Hull had ordered our Coulors to be struck and that it was opposed by Colo Miller, but that he had Sent out a flag of truce to the British to capitulate, and had ordered the whole of the troops into the garrison to stack their Arms The British at this time was marching up the Detroit river by Colums of platons twelve men in front and when the head of their colum had arived within about 5 hundred yards of our line, when a Single Discharge from the 24 poundr must have dispersed them, orders were received from Gnl Hull for all to retreat to the fort and not to fire upon the Enmy one universal burst of indignation was apparent upon the receipt of these orders, our troops was immediately crowded into the fort, and two British officers rode up to the Gnls marke they remained there a short time and retired,—I made inquiry of the caus and what was done I Soon ascertained that the Gnl had Capitulated and had Surrendered the whole army as Prisoners of War. In entering into this capitulation the Gnl only consulted his own feelings, not an officer was consulted, not one antisipated a Surrender

till they Saw the white flag displayed upon the walls. Even the
women was indignant at the Shameful degradation of the
Americ character, and all felt as they should have felt but he who
held in his hands the reins of authority our mornings report
from informati was effectiv men fit for duty 1060, exclusive of
300 Michigan militia on duty,—The whole force of the enemy
both white red and Black was from the best information we
could gain about 1030. They had 29 plattoons twelve in a plat-
toon of men in Uniform, a number of them must have been
Canadian militia,—after enquiring into the principles of the
capitulation, I assertained that all the U. S troops was to be
Sent to Quebeck, and being apprehensive that Gnl Hull would
wish to have me Sent with them, I thought it prudent to leave
the garrison previous to the British taking possession I therefore placed my Sword and uniform clothes in my brother
(Capt J Lucas) Trunk threw my musket and cartridge box
against the wall and left the fort, I went down in the town of
Detroit and passed in the capacity of a citizen, and paid a particular attention to the Proceedings. The British first placed a
peace of Artillery in front of Gnl Hulls Door one at each of
our Battery and placed guards to command the defiles round
the fort previus to our troops being marched out of the fort.
Their order of march into the fort was the Regulars and those
in Uniform in front, the Militia not in Uniform next a Company with handkerchefs round their heads and painted like
Indians next and the Indians in the rear Commanded by British officers Dressed and painted like Indians. The Indians was
not Suffered to go into the fort, I Stood at the corner of the
street and Saw them pass me in this order, with indignant feelings, but when our troops was marched out our Coulors
Struck and the British Coulors hoisted in their Stead, my feelings was affected beyond expression, My God who could bear
the sight without vowing eternal vengeanc against the perpetrators of Such Diabolical acts, and against the Nation that
would employ such Detestable Savage allies. To See our Coulors prostitute to See and hear the firing from our own battery
and the huzzaws of the British troops the yells of the Savages
and the Discharge of small arms, as Signals of joy over our
disgrace was scenes too horrid to meditate upon with any
other view than to Seek revenge—The Indians after the British

had got peaceable possession of the fort, gave themselves up to
plunder they took and bore away at will, horses and Such other
property as fell in their way, they robbed and plundred the
hous of Mr Atwater the Acting Governor and Capt Knaggs the
Indian interpreter of every thing they could find, (the Capitulation to the contrary notwithstanding) and many other attro-
cious acts,—I Saw Major Witherall of the Detroit Volunteers
Brake his Sword and throw it away and Sevral Soldiers broke
their muskets rather than Surrender them to the British—Soon
after the British had taken the fort, and made the arrangements
by placing gards at various places in the town I saw Gnl Hull
walking linked arms, with a British officer, from the fort to his
own hous, Possesing a more pleasing countenanc than I had
ever Seen him, and appeared to be very pleasingly engaged in
conversation with him—While in town I happened in company
with a British officer who was exulting at their conquest. I
could not refrain from telling him that the conquest he was
boasting of they had obtain through treachery, and that in
my opinion they would not maintain it long, as we could have
an army of 10,000 men there in a few months, he appeared to
make light of my observations—after he retired I was advised
by an acquaintan not to speak my mind so free as the British
was Such a haughty people and I was ther in their power, it
might operate against me. I had previously formed a determination not to go with them as a prisoner of war—altho I had
heard it stated that the 4th Rgt and Gnl Lucas was to be Sent
on to Quebeck, I knew they did not know my person, and
being informed by Major Denny that his Detachment was to
be immediately Sent on board a vessel, I thought it desirable
to go aboard lest Some of the inhabitants of Detroit Should
betray me. I communicated my intention to Some of my confidential friends in order that I might not be betrayed about 3
oclock the Detachmt went aboard the Maria of Prisque isle—
I requested Ensign Baird to have Capt J Lucas Trunk taken
aboard, he being absent with Colo McArthur, which he had
done I made Some arrangments in town and went to the warf,
with them. The British Gard that was at the vessel asked me
if I was going aboard I told them I was, he asked me if I
was going to stay aboard I answered him also that I was, he
then Suffered me to pass aboard without asking any further

questions,—I went aboard and requested the boys aboard not
to call me by any title and told them my reason for making
Such request. Soon after I went aboard the vessel dropped
down the rivr about a mile and lay too all night Some time that
Evening Colos. McArthur and Cass returned with their Detachments, and was Surrendered as prisoners

Cornelius Flummerfelt: "The Bold Canadian"

Hull's surrender at Detroit thoroughly discredited him. It made him America's scapegoat for the failure of the campaign in the Old Northwest. It also made Brock "The Hero of Upper Canada," the stuff of legend and barroom ballad. "The Bold Canadian" is one such ballad, a celebration of both the "bold commander" Brock and the "courageous and bold" volunteers who marched into Detroit behind him. Part of Canadian folk tradition to this day, the song is widely attributed to Cornelius Flummerfelt, a private in the 3rd York Militia's First Flank Company, who, the story goes, wrote it while on the road back to York (Toronto). This version, published in Ontario in 1906 by the Niagara Historical Society, was written down from memory by Mrs. Alphaeus Cox, who had it from her mother.

The Bold Canadian

Come all ye bold Canadians,
   I'd have you lend an ear
Unto a short ditty
   Which will your spirits cheer,
Concerning an engagement
   We had at Detroit town,
The pride of those Yankee boys
   So bravely we took down.

Those Yankees did invade us,
   To kill and to destroy,
And to distress our country,
   Our peace for to annoy.
Our countrymen were filled
   With sorrow, grief and woe,
To think that they should fall
   By such an unnatural foe.

At length our brave commander,
   Sir Isaac Brock by name,
Took shipping at Niagara,
   And unto York he came.
Says he, ye valiant heroes,
   Will ye go along with me
To fight those proud Yankees
   In the west of Canada?

And thus we replied,
   We'll go along with you,
Our knapsacks upon our backs,
   Without further adieu.
Our firelocks we did shoulder
   And straight did march away
With firm and loyal purpose
   To show them British play.

At Sandwich we arrived,
   Each man with his supply,
With a determination
   To conquer or to die.
Our General sent a flag to them
   And thus to them did say:
"Surrender up your garrison,
   Or I'll fire on you this day."

They refused to surrender,
   But chose to stand their ground:
We opened on them our great guns,
   And gave them fire all round.
Our troops, they crossed over,
   Our artillery we did land,
And marched up toward their town
   Like an undaunted band.

Those Yankee hearts began to ache,
   Their blood it did run cold
To see us marching forward
   So courageous and so bold.
Their general sent a flag to us,
   For quarter he did call,

Saying, "Stay your hand, brave British boys,
  I fear you'll slay us all."

"Our town, it is at your command,
  Our garrison likewise."
They brought their arms and grounded them
  Right down before our eyes.
Now prisoners we made them,
  On board a ship they went,
And from the town of Sandwich
  Unto Quebec were sent.

We guarded them from Sandwich
  Safe down unto Fort George,
Thence unto the town of York
  All safely we did lodge.
Now we've arrived at home once more,
  Each man is safe and sound.
May the news of this great conquest
  Go all the province round.

Come all ye bold Canadians,
  Enlisted in the cause,
To defend your country,
  And to maintain your laws;
Being all united,
  This is the song we'll sing:
Success unto Great Britain,
  And God save the King.

Moses Smith: *from* Naval Scenes
in the Last War

At the outset of the war, the U.S. Navy consisted of just seventeen ships. The pride of the fleet was its six frigates, of which *Constitution* was one of the finest. (Built in Boston and launched in 1797, she was rated for 44 guns, though during the war she was fitted with as many as 55.) On July 16–19, 1812, under the able command of Captain Isaac Hull, the nephew and adopted son of General William Hull, *Constitution* elegantly eluded five ships of the Halifax squadron in a slow-motion chase through the waters off New Jersey. One month later, on August 19, she was about 750 miles east of Boston when Hull received intelligence that the British frigate *Guerrière* (49 guns), under the command of Captain James R. Dacres, was nearby. Hull's pursuit and capture of *Guerrière* was later recounted by Moses Smith, a crewman who published his memoirs in 1846.

Having learned which way the Guerriere was steering when last seen, we crowded all sail in that direction. We steered a north-east course for several hours, until the morning of the 19th of August, 1812. This was the day of the battle.

We now changed our course, and steered south-east, with a good breeze. At ten o'clock, A.M., the lookout cried:

'Sail ho!'

'Where away?' inquired the lieutenant in command.

'Two points off the larboard bow, sir!' was the reply.

Hull had now come on deck. His first order was to a midshipman:

'Mr. German! take the glass and go aloft. See if you can make out what she is.'

German was soon above us, looking intently in the direction named.

'What do you think?' asked Hull, with animation.

'She's a great vessel, sir! Tremendous sails.'

'Never mind,' coolly added Hull. 'You can come down, sir.

Mr. Adams,' addressing another officer, 'call all hands. Make sail for her!'

But before all hands could be called, there was a general rush on deck. The word had passed like lightning from man to man; and all who could be spared, came flocking up like pigeons from a net bed. From the spar deck to the gun deck, from that to the berth deck, every man was roused and on his feet. All eyes were turned in the direction of the strange sail, and quick as thought studding-sails were out, fore and aft. The noble frigate fairly bounded over the billows, as we gave her a rap full, and spread her broad and tall wings to the gale.

The stranger hauled his wind, and laid to for us. It was evident that he was an English man-of-war, of a large class, and all ready for action. In one of her topsails we read these words:

'NOT THE LITTLE BELT.'

We understood this to mean that the ship we were now approaching was not the 'Little Belt' which had been previously attacked. But we knew that very well; and subsequent events proved that they might have saved themselves the trouble of telling us of it. We saw it was the vessel we wanted to meet, not the 'Little Belt,' but the big Guerriere, of thirty-nine guns.

As we came up she began to fire. They was evidently trying to rake us. But we continued on our course, tacking and half tacking, taking good care to avoid being raked. We came so near on one tack, that a 18 lb. shot came through us under the larboard knight-head, striking just abaft the breech of the gun to which I belonged. The splinters flew in all directions; but no one was hurt. We immediately picked up the shot, and put it in the mouth of long Tom, a large gun loose on deck—and sent it home again, with our respects. ·

Another stray shot hit our foremast, cutting one of the hoops in two. But the mast was not otherwise injured, and the slight damage was soon repaired.

Hull was now all animation. He saw that the decisive moment had come. With great energy, yet calmness of manner, he passed around among the officers and men, addressing to them words of confidence and encouragement.

'Men!' said he, 'now do your duty. Your officers cannot have entire command over you now. Each man must do all in his power for his country.'

At this moment a man was killed on our spar deck. He had run away from us, and was only returned about a fortnight. He fell by the side of long Tom, and never rose again.

Hull determined on closing with the enemy.

'Why don't you fire?' said he.

'We can't get our guns to bear, as she now lies,' was the answer.

'Never mind, my boys!' said he to the men. 'You shall have her as close as you please. Sailing master! lay her along side!'

We came up into the wind in gallant style. As we fell off a little the Guerriere ranged by us her whole length.

The stars and stripes never floated more proudly than they did at that moment. All was silent beneath them, save the occasional order from an officer, or the low sound of the movement of our implements of war. Every man stood firm at his post.

'No firing at random!' cried Hull in a subdued tone of voice. 'Let every man look well to his aim.'

This was the pride of American seamen. Correctness in taking aim did more than anything else in securing the naval victories of the last war.

A shot from the enemy now struck the spar deck, and word was passed that a man was killed.

The long Tom had been capsized, and Ike Kingman got a hoist. But jumping up, with a slap of the hand he said to himself, 'take that.'

'Now close with them!' cried Hull, raising his voice to its sternest note of command, so that it could be heard on the enemy's decks.

'Along side with her, sailing-master.'

A whole broadside from our guns followed this command. The Constitution shook from stem to stern. Every spar and yard in her was on a tremble. But no one was hurt by the recoil of the guns, though several were made deaf by the noise. We instantly followed the thunder of our cannon with three loud cheers, which rang along the ship like the roar of waters, and floated away rapidly to the ears of the enemy.

This was a Yankee style which the British had not adopted. The English officers often spoke of it to ours, after the war was over. They said they were astonished at the spirit of our men in the toil and heat of the battle. Amid the dying and the dead, the crash of timbers, the flying of splinters and falling of spars, the American heart poured out its patriotism with long and loud cheers. The effect was always electrical, throughout all the struggle for our rights.

When the smoke cleared away after the first broadside, we saw that we had cut off the mizzen mast of the Guerriere, and that her main-yard had been shot from the slings. Her mast and rigging were hanging in great confusion over her sides, and dashing against her on the waves.

This discovery was followed by cheers from the Constitution, and the cry;

'Huzza, boys! We've made a brig of her! Next time we'll make her a sloop!'

On board the Guerriere was an American, by the name of Ben Hodges. As the battle commenced he appealed to the captain:

'That is an American frigate,' said he; 'and I cannot fight against my country.'

How different this from the course of many an Englishman during the war! It was a feeling which the commander of the Guerriere respected.

'Go below, my man,' said he. 'Go into the cockpit. You may be of assistance there.'

Hodges obeyed the order. As he stood by one of the surgeons, a voice said:

'I don't see that we've much to do, after all.'

'Hold on a bit sir,' responded Hodges. 'The Yankees haven't begun it. I'm thinking, sir, you'll have plenty to do.'

This was just as the action was commencing. In a moment a red glare followed.

'There!' cried Ben. 'They've begun. Now, look out.' He had hardly spoken before fifteen or twenty wounded men were tumbled into the cockpit.

'Your words were true enough, Ben,' said one of the surgeons as he took up a knife. 'Here's work for us—and plenty of it, too.'

The Guerriere returned our fire with spirit—but it passed too high, and spent its force among our light spars, rigging and sails. Our fore-royal truck was shot away, with two pair of halyards; the flag was hanging down tangled on the shivered mast in the presence of the enemy. This sight inspired one of our men, familiarly called Dan Hogan, to the daring feat of nailing the standard to the mast. He was a little Irish chap, but brim-full of courage. Without a word from any one, he sprang into the rigging and was aloft in a moment. He was soon seen, under the fire of the enemy, who saw him too, at the topmast height, clinging on with one hand, and with the other making all fast, so that the flag could never come down unless the mast came with it. The smoke curled around him as he bent to the work; but those who could see him, kept cheering him through the sulphury clouds. He was soon down again, and at his station in the fight.

Several shot now entered our hull. One of the largest the enemy could command struck us, but the plank was so hard it fell out and sank in the waters. This was afterwards noticed, and the cry arose:

'Huzza! Her sides are made of iron! See where the shot fell out!'

From that circumstance the name of the Constitution was garnished with the familiar title:

'OLD IRONSIDES.'

By this title she is known around the world.

Very soon after the battle commenced, Lieutenant Bush fell, mortally wounded. Lieutenant Morris received a wound in his chest; but he bore himself bravely through until we won the day. Lieutenant Wardsworth came nobly forward, and filled the place made vacant by death with great honor to himself and advantage to the ship.

The braces of both ships were now shot off. The Guerriere swung round into our mizzen rigging, so that a part of her laid right over our taffrail. One might see the whites of the eyes, and count the teeth of the enemy. Our stern guns were pouring in upon them, so that we raked the ship fore and aft. Every shot told well. In a few moments the foremast was gone, and our prediction was fulfilled. The great Guerriere had become a sloop. Soon after the mainmast followed, rendering her a complete wreck. In the fall of the masts some of our boats were swept off, but the Constitution herself was hardly touched, except in some of the yards and sails. Both ships kept firing constantly—our guns continuing to do the most fearful execution.

One of the lieutenants now asked the captain if he should call the boarders?

'No!' replied Hull, 'No! We can take her without losing so many lives.'

The enemy seemed to have been expecting us to board him. He had placed two cannonades on the bowsprit, in such a manner as to sweep off our men as they should attempt to board. These were loaded to the muzzle with musket balls in canvas bags, and would have cut us down like a flock of sheep.

We were preparing for an attack in another quarter, when the Guerriere suddenly dropped to the leeward, and fired a gun for assistance. They tried to haul their colors down; but every man who could be seen attempting it, was shot dead from the tops of the Constitution. We were determined to give them an opportunity to be convinced that we would defend our country's rights to the last; and, besides, we thought these repeated attempts to haul down the flag were intended to deceive us—for we saw the men as busy as ever in continuing the action. I heard the powder boy nearest me on board the Guerriere call to another:

'Work away, there! Huzza! She'll soon be ours!'

The women they had with them were engaged in passing powder, and other munitions of war. Amid such activity on the decks of the enemy, courage and prudence demanded that we should be active on our own.

As an intended insult, the English had hoisted a puncheon of molasses on their main stay, and sent out word:

'Do give the Yankees some switchel. They will need it, when they are our prisoners.'

But we made a very different use of this molasses from what they intended. Our shooting at hogsheads in the Chesapeake Bay, was now turned to good account. We soon tapped their sweet stuff for them, in a way which they little thought of. The Yankee shot tasted the English molasses, and not the Yankee lips. We made the decks of the Guerriere so slippery, that her men could hardly stand! They had more switchel prepared for them than they knew what to do with.

The action was now nearly at its close. The firing had become less frequent on both sides. All felt the necessity of proceeding at once to repair damages. But we dare not trust the enemy. Notwithstanding his disabled condition, it was evident he would attack us again, the first opportunity. His men were still numerous—his ammunition was but partly spent, and his guns had been cleared away from the lower decks, so as to work to the best advantage.

We sent a boat on board, but could get no satisfaction. His colors were down—but still there was danger of his attacking us unawares. This inspired a determined spirit on board the Constitution.

'Let's sink them!' was the cry that ran along our decks—for we felt that we were deceived.

At this moment Captain Dacres appeared in one of our boats, and immediately surrendered himself as a prisoner of war. We did not have any switchel prepared for him as he came on board, because we thought he had had enough already. The delivery of his sword to Hull by Dacres was a scene never to be forgotten by those who witnessed it.

As he placed the hilt in the hand of Hull, his first remark was:

'Captain Hull! what have you got for men?'

'O,' replied Hull, with a sly smile, 'only a parcel of green bush-whackers, Captain Dacres!'

'Bush-whackers! They are more like tigers than men. I never saw men fight so. They fairly drove us from our quarters.'

We remained by the Guerriere all night. The prisoners were taken out and humanely disposed of. We immediately set ourselves at work, repairing damages. Two anchor stocks welded on the foremast, that had been injured by the stray shot, made that as good as new. In one hour's time, we had the gallant frigate as trim as she was when the fight began. But it was not so with the Guerriere. The Yankee wounds made in her sides were incurable. She was kept afloat near us, but with six feet of water in her hold. Lieutenant Reed had command. The prisoners were set at the pumps, but they could not all keep her free. She was soon reported to be in a sinking condition, and we hastened to get all the men out of her.

Some of the captives came on board of us very badly wounded. Their sufferings were greater than can be described, or even imagined. One poor fellow had his under jaw shot off; and while we were watching him, he bled to death. Others, deprived of arms and legs, lingered in the greatest torture, until death put an end to their pains.

There was one of our men—Dick Dunn—who bore the amputation of his leg with a fortitude I shall always bear in mind. 'You are a hard set of butchers,' was all he said to the surgeon, as his torn and bleeding limb was severed from his body. Others, whom I could name, bore their amputations equally well. Some of these brave defenders of the nation are among my friends; and I sometimes meet them stumping it through life. In the midst of all this suffering, Captain Hull was frequently found tendering the consolations needed in such an hour, and showing his humanity to the best advantage. He even looked more truly noble, bending over the hammock of a wounded tar, than when invading and conquering the enemy.

In spite of all the efforts to keep her afloat, we now saw that the Guerriere was rapidly sinking. A council of war was held on board the Constitution, and the decision was that she should be blown up. It was a moment of the deepest interest. After removing every thing thought necessary to be saved, we put a slow match to the magazine, and left her.

There was something melancholy and grand in the sight. Although the frigate was a wreck, floating about a mastless hulk at the sport of the waves, she bore marks of her former greatness. Much of her ornamental work had been untouched; and her long, high, black sides rose in solitary majesty before us, as we bade her farewell. For years she had been the house of thousands of human beings; for years she had withstood the shocks of the winds, the billows and the battle; for years she had borne the insignia of English valor to different and distant climes. But her years were now ended; her course was run; she was about to sink into the deep ocean forever.

Captain Dacres stood by our taffrail as we squared away from the Guerriere. He seemed to brush away a tear from his dark eye, as he took the last look of the vessel he had so lately commanded. But whatever may have been his feelings, it must be admitted that he had done his own duty well—and his men had defended their vessel to the last.

At the distance of about three miles we hove to, and awaited the result. Hundreds of eyes were stretched in that one direction, where the ill-fated Guerriere moved heavily on the deep. It was like waiting for the uncapping of a volcano—or the bursting up of a crater. Scarcely a word was spoken on board the Constitution, so breathless was the interest felt in the scene.

The first intimation we had that the fire was at work was the discharge of the guns. One after another, as the flame advanced, they came booming towards us. Roar followed roar, flash followed flash, until the whole mass was enveloped in clouds of smoke. We could see but little of the direct progress of the work, and therefore we looked the more earnestly for the explosion—not knowing how soon it might occur. Presently there was a dead silence; then followed a vibratory, shuddering motion, and streams of light, like streaks of lightning running along the sides; and the grand crash came! The quarter deck, which was immediately over the magazine, lifted in a mass, broke into fragments, and flew in every direction. The hull, parted in the centre by the shock, and loaded with such masses of iron and spars, reeled, staggered, plunged forward a few feet, and sank out of sight.

It was a grand and awful scene. Nearly every floating thing around her went down with the Guerriere. Scarcely a vestige remained to tell the world that such a frigate had even swept the seas. We immediately squared away, and were again under a crowd of sail for our native land.

Thus ended the capture of the Guerriere.

New-York City Committee of Correspondence: from Address . . . in Support of the Nomination of The Hon. De Witt Clinton

August 17, 1812

The year 1812 brought with it a presidential election. The nominating process had begun in February when the Virginia legislature, following the protocol of the time, chose state electors unanimously committed to Madison. Some two-thirds of Republican legislators in other states followed suit, and on May 18 the Republican caucus in Congress formally nominated Madison for reelection. A vocal group of dissident New York Republicans, however, withheld support for the President. On May 29 these legislators put forth their own nominee, De Witt Clinton, the charismatic forty-three-year-old mayor of New York City. A pro-commerce northerner whose reputation as a "doer" promised, to many, a decisive and favorable end to the war, Clinton was immediately embraced by other dissident Republicans and, in time, by many Federalists as well. In September the Federalist nominating caucus, after rancorous debate, decided to back Clinton (rather than a candidate of their own) as the best chance for ending the "Virginia dynasty" of Jefferson and Madison. A pamphlet published by the New York Republicans was the closest the Clinton coalition came to articulating a national platform.

The state of New-York has now, for the first time, put forward its claim; and examine, we request you, whether some considerations do not strongly mark the propriety of its giving the next president to the union.

The state of Virginia, has for twenty out of the twenty-four years of our present government, enjoyed that honor; she seems desirous of possessing it for another term, and perhaps for as many more as the patience of her sister states will permit. We cheerfully acknowledge the worth and services of the magistrates she has produced, nor do we doubt her competency to furnish a brilliant succession for many years to come; but may be permitted to suggest, that the patriotism and wisdom of the union are not entirely confined within her precincts. If her pretensions be founded on exclusive, or even superior talents, they are offensive to her compeers, and we think unjust. If other states then, can furnish able and intelligent chief magistrates, there are reasons of no light moment, why she should for a time, retire from the competition.

Perhaps if the original framers of our constitution, had inserted a provision for the practical rotation of the presidential office, in the different states, and in some proportion to their population or importance, they would have given an additional proof of their wisdom and foresight. If they had done so, we should not now have occasion to allude to jealousies, the existence of which it is vain to deny, however deeply they may be lamented, as gradually undermining the habitual attachment of many for our confederation. We will abstain from inquiring into their justice; it is unnecessary; since to render them dangerous to our prosperity, it is not essential that they should be well founded; it is sufficient if they exist. They will in that case equally rankle in the heart, bias the understanding, and alienate the affection of whoever feels them. To what are they chiefly owing? Why is *Virginia influence*, a bye-word in the Eastern states, while no one talks of South Carolina or Pennsylvania influence? We are not disposed to facilitate our success, by encouraging those jealousies against Virginia influence. The best interests of the union require that they should be allayed; but we are convinced they never will cease, while the cause or pretext for them remains. Virginia herself, as she values the confederation, should abdicate a situation, which she cannot retain without wounding the feelings of her associates, and weakening their attachments for our union.

Another evil has resulted from the protracted continuance of power in the same quarter. The agriculture and commercial states are beginning to be arrayed against each other, and to feel as if they were not connected by a common bond of interest. The errors of this sentiment we disclaim; but the practical merchants and farmers are prone, in every country, to regard each other as rivals; nor will either party ever patiently submit to be long and exclusively governed by the other, or regulated by its peculiar views or tenets. The population and resources of this state place it in the first rank, while its local situation makes it one of the fit depositories of power, until the distrust and suspicions alluded to shall have subsided, or the evils they complain of shall be remedied. It is a middle state, not deeply tinged with either northern or southern prejudices: it is eminently commercial, and most extensively agricultural: it would be likely to hold the balance even, and to conciliate the interests and good wishes of all.

These considerations would be weighty, even in times of profound peace; but the existence of a war furnishes another and a most powerful argument. New-York is indeed a *middle*, but she is also emphatically a *frontier state*. Whatever disasters may be produced by the war, she will share them as a common calamity, and probably she will also feel them with peculiar severity, as inflicted on herself. We do not utter this in the spirit of querulous repining; nature has placed us in the post of danger, and our hearts and principles determine us to defend it as the post of honor. But if our borders are to be harrassed, and, peradventure, our territory invaded; if our opulent and defenceless capital seems to invite the foe, does not the welfare of the union at large, require that its resources should be directed to the protection of those exposed places, by a statesman to whom their wants are perfectly known, and who would guard them with affectionate zeal? If to this argument of general concern, we added somewhat of personal gratification, should we do wrong? If we said—now that our fortitude is to be peculiarly tried; that our population is to be poured out; that our property may be laid waste; that our individual happiness is put at risk, we offer you a chief magistrate, whose republican principles you cannot doubt; of whose competency and talents to discharge the duties of that station, you are well convinced; gratify us in his election. He enjoys our utmost confidence; he inherits the blood, the principles, and the firmness of that hero, whom ourselves and our fathers long delighted to honor; who was the guide and guardian of his native state, when the same enemy desolated our lands and burnt our towns; who was never appalled in its utmost difficulties, and whose valor and wisdom eminently contributed to the ultimate triumph of America. If we even urged a persuasive like this, is there an American heart, susceptible of feeling or gratitude, that would repel our claim?

There remains to us another subject, which we most reluctantly enter upon, and which we shall endeavor to discuss with candor and forbearance. We are not enemies to Mr. Madison, and should regret exceedingly if we were considered as disparaging his reputation. Much as we esteem Mr. Clinton, and desirous as we are of his success, we should reject it, if it could only be accomplished by vilifying his competitor; but the merits of the one do not require to be set off by censuring the other. Mr. Madison has passed through a life of honor and public services, and has been already exalted to the first office in the union. His friends are desirous of his enjoying it for another term, and allege something like usage in the re-election of his predecessors. It is true Washington, the idol of all parties, was so exalted; it is true Jefferson, the idol of the republicans, obtained the same distinction; but a magistrate may be very meritorious, without deserving the honors conferred upon Washington and Jefferson.

We are not aware of any advantage that can result by establishing the rule, that every President, who is not extremely disapproved of, shall be re-elected. The next step will be, that some favorite public servant, as a proof of our peculiar esteem, will be continued in office for three successive terms; and soon, three times will be the ordinary period for a President whom it is not intended to disgrace: thus we shall imperceptibly slide into an election for life, and perhaps towards an hereditary succession. Eight years are not an improper length of time as a reward for uncommon services; but there is no reason why they should become the ordinary tenure of office. Nevertheless, had there been no sufficiently countervailing motives, and had the times been more tranquil, we should not perhaps object to the re-election of Mr. Madison, if that honor were deemed necessary to fill the measure of his fame. But, much as we respect the feelings of that gentleman, we cannot consent to offer them that tribute under existing circumstances. The present situation of our country excites the deepest anxiety, and renders the choice of its first public officer more important and interesting than ever. This choice involves in effect a question of administration, the appointments of heads of departments, and the institution of principles of policy for conducting our public affairs, of the utmost consequence to the union.

It is a sacred provision of our government, that the President is the responsible officer under the constitution. The prerogative maxim of Britain cannot be applied to him, *that he can do no wrong*. He is answerable to the nation not only for the general system of administration, but also for the prominent public acts and omissions of his Secretaries. The officers are to act under his direction, and cannot be admitted to stand in the same capacity with the ministers of the king of England, interposed between the chief magistrate and the people to bear the burthen of public censure, and screen him from public observation. A severe enforcement of this essential rule, which makes the President responsible to the nation for the acts of his Secretaries, has become indispensable for the restoration of the republic to a healthy condition.

The mode of conducting the war in which we are embarked, is intimately and essentially connected with a satisfactory adjustment of our differences, with the best interests of our country, and with the honor of the American name.

The probability of its taking place could not but have been anticipated; the resources it would require should have been maturely considered, and the means of providing them digested and arranged, the preparations to wage it with effect ought to have been seasonably made. Have those things been done? We do not wish to enter into a minute detail, that might present a disheartening picture to our country; but we are compelled to ask, where are the marks of system or preparation? Our armies have entered upon military service; which of them is properly provided for the present, or when and where have arrangements been made for securing to it the necessary supplies for the future? We fear it will not be found in the army under General Hull; we are sure it is not in the force collected to defend the harbor of New York; nor that organizing on our western border. Supplies for the first should have been furnished through the Lakes, and collected before the British had notice of the war: it is now impossible: and that the last is even as yet provided with tents to cover the men, is entirely owing to the uncommon and unremitted exertions of the governor of this state. Indeed the very impossibility of furnishing our armies with supplies by the Lakes, is in itself a striking proof of incompetency or inattention. We think no administration possessing either foresight or vigor would have omitted strengthening our naval force upon those extensive inland waters, so as to ensure to us the superiority in them. The facility of doing this is nearly equal to its importance; and in time of war, that superiority is of the last importance to the United States, particularly if an attack upon the Canadas be contemplated; besides, the augmentation of our naval force there, is not subject to the objection frequently made against a similar measure in our Atlantic ports, that it would tend to involve us in the maritime contests of Europe.

It is vain to say that these are the errors of the heads of departments. The just and salutary rule of our constitution compels us to place them to the account of our present executive. The Secretaries of the navy and of war, are bound to execute the orders given to them by the president, on all naval and military affairs: either he directed the necessary preparations to be made, or he did not. If he directed them, he is responsible for continuing incapable men in office; if he did not, the blame attaches personally on himself.

But wherefore this lingering preparation, and final inadequacy of the means employed in the contest our government has undertaken? Appropriations were made, in preceding sessions of congress, for the timely provision of munitions of war, in the apprehension that hostilities would grow out of the infringements of our neutral rights. Why has the application of them been neglected, till the conflict was at hand? Do not our raw recruits and vulnerable points in the most valuable and important quarters, declare that recourse has been had to hostilities without a digested system, either of defensive or offensive operations? Neither advice of the declaration of war, nor instructions or orders were received by the commanding officer of our squadron at New York, till general publicity afforded sufficient time for the enemy, most exposed to his operations, to avoid attack, and elude pursuit. An opulent fleet of merchantmen sailed from Jamaica, exactly in time to have been easily intercepted, if the orders of government had been prompt and decisive; but they escaped capture by some negligent delay at Washington; and we should even wish to know, was Commodore Rodgers informed of that fleet by our government, or did he accidentally hear of it at sea?*

If this country be competent to carry on the war, and we are sure it is—if our executive sufficiently foresaw the approach of hostilities, and informed themselves as the best means of conducting them with effect, and shortening their duration by a vigorous commencement, we should have expected to see, not ten or twelve hundred men collecting in the vicinity of Albany, but forces formed, organized, and disciplined; an army invading Nova Scotia, to wrest from England her best naval station in our seas; another acting against the Canadas, and a third attacking the Floridas at the same time.

How shall we characterise the uninterrupted permission to carry on trade with Spain and Portugal? Is it a measure of electioneering policy, or a further proof of the absolute inefficiency that pervades our councils? It undoubtedly affords to England the amplest means of supplying her armies with provisions of every kind, of which they would otherwise be destitute; and therefore gives the most effectual *aid and comfort* to our enemy. It is a trade which cannot be carried on under the American flag; for that will necessarily be excluded by the superiority of the British power in the seas that wash those coasts. It may easily be carried on by British vessels covered by subjects of Spain and Portugal. It affords then to the foe, the means of prolonging the war against us, and promotes the prosperity of British and foreign tonnage, to the ruin of our own ships and merchants. Had the parliament of England legislated for us on this subject, from its policy, its wisdom, and its hatred to our shipping and trade, this arrangement might, perhaps, have been expected; proceeding from our own rulers, it seems almost incomprehensible.

But money has been aptly called the sinews of war, and what system of procuring it has been furnished by our present ad-

---

*The British had intelligence of the war at Fort Malden, Fort George, and Michillimackinac, before the American garrisons in those places, and generally all along the frontier. The American fort at the latter place, was taken in consequence of it. The Governor of this state had not official information of the war, until the Tuesday evening afterwards, altho' it was known in New-York on Saturday. This was a very great neglect, as the frontiers of this state were peculiarly exposed PUBLISHER.

ministration? Where is the republican that was not astonished and confounded at the scheme of taxation proposed through the department of the treasury? It almost seemed intended to damp the public spirit of the country: objects of revenue were presented, odious to the feelings of the citizen, and which, under similar circumstances, formerly occasioned the reprehension of the very person who now revives them. It was not found expedient to adopt this plan; perhaps it was judged cunning to postpone it, till after the presidential election. The credit of the nation is therefore put to the test, by a call for a very large loan, without a specification of security, and impaired, by placing at the disposal of the administration, for instant expenditure, and in order to avoid the immediate resort to direct taxes, monies appropriated to the sinking fund, for the purpose of buying unredeemed debt at a price under par. This injudicious use of that fund, heretofore held sacred by all administrations, cannot fail most injuriously to affect the credit of the other loans at market.

The expenses incident to our situation must, we know, be incurred, and we think that the administration have insulted the patriotism of the people, by declining to take the necessary steps for meeting them; but indeed, considering the conduct hitherto pursued, we are seriously apprehensive lest an immense public debt should be accumulated, without the attainment of any equivalent advantage. The service of the next year may be expected to call for twenty millions, without having made any serious impressions on the enemy, or any advance towards the favorable adjustment of our disputes.

The nomination of De Witt Clinton for the presidency, by the state of New York, proposes to the union, as we firmly believe, a relief from the evils of an inefficient administration, and of an inadequately conducted war. His patriotic and inflexible principles guarantee a firm and unyielding maintenance of the sovereign rights of the United States. Nevertheless, he is not engaged, through any effect of foreign diplomacy, as to the controverted claims of the belligerents of Europe upon each other, in the new, and outrageous species of hostility introduced into the present war.

His qualities, as they have been proved by a long trial in public life, assure us of an able and upright conduct of our national affairs. From his discernment, we infer an excellent selection of the best talents in the nation, to fill the high stations of government, and aid the republic with their counsel and services.

From his energy we anticipate vigor in war, and a determined character in the relations of peace. We believe him to be, in this respect, formed on the model of his venerated uncle, whose decision of mind, constancy and firmness, were almost unequalled.

His attachment to the commercial interests of the union, is founded upon an intimate acquaintance with their beneficial results, and a persuasion of the national advantages accruing from commercial pursuits.

His administration would, we believe, aim at reviving the almost expiring commerce of the country, and extending to it, a naval protection proportioned to its value, and to the revenue poured by it into the national coffers. In fine, we believe, that to maintain the rights of his country, would be his unalterable resolution; to regain peace would be his study; to retain it his desire; and to restore the republic to health and prosperity, his highest ambition.

We therefore earnestly recommend him to the support of the other states, and to the suffrages of the electors for the next president of the union.

WILLIAM W. GILBERT,	SILVANUS MILLER,
MATTHIAS B. TALLMADGE,	THOMAS ADDIS EMMETT,
JOHN McKESSON,	BENJAMIN FERRIS,
PRESERVED FISH,	R. RIKER,
PIERRE C. VAN WYCK,	ELBERT HERRING,
GURDON S. MUMFORD,	P. WILSON,
JACOB DE LA MONTAIGNE,	JOHN H. SICKLES,
BENJAMIN DE WITT,	SAMUEL HARRIS,

SAMUEL A. LAWRENCE.

New York 17th August, 1812

James Madison: Address to the Delegations of Several Indian Nations

Twice in August 1812 the President received delegations of Western Indians in Washington, D.C. The first, consisting mainly of representatives of the Great Osage, Little Osage, Fox, and Sauk tribes, was presented by explorer William Clark, superintendent of Indian affairs for Missouri Territory. On August 16, First Lady Dolley Madison reported to a friend: "A few days ago We had 29 Indians to dinner with us, attended by 5 Interpreters & the Heads of Depts. makeing 40 persons." The second delegation, mainly of Sioux, Winnebagos, and Iowas, was presented around August 19 by Nicholas Boilvin, agent of Indian affairs for Illinois Territory. According to Anna Maria Thornton, wife of the designer of the U.S. Capitol, Madison gave his "Indian Talk" on August 22: "there were 40 of different tribes several of whom made Speeches after the president had done.—The presents were afterwards given the whole lasted six hours."

MY RED CHILDREN, WASHINGTON 1812

You have come thro' a long path to see your father but it is a straight and a clean path kept open for my red children who hate crooked walks. I thank the great spirit that he has brought you in health through the long journey; and that he gives us a clear sky & bright sun, for our meeting. I had heard from General Clarke of the good dispositions of several of the nations on & West of the Mississippi; and that they shut their ears to the bad birds hovering about them for some time past. This made me wish to see the principal chiefs of those bands. I love to shake hands with hearts in them.

The red people who live on the same great Island with the white people of the 18 fires, are made by the great spirit out of the same earth, from parts of it differing in colour only. My regard for all my red children, has made me desirous that the bloody tomahawk should be buried between the Osages, the Cherokees, and the Choctaws. I wish also that the hands of the Shawenoe, & the Osage, should be joined in my presence, as a pledge to cherish & observe the peace made at St. Louis. This was a good peace for both. It is a chain that ought to hold them fast in friendship. Neither blood nor rust should ever be upon it.

I am concerned at the war which has long been kept up by the Sacs & Foxes agst. the Osages; and that latterly a bloody war is carried on between the Osages & Ioways. I now tell my red children now present, that this is bad for both parties. They must put under my feet their evil intentions agst. one another; and henceforward live in peace & good will; each hunting on their own lands, and working their own soils.

Your father loves justice. He extends it to all the red tribes. When they keep the chain of friendship with the 18 fires, bright, he will protect them, and do them good. If any make the chain bloody, it must be broken on their heads. The Winibagoes and some other tribes, between the Mississippi & Lake Michigan & the Wabash, have shut their ears to my councils. They have killed men, women and children, and have plundered the white people. They refuse to give up the murderers, and to return the stolen property. Time enough has been allowed them. When they feel the punishment, they must blame their own folly, and the bad councils to which they have listened. I will not suffer my white children to be killed without punishing the murderers.

A father ought to give good advice to his children, and it is the duty of his children to harken to it. The people composing the 18 fires, are a great people. You have travelled thro' their Country; you see they cover the land, as the stars fill the sky, and are thick as the Trees in your forests. Notwithstanding their great power, the British King has attacked them on the great water beyond which he lives. He robbed their ships, and carried away the people belonging to them. Some of them he murdered. He has an old grudge against the 18 fires, because when he tried to make them dig and plant for his people beyond the great water, not for themselves, they sent out warriors who beat his warriors, they drove off the bad chiefs he had sent among them, and set up good chiefs of their own. The 18 fires did this when they had not the strength they now have. Their blows will now be much heavier, and will soon make him do them justice. It happened when the 13 fires, now increased to 18 forced the British King, to treat them as an independent nation, one little fire did not join them. This he has held ever since. It is there that his agents and traders plot quarrels and wars between the 18 fires and their red brethren, and between one red tribe and another. Malden is the place where all the bad birds have their nests. There they are fed with false tales agst. the 18 fires, and sent out with bloody belts in their bills, to drop among the red people, who would otherwise remain at peace. It is for the good of all the red people, as well as the people of the 18 fires, that a stop should be put to this mischief. Their warriors can do it. They are gone & going to Canada for this purpose. They want no help from their red brethren. They are strong enough without it. The British, who are weak, are doing all they can by their bad birds, to decoy the red people into the war on their side. I warn all the red people to avoid the ruin this must bring upon them. And I say to you my children, your father does not ask you to join his warriors. Sit still on your seats; and be witnesses that they are able to beat their enemies and protect their red friends. This is the fatherly advice I give you.

I have a further advice for my red children. You see how the Country of the 18 fires is filled with people. They increase like the corn they put into the ground. They all have good houses to shelter them from all weathers; good clothes suitable to all seasons; and as for food of all sorts, you see they have enough & to spare. No man woman or child of the 18 fires ever perished of hunger. Compare all this with the condition of the red people. They are scattered here & there in handfuls. Their lodges are cold, leaky, and smokey. They have hard fare, and often not eno' of it. Why this mighty difference? The reason, my red children, is plain. The white people breed cattle and sheep. They plow the earth and make it give them every thing they want. They spin and weave. Their heads, and their hands make all the elements & productions of nature useful to them. Above all; the people of the 18 fires live in constant peace & friendship. No Tomahawk has ever been raised by one agst. another. Not a drop of blood has ever touched the Chain that holds them together as one family. All their belts are white belts. It is in your power to be like them. The ground that feeds one Lodge, by hunting, would feed a great band, by the plow & the hoe. The great spirit has given you, like your white brethren, good heads to contrive; strong arms, and active bodies. Use them like your white brethren; not all at once, which is difficult but by little & little, which is easy. Especially live in peace with one another, like your white brethren of the 18 fires: and like them, your little sparks will grow into great fires. You will be well fed; well cloathed; dwell in good houses, and enjoy the happiness, for which you like them, were created. The great spirit is the friend of men of all colours. He made them to be friends of one another. The more they are so the more he will be their friend. These are the words of your father, to his red children. The great spirit, who is the father of us all, approves them. Let them pass through the ear, into the heart. Carry them home to your people. And as long as you remember this visit to your father of the 18 fires; remember these as his last & best words to you.

As we cannot always see one another, the distance being great, My words from time to time will be delivered by General Clarke and others who may be near you. Your words will always come to me through the same hands. I hope they will always be good words.

Stephen Van Rensselaer to Daniel D. Tompkins

The commander of the American campaign on the Niagara frontier was Major General Stephen Van Rensselaer of the New York militia. A former lieutenant governor of the state, Van Rensselaer was heir to one of the largest personal fortunes in America and the landlord to some twelve hundred tenant farmers in the Albany area; he was, however, an inexperienced soldier, and had never led men into battle. On August 31, from his headquarters at Lewiston, he wrote to Daniel D. Tompkins, the governor of New York, about the sorry state of his "little army" of seven hundred men: many were sick, and most were not properly supplied with clothes and weaponry. Worse yet, Van Rensselaer wrote, the British were growing ever stronger: Isaac Brock had recently returned to Newark (Fort George), bringing with him men from the Detroit campaign. This greatly strengthened the British position at Queenston, directly across the Niagara from Lewiston.

Head-Quarters, Lewiston, August 31, 1812.

Sir,—

Presuming that the surrender of General Hull's army has been officially announced to your Excellency through the proper channel, I shall not enter into any details upon the event so disastrous to our country: its consequence must be felt every where; but they are peculiarly distressing upon these frontiers, both to the citizens, and the little army under my command. Alarm pervades the country, and distrust among the troops. They are incessantly pressing for furloughs, under every possible pretence. Many are without shoes; all clamorous for pay. Many are sick. Swift's regiment at Black Rock are about one-fourth part down. I have ordered Doctor Brown to associate Doctor Chapin with him, and to examine as to the causes producing the diseases, the mode of treating them, &c. and to report to me their opinion of the best mode of restoring the sick, and preserving the health of those who remain well. This duty they are now performing.

Captain Jennings has been tried by a court-martial, and found guilty of such charges as forfeited his commission; and I have approved the sentence. The proceedings, in form, will soon be forwarded to your Excellency.

While we are thus growing daily weaker, our enemy is growing stronger. They hold a very commanding position on the high ground above Queenstown, and they are daily strengthening themselves in it, with men and ordnance. Indeed, they are fortifying almost every prominent point, from Fort Erie, to Fort George. At present we rest upon the armistice; but should hostilities be recommenced, I must immediately change my position. I receive no reinforcements of men, no ordnance, or munitions of war. I must hope, that I shall not long be left in this situation.

Two gentlemen, Messrs Johnson and Bascom, came over in a flag to the garrison, at Niagara, and the first I knew of them they were in my camp. Being satisfied that they were American citizens, men of intelligence, and some standing in society, I permitted them to pass on, with orders to report themselves to your Excellency.

There is one fact, which though not immediately connected with my department, I cannot refrain from mentioning;—the unfortunate soldiers of General Hull's army, who marched by my camp on their way to Lower Canada, are very destitute of clothing. Every consideration would urge that some attention should be paid to their condition.

I have the honour, &c.

His Excellency Governor Tompkins.

Daniel Curtis to Jacob Kingsbury

Daniel Curtis, a young schoolteacher from New Hampshire, was commissioned an ensign of the 1st U.S. Infantry Regiment in January 1812. He began his service at Fort Detroit under Colonel Jacob Kingsbury, an avuncular veteran of the Continental Army. In June he was transferred to Fort Wayne, Indiana Territory, where a hundred-man garrison had been commanded since 1810 by Captain James Rhea. The fort, built in 1794 as a trading outpost at the confluence of the St. Joseph, St. Marys, and Maumee rivers, was at this time in disrepair, and though it was furnished with a good well, its food supplies were low. Fort Wayne had suffered a long and difficult history with the local Indians, who by the late summer of 1812 had been made bold by the recent British and Indian triumphs in the Old Northwest. In August, a group of Miamis and Potawatomis established a camp near the fort, which by September included some five hundred warriors. Curtis addressed this account of the Indians' siege to Colonel Kingsbury, now in command of U.S. forces at Newport, Rhode Island.

———————

Fort Wayne Septr. 21st 1812.

Hond. Sir,

As our difficulties have in some measure subsided, and as I have been so fortunate as to survive the siege, it affords me the highest satisfaction to have it in my power to communicate to you some, among many, of the most important occurrences since my arrival at this place.

I arrived here on the 5th June last, and was, and still continue to be highly pleased with the place and my situation, except, perhaps I might have been better suited with a little more active employment than I have had till about twenty days past.

Nothing worthy of notice has transpired since my arrival here till the 7th Ulto. on which our Capt: received a note from Genl. Hull stating that Fort Dearborn was to be evacuated and requesting him to communicate the same to Capt. Wells and

Mr. Stickney and for them to point out the most expeditious and safe rout possible for Capt. Heald to get to Detroit. The gentlemen were consulted on the subject, and concluded, that by way of this place would be a safe and no doubt as near a rout as could be taken from Chicago to Detroit, except by water, which was intercepted by British vessels then on the lakes. Accordingly on the 8th Capt Wells, with a party of thirty five Indians and their pack horses and one man a private in our comy: with four of our pack horses, sat off for Chicago to assist Capt: Heald in the evacuation of that post. On the 19th one of the party that went with Capt: Wells returned, bringing intelligence that Capt: Heald and his compy: with Capt: Wells, were all killed on the morning of the 15th a short distance from the Fort, the particulars of which he thus related. When they arrived at Chicago there were five hundred Indians encamped near the garrison, of various tribes, some Puttawatamies, Chippewas, Winnebaagoes and some Kickapoos. The next day, which must have been on the 14th a council was called by Capts: Heald and Wells in which they used every exertion to persuade the Indians to let the troops depart in peace: they even agreed to give up all the military arsenal and magazine stores together with the cattle and other stock then there, to which they consented; and the next morning while the blood-thirsty savages were killing and dressing their beeves, the troops left the garrison, the officers marching in front, the baggage waggon next, the women and children next to it, after them the soldiers and the thirty five Indians with their pack horses bringing up the rear. They had not passed half a mile from their little assylum, when looking back they discovered the approach of the enemy about four hundred in number, with their tomahawks raised ready to give the fatal blow. A kind of hollow square was immidiately formed encompassing the women and children, and one round fired at the enemy, but being overpowered by numbers, the brave, the innocent fair, and the helpless, fell a prey to the savage crewilty of the tomahawk and scalping-knife. These are the facts as stated by the first Indian that returned after Capt. Wells left this for Chicago, but we have since been told by others, that Capt. Heald and lady, Lt. Helms and wife, Mr. Kinzie and wife, and nineteen soldiers are made prisoners and sent to Detroit, from whence they are to be conveyed to Montreal. Thus ends the fate of Chicago; the success of this post, and the fate of its late, worthy and intrepid commander I now proceed to relate, and in some instances to particularize. The Indians since the news of Chicago, except some of the Miamies, have expressed and manifested a verry different conduct from anything hitherto observed in them. Several attempts have, within five weeks, been made to send expresses through to Detroit and other places, which have failed either by being killed or driven back by Indians. A Mr. S. Johnston in attempting to go through to Piqua, Ohio, on the evening of the 28th Ulto. and within half a mile from the garrison, was shot, tomahawked, scalped, stabbed in 23 places, and beaten and bruised in the most barbarous manner. The next day an Indian came within hearing of our centinels and hailed, he was answered by our interpreter and asked what he wanted? to which he replied, admittance into the garrison, and through consent of our capt: was ordered to come in. This was the first instance of an Indian hesitating or expressing any fear in approaching the garrison. His business was to request of our capt: a white flag, that some of the Chiefs might come and speak with him and the Indn. agent, a Mr. Stickney. The flag was given out and the chiefs came, but would not acknowledge that they knew anything on the subject of Mr. Johnston's death, or who killed him. They requested the flag for the next day, but it was not returned for several days; during which time, they were constantly killing our hogs, driving away our cattle, robbing and plundering our cornfields and guardains and carrying away the effects of them within point blank musket shot of us, and *we poor soldiers*, (from cowardise or some other agency in our Capt:) were obliged to suffer these repeated insults, to pass with impunity. On the evening of the 4th Instant the flag returned accompanied by Winnemac, five Medals, the long days of June, Chappune and two others, and when asked whether they intended to remain at peace with us or declare themselves in an open state of war fare? Winnemac being the principal chief among them, observed, "I dont know what to tell you, but you know that Mackinac is taken, Detroit is in the hands of the British, and you must expect to fall next, and probably in a few days." Shortly after this, the Capt: invited Winnemac over to his quarters and after having drank three glasses of wine with him, rose from his seat, took the savage rascal by the hand and observed, to the astonishment of every one present, "my good friend I love you, I will fight for you, I will die by your side," and then asked him to come and breakfast with him the next morning. Winnemac retired to his camp, but instead of accepting the invitation to breakfast the next morning, sent five of his young warriors, who secreted themselves behind one of our root houses, and at six oclock A.M., shot at and killed two of our men, as they were returning from the necessary near that place. This made an impression upon the mind of every one in the garrison which will not easily be forgotten. The impression, however, that it made on the mind of Capt: James Rhea commanding, or attempting to command, may be excepted to, for he was as drunk as a fool all night, and had not yet come to his perfect senses, if he ever had any. From the movement of the Indians during the day which we discouvered at a distance, Lt. Ostrander and myself expected some sport before the next morning, and we were not disappointed in our conjectures. Everything remained in perfect tranquility till about eight P.M. when a general shout was heared from the Indians, succeeded by a firing of small arms on every side of us. The alarm post of every man, as well as the respective duties of Mr. Ostrander and myself having been mutually agreed upon in the course of the day, the enemy had not time to fire a second time, before we were prepared and opened two broadsides upon them at the same time. We exchanged three general shots, when I discouvered, from the flash of their guns, that they were secreted behind the buildings, fences, and shrubberies at some distance, and I having command of the musketry below, ordered them to cease firing till further orders, thinking the enemy would conclud that we were frightened or that we were tenacious of ammunition, and would probably venture a little nearer. Mr. Ostrander having charge of the Block rooms, above, as soon as the Indians had collected more in a boddy, sent a few shells among them which caused them soon to disperse, and we presume, must have raked the shins of many. Scattering shots were received for the remainder of the night. They kept up a firing the next day from behind buildings, fences &c. till about three oclock P.M. in order, we presume, to disturb our rest, knowing that we had been all night on the alert. But when night came we were ready and active. And having heared, of old, "that caution is the mother of safty" we had the roofs of our buildings wet, also the pickets on the inside, our water casks all filled and every bucket and kettle arranged in the most convenient places. We had no apprehensions of danger except by fire, which they might have sat to the pickets, by creeping up, of a dark night with a bundle of light combustibles invelloping fire, and got off again without being discouvered till it had taken. In order therefore, to prevent them from approaching undiscouvered, to the pickets, I suggested a plan which readily met the approbation of Mr. Ostrander and others in the garrison and immediately put it in opperation. I procured from the Factor's Store, about thirty Bells of the size of a common half pt: tumbler, and collected a sufficient quantity of Bed cord and other ropes to reach round the garrison, on the outer side, about twelve feet from the pickets. The cord was stretched on crotches about ten inches from the ground, and the Bells suspended from it at convenient distances, so that anything touching the cord at any place round the works would cause the toll of at least two of Bells.

The siege continued from the morning of the 5th till the morning of the 10th without cessation and the fears and troubles of our worthy commander continually drowned in the excessive use of ardent spirits. He committed many abuses upon his subalterns and others, and was heard several times to exclaim "O my money! if I had sent it with my poor wife it might have don her some good, but now it must be lost," and at the moment when the most perfect order and silence were necessary to be obsirved, in order the better to hear and discouver the movement of the enemy without, he was the most troublesome and noysy within the garrison. Our apprehensions from the disorder and confusion he created among the men were our greatest fears; we had every thing prepared at one time during the siege, to silence his clamour and abuses by coersive measures, but fortunately for him (and perhaps for us) he was apprised by some of his friends, that something of that kind was in contemplation against him, which caused him (we presume) to conduct with a little more silence and circumspection; but observed, shortly afterwards, that if the Indians or

British were to bring one or more pieces of cannon from Chicago even of three pound mettal, and plant them near the garrison, we should be obliged to surrender, and when told by his subalterns that the first man or person in the garrison who should offer or propose a surrender to the enemy, at the approach of no heavier mettal than three pounders, should loose his life, he offered no resentment, but remained silent on the subject. After the 10th we remained in tranquillity, but could see frequently large parties of Indians between that time and the 12th running across the river and the paries, and many of them without arms. We were at a loss to determine the cause of this singular movement, but concluded that they must have seen some movement of an army between this and Piqua, as they were running from that quarter. About three oclock P.M. of the 12th to our great joy we beheld the approach of an army of about three thousand men commanded by Genl. Harrison. You may rest assured sir, that we lost no time, after the Genl. had pitched upon and regulated his encampment, in making known to him the meritorious conduct of our intrepid Capt:

The Genl. expressed great astonishment at the breach of confidence in that great man, and requested the particulars to be reduced to writing and presented to him in due form, which was soon done, and about 10 the next morning, the capt: had the honor and sublime pleasure of a visit from one of the Genl's: Aids, requesting him to deliver up his long knife. Shortly afterwards the Genl. sent to us to know whether we would withdraw the arrest, in case the Capt: would resign, to which we consented, on consideration of his having been a long time in the service, and more particularly on account of his young family. His resignation was sent in, to take effect on the 31st of Decr. next and he left this on the 14th for the state of Ohio where he had, some weeks previously, sent his wife and family. The army is to leave this in a few days to descend the Miami to Defyance where they are to fortify and then procede to the foot of rappids, there to be joined by the Pennsylvanians and Virginians making an army in all of about 10,000, a part of which, it is supposed will visit Detroit and Malden this season, Genl. Harrison ranks high in this army, and it is even said that a Washington was never more popular in camp than this young Genl.

Since my appointment in the army I have never had occation till now, of making any communications to my superiors in that establishment; you will therefore have the goodness to excuse any liberties I may have taken in this, and at all events pardon me in the profusion with which I am guilty in the un-limited use of paper.

I omitted in its proper place to tell you that Lt: Whistler has not witnessed any of the scenes at this place since the 15th of July last, being on furlough or permission to Detroit after his wife who was there on a visit. He was to have returned at muster, but we have heared nothing of him personally since.

My best respects to Madam Kingsbury, James, Julia & Cushing.

With a due sense of your goodness Sir,

I subscribe myself
Your Obt: & verry
Humble Servt.
D. Curtis

Col.
J. Kingsbury
commdg:
Newport,
Rhode Island

A. W. Cochran: from a letter
to Rebecca Cochran

Andrew William Cochran, son of the president of King's College, Nova Scotia, was only twenty when, in the summer of 1812, Sir George Prevost, Governor-General of British North America (Canada) and commander-in-chief of its forces, recruited him as his assistant civil secretary. He was in Québec on September 11, 1812, when General Hull, the other American officers, and some of the regulars taken prisoner at Detroit were debarked from the sloop *Queen Charlotte* and paraded into town for processing. The remaining regulars, some five hundred of them, arrived in waves, in smaller boats, throughout the early fall. The sixteen hundred other American prisoners, mostly members of the Ohio and Michigan militias, had been paroled by the British at Fort Detroit and escorted to the Ohio border. Cochran described what he saw in a letter to his mother.

———————————

Part of The American Prisoners taken in Detroit have arrived here the evening before last; I have seen all the officers but do not recognize any of my Boston military acquaintances as I expected I should; Both men and officers are a shabby looking set as ever you set eyes on, and reminded me of Falstaff's men very forcibly.—Some of the officers talked very big, and assured us that before long there would be 100,000 men in Canada and that they would soon have Quebec from us;— They do not speak very respectfully of their *General*, and he in his turn, (Mr Brenton writes me) is or pretends to be very much irritated against his Government who he says have sacrificed him by not complying with his repeated and urgent demands for reinforcements to save him from the fate which has now come on him.—Sir George has let him go home on his Parole (together with such of his officers as were married,) in order that he might further embarass the Government by his complaints and throw his weight into the scale against Madison's party;—But I fear Sir George's hopes on that score will not be realized as Hull is a plausible fellow and little credit is to be given him for sincerity in the violence that he shews against Madison;—No harm however can arise from sending home on his parole, unless he should be dishonourable enough to break it and take up arms again before he is exchanged, and even then his conduct as a General hitherto shews that there is not much to fear from his military prowess;—I should not be at all surprized to hear of his taking some command immediately on his return in spite of his parole, as I believe him to be both rogue and fool;—In one of the letters from him to General Brock when the latter summoned him to surrender, he says (as I suppose you will have seen in the papers before now) that a flag of truce that had been carried by a Captain Brown of his army had been unauthorized by him;—Captain Brown is among the Prisoners who arrived here the other evening and he told my friend Mr. Mure that he could shew General Hull's own order and handwriting, authorizing him to go with the flag of truce;—This will give you some idea of General Hull's regard for his honour; His dwelling house is very near Detroit and also the house of Colonel Baby of the Upper Canada militia, a man of great respectability in that Province; The two families were on the most intimate terms before the War but when the American troops came there Hull allowed them to pillage Colonel Baby's house in the most shameful manner and when Baby expostulated with him and reminded him of their former intimacy Hull answered it was true enough but *circumstances were changed now*;—When Hull surrendered Baby went over to see him in General Brock's tent,—"Well General, says he, *circumstances are changed now indeed.*"

September 13, 1812

John Strachan to John Richardson

In 1812, the Reverend John Strachan was the most influential Anglican clergyman in Upper Canada. As rector of St. James Church in York—he would later become Toronto's first bishop—he was a shaper of conservative opinion in religion and politics. Born and educated in Aberdeen, Scotland, he arrived in North America in 1799, when, at the age of twenty, he was invited by a family connection to become a teacher in Kingston. On his way to Upper Canada, he spent several months in New York City, where he developed a keen antipathy for Americans. (In 1807 he wrote to a friend that "this new nation is *vain* & *rapacious* and without *honour*"; four years later he cosigned a circular urging the implementation of "some check to the admission of strangers from the neighboring States in proper time before their numbers become formidable and the evil incurable.") He frequently corresponded with John Richardson, a fellow Scot and a principal in the Montreal–South West Fur Company, whose connections, intelligence gathering, and initiative played a key role in the taking of Fort Mackinac.

York 30th Septr 1812

My Honble & Dear Sir

I have troubled you with several letters of late & have not had the pleasure of a line in return, but I shall expect that happiness next post. I take the liberty of sending several inclosures which I shall be much obliged to you to distribute. The three letters for Europe may go by the first vessel. The packets for Sir George Prevost & the Bishop contain copies of my sermon & the address of the House of Assembly, which I should have sent much sooner, but various causes interrupted me. You & Mrs Richardson will sympathize with us in the loss of our little Girl who died last week of a severe worm fever—it was a sweet infant 2½ years old, exceedingly interesting. Mrs Strachan finds relief in tears. We are not much pleased with the languid manner in which the war is carried on, forbearance will never answer with our present enemy, it is founded upon a most fallacious idea of the American character, & the situation of parties in that country, & it will, should the war continue, be highly detrimental to this Province and perhaps prove its ruin. An active prosecution of the war along our line now that we are well prepared would produce many solid advantages, but acting merely on the defensive is exceedingly pernicious. I can very well conceive that defensive operations may suit your province better, but it is very different with this, where we come so frequently in contact & where the communications can be easily cut off. Among the advantages resulting from active war I note a few as they occur—

1. A successful attack instead of irritating the Federalists will produce the contrary effect by furnishing them with additional proofs of the incapacity of their present rulers.

2. As the Forces of the enemy at present consist chiefly of three-month men, raw, undisciplined & dismayed by the success which hath already crowned His Majesty's arms & weak from bad nutriment, they are much more disposed to run than to fight.

3. These will soon be replaced by Militia men who have been regularly drilled since the commencement of the war and they will be sent in greater numbers.

4. A successful attack will dispirit the Democrats & ruin their whole plan of operations, for they have allotted the Militia volunteers for the conquest of Upper Canada, reserving the regulars for Lower Canada, where they expect the greater resistance. Another defeat will cut up entirely the Volunteer system.

5. The taking of Niagara would produce more determined opposition among the Militia—their fears would act with the more force, because they might be concealed under the cloak of the unpopularity of the war.

6. Because after taking Niagara & clearing the coast to Black Rock opposite to Fort Erie it will be easy to scour the line down to Ogdensburgh, to take every ship & boat, & thus to secure the command of the waters during the whole war.

7. A general attack of the coast will convince the enemy of the impossibility of conquering Canada, & inspire the inhabitants of this country with invincible courage

8. Because this Province will suffer greatly unless the free navigation of the waters be opened soon, as the usual supplies have not arrived nor are likely to be sent in the present state of the navigation.

9. Because this forbearance is infinitely more advantageous to the enemy than to us—they are hourly augmenting their force & ours is as great as we can expect it to be this season

10. Because this defensive plan of warfare discourages our own troops & elevates the enemy & smells too much of the half measures adopted in the American war.

11. Because before the opening of the navigation it will be in the power of the enemy to send in such reinforcements, as shall give them the command of the waters, especially when the inexperience of our naval Officers is taken into consideration, for ordinance &c of all kinds can be easily transported during the winter.

12. Because a successful attack at present would deprive the enemy of the power of becoming formidable on the lines, for nearly 12 months to come.

13. Because a longer forbearance will enable them to cut off our communication with the Lower Province about or below Ogdensburgh, & how in that event will your troops in Lower Canada be supplied with provisions, flour, pease, pork, &c.

14. Because a successful attack would leave a disposable force afterwards by which we might attack the enemy in the rear should they be able to penetrate into Lower Canada.

15. Because nothing but blows will ever bring our enemy to terms—they call our forbearance cowardice, & as we concede they rise in their demands

We are told that some wise acres find fault with General Brock for employing the Indians, but if he had not done so, he & all his men must have perished—besides if we do not employ these people they will employ themselves—they have been at war with the United States for some years & by attending us, many of their excesses have been restrained. I look for your determination respecting Thomas by the next mail. Mrs Strachan joins me in kind respect to you, Mrs and Miss Richardson.

I always am

Honble John Richardson   My dear & Honble Sir

                                                          Sincerely yours

George McFeely: Diary

The 22nd U.S. Infantry Regiment, created in June 1812, was recruited at the U.S. Army barracks in Carlisle, Pennsylvania. On October 5, 1812, Lieutenant Colonel George McFeely, leading a detachment of two hundred men of the 22nd, began a month long march from Carlisle, in the Susquehanna Valley, to the front at Fort Niagara, 350 miles to the northwest. His men, though young and inexperienced, proved resourceful and determined—though not always along officially sanctioned lines.

October 12th.   Commenced our march this day; crossed the Loyal Sock. A number of our men were drunk this day which retarded our march. Arrived at Williamsport: here we lay two days for the purpose of laying in provisions sufficient for passing the wilderness. The citizens here were remarkably kind in entertaining our men with treating them to coffee; I refused to admit whiskey.

October 15th.   This morning a number of our men were drunk here. I ordered the company officers to search the men and destroy all the whiskey that might be found amongst them; for the remainder of the march no soldier would be permitted to carry whiskey with him on the march. After sending Ensign Cuthbertson with 12 men as a guard with the wagons I marched with the detachment across the hills along an old Indian path to avoid crossing the Lycoming creek. The road this day crosses the Lycoming five times in a day's march. This is a most beautiful water; it is as transparent as glass and contains trout in abundance. Encamped at Rendles.

October 16th.   Cloudy and raining this morning; marched early, bad roads, marched only 7 miles this day owing to the bad roads; encamped at the foot of Lawrel Hill. The road runs this day along the small stream called Tall Trout Run, no doubt from the great quantity of Trout that goes up this stream to spawn. Our soldiers this evening had many fine trout as they could all eat. On the rivers in this run the Trout was in shoals, our men could catch with their hands as many as they pleased. They were about 8 or 9 inches long and of a darker color on the back than any I had ever seen before. This night our men had a frolick, a drunken one, and were at a loss to find where or how they got the whiskey because in the morning every man was searched and all the whiskey emptied out. After some time it was discovered that they had filled their gun barrels with whiskey and had the vent stopped up with a little plug made of hickory wood and a tomkin of cork in the muzzle.

Jared Willson to Alvan Stewart

Jared Willson, a native of Stockbridge, Massachusetts, was a twenty-six-year-old lieutenant in the New York militia in the fall of 1812. His commanding officer at Lewiston was Major General Stephen Van Rensselaer, who, on the advice of his more experienced cousin and aide-de-camp, Lieutenant Colonel Solomon Van Rensselaer, planned an assault on Isaac Brock's forces at Queenston. Before daybreak on October 13, "Sol" led three hundred men across the river, a mission that ended with the Americans seizing the higher ground. Thereafter, reinforcements, including Willson, poured in, and there was a spirited battle for control of Queenston Heights. In one early counterattack, the British suffered an irreplaceable loss when Brock was killed. In the end, the American offensive failed, and Willson was one of 925 Americans captured and later paroled. Back home at Canandaigua, New York, he wrote an account of the battle for his friend Alvan Stewart, a former classmate at the University of Vermont.

CANANDAIGUA, 9th Nov. 1812.

WORTHY FRIEND: The bearer of your letter, dated 23rd ultimo this moment darked the door of my office. He is on his way to the frontier, and inasmuch as that is a dangerous place, and he may never return, I shall, without waiting the uncertain event, write immediately by mail. The former letter you mention has not yet arrived. You expect I am in the army. This is not the case, but to tell you the truth, I have recently returned from a short, but tedious campaign, in which I suffered much fatigue, fought one battle, surrendered my sword to a victorious enemy on the memorable 13th, was a prisoner of war, in Canada, six days and finally sent home on my parole of honor. All this was done in less than four weeks. As the saing is, this campaign was "more short than sweet."

Yes, friend Stewart, I was an actor in the awful tragedy at Queenstown, of which you must have seen the official accounts.

I shall not trouble you with a rehearsal of the events of that day, when after a splendid victory in the morning, we suffered the extreme mortification of a defeat. Little did I think, Sir, at our last interview, that one of the Triumvirate would ever witness such a scene; still less did I think that I should suffer the indignity of surrendering my sword to a British officer, but such is the fate of War, in which we all ought to engage when our country calls.

The Battallion of Rifle-men, to which I belong were sent out after the first engagement, a mile or more from the main body to make discoveries. We had not been gone long, when a party of indian Devils—about two hundred, attacked us in the woods. We were far inferior in numbers and of course compelled to retreat precipitately. The savages, greedy for plunder, and thirsting for blood pursued us closely, firing and yelling, in a most frightful manner. They pursued us close to the main body, but in their turn were compelled to fly for safety. By this time, I thought hell had broken loose and let her dogs of war upon us. In short I expected every moment to be made a "cold Yanky" as the soldiers say. About 4 o'clock P.M. came on the "tug of War." The british forces and indians united, attacked us spiritedly. We obstinately opposed them, against a shower of Grape-Shot and musketry—but at length fatigued and over powered by numbers, we were forced to lay down our arms. Our men fought well. The bloody Heights of Queenstown will bear testimony to the valor & intrepidity of our troops. Thus ended the battle, which commenced before daylight and was almost one continued scene of action untill the surrender in the afternoon. All this transaction took place in fair view of two thousand militia on the opposite shore (poor dastardly wretches) who would not come to our assistance—had they come we might have held our ground untill this time. Oh! shame on them—there surely must be a severe punishment in reserve for these poor, ignoble, base-born wretches. The indian war-hoop even echoed through their camp and still they could not be prevailed upon to mingle with their associates in arms to oppose the inhuman foe.

But still I think our commander in Chief is answerable for our ill success. He knew the militia would not all cross—He ought then to have ordered on Gen. Smyth's regulars in season to help us. He ought to have had more boats in readiness & scows, that we might carry across our field-pieces—but this was not done. Oh! shameful neglect! the Gen'l surely must, for this mismanagement answer to his country & his God, if he can. In fact, Sir, the whole business of that day & the untimely attack were authorized by the commander, at the instigation of his Aid—Sol Van-Rensalaer, who, allured by the prospects of acquiring unfading Laurels, wished to make a firm stand in Canada with a few regulars and a few militia. This ambitious creature was to take the command, but in the first of the engagement, he was carried off the field severely wounded—Thus has the ambition of one man and the folly of another brought disgrace upon our country. This you will find to be a fact.

So you see, Sir, I have agreed not to fight his Royal Highness any more, at present. I am now at my old stand, endeavoring to cultivate the arts of peace. I am no longer a resident in the "tented field." The savage War-Hoop will not again break my slumbers, hoarse clangor of the trumpets call me to the field of Battle. Thanks be to God, that my bones are not now bleaching on the awful Heights of Queenstown. About three hundred of our men were killed and wounded. The enemy must have suffered greater loss. Brock & Aid are among the slain, this adds some splendor to the engagement. 100 Red Devils are supposed to have been killed, among whom were three Chiefs.—I should like to try the Dogs another pull.

It appears you are in this State. I wish I could say in this town. I believe you might get into the Academy here, as the present Preceptor is about to leave it. I should like to know if you have our "Alma Mater" for ever. As for the Law, I know but little about it as yet, but mean now to stick close to my books. L. H. I hope will "puff the vital air" a little longer, and then perhaps I may find time to call on her. Tim has not written me this long time. I think he must be down with the "Flum Fluttocks" or some other nervous complaint. Isham & Hitchcock have never written me, I must needs think they are "Cold Yankys."

You must write me immediately & let me know your intentions as to the future. In the interim, I remain,

Yours sincerely,

JARED WILLSON,
Prisoner of War.

MR. ALVAN STEWART,
    Cherry Valley,
        Otsego Co., N.Y.

John Strachan to William Wilberforce

William Wilberforce is best known today for his decisive role in bringing about the end of the British slave trade in 1807 and for laying the groundwork for the subsequent emancipation of slaves in the British West Indies. Fired by the evangelical spirit, he was an influential voice in Parliament not only for the rights of enslaved people but also for a host of other social reforms, from improving work conditions in factories to preventing cruelty to animals. Like John Strachan, he was gravely concerned with the moral and cultural consequences of the Anglo–Indian encounter in North America, especially the British use of alcohol to control and exploit the Indians. Unlike Strachan, he had to be persuaded that deploying Indians in the war against the United States was both just and necessary.

York Upper Canada 1 Novr 1812

Honble Sir

As the unprovoked war declared by America against Great Britain will produce some debates in the house of Commons, and introduce the question of employing Indians permit a stranger to suggest a few remarks which might not perhaps occur at the moment of such a discussion but may contribute to the formation of a just opinion.

The Indians of North America may be divided into two great classes—1st Those within our territories—2nd Those without.

1. Those within our territories. The greater number of these are such as were driven from their settlements on the Mohawk river during the American war and to whom tracts of land have been assigned in this province of Upper Canada. They must either be with us or against us. Indians said one of their Chiefs lately do not understand the meaning of neutrality, they know nothing but Friend or Foe. These tribes have been solicited & offered bribes by the Americans to desert from us, and one of them the Indians of St Regis were actually induced to join our

enemies for a time, tho' most of them have now returned. And
the reason why the Americans do not succeed better in this
plan of corruption is that the Indians have experienced their
deceptions too often to trust them except in cases of necessity.
The rule of America respecting the Indians is that "might
makes right" and on this rule they act. Were this country in
possession of the United States the Indians as well as the Loyalists would be deprived of their possessions—leading men in
Congress have already declared this. As the Natives have
therefore nothing to expect but the most rigorous treatment,
they have a right to defend their lives and property, and if we
reject their assistance they will turn against us & massacre our
wives & children, while we are on the lines opposing an invading foe. At the commencement of the war, when the Province
appeared incapable of resistance, some of the Indians desired
to be considered neither as friends nor foes, but they were
nevertheless preparing to join the enemy who had invaded us
with a much stronger force than we could bring against them.
Not that they preferred the enemy, but they considered our
case desperate and they thought that by joining the Americans
early they might preserve their lands. After the victory at Detroit they declared for us; and told us that we no longer acted
like women. That they fight in a Savage manner is true but you
are to remember that in this war they are fighting an [   ]
enemy & it is surely better to destroy people marching many of
them nearly two thousand miles to enslave us, than to expose
ourselves to their implacable resentment. We do not seek the
enemy, they come to us. They attack our peaceable shores, and
shall we not use every means which God has given us to repel
them. When you hear of the cruelty of the Savages, think of the
still greater cruelty of the Cabinet at Washington—and then
think of the brave Loyalists of Upper Canada already driven by
rebellion from their native country & plundered of all they
possessed for their love to the King. They are attacked in the
most vindictive manner by their implacable enemies the Demo-
crates, who now rule the United States. The Loyalists have
paramount claim for affection & kindness, and as they have
been left in a manner totally defenceless, it is but just to allow
them the use of the means in their power. The Indians within
our territories destroy none but invaders and as they join our

troops they are restrained from killing any except in battle—
this however is not the case when they act separately, but this
we prevent as much as possible. Add to this the Americans
employ all the Savages that they can get in the war. The reason
of the smallness of their number is this. Instead of assigning
them lands as we do they take them from them and drive them
back into the interior. Hence very few remain within their
settlements, those that do are now employed in the war against
us. In fine the Indians in our territory will not be neutral if war
be near them, they must have a share. Were they disposed to
be Neutral the enemy would not allow them, but be incessantly employed in drawing them away from us. We must
therefore keep them & encourage them, but restrain their excesses as much as possible.

2nd. Indians without our Territories. It is to be premised that
over them we have no controul.

The Indians on the Mississippi, the Ohio and the Wabash,
and all along the Western Frontier have been at war with the
United States for several years, not at the instigation of the
British as the American government have falsely reported, but
for the following reasons which they publicly assign.

1. Because the Americans drive them from their hunting
grounds.
2. Because the American government make fraudulent purchases of their lands from Indians who have no power to sell
—one or two insignificant members of a village for example.
3. Because the American government have connived at their
agents embezzling the small pittance which they give the Indians for lands
4th Because the American government have paid the Indians
only one farthing an acre for lands which they sold immediately after for six dollars making it a most productive article of
revenue and even this miserable pittance of one farthing never
reached the Indians
5. Because the American government have established what
they call trading posts in the Indian territory under the pretence
of supplying them with necessaries instead of money for their
lands at which posts the most scandalous frauds have taken place

6. Because these posts are turned into military stations at the pleasure of the American Government to the annoyance of the Indians & to their ultimate subjugation.

7. Because they are deprived of their usual supplies since the American Government adopted the Anticommercial systm. The non-importation, embargo, and non-intercourse laws have been very detrimental to the Indians.

8. Because the American Government neither attend to the feelings or rights of the poor Indians but as they are independent they have a right to the privileges of independent nations.

These and many other reasons were given as the causes of the war by the Famous Chief Tecumpseh to General Brock when he was lately at Detroit on his expedition against General Hull. This Indian Chief unites the most astonishing wisdom to the most determined valour—he has been employed for several years in uniting all the Indians against the Americans & hearing that General Brock was expected at Detroit to oppose the American General Hull, he came to pay him a visit. It is very easy to lament the massacre of a family or individual, and during such a lamentation we are apt to forget that by driving a tribe from its hunting ground it must either starve or trespass upon the hunting ground of the neighbouring tribe, and a war of extermination is the consequence. Since the United States have seized upon Florida from the Spaniards they have been attacked by the Indians who complain that the Settlers are coming upon their lands. These nations are not in the territories of the United States, but the Americans go to seek them, build houses, & clear lands within their precincts & when such are destroyed they raise a noise & make it a cause of war. Indeed the American government are in my opinion systematically employed in exterminating the Indians, if not always by open force, at least by an insiduous policy. In Kentucky the Americans shoot Indians with as little ceremony as wild beasts, and the farce of their civilizing them is the Cant of Mr Jefferson to gain applause from foreign nations. I might enter more into detail, but I think I have said enough to convince you that the question of employing Indians is not a question of policy but of absolute necessity. Indeed in order to gain a complete command of the Indians, the United States are exerting all their force to subdue Upper Canada. This Province is of infinitely greater importance to them than Lower Canada as it respects their policy with the Indians. But I trespass on your Patience. I have the honor to be

Honble Sir
Your most obedt Humble Servt

Honble Mr Wilberforce

Alexander Smyth: Proclamation

In the fall of 1812, Brigadier General Alexander Smyth, inspector general of the army under William Eustis, was sent to fight on the Niagara frontier. A caricature of haughty self-importance, he refused to meet, let alone take orders from, Stephen Van Rensselaer, a "mere" militia commander and, worse, a Federalist. After Van Rensselaer's disaster at Queenston, Smyth, who had sat out the battle, was given command of the Niagara campaign, but his arrogant behavior crippled his authority, winning nothing from his men but contempt and the nickname "Van Bladder." His high-flown call for volunteers from New York, presented below, was widely mocked and yielded few recruits. He spent weeks devising an elaborate plan of attack on Fort Erie, which his officers then rejected as impracticable. After this his men began to take potshots at his quarters, and at least one publicly denounced him as "a d——d *coward*" who manufactured delay. With winter approaching, operations on the front were suspended, and Smyth requested leave to visit family in Virginia. So ended the Niagara campaign of 1812.

———————

TO THE MEN OF NEW YORK.

For many years you have seen your country oppressed with numerous wrongs. Your Government, although above all others devoted to peace, have been forced to draw the sword and rely for redress of injuries on the valor of the American people.

That valor has been conspicuous; but the nation has been unfortunate in the choice of some of those who directed it. One army has been disgracefully surrendered and lost. Another has been sacrificed by a precipitate attempt to pass it over at the strongest point of the enemy's lines, with most incompetent means. The cause of these miscarriages is apparent. The commanders were popular men, "destitute alike of theory and experience" in the art of war.

In a few days the troops under my command will plant the

American standard in Canada. They are men accustomed to obedience, silence and steadiness. They will conquer or they will die.

Will you stand with your arms folded and look on this interesting struggle? Are you not related to the men who fought at Burlington and Saratoga? Has the race degenerated? Or have you, under the baneful influence of contending factions, forgotten your country? Must I turn from you and ask the men of the Six Nations to support the Government of the United States? Shall I imitate the officers of the British King and suffer our ungathered laurels to be tarnished with ruthless deeds? Shame, where is thy blush? No! where I command, the vanquished and the peaceful man, the child, the maid, and the matron shall be secure from wrong. If we conquer, we will "conquer but to save."

Men of New York!

The present is the hour of renown. Have you not a wish for fame? Would you not choose to be one of those who, imitating the heroes whom Montgomery led, have, in spite of the seasons, visited the tomb of the chief and conquered the country where he lies? Yes, you desire your share of fame. Then seize the present moment; if you do not, you will regret it and say: "The valiant have bled in vain, the friends of my country fell and I was not there."

Advance, then, to our aid. I will wait for you a few days. I cannot give you the day of my departure, but come on. Come in companies, half companies, pairs or singly. I will organize you for a short tour. Ride to this place if the distance is far and send back your horses. But remember that every man who accompanies us places himself under my command and shall submit to the salutary restraints of discipline.

ALEX. SMYTH, Brigade-General.

Camp near Buffalo, Nov. 10, 1812.

A CHRONICLE OF WRETCHEDNESS:
NORTHWESTERN FRONTIER,
SEPTEMBER 1812–JANUARY 1813

William Atherton: from Narrative of the Suffering & Defeat of the North-Western Army

William Atherton was eighteen years old when, in 1812, he enrolled as a private in the 1st Rifle Regiment of Kentucky. The early pages of his memoirs, a small book printed at his own expense thirty years later, detail his part in the scourge on Miami Indian villages that followed the siege of Fort Wayne, a campaign directed by the new commander of the Army of the Northwest, William Henry Harrison. They also chronicle Atherton's winter-long trial at "Fort Starvation," Brigadier General James Winchester's Camp No. 3 on the Maumee River in Ohio. Unlike most soldiers' memoirs of the war, Atherton's are concise in their discussion of military matters but expansive on the subject of daily life among the troops. "History has given us an account of the sufferings of the North-Western Army only in general terms," Atherton wrote in a preface, "but no where . . . has there been given a particular detail of the sufferings and privations of that detachment of the army. . . . [I]t is hoped that what has been said will be sufficient to give the youthful reader some idea of what that 'Spartan band' were called to endure. To the old men of our country these things, perhaps, will not be new."

THE volunteers from Kentucky, under the command of Colonels Allen, Lewis and Scott, left their homes on the 12th of August, 1812, and rendezvoused at Georgetown. Thence took the Dry Ridge road to Cincinnati, where we remained a few days. We then pursued our march through the State of Ohio, by the way of Piqua; from which place we were called to the relief of Fort Wayne.

When we arrived at Fort Wayne, we found that the Indians which had annoyed the fort for some time, had retreated. We were then ordered to march to two Indian towns, for the purpose of burning the houses and destroying their corn. When we had accomplished this, and returned to Fort Wayne, we there met the Kentucky mounted volunteers under the command of Colonel Simrall. We marched from Fort Wayne on the 22d of September, and pursued Wayne's route down the Miami towards old Fort Defiance, where we arrived on the 30th. During the latter part of this march we were frequently annoyed by the enemy. Our advance party of spies fell in with a body of Indians, and a small skirmish ensued, in which one of the spies was slightly wounded, and several of the enemy killed; the exact number could not be ascertained, as the Indians always carry off their dead when practicable.

———

The annoyance from the enemy greatly retarded our movements, as it was impossible, with any degree of certainty, to ascertain either their situation or force. In crossing the river, however, their whole movements were discovered. The British, with their artillery from Detroit, and a large party of Indians, were progressing towards Fort Wayne. After engaging our spies, and annoying our advanced guard, they faced to the right about and retreated precipitately. Owing to the situation of the army (being short of provisions) it was impossible, by forced marches, to intercept them. At this time Captain Bland Ballard showed his skill in Indian fighting, by making good his retreat, for which he deserves much. His Lieutenant, Munday, who had parted with him in the morning, also effected a retreat, by charging upon the Indians, before they ascertained his numbers, and then dashing into camp. The next day our spies had an action—had one wounded—and saw several Indians fall. The day following the Indians showed in front of the spies, and snapped at one of our men—a fire was returned, which left blood where the Indians stood. The Indian spies were on horse back, which rendered it difficult to ascertain their situation. Our spies could not, with propriety, venture far from us, and we could not advance until the country was reconnoitered, consequently our march was slow. A short turn to the right, however, and crossing the river at an unexpected place, gave us the advantage. After crossing the river we saw that the enemy had artillery, and were ahead of us. We were now within six miles of Defiance. It was very bushy for more than a mile before we approached the fort. The army remained at camp that morning, and sent out spies in every direction; when they returned, they reported that the enemy had gone off down the river. It was then deemed inexpedient to move so late in the afternoon. It was supposed there were from one to two hundred British, with from two to five pieces of cannon, and from four to six hundred Indians. The artillery was certainly brought up by water to this place, and re-embarked here again. Their object must have been Fort Wayne.

By this time we became very scarce of provisions, having nothing for some days but the poorest beef. Some of the men began to murmer—and some went so far as to talk of returning home—but when this was known by the officers, measures were taken to put a stop to it. Colonel Allen, in an animated and encouraging address to his men, banished the idea of shrinking in the day of adversity. Captain Simpson, also, was not unemployed. This was the first time we had sensibly felt the want of bread.

General Harrison returned to the army on the second of October. We were greatly animated at seeing him among us once more. He addressed the whole army in a most thrilling speech, which kindled in the breasts of the men, generally, an increased desire to meet the enemy, and a willingness to endure any privations they might be called to suffer. He remained with us but a short time.

———

Before General Harrison left Defiance, he selected a situation for a new fort. A party of men was detailed to procure timber for the buildings. General Winchester, also, moved his camp from the Miami to the Auglaize river.

The command of the left was now confided to General Winchester, who was instructed to occupy the rapids as soon as possible for the purpose of securing a quantity of corn which had been raised by the inhabitants.

Before General Harrison left, he ordered General Tupper to take all his mounted men and proceed down the Miami as far as the Rapids. When this order was issued, General Tupper's command was immediately supplied with provision for eight days, which included all the flour in camp. About 12 o'clock next day a party of Indians fired on the men immediately on the opposite bank of the Miami, one of whom they killed, scalped, and then fled! This, for a moment, produced alarm, and the troops were formed in order of battle. Presently small parties of horsemen began to cross the river in pursuit of the enemy. The horses were mostly at grass, and as soon as they could be caught the owners engaged in the pursuit. Eight or ten parties went, mostly from Colonel Simrall's regiment, in one of which was the Colonel himself. General Tupper ordered that no more should cross, apprehending from the boldness of the Indians that a large body might be lying in ambush. General Winchester now ordered Tupper to commence his expedition towards the Rapids by pursuing these Indians. Tupper had previously sent Logan and six other Indians to reconnoiter, and did not seem willing to go until they returned. They arrived in the evening, stating that they had seen a party of Indians, about fifty strong, ten miles down the river.

Colonel Allen now offered his services to accompany Tupper to the Rapids in any station he thought proper to place him, from a private soldier upwards. He accepted his offer, and caused him to be announced as his aid. General Winchester issued positive orders that General Tupper should proceed; but he declined, saying he would prefer going by the Ottoway towns, &c.

At this time about three hundred of the mounted riflemen, whose terms of service had expired, left the camp and returned home. Colonel Simrall, believing that the orders of General Winchester to General Tupper would not be executed, returned to the settlements to recruit his horses and be in readiness to march when his services should be necessary. It will be sufficient to say this expedition at this time failed.

After the mounted men left us, nothing of importance occurred for some time. We were engaged building the fort, which, through much difficulty, was at length completed. This will appear, when it is known that at that place we had not our full rations. That this fact may be established, I will give some extracts from a letter, written at the time, by James Garrard, Brigade Inspector: "We have not" says he "drawn a full ration since the 8th September. Sometimes without beef—at other times without flour: and the worst of all, entirely without salt, which has been much against the health of the men. They bear it with much patience, although they have been without salt for five or six days." At this time the sick amounted to two hundred and sixteen men, and there was some dissatisfaction in the army against the government because the necessary supplies were not sent on. But when they became acquainted with the true cause of the deficiency, that the fault was not in the government, but in the change of affairs since their march, they were perfectly satisfied. Again Mr. Garrard states: "You would be surprised to see the men appear on the brigade parade. Some without shoes, others without socks, blankets, &c. All the clothes they have are linen; but they discharge their duty with cheerfulness, hoping that their country will supply their wants before the severity of winter comes on." There are many who can testify to the truth of the above. What clothes we took with us when we left our homes had worn very thin. Many left home with their linen hunting-shirts, and some of these were literally torn to rags by the brush. We had heard that General Harrison had made a powerful appeal to the ladies of Kentucky and Ohio, and we were sure it would not be in vain; and about this time we learned that the ladies of Kentucky were exerting themselves to relieve the soldiers of this army. It was highly gratifying to us to know that we were kept in remembrance by the ladies of our own State.

We now began preparations to march towards the Rapids—having completed a new and beautiful fort, situated near the old one, which, like its brave progenitor, had fallen before the irresistible hand of time. We crossed the Miami, and camped a few miles below Defiance.

Very few Indians were seen or heard of for some weeks, neither had any mischief been done, though the men were very careless, and would hunt game and fruit far and near—often strolling miles from the camp without guns. The ground on this side of the river, where we first encamped, being disagreeable, we marched a few miles down the river, remained a short time, and then removed to what is called camp No. 3. There we had a beautiful situation, and an abundance of fine timber.

Although the enemy had now retreated and left us in possession of the Territory, we were still called to contend with the severe weather, which not only prevented the necessary supply of provisions from reaching us, but in our thinly clad condition became very oppressive. We knew that efforts were making to supply us with clothes and rations, but the roads were almost impassable. About the first of November the men became very sickly—the typhus fever raged with violence—three or four would sometimes die in a day. It is said upwards of three hundred was on the sick list at one time.

Towards the latter part of November, or first of December, the rain fell in torrents. We were ordered to build huts, for to advance at that time appeared impossible. Many were so entirely destitute of shoes and other clothing, that had they been compelled to march any distance they must have frozen. What we suffered at Defiance was but the beginning of affliction. We now saw nothing but hunger, and cold, and nakedness, staring us in the face. At one time, for several days, we scarcely had any thing to eat but some poor beef. I have seen the butchers go to a beef and kill it, when lying down and could not get out of the way. This kind of beef, and hickory roots, was our principal subsistence for a length of time. When we had been here a few weeks, and the ground became covered with snow, and we no longer apprehended danger from the enemy, we were permitted to hunt. This we did to some extent, but in a short time there was not a squirrel to be found near the encampment.

————

Soon after this the river was frozen so as to bear us across. This enlarged our hunting ground, for now we were suffering greatly for provisions. At one time, for eleven days, we had nothing but pork, just killed, without salt. These privations were submitted to with astonishing patience—there was scarcely a whisper or a murmur in all the camp—which manifested a patriotism worthy the cause in which they were engaged.

On the 22d of December we were informed, by general order, that we should have flour that day, and that the prospect was fair for a constant supply.

The 24th was the period set for our stay at camp No. 3, which was pleasing intelligence to the whole army. On the 25th, at sunrise, we were commanded to march to the Rapids. Being the vanguard of the North-Western Army, General Harrison instructed us to make a stand there until we should be joined by the North-Western Army. For some time previous we had been engaged in making sleds to haul our baggage, some of which had to be drawn by the soldiers themselves.

A more pleasant and expeditious march than this had been anticipated, for after much fatigue and labor, a great number of canoes had been made, with which we expected our baggage would be taken with great ease and safety down the river; but to our great disappointment, before we could make preparations, or before our provisions reached us—without which we could not move—cold weather set in, and closed up the river. This circumstance at first seemed to present an obstacle insurmountable; many of the men were sick, and that sickness occasioned by being compelled to eat fresh pork without bread or salt, and from being exposed to cold and wet.

But this was not the only difficulty. Many who had not been so provident, perhaps, as the case required, were bare of clothes, and almost barefooted, and were ill prepared to undertake such a march through the snow.

Thus, ill clad, worn down by fatigue and starvation, and chilled by the cold wintry blasts of the north we were compelled to brave—there was no alternative—our condition made it necessary for us to fall upon some other plan to reach the Rapids, where we expected to meet supplies. Under the impulse of this hope we went to work and made sleds sufficient to carry the baggage. But as these were not sufficient to take the sick, many of them had to be left behind. On the 25th, as above stated, we bid adieu to this memorable place, camp No. 3, where lie the bones of many a brave man. This place will live in the recollection of all who suffered there, and for more reasons than one. There comes up before the mind the many times the dead march was heard in the camp, and the solemn procession that carried our fellow sufferers to the grave—the many times we were almost on the point of starvation—and the many sickening disappointments which were experienced by the army from day to day, and from week to week, by the failure of promised supplies, which were daily expected: and, also, that here we parted with the sick, some of whom we were to see no more.

Thus poorly equipped, deeply affected, and yet overjoyed,

we took up the line of march. The reader may ask how such a number of sleds could be drawn, seeing there was not a supply of horses. Some of them were drawn by the *men themselves*— five men were hitched to a sleigh, and, through snow and water, dragged them on at the rate of about ten miles a day. But to our great disadvantage during our march, there was an immense fall of snow. It seemed that the very elements fought against us. But notwithstanding all, we moved slowly on to-wards the destined point. What the men suffered by day, was comparatively nothing to what they experienced by night. The reader can form but a faint idea unless he had been on the spot, and had seen and felt what we saw and felt. Some time was required to arrange the encampment, during which time the men were compelled to keep their places in the lines, and thus become so chilled as to be almost unfit for the necessary exer-tion of preparing a resting place for themselves. The snow, which was about knee deep, had first to be cleared away, then fire to be struck with flint and steel, and when no lynn bark could be had, brush was substituted in its place, which formed our bed. Hard and uncomfortable as it was, yet such was our fatigue that we generally slept soundly. To give a detailed ac-count of individual suffering during this march, from camp No. 3 to the Rapids, would swell this sketch beyond its in-tended limits; and perhaps facts would be related which the present generation, who have but little knowledge of these things only from report, would scarcely believe.

Our little vehicles being made upon a small scale, were too light to carry the burden put upon them, and not sufficiently high to cross the little streams which lay in our way, conse-quently much damage was done to our baggage, and our pro-visions (which were barely sufficient to last us to the Rapids,) was much injured by getting wet. This, it will be plainly seen, was well calculated to increase our sufferings. In fact, the half of what was endured on this slow and painful march has never yet been published to the world, and perhaps never will.

At length, on the 10th of January, we arrived at the Rapids. General Winchester had previously sent forward a detach-ment of six hundred and seventy men, under General Payne, to attack a body of Indians which General Harrison had been informed was lying in an old fortification at Swan creek, a few miles farther down the river. After passing several miles below the old fort, and discovering no appearance of Indians, the whole returned to the position which the army intended to occupy.

About this time the clothes which were sent by the patriotic sons and daughters of Kentucky, began to reach the army. The gratitude of the troops generally was beyond expression. Some had withstood the keen blasts of that cold northern country, until some time in January, with linen hunting shirts and pantaloons, and many almost without either shoes or socks. General Payne in a letter to Governor Shelby, in which he expresses his gratitude, as well as that of the troops, says—"As an *earnest* of her disposition to aid the National Government, Kentucky, at an early period, with a characteristic ardour, sent forth more than her quota required by the Government; and whilst a spark of genuine feeling animates the breasts of her volunteers in the North-Western Army, they can never cease to feel a lively gratitude for the further *earnest* of her anxiety for the cause, manifested in the late abundant supply of clothing." It certainly was a source of heartfelt satisfaction, to express a proper sense of the obligations under which the patriotism of the *sons* of Kentucky had placed her volunteers; but the pleasure was greatly heightened when we reflected that to the *daughters* of Kentucky we were mostly indebted for imperious supplies to meet the blasts of a northern winter.

I hope it is not still too late (though many who engaged in that laudable work have gone from this scene of war and bloodshed,) for me to express my unfeigned gratitude to the daughters of my native State for the blessings bestowed on me as an individual; and as I have never had an opportunity before to express myself, permit me further to say, that these favors, while I possess a spark of feeling, shall never cease to produce a lively sense of gratitude. Help, in real need, is not forgotten.

———

A large storehouse was immediately commenced for the purpose of securing the provisions and baggage. We found a quantity of corn in the fields, which was soon gathered; and before any machinery was prepared to pound and sift it, a quantity was boiled whole, and eaten without even salt. But we quickly arranged to have it made into hommony, and after the hogs came, we fared well upon "hog and hommony." You may judge of our relish for our food, when I tell you that one of our company, whose name I will not give, eat so much corn that he appeared to be actually foundered, and unable to walk for more than a week.

William B. Northcutt: Diary

December 16–25, 1812

Like William Atherton, William Brooks Northcutt took part in Harrison's campaign against the Miamis. A twenty-two-year-old distiller's apprentice in Bourbon County, Kentucky, Northcutt signed up for a yearlong stint with Captain William Garrard's company of mounted volunteers, a unit that soon attached itself to James V. Ball's 2nd Regiment of U.S. Light Dragoons. On December 10, he and some six hundred other mounted troops, under the command of Colonel John B. Campbell, set out from Fort Greene Ville (Greenville, Ohio) to surprise the Miamis along the Mississinewa River, a tributary of the Wabash in Indiana Territory. In the edition of his diary prepared in 1878, Northcutt called Campbell's mission one of the most hazardous undertaken during the War of 1812: "In the depths of winter, with the snow half leg deep, to penetrate an unknown Indian wilderness over one hundred miles against a wiley foe with their numbers to us unknown."

On the night of the 16th of Decbr. 1812 we marched all night in order to get to the Indian town about daylight and take it by surprise, but our guide lost his Bushes a little before daylight and the Col. ordered a halt until the guide found his way again, and this detained us so that we did not get there until about one hour of the sun on the morning of the 17th.

In this night's march a great many of the boys got frost bitten, by getting off thier horses and walking, in order to warm themselves. The fateauge of walking would put them in a perspiration and mounting again would chill off, and frost bite in a very little time. I stuck to my horse and never got off the whole night which was a very trying thing to do, some times being so numbed with cold that I would drop to Sleep in Spite of all that I could do and the first thing that I would Know would be a limb of Brush across my face and eyes making the fire roll, leaving me in no very good humor for I thought that if the Indian that I had to fight the next day had of Been there that I could have given it to him good.

The guide found his way as soon as the day Light made its appearance and we Resumed our march. We were then about 2 miles as near as we could guess, from the first town. We had marched about one mile when our spies let the Commander Know that we were discovered. They were a little ways ahead of the Army when they saw three Indians in the act of cacthing thier horses. The spies and Indians discovered Each other about the same time. The Indians caught and mounted thier horses, and took for the town to give the Alarm and the Spies Came Back to Report to the Commander.

He ordered a line of Battle to be formed when we were within about a mile of the town, he then Ordered a Charge on the town. We then Started on the charge through a tremendious thick peace of woods. We had to pack an Ax to Each mess and we took time about carrying of it, and it fell to my lot that morning to carry the Ax. Our Squadron was on the right of the line and Simmerals on the left and the Infantry on pack horses in the center. They Raised the Yell on the left, and it Extended to the right and put our horses in such a fret that I could not carry the Ax and my gun, and manage my mare and I concluded that the gun would be of more use to me than the Ax so I threw the Ax away marking the place where I threw it so that if I wanted it that I might Know where to find it again.

When our line of battle was formed it Extended for more than one half mile in Length, and our Squadron being on the Extreme Right, missed the town and struck the river a little Below the town, and Simmeral's Rigement which was on the left struck the town and took it before we could wheel to the left and get up there they had taken it, and Killed Eight of the Indians and one big negroe, took forty two prisoners and dispursed the Ballance over the river. We dashed over the river after them, but only Killed one or two of them and took some prisoners. One young man took a Squaw on the other side of the river and put her in a Canoe to Bring her Back to the town, and when he started with her the Canoe turned down Stream and he could not get it straight for the other side with his paddle, when the Squaw put out her hand and at a few liks with her hand she Straitened it and Brought it Right over to the Great merriment of the Boys that was Looking on at them.

When we had taken this town and burned all of the Hutts and Wigwams in it, Except one of the largest Cabins that was Reserved for the accomadation of the prisoners, we went to forming an Encampment in one Edge of the town. Some of the boys says to me, Bill where is that Ax that belongs to the mess? I said that I had thrown it away in the charge on the town. They Said that I had to get it. Well Says I if I must I suppose I must. So I mounted my mare and put Back to the place where I had thrown it away, as I threw it I marked the place. It was where two old trees had fell one across the other, and as I went by the place I pitched it under right where they crossed. So I found the Ax, got down and picked it up and started back with it. I had not gone fifty yards from the place where I picked up the Ax, when I met two men that were going back after Something that they had lost, and I had not got one Hundred Yards further until I heard a gun fire and they came running back and Just after they passed me one of them fell dead from his horse, he being Shot through with a Bullitt. There was a company of men went back to where he was shot but could find no Indian nor no Sign of one so it Remained a mystery how the man got Shot. He was all the man on our side that was Killed on the 17th.

After fixing up a fire and geting Something to eat of which we had very little for our three days Rashion that we drew at fort greenville was about gone, Ball's Squadron were ordered to march three miles lower down the river to another town to destroy it. When we got to the town it was Evacuated by the Indians. There were a great number of dogs and Horses in the town left there by the Indians. We burned the town, Killed thier dogs and caught about forty of thier horses. The horses they were very wild and we had to use stratargey to cacth them. They were principally in an old field and we Surrounded them with the whole Squadron and kept closing in on them until we got them into a Huddle. We then formed a solid line of horse-men around them and some 15 or 20 of the Boys went in to Catching of them, Haltering them and bringing them out. I was one of the guard that Stood around them and I saw three of them Kick one man at the Same time. We Brought them up to the first town, and tied them in lines with our own horses, and that night a great many of them got Killed.

In the second Battle which was fought in the morning before day of the 18th of December 1812 our Squadron got back to the first town about an hour by Sun in the Evening and went into Camp in our usual position which was always the Right of the army. We had Killed some of the Indians cattle that day which I thought was the best beef that I had ever tasted. We cooked some of it with some dried Roasting years that I had got out of an old gum in one of thier Huts before we Burned it down. I got my Cap full of it and divided it with my mess and my mare, for our forage were gone as well as our provisions. With the Indian beef and tosama nona we had a prety good supper that night and it was the last for some days.

The orderly Seargent Came along and says he, Northcutt on guard tonight. Says I, recon that there is a Mistake in the matter. Sir, no mistake whatever says he and if you don't go I will Report you to the Captain. Report away says I for it is not my turn and I am not a going. With that he went to the Captain and made his report, when the old Captain came Bustling along and said Billy what is the matter with you and Mack? Says I, Captain I never refuse to do my duty Sir when it is my time. He says how is it? Why Sir I was on guard last night by being in advance guard all day, and when the orders came to march all night the guard was Called in and I claim that for a tour. You are Right Sir, Seargent Summon a new guard. I happened to stand at the head of the Seargent's old list and before he would write another he was a going to Summon the old one and make it serve, but my refusing to go cleared all the rest of the Boys.

That night about two hours before day on the morning of the 18th we had a false alarm and we were Roused and paraded for battle and that false alarm saved our Bacon for we did not lie down anymore But Roused up our fires and went to prepareing something to eat. We had a few sea Bisket and a little coffe and some of the Indian beef. One of my mesmates and one of the other mess, that always built a fire with us so that one fire might do both our Cooking, had been down to the river and got a tin Bucket of water and sot on the fire to make our coffe when about one half Hour before day the Indians made thier attack on our Camp at the right-angle of the Encampment which was as usual in a hollow square with our horses tied to stakes 20 paces in our Rear. One of my mess mates was on guard where the attack was made and said he saw them coming up in Indian file for some time and Kept snapping his gun at them until another sentinal hailed them when the foremost one of them halted and fired his gun as a Signal, when they raised the yell and formed thier line of battle and made right up to where he was standing and he fell in with them and they run together until they got to within about sixty yards of our line, and they stopped and he ran on into our lines and got shot twice after he came in.

By this time the Indians had formed thier lines and Commenced their attack on us with a terrible yell. They took possion of a Redout at the guard fire, dispersed the guard and Killed Pierce the captain of the guard with a war Hawk. The guard all ran in and left him behind. We were ordered to form in the rear of our fires and put them out which we did, and stood one fire from them in this position, when the officers discovered that they had the advantage of us they being in a thick clump of Woods, and we in an open place in the Edge of thier town with here and there a tree, and we were ordered to retreat and form behind our horses which was tied to stakes twenty paces in our rear.

When we left our first formation to get behind our horses the Indians made a Charge on us and some of them were Killed at our fires that we had left. They fought with desperation yelling all the time like so many fiends. Our watch word was FIGHT ON and we repeated it all the time, when a hoarse voice from thier side Bawled out FIGHT ON and be dam to you. Our Company had to stand the Brunt of the fight. We had two killed dead and a great many wounded. My right hand man was shot through the head and fell flat on his back with his gun cocked across his breast, and my left hand man had his right arm broken close to his right shoulder, and I had four mess mates badly wounded and how I escaped is a Mystery to me, and always will be for I was right in the thickest of the fight and never got a Scratch.

We had a great many of our horses Killed and wounded so

bad that we had to Kill them. Our ranks got so Badly thined that we had to be reinforced by Captain Butler's Company from the center of the Encampment. His was an Infantry company and fired by plattoons. We opened to the right and left and they formed in our lines, and formed in Sexions of Sixteen men in a Sexion, and from the time that they commenced thier fireing the note of the Indian yell began to change, for in a very Short time thier fire became very Scattering, and the smoke of the powder had settled on us so that we could not see them only by the flash of thier guns. When the sun was about one half hour high we oppened our Ranks again and let Trotter's troop of horses from Simmerel's Regiment out to make a charge on them, they haveing begun to retreat. Trotter went out and formed his line in order to make one fire on them. Before he made his Charge on them and while he was doing that the party of Indians that stayed back to cover thier Retreat, fired on his men. They being on thier horses and the Indians behind trees they cut his Company all to pieces, and rendered his charge of no avail.

But the Indians soon cleared out and we were not in a fix to follow them for we were pretyy badly crippled, and they left forty of their dead behind them but none of thier wounded. We took no prisoners in this fight. We had Eight Killed dead on the spot and four died of thier wounds, two coming in and two at Dayton and sixty five wounded. Our Squadron had to bear the Brunt of this fight the other part of the army not being engaged in any part of it. While the fight were going on the prisoners that we had taken the day before Kept up a continual hollowing and gabbering in the Hut that they were Confined in under guard.

When the battle was over we turned our attention to our own dead and wounded. Tom Webster the man that was on guard when the Indians made thier attack on our Camp got shot in the Shoulder. He fell and recovered. Said I to him, Tom are you badly hurt. Says he, d—n them that have Broke my Shoulder. I had just before that taken another one of my messmates that had got shot in the thigh, and put him on a Blanket behind a large tree, immediately in the Rear. I said to him, you can walk, you go where I have Just put Henry Wilson, and Keep out of our way and your own too, showing him the place. He went off and I saw no more of him until the Battle was over. When I went to hunt up my pets Said he to me, Bill they gave it to me again. Said I, how Come it? Why says he, you all Kept such a Hell of a fuss out there, and I Kept peeping around to see what you were after and they have shot me again in the side. But it happened to be a glancing shot and was not Very dangerous. But his Shoulder was Broke all to pieces, and we had to bring him in a horse litter with five more of our Company, but he got well and Joined us again before our time was out, the only one of the Wounded boys that did so.

In hunting up the Wounded I came across a man by the name of Scot that was Shot through his Breast, the ball going in just above the left nipple and coming out under his right Shoulder Blade. When I found him said I to him, are you badly hurt? Says he yes I am mortally wounded. I went off and got a Blanket and three of the boys to go with me to the place that I had left him. I spread out the Blanket and took hold of him to lay him on it when he looked up in my face and says Billy, you go and do something for them that there is some hopes of for as for me there is none. Said I to him where there is life there is hopes and we are going to take you to the doctor's fire. And we four boys took hold of a limb a peace and laid him on the Blanket, and took him to the Doctors, when they drew a silk handkerchief through him and Contrary to his own and Everybody's opinion he got Well, and wrote on to the board of war for a Leut. Commission, got it and went into the Regular Service and Stayed there during the war.

We gathered up the poor wounded boys and took them all to the Doctors quarters, and then we gathered up our dead and buried them all in one grave. We dug it in the floor of the hut that we had left for the prisoners to stay in. We levelled it off even with the other part of the floor, and set it on fire in order to keep the Indians from finding it or finding out how many of us they had Killed. There was one poor fellow that was shot through the head but could not Die, and the Doctors had to give him something to finish him so that we could bury him with the rest of the poor fellows. After dispensing with the Dead we then turned our attention to the poor Wounded boys how we were to Bring them away with us, for we had no

Cariages of any Sort. So we made horse litters to Bring them in in maner following—We cut poles about twelve feet long and took Canvas and sewed it around two of them and put them on horses one before and the other behind and put the wounded in between them, and it took two men to Each litter to manage the horses.

The Indians had Killed so many of our horses and it took so many to bring in the wounded that we were prety near all a foot. We fixed up and left the Battle ground about two o'clock on the Evening of the 18th and marched about two miles and Encamped by makeing of Breast work, for we Expected another attack hourly until we arrived at Fort Greenville, we were prety near out of ammunition. An accident happened to our ammunition a few days before we arrived at the Indian towns. We had two Boxes of Catriges on a pack horse, when he took fright and broke away from the man that was leading him, the package turned under his belly and he Kicked the Boxes to peices, and Scattered the Catriges for one quarter of a mile in the Snow and destroyed them.

We are now on our March back to Greenville, more than the half of us a foot and we had a great many sick and frostbitten. The morning Report this morning the 19th of December was three Hundred and ten fit for duty, the rest being Either wounded sick or frostbitten. We had the prisoners with us the most of them wemen and children. The Commander Ordered the Indian ponies that we had caught on the 17th in the lower town be given up for the Squaws and papooses to ride, which occasioned some hard swearing amongst the Boys that Claimed them as Captured property. There were some of them fine animals, one mare and yearling colt in particular. The man that had the colt refused to give him up and took him home with him to Lexington. He belonged to Trotter's Company from Lexington of six months men and his time was out and he took the colt home with him, but it was a mere streak of good luck for him that he did so, for we were on the point of Starvation and if provisions had not met us as Soon as they did his Colt would have Been Butchered and eaten by the troops, but that saved him and he took the Colt home with him. I lost my mare and had to walk into Dayton and pack my gun and

Sword. I got a soldier that rode a pack horse out to bring in my Saddle and Holsters to Dayton for me.

Our Captain lost both of his horses. There was three horses tied to one sapling and all three of them Killed, the Captain's his waiter boys and Leutenant Hickman's. The second day from the Battleground I overtook the old Captain waddleing along through the snow. He looked up and saw who I was and says he, Billy these are d—n tough times. Says I to him, Captain this is the fate of War and we will have to bear with them, when he swore that he would have a horse the next day. That night Captain Hopkins dismounted one of his men and let the Captain have his Horse, and some time in the day Some of the litters broke down and we had to halt to mend them up and when we went to start on again the Captain led the dragoon's horse up by the side of a log to get on him, got on the log and looked all around him and Bawled out at the top of his Voice, Bourbon Blues mount, when there was not a single Bourbon Blue there to mount but the old Captain himself, which occasioned some meriment for the boys that heard the order.

Today one of our wounded boys died in his litter, and we buried him in the woods by the side of an old log. We had about twenty wounded to bring into Dayton in these litters, and in a great many places the little ponds of water was frozen over so that they would make the horses slip and jolt the poor fellows so that they would Scream so that we would have to take the litters of the horses and carry them over the ice on our Shoulders. We had a very Severe time getting back to Dayton. We had to make Breast Work Every night until we got to Greenville and stand guard every other night which was Enough to try the spunk of the Very Best of us. There was three days and nights that I did not get one hours sleep during the night. It would take us until late in the night to Erect the Breast work, which was done by falling large trees on top of one a nother all around the Encampment and raising them about Breast high. The third night we had to be up all night occasioned by false alarms by the sentenals fireing and running into camp. The Commander ordered the Company to be divided and one half of them to stand one half Hour at the

Breast work while the other half stood by the fire and warmed themselves.

I belonged to our First Leutenant Dr. E Bayse and when our squad was at the Breast work looking out we saw a gun flash and the line of Sentinals broke to run in. I was by the Leut. when he hollowed out to me Shoot Northcutt by g-d they are Coming. Says I, they are our Boys. He ordered me again to Shoot swearing that they were Indians. By this time they had got so Close to the Breast work that he saw himself that they were our boys and told them to cryout the watch word, which was Greenville, when one of them Bawled out Greenfield, Greenfield, for god's Sake don't Shoot. They all Scaled the Breast work and run to the fire, where there was an old Frenchman that belonged to Butler's Company from Pittsburg. Says he to one of them, what you run for? Says the fellow I saw Eleven Indians. Says the Frenchman, how you know there was Eleven Indians? Because I counted them says the fellow. Says the old Frenchman you say you saw Eleven Indians and stop to count Eleven Indians and no shoot yet, to hell with such a Soldier. And they kept up such Sport as that all night and there were no Sleep for any of us that night. The Sentinals was paraded and sent back but just as often they would Break and run in.

One of our boys by the name of Jim Clark was on guard that night when they Kept runing in so that he told the Captain of the guard that he would fight at the guard fire until he died, but he was d—d if he could go Back to his post anymore that night. The next night it fell to my lot to go on guard, and when I started out to go to the guard fire I told my mess mates to go to bed and go to sleep for there should be no false alarms that night when I was on post. My time to go on duty was the Second Relief and the sentinal that I had to relieve was fast a sleep and I took his place Knowing that he had been asleep which made me look out with all the Eyes that I had.

I had not stood there long before I saw in the head of a hollow Right before me Something moving to wards me. I Sprung the triggers of my gun to be ready to shoot if an Enemy approached and when I set my triggers I heard two more Sentinals one to my right and the other to my left set thiers. The main Spring of our locks were so Strong that they could be heard to set a good ways off. Well when I heard thier locks set thinks I there is two of you not asleep anyhow, and when we came in off the guard we three had the Same tale to tell. I kept watching the object thinking about what I had told the boys in Camp about false alarms when I heard an Owl hollow Right opposite me and a nother one answer it right back of the Encampment. Then I remembered hearing old Indian fighters talking about them hollowing like owls. I then had it all fixed up that they were surrounding of the Camp and giving one another the Signal by the owl's hollow, and the object before me was one of thier Spies.

It Kept coming gradualy to wards me and I should certainly have fired had it not been for the promise made to the boys. I was determined to let it get close enough to me before I shot to make a sure shoot, and when that occured it turned out to be an old horse that had got out of the Camp, and was Boosing his way back.

The sentinal that was found asleep was Reported to his Captain by the Seargent of the guard and the next morning was punished for it by being tied across the Breast work and given fifteen licks well laid on, with a paddle made for the purpose.

That morning when the guard was Called in I was detailed as one of the Road cutters for the litters to pass along. About 10 oclock some of the litters Broke down and we were ordered to halt until they were mended up again. When we halted I pulled a peice of bark off an old dead hickry tree and the last thing that I Remembered was throwing it down at the foot of the tree. They mended up the litters and had all gone on, Road cutters and all, and left me sitting there fast asleep, when one of my mess mates that was in the rear guard caught me by the top of the head and asked me what I was doing there. I told him that I was Sleeping and by that time my company of Road cutters was a half mile Ahead, so I fell in with the rear guard and there marched the ballance of the day and when the Army halted for the night, I Slipt up and answered to my name so there was nothing more Said about it. I had got so worn out for want of Sleep that I was more like a dead man than a living one. A man can do about as well without Eating as he can without Sleeping.

We had forty two prisoners with us the most of them women and children and when Encamped at night the Squaws would have the wood to cut to make thier fires, the men standing by looking on. I saw six Squaws cutting down a tree not more than a foot and a half over. They had what they called Squaw axes and they commenced choping on the tree and Kept going Backwards one afeter the other all around the tree until it fell, and they all jumped on to it and Commenced cutting it up to make thier fire with.

Today another one of our poor wounded boys died in his litter and we had to bury him like we did the other by the side of a log in the wild woods. Today some provisions met us from the fort but it was so little it hardly gave us all a taste. It took us six or seven days to get from the battle ground to the fort. We left it on the 18th and got to the fort on the 24th of December, it being Christmas Eve. We had a hard time of it getting in for we had to build a Breast work Every night clear until we got to the fort, but when we got to the fort we had a Jubule for there we found a plenty to Eat and drink, and we had a merry Christmas of it.

We Encamped at one Edge of the fort without puting out a regular guard and had a real old fasheoned Christmas frolick. We had One old Squaw with us that Could Speak a little Broken English and I sopposed that Some of the boys had put her up to it, for about day light She Came along the lines Saying Clisamas gift, Clisamas gift which produced considerable mirth with the boys. Some would give her money and Some of them gave her Some Curses. We staid here all Christmas day and rested, a thing that we greatly needed, and here the Commander dispensed with the prisoners by giving Them up to the Indian Agent, and saw no more of them.

Elias Darnell: Journal

As the Northwestern campaign of 1812 drew to a close, Harrison decided to winter in a camp by the Maumee Rapids in Ohio. He ordered his second-in-command, Brigadier General Winchester, to join him there, but Winchester, then leading about a thousand troops to Detroit, elected first to push on to Frenchtown (Monroe, Michigan) to aid American settlers defending their homes from British assault. On January 22, 1813, Winchester was surprised at the River Raisin by a British and Indian force of about twelve hundred under the command of Colonel Henry Procter. During the ensuing Battle of Frenchtown, Winchester was captured and persuaded to surrender what remained of his army. Misinformed that Harrison's troops were marching behind Winchester's, Procter withdrew with most of his five hundred prisoners to Fort Amherstburg. This left some one hundred wounded Americans at the mercy of the Indians, who, the next day, scalped about thirty of them. In 1854 Elias Darnell, a Kentucky militiaman, published a vivid account of Frenchtown and the River Raisin Massacre, the bloodiest series of events in the annals of the Army of the Northwest.

———————

17*th.* A Frenchman came yesterday from the river Raisin; he said two companies of British had just arrived from Canada, and the Indians were collecting, and intended to burn Frenchtown in a few days. By the repeated solicitations of the French, and being counselled by some of the field-officers, the General has been induced to order out a detachment of five hundred and seventy men, destined to the river Raisin; it was said, contrary to the instructions of Gen. Harrison. The detachment started* early with three days' provisions, and proceeded on twenty miles near to Presqu' Isle, a French village on the south side of the Maumee River. The sight of this village filled each heart with emotions of cheerfulness and joy; for we had been

———————

*The French, who were looking at us when we started, were heard to say, we were not men enough.

nearly five months in the wilderness, exposed to every inconvenience, and excluded from everything that had the appearance of a civilized country. When the inhabitants of the village discovered us, they met us with a white flag, and expressed particular friendship for us. They informed us the British and Indians had left Frenchtown a few days ago, and had gone to Brownstown. About three hours after dark, a reinforcement of one hundred and ten men overtook us, commanded by Col. Allen. Some time in the latter part of the night an express came from the river Raisin, informing Col. Lewis there were four hundred Indians and two companies of British there, and that Colonel Elliott was to start the next morning from Malden with a reinforcement.

18th. We started early, in order to get there before Col. Elliott; after travelling fifteen miles, mostly on the ice, we received information of the enemy being there waiting for us; we were then within three miles of Frenchtown; we proceeded on with no other view than *to conquer or die*. When we advanced in sight of the town, and were about a quarter of a mile from it, the British saluted us by the firing of a piece of cannon; they fired it three times, but no injury was sustained. During this time we formed the line of battle, and, raising a shout,* advanced on them briskly; they soon commenced the firing of their small arms, but this did not deter us from a charge; we advanced close and let loose on them; they gave way, and we soon had possession of the village without the loss of a man! Three were slightly wounded. Twelve of their warriors were slain and scalped, and one prisoner taken before they got to the woods. In retreating, they kept up some firing. We pursued them half a mile to the woods, which were very brushy and suited to their mode of fighting. As we advanced, they were fixing themselves behind logs, trees, &c. to the best advantage;

---

*A Frenchman who lived in this village said when the word came the Americans were in sight, there was an old Indian smoking at his fireside; the Indian exclaimed, "*Ho, de Mericans come; I suppose Ohio men come, we give them another chase:*" (alluding to the time they chased Gen. Tupper from the Rapids.) He walked to the door smoking, apparently very unconcerned, and looked at us till we formed the line of battle, and rushed on them with a mighty shout! he then called out "*Kentuck, by God!*" and picked up his gun and ran to the woods like a wild beast.

our troops rushed on them resolutely, and gave them Indian play, took the advantage of trees, &c. and kept them retreating a mile and a half in the woods. During this time a heavy fire was kept up on both sides; at length, after a battle of three hours and five minutes, we were obliged to stop the pursuit on account of the approach of night, and retire to the village; we collected our wounded and carried them to the village, leaving our dead on the ground. In this action the Kentuckians displayed great bravery, after being much fatigued with marching on the ice; cowardice was entirely discountenanced; each was anxious to excel his fellow-soldiers in avenging his injured country; those only fell in the rear who were most fatigued. Our loss in this action was eleven killed and fifty wounded.* Although the enemy had the advantage of the village in the first attack, and of the woods in the second, their loss, by the best information, far exceeded ours. A Frenchman stated they had fifty-four killed and a hundred and forty wounded, part of whom were carried to his house, on Sand Creek, a few miles from the village. An express and the Indian prisoner were sent immediately to the Rapids. Some dispute arose between the Indians and some of the French on Sand Creek; the Indians killed an old man and his wife; in consequence of this the French were enraged, and resolved to get revenge. They applied to us for assistance, but it was thought improper to leave the village, though some of them had assisted us and fought in the front of the battle.

19th.   A party was sent out to the battle-ground to bring in the dead, which were found scalped and stripped except one. In going over the battle-ground, great signs were seen (by the blood and where they had been dragged through the snow) of a considerable loss on the part of the enemy. Two of the wounded died. The British left a considerable quantity of provisions and some store goods, which answered us a valuable purpose. The wounded could have been as well accommodated here with every necessary as in any part of Kentucky. Apples, cider, sugar, butter, and whiskey appeared to be plenty. The river Raisin runs an east course through a level country, interspersed

---

*It would have been better for us if we had been contented with the possession of the village, without pursuing them to the woods.

with well-improved farms, and is seventy or eighty yards wide; the banks are low. Frenchtown is situated on the north side of this river, not more than three miles from the place it empties into Lake Erie. There is a row of dwelling-houses, about twenty in number, principally frame, near the bank, surrounded with a fence made in the form of picketing, with split timber, from four to five feet high; this was not designed as a fortification, but to secure their yards and gardens.

21st. A reinforcement of two hundred and thirty men arrived in the afternoon; also Gen. Winchester, Col. Wells, Major M'Clanahan, Capt. Hart, surgeons Irvin and Montgomery, and some other gentlemen, who came to eat apples and drink cider, having been deprived of every kind of spirits nearly two months. The officers having viewed and laid off a piece of ground for a camp and breastworks, resolved that it was too late to remove and erect fortifications that evening; farther, as they resolved to remove early next day, it was not thought worth while, though materials were at hand, to fortify the right wing, which therefore encamped in the open field,* and Col. Wells, their commander, set out for the Rapids late in the evening. A Frenchman arrived here late in the evening from Malden, and stated that a large number of Indians and British were coming on the ice with artillery to attack us; he judged their number to be three thousand; this was not believed by some of our leading men, who were regaling themselves with whiskey and loaf sugar; but the generality of the troops put great confidence in the Frenchman's report, and expected some fatal disaster to befall us; principally because Gen. Winchester had taken up his head-quarters nearly half a mile from any part of the encampment, and because the right wing was exposed. Ensign Harrow was sent with a party of men, some time after night, by the orders of Col. Lewis, to bring in all the men, either officers or privates, that he might find out of their quarters. After finding some and giving them their orders, he went to a brick house, about a mile up the river, and entered a room; finding it not occupied, he immediately went above stairs and saw two men, whom he took to be British officers, talking with the landlord. The landlord asked him to walk

*This want of precaution was a great cause of our mournful defeat!

down into a stove room, and handing his bottle, asked him to drink, and informed him "there was no danger, for the British had not a force sufficient to whip us." So Harrow returned about 1 o'clock and reported to Col. Lewis what he had seen. Col. Lewis treated the report with coolness, thinking the persons seen were only some gentlemen from town; just at daybreak the reveille began to beat, as usual; this gave joy to the troops, who had passed the night under the apprehensions of being attacked before day. The reveille had not been beating more than two minutes before the sentinels fired three guns in quick succession; this alarmed our troops, who quickly formed and were ready for the enemy before they were near enough to do execution. The British immediately discharged their artillery, loaded with balls, bombs, and grape-shot, which did little injury; they then attempted to make a charge on those in the pickets, but were repulsed with great loss. Those on the right being less secure for the want of fortification, were overpowered by a superior force, and were ordered to retreat to a more advantageous piece of ground. They got in disorder and could not be formed.* The Indians pursued them from all quarters, and surrounded, killed, and took the most of them. The enemy again charged on the left with redoubled vigor, but were again forced to retire. Our men lay close behind the picketing, through which they had portholes, and every one having a rest took sight, that his ammunition might not be spent in vain. After a long and bloody contest, the enemy finding they could not, either by stratagem or force, drive us from our fortification, retired to the woods, leaving their dead on the ground, except a party that kept two pieces of cannon in play on our right. A sleigh was seen three or four hundred yards from our lines going towards the right, supposed to be laden with ammunition to supply the cannon. Four or five men rose up and fired at once, and killed the man and wounded the horse. Some Indians who were hid behind houses continued to annoy us with scattering balls. At this time bread from the commissary's

---

*When the right wing began to retreat, it is said orders were given by some of the officers to the men in the eastern end of the picketing to march out to their assistance. Capt. Price and a number of men sallied out. Capt. Price was killed, and most of the men.

house was handed round among our troops, who sat composedly eating and watching the enemy at the same time. Being
thus refreshed, we discovered a white flag advancing toward
us; it was generally supposed to be for a cessation of arms that
our enemies might carry off their dead, which were numerous,
although they had been bearing away both dead and wounded
during the action; but how were we surprised and mortified
when we heard that Gen. Winchester, with Col. Lewis, had
been taken prisoners by the Indians in attempting to rally the
right wing, and that Gen. Winchester had surrendered us
prisoners of war to Col. Proctor! Major Madison, then the
highest in command, did not agree to this until Col. Proctor
had promised* that the prisoners should be protected from
the Indians, the wounded taken care of, the dead collected and
buried, and private property respected. It was then with extreme reluctance our troops accepted this proposition; there
was scarcely a person that could refrain from shedding tears!
Some plead with the officers not to surrender, saying they
would rather die on the field! We had only five killed, and
twenty-five or thirty wounded, inside of the pickets. The British asked, when they came in, what we had done with our
dead, as they saw but few on the ground. A barn being set on
fire to drive the Indians from behind it, they concluded that,
to conceal our dead, we had thrown them into these flames.

One of the houses that the wounded were in, was much
shattered by the cannon balls, though only a few struck as low

*Col. Proctor had informed Gen. Winchester he would afford him an op-
portunity of surrendering his troops, and if not accepted he would let loose
the Indians on us, who would burn the town, and he would not be account-
able for their conduct. Gen. Winchester, not knowing how we had resisted
their efforts, thought probably it would be the case.

But why did not Col. Proctor make this proposition before he had exerted
all his skill in trying to burn the town and to set the Indians on us? Proctor
knew very well he had done all that was in his power with the force he had
then, and he was then less able to rout us from the town than he was at first.

The British informed us afterwards that Col. Proctor had ordered a general
retreat to Malden, and that they had *spiked four pieces of their cannon!* but he
thought he would demand a surrender, according to custom.

Our officers, knowing that we had but little ammunition, and the troops
being still exposed to the fire of the cannon, thought proper to surrender.

as a man's head. The bombs flew over. Some bursted fifty feet above the ice, some fell on the ice, and some fell over the river. Notwithstanding all their exertions, their six cannon (which were all said to be six-pounders) did but little damage.

In this battle, officers and privates exhibited the utmost firmness and bravery. Whilst the men were at their posts firing on the enemy, the officers were passing along the lines supplying them with cartridges. Major Graves, in passing around the line, was wounded in the knee. He sat down in a tent, bound up his wound, and cried: "BOYS, I AM WOUNDED; NEVER MIND ME, BUT FIGHT ON!"

The British collected their troops, and marched in front of the village. We marched out and grounded our arms, in heat and bitterness of spirit. The British and Indians took possession of them. But all the swords, dirks, tomahawks, and knives were given up with promise that they should be restored again. [This promise was broken.]

All the prisoners, except those that were badly wounded, Dr. Todd, Dr. Bowers, and a few attendants, were marched towards Malden. The British said, as they had a great many of their wounded to take to Malden that evening, it would be out of their power to take ours before morning, but they would leave a sufficient guard, so that they should not be interrupted by the Indians. You will presently see with what aggravating circumstances the breach of this promise was attended.

Brother Allen Darnall having been badly wounded in the right shoulder on the 18th, and I being appointed to attend on the wounded, I continued with them.

Before the British and prisoners marched, the Indians ransacked the camp, and got all the plunder that was remaining— namely, tents, kettles, buckets, pans, &c.; then coming amongst the wounded, greatly insulted them, and took some of their plunder. After they went out I bolted the door. They came again and broke it open with their tomahawks. I immediately applied to a British officer, and told him the Indians were interrupting the wounded. He turned round, and called to another officer to send the guard. The Indians at that time had plundered the commissary's house (which was near the house in which the wounded were) of everything they wanted, and

piled rails against it and set them on fire: I, with the assistance
of two British officers, put it out. One of the British officers
(Maj. Rundels) inquired where the ammunition was. I told
him, if there was any, it was above stairs. We went up, but
could find none. There was a large quantity of wheat on the
loft; he said it was a pity it was there, for the Indians would
burn the house. I apprehended by that, the town was to be
burned, and began to lament our wretched condition. After
we went down stairs, Rundels asked me how many we had
killed and wounded on the 18th. I told him, but he very
haughtily disputed it. I had the return in my pocket. He read
it, but made no reply.

Those that remained of us being hungry, I applied to one of
the British in the evening for some flour, as there were a good
many barrels in the commissary's house, which I considered to
belong to them. He told me to take as much as I wanted. I
asked him if there was a guard left? He said there was no necessity for any, for the Indians were going to their camp, and
there were interpreters left who would walk from house to
house and see that we should not be interrupted. He kept
walking about and looking towards the road. He told me I had
better keep in the house, for the Indians would as soon shoot
me as not, although he had just told me we should not be interrupted! I suspected he was looking for Gen. Harrison. Oh!
if we had seen General Harrison coming with his troops, the
wounded would have leaped for joy! but I did not expect him.

As they did not leave the *promised guard*, I lost all confidence in them, and expected we would be all massacred before
morning. I being the only person in this house not wounded,
with the assistance of some of the wounded, I prepared something for about thirty to eat. The Indians kept searching about
town till after dark. One came in the house who could talk
English, and said he commanded a company after the retreating party, and that most of that party were slain. He said the
men gave up their guns, plead for quarters, and offered them
money if they would not kill them; but his boys, as he called
them, would tomahawk them without distinction. He said the
plan that was fixed on by the Indians and British, before the
battle commenced, was that the British were to attack in front
to induce us to charge on them; 500 Indians were placed on

the right hand and 500 on the left, to flank round and take possession of the town; but he said we were too cunning for them; we would not move out of the pickets.

We passed this night under the most serious apprehensions of being massacred by the tomahawk or consumed in the flames. I frequently went out during the night to see if the house was set on fire. At length the long wished-for morn arrived, and filled each heart with a cheerful hope of being delivered from the cruelty of those merciless savages. We were making every preparation to be ready for the promised sleighs; but, alas! instead of the sleighs, about an hour by sun a great number of savages, painted with various colors, came yelling in the most hideous manner! These bloodthirsty, terrific savages (sent here by their more cruel and perfidious allies, the British) rushed into the houses where the desponding wounded lay, and insolently stripped them of their blankets and all their best clothes, and ordered them out of the houses! I ran out of the house to inform the interpreters* what the Indians were doing. At the door, an Indian took my hat and put it on his own head. I then discovered the Indians had been at the other house first, and had used the wounded in like manner. As I turned to go back into the house, an Indian, taking hold of me, made signs for me to stand by the corner of the house. I made signs to him I wanted to go in and get my hat; for I desired to see what they had done with the wounded. The Indians sent in a boy who brought out a hat and threw it down to me, and I could not get in the house. Three Indians came up to me and pulled off my coat. My feeble powers cannot describe the dismal scenes here exhibited. I saw my fellow soldiers, naked and wounded, crawling out of the houses to avoid being consumed in the flames. Some that had not been able to turn themselves on their beds for four days, through fear of being burned to death, arose and walked out and about through the yard. Some cried for help, but there were none to help them. "Ah!" exclaimed numbers, in the anguish of their spirit, "what shall we do?" A number, unable to get out,

---

*I was since informed that Col. Elliott instructed the interpreters to leave the wounded, after dark, to the mercy of the savages. They all went off, except one half-Indian.

miserably perished in the unrelenting flames of the houses, kindled by the more unrelenting savages. Now the scenes of cruelty and murder we had been anticipating with dread, during last night, fully commenced. The savages rushed on the wounded, and, in their barbarous manner, shot, and tomahawked, and scalped them; and cruelly mangled their naked bodies while they lay agonizing and weltering in their blood. A number were taken towards Malden, but being unable to march with speed, were inhumanly massacred. The road was, for miles, strewed with the mangled bodies, and all of them were left like those slain in battle, on the 22d, for birds and beasts to tear in pieces and devour. The Indians plundered the town of everything valuable, and set the best houses on fire. The Indian who claimed me, gave me a coat, and when he had got as much plunder as he could carry, he ordered me, by signs, to march, which I did, with extreme reluctance, in company with three of the wounded and six or seven Indians. In travelling about a quarter of a mile, two of the wounded lagged behind about twenty yards. The Indians, turning round, shot one and scalped him. They shot at the other and missed him; he, running up to them, begged that they would not shoot him. He said he would keep up, and give them money. But these murderers were not moved with his doleful cries. They shot him down; and, rushing on him in a crowd, scalped him. In like manner my brother Allen perished. He marched with difficulty after the wounded, about two or three hundred yards, and was there barbarously murdered. My feelings at the sight and recollection of these inhuman butcheries cannot be described. In addition to these deep sorrows for the mournful fate of my companions, and the cruel death of a dear brother, I expected every moment, for a considerable time, that the same kind of cruelty and death would be my portion. The Indians that guarded me and one of the wounded, observing our consternation, one that could talk English said, "We will not shoot you." This a little revived our hopes, that were almost gone;* and he, having cut a piece, hide and all, of a dead cow,

---

*Upon taking a view of these scenes of woe, who can avoid some such exclamation as the following? Why has the all-seeing, beneficent Ruler of the universe delivered so many of our choice officers and brave soldiers into the

started. It is their common practice to kill a cow or hog, and take a piece, and leave the rest. In travelling two miles, we came to a house where there were two British officers; the Indian made a halt, and I asked one of the officers what the Indian was going to do with me; he said he was going to take me to Amherstburg (or Malden). I judged these villains had instructed the Indians to do what they had done. A few miles farther, we came to the Indian encampment, where there were a great many hallooing and yelling in a hideous manner. I thought this my place of destiny. The Indian took off my pack, broiled a piece of meat and gave me part; this I ate merely in obedience to him. Then we started and arrived at Amherstburg, eighteen miles from Frenchtown. The other prisoners had just arrived. The British were firing their salute. The Indian took me into a house not far from the fort; it was probably their council house; it would have held 500. It was inhabited by a large number of squaws, children, and dogs. They welcomed me by giving me some bread, meat and hominy to eat. After this an Indian asked me if I had a squaw; I told him not; he immediately turned round and talked to the squaws in Indian, while I sat in a pensive mood observing their motions. I discovered the squaws were pleased, by their tittering and grinning; one, I observed, had a great desire to express her joy by showing her teeth; but the length of time she had lived in this world had put it out of her power. I suspected, from their manœuvres, I would have to undergo a disagreeable adoption (as other prisoners had done)—and, what was a task still more unpleasant, to be united in the conjugal band to one of these swarthy, disgustful animals. The Indian asked me a few questions—where we had come from—how far it was—when we started—and if there were any more coming. In reply to these questions, I gave him but little satisfaction. After this they spread blankets down, and made

---

hands of our enemies, to be slain in battle, and to lie unburied, to be dragged away in the galling chains of captivity, and to be put to torturing deaths by monsters of cruelty? Not, I presume, because of infidelity and injustice towards our enemies; but owing to our ingratitude towards the God of armies; and to our want of confidence in Jehovah—our pride, our too great confidence in our own wisdom, valor, and strength; our unbelief—and a catalogue of vices too tedious to enumerate. Aggravated national crimes have involved us in heavy and complicated judgments!

signs for me to go to bed. I did, and soon fell asleep, as I was much fatigued and had not slept much for four nights past. Early next morning, the Indian collected his family and all his property, and started: I knew not where he was going; he gave me a knapsack and gun to carry. Now I despaired of getting with the other prisoners, unless I could desert from the Indians! I expected I would be taken to an Indian town, there to undergo a disagreeable adoption, or to be burned to death with firebrands. As he took me near Fort Malden, I took as good a view of it as I could while I passed it. It stands about thirty yards from the river bank. I judged it to be seventy or eighty yards square; the wall appeared to be built of timber and clay. The side, from the river, was not walled, but had double pickets, and entrenched round, about four feet deep; and in the entrenchment was the second row of pickets. As we went on through the edge of town (Amherstburg) I asked an Englishman where the other prisoners were? He said they were in town, in a wood-yard; the Indian hurried me along and would not let me talk to the Englishman. The Indian had a little horse, packed with his plunder, which I resolved to take, if possible, and ride into town that night.

He took me to his place of residence, about three miles from Malden. I was anxious for the approach of night, so that I might make my escape. While I was consoling myself with the anticipation of seeing my fellow sufferers at Malden, night made its approach. Some time after dark the Indian spread blankets down, and made signs for me to lie down, and put my coat, shoes, and socks, under his own head. I wanted him to leave my socks on, for my feet would get cold; he made signs to warm them by the fire. Thus I was sadly disappointed.

Next day he examined all his plunder. He had a very good suit of clothes, besides several other coats, socks, shoes, &c.; among these were Wesley's Sermons and a great many papers, which he gave me to read. I found several old letters, but nothing of value. He discovered I wanted to shave, and got his razor, shaving-box, and a piece of glass, and made signs for me to shave. After this, I lay down on some blankets and fell asleep. He came and awoke me, and gave me a twist of tobacco, which I received as a token of friendship. In a short time after, he started to Malden, and made signs for me to stay there till he would come back. He returned in the evening with a blanket, tied full of loaves of bread, just out of the oven, besides some meat. The Indians always gave me a plenty to eat; and served me before any of the family, with more politeness than I expected to find amongst them. He had drawn some money. I asked him to let me look at it. I found it to be pieces of cards with the number of livres written on them.

The third night at length arrived; and he made my bed as usual; and took my coat and shoes, but accidentally left my socks on. I lay down with the determination to leave him before morning. I slept very well for awhile. When I awoke, the house was dark. I thought this as good an opportunity of deserting as I could get, but with considerable timidity I made the attempt. I crawled to the door very easily, and raised the blanket that hung up at the door; just as I was going out he coughed, and I stopped until I thought he was asleep, and then started, without shoes or coat, to Amherstburg. When I got there, I examined several yards and gardens to see if there was any fire. After going through many streets, I turned my course towards the river, and accidentally came to the house where the prisoners were. The sentinel, who was standing at the door, let me in without much ceremony. Providence smiled on this attempt to extricate myself from the Indians. Thus, through mercy, I escaped from the savages, and was delivered from the doleful apprehensions of being sacrificed in some barbarous and cruel manner, to gratify their bloodthirsty souls. I got in between two of my comrades who were lying next to the door. My feet were almost frozen before morning.

During my captivity with the Indians, the other prisoners were treated very inhumanly. The first night, they were put in a wood-yard; the rain commenced early in the night, and put out all their fires. In this manner they passed a tedious night, wet, and benumbed with cold. From this place they were taken to a cold warehouse, still deprived of fire, with their clothes and blankets frozen, and nothing to eat but a little bread. In this wretched condition they continued two days and three nights!

26th.   The Indians came early in the morning to search for me, but they were not admitted into the house. The guard said it would be well for me to keep as much concealed as possible, for if the Indian I had left could get me he would kill me. He came to the door, and made motions to show how he would scalp me. I disguised myself by changing my clothes and tying up my head, so that he did not know me.

The prisoners being destined to Fort George, were divided in two divisions, the first to keep a day's march before the second, in order, probably, to be better supplied with provisions on the way.

I being attached to the first division, the Indians examined the lines very closely for me, but not possessing discernment sufficient to know me, I fortunately escaped.

Malden, or Amherstburg, is situated on the east side of Detroit River, near its junction with Lake Erie, and contains about one hundred houses, mostly frame; in lat. 42° 22′ N., long. 8° 3′ W. from Philadelphia.

We set out from this town, and marched seventeen miles to Sandwich, a small town on the east side of Detroit River, and one mile below Detroit; it contains perhaps about three hundred inhabitants. We were divided in small companies, and put into different houses, where we had the happiness once more to see fire.

James Madison: Second Inaugural Address

March 3, 1813

The presidential election of 1812 was determined through staggered state balloting during November and December. The returns followed much the same sectional pattern as Congress's vote on the war, with Madison carrying the South and the West and De Witt Clinton most of the North. Madison received 128 electoral votes from eleven states, and Clinton 89 electoral votes from the other seven. (Had pivotal Pennsylvania, with twenty-five votes, gone to Clinton, he would have unseated the incumbent.) In the end, Madison won 58.7 percent of the electoral vote, down from 1808, when he won 69.3 percent. On March 3, 1813, the President delivered his second inaugural address in the House Chamber of the U.S. Capitol.

———————

ABOUT to add the solemnity of an oath to the obligations imposed by a second call to the station in which my country heretofore placed me, I find in the presence of this respectable assembly an opportunity of publicly repeating my profound sense of so distinguished a confidence and of the responsibility united with it. The impressions on me are strengthened by such an evidence that my faithful endeavors to discharge my arduous duties have been favorably estimated, and by a consideration of the momentous period at which the trust has been renewed. From the weight and magnitude now belonging to it I should be compelled to shrink if I had less reliance on the support of an enlightened and generous people, and felt less deeply a conviction that the war with a powerful nation, which forms so prominent a feature in our situation, is stamped with that justice which invites the smiles of Heaven on the means of conducting it to a successful termination.

May we not cherish this sentiment without presumption when we reflect on the characters by which this war is distinguished?

It was not declared on the part of the United States until it had been long made on them, in reality though not in name; until arguments and expostulations had been exhausted; until a positive declaration had been received that the wrongs provoking it would not be discontinued; nor until this last appeal could no longer be delayed without breaking down the spirit of the nation, destroying all confidence in itself and in its political institutions, and either perpetuating a state of disgraceful suffering or regaining by more costly sacrifices and more severe struggles our lost rank and respect among independent powers.

On the issue of the war are staked our national sovereignty on the high seas and the security of an important class of citizens, whose occupations give the proper value to those of every other class. Not to contend for such a stake is to surrender our equality with other powers on the element common to all and to violate the sacred title which every member of the society has to its protection. I need not call into view the unlawfulness of the practice by which our mariners are forced at the will of every cruising officer from their own vessels into foreign ones, nor paint the outrages inseparable from it. The proofs are in the records of each successive Administration of our Government, and the cruel sufferings of that portion of the American people have found their way to every bosom not dead to the sympathies of human nature.

As the war was just in its origin and necessary and noble in its objects, we can reflect with a proud satisfaction that in carrying it on no principle of justice or honor, no usage of civilized nations, no precept of courtesy or humanity, have been infringed. The war has been waged on our part with scrupulous regard to all these obligations, and in a spirit of liberality which was never surpassed.

How little has been the effect of this example on the conduct of the enemy!

They have retained as prisoners of war citizens of the United States not liable to be so considered under the usages of war.

They have refused to consider as prisoners of war, and threatened to punish as traitors and deserters, persons emigrating without restraint to the United States, incorporated by naturalization into our political family, and fighting under the authority of their adopted country in open and honorable war for the maintenance of its rights and safety. Such is the avowed purpose of a Government which is in the practice of naturalizing by thousands citizens of other countries, and not only of permitting but compelling them to fight its battles against their native country.

They have not, it is true, taken into their own hands the hatchet and the knife, devoted to indiscriminate massacre, but they have let loose the savages armed with these cruel instruments; have allured them into their service, and carried them to battle by their sides, eager to glut their savage thirst with the blood of the vanquished and to finish the work of torture and death on maimed and defenseless captives. And, what was never before seen, British commanders have extorted victory over the unconquerable valor of our troops by presenting to the sympathy of their chief captives awaiting massacre from their savage associates.

And now we find them, in further contempt of the modes of honorable warfare, supplying the place of a conquering force, by attempts to disorganize our political society, to dismember our confederated Republic. Happily, like others, these will recoil on the authors; but they mark the degenerate counsels from which they emanate: and if they did not belong to a series of unexampled inconsistencies, might excite the greater wonder, as proceeding from a Government which founded the very war in which it has been so long engaged, on a charge against the disorganizing and insurrectional policy of its adversary.

To render the justice of the war on our part the more conspicuous, the reluctance to commence it was followed by the earliest and strongest manifestations of a disposition to arrest its progress. The sword was scarcely out of the scabbard, before the enemy was apprized of the reasonable terms on which it would be resheathed. Still more precise advances were repeated, and have been received in a spirit forbidding every reliance not placed on the military resources of the nation.

These resources are amply sufficient to bring the war to an honorable issue. Our nation is, in number, more than half that of the British isles. It is composed of a brave, a free, a virtuous, and an intelligent people. Our country abounds in the necessaries, the arts, and the comforts of life. A general prosperity is visible in the public countenance. The means employed by the British Cabinet to undermine it, have recoiled on themselves; have given to our national faculties a more rapid development; and draining or diverting the precious metals from British circulation and British vaults, have poured them into those of the United States. It is a propitious consideration, that an unavoidable war should have found this seasonable facility for the contributions required to support it. When the public voice called for war, all knew and still know, that without them it could not be carried on through the period which it might last; and the patriotism, the good sense, and the manly spirit of our fellow-citizens, are pledges for the cheerfulness with which they will bear each his share of the common burden. To render the war short, and its success sure, animated, and systematic exertions alone are necessary; and the success of our arms now may long preserve our country from the necessity of another resort to them. Already have the gallant exploits of our naval heroes proved to the world our inherent capacity to maintain our rights on one element. If the reputation of our arms has been thrown under clouds on the other, presaging flashes of heroic enterprise assure us that nothing is wanting to correspondent triumphs there also, but the discipline and habits which are in daily progress.

Henry, Earl Bathurst
to Sir Thomas Sidney Beckwith

On August 3, 1812, Admiral Sir John Borlase Warren was placed in charge of the "hitherto separate commands of the Halifax, Jamaica, and Leeward Island Stations." Over the course of his first months in the new consolidated post he established a blockade from Spanish Florida to Charleston, South Carolina, which in early 1813 he extended northward to the Chesapeake and Delaware Bays. By March, Henry, Earl Bathurst—formerly a lord on the Board of Admiralty and now, as secretary of state for war and the colonies, the chief liaison between the cabinet and the Admiralty—was prepared to authorize amphibious raids on coastal towns with the aim of drawing off U.S. troops from Upper and Lower Canada and of bringing the war home to the Americans. These raids were to be planned and conducted by Warren's second-in-command, Rear Admiral Sir George Cockburn, and by Army Colonel Sir Thomas S. Beckwith, assistant quartermaster general to the British forces in North America.

Most Secret.

Downing Street   20th March 1813

Sir,

It having been judged expedient to effect a diversion on the Coasts of the United States of America, in favour of Upper and Lower Canada, which the American Government have declared it to be their intention to wrest from His Majesty in the course of the ensuing Campaign, Sir J. B. Warren will receive Instructions to direct a Squadron to proceed with the Troops named in the Margin, towards those places on the Coast, where it may appear to him most adviseable that a descent should be made— And His Royal Highness the Prince Regent confiding in your Valour, Enterprize and Discretion, has been generously pleased to commit to you the Command of these Troops, in such Operations as you may judge it expedient when on shore to undertake.

The number and description of the Force placed under your Command, as well as the object of the Expedition itself, will point out to you that you are not to look to the permanent possession of any place, but to the reembarking the Force as soon as the immediate object of each particular attack shall have been accomplished.

While afloat, you will consider yourself as under the Command of the Naval Officer Commanding this Expedition. The Disembarkation of the Troops, and their Re:embarkation, will be directed by him; but he will be instructed to concert with you as to the best mode of effecting the same respectively. You will decide as to the time of re:embarking the Troops, as that must in a great measure be regulated by the success of your undertaking, and by the approach of the Enemy's Force; but you will previously ascertain, whether, in the opinion of the Commander of the Naval Force, there is any time peculiarly unfavourable for Re:embarkation.

As the object of the Expedition is to harrass the Enemy by different attacks, you will avoid the risk of a general action, unless it should become necessary to secure your retreat.

When the object of the Descent is to take possession of any Naval or Military Stores, you will not delay the destroying them, if there is reasonable ground of apprehension that the Enemy is advancing with a superior force to effect their recovery.

If you shall be enabled to take such a position as to threaten the Inhabitants with the destruction of their property, you are hereby authorized to levy upon them Contributions in plate and Money in return for your forbearance. But you will not by this understand that the Magazines belonging to the Government, or their Harbours, or their Shipping are to be included in such arrangement.

You will on no account give encouragement to any disposition which may be manifested by the Negroes to rise against their Masters. The Humanity which ever influences His Royal Highness must make Him anxious to protest against a system of Warfare which must be attended by the atrocities inseparable from commotions of such a description. If any Individual Negroes shall in the course of your operations have given you assistance, which may expose them to the vengeance of their Masters after your retreat, you are at liberty on their earnest desire to take them away with you. You are authorized to enlist them in any of the Black Corps if they are willing to enlist; but you must distinctly understand that you are in no case to take slaves away as Slaves, but as free persons whom the public become bound to maintain. This circumstance as well as the difficulty of transport, will make you necessarily cautious how you contract engagements of this nature, which it may be difficult for you to fulfill. I am Sir Your most obedient Humble Servant

Bathurst

Patrick Finan: from
"Recollections of Canada"

Patrick Finan Jr. was twelve years old in 1812, when he, his siblings, and his mother made the transatlantic passage from Ulster to Upper Canada to live for a while near his father, an Irish officer stationed in Kingston, the major British base on Lake Ontario. On the way the family had been reunited by chance in Montreal when Finan Sr. and others of the 8th Regiment paraded General Hull through the town. Patrick later recalled with shame his jeering at Hull: "My youthful heart, too inconsiderate to sympathize with misfortunes of this description, triumphantly exalted in the sight of a fallen enemy." The boy would soon learn firsthand what it was to have one's "patriotic pride humbled," as evidenced in this memoir of the American capture of York, published when the author was twenty-eight.

On the 25th of April the grenadier company of the 8th regiment arrived in batteaux, from Kingston, on their way up the country. They were allowed to remain during the 26th to refresh themselves after a long journey, and were to have proceeded on the 27th. During the 26th my father and I were in town, and while returning to the garrison in the evening, we were overtaken by Captain M'Neile, of that company, who was also going there. On our way he informed my father of the various arrangements he had made for the remainder of his journey to the place of his destination, and spoke as confidently of being in Fort George, the next town, on a certain day, as if no untoward circumstance could intervene; or as if uncertainty and disappointment were not, alas! too constantly, the companions of man. When we arrived at the garrison all was bustle and activity; the American fleet had appeared off the harbour, and from its manœuvres it was supposed that York was the place of its destination.

The troops were under arms, and although the greatest activity prevailed in making the necessary dispositions for the defense of the place, very little apprehension was entertained for its safety; which was rather surprising, since the whole amount of the regular forces, including the grenadiers of the 8th regiment, did not exceed 300; the militia, &c. composing a few hundreds more.

Early on the morning of the 27th the enemy's fleet appeared, steering directly for the harbour: the troops were again formed in the barrack square, and kept in readiness to march off to oppose the landing of the enemy, when it should appear what point they would choose for that purpose. We had a small battery at the garrison, another at the governor's house, a short distance farther up the lake shore, and a third about half a mile beyond it, in the same direction.

About seven o'clock the fleet, consisting of a frigate of 24 guns, a brig of 18, and fifteen armed schooners, sailed round Gibraltar Point, steering towards the uppermost battery. The morning was very fine; the lake quite calm; and the fleet, gliding slowly upon its surface with a gentle breeze, and in regular order, the frigate leading, the others following in a line, and each towing several large boats for the purpose of landing the troops, had an elegant and imposing appearance.

As soon as it became evident where the enemy intended to attempt a landing, our forces were ordered off to oppose them.—Well do I yet remember that fatal morning.—Oh! how my heart bleeds, even at this distant period, when memory represents to my view the devoted band cheerfully marching to offer themselves a useless, but honourable sacrifice at their country's shrine! What could a few hundreds, even of *British* soldiers, be supposed to effect against the overwhelming superiority of force that their adversaries opposed to them, consisting of a greater number of thousands than they had of hundreds?—But as it is not the part of British soldiers to surrender at discretion, or quietly to resign the post of honour, without at least making an effort to repel their invaders, the desperate experiment must of necessity be made, and melancholy indeed was the result!

The grenadier company of the 8th regiment consisted of 119 as fine men as the British army could produce, commanded by the brave and elegant Captain M'Neile. I saw the generous hero, at the head of his valiant company, in the prime of life, and prompt to obey the call of honour, march off—but, ah! I saw him, and the most of his little band, return no more! thirty alone escaped the havoc of that day!

All the regulars that could be spared from the batteries advanced beyond the uppermost one, and as the enemy attempted to land, opened a spirited fire upon them; but, as the latter were so numerous that it was impossible to oppose them all, some landed above where our little force was posted, got into the woods, and coming down in their rear cut them off in great numbers. Captain M'Neile was the first who fell upon this melancholy occasion; the sergeant-major of the 8th, a remarkably fine looking man, was the next, and the carnage soon became general.

While this part of our force was contending with the enemy in the woods, an unfortunate accident occurred in the battery opposed to the fleet, which proved a death-blow to the little hope that might have been entertained of a successful issue to the proceedings of the day. A gun was aimed at one of the vessels, and the officers, desirous of seeing if the ball would take effect, ascended the bastion: in the mean time the artillery man, waiting for the word of command to fire, held the match behind him, as is usual under such circumstances; and the travelling magazine, a large wooden chest, containing cartridges for the great guns, being open just at his back, he unfortunately put the match into it, and the consequence, as may be supposed, was dreadful indeed! Every man in the battery was blown into the air, and the *dissection* of the greater part of their bodies was inconceivably shocking! The officers were thrown from the bastion by the shock, but escaped with a few bruises: the cannons were dismounted, and consequently the battery was rendered completely useless.

I was standing at the gate of the garrison when the poor soldiers, who escaped the explosion with a little life remaining, were brought in to the hospital, and a more afflicting sight could scarcely be witnessed. Their faces were completely black, resembling those of the blackest Africans; their hair frizzled like theirs, and their clothes scorched and emitting an effluvia so strong as to be perceived long before they reached one. One man in particular presented an awful spectacle: he was brought in a wheel-barrow, and from his appearance I should be inclined to suppose that almost every bone in his body was broken; he was lying in a powerless heap, shaking about with every motion of the barrow, from which his legs hung dangling down, as if only connected with his body by the skin, while his cries and groans were of the most heart-rending description.

Although Spartan valour was evinced by our little party, it proved unavailing against the numbers that pressed them upon all sides; and in consequence of the loss of the battery, and the reduction that had been made in the number of our troops, their ground was no longer tenable; but after nobly and desperately withstanding their enemies for several hours, a retreat towards the garrison became inevitable, although every inch of the ground was obstinately disputed.

The governor's house, with some smaller buildings, formed a square at the centre battery, and under it the grand magazine, containing a large quantity of powder, was situated. As there were only two or three guns at this battery, and it but a short distance from the garrison, the troops did not remain in it, but retreated to the latter. When the Americans, commanded by one of their best generals, Pike, reached this small battery, instead of pressing forward, they halted, and the general sat down on one of the guns: a fatal proceeding—for, in a few minutes, his advance guard, consisting of about 300 men, and himself, were blown into the air by the explosion of the grand magazine.

Some time before this horrible circumstance took place, the vessels had commenced firing upon the garrison, which obliged the females, children, &c. to leave it; we therefore retired into the country, to the house of an officer of the militia, where we remained a short time; but, feeling anxious to know the fate of the day, I left the house without the knowledge of my mother, and was proceeding towards the garrison, when the explosion took place. I heard the report, and felt a tremulous motion in the earth, resembling the shock of an earthquake; and looking towards the spot I saw an immense cloud ascend into the air. I was not aware at the moment what it had been occasioned by, but it had an awfully grand effect: at first it was a great confused mass of smoke, timber, men, earth, &c. but as it rose, in a most majestic manner, it assumed the shape of a vast balloon. When the whole mass had ascended to a considerable height, and the force by which the timber, &c. were impelled upwards became spent, the latter fell from the cloud, and spread over the surrounding plain. I stopped to observe the cloud, which preserved its round shape while it remained within my view. I then advanced towards the garrison, but had not proceeded much farther until I discovered our little party collected in a close body between the town and that place, which latter they had been obliged to evacuate. After observing their motions for a short time, I looked towards the garrison, when I became the melancholy spectator of what I had never witnessed upon any former occasion, and what I had little anticipated upon this. Just as the flag-staff caught my eye I saw—and oh! how my young feelings were harrowed, and my patriotic pride humbled at the sight!—I saw the "meteor flag" of England bow, by impious, traitorous hands,* to the then triumphant, "star-spangled" banner of America!

Finding that the garrison, which was very near me, was in the possession of the Americans, and, consequently, that all was over, I returned to the house where I had left my mother, and shortly after I reached it a soldier came to us, with directions to proceed to the town as fast as possible.

We had a 26 gun frigate upon the stocks at York at the time, the capture or destruction of which was probably the principal object the Americans had in view in this expedition: the yard where it was building was about mid-way between the town and the garrison; and as the enemy were not sufficiently good soldiers to improve the advantage they had obtained, by following our troops immediately after they got possession of the garrison, but, on the contrary, remained in it for sometime afterwards—the second error highly disadvantageous to them this day—our people had fortunately an opportunity of consuming the ship, and thereby preventing it from falling into their hands. This was a particularly happy circumstance, since the possession of it would have rendered them complete masters of the lake for a long time, and most probably during the remainder of the war.

---

*The English flag was hauled down, and the American substituted, by a sergeant who had deserted from the British army.

On reaching the town we found the soldiers evacuating it, on their retreat towards Kingston; and there being no other alternative, we joined them, just as we were, and left the town.

As in the morning we had very foolishly entertained no apprehension whatever of being defeated, but left our quarters confident of soon returning, and walked out from the breakfast table as if to look at some curiosity, we brought no clothing with us more than we wore at the moment; and, consequently, left York about 4 o'clock in the afternoon, to commence a journey of 200 miles through the woods of America, at an inclement season, without an outside garment of any description, or a second pair of shoes. The snow had just thawed also, which, with the heavy and copious rains, usual at this season, rendered the roads, that are bad at best, almost impassable.

John Richardson:
from "A Canadian Campaign"

When campaigning resumed in the spring of 1813, the British still dominated the Old Northwest. Ordered by John Armstrong, the new secretary of war, to stay on the defensive until the U.S. Navy gained control of Lake Erie, Harrison concentrated his efforts on building a fort on the Maumee Rapids that would serve as supply depot and staging area for a fresh assault on Detroit. Named in honor of Return J. Meigs Jr., the governor of Ohio, Fort Meigs was exceptionally strong and well designed, defended on all sides by fences, block-houses, and batteries and fortified by interior earthworks. Upon learning of its construction, Henry Procter resolved to destroy the fort before it could be completed. He left Fort Amherstburg with a thousand troops and on April 26 met Tecumseh and fifteen hundred Indians at the mouth of the Maumee. John Richardson, who in 1813 was a sixteen-year-old volunteer in Britain's 41st Regiment of Foot, wrote this memoir of the siege of Fort Meigs for a London magazine in 1827.

Far from being discouraged by the discomfiture of their armies under Generals Hull and Winchester, the Americans despatched a third and more formidable under one of their most experienced commanders, General Harrison, who, reaching Fort Meigs shortly subsequent to the affair at Frenchtown, directed his attention to the construction of works which rendered his position in some measure impregnable. Determined if possible to thwart the views of the enemy, and give a finishing stroke to his movements in that quarter, General Procter (lately promoted) ordered an expedition to be in readiness to move for the Miami. Accordingly, towards the close of April, a detachment of the 41st, some militia, and 1500 Indians, accompanied by a train of battering artillery, and attended by two gun-boats, proceeded up that river, and established themselves on the left bank at the distance of a mile from the site selected for our batteries. The season was unusually wet, yet, in defiance of every obstacle, they were erected the same night in front of the American fortress, and the guns transported along a road in which the axle-trees of the carriages were frequently buried in mud. Among other battering pieces were two 24-pounders, in the transportation of which 200 men with several oxen were employed from nine o'clock at night until daybreak in the morning. At length every preparation having been made, a gun fired from one of the boats was the signal for their opening, and early on the morning of the 1st of May, a heavy fire was commenced, and continued for four days without intermission, during which period every one of the enemy's batteries within our range were silenced and dismantled. The fire of the 24-pounder battery was principally directed against the powder magazine, which the besieged were busily occupied in covering and protecting from our hot shot. It was impossible to have artillery better served: every shot that was fired sank into the roof of the magazine, scattering the earth to a considerable distance, and burying many of the workmen in its bed, from whence we could distinctly perceive the survivors dragging forth the bodies of their slaughtered comrades. Meanwhile the flank companies of the 41st, with a few Indians, had been detached to the opposite shore within a few hundred yards of the enemy's works, and had constructed a battery, from which a galling cross-fire was maintained. Dismayed at the success of our operations, General Harrison, already apprised before our arrival of the approach of a reinforcement of 1500 men, then descending the Miami under General Clay, contrived to despatch a courier on the evening of the 4th, with an order for that officer to land immediately and possess himself of our batteries on the left bank, while he (General Harrison) sallied forth to carry those on the right. Accordingly, at eight o'clock on the morning of the 5th, General Clay pushed forward the whole of his force, and meeting with no opposition at the batteries, which were entirely unsupported, proceeded to spike the guns in conformity with his instructions; but elated with his success, and disobeying the positive order of his chief, which was to retire the instant his object was effected, continued to occupy the position. In the mean time the flying artillerymen had given the alarm, and three companies of the 41st, several of militia, and a body of

Indians, the latter under their celebrated chieftain Tecumseh, were ordered to move on the instant, and repossess themselves of the works. The rain, which had commenced early in the morning, continued to fall with violence, and the road, as has already been described, was knee-deep with mud, yet the men advanced to the assault with the utmost alacrity and determination. The enemy on our appoach had sheltered themselves behind the batteries, affording them every facility of defence, yet they were driven at the point of the bayonet from each in succession, until eventually not a man was left in the plain. Flying to the woods, the murderous fire of the Indians drove them back upon their pursuers, so that they had no possibility of escape. A vast number were killed, and independently of the prisoners taken by the Indians, 450, with their second in command, fell into our hands. Every man of the detachment acquitted himself on this occasion to the entire satisfaction of his superiors. Among the most conspicuous for gallantry was Major Chambers of the 41st, acting deputy quarter-master-general to the division. Supported merely by four or five followers, this meritorious officer advanced under a shower of balls from the enemy, and carried one of the batteries sword in hand. A private of the same regiment being opposed in an isolated situation to three Americans, contrived to disarm and render them his prisoners. On joining his company towards the close of the affair, he excited much mirth among his comrades, in consequence of the singular manner in which he appeared, sweating beneath the weight of arms he had secured as trophies of his victory, and driving his captives before him with an air of indifference and carelessness which contrasted admirably with the occasion. Of the whole of the division under General Clay, scarcely two hundred men effected their escape. Among the fugitives was that officer himself. The sortie made by General Harrison at the head of the principal part of the garrison had a different result. The detachment supporting the battery already described, were driven from their position, and two officers, Lieutenants Mac Intyre and Hailes, and thirty men, were made prisoners. Meanwhile it having been discovered that the guns on the left bank, owing to some error on the part of the enemy, had been spiked with the ramrods of their musquets, instead of the usual instruments, they were speedily rendered serviceable, and the fire from the batteries was renewed. At this moment a white flag was observed waving on the ramparts of the fort, and the courage and perseverance of the troops appeared at length as if about to be crowned by the surrender of a fortress, the siege of which had cost them so much toil and privation. Such, however, was far from being the intention of General Harrison. Availing himself of the cessation of hostilities which necessarily ensued, he caused the officers and men just captured to be sent across the river for the purpose of being exchanged; but this was only a feint for the accomplishment of a more important object. Drawing up his whole force both of cavalry and infantry in the plain beneath the fortress, he caused such of the boats of General Clay's division as were laden with ammunition, of which the garrison stood much in need, to be dropped under the works, and the stores to be immediately disembarked. All this took place during the period occupied in the exchange of prisoners. The remaining boats, containing the baggage and private stores of the division, fell into the hands of the Indians still engaged in the pursuit of the fugitives, and the plunder they acquired was immense. General Harrison having secured his stores and received the officers and men exchanged for his captives, withdrew into the garrison, and the bombardment was recommenced.

The victory obtained at the Miami was such as to reflect credit on every branch of the service; but the satisfaction arising from the conviction was deeply embittered by an act of cruelty, which, as the writer of an impartial memoir, it becomes my painful duty to record. In the heat of the action a strong corps of the enemy which had thrown down their arms, and surrendered themselves prisoners of war, were immediately despatched, under an escort of fifty men, for the purpose of being embarked in the gun-boats, where it was presumed they would be safe from the attacks of the Indians. This measure, however, although dictated by the purest humanity, and apparently offering the most probable means of security, proved one of fatal import to several of the prisoners. On reaching our encampment, then entirely deserted by the troops, they were met by a band of cowardly and treacherous Indians, who had borne no share in the action, yet who now, guided by the savage instinct of their nature, approached the column, and, selecting their victims, commenced the work of blood. In vain did the harassed and indignant escort attempt to save them from the fury of their destroyers; the phrenzy of these wretches knew no bounds, and an old and excellent soldier of the name of Russell, of the 41st, was shot through the heart while endeavouring to wrest a victim from the grasp of his murderer. Forty of these unhappy men had already fallen beneath the steel of the infuriated party, when Tecumseh, apprised of what was doing, rode up at full speed, and raising his tomahawk threatened to destroy the first man who resisted his injunction to desist. Even on those lawless people, to whom the language of coercion had hitherto been unknown, the threats and tone of the exasperated chieftain produced an instantaneous effect, and they retired at once humiliated and confounded. Never did Tecumseh shine more truly himself than on this occasion; and nought of the savage could be distinguished save the colour and the garb. Ever merciful and magnanimous as he was ardent and courageous, the voice of the suppliant seldom reached him in vain; and although war was his idol, the element in which he lived, his heart was formed to glow with all the nobler and more generous impulses of the warrior; and his character was not less esteemed by ourselves than reverenced by the various tribes over which, in his quality of brother to the prophet, he invariably presided. In any other country, and governing any other men, Tecumseh would have been a hero; at the head of this uncivilized and untractable people he was a savage; but a savage such as Civilization herself might not blush to acknowledge for her child. Constantly opposed to the encroachments of the Americans for a series of years previous to their rupture with England, he had combated their armies on the banks of the Wabash with success, and given their leaders proofs of a skill and judgment in defence of his native soil, which would not have disgraced the earlier stages of military science in Europe. General Harrison himself, a commander with whom he had often disputed the palm of victory, with the generous candour of the soldier subsequently ascribed to him virtues as a man and abilities as a warrior, commanding at once the attention and admiration of his enemies.

The survivors of this melancholy catastrophe were immediately conveyed on board the gun-boats moored in the river; and every precaution having been taken to prevent a renewal of the scene, the escorting party proceeded to the interment of the victims, to whom the rites of sepulture were afforded even before those of our own men who had fallen in the action. Colonel Dudley, second in command of General Clay's division, was among the number of the slain.

On the evening of the second day after this event, I accompanied Major Muir of the 41st, in a ramble throughout the encampment of the Indians, distant a few hundred yards from our own. The spectacle there offered to our view was at once of the most ludicrous and revolting nature. In various directions were lying the trunks and boxes taken in the boats of the American division, and the plunderers were busily occupied in displaying their riches, carefully examining each article, and attempting to divine its use. Several were decked out in the uniforms of the officers; and although embarrassed to the last degree in their movements, and dragging with difficulty the heavy military boots with which their legs were for the first time covered, strutted forth much to the admiration of their less fortunate comrades. Some were habited in plain clothes; others had their bodies clad in clean white shirts, contrasting in no ordinary manner with the swarthiness of their skins; all wore some article of decoration, and their tents were ornamented with saddles, bridles, rifles, daggers, swords, and pistols, many of which were handsomely mounted and of curious workmanship. Such was the ridiculous part of the picture; but mingled with these, and in various directions, were to be seen the scalps of the slain drying in the sun, stained on the fleshy side with vermilion dyes, and dangling in air as they hung suspended from the poles to which they were attached, together with hoops of various sizes, on which were stretched portions of human skin taken from various parts of the body, principally the hand and foot, and yet covered with the nails of those parts, while scattered along the ground were visible the members from which they had been separated, and serving as nutriment to the wolf-dogs by which the savages were accompanied. As we continued to advance into the heart of the encampment, a scene of a more disgusting nature arrested our attention. Stopping at the entrance of a tent occupied by a part

of the Minoumini tribe we observed them seated round a large
fire, over which was suspended a kettle containing their meal.
Each warrior had a piece of string hanging over the edge of the
vessel, and to this was suspended a food, which, it will be presumed we heard not without loathing, consisted of part of an
American. Any expression of our feelings, as we declined the
invitation they gave us to join in their repast, would have been
resented by the Indians without much ceremony. We had,
therefore, the prudence to excuse ourselves under the plea that
we had already taken our food, and we hastened to remove
from the contemplation of a sight so revolting to humanity.
This was the only instance in which the natives ever appeared
to us in the character of Anthropophagi, and the obloquy must
in justice fall on this tribe alone. They were the most barbarous
of the whole Indian race; and no example can be adduced of a
similar disposition being manifested by any one other tribe
during the course of our struggle with America.

Since the affair of the 5th the enemy continued to keep
themselves shut up within their works, and the bombardment,
although followed up with vigour, had effected no practicable
breach. From the account given by the officers captured during
the sortie, it appeared that, with a perseverance and toil peculiar to themselves, the Americans had constructed subterranean
passages to protect them from the annoyance of our shells,
which, sinking into beds of clay softened by the incessant rains
that had fallen, instead of exploding, were speedily extinguished. Impatient of longer privation, and anxious to return
to their families and occupations, numbers of the militia withdrew themselves in small bodies, and under cover of the night:
while the majority of the Indians, enriched by plunder, and
languishing under the tediousness of a mode of warfare so different from their own, with less ceremony and caution left us
to prosecute the siege as we could. Tecumseh at the head of
his own tribe (the Shawanees) and a few others, in all amounting to about four hundred warriors, continued to remain. The
troops also were worn down by constant fatigue; for here, as in
every other expedition against the enemy, few even of the officers had tents to shield them from the weather. A few pieces
of bark torn from the trees, and covering the skeleton of a hut,
was their only habitation, and they were merely separated from

the damp earth on which they lay by a few scattered leaves, on which was generally spread a blanket by the men, and a cloak by the officers. Hence frequently arose dysentery, ague, and the various ills to which an army, encamped on a wet and unhealthy ground, is inevitably subject; and fortunate was he who possessed the skin of the bear or buffalo, on which he could repose his wearied limbs after a period of suffering and privation, which those who have never served in the wilds of America can with difficulty comprehend. Such was the position of the contending parties towards the middle of May, when General Procter, despairing to effect the reduction of the fort, caused preparations to be made for raising the siege. Accordingly the gun-boats ascended the river, and anchored under the batteries, the guns of which were conveyed on board under a heavy fire from the enemy. The whole being secured, the expedition returned to Amherstburg, the Americans remaining tranquil within their works, and suffering us to depart unmolested.

Thomas Jefferson to Madame de Staël

The novelist and essayist Anne-Louise Germaine Necker, Baroness de Staël-Holstein, presided over one of the leading salons of Revolutionary France. Daughter of the minister of finance to Louis XVI and wife of the Swedish ambassador to France, she had entrée to the intellectual and political elite of Paris, including Thomas Jefferson, who became her friend during the 1780s, when he was American minister to France. As an outspoken philosopher of personal and political freedom, Madame de Staël suffered under Napoleon, who banished her from Paris in 1803. In a letter to Jefferson of November 10, 1812, she protested America's declaration of war against Great Britain, the country that for ten years had been the "sole barrier" against Napoleon's ambition to establish a "universal monarchy." She punctuated her letter with a warning: "the greatest misfortune which could come to the American people in the present war would be to do real damage to their enemies, for then the English would no longer be in a condition to serve you as a bulwark against the despotism of the Emperor of France, or rather of Europe. When he shall have overthrown the liberty of England it will be yours that he will next attack."

United States of America, May 24, 1813

I received with great pleasure, my dear Madam and friend, your letter of November the 10th, from Stockholm, and am sincerely gratified by the occasion it gives me of expressing to you the sentiments of high respect and esteem which I entertain for you. It recalls to my remembrance a happy portion of my life, passed in your native city; then the seat of the most amiable and polished society of the world, and of which yourself and your venerable father were such distinguished members. But of what scenes has it since been the theatre, and with what havoc has it overspread the earth! Robespiere met the fate, and his memory the execration, he so justly merited. The rich were his victims, and perished by thousands. It is by millions that Buonaparte destroys the poor, and he is eulogised and deified by the sycophants even of science. These merit more than the mere oblivion to which they will be consigned; and the day will come when a just posterity will give to their hero the only pre-eminence he has earned, that of having been the greatest of the destroyers of the human race. What year of his military life has not consigned a million of human beings to death, to poverty and wretchedness! What field in Europe may not raise a monument of the murders, the burnings, the desolations, the famines and miseries it has witnessed from him! And all this to acquire a reputation, which Cartouche attained with less injury to mankind, of being fearless of God or man.

To complete and universalise the desolation of the globe, it has been the will of Providence to raise up, at the same time, a tyrant as unprincipled and as overwhelming, for the ocean. Not in the poor maniac George, but in his government and nation. Buonaparte will die, and his tyrannies with him. But a nation never dies. The English government and its piratical principles and practices, have no fixed term of duration. Europe feels, and is writhing under the scorpion whips of Buonaparte. We are assailed by those of England. The one continent thus placed under the gripe of England, and the other of Buonaparte, each has to grapple with the enemy immediately pressing on itself. We must extinguish the fire kindled in our own house, and leave to our friends beyond the water that which is consuming theirs. It was not till England had taken one thousand of our ships, and impressed into her service more than six thousand of our citizens; till she had declared, by the proclamation of her Prince Regent, that she would not repeal her aggressive orders *as to us*, until Buonaparte should have repealed his *as to all nations*; till her minister, in formal conference with ours, declared, that no proposition for protecting our seamen from being impressed, under color of taking their own, was practicable or admissible; that, the door to justice and to all amicable arrangement being closed, and negotiation become both desperate and dishonorable, we concluded that the war she had been for years waging against us, might as well become a war on both sides. She takes fewer vessels from us since the declaration of war than before, because they venture more cautiously; and we now make full reprisals where before we made none. England is, in principle, the enemy of all maritime nations, as Buonaparte is of the continental; and I place in the same line of insult to the human understanding, the pretension of conquering the ocean, to establish continental rights, as that of conquering the continent, to restore maritime rights. No, my dear Madam; the object of England is the *permanent dominion of the ocean*, and the *monopoly of the trade of the world*. To secure this, she must keep a larger fleet than her own resources will maintain. The resources of other nations, then, must be impressed to supply the deficiency of her own. This is sufficiently developed and evidenced by her successive strides towards the usurpation of the sea. Mark them, from her first war after William Pitt the little, came into her administration. She first forbade to neutrals all trade with her enemies in time of war, which they had not in time of peace. This deprived them of their trade from port to port of the same nation. Then she forbade them to trade from the port of one nation to that of any other at war with her, although a right fully exercised in time of peace. Next, instead of taking vessels only *entering* a blockaded port, she took them over the whole ocean, if destined to that port, although ignorant of the blockade, and without intention to violate it. Then she took them returning from that port, as if infected by previous infraction of blockade. Then came her paper blockades, by which she might shut up the whole world without sending a ship to sea, except to take all those sailing on it, as they must, of course, be bound to some port. And these were followed by her orders of council, forbidding every nation to go to the port of any other, without coming first to some port of Great Britain, there paying a tribute to her, regulated by the cargo, and taking from her a license to proceed to the port of destination; which operation the vessel was to repeat with the return cargo on its way home. According to these orders, we could not send a vessel from St. Mary's to St. Augustine, distant six hours' sail, on our own coast, without crossing the Atlantic four times, twice with the outward cargo, and twice with the inward. She found this too daring and outrageous for a single step, retracted as to certain articles of commerce, but left it in force as to others which constitute important branches of our exports. And finally, that her views may no longer rest on inference, in a recent debate, her minister declared in open parliament, that the object of the present war is a *monopoly of commerce.*

In some of these atrocities, France kept pace with her fully in speculative wrong, which her impotence only shortened in practical execution. This was called retaliation by both; each charging the other with the initiation of the outrage. As if two combatants might retaliate on an innocent bystander, the blows they received from each other. To make war on both would have been ridiculous. In order, therefore, to single out any enemy, we offered to both, that if either would revoke its hostile decrees, and the other should refuse, we would interdict all intercourse whatever with that other; which would be war of course, as being an avowed departure from neutrality. France accepted the offer, and revoked her decrees as to us. England not only refused, but declared by a solemn proclamation of her Prince Regent, that she would not revoke her orders *even as to us,* until those of France should be annulled *as to the whole world.* We thereon declared war, and with abundant additional cause.

In the mean time, an examination before parliament of the ruinous effects of these orders on her own manufacturers, exposing them to the nation and to the world, their Prince issued a palinodial proclamation, *suspending* the orders on certain conditions, but claiming to renew them at pleasure, as a matter of right. Even this might have prevented the war, if done and known here before its declaration. But the sword being once drawn, the expense of arming incurred, and hostilities in full course, it would have been unwise to discontinue them, until effectual provision should be agreed to by England, for protecting our citizens on the high seas from impressment by her naval commanders, through error, voluntary or involuntary; the fact being notorious, that these officers, entering our ships at sea under pretext of searching for their seamen, (which they have no right to do by the law or usage of nations, which they neither do, nor ever did, as to any other nation but ours, and which no nation ever before pretended to do in any case,) entering our ships, I say, under pretext of searching for and taking out their seamen, they took ours, native as well as naturalised, knowing them to be ours, merely because they wanted them;

insomuch, that no American could safely cross the ocean, or venture to pass by sea from one to another of our own ports. It is not long since they impressed at sea two nephews of General Washington, returning from Europe, and put them, as common seamen, under the ordinary discipline of their ships of war. There are certainly other wrongs to be settled between England and us; but of a minor character, and such as a proper spirt of conciliation on both sides would not permit to continue them at war. The sword, however, can never again be sheathed, until the personal safety of an American on the ocean, among the most important and most vital of the rights we possess, is completely provided for.

As soon as we heard of her partial repeal of her orders of council, we offered instantly to suspend hostilities by an armistice, if she would suspend her impressments, and meet us in arrangements for securing our citizens against them. She refused to do it, because impracticable by any arrangement, as she pretends; but, in truth, because a body of sixty to eighty thousand of the finest seamen in the world, which we possess, is too great a resource for manning her exaggerated navy, to be relinquished, as long as she can keep it open. Peace is in her hand, whenever she will renounce the practice of aggression on the persons of our citizens. If she thinks it worth eternal war, eternal war we must have. She alleges that the sameness of language, of manners, of appearance, renders it impossible to distinguish us from her subjects. But because we speak English, and look like them, are we to be punished? Are free and independent men to be submitted to their bondage?

England has misrepresented to all Europe this ground of the war. She has called it a new pretension, set up since the repeal of her orders of council. She knows there has never been a moment of suspension of our reclamations against it, from General Washington's time inclusive, to the present day: and that it is distinctly stated in our declaration of war, as one of its principal causes. She has pretended we have entered into the war to establish the principle of 'free bottoms, free goods,' or to protect her seamen against her own right over them. We contend for neither of these. She pretends we are partial to France; that we have observed a fraudulent and unfaithful neutrality between her and her enemy. She knows this to be false, and that if there has been any inequality in our proceedings towards the belligerents, it has been in her favor. Her ministers are in possession of full proofs of this. Our accepting at once, and sincerely, the mediation of the virtuous Alexander, their greatest friend, and the most aggravated enemy of Buonaparte, sufficiently proves whether we have partialities on the side of her enemy. I sincerely pray that this mediation may produce a just peace. It will prove that the immortal character, which has first stopped by war the career of the destroyer of mankind, is the friend of peace, of justice, of human happiness, and the patron of unoffending and injured nations. He is too honest and impartial to countenance propositions of peace derogatory to the freedom of the seas.

Shall I apologise to you, my dear Madam, for this long political letter? But yours justifies the subject, and my feelings must plead for the unreserved expression of them; and they have been the less reserved, as being from a private citizen, retired from all connection with the government of his country, and whose ideas, expressed without communication with any one, are neither known, nor imputable to them.

The dangers of the sea are now so great, and the possibilities of interception by sea and land such, that I shall subscribe no name to this letter. You will know from whom it comes, by its reference to the date of time and place of yours, as well as by its subject in answer to that. This omission must not lessen in your view the assurances of my great esteem, of my sincere sympathies for the share which you bear in the afflictions of your country, and the deprivations to which a lawless will has subjected you. In return, you enjoy the dignified satisfaction of having met them, rather than be yoked with the abject, to his car; and that, in withdrawing from oppression, you have followed the virtuous example of a father, whose name will ever be dear to your country and to mankind. With my prayers that you may be restored to it, that you may see it re-established in that temperate portion of liberty which does not infer either anarchy or licentiousness, in that high degree of prosperity which would be the consequence of such a government, in that, in short, which the constitution of 1789 would have insured it,

if wisdom could have stayed at that point the fervid but impru-
dent zeal of men, who did not know the character of their own
countrymen, and that you may long live in health and happiness under it, and leave to the world a well educated and virtuous representative and descendant of your honored father, is
the ardent prayer of the sincere and respectful friend who
writes this letter.

George McFeely: Diary

On March 15, 1813, Major General Dearborn put Lieutenant Colonel Winfield Scott in charge of planning the Niagara campaign. With Oliver Hazard Perry, commander of the U.S. naval forces on Lake Erie, Scott conceived an amphibious attack on Brigadier General John Vincent and his fourteen hundred British troops at Fort George, in Upper Canada, where the Niagara River empties into Lake Ontario. By early spring, Scott had assembled a force of four thousand troops just across the Niagara from the fort, and on May 25–26 he began the attack with cannon fire from the river. At daybreak on May 27, the United States landed waves of troops on the fort's lake side, and Scott led a well-executed surprise attack on the fort from the rear. One of Scott's companies was led by Lieutenant Colonel George McFeely, of the 22nd U.S. Infantry Regiment.

May 27th. The Light troops were formed and marched from camp at two o'clock this morning; embarked on board of the boats and put out at three. This morning was calm, not a ripple on the lake, and a thick heavy fog. This gave us great spirits as the fog was much in our favor. We passed the fleet and within a mile and a half of the Canada shore, were ordered to hold and lay off out oars. Here three schooners came up and passed up, one ran into the mouth of the river, the other stood round Massesauga point to the mouth of the Two Mile creek. After sunrise clear away and the cannon commenced from Fort Niagara and all her detached batteries. The schooner in the river opened fire on the Lighthouse battery, the other two opened on a one gun battery at the mouth of Two Mile creek: this was the point of landing. Here we lay waiting for the Grand Army to come up, but it appears that great confusion took place at the place of embarkation, the different brigades and regiments became all mixed into a confused mass, and it was eleven o'clock in the day before Boyd's division came up, followed by Winder's and Chandler's.

Orders were given for the light troops to make for the shore. Our boats formed a line and pulled away for the shore. The two schooners covered our landing. The enemy about 1500 strong lay in waiting in a ravine forty yards from the shore. They reserved their fire until our boats were within one hundred and fifty yards when they opened a heavy and galling fire. The fire was returned from our boats, the men at the oars quit rowing and took to their muskets. All appeared to be in confusion, some of our boats swung around broadside to the shore, but with the exertions of the officers we soon got under way again. As we approached near the shore their firing ought to have been very destructive, but we suffered less owing to their firing too high in consequence of their cartridges being so heavy that no man dare lay the butt of his musket to his shoulder, or if he does do it once he will not like very well to try it again, and consequently will hold his musket in such a way as not to knock the shoulder off himself. He will put the butt down along his side under his arm and in this case the muzzle when the soldiers thinks his piece is level will always be elevated.

The action was very close and warm for about ten minutes after we landed, when the army gave way and retreated in confusion. Gen'l Boyd's division landed at the same point and at the heels of the van about the close of the action and in place of extending the line to the right or the left they rushed up the bank among the light troops and all became one solid mass of confusion. It was well for us that the enemy was beaten before this took place for our superior numbers were rendered useless for the space of about 20 minutes. After great exertions by the officers, the light troops were gotten formed in line of battle on the ground where the enemy's dead and wounded lay. I had two riflemen selected to keep close along side of me during the action, the one named Shoops and the other Devor. They were first-rate marksmen. Devor in the confusion of landing got lost from me, I did not see him until after the action, but Shoops kept close to me nor did he fire until he asked for permission. This man possessed the most cool and determined bravery that I have ever seen. When some of our men were firing into the air at an angle of forty-five degrees, others in their confusion did not ram the cartridge half way home, dropped their ramrods on the ground and indeed some rendered their muskets useless during the fight by firing away their hammers, Shoops remained cool and collected, he lowered his rifle and took his aim as deliberately as if he had been shooting at a mark. I saw him in the heat of the action taking aim long enough to fire then move his rifle off to the right, take a new and steady aim and fire. I supposed at the time that his eye had caught an officer, but this was not the case. The next day I had an opportunity to ask him the cause of changing his mark, if he was picking out the officers. He replied that he had picked out several officers, but in the case I alluded to the first man he was aiming at fell just as he was moving his finger to pull the trigger, that he thought there was no use in shooting at that fellow, and so he moved his piece off to the right and caught another. I said, well did that fellow go down, he replied, "Yes, Sir, all that I took aimed went down when I fired, but perhaps some of the other boys put them down as they were all shooting as fast as they could load, and that in one case about which you asked the fellow before I shot. If I had shot at that instant I would have thought that I had killed him when in fact it was some other one." I have no doubt but that every ball that this brave fellow fired took effect as the distance was only forty yards; I stepped the distance the day after the action. My other soldier Devor committed a most shocking outrage on a wounded soldier. This circumstance was communicated to me in the evening by Sergeant Pratt as follows: "A poor fellow was wounded in the main artery of the thigh. He was sitting on the ground holding his wound with both hands, the blood was shooting out at jerks as thick as a finger; I was looking at him when Devor came up, he cocked his rifle, and blew out his brains." This was confirmed by two or three other men; I sent for Devor the next morning and told him what I had heard and asked him if it were true. He appeared to be embarrassed and muttered that the fellow was reaching for his gun and he thought he was going to shoot some of the men. I told him that that was murder & that I had a good mind to send him to the Prevost Guard and prefer charges against him. He deserted the next morning and was never heard of.

The light troops were ordered to pursue the enemy: their track was easily followed, the ground was covered with muskets, knapsacks, blankets, and cartridge boxes, &c. &c. When we got through the woods onto the plains of Newark, we saw the enemy forming on the back of the town. I suggested to Col. Scott to fall back until we could gain the woods, take a circuitous route under the cover of the woods, and gain the rear of the enemy while the main army would come up in their front, thus cutting of their retreat, they would surrender. Scott agreed to this and our column was to the right when the enemy opened a battery of four six pounders upon us. Scott ordered the column to wheel to the left and march at quick time direct for the battery. They continued a brisk fire until we approached within two hundred yards, when they retreated in great confusion. Every shot passed over our heads and not a shot took effect, however, several men were killed and wounded in the main army three quarters of a mile in our rear.

We passed on skirting the back part of the town of Newark when we halted at a church where a black flag was flying. Scott, Hindman, and myself entered the church which was occupied as a hospital; a number of wounded had been brought from the field of battle to this place, several British surgeons were employed in dressing their wounds. A British Colonel Myers was just then under the hands of the doctors, they had him bolstered up in bed and were wrapping a bandage around his body. He was wounded in four different places, he looked very pale and sick. We drank some wine and water at the invitation of the colonel. A guard was left to protect the hospital and we took our leave and marched off. We had not gone far when two British came out to a house. Scott halted the column and commenced a conversation with them. I advanced from the center to the front to hear what was said. When I came up Scott said: "I'll go see, you shall go along, and if you are lying by God I will sacrifice you on the spot." He turned round to me and said that these men said that the enemy had vacated Fort George and that he would go with the two front companies to the fort, that I should proceed with the remainder of the column along in the direction we were then in until we would intersect the river about three quarters to the left of the fort, which was then about 300 yards off and only obstructed from our view by the town. Soon after a tremendous explosion took place and in a few minutes more another, more tremendous than the first. Scott marched on to the fort and entered, cut down the flag staff and took the matches out of two other magazines that would have exploded in a few seconds. I proceeded with the column until I came to the river, our men complained much for want of water. I ordered the one half to go down the bank of the river and fill their canteens with water. When this was done I permitted the other half to go and water. On our way here we took about twenty prisoners, they were all Irishmen and had concealed themselves in houses and other places when on the retreat. In half an hour Scott came up riding a British officer's horse with the flag from Fort George hanging across the saddle before him. He swore he would sleep in it that night. He said the General's orders were to pursue the enemy. We marched in pursuit of the enemy about five miles, when orders came for the light troops to return to Fort George. I should have mentioned that Col. Miller with his regiment joined us at the place where we halted for water. We returned with reluctance from our pursuit. This was in my opinion very censurable on our generals. We ought to have pursued the enemy night and day while they were under the panic. We could have captured all their stores and baggage that evening and the greater number of their army. Many of their men came in from the woods and gave themselves up claiming the right of deserters. That night the stores at Queenston and Fort Erie were burned and their scattered remains marched for Burlington Heights at the head of Lake Ontario. We retired and encamped in Fort George and lay on the ground having no tents or straw. This was on the 27th of May, 1813, and our Generals appeared to act as if Canada were conquered.

John Le Couteur: Journal

In November 1811, John Le Couteur, a seventeen-year-old ensign in the 96th Regiment of Foot (Jersey), was sent to British North America as a lieutenant in the 104th Regiment (New Brunswick). One year later, George Prevost ordered the 104th to make a winter's trek of seven hundred miles from Fredericton, New Brunswick, to Kingston, to help him defend the shores of Lake Ontario. No sooner had Le Couteur reached Kingston than he was ordered to join Prevost's attack on Sackets Harbor, New York, the American naval base on the eastern shore of the lake. Prevost's goal was threefold: to destroy a precious U.S. asset, to force a recall of American troops from the Niagara front, and to avenge the attack on York. Sailing from Kingston, Commodore James Yeo led a squadron of thirty-three vessels carrying nearly a thousand British and Indian troops, including Le Couteur and Prevost himself. They were met at Sackets Harbor by Brigadier General Jacob Brown of the New York militia, commanding a garrison of fourteen hundred men.

---

27 May
We were suddenly ordered to march from Point Frederick to Kingston—to our great relief. The Captain left me behind to see the baggage forwarded and I never thought of hurrying and meant to take my pleasure when to cross when a light bob came running to me: "Oh Sir, the troops and our men are parading in Kingston, the Bugles are sounding and Drums rolling—there is some great move, for the Men of War's boats are pulling to Kingston." I ran down with Him to the edge of the Lake—not a boat or Canoe to be seen but one with its stern stove in. He was a thorough Canoe-man, a New Brunswicker, and offered to paddle me over with a bit of plank taken from the dock yard.

We both sat on the sound end of the wooden Canoe, cocked her broken bow over the water and launched our bark for fame and glory. It was, in vulgar parlance, a funky affair but we got over safe. I got over in time to run for my haversack and to parade the company in Haversacks and light marching order with Sixty rounds of Ball Cartridge. At twelve we began to embark in Boats—detachments of the 8th, 100th, 104th, Glengarry Light Infantry, Candn Voltigeurs, and Newfoundland Regiments—when it leaked out that we were destined for Sackets Harbor, as a set-off for the damage they had done us at York.

28 May

On Tuesday morning the 28th, a beautiful morning, we were about Seven miles from the harbour. The fleet stood in close to reconnoitre the batteries—it was supposed they were thought too strong, for we stood off again. About 8 A.M., our fire eater, Major Drummond, had got us into the bateaux to practice pulling, as He said, and was pulling toward the landing place when Sir George Prevost sent an ADC to order Him to re-embark his Men instantly. Drummond said He would engage to take the place with his own Regiment if allowed because it was evidently a surprise—the enemy were quite unprepared for an attack. In standing off, however, we cut off a brigade of bateaux, with a reinforcement of three hundred men that was en route to Sackets. It had come on to rain hard, and we were all thoroughly soaked, cold and shivering—having no great coats. Sir George gave the Americans all that day and the next night ample time for a fair stand up fight, like the old French Guards, who never fired first, however.

29 May

On the 29th May, the fleet was pretty close in at day break. At 4 A.M., we got into bateaux, formed in line, and pulled steadily for the Shore. The American troops were formed in Line, about a hundred yards from the beach. As we neared, they plied us with round shot from a Battery on our left. Just before we touched the shore, a round shot passed close over our boat, and plumped into the Grenadier boat on our right—Killed and wounded a couple of men—cut the boat nearly in two, and down she went. The Grenadiers behaved admirably, raised their firelocks high, and could just touch the bottom, we little fellows would half of us been drowned. We cheered lustily, so did they, soon Old Dick their Veteran Captain formed them, so did we form. The whole line was soon landed & formed under a roll of musquetry, when we charged and the Americans ran. We drove them at a skirmishing run a mile and a half.

Sir James Yeo, was running in front of and with our men, in a round Jacket and waving his cap, cheering the men on, without sword or pistol. His cockswain was hit by a musket bullet in the head—the Commodore desired him to go to the rear, to the Doctors. Not a bit, He swore He would not leave his Captain in a fight.

Our gallant Drummond was also running on Sword in hand, like Roderick Dhu in a foray. An American Soldier, who was skirmishing very gallantly, saw the effect of his presence. He quietly waited until Drummond was about twenty yards from Him, amidst shot and Yells of fury, levelled his piece and knocked the Major over, apparently stone dead. Our men bayoneted the gallant fellow in an instant. Drummond was lifted, said "tis not mortal, I can move my legs." No blood appeared. "Charge on Men!" He shouted. We had induced Him to remove his Epaulettes. He had deposited them in the front pockets of his overalls, which saved his life. The ball had struck the pad and steel plate—it was a dreadful bruise that He received.

Jobling, my Senior Sub., made a dash with half the Light Company at a Battery but lost half his men. We had then reached the Town. We saw the *Pike*, a ship of war, on the Stocks in flames or rather smoke. We had turned the battery, and got up to the Stockade round the barracks I believe. It was ticklish work, for as I had nothing but a sword, there was nothing to do. The Yankees were poking the muzzles of their guns, on each side of me while I made myself as flat as I could edgewise behind one of the posts of the stockade. It was a really uncomfortable position there was neither glory nor pleasure in being riddled, or rather fringed, with balls. This did not last long, our men got round the flank and soon cleared the space.

Major Moodie & I with my Servant Mills then tried to turn a small howitzer on the blockhouse in which a handful of men were keeping us at bay. My servant was slightly hit in five places, and Moodie was wounded in this operation. Moodie told me "it won't do." I said: "What is that Sir?" "The retreat is sounding, See our Men are forming, are you much hurt?"

"No. It must be a mistake, there are the Americans running away en Masse to the left", which we both distinctly saw.

The Bugles continued to sound the recall so we formed in good Line, just out of range of the block house. Major Drummond immediately offered, wounded as He was, to proceed to summon the Americans to surrender which Sir George permitted. But brother Jonathan was too grass sharp. "Why do you retreat, if you wish us to surrender?" "Only to form a fresh attack and to save a further effusion of blood." "Then tell Sir George Prevost, we will await the issue of his attack." Poor Sir George, if no worse, mistook the body of three thousand Americans Moodie & I saw in retreat for a fresh reinforcement. We continued our own retreat and embarked unmolested, save by a few straggling shot.

Our young troops went into action admirably, formed and advanced as on field day. It is a strange, an awful sense that first feeling of deadly encounter—it is not fear We feel, but a glorious sense of awe, the spirit desiring to urge the flesh to aid its fellow man. Strange to witness death and wounds on every side—still to rush into the very Jaws of danger.

As we charged, a fine young American Soldier fell and was caught by our light bobs, two or three bayonets were flourishing over his handsome imploring face, with hands uplifted. "For Gods sake spare me!" "For shame men, never kill an unarmed man who begs for quarter!" I struck their Bayonets aside, and sent the poor fellow to the rear.

A sad scene disturbed us much as were embarking. The DQMG had been killed in the action, and his Son a Youth of eighteen, an Ensign in our Regiment, was in the saddest state of grief—desiring to remain by his Father's body. There was no *step* in our Regiment but Maj. Drummond, Major Moodie, Captains Leonard & Shore, Lieutenants Rainsford, Moore, and De Lancey were wounded —25 men killed & 75 wounded of our Regt. Our force in all amounted to 870 men, and our loss was 48 killed & 195 wounded.

It was a scandalously managed affair. We gained a surprise and threw it away to allow the enemy to gain time. The murmurs against Sir George were deep, not loud. Our sweet little Band was sadly cut up, three of them being killed in this affair. It was a folly to take them.

Dear Wm and Miss Robison told me that their anxiety and alarm was indescribable. All the Ladies, who had relatives in the attacking force, with those who had only friends, were listening in breathless trepidation to the distant roar of Guns & musquetry while the action lasted.

My friend Moore was shot in the left Jaw, the ball had passed through the Cheek and horribly disfigured Him. I fed Him with a spoon for several days & nights and took his hand to mine in order to prevent his touching his bandages.

Joseph Penley Jr.: from The Sanguinary and Cruel War of 1812–14

Captured American soldiers and sailors were treated variously by the British. Officers were considered gentlemen and enjoyed special privileges. Some were given the freedom of a town; others, like General Hull, were sent home on extended parole and required to refrain from fighting until officially exchanged. Militia were sometimes sent home, too, as they were only part-time soldiers. Enlisted men, however, were generally confined until they were actually exchanged. The British principally housed them on Melville Island, near Halifax, Nova Scotia; at Dartmoor Prison in England, or on rotting hulks or converted store ships. One such floating prison was HMS *Malabar*, a 56-gun fourth-rate formerly belonging to the East India Company, anchored in the St. Lawrence River just south of the city of Québec. Private Joseph Penley Jr. of the Maine militia, captured on the Richelieu River during the taking of USS *Growler* (June 3, 1813), spent six months aboard *Malabar*, then another six months on Melville Island. He published his prison memoirs in 1853.

The next day after our capture, we were taken down the St. John's river in row-boats, about twenty miles to the town of St. Johns. On arriving, it being King George's birth-day, the fourth of June, our guards gave each of us a glass of Old Jamaica, and requested us to drink to the health of the King. We drank with thankful hearts, but the King we choose to say nothing about.

The 5th day of June, we were taken by land to Chamble, a village situated on the St. Johns, which here takes the name of Sorrell. On account of rocks and rapids in the river from St. Johns to this place, it is not boatable, consequently we had to foot it, except the sick, lame and halt, who were provided with horses and horse-carts.

On our arrival, we were put into some old stone barracks and confined there until about noon the next day, when we were again started for Montreal, distant from Chamble about fifteen miles, and from St. Johns thirty. On account of my old lameness, I had the offer of a ride the whole distance, which I gladly accepted. There were about ten of us who rode in the two horse carts, one of whom was a young lady who was captured on board the Growler with us. She had the offer of being carried back with the wounded over the lines, but she refused; choosing she said, to go with the men, and return home when they did. She was naturally a pretty decent looking woman, but she was a deluded character.

We arrived at a hotel on the banks of the St. Lawrence, nearly opposite Montreal, about five o'clock in the afternoon. Here we were put into open boats and rowed over the river by hired Canadians, and then passed down the river on the West side. Two boats also accompanied us, containing about twenty-five soldiers with loaded muskets, ready to fire upon us if we should attempt to make ourselves masters of the boats and run away with the boatmen.

We passed rapidly down this mighty river until near dark, when the boatmen put ashore and moored the boats a few fathoms from the water's edge. The soldiers built a fire on shore and stood guard over us all night. Not one of the prisoners was permitted to leave the boat, nor was there the least possible chance for us to get any rest, except what we could obtain by standing or sitting in the boats.

Early the next morning, the 7th of June, the boatmen came on board, took in their mud-hooks, and were again passing rapidly down the river. On, on we went, where many of our number were doomed never to return: never more to behold the friends and happy homes they had left far behind; and little did they think of the suffering that awaited them,—that before that short summer should pass away, near one third of our high-spirited, noble crew, would be mouldering in the dust of a foreign land! Alas! such was their fate.

Our boatmen rowed all day, until near dark, when they again moored the boats in a small cove and near the shore. A guard was placed over us, as the night before, and we passed a second night without any of us obtaining rest or sleep.

Early the next morning we were again on our way, but where we knew not. About dark we were landed at a village called

Three Rivers, and conducted into some old barracks, which was gladly accepted as a resting place for the night. Although we had nothing better to stretch our weary limbs upon, than the soft side of a board, yet we had a pretty good night's rest, and we were very much in need of it, for, being in open boats the two nights before, with nothing but the canopy of the heavens to cover or screen us from the chilly air and heavy night dews, to sleep was impossible: nor was there room in the boat for a man to lay down. We had nothing to eat but raw pork and bread, and as for drink, we had the river water we floated in, from the time we went on board the boats at Montreal, until the first day of the next November. The tide was always running at the rate of four or five miles an hour, and although the water was sweet to the taste, yet it being always a little turbid, the effect on our bowels and health may easily be imagined.

On the morning of the 9th of June, we took another start, and about two o'clock in the afternoon we arrived within about one mile of the city of Quebec, and were ordered on board a transport ship of 620 tons burthen, called the Malabar. She had recently arrived from England with troops, munitions of war, &c., and was then lying at anchor about one mile above the city and about that distance from the West shore, the river there being about three miles wide. As we ascended the rope ladder and went over the side of the ship, we found to our sorrow, upon her deck and before our eyes, about three hundred American prisoners. Although they had been there but a few weeks, yet their sorrowful and haggard looks told a tale of suffering and woe.

Our crew numbered about 90 men, the guard and ship's crew about 40 more, making in all about 430 men on board that ship.

By day we had only about one-half the deck, it being barred across at the middle mast, and sentries placed to prevent us from going any further aft, consequently we were badly crowded and about as thick as we could stand. At sunset, we were counted down between decks, and remained there until sunrise the next morning, and then counted again as we came on deck. None were allowed to go between decks during the day, except one mess, of six men, who were called by turns every day, to go below and clean up, which was no small job, you may depend. They used three-cornered scrapers, shovels, scrub-brooms, buckets of water, mops, &c.

The ship had two tier of berths, one above the other, built of rough boards around the lower deck. They were intended each to hold four men, but we were obliged to crowd five into each berth, and then had to lay spoon fashion, and when one turned or shifted sides, all had to change too. For the want of berths, thirty or forty men had to lie upon the bare deck during the whole time we were on board the Malabar. We were in Egyptian dark also, and many having occasion to go upon the upper deck during the night, would tread on and tumble over those who were stretched out on the deck, which was the occasion of many horrible oaths and bitter curses. Some had blankets and some had none, and the suffering we endured on board that horrible ship, nearly six months, was enough to excite pity in the most savage breast. Our provisions were of the most loathsome kind. We had half a pound of what they called pork, but it was much the poorest of any thing of the kind I ever saw before, also one pound and a half of bread and one gill of peas per day, each. What we lacked in meat alone, we had in meat and bread together, for nearly all our bread was full of live worms! about half an inch long, but a great part of it was so mouldy that worms could not live in it. It had the appearance of being made of barley meal, without bolting or sifting. It was put into coarse bags and kept in the ship's hold, and had the appearance of having been baked some years.

As we had to sleep upon hard boards, with nothing under us but a blanket, the continual rolling and motion of the ship soon wore the skin from our hips. We were kept in dirt and filth, had no clothing except what we stood in when we were captured, had no chance to wash a shirt or any thing else, and no such privilege allowed us while on board that floating prison. And I will further say, although it may cause a shudder, or a qualmish feeling to come over the delicate and sensitive reader, (and well it may.) yet as it is true, and that the reader may form some faint idea of our situation and suffering, I will not pass it over in silence, and here it is, kind reader,—we were all lousy! Yes, these horrible vermin were in our blankets, shirts, and every part of our clothing and swarming in every article. Their presence was caused by our being confined so close together and kept in dirt and filth, without a change of clothing. They had no respect of persons, all had a full share of their company. Day times they would hide themselves under the patches, pleats and seams on our clothing, and at night would come forth from their hiding places and prey upon our emaciated bodies, and although we slew vast numbers daily, yet those that eluded our search, greatly outnumbered us.

Two of our number were set to do the cooking, that is, to boil our meat and peas. It was done in large square copper boilers, set in a cast iron fire-place. The boiler was several inches higher than the iron jambs that surrounded it on three sides, and it also set far enough from the jambs to allow the fire to blaze up around it, and here all those that had a tin cup, or tin quart, would fill it with water and then set it on the fire-frame, resting it against the boiler, and then take some of their miserable, loathsome bread, such as they could not eat, burn it to a crust and make coffee of it. That we relished highly.

We were classed in messes of six, and some messes received their daily portions together; their meat was boiled in little bags of net work made of rope yarn, and then eat together. They would frequently loose, however, that way, for portions of their meat would boil to pieces and fall through the netting. and on that account far the greatest number of us would have our portions divided, and each man take his part seperate, and to make sure of the whole, would devour it raw. Many of us, frequently fifty or sixty, would, if possible, procure a little stick or splinter, and stick on an ounce or two of lean pork, and when the cooks took off the boiler, there would be a rush made for the fire by some scores of men, to broil their meat on the few remaining coals that were left; but the weak, the timid, and the feeble, stood but a poor chance. All were selfish; none, or but a very few, seemed to show, or have any feeling for their fellow prisoners. They would be crowded and wedged in five or six deep, with bits of meat on their skewers, and in their scrambling and pushing, it would frequently get knocked off the skewer, which would often cause bloody noses,—it would be but a word and a blow, and the blow very frequently come first.

In the month of August we were visited by Gen. Chandler

Gen. Winder, and Col. Baerstler, who were prisoners of war, on a limited parole, at the town of Bowport, four or five miles below Quebec. They were accompanied by several British officers and the U. S. Agent. They made us a present of four dollars each in hard money, an article very much needed by us. The next day a French Canadian came off to the ship in a bumboat, to trade with us. He had cakes, pies, smoked herring, fruits, vegetables, &c., for all of which he asked twice or three times as much as they were worth: but his price had to be paid, or no trade. He was not allowed to come on deck, nor were we allowed to go over the side of the ship to trade with him, so we let down our money in a pail or basket, made fast to a line, and he would return just as much of the article we wanted, as he pleased, and no more.

One time while John, for that was his name, was busily engaged, with his back turned towards the ship, some one let down a line with a hook attached to it, and drew up a small basket containing a quantity of smoked herring, &c. John soon missed them, but knowing they were forever gone from him, comforted himself by singing out at the top of his voice, "Sacra non ge! Sacra non ge! begare." The English of which needs no interpretation, but may easily be imagined. John continued his visits daily while our money lasted, and after he had got it all, he took our lady prisoner on shore with him, and that was the last I saw of either of them.

In the months of July and August, eight of the prisoners attempted to gain their liberty by swimming on shore in the night. The two first that left the ship, we supposed were successful, for we never heard from them again. Their names were Smith and Hutchinson. They went on deck in a dark night and let themselves down into the water by a rope, unobserved by the sentries. The nearest land they could possibly reach by swimming, was a point that made round Wolf's Cove, and was about three miles above where our ship lay at anchor.

But a few nights after Smith and Hutchinson left the ship, two others made the attempt; but their strength failing them long before they reached the shore, they called loudly for help, and a boat put off from a ship lying at anchor not far from them, with an intent to save them, but before the boat reached them, they sank and were both drowned. Their bodies were picked up some days after, and buried. One of them was a drummer, his name was Haywood, and he belonged in the State of New York. The name of the other was Webber, and he belonged in the District, now State of Maine.

What, but the most intense suffering and anxiety of mind, could induce men to risk their lives by plunging into the deep, foaming river, on a dark night, knowing they must swim three miles before they could reach land, or be drowned.

After that but two prisoners were permitted to go on deck at once in the night, and the sentry was obliged to see them below before others were allowed to go up, and being thus closely watched, there was no more chance to leave the ship in that way. But there was a scuttle in the side of the ship, about eighteen inches square, strongly fastened with cross-bars of hard wood, and small holes left to let in air to prevent the prisoners from suffocating with heat. To get out that scuttle was the next thing to be tried. We operated in the night with our knives, and cut every bar nearly off upon the inside, and then watched a favorable opportunity to go out, which must be in a still, calm night, with the tide coming in. Soon a favorable opportunity occurred, and four stout hearted young men got ready for their perilous voyage, and surely none other than men of courage would have attempted it. Three of them went out together, but the fourth man, whose name was Hanway, put his head out through the scuttle, and seeing the surrounding darkness and gloom of night, and hearing the agitated waters as they foamed and dashed against the side of the vessel, and realising the danger he was exposing himself to, drew back with fear; but after waiting a few minutes, he said he had made up his mind to leave the infernal ship that night, and sink or swim, die or live, he would make the attempt. About fifteen minutes after the others had left, he went out with the flood tide, but long before he could see the shore he became weary, his strength began to fail him, and he called for help. A boat with three men was sent from a ship, lying at anchor near by, to his relief, before they came up with him he had reached the shore, but in so exhausted a state that he could not get out of their way. After telling them who he was, and seeing his naked condition, they furnished him with a part of their own clothing, together with a hat, shoes, &c., and told him to get clear if he could: but after being gone about three days, he was captured and brought back to the ship again.

The other three men were gone about fourteen days, and then captured and brought back by some armed Canadians who were in pursuit of them for the sake of the reward of five dollars a head, that was offered for their apprehension and return to the ship. They said that when they were taken, they were within a few miles of the lines.

We had resolved that dishonesty of one prisoner towards another, should be punished. That we knew could not well be dispensed with. There was a set of desperate men among us, who seemed to take delight in cruelty and tyarannizing over their fellow prisoners, and about a half dozen of these rabbid fellows, made that resolve a plea for carrying out their own rabbid principles. They fell upon one man and flogged him so severely that he had to be sent to the hospital, where he soon after died. He was a dragoon; his name was Shed, and he belonged in Salem, Massachusetts.

Some days after this, they accused a young man of Capt. Herrick's company, by the name of Emery, of stealing from his mess, and began to prepare to "cob" him. Myself and many others, knowing that Emery was an honest fellow, and that the charge was false, determined that he should not be hurt if we could prevent it. But they took poor Emery and dragged him to one of the ship's guns, set him astride of it, and then four or five of them held him down, while one Webber, a large, powerful man, stood by with a bat-board in his hand to battel him with. Four or five of us, Emery's friends, crowded around, told them that Emery was innocent and that their charge was false, and that he must not be hurt; but they heeded it not. Webber raised his cudgel and struck Emery a cruel blow upon his breech, without our being able to prevent it by reason of the crowd; he raised his weapon to strike again,—Emery begging for help,—in an instant I rushed into the crowd and sprang upon Webber, wrenched the cudgel out of his hand and threw it overboard, before he could inflict another blow. Webber, Smith, Peterson, Blanchard, Bill Evaton, or Saucy Bill as we used to call him, and Peter McDaniels an Irishman, came at me like tigers, but I was prepared for them, and gave them several well directed shots of bone and sinew, which brought two or three of them down sprawling upon the deck. The others closed in with me, but my friends being on hand, we had it rough and tumble for a short time. The officers of the ship hearing and seeing the rumpus, were soon at the scene of action, and inquiring into the cause of the tumult. We told them of the cruel conduct of the rowdies, at which they ordered the guard to drive them into the ship's hold, where they were kept until the next morning, which put a final stop to such reprehensible conduct, and Webber was soon after drowned in attempting to swim ashore, as I have before stated.

While we were on board that ship it was very sickly among the prisoners, and for several weeks in the latter part of June and the first of July, some days two, three, and sometimes, four men would die. One man died the next day after we were put on board the ship. Volunteers being called for to go on shore and bury him, myself with several other prisoners, offered our services. We went under a guard of British soldiers, landed at a wharf and passed through the upper part of the city. The ascent was quite steep from the wharf, and I noticed one street so steep that it was not passable except for foot people, and then only on stone steps. The houses were mostly built but one story high, and were of undressed stone, which gave them a rough, ragged appearance. The buildings were very compact, and the streets narrow, and as we passed out of the city to the burying ground, which is on the border of the Plains of Abraham, we passed through two ponderous iron gates, in the two massive stone walls that encircle that part of the city. We dug a grave in the common burying ground and there deposited the mortal remains of our fellow-prisoner, and returned to the ship.

On our visit to the city, we were accompanied by Capt. Askow, the commander of the prison ship. He had no control over us prisoners, but he seemed to be a kind hearted man, and appeared to pity our situation. He told us while on our way to the city, that he hoped before many weeks his ship would be made a cartel of, to take us to the States, but the kind wishes of the good man were never realised by us.

About twenty of our men died on board of that horrible ship within a few days after we arrived on board. They had no more nursing and but little more attention paid them, then would so many brute beasts. Their dead bodies were put into coffins made of rough boards, sawed by the prisoners on board the ship with whip-saws.

Some time in the month of July, the sick, about thirty in number, were transferred on board of a brig that had been fitted up for a Hospital, and was then lying at anchor not far from the Malabar. I soon after reported myself sick, and sick I was. I was sick of my horrible situation, and I did not think I could find such a dirty, loathsome, horrible place on board the brig, as I was then in, and so it proved. The sick there were poorly provided for, had bad accommodations, and bad nurses. We were on board the brig about three weeks, and in that short time many of our men breathed their last. Corporal Herrick, a cousin to our Captain, died there, also, a man who belonged in Greene, a member of our company, a man by the name of Churchill, who belonged in Paris, and a man by the name of Pratt, are all that I now recollect.

The Doctor ordered all that were able to walk, to go on deck every pleasant day, and those that were not too feeble, to be helped on deck. The head nurse, whose name was Cornel, got a rope and put it around a sick man's body, who was as helpless as an infant, drew him up and lay him upon deck, and the poor fellow died in less than one-half hour after. A cruel nurse surely.

Some time in August, the British had got a Hospital fitted up, a short distance above the city upon the border of the Plains of Abraham, and nearly opposite where our ship lay, to which place the sick were immediately sent, and where great numbers of them died. Five of those that died here, belonged to the small remnant of Capt. Herrick's company.

When I left the brig, with some others, I was ordered back to the prison ship, where we were doomed to remain about three months longer. Soon after my return, one of my berth mates, who slept with me, was suddenly seized in the night with powerful delirium. His talk was frantic, wild and incoherent, but I contrived to keep him in the berth until morning. After we were counted up, out of the dirty hold, on to the deck, I took him by the arm and led him to the sentry, who was always on guard to keep the prisoners from going on to the quarter deck, and asked him to be so kind as to speak to Capt. Askow and ask him if he would not come there. He complied with my request, and soon the Capt. came. I pointed to the young man that was bereft of reason, and asked if there could be anything done for him. The Capt. put his hand on his shoulder and bid him follow; he took him as far as the cabin door, and then brought him a tumbler of wine; the poor fellow grasped it with both hands, drank it off at a draught, and returned to me, apparently better. I assisted him all I could, and that was but little. Soon after noon the Doctor came on board and ordered this man, with some others, to be sent on shore to the hospital. Before they reached the shore, however, it began to rain, and poured down in torrents. Surely, thought I, this is too bad weather for a sick man to be out in, and it was. The man died in a few days after he got to the hospital. He was a kind hearted, noble spirited young man, and was one of Herrick's company. His name was Frost and was a townsman of mine. The names of the other four who belonged to Herrick's company, that died in the hospital, were Edward Parker, Jacob Sinclair, of Greene, Me., and two young men who were brothers, by the name of Pratt, who belonged in Livermore, Me.

One poor fellow by the name of Eames, attempted to run away from the hospital, but did not get far. A Canadian seeing him crossing some fields, went at him with his hoe-handle, and Eames being too weak to resist, had to surrender, and was sent back to the ship.

There were more than one thousand American prisoners sent to Quebec during the summer, and as they died off on board the ship and in the hospital, our number was kept good on board the ship, by new comers, of which there were more or less every week.

Philip B. V. Broke
to John Borlase Warren

On June 1, 1813, in the middle of Massachusetts Bay, the British frigate
Shannon (52 guns) met the U.S. frigate *Chesapeake* (50 guns) barreling
out of Boston Harbor. For *Shannon*'s captain, Philip Broke, a duel with
an evenly matched enemy was the long-awaited payoff for seven years
of gunnery drills with live ammunition. For *Chesapeake*'s captain, James
Lawrence, engaging *Shannon* was a matter of national honor and personal glory. In the bloody, close-range battle that ensued, precision
gunnery won the day: *Chesapeake* was disabled, subjected to murderous fire, and then boarded—all within fifteen minutes. Lawrence,
mortally wounded, cried out to his men, "*Don't give up the ship!*" but
they had little choice but to surrender. Broke, though he sustained a
severe head wound from which he never fully recovered, became a British national hero, the vindicator of the Royal Navy. The official account
of the battle, though signed by the incapacitated Broke, was in fact
written by three captains at Halifax, including the station chief, Thomas
B. Capel, in order to get news of the victory to London as soon as
possible.

Copy   Thos. Bladen Capel   *Shannon*   Halifax
                                          June 6th 1813

Sir,
    I have the honor to inform you that being close in with
Boston Light House in His Majestys Ship under my Com-
mand on the 1st inst.—I had the pleasure of seeing that the
United States Frigate *Chesapeake* (whom we had long been
Watching) was coming out of the Harbour to engage the
Shannon— I took a position between Cape Ann and Cape
Cod, and then hove to for him to join us—the Enemy came
down in a very handsome manner, having three American
Ensigns flying—when closing with us he sent down his royal
Yards— I kept the *Shannons* up, expecting the breeze would

die away— At half past five P.M. the Enemy hauled up within hail of us, on the Starb. side & the Battle began—both Ships steering full under the Topsails; after exchanging between two and three Broadsides, the Enemys Ship fell on board of us— her mizen channels locking in with our fore rigging— I went forward to ascertain her position, and observing that the Enemy were flinching from their Guns, I gave orders to prepare for boarding— Our gallant bands appointed to that Service immediately rushed in under their respective Officers, upon the Enemys Decks driving every thing before them with irresistable fury.— the Enemy made a desperate, but disorderly Resistance— The firing continued at all the Gangways and between the Tops, but in two minutes time the Enemy were driven, Sword in hand from every Post. The American flag was hauled down and the proud old British Union floated triumphant over it— in another minute they ceased firing from below and called for quarter— the whole of this Service was atchieved in fifteen minutes from the commencement of the Action.

I have to lament the loss of many of my gallant Shipmates, but they fell exulting in their Conquest.

My brave first Lieutenant Mr. Watt was slain in the moment of Victory, in the act of hoisting the British Colours—his Death is a severe loss to the Service— Mr. Aldham the Purser, who had spiritedly Volunteered the charge of a Party of small armed men, was killed at his Post on the Gangway— My faithful Old Clerk Mr. Dunn was Shot by his Side.— Mr. Aldham has left a Widow to lament his loss— I request the Commander in Chief will recommend her to the protection of the Lords Commissioners of the Admiralty.—

My Veteran Boatswain, Mr. Stephens has lost an Arm—he fought under Lord Rodney on the 12th April. I trust his Age and Services will be duly rewarded— I am happy to say that Mr. Samwell a Midshipman of much merit, is the only other Officer Wounded besides myself, and he not dangerously. Of my gallant Seamen & marines We had twenty three Slain, and fifty six Wounded— I subjoin the Names of the former— No expressions I can make use of can do justice to the merits of my Valiant Officers and Crew.— the calm courage they displayed during the Cannonade, and the tremendous precision of their fire, could only be equalled by the ardour with which they rushed to the assault.— I recommend them all warmly to the protection of the Commander in Chief—

Having received a severe Sabre Wound at the first onset, whilst charging a party of the Enemy who had rallied on their forecastle, I was only capable of giving Command 'till assured our Conquest was Complete, and then, directing Second Lieutenant Wallis to take charge of the *Shannon*, and secure the Prisoners, I left the third Lieutenant Mr. Falkiner (who had headed the Main Deck boarders) in charge of the Prize— I beg to recommend these Officers most strongly to the Commander in Chiefs patronage, for the gallantry they displayed during the Action, and the Skill and judgment they evinced in the anxious duties which afterwards devolved upon them—

To Mr. Etough the acting Master—I am much indebted, for the steadiness in which he Conn'd the Ship into Action— The Lieutenants Johns and Law of the Marines bravely boarded at the head of their respective Divisions.

It is impossible to particularize every brilliant deed performed by my Officers and Men, but I must mention when the Ships Yard Arms were locked together, that Mr. Cosnahan who Commanded in our Main Top, finding himself screened from the Enemy by the foot of the Topsail, laid out at the Main Yard Arm to fire upon them, and Shot three men in that situation— Mr. Smith who Commanded in our foretop, & stormed the Enemys foretop from the fore Yard Arm, and destroyed all the Americans remaining in it— I particularly beg leave to recommend Messrs. Etough the acting Master, Smith & Leake midshipmen as having already passed their examination for Lieutenants and Messrs. Clavering, Raymond and Littlejohn as equally qualified, and being within a few weeks of their time—this latter Officer is a Son of Captain Littlejohn who was Slain in the *Berwick*.

The loss of the Enemy was about Seventy killed, and One hundred Wounded—amongst the former were the fourth Lieutenant, a Lieut. of marines, the Master and many other Officers— Captain Lawrence is since Dead of his Wounds.—

The Enemy came into Action with a Compliment of four

hundred and forty men— the *Shannon* having picked up some re Captured Seamen had three hundred and thirty.

The *Chesapeake* is a fine frigate, and mounts forty nine Guns—Eighteens on her main Deck—two and thirties on her quarter Deck & forecastle—both Ships came out of Action in the most beautiful order—their Rigging appearing as perfect as if they had only been Exchanging a Salute.— I have the honor to be Sir, Your most Obedient humble Servant

P. B V. Broke

John C. Calhoun to James Macbride

The Thirteenth Congress opened on March 4, 1813. Henry Clay was again elected Speaker of the House, and again he packed the key committees with pro-Madison war men. But the Republican Party was in a less dominant position than it had been before. As a result of the elections of 1812, the Federalists had increased their numbers, talent, and voice in both houses. The President, who was gravely ill, was unable to provide forceful leadership, and certain of his second-term appointments were rejected. His proposals for new trade restrictions, militia reform, and the enlistment of minors came to nothing, and his efforts to raise taxes were borne at great political cost by a fraying Republican front. "Party sperit," wrote John C. Calhoun to his friend the botanist James Macbride, "is more violent than I ever knew." So violent, in fact, that Calhoun nearly engaged in pistol duels with two Federalist congressmen: Thomas P. Grosvenor of New York, who stridently contested every Republican measure, and William Gaston of North Carolina, Calhoun's "fiery" opponent on the House Ways and Means Committee.

Washington 23d. June 1813

Dr Sir, I regret exceedingly I had not an opportunity of seeing you, when I was last in St. Johns. It is impossible for me in the shape or extent of an ordinary letter, to communicate half the observations and speculations which I have made since the commencement of my publick life.

Party sperit is more violent than I ever knew. In what it will terminate it is impossible to conjecture. For my part my resolve is taken. No menace, no threat of disunion shall shake me, from persuing that course of measures, which I know to be for the honor and best interest of this nation. I wish them to be persued with every possible vigour; and to put it home fairly to the people, whither they will or will not make the necessary sacrafices.

I know the difficulties which oppose the best wishes of the patriot. To me they are nothing. I speak personally. I by no means dispair of the destiny of our nation or government. National greatness and perfection are of slow groth, often checked often to appearance destroied. The intelligence, the virtue and the tone of publick sentiment are too great in this country to permit its freedom to be destroied by either domestick or foreign foes.

The application of your friend shall be attended to.

I am with esteem yours &c

J. C. CALHOUN

*Laura Ingersoll Secord:
Incident at Beaver Dams*

Born in Massachusetts in 1775 to loyalist parents, Laura Ingersoll moved with her family to Queenston, Upper Canada, in 1795. There she married James B. Secord, sergeant of the 1st Lincoln Militia, who at Queenston Heights helped carry Isaac Brock's body from the field. Later in the battle, James Secord was seriously wounded by a musket ball and Laura Secord found him and brought him home to convalesce. Six months later, on June 21, 1813, Laura learned—how she does not say—of American plans for an attack on the British post at Beaver Dams, some twelve miles southwest of Queenston, and resolved to take action. She wrote the following account of her adventure for a Toronto magazine in 1853.

I shall commence at the battle of Queenston, where I was at the time the cannon balls were flying around me in every direction. I left the place during the engagement. After the battle I returned to Queenston and there found that my husband had been wounded, my house plundered and property destroyed. It was while the Americans had possession of the frontier that I learned the plans of the American commander and determined to put the British troops under FitzGibbon in possession of them, and if possible to save the British troops from capture or perhaps total destruction. In doing so I found I should have great difficulty in getting through the American guards, which were out ten miles in the country. Determined to persevere, I left early in the morning, walked nineteen miles in the month of June over a rough and difficult part of the country, when I came to a field belonging to a Mr. Decamp in the neighborhood of the Beaver Dam. By this time daylight had left me. Here I found all the Indians encamped; by moonlight the scene was terrifying and to those accustomed to such scenes might be considered grand. Upon advancing to the Indians they all rose and with some yells said, "Woman," which made me tremble. I cannot express the awful feeling it gave me, but I did not lose my presence of mind. I was determined to persevere. I went up to one of the chiefs, made him understand that I had great news for Capt. FitzGibbon and that he must let me pass to his camp or that he and his party would all be taken. The chief at first objected to let me pass, but finally consented, after some hesitation, to go with me and accompany me to FitzGibbon's station, which was at the Beaver Dam, where I had an interview with him. I then told him what I had come for and what I had heard—that the Americans intended to make an attack upon the troops under his command and would, from their superior numbers, capture them all. Benefitting by this information, Capt. FitzGibbon formed his plans accordingly and captured about five hundred American infantry, about fifty mounted dragoons, and a field piece or two was taken from the enemy. I returned home next day exhausted and fatigued. I am now advanced in years and when I look back I wonder how I could have gone through so much fatigue with the fortitude to accomplish it.

John Le Couteur: Journal

The post at Beaver Dams, commanded by Lieutenant James FitzGibbon, was one of several from which British soldiers harassed the Americans occupying Fort George. Major General Dearborn resolved to destroy the post, and ordered Colonel Charles G. Boerstler to do the job. On the evening of June 23, 1813, Boerstler and some 600 troops began the twenty-mile march from Fort George in preparation for an early-morning surprise attack. But Laura Secord had already arrived at Beaver Dams, as had intelligence from Indian scouts, so FitzGibbon and his fifty men were ready for them, as were a nearby camp of Caughnawagas and Mohawks. Before Boerstler could reach the post, four hundred Indians were upon him; some three hours later FitzGibbon arrived on the scene and easily convinced Boerstler to surrender. The resourceful John Le Couteur, marching under Major P. W. De Haren of the 104th, was present for the capitulation. FitzGibbon always thought of Beaver Dams as an Indian victory, but as the Mohawk chief John Norton wryly observed: "The *Cognawaga Indians* fought the *battle*, the *Mohawks* . . . got the *plunder*, and *Fitzgibbon* got the Credit."

———————

24 June

About half an hour before day break, an Indian brought me a message from their Chief intimating that a strong force of the Enemy with Guns and Cavalry were moving upon us by De Cew's. I instantly ordered the turn out, as silently as possible, and ran to Major De Haren who desired the men to be formed instantly. The Indians had all gone off after their own Mode of warfare acting quite independently—we moved after them in a run towards the Beech woods.

Presently we heard one rapid, yet steady, roll of musquetry then a terrific Yell which sounded high above a roll of Artillery & small arms. The Major ordered me to gallop on and see how the affair stood, then return to bring the Light Division up to the best position. In a quarter of an hour, I got to the scene of action—some round shot came plunging along the road but the Indian yells were awful and ringing all around an extensive clearing—they concealed and lying down along the edges of the wood, the American force in the clearing in Line with their Guns on their Right and their Cavalry in reserve. The 49th I perceived to be to the Right of the Americans turning it. To these I rode when, immediately, a flag of truce was sent in with an offer to surrender to a British force.

Fitzgibbon wished them to surrender to Him but the American officer said He would not to so small a force. I observed that "the Light Division, Seven hundred men under Major De Haren, was here." "The moment they are here and can protect us from the Indians, we will surrender." They came up in less than twenty minutes and Major De Haren ratified the treaty which Fitzgibbon had entered on. The Yankee Horsemen made a dash through the Indian fire and got off but we took Two Guns, a number of Volunteer officers, and 550 men.

The Indians were very savage—one tomahawked an American close to me during the parley—they would have destroyed them all but for us. All the dead were scalped. Their heads divested of the scalp looked white and clean, some as if they had been washed. I got a capital black horse for a charger on this occasion, saddle & Bridle & Pistols and all.

Major De Haren gave me charge of the Comd officer, Colonel Boerstler, and the Field officers. Our Division was drawn up in line and presented arms to Him as He rode by. He admired the men greatly: "what fine, smart, well-disciplined Young Men." Then, as he passed the Indians and saw numbers of his poor men Scalped, He first asked: "Oh! What are those? What is that?" I made no answer but turned away my head for I felt for Him. He was badly wounded and seemed horror struck, the tears rolled down his handsome countenance. He was exceedingly sensible of the poor Courtesy which I had occasion to show Him and, when I left Him in the quarters allotted to Him, He was most friendly—a fine Gentlemanly Young man.

The Indians were ticklish friends to deal with. I had for a few days been acting Commissary and Quartermaster as well as Adjutant to the Light Division, having to ride about the Country with an escort, buy Oxen, flour & Rum where I could get them, then do the distribution myself. One day, I refused to give a half-drunken Indian a Hide which He coveted over and above the Meat which had been issued to his tribe when he snatched his Tomahawk and made a motion as if to cut me down. In an instant, however, self-preservation had instinctively made me place my drawn Sword to his throat and He pretended it was a mere faint and, after a growl, "Sago Nitchie." Of course I shook hands with Him but my men would have bayoneted Him, if I had not prevented it. I complained to his Chief and He met with some Indian rebuff.

There was a poor unfortunate American Soldier, a Prisoner in the Indian camp. An old Mohawk Chief had lost his only Son in one of the late engagements and He kept this Young Man as a Victim—it was said to be immolated when He got Him into the back woods. The poor fellow implored us to ransom or rescue Him from his sad fate and shed many tears at the idea of being taken away from civilized man. We settled on a Subscription and offered the Old Chief a Considerable Sum to give Him up to us. No Sum would tempt Him—if the young Man behaved well, He would adopt Him as his Son! A delightful Compliment! Rescue Him we dared not, it would have lost us an alliance of seven hundred Indians, most invaluable allies they were—no surprises with Nitchie on the lookout.

After a few days Our Yankee friend was stripped of his Uniform and toggery of all sorts and clothed in an Indian dress. His hair was shaven, a tuft left on it which was ornamented with Feathers and Horse hair and, though it was very lamentable to Him and excited our Sympathy, He looked irresistibly ludicrous. However we got the Old Chief, by Good humour and presents, to adopt Him as his Son which insured his life. He was, notwithstanding, incessantly watched both by night and day. We advised not to attempt to escape till he had a year or two with them as any trick of the sort would cost his life.

James Monroe to Thomas Jefferson

The pale and delicate James Madison—"Little Jemmy" to his detractors —was never an imposing figure. He was five foot four, weighed only a hundred pounds, and was prey to worry and depression. (When Washington Irving met Madison in January 1811, he remarked in a letter to a friend: "Ah! poor Jemmy!—he is but a withered little apple-john.") His near-fatal illness of the summer of 1813, possibly mosquito-borne malaria from the Washington swamps, occurred at the height of the year's military campaigning and congressional activity, and further compromised his image as a capable chief executive. Thomas P. Grosvenor prayed for a speedy end to the President, that he might "soon appear at the bar of Immortal Justice" and be judged for his "bloody crime." Major John Lovett wished good riddance to both him and his vice president, the "scant-patterned skeleton" Elbridge Gerry, then sixty-nine and struggling back from a stroke. On June 28th, Secretary of State James Monroe informed Thomas Jefferson of the President's illness and lamented that the administration's adversaries in the Senate were capitalizing on it by blocking two of Madison's diplomatic appointments, John Russell to Sweden and Albert Gallatin to the Russian peace mission.

WASHINGTON June 28th 1813

DEAR SIR,—From the date of my last letter to you the President has been ill of a bilious fever; of that kind called the remittent. It has perhaps never left him, even for an hour, and occasionally simptoms have been unfavorable. This is I think the 15th day. Elzey of this place, & Shoaff of Annapolis, with Dr. Tucker, attend him. They think he will recover. The first mention'd I have just seen, who reports that he had a good night, & is in a state to take the bark, which indeed he has done on his best day, for nearly a week. I shall see him before I seal this, & note any change, should there be any, from the above statement.

The federalists aided by the malcontents have done, and are

doing, all the mischief that they can. The nominations to Russia, & Sweden, (the latter made on an intimation that the Crown prince would contribute his good offices to promote peace on fair conditions) they have embarrassed, to the utmost of their power. The active partizans are King, Giles and (as respects the first nomination) S. Smith. Leib, German and Gilman, are habitually in that interest, active, but useful to their party by their votes only. The two members from Louisiana, Gailliard, Stone, Anderson, & Bledsoe, are added to that corps, on those questions. They have carried a vote 20. to 14. that the appointment of Mr. Gallatin to the Russian mission, is incompatable, with his place in the treasury, & appointed a committee, to communicate the resolution to the President. They have appointed another committee to confer with him on the nomination to Sweden. The object is to usurp the Executive power in the hands of a faction in the Senate. To this, several mention'd are not parties, particularly the four last. A committee of the Senate ought to confer with a committee of the President, that is a head of a dept. and not with the ch: Majistrate, for in the latter case a committee of that house is equal to the Executive. To break the measure, & relieve the President from the pressure, at a time when so little able to bear it, indeed when no pressure whatever should be made on him, I wrote the committee on the nomination to Sweden, that I was instructed by him to meet them, to give all the information they might desire of the Executive. They declin'd the interview. I had intended to pursue the same course respecting the other nomination, had I succeeded in this. Failing, I have declined it. The result is withheld from the President. These men have begun, to make calculations, & plans, founded on the presum'd death of the President & Vice-President, & it has been suggested to me that Giles, is thought of to take the place of the President of the Senate, as soon as the Vice President withdraws.

Genl. Dearborn is dangerously ill, & Genl. Lewis doing little. Hampton has gone on to that quarter, but I fear on an inactive command. Genl. Wilkinson is expected soon, but I do not know what station will be assign'd him. The idea of a comr. in Ch: is in circulation, proceeding from the War dept., as I have reason to believe. If so, it will probably take a more decisive form, when things are prepar'd for it. A security for his (the Secys.) advancement to that station, is I presume the preparation desir'd.

Your friend, etc.

"P." (*Richard E. Parker*) *to the* Richmond Enquirer

July 16, 1813

By the end of April 1813, British harassment of Chesapeake Bay was in full swing. Rear Admiral Cockburn led fiery raids on several Maryland towns: Frenchtown, Havre de Grace, Georgetown, Fredericktown, Elkton, Queenstown, and St. Michaels. On June 1st, Colonel Beckwith joined the fray, but his forces were repulsed at Craney Island, Virginia, which protected the approaches to Norfolk. Then, on June 25, a large raiding party—some twenty-four hundred men, mostly British but also many companies of French "Independent Foreigners" recruited from British prison hulks and brought with Beckwith from Bermuda—laid waste to Hampton, Virginia. "Every horror was committed with impunity," wrote one British observer, Lieutenant Colonel Charles Napier: "rape, murder, pillage—and not a man was punished!" The unruly companies of Foreigners were then shipped by Admiral Warren to Halifax, where they continued to make trouble until sent to Europe and disbanded. Richard E. Parker, lieutenant colonel of the 111th Virginia militia regiment, was present at Hampton, and is widely accepted as author of this letter to the editor of the *Richmond Enquirer.*

To the Editor of the Enquirer.

SIR:

Having just returned from Hampton, where I made myself acquainted with all the particulars of British outrage, whilst that place was in their possession, I am requested, by many persons, to communicate, through you, to the public, the information I have given them. I do this with no hope or expectation of satisfying those who required other testimony than Major Crutchfield's or Captain Cooper's. I too well know there are those among us, who will still doubt, or pretend to doubt. But as I believe this class to be few in number, and insignificant in the public estimation; as I firmly believe that a large majority of all political persuasions are open to conviction, and feelingly alive to their country's wrongs; I cannot withhold from them the facts, whose simple recital will, according to their different temperaments, inflame them with rage, or fill them with horror.

My name you are at liberty to give to the public, or only to those who may inquire for it, as you think proper. I have reason to believe that those who know me, whether federal or republican, will know and acknowledge that I am incapable of publishing a falsehood; and I aver, that every statement inconsistent with the following, no matter on whose authority it is made, is untrue; in proof of which I solemnly undertake, before the world, to establish every fact contained in it, provided any *gentleman* will sign his name to a denial of either of them.

I went to Hampton with a determination of inquiring minutely into the truth of reports, which I *hoped*, for the honor of a soldier's profession, and of human nature, to have found exaggerated. In the investigation, I resolved to depend on the second hand relation of no one, where I could mount to the original source of evidence; but since, in some cases, this was impracticable, I feel it a duty carefully to distinguish the one class from the other.

That the town and country adjacent was given up to the indiscriminate plunder of a licentious soldiery, except, perhaps, the house where the head quarters were fixed, is an undeniable truth. Every article of valuable property was taken from it. In many houses not even a knife, a fork, or plate was left. *British officers* were seen by Dr. Colton in the act of plundering a Mr. Jones's store. His house, although he remained in town, was rifled, and his medicine thrown into the public street, just opposite where many officers took up their quarters, who must have been eye-witnesses of the scene. The church was pilaged, and the plate belonging to it taken away, although inscribed with the donor's name. The wind-mills in the neighorhood were stript of their sails. The closets, private drawers, and trunks of the inhabitants, were broken open, and scarcely any thing seemed to be too trifling an object to excite the cupidity of these robbers. Several gentlemen informed me that much of their plunder was brought into the back yard of Mrs. Westwood's house, where Sir Sidney Beckwith and Admiral Cockburn resided. But I had no opportunity of seeing this lady, who, *it was said*, *would* testify to the fact. In short, Hampton exhibits a dreary and desolate appearance, which no *American* can witness unmoved. Doctor Wardlaw and Mr. John G. Smith, of this city, visited it in company with me; and their indignation was equal. They, and every one who saw and heard what I have stated, united in execrating the monsters who perpetrated these enormities; and political distinctions, if any existed, were lost in the nobler feelings of pity for the sufferers, and a generous ardor to avenge their wrongs.

Here it may be necessary to notice a publication I have this moment read in the Alexandria Gazette of the 19th, where, among other things, it is said, on the authority of a "gentleman who was in Hampton the day after the evacuation by the enemy," that it was believed there "that nearly all the plundering was committed by the negroes;" and that he saw many "articles brought to the magistrates which had been secreted in negro houses." That *some* plundering may have been committed by the negroes, who, (as I was told) were embodied and paraded through the streets, is probable enough; that the expression of *such an* opinion may have been heard in Hampton is likewise probable; but I do utterly deny, that it is believed there, by any person worthy of credit, that "nearly all the plundering was committed by them." Let the gentleman, then, who gives this account, state from whom he derived his information. Let him give the names of the magistrates who received the plunder thus found and his *own*; and let him declare what were the main articles he saw brought in. I will not directly hazard the assertion, but I am very much inclined to believe, there were no magistrates in the town at the time spoken of, unless Parson Holsen, Dr. Colton, or Captain Wills, are magistrates; and with all these gentlemen I conversed, and heard not a whisper countenancing the statement in the Alexandria paper. How it is known that the negroes "had the address," first to impose on the British commanders, and then on the American troops, which "induced them to retreat to York," and leave Hampton to be plundered by these artful rogues, that *gentleman* is left to say; but that the American troops did not retire to York, in consequence of such information, is undoubtedly true. Nor is it less true that Captain Cooper's troop arrived in time to prevent any plundering of the least consequence, after the evacuation; and in time to prevent, what many gentlemen there believed to have been a plan concerted between the black and white allies—the firing of the town.

That "Admiral Warren expressed his regret that the inhabitants of Hampton had not all remained, as in that case no plundering would have happened," is possible enough; since it admits the fact of the plundering, and is conformable with the answer given to Captain Wills, who complained to Cockburn and Beckwith of the destruction of his private property. "Why did you quit your house?" said these *honorable* men. "I remained in my house," *answered* Doctor Colton, "and have found *no better* treatment."

That Kirby, who, for seven weeks or more, had been confined to his bed, and whose death the savages only a little hastened, was shot in the arms of his wife, is not denied. Those who wish for further confirmation may go and take him from his grave, and weep, if they can feel for an American citizen, over his mangled body. They may go to his wounded wife, and hear her heart-rending tale, and then they may turn to the account of the *gentleman*, and derive consolation from the excuse (*which I never heard*) "that it was done in revenge for the refusal of the militia to give quarter to some Frenchmen, who were on board a barge that was sunk by our troops, who continued to fire on the almost drowning men, when making for the shore." This vile slander on our troops will, I have no doubt, be met, in the proper manner, by the gallant officer who commands them at Norfolk. But the worst is to come.

I conversed with a lady whose name is mentioned in Captain Cooper's letter, in company with Parson Holson, Doctor Colton, and Captain Wills. Her story was too shocking in its details to meet the public eye. When I had convinced her of the object I had in view in visiting her—that it was dictated by no impertinent curiosity, but a desire to know the whole truth, to enable me, on the one hand, to do justice even to an enemy, or, on the other, to electrify my countrymen with the recital of her sufferings, she discovered every thing which her convulsive struggles between shame and a desire to expose her brutal assailants would permit. This woman was seized by five or six

ruffians, some of them *dressed in red* and *speaking correctly the
English language, and stripped naked*. Her cries and her prayers
were disregarded, and her body became the subject of the
most abominable indecencies. She at one time made her escape, and ran into a creek hard by, followed by a young daughter; whence she was dragged by the monsters in human shape,
to experience new and aggravated suffering. In this situation
she was kept the whole night, whilst her screams were heard at
intervals by some of the Americans in town, who could only
clasp their hands in hopeless agony.

Virginian! American! Friend or enemy of the administration,
or of the war! go, as I have done, to this woman's house, and
hear and see her. See too her young daughter on the bed of
sickness, in consequence of the abuses of that night! and your
heart, if it be made of "penetrable stuff," will throb with indignation, and a thirst for revenge, and your hand instinctively
grasp the weapon for inflicting it.

A Mrs. Briggs related to us, that a woman who had come to
Hampton, to visit her husband, who was in the militia, was
taken forcibly from her side by four soldiers in green, and with
her young child, which one of them snatched from her arms,
borne to the hospital, in spite of her screams. They had previously robbed them of their rings, and attempted to tear open
their bosoms. A Mrs. Hopkins, who was not in town when I
was there, obtained the assistance of an officer, and rescued the
woman from her ravishers, but not until one of them had
gratified his abominable desires. I was told by the gentleman
who accompanied me, that Mrs. Hopkins confirmed this statement, and would swear to at least two other cases of a similar
kind, without, however, giving up the names of the *young and
respectable* women who suffered.

Doctor Colton and Captain Wills, assisted by an officer, rescued another lady from the greatest of calamities.

Old Mr. Hope, aged, as he told Major Crutchfield, (in my
presence) sixty-four or five years, was seized by these wretches
and stripped of all his clothing, even of his shoes and his shirt.
A bayonet was run a little way into his arm behind, as if in cruel
sport; while several were held to his breast. In this situation he
was kept for a considerable time, and would probably have
been another victim of their rage, if their attention had not

been diverted to a woman, who had sought refuge in his house. They followed her into the kitchen, whither she had run for safety. Mr. Hope made off amidst her agonizing screams, and when he returned to his house, he was told by his domestics that their horrid purposes were accomplished. This I had from him.

How far this violation extended will never be known. Women will not publish what they consider their own shame, and the men in town were carefully watched and guarded. But enough is known to induce the belief of the existence of many other cases, and enough to fire every manly bosom with the irrepressible desire of revenge.

I am not disposed to tire the public patience, or I could tell of enormities little inferior to the above. But the enemy are convicted of robbery, rape, and murder, and it is unnecessary to add to the catalogue of their crimes.

Men of Virginia! will you permit all this? Fathers, and brother, and husbands, will you fold your arms in apathy, and only curse your despoilers? No, you will fly with generous emulation to the unfurled standard of your country. You will imitate the example of those generous spirits who are, even now, in crowds, tendering their services to the commander-in-chief; who are pouring from their native mountains, and soliciting to be led against the enemy wherever he dares to show his face. You will prove yourselves worthy of the immortal honor that the enemy has conferred upon you in selecting you as the object of his vengeance. You will neglect, for a time, all civil pursuits and occupations, and devote yourselves to the art, a knowledge of which the enemy has made necessary. You will learn *to command*, *to obey*, and, with "Hampton" as your watch word—*to conquer*.

P.

Blackbird: Message from the Ottawa Nation to William Claus

July 15, 1813

On July 5, 1813, Chief Blackbird and 150 other Ottawa warriors from Michigan joined the British army during the siege of Fort George. Three days later a party of Ottawas ambushed an American patrol near the fort, and Lieutenant Joseph C. Eldridge of the 13th U.S. Infantry was killed. American witnesses claimed that Eldridge was taken prisoner by the Ottawas and was tortured, murdered, scalped, and then butchered. George McClure, the U.S. commander at Fort George, asked Colonel William Claus, a deputy superintendent of the Indian Department for Upper Canada, to investigate the incident. Claus, who was fluent in the Ottawa language, visited Blackbird to express concern about the tribe's treatment of prisoners and to announce that henceforth the British would pay the chief five U.S. dollars for each American prisoner his warriors took alive. Blackbird, whose people had suffered at the hands of the United States earlier that year, told Claus exactly what he thought of the Americans ("Big Knives") and the British bounty. "Our father" in Blackbird's response refers to the British king and his agents in Canada.

Brother,—We have listened to your words, which words come from our father. We will now say a few words to you. At the foot of the Rapids last spring we fought the Big Knives, and we lost some of our people there. When we retired the Big Knives got some of our dead. They were not satisfied with having killed them, but cut them into small pieces. This made us very angry. My words to my people were: "As long as the powder burnt, to kill and scalp," but those behind us came up and did mischief.

Brother,—Last year at Chicago and St. Joseph's the Big Knives destroyed all our corn. This was fair, but, brother, they did not allow the dead to rest. They dug up their graves, and the bones of our ancestors were thrown away and we never could find them to return them to the ground.

Brother,—I have listened with a good deal of attention to the wish of our father. If the Big Knives, after they kill people of our colour, leave them without hacking them to pieces, we will follow their example. They have themselves to blame. The way they treat our killed, and the remains of those that are in their graves in the west, makes our people mad when they meet the Big Knives. Whenever they get any of our people into their hands they cut them like meat into small pieces. We thought white people were Christians. They ought to show us a better example. We do not disturb their dead. What I say is known to all the people present. I do not tell a lie.

Brother,—It is the Indian custom when engaged to be very angry, but when we take prisoners to treat them kindly.

Brother,—we do not know the value of money; all I wish is that our people receive clothing for our prisoners. When at home we work and hunt to earn those things; here we cannot. Therefore, we ask for clothing.

Brother,—The officer that we killed you have spoken to us before about. I now tell you again, he fired and wounded one of our colour; another fired at him and killed him. We wished to take him prisoner, but the officer said "God damn," and fired, when he was shot. This is all I have to say.

William B. Northcutt: Diary

Fort Stephenson, thirty miles southeast of Fort Meigs, was a supply depot on the Sandusky River. Convinced that it was indefensible, William Henry Harrison ordered it abandoned and destroyed, but its commander, twenty-one-year-old Major George Croghan (pronounced "Crawn"), respectfully refused: "We have determined to maintain this place," he replied, "and by heavens we can." Incensed by his insubordination, Harrison sent a squadron to bring Croghan to him at his camp, nine miles south of Fort Stephenson. Among the squadron's number was Kentucky private William B. Northcutt, whose diary reveals that the mission was not without its complications.

About the last of July 1813 Harrison sent an Express after us to come to him at his head quarters on the Sandusky river about nine miles above fort Stepenson on lower Sandusky. We got there by a forced march about the last day of July and here he had one soldier shot for Deserting and Another tried and Condemned to be Shot for Charging baynet on his Leutenant on thier march into Camp. The Soldier was sick and could not Keep up with his Company, when the officer Drew his Sword and put at him with it to make him keep up, when the Soldier Charged baynet on him and made him Back out. But they court marshalled him and condemned him to be shot, and had him marched out into an old field for that purpose. But after all the menuvering had been gone through with Except the word fire, Harrison Reprieved him to the Joy of the Whole army and poor Culprit in particular, for it did appear to me that he was as good as dead until the genls. Aid rode up and read his Reprieve and then he appeared to revive and live again, and the troops that were formed in A hollow square Wheeled Out into line and marched back to camp in quite a different maner to that in which they marched out, for they went out with Reversed arms and the Dead march with muffled musick.

When our squadron arived at Harrisons head quarters there
was not any forage there for our horses, and he ordered them
to take thier forage bags and go down to lower Sandusky and
get them full of oats for our horses and to Bring back with us
to his Camp George Chron the commander at lower Sandusky
to answer to him for disobedience of orders, for he had ordered him Col. Chron to Evacuate that post and he and his
Command to come to him and Chron had not done it according to orders. We started to the fort with our forage Sacks after
the oats, and when within two miles of the fort as we were
marching along very Soberly, our advance guard being about
One Hundred yards in advance of the Squadron, and composed of six men, there was lying conceiled in the high grass
by the road side, thirteen Indians who rose up out of thier
ambush and fired simmultaniously on the six men, that formed
the guard and Killed three of thier horses, and wounded two
men. As it happened the wounded mens horses were not hurt
and they all wheeled and run back to the Squadron, with the
Indians close after them and the first thing that the Indians
new of the Squadron they were right under our Broad Swords
and we made thier heads Rattle like old gourds. They caught
thier guns in both hands and held them over thier heads and
gabbered Something—Something I suppose about quarters,
but we were Kentuckians and did not under Stand one word
about the Indian language, and we gobled them right up on
the spot.

I happened to be in front of the Squadron when the thing
ocured, and saw the whole of the Sport. The Indians appeared
panic Stricken for there was but one of them that attempted to
run. I had cut one fellow down with my Sword and took after
the one that broke to run. There was one of the boys by the
name of Wilson that started with me after the Indian that
broke to run. I was before Wilson and had raised in my Stirups
several times to cut him down, but Every time he was a little
too far off. At length we came to an old log that had fallen and
the Indian Loped it. My horse made a stop to gather himself
up for the lope, and Wilsons horse cleared it at the Charge,
and he got in before me and the moment that he did so he
drew his pistol and shot the Indian and he fell dead. I was so
anxious to cut him with my Sword that I had never thought of

my pistols until I saw Wilson draw his and then it was too late. When the Indian fell Wilson turned around to me and says Bill, shall I Scalp him? Says I no John don't do that for if you want his Scalp for a witness that you have Killed him I am a living one.

After the fracas was over we went on to the fort and left the Indians a lying there. We drew our forage and took Chron the commander of the fort and Brought him up to Harrison, and as we came Back our Commander ordered a line to be formed and we made a rake over the ground that we had had the Skirmish on, in order to see how many of the Indians we had killed, and we found thirteen of them laying stretched out on thier cooling boards. But we had not time to bury them, but the next day some of our pet Indians that Harrison had with him went down and Buried them and came back and Reported that one of the Hostile Indians had Got Away Wounded. In Makeing the Rake over the Battle ground I found one of thier hopperses. It was a new Mackanaw Blanket, Roled up with part of a dryed deer Skin in it and with about one pound of the best double of glazed powder in it and two pair of mocasons cut out but not made, a Bladder of paint and another of Indian medicine. When we got back to the Camp I oppened the Blanket, and there was one of the pet Indians Standing by, and I asked him what the medicine was. Says he good for sick Indian. I asked him if he wanted it when he said that he did so I gave the medicine to him but kept the Ballanc of the prise and Brought it home with me.

George Croghan to William Henry Harrison

Having retreated to Canada after lifting the siege of Fort Meigs, Henry Procter returned to the Maumee River in July 1813 with five hundred British and three thousand Indians. After toying with plans for a second attack on the fort, he detached four hundred troops to take Fort Stephenson. On August 1, the day after Harrison's conference with Croghan, the British attacked, but Croghan, back at the fort, was ready for them. William B. Northcutt, from the safety of Harrison's camp, heard every cannon fired that day. He wrote in his diary that he "did think it an extreme hard case, that Chron should be cooped up with a hand full of men to be massacred by the British while Harrison was lying in hearing of him with fifteen hundred men." As it turned out, Croghan was underestimated by everyone—Harrison, Northcutt, and especially Henry Procter.

LOWER SANDUSKY, August 5, 1813

DEAR SIR,

I have the honour to inform you that the combined forces of the enemy, amounting to at least 500 regulars and 700 or 800 Indians, under the immediate command of general Proctor, made its appearance before this place early on Sunday evening last, and so soon as the general had made such disposition of his troops as would cut off my retreat, should I be disposed to make one, he sent colonel Elliott, accompanied by major Chambers, with a flag, to demand the surrender of the fort, as he was anxious to spare the effusion of blood, which he should probably not have in his power to do, should he be reduced to the necessity of taking the place by storm. My answer to the summons was, that I was determined to defend the place to the last extremity, and that no force, however large, should induce me to surrender it. So soon the flag had returned, a brisk fire was opened upon us from the gun-boats in the river, and from a 5½ inch howitzer on shore, which was kept up with little intermission throughout the night. At an early hour next morning, three sixes (which had been placed during the night within 250 yards of the pickets) began to play upon us with little effect. About four o'clock, P.M., discovering that the fire from all his guns was concentrated against the northwestern angle of the fort, I became confident that his object was to make a breach, and attempt to storm the works at that point, I therefore ordered out as many men as could be employed for the purpose of strengthening that part, which was so effectually secured by means of bags of flour, sand, etc. that the picketing suffered little or no injury; notwithstanding which the enemy, about 500, having formed in close column, advanced to assault our works at the expected point, at the same time making two feints on the front of captain Hunter's lines. The column which advanced against the northwestern angle, consisting of about 350 men, was so completely enveloped in smoke, as not to be discovered until it had approached within 18 or 20 paces of the lines, but the men being all at their posts and ready to receive it, commenced so heavy and galling a fire as to throw the column a little into confusion; being quickly rallied, it advanced to the outer works, and began to leap into the ditch. Just at that moment a fire of grape was opened from our six-pounder (which had been previously arranged so as to rake in that direction) which, together with the musketry, threw them into such confusion that they were compelled to retire precipitately to the woods.

During the assault, which lasted about half an hour, an incessant fire was kept up by the enemy's artillery (which consisted of five sixes and a howitzer) but without effect. My whole loss during the siege, was one killed and seven wounded, slightly. The loss of the enemy in killed, wounded and prisoners, must exceed 150: one lieutenant-colonel, a lieutenant, and 50 rank and file were found in and about the ditch, dead or wounded. Those of the remainder who were not able to escape were taken off during the night by Indians. Seventy stand of arms, and several brace of pistols have been collected near the works. About three in the morning the enemy sailed down the river, leaving behind them a boat, containing clothing and considerable military stores.

Too much praise cannot be bestowed on the officers, non-commissioned officers, and privates under my command, for their gallantry and good conduct during the siege.

G. CROGHAN, *Major 17 United States Infantry*
Major General HARRISON, *commanding N.W. Army*

Black Hawk: from Life of Ma-ka-tai-me-she-kia-kiak or Black Hawk . . . Dictated by Himself

Some two hundred Sauk Indians fought for Henry Procter during the 1813 campaign. Their leader was Black Hawk, a warrior highly prized by the British as an effective recruiter and military strategist. Though present at Fort Stephenson, Black Hawk would not lead his men into battle, for he correctly saw that they and the British could not gain advantage in the situation. In his memoirs, dictated to a U.S. Army interpreter in 1833, Black Hawk recalled that on the evening after the American victory, he resigned his command in disgust and with twenty of his braves set out for home—the village of Saukenuk, on the Rock River, in present-day Rock Island, Illinois. There, as he later recalled in his autobiography, he treated his people to a scathing analysis of the Anglo-American approach to war.

On my arrival at the village, I was met by the chiefs and braves, and conducted to a lodge that had been prepared to receive me. After eating, I gave an account of what I had seen and done. I explained to them the manner the British and Americans fought. Instead of stealing upon each other, and taking every advantage to *kill the enemy* and *save their own people*, as we do, (which, with us, is considered good policy in a war chief,) they march out, in open daylight, and *fight*, regardless of the number of warriors they may lose! After the battle is over, they retire to feast, and drink wine, as if nothing had happened; after which, they make a *statement in writing*, of what they have done—*each party claiming the victory!* and neither giving an account of half the number that have been killed on their own side. They all fought like braves, but would not do to *lead a war party* with us. Our maxim is, "*to kill the enemy*, and *save our own men*." Those chiefs would do to *paddle* a canoe, but not to *steer* it. The Americans shoot better than the British, but their *soldiers* are not so well clothed, or provided for.

James Fenimore Cooper: from
Ned Myers; or, A Life Before the Mast

Born in Canada in 1793, Edward "Ned" Myers left home at age twelve
to work as a cabin boy on the U.S. merchant ship *Stirling*. By the
time of his death at age fifty-six, he had served on the crew of scores
of vessels and had spent "a full twenty-five years out of sight of land."
In the winter of 1806, on one of *Stirling*'s passages from New York to
Liverpool, Myers met a young James Fenimore Cooper, who in 1842
penned his memoirs. In two early chapters, Myers describes his adventures aboard USS *Scourge* on Lake Ontario in the summer of
1813. He recalls that the schooner, launched in 1811, was "unfit for
[military] duty, but time pressed, and no better offered. . . . Her
accommodations were bad enough, and she was so tender, that we
could do little or nothing with her in a blow." The "blow" described
here came in the early hours of August 8, 1813, near present-day Hamilton, Ontario, after a long day's patrol of the lake.

I was soon asleep, as sound as if lying in the bed of a king.
How long my nap lasted, or what took place in the interval, I
cannot say. I awoke, however, in consequence of large drops of
rain falling on my face. Tom Goldsmith awoke at the same
moment. When I opened my eyes, it was so dark I could not
see the length of the deck. I arose and spoke to Tom, telling
him it was about to rain, and that I meant to go down and get
a nip, out of a little stuff we kept in our mess-chest, and that I
would bring up the bottle if he wanted a taste. Tom answered,
"this is nothing; we're neither pepper nor salt." One of the
black men spoke, and asked me to bring up the bottle, and
give him a nip, too. All this took half a minute, perhaps. I now
remember to have heard a strange rushing noise to windward
as I went towards the forward hatch, though it made no impression on me at the time. We had been lying between the
starboard guns, which was the weather side of the vessel, if

there were any weather side to it, there not being a breath of air, and no motion to the water, and I passed round to the larboard side, in order to find the ladder, which led up in that direction. The hatch was so small that two men could not pass at a time, and I felt my way to it, in no haste. One hand was on the bitts, and a foot was on the ladder, when a flash of lightning almost blinded me. The thunder came at the next instant, and with it a rushing of winds that fairly smothered the clap.

The instant I was aware there was a squall, I sprang for the jib-sheet. Being captain of the forecastle, I knew where to find it, and throw it loose at a jerk. In doing this, I jumped on a man named Leonard Lewis, and called on him to lend me a hand. I next let fly the larboard, or lee topsail-sheet, got hold of the clew-line, and, assisted by Lewis, got the clew half up. All this time I kept shouting to the man at the wheel to put his helm "hard down." The water was now up to my breast, and I knew the schooner must go over. Lewis had not said a word, but I called out to him to shift for himself, and belaying the clew-line, in hauling myself forward of the foremast, I received a blow from the jib-sheet that came near breaking my left arm. I did not feel the effect of this blow at the time, though the arm has since been operated on, to extract a tumour produced by this very injury.

All this occupied less than a minute. The flashes of lightning were incessant, and nearly blinded me. Our decks seemed on fire, and yet I could see nothing. I heard no hail, no order, no call; but the schooner was filled with the shrieks and cries of the men to leeward, who were lying jammed under the guns, shot-boxes, shot, and other heavy things that had gone down as the vessel fell over. The starboard second gun, from forward, had capsized, and come down directly over the forward hatch, and I caught a glimpse of a man struggling to get past it. Apprehension of this gun had induced me to drag myself forward of the mast, where I received the blow mentioned.

I succeeded in hauling myself up to windward, and in getting into the schooner's fore-channels. Here I met William Deer, the boatswain, and a black boy of the name of Philips, who was the powder-boy of our gun. "Deer, she's gone!" I said. The boatswain made no answer, but walked out on the fore-rigging, towards the mast-head. He probably had some vague notion that the schooner's masts would be out of water if she went down, and took this course as the safest. The boy was in the chains the last I saw of him.

I now crawled aft, on the upper side of the bulwarks, amid a most awful and infernal din of thunder, and shrieks, and dazzling flashes of lightning; the wind blowing all the while like a tornado. When I reached the port of my own gun, I put a foot in, thinking to step on the muzzle of the piece; but it had gone to leeward with all the rest, and I fell through the port, until I brought up with my arms. I struggled up again, and continued working my way aft. As I got abreast of the main-mast, I saw some one had let run the halyards. I soon reached the beckets of the sweeps, and found four in them. I could not swim a stroke, and it crossed my mind to get one of the sweeps to keep me afloat. In striving to jerk the becket clear, it parted, and the forward ends of the four sweeps rolled down the schooner's side into the water. This caused the other ends to slide, and all the sweeps got away from me. I then crawled quite aft, as far as the fashion-piece. The water was pouring down the cabin companion-way like a sluice; and as I stood, for an instant, on the fashion-piece, I saw Mr. Osgood, with his head and part of his shoulders through one of the cabin windows, struggling to get out. He must have been within six feet of me. I saw him but a moment, by means of a flash of lightning, and I think he must have seen me. At the same time, there was a man visible on the end of the main-boom, holding on by the clew of the sail. I do not know who it was. This man probably saw me, and that I was about to spring; for he called out, "Don't jump overboard!—don't jump overboard! The schooner is righting."

I was not in a state of mind to reflect much on anything. I do not think more than three or four minutes, if as many, had passed since the squall struck us, and there I was standing on the vessel's quarter, led by Providence more than by any discretion of my own. It now came across me that if the schooner should right she was filled, and must go down, and that she might carry me with her in the suction. I made a spring, therefore, and fell into the water several feet from the place where I had stood. It is my opinion the schooner sunk as I left her. I went down some distance myself, and when I came up to the surface, I began to swim vigorously for the first time in my life. I think I swam several yards, but of course will not pretend to be certain of such a thing, at such a moment, until I felt my hand hit something hard. I made another stroke, and felt my hand pass down the side of an object that I knew at once was a clincher-built boat. I belonged to this boat, and I now recollected that she had been towing astern. Until that instant I had not thought of her, but thus was I led in the dark to the best possible means of saving my life. I made a grab at the gunwale, and caught it in the stern-sheets. Had I swum another yard, I should have passed the boat, and missed her altogether! I got in without any difficulty, being all alive and much excited.

My first look was for the schooner. She had disappeared, and I supposed she was just settling under water. It rained as if the flood-gates of heaven were opened, and it lightened awfully. It did not seem to me that there was a breath of air, and the water was unruffled, the effects of the rain excepted. All this I saw, as it might be, at a glance. But my chief concern was to preserve my own life. I was cockswain of this very boat, and had made it fast to the taffrail that same afternoon, with a round turn and two half-hitches, by its best painter. Of course I expected the vessel would drag the boat down with her, for I had no knife to cut the painter. There was a gang-board in the boat, however, which lay fore and aft, and I thought this might keep me afloat until some of the fleet should pick me up. To clear this gang-board, then, and get it into the water, was my first object. I ran forward to throw off the lazy-painter that was coiled on its end, and in doing this I caught the boat's painter in my hand, by accident. A pull satisfied me that it was all clear! Some one on board must have cast off this painter, and then lost his chance of getting into the boat by an accident. At all events, I was safe, and I now dared to look about me.

My only chance of seeing, was during the flashes; and these left me almost blind. I had thrown the gang-board into the water, and I now called out to encourage the men, telling them I was in the boat. I could hear many around me, and, occasionally, I saw the heads of men, struggling in the lake. There being no proper place to scull in, I got an oar in the after rullock, and made out to scull a little, in that fashion. I now saw a man quite near the boat; and, hauling in the oar, made a spring amidships, catching this poor fellow by the collar. He was very near gone; and I had a great deal of difficulty in getting him in over the gunwale. Our joint weight brought the boat down, so low, that she shipped a good deal of water. This turned out to be Leonard Lewis, the young man who had helped me to clew up the fore-topsail. He could not stand, and spoke with difficulty. I asked him to crawl aft, out of the water; which he did, lying down in the stern-sheets.

I now looked about me, and heard another; leaning over the gunwale, I got a glimpse of a man, struggling, quite near the boat. I caught him by the collar, too; and had to drag him in very much in the way I had done with Lewis. This proved to be Lemuel Bryant, the man who had been wounded by a hot shot, at York, as already mentioned, while the commodore was on board us. His wound had not yet healed, but he was less exhausted than Lewis. He could not help me, however, lying down in the bottom of the boat, the instant he was able.

For a few moments, I now heard no more in the water; and I began to scull again. By my calculation, I moved a few yards, and must have got over the spot where the schooner went down. Here, in the flashes, I saw many heads, the men swimming in confusion, and at random. By this time, little was said, the whole scene being one of fearful struggling and frightful silence. It still rained; but the flashes were less frequent, and less fierce. They told me, afterwards, in the squadron, that it thundered awfully; but I cannot say I heard a clap, after I struck the water. The next man caught the boat himself. It was a mulatto, from Martinique, who was Mr. Osgood's steward; and I helped him in. He was much exhausted, though an excellent swimmer; but alarm nearly deprived him of his strength. He kept saying, "Oh! Masser Ned—Oh! Masser Ned!" and lay down in the bottom of the boat, like the two others; I taking care to shove him over to the larboard side, so as to trim our small craft.

I kept calling out, to encourage the swimmers, and presently I heard a voice, saying, "Ned, I'm here, close by you." This was Tom Goldsmith, a messmate, and the very man under whose rug I had been sleeping, at quarters. He did not want much help, getting in, pretty much, by himself. I asked him, if he were able to help me. "Yes, Ned," he answered, "I'll stand by you to the last; what shall I do?" I told him to take his tarpaulin, and to bail the boat, which, by this time, was a third full of water. This he did, while I sculled a little ahead. "Ned," says Tom, "she's gone down with her colours flying, for her pennant came near getting a round turn about my body, and carrying me down with her. Davy has made a good haul, and he gave us a close shave; but he didn't get you and me." In this manner did this thoughtless sailor express himself, as soon as rescued from the grasp of death! Seeing something on the water, I asked Tom to take my oar, while I sprang to the gunwale, and caught Mr. Bogardus, the master's mate, who was clinging to one of the sweeps. I hauled him in, and he told me, he thought, some one had hold of the other end of the sweep. It was so dark, however, we could not see even that distance. I hauled the sweep along, until I found Ebenezer Duffy, a mulatto, and the ship's cook. He could not swim a stroke; and was nearly gone. I got him in, alone, Tom bailing, lest the boat, which was quite small, should swamp with us.

As the boat drifted along, she reached another man, whom I caught also by the collar. I was afraid to haul this person in amidships, the boat being now so deep, and so small, and so I dragged him ahead, and hauled him in over the bows. This was the pilot, whose name I never knew. He was a lake-man, and had been aboard us the whole summer. The poor fellow was almost gone, and like all the rest, with the exception of Tom, he lay down and said not a word.

We had now as many in the boat as it would carry, and Tom and myself thought it would not do to take in any more. It is true, we saw no more, everything around us appearing still as death, the pattering of the rain excepted. Tom began to bail again, and I commenced hallooing. I sculled about several minutes, thinking of giving others a tow, or of even hauling in one or two more, after we got the water out of the boat; but we found no one else. I think it probable I sculled away from the spot, as there was nothing to guide me. I suppose, however, that by this time, all the Scourges had gone down, for no more were ever heard from.

Tom Goldsmith and myself now put our heads together as to what was best to be done. We were both afraid of falling into the enemy's hands, for, they might have bore up in the squall, and run down near us. On the whole, however, we thought the distance between the two squadrons was too great for this; at all events, something must be done at once. So we began to row, in what direction even we did not know. It still rained as hard as it could pour, though there was not a breath of wind. The lightning came now at considerable intervals, and the gust was evidently passing away towards the broader parts of the lake. While we were rowing and talking about our chance of falling in with the enemy, Tom cried out to me to "avast pulling." He had seen a vessel, by a flash, and he thought she was English, from her size. As he said she was a schooner, however, I thought it must be one of our own craft, and got her direction from him. At the next flash I saw her, and felt satisfied she belonged to us. Before we began to pull, however, we were hailed "boat ahoy!" I answered. "If you pull another stroke, I'll fire into you"—came back—"what boat's that? Lay on your oars, or I'll fire into you." It was clear we were mistaken ourselves for an enemy, and I called out to know what schooner it was. No answer was given, though the threat to fire was repeated, if we pulled another stroke. I now turned to Tom and said, "I know that voice—that is old Trant." Tom thought "we were in the wrong shop." I now sung out, "This is the Scourge's boat—our schooner has gone down, and we want to come alongside." A voice next called from the schooner— "Is that you, Ned?" This I knew was my old ship-mate and school-fellow, Jack Mallet, who was acting as boatswain of the Julia, the schooner commanded by sailing-master James Trant, one of the oddities of the service, and a man with whom the blow often came as soon as the word. I had known Mr. Trant's voice, and felt more afraid he would fire into us, than I had done of anything which had occurred that fearful night. Mr. Trant, himself, now called out—"Oh-ho; give way, boys, and come alongside." This we did, and a very few strokes took us up to the Julia, where we were received with the utmost kindness. The men were passed out of the boat, while I gave Mr. Trant an account of all that had happened. This took but a minute or two.

Mr. Trant now inquired in what direction the Scourge had gone down, and, as soon as I had told him, in the best manner

I could, he called out to Jack Mallet—"Oh-ho, Mallet—take four hands, and go in the boat and see what you can do—take a lantern, and I will show a light on the water's edge, so you may know me." Mallet did as ordered, and was off in less than three minutes after we got alongside. Mr. Trant, who was much humoured, had no officer in the Julia, unless Mallet could be called one. He was an Irishman by birth, but had been in the American navy ever since the revolution, dying a lieutenant, a few years after this war. Perhaps no man in the navy was more generally known, or excited more amusement by his oddities, or more respect for his courage. He had come on the lake with the commodore, with whom he was a great pet, and had been active in all the fights and affairs that had yet taken place. His religion was to hate an Englishman.

Mr. Trant now called the Scourges aft, and asked more of the particulars. He then gave us a glass of grog all round, and made his own crew splice the main-brace. The Julias now offered us dry clothes. I got a change from Jack Reilly, who had been an old messmate, and with whom I had always been on good terms. It knocked off raining, but we shifted ourselves at the galley fire below. I then went on deck, and presently we heard the boat pulling back. It soon came alongside, bringing in it four more men that had been found floating about on sweeps and gratings. On inquiry, it turned out that these men belonged to the Hamilton, Lt. Winter—a schooner that had gone down in the same squall that carried us over. These men were very much exhausted, too, and we all went below, and were told to turn in.

I had been so much excited during the scenes through which I had just passed, and had been so much stimulated by grog, that, as yet, I had not felt much of the depression natural to such events. I even slept soundly that night, nor did I turn out until six the next morning.

When I got on deck, there was a fine breeze; it was a lovely day, and the lake was perfectly smooth. Our fleet was in a good line, in pretty close order, with the exception of the Governor Tompkins, Lieutenant Tom Brown, which was a little to lee-ward, but carrying a press of sail to close with the commodore. Mr. Trant perceiving that the Tompkins wished to speak us in passing, brailed his foresail and let her luff up close under our lee. "Two of the schooners, the Hamilton and the Scourge, have gone down in the night," called out Mr. Brown; "for I have picked up four of the Hamilton's." "Oh-ho!"—answered Mr. Trant—"That's no news at all! for I have picked up *twelve*; eight of the Scourge's, and four of the Hamilton's—aft fore-sheet."

These were all that were ever saved from the two schooners, which must have had near a hundred souls on board them. The two commanders, Lieutenant Winter and Mr. Osgood were both lost, and with Mr. Winter went down I believe, one or two young gentlemen. The squadron could not have moved much between the time when the accidents happened and that when I came on deck, or we must have come round and gone over the same ground again, for we now passed many relics of the scene, floating about in the water. I saw spunges, gratings, sweeps, hats, &c., scattered about, and in passing ahead we saw one of the latter that we tried to catch; Mr. Trant ordering it done, as he said it must have been Lieutenant Winter's. We did not succeed, however; nor was any article taken on board. A good look-out was kept for men, from aloft, but none were seen from any of the vessels. The lake had swallowed up the rest of the two crews; and the Scourge, as had been often predicted, had literally become a coffin to a large portion of her people.

James Inderwick: Journal

The American brig *Argus*, under Captain William Henry Allen, left New York Harbor on June 18, 1813, to deliver William H. Crawford, the former president pro tempore of the Senate, to his new post as minister to France. That mission accomplished, she left Lorient, Brittany, on July 11, and embarked upon a brief but remarkable career in the English Channel and the Irish Sea, capturing and burning some twenty ships within a month. Then, on the morning of August 14, *Argus* met the British brig *Pelican* in St. George's Channel, near Pembrokeshire, Wales. *Pelican*, under Captain John Fordyce Maple, returned fire and, at the conclusion of a closely matched fifty-minute contest, brought her bow against *Argus*'s quarter. Before the British could board, *Argus* struck her colors. The *Argus*'s surgeon, James Inderwick, recorded the human cost of the battle in his journal.

August 14th Saturday   St George's Channel
Early this morning came to action with a large English Brig She captured us after an action of 45 minutes She proved to be the *Pelican*.

August 15th Sunday   at sea
The following list comprehends the number of killed and wounded on board of our vessel as far as can be at present ascertained.
Mr Wm W Edwards Midshipman.   Killed by shot in the head.
Mr Richd Delphy Midshipman.   Do   Had both legs nearly shot off at the knees — he survived the action about 3 hours
Joshua Jones   Seaman — Killed.
Geo Gardiner   Seaman — His thigh taken off by a round shot close to his body.   he lived about ½ an hour
Jno Finlay   Seaman — His head was shot off at the close of the action.
Wm Moulton   Seaman — Killed.
Total 6.

The following were wounded   viz

Wm H Allen Esq — Commander — His left knee shattered by a cannon shot. Amputation of the thigh was performed about 2 hours after the action — An anodyne was previously administered — An anodyne at night.

Lieut Watson — 1st — Part of the Scalp on the upper part of the head torn off by a grape shot — the bone denuded.   It was dressed lightly and he returned and took command of the deck.   Now on board the *Pelican*.

Mr Colin McCloud — Boatswain — Received a severe lacerated wound on the upper part of the thigh, a slight one on the face and a contusion on the right shoulder.   Dressed simply with lint and roller Bandage.

Mr James White — Carpenter — Shot near the upper part of the left thigh — bone fractured.   Hemmorrhage considerable — Dressed the wound with lint imbued with ol olivar — applied bandage and Splints — anodyne at night   has also an incised wound in the head — Dressing — Suture — Adhesive plaster & double headed roller —

Joseph Jordan — Boatswains Mate.   Has a large wound thro the left thigh the bone fractured and splintered, — the back part of the right thigh carried off and nearly the whole of the fleshy nates carried away — Dressed with lint imbued with ol olivar — gave him a large anodyne — repeated it at night — Case hopeless.

Jno. Young — Quarter Master — Received a severe shot wound in the left breast seemingly by a glancing shot.   The integuments and part of the extensor muscles of the hand torn away — Dressed lightly with oil and lint with appropriate bandages — gave him an anodyne at night.

Francis Eggert — Seaman — Has a very severe contusion of the right leg with a small gun shot wound a little above the outer ancle no ball discoverable — Dressed the wound with lint & bandage & directed the leg to be kept constantly wet with Aq. Veg. Mineral — 3 hours after reception the leg was swelled and very painful gave him an anodyne — Proposed Amputation but he would not consent.   This morning the leg excessively tense — swelled — vesicated — and of a dark color about the outer ancle — Has considerable fever   Directed the saline mixture with occasional anodyne   To continue the lotion.

John Nugent — Seaman — Gun shot wound in the superior part of the right thigh about 2 inches from the groin — Thigh bone fractured and much splintered — ball supposed to be in — Several pieces of bone were extracted but the ball was not found — Dressed lint Bandage with splints — Anodyne — Rested considerably well last night but there has been a large oozing from the wound — Applied fresh lint.   No fever.

Charles Baxter — Seaman — Has a lacerated wound of the left ancle — The lower part of the fibula splintered — apparently affecting the joint. Has much hemmorhage from this wound.   He has also a gun shot wound of the right thigh.   The ball has passed obliquely downwards thro the back part of the thigh.   I proposed the amputation of his left leg but he would not give his consent.   Dressed both wounds with lint & Roller Bandages — Made considerable compression on the left foot in order to restrain the bleeding — Has some fever this morning.   H. Mist. Salin — Tamarind water for drink — low diet.

James Kellam — Seaman — Lacerated wound of the calf of the right leg — also a wound in the ham of the same Extremity — Dressing simple — To day the leg somewhat swelled and painfull — slackened the bandage.

Wm Harington — Seaman — Complains much of pain & soreness in the small of the back and nates.   It is suspected that he has received a severe contusion on the parts   H. Anodyne at night — N. S. ad ℥xvi   Apply continually Aq. Veg. Min to the parts.

Jas Hall — Seaman — Has a slight wound above the left eye — I suspect caused by a splinter — Dressing simple.

Total ascertained — 12.

Owing to the disordered state of the vessel the wounded have wretched accommodation — if that term may be used — I endeavoured to make their condition as comfortable as possible — Divided, those of our people who remained on board, and were well, into watches — in different parts of the vessel — Mr Hudson Mr Dennisson & myself sitting up with the Captain — Directed Lemonade & Tamarind water to be kept made and served to the Wounded.

August 16th Monday   arrived at Plymouth

Capt Allen — Morn — No fever — has had some slight spasms in the stump — on which account an anodyne was occasionally administered — He has been for some time troubled with a dyspeptic complaint which is peculiarly disagreeable in his present state   H. Mist Salina with rather an excess of the alkali.

Eve — an exudation of the thinner parts of the blood now begins to appear thro' the dressings — stump as easy as can be expected — Enjoined a light diet — Chicken broath, Panada &c — Administerd a purg. but it was not retained.

Colin McLeod — Thigh but little swelled.   No febrile action in his pulse — He is in the best of spirits.

Mr White — Morn — Rested considerably last night in consequence of the anodyne — Some oozing from the posterior orifice — Is extremely weak & is troubled with spasmodic twitches — Gave him wine & water as drink — Soup occasionally.

Eve — very restless — delirium — Gave him a large anodyne which was repeated in the night with no good effect.

Joseph Jordan — Died this morning.

John Young — His Breast easy — arm painfull   apparently in consequence of the swelling which has taken place — Loosened the Bandage — Pulse frequent and rather hard — Directed Sulph Sod — and an anodyne at night — Eve.   A poultice was directed

Francis Eggert — this morning H. Sulph. Sod.   Is easier — but the leg is still excessively swelled — Cap pil opii gr i 4ta quaq hor. — Contin the lotion — H. mist Salin. ℥viii adde Tart Emet gr ii cap lact mag 2 quaq hor.

John Nugent — Is easier than could have been expected   Has some fever to day — H mist Salin cum Tart Emet.

Charles Baxter — Considerable oozing yet from the ancle Pulse frequent — Contin mist Salin.

Jas Kellam — Has some fever to day — Complains much of soreness — Directed a cataplas.

Wm Herington — The same — Contin. the application.

Jas Hall — Eye a little sore — No complaint.

Our wounded are in a distressed condition. The riotous behaviour of the captors is such that they have no rest whatever and are frequently trodden upon and bruisd by them.

Directed to day thin Chicken broth to be served out to them with their light Nourishment.

August 17th Tuesday   Plymouth

The wounded and sick Seamen were this morning carried to the hospital — Mr Hudson attended them thither — I request'd him to enquire what accommodation he could find for the captain at the Town as the noise & tumult on board is very disagreeable.

Capt Allen — Stump in a good state — but little soreness — but has some fever this morning — Took an anodyne last night — dosed at times — the sickness of stomach & vomiting continues — He takes the Saline mist occasionally — but without relief — He is allowed wine in his drink — Diet Chicken broath — Panada &c — Injected a Cathartic enema.

This afternoon I obtained permission to go to town for the purpose of hiring private lodgings for the Captain. On return found him worse. Vomiting more frequent. Pulse weak and frequent — Skin cold — now & then troubled with Hiccup — Mind, at times, wandering — false vision — Directed ½ a wine glass full of Wine every hour — Ether & Tinct of Opii occasionally for the hiccup which did not often after recur — Lime water & milk was administered as an anti emitic but with little relief. Soda water was also occasionally given — Applied hot fomentations to the region of the stomach with anodyne liniment.

August 18th Wednesday

Capt Allen — Passed a very restless night — vomiting continues, altho' wine & occasional anodynes seemed to relieve it.

This morning I dressed the Stump assisted by the Surgeon of the *San Salvadore* Flag Ship. Found the incision united but a little at the inner angle — Surface flabby Discharge thin, sanious — Whole appearance exhibiting a want of action in the parts.

On consultation with the Surgeon of the Flag Ship and, with Dr Magrath of the Mill Prison Hospital, it was agreed to have him removed thither — Mr Denison, Mr Hudson, & myself were to be favoured with the liberty of remaining with him untill the event of his case was determined. — The disagreeable condition of the vessel, — his danger, and the eminent medical assistance at the Hospital concur in inducing us to adopt this plan.

11 A.M.   Capt Nash of the *San Salvador*, sent his launch with a large cot slung in it.

12 M   Arrived at the Hospital and found a neat & commodious apartment ready — on arrival he complained of languor & appeared somewhat fatigued — a glass of wine reviv'd him — vomiting continues — By the direction of Dr Magrath a mist Ether & laud with an Infusion of P Peruv. was given him & a Liniment composed of Camph, opium and oil was rubbed on the Epigrastric region, but without effect — Skin moist & cold — A blister was applied to the stomach and bottles of warm water to his foot — Abdomen humid — Has had no passage from his bowels, except 2 evacuations yesterday, in consequence of the Enema   Dr Magrath advised a purg — Cal. et P Rhei was given in balm — It was soon afterward rejected.

9 P.M. — Pulse feeble, frequent, interrupted, skin covered with a clammy moisture — Vomiting continues unabated notwithstanding the use of anti Emetic remedies. — Since last report has taken Alkali & lime juice administered seperately — is now using Soda Water supersaturated with Carb. Acid Gas. — He is extremely restless, desireing often to have his position altered — Comatose Delirium with startings — subsultus tendinum.

11 oClk P.M.   He died.

To the time of Capt Allen's death, Dr Magrath & his assistant Mr Allan remain'd with us and afforded every assistance possible.

                        August 21st Saturday — Mill Prison
Attended the funeral of Capt Allen with Mr Denison Mr Hudson & Mr Snelson as Mourners.

Thomas Hart Benton: Broadside

In 1812, Major General Andrew Jackson named his admiring protégé Thomas Hart Benton, of Franklin, Tennessee, his aide-de-camp and personal liaison to Washington. In June 1813, Benton's admiration of Jackson cooled to freezing when he learned that his younger brother Jesse had been challenged to a duel by another of Jackson's officers, William Carroll, and that Jackson had accepted Carroll's request to act as his second. In the duel, on June 14, Carroll lost the tip of his thumb and Jesse received a grazing wound to his hip and buttock. After this, Benton lost no opportunity to defame Jackson throughout Franklin and Knoxville. When word of this invective reached Jackson, he warned Benton that should he ever again set foot in Nashville he would suffer a horsewhipping. The following broadside presents Benton's account of what occurred on September 4, 1813, when he and Jesse checked in at Nashville's City Hotel.

FRANKLIN, TENNESSEE, SEPT. 10, 1813.

A difference which had been for some months brewing between General Jackson and myself, produced on Saturday the 4th inst. in the town of Nashville, the most outrageous affray ever witnessed in a civilized country. In communicating this affair to my friends and fellow citizens, I limit myself to the statement of a few leading facts, the truth of which I am ready to establish by judicial proofs.

1. That myself and my brother Jesse Benton arriving in Nashville on the morning of the affray, & knowing of Gen. Jackson's threats, went and took lodgings in a different house from the one in which he staid, on purpose to avoid him.

2. That the general and some of his friends came to the house where we had put up, and commenced the attack by levelling a pistol at me, *when I had no weapon drawn*, and advancing upon me at a quick pace, *without giving me time to draw one.*

300

3. That seeing this my brother fired upon Gen. Jackson when he had got within eight or ten feet of me.

4. That four other pistols were fired in quick succession: one by Genl. Jackson at me: two by me at the General: and one by Col. Coffee at me. In the course of this firing Gen. Jackson was brought to the ground; but I received no hurt.

5. That daggers were then drawn. Col. Coffee and Mr. Alexander Donelson made at me, and gave me five slight wounds. Capt. Hammond and Mr. Stokley Hays engaged my brother, who being still weak from the effect of a severe wound he had lately received in a duel, was not able to resist two men. They got him down; and while Captain Hammond beat him on the head to make him lay still, Mr. Hays attempted to stab him, and wounded him in both arms, as he lay on his back parrying the thrusts with his naked hands. From this situation a generous hearted citizen of Nashville, Mr. Sumner, relieved him. Before he came to the ground my brother clapped a pistol to the body of Mr. Hays to blow him through, but it missed fire

6. My own and my brothers pistols carried two balls each: for it was our intention, if driven to arms, to have no childs play. The pistols fired at me were so near that the blaze of the muzzle of one of them burnt the sleeve of my coat, and the other aimed at my head, at little more than arms length from it.

7. Capt. Carroll was to have taken part in the affray, but was absent by the permission of General Jackson, as he has since proved by the Generals certificate: a certificate which reflects I know not whether less honor upon the General or upon the Captain.

8. That this attack was made upon me in the house where the judge of the district Mr. Searcy, had his lodgings! So little are the laws and its ministers respected! Nor has the civil authority yet taken cognizance of this horrible outrage.

These facts are sufficient to fix the public opinion. For my own part I think it scandalous that such things should take place at any time, but particularly so at the present moment when the public service requires the aid of all its citizens. As for the name of *courage*, God forbid that I should ever attempt to gain it by becoming a bully. Those who know me, know full well that I would give a thousand times more for the reputation of *Croghan* in defending his fort, than I would for the reputations of all the duellists and gladiators that ever appeared upon the face of the earth.

THOMAS HART BENTON.
Lieutenant Colonel 39th Infantry.

Philip Freneau: *"The Battle of Lake Erie"*

In the battle for the Old Northwest, control of Lake Erie was a chief aim of both navies in the summer of 1813. The commander of the British squadron was Robert H. Barclay; his six ships were anchored near Fort Amherstburg, and the weight of his broadside—that is, the weight of shells that his ships could bring to bear in a single firing—was 494 pounds. The commander of the American squadron was Oliver Hazard Perry; his nine ships were anchored near Presque Isle, in Pennsylvania, and the weight of his broadside was 912 pounds. On September 10, the two squadrons faced each other near Put-in-Bay, on South Bass Island, at the western end of the lake. Perry captained the brig *Lawrence* (20 guns), which was seconded by her identical sister *Niagara*; Barclay captained the sloop *Detroit* (19 guns), which was seconded by *Queen Charlotte* (17 guns). After a three-hour battle, in which 80 percent of his crew was killed or injured, Perry emerged victorious. His skill and daring made him a legend, as did his succinct battle report to William Henry Harrison: "We have met the enemy and they are ours: two ships, two brigs, one schooner & one sloop." Of the many poetic tributes inspired by Perry's exploits, Philip Freneau's, published in 1815, remains the most memorable.

THE BATTLE OF LAKE ERIE

September 10, 1813

"To clear the lake of Perry's fleet
 And make his flag his winding sheet
 This is my object—I repeat—"
   —Said Barclay, flush'd with native pride,
 To some who serve the british crown:—
 But they, who dwell beyond the moon,
 Heard this bold menace with a frown,
   Nor the rash sentence ratified.

Ambition so bewitch'd his mind,
 And royal smiles had so combined
 With skill, to act the part assign'd

He for no contest cared, a straw;
The ocean was too narrow far
To be the seat of naval war;
He wanted lakes, and room to spare,
   And all to yield to Britain's law.

And thus he made a sad mistake;
Forsooth he must possess the lake,
As merely made for England's sake
   To play her pranks and rule the roast;
Where she might govern, uncontrol'd,
An unmolested empire hold,
And keep a fleet to fish up gold,
   To pay the troops of George Provost.

The ships approach'd, of either side,
And Erie, on his bosom wide
Beheld two hostile navies ride,
   Each for the combat well prepared:
The lake was smooth, the sky was clear,
The martial drum had banish'd fear,
And death and danger hover'd near,
   Though both were held in disregard.

From lofty heights their colors flew,
And Britain's standard all in view,
With frantic valor fired the crew
   That mann'd the guns of queen Charlotte.
"And we must Perry's squadron take,
And England shall command the lake;—
And you must fight for Britain's sake,
   (Said Barclay) sailors, will you not?"

Assent they gave with heart and hand;
For never yet a braver band
To fight a ship, forsook the land,
   Than Barclay had on board that day;—
The guns were loosed the game to win,
Their muzzles gaped a dismal grin,
And out they pulled their tompion pin,
   The bloody game of war to play.

But Perry soon, with flowing sail,
Advanced, determined to prevail,
When from his bull-dogs flew the hail
    Directed full at queen Charlotte.
His wadded guns were aim'd so true,
And such a weight of ball they threw,
As, Barclay said, he never knew
    To come, before, so scalding hot!

But still, to animate his men
From gun to gun the warrior ran
And blazed away and blazed again—
    Till Perry's ship was half a wreck:
They tore away both tack and sheet,—
Their victory might have been complete,
Had Perry not, to shun defeat
    In lucky moment left his deck.

Repairing to another post,
From another ship he fought their host
And soon regain'd the fortune lost,
    And down, his flag the briton tore:
With loss of arm and loss of blood
Indignant, on his decks he stood
To witness Erie's crimson flood
    For miles around him, stain'd with gore!

Thus, for dominion of the lake
These captains did each other rake,
And many a widow did they make;—
    Whose is the fault, or who to blame?—
The briton challenged with his sword,
The yankee took him at his word,
With spirit laid him close on board—
    They're ours—he said—and closed the game.

Washington Irving: "Biographical Memoir of Commodore Perry"

By 1812 Washington Irving—later famous as the creator of Rip Van Winkle and Ichabod Crane—had earned a significant literary reputation as the author of *A History of New York, by Diedrich Knickerbocker* (1809), a satirical chronicle of Manhattan "from the beginning of the world to the end of the Dutch Dynasty." His talents were sought by the publisher Moses Thomas, who, shortly after war was declared, hired him to edit a new monthly, the *Analectic Magazine*. Among Irving's many contributions to the first volume was a series of profiles of naval heroes of the war, the most memorable of which is the following portrait of Oliver Hazard Perry, published in the December 1813 issue. Like all of Irving's naval articles, it reveals the author's ambivalence about the war, his support of all who served, and his gift for American mythmaking.

In taking up the pen to commemorate another of our naval victories, we solicit the patience of our readers if we indulge in a few preliminary reflections, not strictly arising out of the subject of this memoir, though, we trust, not wholly irrelevant.

Indeed, we do not pretend to the rigid precision and dispassionate coolness of historic narrative. Excited as we are by the tone and temper of the times, and the enthusiasm that prevails around us, we cannot, if we would, repress those feelings of pride and exultation, that gush warm from the heart, when the triumphs of our navy are the theme. Public joy is at all times contagious; but in the present lowering days of evil, it is a sight as inspiring as it is rare, to behold a whole nation breaking forth into gladness.

There is a point, however, beyond which exultation becomes insulting, and honest pride swells into vanity. When this is exceeded even success proves injurious, and, instead of begetting a proper confidence in ourselves, produces that most disgusting of all national faults, boastful arrogance. This is the evil against the encroachments of which we would earnestly caution our countrymen; it comes with such an open and imposing front of worthy patriotism, and at such warm and incautious moments, that it is apt to take possession of us before we are aware. We have already noticed some symptoms of its prevalence. We have seen many of our papers filled with fulsome and extravagant paragraphs, echoing the vulgar joy and coarse tauntings of the rabble: these may be acceptable to the gross palates of the mean minded; but they must grieve the feelings of the generous and liberal; and must lessen our triumphs in the eyes of impartial nations. In this we behold the striking difference between those who fight battles, and those who merely talk about them. Our officers are content modestly to announce their victories; to give a concise statement of their particulars, and then drop the subject: but then the theme is taken up by a thousand vaunting tongues and vaunting pens; each tries to outvie the other in extravagant applause, until the very ear of admiration becomes wearied with excessive eulogium.

We do not know whether, in these remarks, we are not passing censure upon ourselves, and whether we do not largely indulge in the very weakness we condemn: but of this we are sure, that in our rejoicings no feelings enter insulting to the foe. We joy, indeed, in seeing the flag of our country encircled with glory, and our nation elevated to a dignified rank among the nations of the earth; but we make no boastful claims to intrinsic superiority, nor seek to throw sneer or stigma on an enemy, whom, in spite of temporary hostility, we honour and admire.

But, surely, if any impartial mind will consider the circumstances of the case, he will pardon our countrymen for overstepping, in the flush of unexpected and repeated success, the modest bounds of propriety. Is it a matter of surprise that, while our cheeks are yet scarce cool from the blushes—the burning blushes—of wounded pride and insulted patriotism, with which we have heard our country ridiculed and set at naught by other nations—while our ears still ring with the galling terms in which even British statesmen have derided us, as weak, pusillanimous and contemptible—while our memories are still sore with the tales of our flag insulted in every sea, and our countrymen oppressed in every port—is it a matter of surprise that we should break forth into transports at seeing these foul aspersions all suddenly brushed away—at seeing a continued series of brilliant successes flashing around the national standard, and dazzling all eyes with their excessive brightness? "Can such things be, and overcome us, like a summer cloud," without, not merely our "special wonder," but our special exultation? He who will cast his eye back, and notice how, in little more than one short year, we have suddenly sprung from peaceful insignificance to proud competition with a power whose laurels have been the slow growth of ages, will easily excuse the temporary effervescence of our feelings.

For our parts we truly declare that we revere the British nation. One of the dearest wishes of our hearts is to see a firm and well grounded friendship established between us. But friendship can never long endure, unless founded on mutual respect, and maintained with mutual independence; and however we may deplore the present war, this double good will spring out of it, we will learn our own value and resources, and we will teach our antagonist and the world at large to know and estimate us properly. There is an obsequious deference in the minds of too many of our countrymen towards Great Britain, that not only impairs the independence of the national character, but defeats the very object they would attain. They would make any sacrifices to maintain a precarious, and patched up, and humiliating, connexion with her; but they may rest assured that the good opinion of Great Britain was never gained by servile acquiescence; she never will think the better of a people for thinking despicably of themselves. We execrate that lowliness of spirit that would flatter her vanity, cower beneath her contumely, and meanly lay our honours at her feet. We wish not her friendship gratuitously; but to acquire it as a right; not to supplicate it by forbearance and long-suffering, but gallantly to win and proudly to maintain it. After all, if she will not be a friend, she must be content to become a rival; she will be obliged to substitute jealousy for contempt, and surely it is more tolerable, at any time, to be hated than despised.

Such is the kind of feeling that we avow towards Great Britain—equally removed, we trust, from rancorous hostility on the one side, and blind partiality on the other.

Whatever we may think of the expediency or inexpediency of the present war, we cannot feel indifferent to its operations. Whenever our arms come in competition with those of the enemy, jealousy for our country's honour will swallow up every other consideration. Our feelings will ever accompany the flag of our country to battle, rejoicing in its glory—lamenting over its defeat. For there is no such thing as releasing ourselves from the consequences of the contest. He who fancies he can stand aloof in interest, and by condemning the present war, can exonerate himself from the shame of its disasters, is wofully mistaken. Other nations will not trouble themselves about our internal wranglings and party questions; they will not ask who among us fought, or why we fought—but *how* we fought. The disgrace of defeat will not be confined to the contrivers of the war, or the party in power, or the conductors of the battle; but will extend to the whole nation, and come home to every individual. If the name of American is to be rendered honourable in the fight, we shall each participate in the honour; if otherwise, we must inevitably support our share of the ignominy. For these reasons do we watch, with anxious eye, the various fortunes of this war; a war awfully decisive of the future character and destinies of the nation. But much as we are gladdened by the bright gleams that occasionally break forth amid the darkness of the times, yet joyfully, most joyfully, shall we hail the period, when the "troubled night" of war shall be passed, and the "star of peace" again shed its mild radiance on our country.

We have seized this opportunity to express the foregoing sentiments, because we thought that if of any value, they might stand some chance of making an impression, when accompanied by the following memoir. And, indeed, in writing these naval biographies, it is our object not merely to render a small tribute of gratitude to these intrepid champions of our honour; but to render our feeble assistance towards promoting that national feeling which their triumphs are calculated to inspire.

Oliver Hazard Perry is the eldest son of Christopher Raymond Perry, Esq. of the United States navy. He was born at Newport, Rhode Island, in August, 1785, and being early destined for the navy, he entered the service in 1798, as midshipman, on board the sloop of war General Greene, then commanded by his father. When that ship went out of commission he was transferred to a squadron destined to the Mediterranean, where he served during the Tripolitan war. His extreme youth prevented his having an opportunity of distinguishing himself; but the faithfulness and intelligence with which he discharged the duties of his station, recommended him greatly to the favour of his superior officers; while his private virtues, and the manly dignity of his deportment, commanded the friendship and respect of his associates.

On returning from the Mediterranean he continued sedulously attentive to his profession, and though the reduction of the navy, and the neglect into which it fell during an interval of peace, disheartened many of the officers, and occasioned several to resign, yet he determined to adhere to its fortunes, confident that it must at some future period rise to importance. It would be little interesting to enumerate the different vessels in which he served, or to trace his advances through the regular grades. In 1810, we find he was ordered to the United States schooner Revenge, as lieutenant commandant. This vessel was attached to the squadron of Commodore Rodgers, at New London, and employed in cruising in the Sound, to enforce the embargo act. In the following spring he had the misfortune to lose the Revenge on Watch Hill Reef, opposite Stoney Town. He had sailed from Newport, late in the evening, for New London, with an easterly wind, accompanied by a fog. In the morning he found himself enveloped in a thick mist, with a considerable swell going. In this situation, without any possibility of ascertaining where he was, or of guarding against surrounding dangers, the vessel was carried on the reef, and soon went to pieces. On this occasion Perry gave proofs of that admirable coolness and presence of mind for which he is remarkable. He used every precaution to save the guns and property, and was in a great measure successful. He got off all the crew in perfect safety, and was himself the last to leave the wreck. His conduct in respect to this disaster underwent examination by a court of inquiry, at his own request, and he was not merely acquitted of all blame, but highly applauded for the judgment, intrepidity, and perseverance he had displayed. The secretary of the navy, Mr. Hamilton, also wrote him a very complimentary letter on the occasion.

Shortly after this event he returned to Newport, being peculiarly attracted thither by a tender attachment for Miss Mason, daughter of Dr. Mason, and niece of the Hon. Christopher Champlin of the United States senate; a lovely and interesting young lady, whom he soon after married.

At the beginning of 1812 he was promoted to the rank of master and commander, and ordered to the command of the flotilla of gun-boats stationed at the harbour of New-York. He remained on this station about a year; during which time he employed himself diligently in disciplining his crew to serve either as landsmen or mariners; and brought his flotilla into an admirable state of preparation for active operations.

The gun-boat service, however, is at best but an irksome employ. Nothing can be more dispiriting for ardent and daring minds than to be obliged to skulk about harbours and rivers, cramped up in these diminutive vessels, without the hope of exploit to atone for present inconvenience. Perry soon grew tired of this inglorious service, and applied to the secretary of the navy to be ordered to a more active station, and mentioned the Lakes as the one he should prefer. His request was immediately complied with, and he received orders to repair to Sackett's Harbour, Lake Ontario, with a body of mariners to reinforce the squadron under Commodore Chauncey. So popular was he among the honest tars under his command, that no sooner was the order known than nearly the whole of the crews volunteered to accompany him.

In a few days he was ready to depart, and tearing himself from the comforts of home, and the endearments of a young and beautiful wife and blooming child, he set off at the head of a large number of chosen seamen, on his expedition to the wilderness. The rivers being completely frozen over, they were obliged to perform the journey by land, in the depth of winter. The greatest order and good humour, however, prevailed throughout the little band of adventurers, to whom the whole expedition seemed a kind of frolic, and who were delighted with what they termed a land cruise.

Not long after the arrival of Perry at Sackett's Harbour,

Commodore Chauncey, who entertained a proper opinion of his merits, detached him to Lake Erie, to take command of the squadron on that station, and to superintend the building of additional vessels. The American force at that time on the Lake consisted but of several small vessels; two of the best of which had recently been captured from the enemy in a gallant style by Captain Elliot, from under the very batteries of Malden. The British force was greatly superior, and commanded by Commodore Barclay, an able and well tried officer. Commodore Perry immediately applied himself to increase his armament, and having ship carpenters from the Atlantic coast, and using extraordinary exertions, two brigs of twenty guns each were soon launched at Erie, the American port on the Lake.

While the vessels were constructing, the British squadron hovered off the harbour, but offered no molestation. At length, his vessels being equipped and manned, on the fourth of August Commodore Perry succeeded in getting his squadron over the bar at the mouth of the harbour. The water on the bar was but five feet deep, and the large vessels had to be buoyed over: this was accomplished in the face of the British, who fortunately did not think proper to make an attack. The next day he sailed in pursuit of the enemy, but returned on the eighth, without having encountered him. Being reinforced by the arrival of the brave Elliot, accompanied by several officers and eighty-nine sailors, he was enabled completely to man his squadron, and again set sail on the twelfth, in quest of the enemy. On the fifteenth he arrived at Sandusky Bay, where the American army under General Harrison lay encamped. From thence he cruised off Malden, where the British squadron remained at anchor, under the guns of the fort. The appearance of Perry's squadron spread great alarm on shore; the women and children ran shrieking about the place, expecting an immediate attack. The Indians, we are told, looked on with astonishment, and urged the British to go out and fight. Finding the enemy not disposed to venture a battle, Commodore Perry returned to Sandusky.

Nothing of moment happened until the morning of the tenth of September. The American squadron were, at that time, lying at anchor in Put-in-Bay, and consisted of

Brig Lawrence,	Commodore Perry,	20 guns.
Niagara,	Captain Elliot,	20
Caledonia,	Purser M'Grath,	3
Schooner Ariel,	Lieutenant Packet,	4
Scorpion,	Sailing-Master Champlin,	2
Somers,	Almy,	2 and 2 swivels.
Tigress,	Lieutenant Conklin,	1
Porcupine,	Midshipman G. Senat,	1
Sloop Trippe,	Lieutenant Smith,	1
		54 guns.

At sunrise they discovered the enemy, and immediately got under way and stood for him with a light wind at southwest. The British force consisted of

Ship Detroit,	19 guns,	1 on pivot, and 2 howitzers.
Queen Charlotte,	17	1 on pivot.
Schooner Lady Prevost,	13	1 do.
Brig Hunter,	10	
Sloop Little Belt,	3	
Schooner Chippeway,	1	2 swivels.
	63 guns.	

At 10 A.M. the wind haled to the southeast and brought our squadron to windward. Commodore Perry then hoisted his Union Jack, having for a motto, the dying words of the valiant Lawrence, "Don't give up the ship!" It was received with repeated cheerings by the officers and crews. And now having formed his line he bore for the enemy; who likewise cleared for action, and haled up his courses. It is deeply interesting to picture to ourselves the advances of these gallant and well-matched squadrons to a contest, where the strife must be obstinate and sanguinary, and the event decisive of the fate of almost an empire.

The lightness of the wind occasioned them to approach each other but slowly, and prolonged the awful interval of suspense and anxiety that precedes a battle. This is the time when the stoutest heart beats quick, "and the boldest holds his breath;" it is the still moment of direful expectation; of fearful looking out for slaughter and destruction; when even the glow of pride and ambition is chilled for a while, and nature shudders at the awful jeopardy of existence. The very order and regularity of naval discipline heighten the dreadful quiet of the moment. No bustle, no noise prevails to distract the mind, except at intervals the shrill piping of the boatswain's whistle, or a murmuring whisper among the men, who, grouped around their guns, earnestly regard the movements of the foe, now and then stealing a wistful glance at the countenances of their commanders. In this manner did the hostile squadrons approach each other, in mute watchfulness and terrible tranquillity; when suddenly a bugle was sounded from on board the enemy's ship Detroit, and loud huzzas immediately burst forth from all their crews.

No sooner did the Lawrence come within reach of the enemies' long guns, than they opened a heavy fire upon her, which, from the shortness of her guns, she was unable to return. Commodore Perry, without waiting for his schooners, kept on his course in such gallant and determined style that the enemy supposed it was his intention to board. In a few minutes, having gained a nearer position, he opened his fire. The length of the enemies' guns, however, gave them vastly the advantage, and the Lawrence was excessively cut up without being able to do any great damage in return. Their shot pierced her sides in all directions, killing our men on the birth deck and in the steerage, where they had been taken down to be dressed. One shot had nearly produced a fatal explosion; passing through the light room it knocked the snuff of the candle into the magazine; fortunately the gunner happened to see it, and had the presence of mind to extinguish it immediately with his hand.

Indeed, it seemed to be the enemies' plan to destroy the commodore's ship, and thus throw the squadron into confusion. For this purpose their heaviest fire was directed at the Lawrence, and blazed incessantly upon it from their largest vessels. Finding the hazard of his situation, Perry made sail, and directed the other vessels to follow for the purpose of closing with the foe. The tremendous fire, however, to which he was exposed, soon cut away every brace and bowline, and the Lawrence became unmanageable. Even in this disastrous plight she sustained the action for upwards of two hours, within canister distance, though for a great part of the time he could not get more than three guns to bear upon her antagonists. It was admirable to behold the perfect order and regularity that prevailed among her valiant and devoted crew, throughout this scene of horror. No trepidation, no confusion occurred, even for an instant; as fast as the men were wounded they were carried below and others stept into their places; the dead remained where they fell until after the action. At this juncture the fortune of the battle trembled on a point, and the enemy believed the day their own. The Lawrence was reduced to a mere wreck; her decks were streaming with blood, and covered with mangled limbs and the bodies of the slain; nearly the whole of her crew was either killed or wounded; her guns were dismounted, and the commodore and his officers helped to work the last that was capable of service.

Amidst all this peril and disaster the youthful commander is said to have remained perfectly composed, maintaining a serene and cheerful countenance, uttering no passionate or agitated expression, giving out his orders with calmness and deliberation, and inspiriting every one around him by his magnanimous demeanour.

At this crisis, finding the Lawrence was incapable of further service, and seeing the hazardous situation of the conflict, he formed the bold resolution of shifting his flag. Giving the ship, therefore, in charge to Lieutenant Yarnall, who had already distinguished himself by his bravery, he haled down his union, bearing the motto of Lawrence, and taking it under his arm, ordered to be put on board of the Niagara, which was then in close engagement. In leaving the Lawrence he gave his pilot choice either to remain on board, or accompany him; the faithful fellow told him "he'd stick by him to the last," and jumped into the boat. He went off from the ship in his usual gallant manner, standing up in the stern of the boat, until the crew absolutely pulled him down among them. Broadsides were levelled at him, and small arms discharged by the enemy, two of whose vessels were within musket shot, and a third one nearer. His brave shipmates who remained behind, stood watching him, in breathless anxiety; the balls struck around him and flew over his head in every direction; but the same

special providence that seems to have watched over the youthful hero throughout this desperate battle, conducted him
safely through a shower of shot, and they beheld with transport
his inspiring flag hoisted at the mast head of the Niagara. No
sooner was he on board than Captain Elliot volunteered to put
off in a boat and bring into action the schooners which had
been kept astern by the lightness of the wind; the gallant offer
was accepted, and Elliot left the Niagara to put it in execution.

About this time the commodore saw, with infinite regret,
the flag of the Lawrence come down. The event was unavoidable; she had sustained the whole fury of the enemy, and was
rendered incapable of defence; any further show of resistance
would but have been most uselessly and cruelly to have provoked carnage among the relics of her brave and mangled
crew. The enemy, however, were not able to take possession of
her, and subsequent circumstances enabled her again to hoist
her flag.

Commodore Perry now made signal for close action, and
the small vessels got out their sweeps and made all sail. Finding
that the Niagara was but little injured, he determined, if possible, to break the enemy's line. He accordingly bore up and
passed ahead of the two ships and brig, giving them a raking
fire from his starboard guns, and also to a large schooner and
sloop from his larboard side at half pistol shot. Having passed
the whole squadron, he luffed up and laid his ship along side
the British commodore. The smaller vessels under the direction of Captain Elliot having, in the mean time, got within
grape and canister distance, and keeping up a well directed fire,
the whole of the enemy struck excepting two small vessels
which attempted to escape, but were taken.

The engagement lasted about three hours, and never was
victory more decisive and complete. The captured squadron,
as has been shown, exceeded ours in weight of metal and
number of guns. Their crews were also more numerous; ours
were a motley collection, where there were some good seamen, but eked out with soldiers, volunteers and boys, and
many were on the sick list. More prisoners were taken than we
had men to guard. The loss on both sides was severe. Scarcely
any of the Lawrence's crew escaped unhurt. Among those slain
was Lieutenant Brooks of the marines, a gay and elegant young

officer, full of spirit, of amiable manners, and remarkable for his personal beauty. Lieutenant Yarnall, though repeatedly wounded, refused to quit the deck during the whole of the action. Commodore Perry, notwithstanding that he was continually in the most exposed situations of the battle, escaped uninjured; he wore an ordinary seaman's dress, which, perhaps, prevented him from being picked off by the enemies' sharp shooters. He had a younger brother with him, on board the Lawrence as midshipman, who was equally fortunate in receiving no injury, though his shipmates fell all round him. Two Indian chiefs had been stationed in the tops of the Detroit to shoot down our officers, but when the action became warm, so panic struck were they with the terrors of the scene, and the strange perils that surrounded them, that they fled precipitately to the hold of the ship, where they were found after the battle in a state of utter consternation. The bodies of several other Indians are said to have been found the next day on the shores of the Lake, supposed to have been slain during the engagement and thrown overboard.

It is impossible to state the number of killed on board the enemy. It must, however, have been very great, as their vessels were literally cut to pieces; and the masts of their two principal ships so shattered that the first gale blew them overboard. Commodore Barclay, the British commander, certainly did himself honour by the brave and obstinate resistance which he made. He is a fine looking officer, of about thirty-six years of age. He has seen much service, having been desperately wounded in the battle of Trafalgar, and afterwards losing an arm in another engagement with the French. In the present battle he was twice carried below, on account of his wounds, and had the misfortune to have his remaining hand shot away. While below the second time, his officer came down and told him that they must strike, as the ships were cut to pieces, and the men could not be kept to their guns. Commodore Barclay was then carried on deck, and after taking a view of their situation, and finding all chance of success was over, reluctantly gave orders to strike.

We have thus endeavoured to lay before our readers as clear an account of this important battle as could be gathered from the scanty documents that have reached us; though sketched out, we are sensible, with a hand but little skilled in naval affairs. The leading facts, however, are all that a landsman can be expected to furnish, and we trust that this glorious affair will hereafter be recorded with more elaborate care and technical precision. There is, however, a distinctness of character about a naval victory, that meets the capacity of every mind. There is such a simple unity in it; it is so well defined; so complete within itself; so rounded by space; so free from those intricacies and numerous parts that perplex us in an action on land, that the meanest intellect can fully grasp and comprehend it. And then, too, the results are so apparent; a victory on land is liable to a thousand misrepresentations; retreat is often called falling back, and abandoning the field called taking a new position; so that the conqueror is often defrauded of half the credit of his victory; but the capture or destruction of a ship is not to be mistaken, and a squadron towed triumphantly into port, is a notorious fact that admits of no contradiction.

In this battle, we trust, incontrovertible proof is given, if such proof were really wanted, that the success of our navy does not arise from chance, or superiority of force; but from the cool, deliberate courage, the intelligent minds and naval skill of our officers, the spirit of our seamen, and the excellent discipline of our ships; from principles, in short, which must insure a frequency of prosperous results, and give permanency to the reputation we have acquired. We have been rapidly adding trophy to trophy, and successively driving the enemy from every excuse in which he sought to shelter himself from the humiliation of defeat; and after having perfectly established our capability of fighting and conquering in single ships, we have now gone further and shown that it is possible for us to face the foe in squadron, and vanquish him even though superior in force.

In casting our eye over the details of this engagement, we are struck with the prominent part which the commander takes in the contest. We realize in his dauntless exposure and individual prowess, what we have read in heroic story, of the warrior, streaming like a meteor through the fight, and working wonders with his single arm. The fate of the combat seemed to rest upon his sword; he was the master spirit that directed the storm of battle, moving amid flames, and smoke, and death, and mingling wherever the struggle was most desperate and deadly. After sustaining in the Lawrence the whole blaze of the enemy's cannonry; after fighting until all around him was wreck and carnage; we behold him, looking forth from his shattered deck, with unruffled countenance, on the direful perils that environed him, calculating with wary eye the chances of the battle, and suddenly launching forth on the bosom of the deep, to shift his flag on board another ship, then in the hottest of the action. This was one of those master strokes by which great events are achieved, and great characters stamped, as it were, at a single blow—which bespeak the rare combination of the genius to conceive, the promptness to decide, and the boldness to execute. Most commanders have such glorious chances for renown, some time or another, within their reach; but it requires the nerve of a hero to grasp the perilous opportunity. We behold Perry following up his daring movement with sustained energy—dashing into the squadron of the enemy—breaking their line—raking starboard and larboard—and in this brilliant style achieving a consummate victory.

But if we admire his presence of mind and dauntless valour in the hour of danger, we are no less delighted with his modesty and self command amidst the flush of triumph. A courageous heart may carry a man stoutly through the battle, but it argues some strong qualities of head, to drain unmoved the intoxicating cup of victory. The first care of Perry was to attend to the comfort of the suffering crews of both squadrons. The sick and wounded were landed as soon as possible, and every means taken to alleviate the miseries of their situation. The officers who had fallen, on both sides, were buried on Sunday morning, on an island in the lake, with the honours of war. To the surviving officers he advanced a loan of one thousand dollars, out of his own limited purse—but, in short, his behaviour in this respect is best expressed in the words of Commodore Barclay, who, with generous warmth and frankness, has declared, that "the conduct of Perry towards the captive officers and men, was sufficient, of itself, to immortalize him!"

The letters which he wrote announcing the intelligence were remarkably simple and laconic. To the secretary of the navy he observes, "It has pleased the Almighty to give to the arms of the United States a signal victory over their enemies on this lake. The British squadron, consisting of two ships, two brigs, one schooner, and one sloop, have this moment surrendered to the force under my command, after a sharp conflict." This has been called an imitation of Nelson's letter after the battle of the Nile; but it was choosing a noble precedent, and the important national results of the victory justified the language. Independent of the vast accession of glory to our flag, this conquest insured the capture of Detroit—the rout of the British armies—the subjugation of the whole peninsula of Upper Canada, and, if properly followed up, the triumphant success of our northern war. Well might he say "it had pleased the Almighty," when, by this achievement, he beheld immediate tranquillity restored to an immense extent of country. Mothers no longer shrunk aghast, and clasped their infants to their breasts, when they heard the shaking of the forest or the howling of the blast—the aged sire no longer dreaded the shades of night, lest ruin should burst upon him in the hour of repose, and his cottage be laid desolate by the firebrand and the scalping knife—Michigan was rescued from the dominion of the sword, and quiet and security once more settled on the harassed frontiers, from Huron to Niagara.

But we are particularly pleased with his subsequent letter giving the particulars of the battle. It is so chaste, so moderate and perspicuous; equally free from vaunting exultation and affected modesty; neither obtruding himself upon notice, nor pretending to keep out of sight. His own individual services may be gathered from the letter, though not expressly mentioned; indeed, where the fortune of the day depended so materially upon himself, it was impossible to give a faithful narrative without rendering himself conspicuous.

We are led to notice these letters thus particularly, because that we find the art of letter writing is an accomplishment as rare as it is important among our military gentlemen. We are tired of the valour of the pen and the victories of the inkhorn. There is a common French proverb, "Grand parleur, mauvais combattant," which we could wish to see introduced into our country, and engraven on the swords of our officers. We wish to see them confine themselves in their letters to simple facts, neither swaggering before battle, nor vaunting afterwards. It is unwise to boast before, for the event may prove disastrous—and it is superfluous to boast afterwards, for the event speaks for itself. He who promises nothing, may with safety perform nothing, and will receive praise if he perform but little; but he who promises much will receive small credit unless he perform miracles. If a commander have done well, he may be sure the public will find it out, and their gratitude will be in proportion to his modesty. Admiration is a coin which, if left to ourselves, we lavish profusely, but we always close the hand when dunned for it.

Commodore Perry, like most of our naval officers, is yet in the prime of youth. He is of a manly and prepossessing appearance; mild and unassuming in his address, amiable in his disposition, and of great firmness and decision. Though early launched among the familiar scenes of naval life, (and nowhere is familiarity more apt to be licentious and encroaching,) yet the native gentility and sober dignity of his deportment, always chastened, without restraining, the freedom of intimacy. It is pleasing thus to find public services accompanied by private virtues; to discover no drawbacks on our esteem; no base alloy in the man we are disposed to admire; but a character full of moral excellence, of high-minded courtesy, and pure unsullied honour.

Were any thing wanting to perpetuate the fame of this victory, it would be sufficiently memorable from the scene where it was fought. This war has been distinguished by new and peculiar characteristics. Naval warfare has been carried into the interior of a continent, and navies, as if by magic, launched from among the depths of the forest. The bosoms of peaceful lakes which, but a short time since, were scarcely navigated by man, except to be skimmed by the light canoe of the savage, have all at once been ploughed by hostile ships. The vast silence that had reigned for ages on those mighty waters, was broken by the thunder of artillery, and the affrighted savage stared with amazement from his covert, at the sudden apparition of a seafight amid the solitudes of the wilderness.

The peal of war has once sounded on that lake, but probably will never sound again. The last roar of cannonry that died along her shores, was the expiring note of British domination.

Those vast internal seas will, perhaps, never again be the separating space between contending nations; but will be embosomed within a mighty empire; and this victory, which decided their fate, will stand unrivalled and alone, deriving lustre and perpetuity from its singleness.

In future times, when the shores of Erie shall hum with busy population; when towns and cities shall brighten where now extends the dark and tangled forest; when ports shall spread their arms, and lofty barks shall ride where now the canoe is fastened to the stake; when the present age shall have grown into venerable antiquity, and the mists of fable begin to gather round its history; then will the inhabitants of Canada look back to this battle we record, as one of the romantic achievements of the days of yore. It will stand first on the page of their local legends, and in the marvellous tales of the borders. The fisherman, as he loiters along the beach, will point to some half buried cannon, corroded with the rust of time, and will speak of ocean warriors that came from the shores of the Atlantic—while the boatman, as he trims his sail to the breeze, will chant in rude ditties the name of Perry—the early hero of Lake Erie.

Tecumseh: Speech to Henry Procter

With the defeat of Barclay's squadron, Fort Amherstburg and its supply lines to Detroit became defenseless against American attack. "The Loss of the Fleet is a most calamitous Circumstance," Procter wrote just two days after Perry's victory to Major General Baron Francis de Rottenburg, who in June had become the new commander of British forces in Upper Canada. "I do not see the least Chance of occupying to advantage my present extensive Position." He resolved to burn the fort, the naval yard, and the rest of the British installation at Amherstburg and then remove his troops to Burlington Heights, two hundred miles east, on the west end of Lake Ontario. The Indians opposed the British abandonment of the Detroit frontier, and Tecumseh made a speech in bitter protest.

———————

AMHERSTSBERG, Sept. 18, 1813
In the name of the Indian chiefs and warriors, to major-general Proctor, as the representative of their great father—the king.

FATHER, listen to your children! You have them now all before you.

The war before this, our British father gave the hatchet to his red children, when our chiefs were alive. They are now dead. In that war, our father was thrown on his back by the Americans, and our father took them by the hand without our knowledge; and we are afraid that our father will do so again at this time.

Summer before last, when I came forward with my red brethren, and was ready to take up the hatchet in favor of our British father, we were told not to be in a hurry, that he had not yet determined to fight the Americans.

Listen! When war was declared, our father stood up and gave us the tomahawk, and told us that he was then ready to strike the Americans; that he wanted our assistance and that he would certainly get us our lands back, which the Americans had taken from us.

Listen! You told us, at that time, to bring forward our

323

families to this place; and we did so; and you promised to take care of them, and that they should want for nothing, while the men would go and fight the enemy. That we need not trouble ourselves about the enemy's garrison; that we knew nothing about them, and that our father would attend to that part of the business. You also told your red children, that you would take care of your garrison here, which made our hearts glad.

Listen! When we were last to the Rapids, it is true we gave you little assistance. It is hard to fight people who live like ground hogs.

Father listen! Our fleet has gone out; we know they have fought; we have heard the great guns; but know nothing of what has happened to our father with one arm. Our ships have gone one way, and we are much astonished to see our father tying up everything and preparing to run away the other, without letting his red children know what his intentions are. You always told us to remain here and take care of our lands; it made our hearts glad to hear that was your wish. Our great father, the king, is our head, and you represent him. You always told us, that you would never draw your foot off British ground; but now, father we see you are drawing back, and we are sorry to see our father doing so without seeing the enemy. We must compare our father's conduct to a fat animal, that carries its tail upon its back, but when affrighted, he drops it between his legs and runs off.

Listen Father! The Americans have not yet defeated us by land; neither are we sure that they have done so by water; we, therefore, wish to remain here, and fight our enemy, if they should make their appearance. If they defeat us, we will then retreat with our father.

At the battle of the Rapids last war, the Americans certainly defeated us; and when we retreated to our father's fort at that place the gates were shut against us. We were afraid that it would now be the case; but instead of that we now see our British father preparing to march out of his garrison.

Father! You have got the arms and ammunition which our great father sent for his red children. If you have an idea of going away, give them to us, and you may go and welcome, for us. Our lives are in the hands of the Great Spirit. We are determined to defend our lands, and if it be his will we wish to leave our bones upon them.

John Richardson: from War of 1812

John Richardson, of Britain's 41st Regiment, was present at Fort Amherstburg when Tecumseh, with "powerful energy and gesticulation," rebuked Henry Procter. The admiration of the sixteen-year-old volunteer for the great warrior, "whose gallant and impetuous spirit could ill brook retiring before his enemies," was complete and abiding; he would later recall "that ardour of expression" in Tecumseh's eye, a look "so anticipatory of coming success" that it "could not fail to endear him to the soldier hearts of those who stood around, and inspire in them a veneration and esteem, not even surpassed by what they entertained for their own immediate leader." Here, from a personal history of the war published in 1842, Richardson records the moments immediately following Tecumseh's speech, when Procter chose a course that, within two weeks, would end both his own military career and Tecumseh's life.

─────────────

No sooner had the last words of this startling speech died away upon his lips, than the various chieftains started up to a man, and brandishing their tomahawks in the most menacing manner, vociferated their approbation of his sentiments. The scene altogether was of the most imposing character. The council room was a large, lofty building, the vaulted roof of which echoed back the wild yell of the Indians; while the threatening attitude and diversified costume of these latter formed a striking contrast with the calm demeanor and military garb of the officers grouped around the walls. The most prominent feature in the picture, however, was Tecumseh. Habited in a close leather dress, his athletic proportions were admirably delineated, while a large plume of white ostrich feathers, by which he was generally distinguished, overshadowing his brow, and contrasting with the darkness of his complexion and the brilliancy of his black and piercing eye, gave a singularly wild and terrific expression to his features. It was evident that he could be terrible. Tranquillity being at length restored, General Procter, through the medium of his interpreters, entered into a more detailed account of the motives by which he was influenced, and finally succeeded in prevailing on the warrior to assent to a second proposal, which was to retire on the Moravian village, distant nearly halfway between Amherstburg and the outposts of the Centre Division, and there await the approach of the enemy.

It having been resolved to move without loss of time, the troops were immediately employed in razing the fortifications, and committing such stores as it was found impossible to remove to the flames, kindled in the various public buildings; and the ports of Detroit and Amherstburg for some days previous to our departure presented a scene of cruel desolation. At length, the baggage waggons and boats having been sent in advance, the troops of the latter garrison commenced their march early in the last week of September, and being joined by those of Detroit, proceeded up the mouth of the Thames, a river navigable for small craft, and separated from that of Detroit by the Lake St. Clair, into which it empties itself. Our movements were extremely dilatory; and although the bridge near Amherstburg, already described in the early part of this narrative, had been destroyed by our rear-guard, it was speedily repaired by the American general who, on the third day after our departure from Amherstburg, crossed the lake in boats; and hastening to overtake us with a corps of five thousand men, was within a few leagues at the moment we approached the position where it was originally intended the little army should entrench itself.

The Moravian village, situated in a small plain, offered every facility of defence, being bounded on one flank by a thick wood, highly favorable to the operations of the Indians, and on the other, by the river Thames, while immediately in front, a deep ravine, covered with brushwood, and commanded by our guns, presented an obstacle peculiarly unfavorable to the passage of cavalry, of which, we were sufficiently informed, a large portion of the advancing columns consisted. Yet, notwithstanding the excellence of the position, from some singularly selfish motive, the project was entirely abandoned. On the evening of the 4th, the enemy had captured our boats and, with them, the guard by which they were accompanied. Lieut. Holmes, of the Provincial Dragoons, an active and enterprising officer, who, with a small detachment of men, was of great service to the army during its retreat, also fell into the hands of the enemy on this day, having been taken while in the act of swimming his horse across the Chatham river, on his return from destroying some bridges. On the 5th, at one o'clock in the afternoon, we were within two miles of the Moravian village, but in defiance of that repeated experience which should have taught us the hopelessness of combating a concealed enemy, the troops were ordered to defile into the heart of a wood, not very close it is true, yet through the interstices of which it was impossible for the view to extend itself beyond a distance of twenty paces, much less to discover objects bearing so close a resemblance to the bark and foliage of the trees and bushes as the costume of the Americans; whereas, on the contrary, the glaring red of the troops formed a point of relief on which the eye could not fail to dwell. In this position we continued to remain during two hours, our left wing extending to the road, in which a solitary six pounder was posted, and the right flanked by the Indians to the number of 1,000 under Tecumseh; when the bugles of the enemy sounding at length to the attack, the engagement commenced. The result of an affair, against a body of such numerical superiority, and under such circumstances, may easily be anticipated. Closely pressed on every hand, and principally by a strong corps of mounted riflemen, the troops were finally compelled to give way, and completely hemmed in by their assailants, had no other alternative than to lay down their arms—about fifty men only, with a single officer of the regiment, (Lieut. Bullock), contriving, when all was lost, to effect their escape through the wood. General Procter, mounted on an excellent charger, and accompanied by his personal staff, sought safety in flight at the very commencement of the action, and being pursued for some hours by a detachment of mounted Kentucky riflemen, was in imminent danger of falling into their hands.

In this affair, I had an opportunity of witnessing the cruel dexterity and despatch with which the Indians use the tomahawk and scalping knife. A Kentucky rifleman, who had been dismounted within a few yards of the spot where I stood,—and the light company, to which I was attached, touched the left flank of the Indians—was fired at by three warriors of the Delaware tribe. The unfortunate man received their several balls in his body, yet, although faint from loss of blood, he made every exertion to save himself. Never was fear so strongly depicted on the human countenance, and the man's hair (for he was uncovered) absolutely seemed to me to stand on end, as he attempted to double a large fallen tree, in order to elude the weapons of his enemies. The foremost of his pursuers was a tall powerful man—a chief whom I well knew, having, only a few days before we commenced our retreat, obtained from him a saddle in exchange for a regimental coat, purchased at the sale of the effects of Lieut. Sutherland, wounded at Maguaga. When within twelve or fifteen paces of the rifleman, he raised and threw his tomahawk, and with such precision and force, that it immediately opened the skull, and extended him motionless on the earth. Laying down his rifle, he drew forth his knife, and after having removed the hatchet from the brain, proceeded to make a circular incision throughout the scalp. This done, he grasped the bloody instrument between his teeth, and placing his knees on the back of his victim, while at the same time he fastened his fingers in the hair, the scalp was torn off without much apparent difficulty and thrust, still bleeding, into his bosom. The warrior then arose, and after having wiped his knife on the clothes of the unhappy man, returned it to its sheath, grasping at the same time the arms he had abandoned, and hastening to rejoin his comrades. All this was the work of a few minutes.

While this brief scene was enacting, the main body of the enemy, who had by this time succeeded in breaking through our centre, and had wheeled up, in order to take the Indians in flank, moved rapidly upon us in every direction; so that the resistance the light company had hitherto opposed, was now utterly hopeless of any successful result. Persuaded moreover, from the sudden cessation of the firing in that direction, that our centre and left (for the wood intercepted them from our view), had been overcome, we, at the suggestion and command of Lieutenant Hailes, the only officer with us, prepared to make good our retreat, but, instead of going deeper into the wood as we purposed, we mistook our way, and found ourselves unexpectedly in the road; when, on glancing to the right, we beheld, at a distance of about five hundred yards, the main body of our men disarmed—grouped together, and surrounded by American troops. On turning to the left, as we instinctively did, we saw a strong body of cavalry coming toward us, evidently returning from some short pursuit, and slowly walking their horses. At the head of these, and dressed like his men, in Kentucky hunting frocks, was a stout elderly officer whom we subsequently knew to be Governor Shelby, and who the moment he beheld us emerging from the wood, galloped forward and brandishing his sword over his head, cried out with stentorian lungs "Surrender surrender, it's no use resisting, all your people are taken, and you had better surrender." There was no alternative. The channel to escape had been closed by the horsemen in the wood, as well as those in the road, and a surrender was unavoidable. We accordingly moved down to join our captured comrades, as directed by Governor Shelby, yet I well recollect burying my musket in the mud, which was very deep, in order to avoid giving it up to the enemy. Perfectly also do I recollect the remark made by a tall Kentuckian as I passed by him to the group—"Well I guess now, you tarnation little Britisher, who'd calculate to see such a bit of a chap as you here?" But I heeded not the sneer of the Kentuckian. My eye had fallen and rested upon a body of American Indians, about fifty in number, from some one of whose tomahawks, I apprehended the deathblow—I had seen their weapons too often exercised (and indeed, as has been seen, only a few minutes before) to feel anything like security. But my fear was without foundation. As I watched them more narrowly, I found that their countenances wore an expression of concern, and that, so far from seeking to injure us, they seemed rather to regret our fate. Nor is this at all unlikely, as it was well known that the greater portion of the warriors who had taken up the hatchet in favor of the United States, had been induced to do so from compulsion alone. This little anecdote, otherwise too personal perhaps, affords another in support of the many striking evidences of the strong attachment of the Indians for the British.

The most serious loss we sustained on this occasion was that of the noble and unfortunate Tecumseh. Only a few minutes

before the clang of the American bugles was heard ringing
through the forest, and inspiriting to action, the haughty
Chieftain had passed along our line, pleased with the manner
in which his left was supported, and seemingly sanguine of
success. He was dressed in his usual deer skin dress, which admirably displayed his light yet sinewy figure, and in his handkerchief, rolled as a turban over his brow, was placed a
handsome white ostrich feather, which had been given to him
by a near relation of the writer of this narrative, and on which
he was ever fond of decorating himself, either for the Hall of
Council or the battle field. He pressed the hand of each officer
as he passed, made some remark in Shawnee, appropriate to
the occasion, which was sufficiently understood by the expressive signs accompanying them, and then passed away forever
from our view. Towards the close of the engagement, he had
been personally opposed to Colonel Johnson, commanding
the American mounted riflemen, and having severely wounded
that officer with a ball from his rifle, was in the act of springing
upon him with his tomahawk, when his adversary drew a pistol
from his belt, and shot him dead on the spot. It has since been
denied by the Americans that the hero met his death from the
hand of Colonel Johnson. Such was the statement on the day
of the action, nor was it ever contradicted at that period. There
is every reason to infer then that the merit (if any merit could
attach to the destruction of all that was noble and generous in
savage life), of having killed Tecumseh, rests with Colonel
Johnson. The merit of having flayed the body of the fallen
brave, and made razor strops of his skin, rests with his immediate followers. This too has been denied, but denial is vain. On
the night of the engagement, when seated around a fire kindled
in the forest, partaking, on the very battle ground, of the meat
which Gen. Harrison's aids-de-camp were considerately and
hospitably toasting for us on long pointed sticks, or skewers,
and which, half-famished as we were, we greedily ate without
the accompaniment of either salt or bread, the painful subject
was discussed, and it is not less an eulogy to the memory of the
high-minded Tecumseh, than a justice to that of General Harrison to add, that that officer was the first to deplore his death;
while the sentiments he expressed, when the circumstance and

manner of his fall were made known, were such as to reflect credit on himself, both as a man, a Christian, and a soldier.

Doubts as to the fact of Tecumseh having fallen at all at the Moraviantown, have, in the same spirit of party which has denied to Colonel Johnson the act of having shot him, been entertained; and it has even been asserted that the mutilated remains which were supposed to have been his, were in reality those of another Chief. Would for the honor of humanity it had been so: but this is incorrect. Several of the officers of the 41st, on being apprized of his fall, went, accompanied by some of General Harrison's Staff, to visit the spot where Tecumseh lay, and there they identified (for they knew well) in the mangled corpse before them, all that remained of the late powerful and intelligent chieftain. Of the pain with which the sight was viewed, and the deep regret with which his death was regarded, no stronger evidence can be given than in the fact that there was scarcely an officer of the captured Division who, as he reposed his head upon the rude log, affording him the only pillow that night, did not wholly lose sight of his own unfortunate position in the more lively emotion produced by the untimely fate of the lamented and noble Indian. It has ever been a source of profound regret to me that I was not present at this inspection, for although the sight of the mutilated hero could not have failed to inflict upon my heart pain of the most poignant kind, it would have been at least a consolation to have seen the last of his remains on earth: and this not more from the reverence and honor in which I had, and have, ever held the Warrior, than from the opportunity I should now possess of bearing attestation to the fact and manner of his fall, from my own positive and personal observation. I was not, however, aware of the purposed visit until the party had returned, and made it the subject of conversation, in presence of General Harrison, as already stated. Nor was there time afforded for remedying the unintentional omission.

William Henry Harrison: Proclamation

The Battle of the Thames was a significant victory for the United States. Although casualties on both sides were light, some six hundred British were captured, Procter was disgraced, and Tecumseh was killed. British power and influence in the Old Northwest declined precipitously, and the Indian confederacy was shattered. On October 14, at Fort Detroit, William Henry Harrison concluded an armistice with the Indians, laying the groundwork for a binding treaty. For the rest of the war the United States would control the northwestern frontier and exercise a decisive influence over its Indian population.

A PROCLAMATION

DETROIT Oct. 16, 1813

An Armistice having been concluded between the United States and the tribes of Indians called Miamies, Potawatamies, Eel river Miamies, Weas, Ottoways, Chippeways, and Wyandots, to continue until the pleasure of the government of the former shall be known; I do hereby make known the same to all whom it may concern. The armistice is preparatory to a general council, to be held with these different tribes; and, until its termination, they have been permitted to retire to their hunting-grounds, and there to remain unmolested, if they behave themselves peaceably. They have surrendered into our hands hostages from each tribe; and have agreed immediately to restore all our prisoners in their possession, and unite with us in the chastisement of any Indians who may commit any aggression upon our frontiers. Under these circumstances, I exhort all citizens living upon the frontiers to respect the terms of said armistice, and neither to engage in nor countenance any expedition against their person or property; leaving to the government, with whom the constitution has left it, to pursue such course, with respect to the Indians as they may think most compatible with sound policy and the best interests of the country.

WM. H. HARRISON

Red Jacket: Message to Erastus Granger

October 21, 1813

Red Jacket, the aging chief of the Wolf tribe of the Seneca nation, was spokesman for the Seneca and Onondaga Indians residing on Buffalo Creek in upstate New York. In 1813 he and some five hundred fellow warriors joined the Americans on the Niagara in several battles against the British. General Peter B. Porter of the New York militia admired Red Jacket, writing that he was "endowed with great intellectual powers, and . . . as an orator, was not only unsurpassed, but un-equalled . . . by any of his contemporaries." Here Red Jacket, ad-dressing U.S. Indian agent Erastus Granger, demands fair payment for services provided by his people to Porter and his successors at Fort George.

––––––––––––––

Brother, we are rejoiced to meet you in health, for which we are grateful to the Great Spirit. Brother, our feelings were hurt, that after the willingness we have shown to assist our brethren of the United States in the war in which they are en-gaged, our friendship should be suspected. Our dissatisfaction arose from another cause.

Brother: General Porter and myself had promised our war-riors that they should have pay for one month's services for guarding the lines. General Wilkinson also promised them pay for their services, but went away and told them that General McClure would fulfil the promise made to them. We have not received pay according to promise. We think you were not au-thorized to promise us. We think we are trifled with. We were promised that all horses and cattle should be free plunder. We took horses; we had to give them up. We have been deceived. We, the Senecas and Onondagas, gave up the property we took. The Oneidas, whom you have educated and taught your habits, gave up nothing. We want you to state this to the President. We want permission to go to Washington. We are an independent nation. We have taken up arms in your favor. We want to know on what footing we stand. We know not how long the war will last. It was agreed by all at Fort George that we should send word. We want a small deputation from the friendly Indians at the westward to meet us at Washington. Let us unite, and in one season more we will drive the red coats from this island. They are foreigners. This country belongs to us and the United States. We do not fight for conquest, but we fight for our rights—for our lands—for our country. We hope our request will be granted. We trust that you will make our request known to the President and that we shall not be deceived.

John Le Couteur to Philip Bouton

October 1813 found Lieutenant John Le Couteur, of the 104th British Regiment of Foot, on garrison duty in Kingston, and a boarder in the home of a well-to-do widow. On the 21st, he wrote in his journal, "I entered my nineteenth year" by reading passages from favorite English novels "to a coterie of sweet girls, three or four, whom the old Lady permitted to listen to me." That evening his commander, Major Thomas Hunter, called to see him. "There are thirteen thousand American troops at Sackets Harbor with a design to attack this place," Hunter told him, not knowing that the Americans had their eye on Montreal, 180 miles down the St. Lawrence River. Three days later Le Couteur wrote the following letter to his uncle Philip Bouton, who lived near Le Couteur's family home on the isle of Jersey, in the English Channel.

———————

Kingston, 24th October, 1813

My Dear Bouton,

How to set about framing an excuse for my long silence to you, I know not. I shall trust to your generosity, and return you my Sincerest thanks for yours of the 11th June. I received it last month at Niagara and would have answered it from thence, had not an order from Sir George, for our proceeding to Kingston with the utmost dispatch, prevented it. You can not conceive how happy we all were at the Idea of leaving that detested place, where, only misery, wretchedness, Broken heads and no honour or credit can be met with.

I had not mentioned to any one of the family that we were employed against the Enemy's Indians, and although deserted by our own, owing to the mismanagement of our affairs of this at all events I am not a competent Judge, but I can assure you, that neither to us or our enemies, is the Death whoop an agreeable sound. The Indians are cunning, cowardly and revengeful in the highest degree, *brave* only when their enemy is Broken or flying, and then the tomahawk and scalping knife are liberally made use of. I have witnessed it with horror, but an Indian if you face him, will never stand, this, we have well impressed on the minds of our men, and they fear them not. The Americans on the Ohio and Kentucky lands, are nearly Indians, they use the Scalping knife and Tomahawk, and are merely a civilized Savage, or rather without the Virtues of an Indian and all the vice and evil which civilized life sets forth. Some of the tribes, I have met with, are Brave, generous and honorable such as the Otawas, Cocknawagas and some others whose Jaw-breaking names I do not recollect. The Mohawks of whom we have all heard so much, are mostly cowards, thieves and dirty. They do not however make a practice of scalping which the others do, I shall endeavour to procure one as a *relic*.

One morning in a Skirmish after they had scalped 45 and taken 14, who were in no small terror of being similarly treated, they were dressing their scalps and some of them after picking of the flesh, eat it. This a fact. Let the Ladies pass their comments, and rejoice that they are blessed in a country where such deeds were never heard of; happy little Island.

I had the pleasure, [   ] of seeing the Grand Falls of Niagara. They gave me an impression I shall never forget or ever feel again, so sublimely grand you feel a terrible delight, a kind of horror, at the immense body of water forever falling, and the great lakes from which it flows. I crept to the edge of Table rock and looked over and almost shrunk back at the dreadful depth below me. The air was beautiful and the Sun shining on the Spray, made the beautiful rainbow. I had so much wished to see the charms of the Naiad of the Falls, Miss Willson, and her sprightly wit were the next object of our attention; after a cold collation prepared for us by the said Lady and well partaken of by your humble servant, We returned and 13 miles off, near the camp, we still heard the roaring Falls.

I am now, my dear Bouton, in about as comfortable quarters as a poor, wandering Soldier of fortune need be, at a Widow Lady's who has an agreeable daughter and lives in the handsome Style in Kingston. Thanks to my impudence & [   ], and the kind hospitality of my Landlady Mrs. Robison. They are a Yankee family, and have several relatives in the American army and navy. Some hard, hitherto I have been fortunate in my acquaintances, I hope I shall continue so. I am just now, confined to the house by an inflammation on my knee which the Ladies have been very careful of, was much as I can walk about pretty well but have been in great distress for fear the enemy should make their attack before I can run about as usual.

By the by, the Americans have assembled a force of 13,000 men at Sackets Harbor under Genl. Wilkinson and intend attacking this, I trust we shall give them a warm and spirited reception, as they have no right or pretension whatever in attacking and disturbing the peaceable inhabitants of Kingston. The rascals, they are worse than Frenchmen, I would not give quarter to a [   ] of them. Pardon my warmth. Their repulse I hope soon to write you an account of, perhaps they mean it only as a diversion and will attack Montreal.

It is very singular our Fleet and theirs have not yet come to a decisive engagement, all summer have they been growling and snapping at one another [   ] Chauncey engaged Sir James last month; We saw the engagement take place and were not a little in expectation, it lasted nearly three hours and nothing on either side terminated. Chauncey had the weather gage, his long guns carried away the Wolfe's Main and fore top masts, and they fell by the board, which for the time so disabled him, he could only make use of 5 guns, and the Navy say, Chauncey must either be a coward or a Jackass, for not capturing all our fleet which they have already done on the Upper Lakes after [   ] battle. You will have heard the particulars long ago, I do not like repeating them, as I feel indignant at our proceedings. It will be a miracle if Poor Sir James does not get thrashed here also. He is not well supported—enough of Politics.

I feel proud, to hear of the progress in arms, made by the youth of my dear native Isle. Oh, if ever it is attacked, may I be there to share the honour of defending it. Pray give my kind regards and congratulations to Col. Touzel, on the Subject nay, even to my friends the Inspectors, whom I hope to breakfast with again at Mrs. LaPerise. [   ] of the deeds of the 104th, Bouton, as yet they have ever behaved gallantly, I am proud to say, but it is the Skeleton of a Regt., my own compy. marched 95, fine lads from Fredericton and are now 25, The remains of as pretty a Light company as most regts. can boast of, I sicken when I think of it, it is truly mortifying. If DeCarteret of the 96th is in Jersey yet, remember me most kindly to him, I expected to have seen him in this country, a report having reached us they were ordered out here.

I hope my Dear Grandpa and all the Family continues well in health, give them my kindest love and regards, as well as to all my fine friends in St. Aubins. [   ] will have received my letter long since, I expect one from him soon. The day I received yours, I was greeted with one from my Mother dated 10th May and another June. They were all very well, Thank God, and had received your gazette which was a most agreeable treat.

Adieu my Dear Bouton, with my best wishes for your health and happiness, Believe me, ever yours faithfully and affectionately yours,

Le Couteur

Robert Purdy to James Wilkinson

October 26, 1813

In 1813, Montreal, with a population of about 15,000, was the largest city in British North America and a crucial base for the British forces on the St. Lawrence River. Late in the year's campaign, Secretary of War John Armstrong conceived an ambitious two-pronged assault on the city, one that would marshal the largest assemblage of U.S. regulars prior to the Civil War. One army, starting from Sackets Harbor, was led by Major General James Wilkinson, a skilled self-promoter prone to quarrels, intrigue, and controversy. The other army, starting from Cumberland Head, New York, was led by Major General Wade Hampton, who refused to serve under Wilkinson and asked to be directed from Washington. Wilkinson's army was routed at the Battle of Crysler's Farm, which was fought just north of the St. Lawrence a hundred miles southwest of Montreal. Hampton's army came within forty miles of the city, but was stymied by cold, wet weather, and a well-prepared British and French Canadian force along the Châteauguay River, near present-day Ormstown, Quebec. Colonel Robert Purdy, who led one flank of Hampton's army, reconstructs the American defeat.

I arrived at Cumberland-head September 16th, 1813, and on the 18th took command of the 4th regiment of infantry, stationed at that place. The army, consisting of about four thousand men, was composed principally of recruits who had been but a short time in service, and had not been exercised with that rigid discipline so essentially necessary to constitute the soldier. They had, indeed, been taught various evolutions, but a spirit of subordination was foreign to their views. On the 19th, orders were issued for the whole army, except a squadron of horse and the artillery, to embark in bateaux. The army got under way, preceded by the light corps, and flanked on the right by the navy, and arrived at Chazy at 12 o'clock at night, lay on their arms, embarked again soon after sunrise the next morning, proceeded down the lake as far as Champlain, and up Champlain river the distance of four miles, where we landed, and immediately marched to Odletown. The light corps, who preceded the other troops some hours, surprised and defeated a guard of the enemy at that place. We remained at Odletown until the middle of the next day, during which time a want of system in the management of the army was readily discovered by every military man, that led to apprehensions for the safety of the troops, should the enemy oppose with any considerable force. The army returned to Champlain the 21st, the 22d to Chazy, and the day following commenced the route to Chateaugay. The whole of this march, a distance of more than seventy miles, was very disagreeable; the officers were not permitted to take with them the necessaries, much less the conveniences of life, and were compelled to abandon clothing and other things essentially necessary to preserve the body in health. We forebore complaint, endured every privation, presuming the commanding officer had sufficient reasons for his conduct, and concluding it was pro bono publico. The scene has past, and time sufficient has elapsed to have discovered those reasons, had they existed; none have been found; on the contrary, circumstances have demonstrated that it was a useless and unnecessary sacrifice of both public and private property. The army remained at Chateaugay twenty-six days, and on the 21st October commenced an excursion into the enemy's country. The first brigade followed the course of the Chateaugay river to Spear's, the distance of eighteen miles and upwards, and there met the second brigade, which had taken a nearer and more convenient route. The march was very fatiguing, equalled only by another that soon followed. Credit is due to both the officers and soldiers for their orderly conduct, patience, and perseverance, in surmounting the incredible obstacles the enemy threw in their way. On the 25th, a difficult and very fatiguing expedition was planned, and the execution of it assigned to the first brigade, which had been for some time previous, and still remained, under my command. The design was to cut off the retreat of a body of the enemy, supposed to be encamped on the banks of the Chateaugay, six miles distant. With this intention the first brigade was ordered to cross the river at night, march silently down, and recross at a ford two miles below the enemy, and attack them in rear, giving a preconcerted signal, while the second brigade moved down the road in front. We commenced the march at sundown, and by sun-rise the next morning had gained only six miles. Here we were discovered by the enemy, and fired on from the opposite side of the river. During that night we were repeatedly misled by the guides, who knew nothing of the country, having never been that way, and at the time we were attacked, they had led us into a thick cedar growth or swamp on the banks of the river, and immediately opposite the enemy's position, and knew not how to extricate us. Incredible as it may appear, General Hampton entrusted nearly one half of his army, and those his best troops, to the guidance of men, each of whom repeatedly assured him that they were not acquainted with the country, and were not competent to direct such an expedition. At the same time General Hampton told me he had a man by the name of Smith, who had a perfect knowledge of the country, and whom he promised to send me, but which he neglected to do. The defeat of the expedition was the consequence of this neglect of the Major General. About two o'clock, while receiving an order from Colonel King, Adjutant General, upon the opposite side of the river, to march back four miles, and then ford the river and join the 2d brigade, the enemy made a furious attack on the column by a great discharge of musketry, accompanied by the yells of the savages. Unfortunately, the word "retreat" was heard, which, for a short time, spread confusion among the several corps. A sufficient number, however, remained firm, and the enemy was soon compelled to retire. Towards sun-down I sent General Hampton a request that a regiment might be ordered down to cover my landing on the opposite side of the river; but judge my surprise, on receiving intelligence that he had retreated with the second brigade nearly three miles. Thus was I deserted, without the smallest guard to cover my landing. To what cause shall it be attributed, that the General ordered a retreat, and that too at the moment when the presence of the second brigade was required, or could be useful, as soon afterwards he declared "he should be willing to compound with the first brigade for five hundred men." The wounded had previously been conveyed across on rafts, which made a removal of my brigade absolutely necessary for their protection.

An attempt was accordingly made, and a floating bridge soon constructed of old logs, found on the margin of the river. The enemy discovering our disposition, commenced a firing from the opposite side, and killed several while crossing. Major Snelling, with about a hundred men, effected a landing, and joined the main body. The remainder of my force, exhausted by the excessive exertions of the preceding night, and weary with the fatigues of the day, not having had a moment either for rest or refreshment, were compelled to endure the privation of sleep another night. We retired two or three miles and took a position. At about twelve o'clock the enemy came up and made an attack upon us, but were soon routed. The men at this time were formed, and lying on the ground they were to occupy in case of an attack, and were ordered to, and did immediately rise, seize their arms, and remain under them the residue of the night. An excessively heavy rain prevented the firing both of the enemy and ourselves, except occasionally a single gun from the former. Our troops were ordered not to fire, but, in case of a repetition of attack, to charge bayonets; this was accordingly done. The enemy charged several times, and as often were put to flight. It is observable in this place, that, so greatly were the men overpowered by fatigue, though in a situation every way dangerous, and in which they had every reason to believe they should be sallied upon by the enemy every moment, many were unable to conquer their disposition to sleep, and it was not in the power of the officers to keep them awake. It was on the morning of this last attack that the General expressed his apprehensions for the first brigade, and made the declaration above quoted. The next morning we crossed the river, and joined General Hampton; on the 28th the army retreated four miles, and on the 30th and 31st marched back to Chateaugay. The troops, at the times of the attack, were not in a situation to endure further fatigue; and it is an indubitable fact, that many of them were so debilitated they were unable to proceed with the brigade on its march from the place of its last attack, and actually did not reach the main body until the day after the brigade had joined it, and some not even until the army had reached the Four Corners of Chateaugay.

Never, to my knowledge, during our march into Canada, and while we remained at the Four Corners, a term of twenty-

six days, did General Hampton ever send off a scouting or reconnoitering party, (except in one or two cases at Spear's, in
Canada, when he detached a few dragoons for this duty) nor
did he, from the time we commenced our march from Cumberland head, to our arrival at Plattsburg, ever order a front,
flank, or rear guard to be kept up, though a great part of the
time we were in situations which evidently required it. True it
is, these guards were occasionally sent out, not, however, by his
order, but by the orders of the officers commanding brigades.

By a general order, dated Chateaugay, November 5, the
General says he has paid the first attention to the sick, and has
granted them indulgences, which created murmurings on the
part of some officers at their posts. It is only necessary here to
observe, that every officer of the army can testify that the sick
were very much neglected as far as regards comfortable quarters and transportation, and that they were strewed along the
roads through which we marched without care or attendance;
and it is presumable that many have died in consequence of
this who might have been saved to themselves if not to the
service. The General, indeed, at the time this order was issued,
which was after our return to the Four Corners, did order
transportation for the sick to Burlington, but this is the only
instance to my knowledge.

The Commissary's Department is worthy of notice. My
order for provision was not sufficient; nor could I obtain any
but by special licence of General Hampton. The commissary
of issues has been constantly in the habit of selling the livers,
&c. of the beeves to officers; and though I represented this to
General Hampton as unusual and improper, he refused to take
any other notice of it than saying, "the Commissary is ac-
countable for all parts of the beef, even to a pound or ounce of
tallow;" nor did he take any notice of another piece of misconduct of the Commissary, that of acting in the capacity of sutler,
but sanctioned it by purchasing of him.

The common practices with General Hampton, of arresting
officers and releasing them without their consent; of releasing
arrested officers without the knowledge or consent of the officers by whom they were arrested (the case of Lieutenant
Morris of the 33d regiment, who was arrested by me on the
charge of cowardice and misconduct before the enemy on

the 26th October, 1813, the time of the skirmish with the enemy at Ormstown, or Chateaugay river, being an instance;) of refusing to arrest officers whom I reported to him as having deserted their posts in time of action; of daily issuing orders and countermanding them, and of interfering in an improper manner with the subordinate commands of the army, as a reference to the orders issued by him will show, mark very strongly the capriciousness of his conduct and the total want of steadiness in his intentions.

Such has been the General's conduct on some occasions, that I have, in common with other officers, been induced to believe that he was under the influence of a too free use of spirituous liquors.

I must, in justice to General Hampton, say, that the expedition he planned, and which I have called "difficult and fatiguing," did, at the time it was suggested to me by him, meet my full approbation, and that I have since seen no reason for changing my opinion of its practicability or usefulness; but I must also say that it required competent guides; and these (as I said before) he promised to furnish me, but did not.

I am of opinion no officer that has served under Major General Hampton, on the late campaign, can, or will contradict this statement.

ROBERT PURDY, *Colonel 4th Infantry.*

A true copy.

R. H. M'PHERSON, *Captain and Secretary.*

November 1813

Charles Ball: from Slavery in the United States: A Narrative of the Life and Adventures of Charles Ball

Charles Ball was born a slave in Calvert County, Maryland, shortly after the American Revolution. In 1805 he was sold to a South Carolina cotton planter, from whom he escaped four years later. He made his way back to the Chesapeake region, where, ever fearful of discovery by bounty hunters, he worked odd jobs, describing himself as a free man of color. When the British occupied Chesapeake Bay in 1813, Ball briefly considered their offer to enlist as a sailor or to settle as a freeman in the West Indies. In the end, he decided to defend the United States by joining the Chesapeake Bay Flotilla under Commodore Joshua Barney. "I did not enlist . . . until December, 1813," Ball recalled in his memoirs, published in 1836. "But as I resided in Calvert County, in the summer of 1813, I had an opportunity to witness many of the evils that followed in the train of war, before I assumed the profession of arms myself."

In the spring of the year 1813, the British fleet came into the bay, and from this time, the origin of the troubles and distresses of the people of the Western Shore, may be dated. I had been employed at a fishery, near the mouth of the Patuxent, from early in March, until the latter part of May, when a British vessel of war came off the mouth of the river, and sent her boats up to drive us away from our fishing ground. There was but little property at the fishery that could be destroyed; but the enemy cut the seines to pieces, and burned the sheds belonging to the place. They then marched up two miles into the country, burned the house of a planter, and brought away with them several cattle, that were found in his fields. They also carried off more than twenty slaves, which were never again restored to their owner; although, on the following day, he went on board the ship, with a flag of truce, and offered a large ransom for these slaves.

These were the first black people whom I had known to desert to the British, although the practice was afterwards so common. In the course of this summer, and the summer of 1814, several thousand black people deserted from their masters and mistresses, and escaped to the British fleet. None of these people were ever regained by their owners, as the British naval officers treated them as free people, and placed them on the footing of military deserters.

In the fall of this year, a lady by the name of Wilson, who owned more than a hundred slaves, lost them all in one night, except one man, who had a wife and several children on an adjoining estate, and as he could not take his family with him, on account of the rigid guard that was kept over them, he refused to go himself.

The slaves of Mrs. Wilson effected their escape in the following manner. Two or three of the men having agreed amongst themselves, that they would run away and go to the fleet, they stole a canoe one night, and went off to the ship that lay nearest the shore. When on board, they informed the officer of the ship, that their mistress owned more than a hundred other slaves, whom they had left behind them. They were then advised to return home, and remain there until the next night, and then bring with them to the beach, all the slaves on the plantation—the officer promising that he would send a detachment of boats to the shore, to bring them off. This advice was followed, and the fugitives returned before day to their cabins, on the plantation of their mistress.

On the next night, having communicated their plans to some of their fellow-slaves, they rose about midnight, and partly by persuasion, partly by compulsion, carried off all the slaves on the plantation, with the exception of the man already named. When they reached the beach, they kindled a fire, as had been concerted with the British officers, and the boats of the fleet came off, and removed this whole party on board. In the morning, when the overseer of Mrs. Wilson arose, and went to call his hands to the field, he found only empty cabins in the quarter, with a single man remaining, to tell what had become of his fellows.

This was the greatest disaster that had befallen any individual in our neighborhood, in the course of the war; and as the sufferer was a lady, much sympathy was excited in her favor. A large number of gentlemen met together, for the purpose of endeavoring to devise some means of recovering the fugitive slaves. Their consultations ended in sending a deputation of gentlemen on board the fleet, with a flag of truce, to solicit the restoration of the deserters, either as a matter of favor, or for such ransom as might be agreed upon. Strong hopes were entertained, that the runaways might be induced voluntarily to return to the service of their mistress, as she had never treated them with great severity.

To accomplish, if possible, this latter end, I was spoken to, to go along with the flag of truce, in the assumed character of the servant of one of the gentlemen who bore it; but in the real character of the advocate of the mistress, for the purpose of inducing her slaves to return to her service.

We went on board the ship in the afternoon, and I observed, that the gentlemen who went with me, were received by the British officers with very little ceremony. The captain did not show himself on deck, nor were the gentlemen invited into his cabin. They were shown into a large square room under the first deck of the ship, which was a 74, and here, a great number of officers came to talk to them, and ask them questions concerning the war, and the state of the country.

The whole of the runaways were on board this ship, lounging about on the main deck, or leaning against the sides of the ship's bulwarks. I went amongst them, and talked to them a long time, on the subject of returning home; but found that their heads were full of notions of liberty and happiness in some of the West India islands.

In the afternoon, all the gentlemen, except one, returned home in the boat that they had come off in. The gentleman who remained on board, was a young man of pleasing manners and lively conversation, who appeared, even before the other gentlemen who had come with the flag had left the ship, to have become quite a favorite with the younger British officers. Permission was obtained of the British captain, for this young gentleman to remain on board a few days, for the purpose, as he alleged, of seeing the curiosities of the ship. He had permission to retain me with him as his servant; and I was instructed to exert myself to the utmost, to prevail on the runaway slaves to return to their mistress. The ship lay at anchor off the shore of Calvert county, until the second night after I came on board, when, from some cause which I was not able to understand, this ship and all the rest of the fleet, got under weigh, and stood down the Bay to the neighborhood of Tangier Islands, where she again cast anchor, soon after sunrise the next morning, in ten fathoms water. I was now at least seventy or eighty miles from home, in a ship of the public enemies of the country, and liable to be carried off to sea, and to be conveyed to the most distant part of the world.

To increase my alarm, about noon of this day, a sloop of war cast anchor under the stern of our ship; and all the black people that were with us, were immediately removed on board the sloop. I was invited, and even urged to go with the others, who, I was told, were bound to the Island of Trinidad, in the West Indies, where they would have lands given to them, and where they were to be free. I returned many thanks for their kind offers; but respectfully declined them; telling those who made them, that I was already a freeman, and though I owned no land myself, yet I could have plenty of land of other people to cultivate.

In the evening, the sloop weighed anchor, and stood down the Bay, with more than two hundred and fifty black people on board. I watched her as she sailed away from us, until the darkness of the night shut her out from my sight. In the morning she was not to be seen. What became of the miserable mass of black fugitives, that this vessel took to sea, I never learned.

My mission was now at an end, and I spoke this day to the young gentleman, under whose care I was, to endeavor to procure some means of conveying both him and me back again to Calvert. My protector seemed no less embarrassed than I was, and informed me, that the officers of the ship said they would not land us on the Western Shore, within less than two weeks. I was obliged to content myself in the best way I could, in my confinement on ship-board; and I amused myself by talking to the sailors, and giving them an account of the way in which I had passed my life on the tobacco and cotton plantations; in return for which, the seamen gave many long stories of their adventures at sea, and of the battles they had been engaged in.

I lived well, whilst on board this ship, as they allowed me to share in a mess. In compensation for their civility, I gave them many useful instructions in the art of taking fish in the Bay. This great ship lay at anchor like a vast castle, moored by the cable; but there were many small vessels, used as tenders to the fleet, that were continually sailing up and down the Bay, by night, as well as by day, in pursuit of anything that they might fall in with, that they could take from the Americans. Whilst I was on board, I saw more than thirty vessels, chiefly Bay craft, brought to our anchorage, and there burned, after being stripped of everything valuable that could be taken from them.

The people who manned and navigated these vessels, were made prisoners, and dispersed amongst the several ships of the fleet, until they could be removed to Halifax, or the West Indies. One day a small schooner was seen standing out of the mouth of Nanticoke river, and beating up the Bay. Chase was immediately given by several of the light vessels belonging to the fleet, and continued until nightfall, when I could no longer see the sails; but the next day, the British vessels returned, bringing in their company, the little schooner, which was manned by her owner, who acted as captain, and two boys. On board the schooner, besides her crew, were several passengers, seven in number, I believe. The people were taken out of this vessel, which was laden with Indian corn, and after her cargo had been removed, she was burned in view of her owner, who seemed much affected at the sight, and said that it was all the property he owned in the world, and that his wife and children were now beggars. The passengers and crew of this little vessel, were all retained as prisoners of war, on board the 74, in which I was; and were shut up every night in a room on the lower gun-deck. In this room there were several port-holes, which were suffered to remain open for the benefit of the air.

After these people had been on board three or four days, a boat's crew, that had been out somewhere in the evening, when they returned to the ship, tied the boat with a long rope to one of the halyards of the ship, and left the boat floating near the ship's bows. Some time after night, the tide turned, moved the boat along the side of the ship, and floated it directly under the port-holes of the prisoner's room. The night was dark and warm, and I had taken a station on the upper deck, and was leaning over the bulwarks, when my attention was drawn towards the water, by hearing something drop into the boat that lay along side. Dark as it was, I could see the forms of men passing out of the port-holes into the boat. In less than two minutes, nine persons had entered the boat; and I then heard a low whisper, which I could not understand, but immediately afterwards, saw the boat drifting with the tide; which convinced me that she was loose, and that the prisoners were in her. I said nothing, and in a short time the boat was out of sight. She had, however, not been long gone, when the watch on deck passed near me, and looking over the side of the ship, called to the officer on deck, that the yawl was gone. The officer on deck instantly called to some one below to examine the room of the prisoners; and received for answer, that the prisoners had fled. A gun was immediately fixed under me, on one of the lower decks; the ship's bells were tolled; numerous blue lights were made ready, and cast high into the air, which, performing a curve in the atmosphere, illuminated the face of the water all the way from the ship to the place where they fell. The other ships in the fleet all answered, by firing guns, casting out lights, and ringing their large bells. Three boats put off from our ship, in search of the fugitives, with as little delay as possible; and, after being absent more than an hour, returned without finding those who had escaped.

This affair presented one of the finest night scenes that can well be imagined. The deep thunder of the heavy artillery, as it broke upon the stillness of the night, and re-echoed from the distant shores; the solemn and mournful tones of the numerous bells, as they answered each other from ship to ship, as the sounds rose in the air, and died away in the distance, on the wide expanse of waters; with the shouts of the seamen, and the pale and ghastly appearance of the blue lights, as they rose into the atmosphere, and then descended and died away in the water—all combined together, to affect both the eye and the ear, in a manner the most impressive.

One of the prisoners remained in the ship; not having courage to undertake, with his companions, the daring and dangerous exploit of escaping from the ship in her own boat. When the morning came, this man explained to the officers of the ship, the whole plan that had been devised, and pursued by his companions. When they found that the boat had floated under the port-holes of their room, some one of the number proposed to the rest, to attempt to escape, as the oars of the boat had been left in her; but a difficulty suggested itself, at the outset, which was this; the oars could not be worked on the boat without making a great noise, sufficient to alarm the watch on deck. To avoid this, one of the prisoners said he would undertake to pull off his coat, and muffle one of the oars with it, and scull the boat until they should be clear of the fleet; when they could lay both oars on the boat, and row to shore. We lay much nearer to the Western Shore, than we were to the Eastern, but this man said, the design of the prisoners was to pull to the Eastern Shore. All the boats that went from our ship pulled for the Western Shore, and by this means the prisoners escaped, without being seen.

The captain of the ship was much enraged at the escape of these prisoners, and swore he would be avenged of the Yankees in a short time. In this, he was as good as his word; for the very next day, he fitted out an expedition, consisting of eleven long boats, and more than two hundred men, who landed on the Western Shore, and burned three houses, with all their furniture, and killed a great number of cattle.

The officer who headed this expedition, brought back with him a large silk handkerchief full of silver spoons, and other articles of silver plate. I saw him exhibit these trophies of his valor amongst his brother officers, on the deck of the ship. After I had been on board nearly a week, a furious north-east storm came on and blew for three days, accompanied with frequent gusts of rain. In the evening of the second day, we saw two schooners standing down the Bay, and sailing close on the wind, so as to pass between the fleet and the Eastern Shore. As it was dangerous for large ships to approach much nearer the Eastern Shore than where we lay, several of the tenders of the fleet, amounting in all to more than a dozen, were ordered, by signal, to intercept the strange sails, and bring them to the fleet.

The tender got under weigh and stood before the wind, for the purpose of encountering the schooners, as they came down the Bay. These schooners proved to be two heavy armed American privateers, and when the tenders approached them a furious battle commenced, with canon, which lasted more than an hour, and until the privateers had passed quite below the anchorage, of the fleet.

Several of the tenders were much damaged in their hulls and rigging; and it was said that they lost more than twenty men. I could not perceive that the privateers sustained the least injury, as they never shortened sail, nor altered their course, until they had passed to the windward of all the ships of the fleet, when they changed their bearing, and stood for the Capes of Virginia. There were nearly forty vessels in the fleet, great and small; and yet these two privateers braved the whole of them in open day-light, and went to sea in spite of them.

On the ninth day after we came on hoard, the fleet again moved up the bay, and when we were off the mouth of the Potomac, the captain sent the young gentleman, in whose service I was, together with myself, on shore in his own gig.

The lieutenant who had command of the gig, after he set us on shore, went up to the house of a farmer, whose estate lay open to the bay, and after pilfering the premises of every thing that he could carry away, set fire to the house, and returned to his boat. In the course of the summer and fall of the year 1813, I witnessed many other atrocities, of equal enormity.

I continued with the army after the sack of Washington, and assisted in the defence of Baltimore; but in the fall of 1814, I procured my discharge from the army, and went to work in Baltimore, as a free black man.

James Scott: from Recollections of a Naval Life

James Scott, a lieutenant of the British squadron in Chesapeake Bay, had qualified praise for American seamen. He readily acknowledged that they were brave, yet dismissed their bravery as the high-spirited recklessness of mariners "unused to the fatigue, dangers, and discipline of regular warfare." In his memoirs, published in 1834, he observed that "too great and ridiculous a sense of freedom and liberty on the part of Americans made them spurn the necessary restraint and obedience requisite to ensure success," a trait that almost always gave British "discretion" the upper hand. But if Scott's verdict on American sailors was mixed, his opinion of common American citizens was unequivocally negative, as revealed in this account of his dealings with two Maryland brothers.

I have had no very great intercourse with the Americans, except upon the coast, during the war, therefore my observations are to be considered as not applying to the Union at large; but I confess I was not imbued with any very high idea of their patriotism, whenever their own interest intervened between them and the public weal, nor did I ever observe, except in one or two instances, that they ever hesitated a moment to throw the burden off their own shoulders and lodge it on those of their nearest kin, if they could, or fancied they could, gain a dollar by the transfer. Nor were these instances solitary; they occurred unpleasantly often in my numerous foraging excursions.

A tender with a carronade on board generally accompanied the boats. If the vicinity of our intended landing afforded shelter or ambush for foes, a round shot fired into them previously to disembarking, would at once discover the true state of affairs. These tyros in war (the militia-men) never waited for a second *avant courier* without betraying themselves. Thus assured we landed, and securing our flanks by throwing out pickets to the right and left, we advanced to the farm-house marked out for visitation in comparative security. The farms situated upon peninsulas were preferred, as affording the better means of defence and safety. By adopting these precautions I never was surprised, and our missions were generally peaceably and satisfactorily accomplished; but occasionally a hotheaded bully would arm himself and people, quietly waiting our approach till we were within that distance which enabled each man to make sure of his bird,—they would then let fly a volley, and retreat as fast as the legs of their horses could carry them. This act of treachery was punished by taking the stock without paying for it; but, finding that this system had not the desired effect, and that we lost some valuable lives by this poltroon mode of avenging themselves, we adopted other and severer measures, which speedily brought them to a sense of their own interest, the most powerful lever we met with in bringing them to reason. Whenever this villainous mode was resorted to, we not only took what we required, but, on quitting, set fire to the whole establishment of dead stock, by way of enlightening the proprietor upon his erroneous tactics. This speedily crushed such proceedings; even the most violent democrats (demys, as they styled themselves,) came to the conclusion that it was better to allow the Britishers to deposit their dollars on the table; or, if the poor man's conscience was troublesome, we would indulge him by placing them in a cupboard, the key of which he would composedly turn, and putting it into his pocket, mutter to himself, "It is better than being deprived of my stock, and a blaze made of my habitation, for the sake of having a shot at those G—— d——d Britishers."

I once landed on the eastern shore of Virginia, in Pokomoke Bay, for cattle, at a farmer's who, from the information I had previously obtained, I was aware had a large stock to dispose of. The said farmer was perfectly sensible that no assistance of his military friends could avail him in time to prevent us from executing our intention; but he had observed us from afar, and had ample leisure to cogitate and mature his plans, in which he so completely succeeded that he fairly outwitted himself. I found the farmer quietly seated before his own door, with a face as long as a methodist parson's, and apparently absorbed in melancholy reverie. I accosted him in a most propitiatory tone. "Good morning to you, farmer." Remaining seated, he returned the salutation in a voice so sepulchral that it might have startled any person less decided upon the prosecution of his errand than I was.

"I am come for some stock; how many head of cattle have you?"

"Me! why, my God Almighty! you'll not deprive me of all I've got in this blessed world, I guess?"

"No, no, you shall be well paid for all I take."

"You'll find they are but poor beasts, and not worth your taking, and you'll ruin me: I vow to God I've but three," and at the same time he pointed out precisely that number of half-starved looking animals, which fully corroborated his assertion. Knowing the character of the class I had to deal with, and suspecting that his evasion was merely to gain time, I at once brought the matter to issue by declaring that I was apprized of the number of his cattle, and ready to pay him his price, provided they were immediately brought forward; but, if he gave me the trouble of searching for them, not a cent should he receive, and that I would take him off as a prisoner for his contumacy. He was ready with a string of protestations, which I cut short by calling for his decision. Seeing me determined, and that there was no appeal, he took me on one side from my men, and informed me, in a confidential whisper, that I had certainly mistaken him for his brother, who lived not half a mile distant. He swore by his Maker that he himself was a poor man, but that his brother Zachariah was mighty well to do in the world, and had at least eighty head of cattle, and from two to three hundred sheep. I began to believe that I might have been deceived as to my man, and assured him that, if it was so, and he would direct me where to find his brother's stock, I would promise not to take any of his. Thus secure of my word, he bargained for profound secrecy as to the manner in which I obtained my information. Satisfied on this head, he gave me a full and true account of the whole of his brother's property, with the correct bearings and distance to the place where they were concealed, terminating his treachery by stating that his brother Zachariah would call all the saints in heaven to witness that he was not the proprietor of a single horned beast, but that, if I followed his directions, I could not fail in discovering them.

Armed with this intelligence I proceeded to brother Zac.'s mansion, and, as I had been forewarned by his affectionate brother, he stoutly maintained his poverty, and swore he had not even one four-footed animal belonging to him. Drawing out my watch, I told him I allowed him twenty minutes to bring me as many oxen, for which I should pay him; that, if he did not know where to find them, I would direct my men to their hiding-place, indicating the spot with my finger; adding that, if they were not forthcoming at the stipulated time, I should take the whole of them without payment. These arguments were conclusive: Zachariah went in search of the cattle; I selected the given number, and a few sheep, desiring that they might be driven down to the boats, whither I invited the veracious farmer to accompany me for the purpose of payment. The latter part of the business he appeared to think equivocal, but, addressing me, he exclaimed, "Now I calculate my tarnation brother has told you all about this affair: he is just about as pretty considerable d——d a rogue as there is in the States, I guess."

"He is a poor man, is he not?"

"Now, if you'll believe me, he has more than I have, and by the Lord of heaven, I'll tell you where you may find them;" and I received a circumstantial detail of the quantity, quality, and hiding-place of my first informer's stock. But I had pledged my word, and was bound not to molest the arch hypocrite, for which, I confess, I was heartily sorry.

At the beach these loving sons of the same parents met: never shall I forget the malicious grin that settled upon the countenance of the one, and the conscience-stricken physiognomy of the other as I handed over the dollars. The former then assumed an air of triumph, the latter that of astonishment and disappointment. The sneaking scoundrel, with a face of brass, requested I would not take so many from poor Zachariah, and he would endeavour to obtain some from his neighbours to replace them; but poor Zac. required no such amiable interference, and loudly offered to double the number if I wished it. Having embarked my purchase, I bade adieu to this amiable sample of fraternal love and affection. The authorities, it is to be suspected, were duly favoured with the information that brother Zac. had been guilty of the unpatriotic crime of fingering the Britishers' pelf.

Such, I am sorry to say, is a specimen of the greater part of the inhabitants on the shores of the Chesapeake and its tributary streams. "It is an ill wind that blows nobody good," and in this total disorganization of the bonds that bind man to man, we reaped the benefit that must ever accrue to one of the belligerent parties when disunion and sordid feelings govern the actions of the other. The men who most vehemently proclaimed their patriotism and devotion to their country's service, and a proportionable degree of hatred to the Britishers, when subjected to the scrutiny of Argus' eyes and hearing of jealous ears, were the very men who were privately our best friends, and whose adherence we never doubted so long as we could administer to their self-interest. I cannot therefore be supposed to entertain any very high idea of the inhabitants of the land of liberty, or their integrity of purpose; but in making this avowal it is but justice to declare, as I have before stated, that my experience was circumscribed to within ten miles of the shores of that finest piece of water in the world, the Chesapeake, and its magnificent rivers.

Francis Jeffrey: A Conversation with James Madison

November 18, 1813

In the summer of 1813, Francis Jeffrey, editor of the Whiggish intellectual quarterly *Edinburgh Review*, came to the United States to marry Charlotte Wilkes, daughter of the president of the Bank of New-York. Jeffrey, then a decade into his editorship of the *Review*, was popular among America's political and intellectual elite for his opposition to his government's policies toward the United States, and was received graciously in New York, Philadelphia, Boston, and Washington. The purpose of his visit to Washington was twofold: to interview the President and James Monroe—the latter an admirer and sometimes correspondent—and to obtain safe passage home for himself and his bride. Jeffrey's journal records two meetings with Monroe, during which they discussed the problems of search-and-seizure and of impressment. He met with the President three times, the first two being social calls, the third the private interview recorded here. Jeffrey's first impression of Madison was of "a little mean-looking yellow cunning sour awkward personage—attired in proper black . . . He had altogether the air of a country schoolmaster in mourning for one of his pupils whom he had whipped to death." Such drollery, which Jeffrey shared with Federalist friends in Washington and Boston, became the stuff of transatlantic gossip even before he sailed for England, aboard the cartel ship *Fair American*, in early 1814.

On the 18th we had the honor of dining with the President and having previously learned from Mr. M that it would be proper to take some notice of the indulgence I had met with in the matter of the cartel I took occasion when preparing to take leave in the evening to make my acknowledgments in a short and common place manner enough. This was received in a composed civil way—and then his Excellency proceeded to say that it was the wish of his govt to set an example of the utmost liberality in everything, and to prove to the world that nothing but absolute necessity should ever induce them to adopt those principles of warfare which had been directed against them. I said I trusted the English nation stood in need of no lessons in these particulars and that her present unfortunate hostilities with America would show the same spirit of generosity which had distinguished even her most impolitic wars. He took this up a little warmly—and said that the way in which she had attacked the defenceless villages—threatened the citizens with the fate of traitors and broken off the agreements entered into by their own agents as to the exchange of prisoners did not say much for their spirit of generosity. But that the very practice in which the war originated, the obstinacy and insolence with which all satisfaction had been refused, and the extraordinary form in which negotiation was ultimately offered could leave little doubt in any impartial mind as to the temper by which this war had been provoked and in which it was carried on on the part of England. I was a little surprised at this sort of challenge to discussion thrown out by a Sovereign to a private individual in his own drawing room. I felt however that it was not my part to decline it—and being somewhat *au fait* of the matter by my discussion with the Secretary I did not hesitate to accept. We entered accordingly upon a discussion which lasted nearly two hours and embraced all the topics which I had gone over with Mr. M. very nearly upon the same grounds and to the same results—tho maintained on the part of the President with rather more caution and reserve—more shyness as to concessions—and a tone considerably more acrimonious towards England—tho perfectly civil and even courteous to myself. I shall not repeat what was substantially the same in the two discussions—but there were some additions and variations which it is both fair and important to notice. He enlarged a good deal for example upon the unprecedented measure of England at last sending a proposal for an arrangement by the admiral commanding the hostile squadron on the coast and directing all the predatory excursions on the coast. He asked whether there was any precedent for such a mode of negotiation or whether it was at all unfair to suppose that nothing serious could be meant by the nation who offered it. Would Sir J. B. Warren come to Washington—or were they to send a plenipotentiary aboard his ship. If they were where were they

to find him—today off the Chesapeake—tomorrow at Bermuda
—at Halifax—or at New London. If they really wished to negotiate there were no obstacles in the way of their doing so
regularly—and no apology for a proceeding so tardy and insulting. I answered to this that I really did not see anything so
objectionable in putting the sword and the olive branch into
the hand of the same man—and that all commanders in chief
in fact had powers to negotiate—that the negotiation might be
very well managed by correspondence and that I really did not
imagine that it was intended that the admiral should conclude
a final treaty of peace—but rather arrange an armistice upon
such general grounds as would probably lead to peace—and
that to settle an armistice was among the ordinary duties of
military commanders. In the course of this conversation he
observed that what he had seen in public life had disposed him
to doubt very much whether all negotiation ought not to be
settled by correspondence alone—and whether ambassadors
did not for the most part do more harm than good. Without
imputing any bad motives to them he said it was natural for
them almost unconsciously to represent things to their own
court in too favorable a point of view, to hold out unreasonable hopes and to give a partial colouring to all their statements
of what took place between them and the govt. with whom
they had to transact. The ultimate issue of all which was that
when matters came to be practically settled their courts were
quite disappointed and irritated—and great discontent and
dissension often existed which might have been prevented, if
they had been prepared by a timely and full explanation of the
truth. I admitted the fact—but said it was a necessary evil—
and that it might be remedied by a more liberal and regular
use of official notes upon all matters of importance. He spoke
civilly of all our late ministers at Washington—but said that Mr
Rose had an unfortunate awkwardness of manner. Mr. Liston
he said was an agreeable and judicious man—but that an un-
lucky disclosure of some of his dispatches by accident had excited such an animosity against him that he believed he could
not have been usefully employed as a minister in this country.
Upon the subject of impressment he took a higher and more
unaccommodating tone than Mr. M. He said that there was
great room for questioning the right which the English had

assumed of searching neutrals for contraband or hostile property but that the pretence of searching for seamen lawfully and publicly engaged in the service of a friendly merchant was altogether peculiar to them, and must be resisted, if there was to be any end to their usurpations. I said I conceived the right to search for contraband and enemies property had been admitted all over Europe for many years, and had even been expressly recognised on former occasions by America. The right in question I defended as I had done to Mr. Monroe—but could not help asking why instead of going to war he had not retorted on us by making his frigates search some of our traders and take out any Americans he found in them? He answered that as they did not impress their own seamen they would have scarcely any pretext for searching any ships to recover them—but that at all events they would not adopt a practice against which they had protested as illegal and unjust. I said it was not quite as bad at any rate as shedding blood—and that the principle of retaliation implied a protest against all the acts in which it consisted.

I did not chuse to say much on the painful subject of retaliation as it regarded the prisoners lately seized in Canada—but I could not help hinting that to make a proper *retaliation* they ought to have taken American natives who had been naturalised in England and were found fighting against their original country—as there was no *parity* in any other case. He said there were none such and they were entitled to take any of the enemy when any of their subjects were treated against the law of nations.

He spoke in a very sanguine way of the conquest of Canada and said they must sweep us up to Quebec if not this campaign at least the next—and then went on in a paltry long discourse to convince me that we should be much better without Canada than with it. The expense of governing and defending it he said was more than it could ever produce. In time of peace we might at all times get what we wanted of its produce much cheaper if it were not our own than if it were—and in time of war our intercourse with it would be nearly as much obstructed altho' the territory were in our hands as if it were not —while the connection with the Indians on their backs which its possession enabled us to keep up almost ensured perpetual heartburning and jealousy between us and America so long as those Indians continued formidable to their back settlements. To this extraordinary statement I answered that considering the capabilities of Canada the pledges we had given to its natives, its importance in the event of war in the North in supplying us with naval stores I had no idea that we should be much *better* for wanting it—as I really did not understand how we could obtain those supplies in the event of our being at war with America as readily if it were in their hands as if it continued our own. However convincing the arguments on this point might be however I was clearly of opinion that we should be much more apt to listen to them at any time than when we were at war—that the English were very little disposed to be convinced by the reassurings of those who came to the debate with arms in their hands—and that he might be quite sure that the most demonstrative argument would make no impression when it was preceded by a violent attack on the place which it was proposed to convince us we ought to give up. He said the war had been forced upon them—and that while possession (if they could attain it) might help to force us to listen to reason it ought not to offer any obstruction to its efficacy.

We had a curious discussion—considering the parties—on the good and bad effects of *party* in a free country—in the course of which he *admitted* that as there must be many ignorant and violent in all parties and as where they were at all nearly balanced the aid of all must be received it almost necessarily happened that the popular advocates and warmest supporters of the *ruling* party pushed things so far both in their pretensions and their abuse—that when the sober and leading minds that had the ultimate determination were themselves satisfied with the terms that could be obtained they were often deterred from accepting them by the dread of disowning and deserting those abettors whose aid they had accepted and without whom it might not be clear that they could go on.

He spoke with extravagant and I think sincere tho' rather narrow minded partiality of his country—their future greatness and the genius and virtue and general intelligence of the people. He enlarged as Monroe had done—but in a more sanguine and triumphant tone on the ultimate advantages that the war would bring to America.

Henry Clay to Thomas Bodley

As parts of western Upper Canada came under U.S. control, the Madison administration faced the problem of how to govern this territory. At the outset of the war, the administration and its supporters in Congress had insisted that Canada was not an end in itself; it was to be won and used as a bargaining chip to secure concessions from Britain on the issues of "free trade and sailors' rights." But as the war progressed, Republicans grew more open in their calls for the annexation of Canada. In November 1813, a party newspaper in Boston argued that "too much valuable blood has already been shed, and too much treasure expended, for us to indulge for a moment the idea of resigning this country." Federalists, on the other hand, rejected the idea that Canada could be a legitimate spoil of war: "Canada has issued no Orders in Council," said Congressman Samuel Taggart of Massachusetts. "She has not impressed our seamen . . . nor in any other respect treated us ill. All the crime alleged against . . . the Canadians is that . . . they are connected with, and under the protection of, a nation which has injured us on the ocean." Here, in a letter to his friend Thomas Bodley, a quartermaster in the Army of the Northwest, Henry Clay speaks his mind on the Canadian matter.

Dr. Bodley   Wash. 18h. Decr. 1813

When your favor giving me an account of the glorious result of the Campaign in the N.W. reached me, I was in Philada. where we spent very agreeably two weeks. I had heard of your success on my way to this place from K. and heard of it with emotions of pleasure which it is impossible for me to describe. In another quarter our success has not been equal to our expectations, but we must have patience, and all will turn out well.

You describe that portion of the Country which Kentucky has conquered as extremely fine, and say that a very unpopular opinion has been attributed to me that it ought to be given up, as the price of peace. During the last summer when, so far from having reduced any portion of the Territories of the enemy, the enemy had possession of the Michigan Territory, I did say that if we could make a peace securing to us all the points in controversy, I should for one be willing not to give up Canada (for we had it not to give up) but to forego for the present its conquest. I was totally unapprized of the views of Administration on this subject, and expressed the sentiment in casual conversation. When the War was commenced Canada was not the end but the means; the object of the War being the redress of injuries, and Canada being the instrument by which that redress was to be obtained. But it has ever been my opinion that if Canada is conquered it ought never to be surrendered if it can possibly be retained. Relations and connexions will take place which ought not to be broken, in the event of its conquest. You know however that I do not belong to that branch of the Government with which the power of making peace is lodged; and perhaps after all it is premature to say any thing at present about the terms of a peace, which may not be made for years to come. The *state* of things is undergoing continual changes, and we must judge of the conditions of peace, when peace comes, not by the present state, but by that state of things which shall exist when it is negociated. That government is sensible of the advantages which will accrue from the possession of Canada, you may be well assured; and that it will get all it can in making a peace its desire of fame, to say nothing of its love of country, affords a sufficient guarrantee.

Congress has been chiefly engaged in confidential business, since it met. I am not yet at liberty to say what it is, but it will be disclosed in a day or two.

Judge Todd is here. He and Genl. Harrison dine with me to day.

We shall have to pay $2.000 as Jordan's sureties. That is the penalty of our bond. When Granger arrives (for he has been detained on the road to this place by illness) I shall get him to direct the Atto. of the U.S. to investigate Jordan's circumstances. I hope our friend Fowler has by this time got the appointment of P. Master.

I have recommended Davis and Young for subaltern commissions in the army.

There is a rumor that one of our frigates has arrived to the

Eastward. Genl. Floyd and the Georgia Militia have defeated a party of the creeks killing 200 of them, besides the wounded, and losing only 11 killed and 54 wounded Yr friend

H

Cyrenius Chapin to the Buffalo Gazette

In the summer of 1813, the British sought to retake Fort George, the American toehold on the Canadian side of the Niagara River. By then most of the U.S. regulars had been transferred east for the Montreal campaign, leaving only 250 New York militiamen, under Brigadier General George McClure, to defend the fort and adjacent frontier. On December 10, acting on intelligence that British troops were advancing on his position, McClure ordered Fort George abandoned. He directed his men to burn not only the installation but also the neighboring town of Newark, home to many British soldiers and their families. In response, the British quickly captured Fort Niagara and burned the New York towns of Lewiston, Manchester, Tuscarora, Black Rock, and Buffalo. A spirited resistance, led in part by Lieutenant Colonel Cyrenius Chapin, defended Buffalo, but dissolved when the colonel was captured. Six months later, upon his release from a Montreal jail, Chapin published the following indictment of McClure's command in the June 13 edition of the *Buffalo Gazette*.

The distressing scenes exhibited on the Niagara frontier last fall and winter having excited many painful reflections and anxious inquiries for the causes which led to those disgraceful disasters, have induced me to lay before the public some of the most conspicuous actors of those base exploits.

While the American regular forces continued at Fort George nothing occurred to affect our security till that strange phenomenon, George McClure, appeared. He, with much pomp and parade, however, kept out of harm's way by riding up and down upon the east side of the streights of Niagara till I had, with a small body of volunteers, militia and Indians, routed the enemy from his encampment at the Four Mile Creek. Then this mighty man crossed the river with all the wind of a Hull or a Smyth (aided by the fœtid breath of a J. C. Spencer,) who burst forth with terror and rage upon the defenceless inhabitants of

Canada. These terrible heroes, however, very cautiously avoided any engagement with the enemy. They conceived it sufficient for them to war with women and children; to lay waste their dwellings, "to burn up the d————d rascals" was their favorite motto.

Their march from the Beaver Dam to Queenston will be long remembered by the distressed victims of that march. Property of almost every description was plundered and buildings burned under his own eye. This, however, was a mere prelude to the tragedy he was destined to enact.

The ill-fated town of Newark was burnt, under his orders, the night of the 10th of December, 1813. Here was exhibited a scene of distress which language would be inadequate to describe. Women and children were turned out of doors in a cold and stormy night; the cries of infants, the decrepitude of age, the debility of sickness, had no impression on this monster in human shape; they were consigned to that house whose canopy was the heavens and whose walls were as boundless as the wide world. In the destruction of this town he was aided by the most active exertions of Joseph Wilcox, who had for a number of years resided in this pleasant village and had been patronized far beyond his merits; and at that time, when it became his duty as a man of justice and as a subject of His Majesty, whose government he had sworn to protect and defend, he, like a cowardly sycophant, deserted the cause of his country and actually led a banditti through the town, setting fire to his neighbors' dwellings and cursing every American—applying the epithet of tory to everyone who disapproved of this act of barbarity. It will be remembered that this town was burned when the British forces were not in any considerable force within a distance of thirty miles.

The General next selected the American side of the river for the theatre of operations. He took up his quarters at Buffalo. A small force of about two hundred regulars was called from Canandaigua, which we should have supposed ought to have been sent to the protection of Fort Niagara, as that place was menaced by the enemy. Instead of this the General ordered them to remain at Buffalo. Fort Niagara was taken on the morning of the 19th of December, 1813. The day previous the General was informed by a citizen who had made his escape from Canada, that an attack would be made on Fort Niagara at the time it was made. Here then is something very remarkable in the conduct of General McClure: instead of despatching an express with this very important intelligence he omitted it, if not altogether, until it was too late for the express to get there.

As soon as the capture of that fort was known at Buffalo, the General removed himself and men from Buffalo to Cold Springs, a distance of two miles. This movement appeared to be made that the redoubtable General should have time to re- treat without hearing the whistle of British balls, which, by- the-bye we suppose would have been very unpleasant to the General's organs of hearing, as he was totally unused to such sounds. Here he remained for a few days, but finding from intelligence which he received from Canada that the enemy were preparing to attack Buffalo, he took up his line of march to Batavia, a distance of forty miles, no doubt conceiving that a place of greater safety, as there he could not hear the report of the enemy's guns. From Batavia I was told he made good his retreat to his own home in Steuben County, having covered himself and his associates with laurels of disgrace. As to his as- sertion that he was fired upon by men who he said were under my command, I believe it to be utterly false. The inhabitants of Buffalo all felt deeply interested in the protection of that place, apprehending full well the consequences of an invasion of it by an enemy whose character had been marked by acts of out- rage and cruelty, and who was now stimulated to the most desperate measures of retaliation by the conduct of McClure in the burning of Newark. They repeatedly requested him to afford them the necessary protection. The ruins of the Niagara frontier, the tears of the widows and the cries of orphan chil- dren, still testify to his cowardice and villany. As it regards myself and the command I held in the army while it was under General McClure, I think proper to state the principal reason that induced me to resign, after having been repeatedly ex- posed to much danger by his orders, especially when he or- dered me to Forty Mile Creek in Upper Canada, and while I remained there under his orders, with about forty men, he said in presence of Mr. Curtiss, whose affidavit I procured, "that he regretted that I had not been taken by the enemy, that he wished I had been and that he hoped the damned rascal would be."

Now the public will observe that I was acting under the orders of Gen. McClure and had taken a commanding position at that place. He ordered Col. Hopkins to command the men in rear of me, who were twelve miles from that place. I was ordered to remain at the Forty Mile Creek until I was reinforced, but, contrary to the assurances which McClure gave me, Colonel Hopkins was ordered to remain twelve miles in rear of me. Should any person concerned reply to these observations further facts will be developed; meanwhile the public are requested to peruse the subjoined documents. Others are in my possession and will be published next week.

JUNE 13th.   CYRENIUS CHAPIN.

Eber D. Howe: from
"Recollections of a Pioneer Printer"

The combatants along the Niagara frontier fought across a once-open border that had seen much traffic in the decades before the war. Of the seventy-seven thousand white inhabitants of Upper Canada in 1812, three-fifths had been born in the United States, and war put their loyalties to the test. Eber Dudley Howe was a case in point. Born in Saratoga County, New York, in 1798, Howe, who grew up to become a frontier journalist and printer, moved with his family near Fort George when he was thirteen. The early chapters of Howe's memoirs, published in 1878, recall events as they played out on the Canadian side of the Niagara in 1811–13, culminating in the burning of Newark and its aftermath. As a result of the events he witnessed, Howe, at the age of sixteen, forsook Canada and joined the New York militia.

About 100 regular soldiers, mostly invalids, had been left in Fort Niagara for its defense, under command of a Captain Leonard, who retired every night to a private residence four miles out on the lake shore. The military strategy in this procedure of the captain is not very apparent at the present day, but was in keeping with a good share of the strange movements of that war.

Thus stood matters till the night of the 18th December, when the British with their Indian allies crossed the river, passed the sentinels (if any there were), entered the gates and took possession of the old fort without firing a gun. They then sent a file of men down to the captain's quarters with a request that he appear at the fort without any unnecessary delay. He still holding to his previous notions that "prudence was the better part of valor," did not stand upon the manner of his going, but obeyed the summons forthwith. I think his name was never again heard of in connection with the military service.

The Indians immediately took the line of march up the river, and arrived at the village of Lewiston about sunrise, where they found most of the people in their beds. The first warning they had of their danger was the Indian war-whoop as they emerged from a piece of woods which skirted the whole length of the town, and about thirty rods distant. The consternation that followed this sudden eruption of a savage foe, can hardly be imagined. Each one from instinct supposed their safety depended upon flight. It so happened that on this occasion the savage appetite for plunder outweighed his appetite for blood. Therefore, they were so long detained at a few of the first dwellings that a large share of the people got well under way before pursuit commenced. I think but one man and a woman were killed at this time. A Dr. Alvord, who was a cripple, attempted to mount his horse and ride away, but was shot. The ground was frozen and covered with a light snow. The main and almost only road that led from the town ran directly east, and was somewhat thickly settled; and as the alarm went far ahead of the main body, carried by a few who had the good luck to find horses, the inhabitants were instantly wheeling into line in front of those who first started. Three miles out, I with my father's family fell into the fugitive cavalcade. By this time the road was getting pretty well filled up with men, women and children, horses, oxen, carts, wagons, sleds, in fine, everything that could facilitate the movement of women and children; and after filling up all these many were carried in the arms of those most able to endure fatigue.

Very few of the vast throng thus suddenly thrown together had eaten anything that morning. I well remember the breakfast that was on the table that morning as the frightened rider passed our door. The frying-pan went one way and the teakettle the other. The horses and sled were soon at the door—feather beds, blankets, and whatever eatables were nearest at hand were hurled in, the women and children on top, and away they went over the rough and frozen ground. As the frightened procession advanced, its numbers increased, until neither end could be discovered by those in the center. It was supposed to be about five miles in length, resembling somewhat the serpentine movements of a huge black snake—rendered more distinctly visible by the snow on the ground.

There was no halt for the distance of about fifteen miles, except to cast an "anxious lingering look behind," to get the first glimpse of the savage foe, with his uplifted tomahawk and bristling scalping-knife; but he only followed on the trail for about three miles, securing the plunder and firing the now deserted dwellings. There were, however, two of the red men more fearless than their fellows. Being mounted on fleet horses they followed in the rear for about five miles, and came up with two men, one of whom they shot, took his rifle and retreated, while the other escaped into the bush. These men both had their rifles pointed at the Indians, but concluded they were friendly—as the Tuscorora tribe resided in that neighborhood—took down their guns and awaited their approach until it was too late to retrieve their mistake.

As night approached the procession arrived at the forks of the roads (near where Lockport now stands) one leading to Batavia and the other to Rochester. Here some of the most weary, and perhaps the most courageous, bivouacked for the night—finding shelter for the women and children as best they could, the men standing guard and putting themselves in the best position for defense; while others again pursued their course to the right or the left. I took the road leading to Rochester, and soon entered what was then called the Eleven-mile woods, there being then but one solitary house for that distance, seven miles of which was covered with a thick growth of timber, having only the small brush cut away just sufficient to keep on the direction. At this juncture a brisk snowstorm set in—but on, on wended the cavalcade, over a corduroy bridge laid down in the mud and water for the distance of about four miles, some, of course, occasionally giving out, but others pursuing the even tenor of their way the whole night. Somehow, at present unknown, I found myself on board an old ricketty wagon, drawn by a half-starved pair of oxen, plodding along through the last seven miles, almost every minute in collision with a tree, first on one side and then on the other, constantly "hawing" and "geeing," as the case might be. The next morning I found myself enjoying a quiet snooze at the eastern end of the "woods" under a blanket, with nearly a foot of snow thereon.

The Indians and redcoats tarried thereabouts for two days, reveling in whiskey and plunder, and then "departed for their own coast," carrying with them a few prisoners to their wigwams on Grand river. Among these was a man by the name of Phillips, who had resided in Canada about six months before the war commenced, and had taken the oath of allegiance to His Majesty, while in his dominions. The first opportunity that was offered he left and became a soldier on the American side. Under these circumstances he concluded that his best chance for life would be to remain with the Indians in as much privacy as possible. After arriving at their village many of the tribe became clamorous for the sacrifice of a Yankee, in propitiation for some of their braves who had recently been killed, and proceeded with all due ceremony to prepare the place of execution by bringing together all the pine limbs, knots and faggots, that were most convenient. Before they had time to carry out and execute their plans, however, some British officers made their appearance upon the ground, and by dint of entreaty they were induced to stay the savage procedure. The old chief took Phillips to his hut and set him to work, and finding him an expert at divers things, especially at making shoes, moccasins, etc., he soon became a favorite in the camp. After serving them in this manner for about three months, the chief proposed that he should marry a squaw, and even proposed his own daughter, and urged the proposition with so much tenacity that he concluded to let them know that he had a wife and children in Canada. This soon led to an arrangement whereby they were to liberate him for five gallons of whiskey and ten pounds of tobacco. Phillips soon found means of conveying the intelligence to his wife, who was then about forty miles from the place. After many difficulties and hardships she procured the articles with which to pay the ransom and carried them to the Indian headquarters on Grand river, and brought away her husband in safety. The following November, just at the close of the war, Phillips and his family crossed the lines and came to Buffalo, from thence to Ontario County, where he died at the age of ninety years. The woman above spoken of was a sister to the writer hereof.

THE BURNING OF BLACK ROCK AND BUFFALO:
NIAGARA FRONTIER, DECEMBER 1813

Amos Hall to Daniel D. Tompkins

The wholesale destruction of the towns on the New York side of the river brought a shocking end to the Niagara campaign of 1813. What had begun with such promise for the United States with the British abandonment of Fort George had ended with the British in control of all the key forts on both sides of the river and almost all the American settlements in ashes. In this letter, Major General Amos Hall, the American commander at Black Rock and Buffalo, describes the battle and conflagration for the governor of New York. "The whole frontier from Lake Ontario to Lake Erie," Governor Tompkins later summarized to Secretary of War Armstrong, "is depopulated & the buildings & Improvements, with a few exceptions, destroyed."

HEADQUARTERS, NIAGARA FRONTIER, Jan. 6th, 1814.
DEAR SIR:—

The confusion into which everything was thrown by the events of the 30th December and the imperious necessity of taking precautionary measures against the advance of the enemy, put it out of my power to furnish at an earlier period a detailed account of the operations on this frontier during my hitherto unfortunate and embarrassing command. Add to this the extreme difficulty of collecting facts relative to our loss, since the forces under my command were of that multiform description which they necessarily were, being composed almost wholly of volunteer militia and exempts hastily and confusedly assembled in the moment of alarm and dissipated by the events of the battle.

The storming of Fort Niagara and the burning of Lewiston presaging further devastation, threw the whole country into the most violent agitation. On the moment and without any previous preparation I hastened to Batavia with a view to take such measures as might be within my power to repel the enemy and protect the frontier. I hastily collected from the militia and volunteers of Genesee County and the brigade of General

Wadsworth in Ontario, a considerable force, but generally deficient in arms and ammunition, and the necessary conveniences of a camp.

In the evening of the 22nd December General McClure with the regulars under command of Major Riddle arrived in Batavia and on the morning of the 23rd signified by letter his desire that I would take the command during the moment of general alarm. I accordingly proceeded to organize in the best manner in my power the forces then at Batavia, and with the arms and ammunition collected from different sections of the country and what little could be procured from the arsenals at Canandaigua and Batavia, I was enabled to get under march on the 25th, for Lewiston, a body of infantry about 150 strong, under Lieutenant-Colonel Lawrence, supported by one company of cavalry under command of Captain Marvin, with orders to proceed to join a corps of militia, said to be 200 men under command of Lieut.-Colonel Achinson, which was stationed at Forsyth's, on the Ridge Road, 15 miles east of Lewiston, to collect and save all the ammunition in his power, which had been moved from the arsenal at Lewiston and was then dispersed on the road and in different parts of the country, and with instructions to act as circumstances and the nature of his force would permit against the enemy, and, if practicable, to effect a junction with the main force at Buffalo, by the way of Manchester, Schlosser, and thence up the river to Black Rock, leaving as a reserve the corps under Colonel Achinson at the station near Lewiston. I then ordered the remainder of the troops to Buffalo, with the exception of the regular forces, over whom I assumed no command. On the morning of the 25th I proceeded to Buffalo, leaving General McClure at Batavia with instructions to organize such detachments of volunteers as might arrive, and direct their march for Buffalo. I arrived in Buffalo on the morning of the 26th and there found a considerable body of irregular troops of various descriptions, disorganized and confused. Everything wore the appearance of consternation and dismay. On the same day I issued an order to the several commandants for a return of the number of effective men under their command and an order to Captain Camp, Assistant Deputy Quartermaster General, for a return of the ordnance and ordnance stores in the quartermaster's department, a copy of which return I have heretofore had the honor to forward Your Excellency and which sufficiently exhibits the destitute condition of that department. On the 27th I ordered a review of all troops under my command at Buffalo and Black Rock, when I found my force to be as follows:—

At Buffalo, Lieut.-Colonel Boughton, of the cavalry and mounted volunteers, 129; Lieut.-Colonel Blakesley, of the Ontario exempts and volunteers, 433; Lieut.-Colonel Chapin, of the Buffalo militia, 136; Lieut.-Colonel Mallory, of the Canadian volunteers, 97; Major Adams, of the Genesee militia, 382. At the Rock were stationed, under the command of Brigadier General Hopkins, 382 effective men, composed of the corps commanded by Lieut.-Colonel Warren and Lieut.-Colonel Churchill, exclusive of a body of 37 mounted infantry, under command of Captain Ransom, 83 Indians, under command of Lieut.-Colonel Granger, and one piece of field artillery, a six pounder, and 25 men commanded by Lieut. Seeley, making my aggregate force on the 27th to be 1,711 men. Add to this a regiment of Chautauqua militia, under the command of Lieut.-Colonel McMahon, which arrived at Buffalo on the 29th, about 300, swells my force to 2,011, which was reduced on the morning of the alarm to less than 1,200, and so deficient were my supplies of ammunition that a greater part of the cartridges of Lieut.-Colonel McMahon's regiment were made and distributed after they were paraded on the morning of the battle.

The movements of the enemy already indicated their intention of attacking the village of Buffalo or Black Rock, which left me not a moment from the arduous duty of preparing the most effective means in my power of meeting the enemy with the crude force under my command. On the 28th I was so fortunate as to procure information as to the enemy's movements, from a citizen who made his escape from Canada, as to leave me no doubt as to his intentions.

In the evening of the 29th, at about 12 o'clock, I received information that our horse patrol had been fired on a short distance below Conjockatie's Creek, and one mile below Black Rock. Lieut. Boughton, an enterprising and brave officer, had his horse shot under him. The enemy advanced and took possession of the Sailors' Battery, near Conjockatie's Creek. The troops were immediately paraded and stood by their arms. I was yet uncertain as to what point the enemy would attack me, the darkness of the night was not favorable for making observations. I was apprehensive the enemy designed to make a feigned attack below Black Rock, for the purpose of drawing off my force from the village of Buffalo, preparatory to landing above the village, intending thereby to take it by surprise. At the same time being anxious to anticipate the enemy's landing and meet them at the water's edge, I gave orders that the troops at the Rock, commanded by Colonels Warren and Churchill, (General Hopkins being at that time absent from camp,) attack the enemy and endeavor to dislodge them from the battery and drive them to their boats. The attempt failed through the confusion the militia were thrown into at the first fire of the enemy and the darkness of the night. They were dispersed and not again embodied under their proper officers through the day. I then ordered the corps under Major Adams and the corps under Colonel Chapin to make the attack. This was attended with no better effect. The men were thrown into confusion by the enemy's fire and after skirmishing a short time, fled and were not again embodied during the day. I then ordered the corps under command of Colonel Blakeslee to advance to the attack, and at the same time I put the remainder of my troops in motion for the same point and proceeded by the hill road to Black Rock. On approaching the village of Black Rock, I discovered a detachment of the enemy's boats crossing to our shore and bending their course to the rear of General Porter's house. The day was now beginning to dawn. I immediately countermanded the order given to Colonel Blakeslee to attack the enemy's left and directed him to form and attack the enemy's centre at the water's edge.

I now became satisfied as to the disposition of the enemy and their object, which I ascertained to be as follows:—

Their left wing, composed of about 800 regular troops and the Incorporated Militia and 150 or 200 Indians, were disposed below Conjockatie's Creek and had been landed under cover of the night. With this force the enemy designed to cover their left, outflank our right, and cut off our retreat by the woods. With their centre, consisting of about 400 Royal Scots, commanded by Colonel Gordon, the battle was commenced. Their right, which was purposely weak, was landed near our main battery under cover of a high bank and was merely intended to divert our force from the principal attack. The whole, under the command of Lieut.-General Drummond, conducted to the attack by Major General Riall. I therefore ordered the enemy's left wing, which was discovered to be wheeling upon our right, to be attacked by the Indians, under command of Lieut.-Colonel Granger, and the Canadian Volunteers, under command of Col. Mallory, at the same time I posted the regiment under command of Col. McMahon, at the battery, as a reserve, to act as emergencies should require. The attack was commenced by a fire from our six-pounder under Lieut. Seeley, below General Porter's house, and one 24 and two 12-pounders at the battery, under command of Lieut. Farnum of the 21st United States Infantry, acting as a volunteer. At the same time the enemy opened a heavy fire from the batteries on the other side of the river, of shells, spherical shot, and ball. The regiment under command of Colonel Blakeslee, about 400 strong, were regularly in the line, together with detached bodies from other corps, amounting, according to the best estimate I can make, in all about 600 men. These few but brave men commenced the attack with musketry upon the enemy in their boats and poured upon them a most destructive fire. Every inch of ground was disputed with the steady coolness of veterans and at the expense of many valuable lives. Their bravery at the same time it casts a lustre over their names reflects equal disgrace on those who fled at the first appearance of danger, and who neither entreaties nor threats could turn back to the support of their commanders. Perceiving that the Indians, on whom I had relied for attacking the enemy's flank, were offering no assistance, and that our right was endangered by the enemy's left, I gave directions for the reserve under Colonel McMahon to attack the enemy in flank, but terror had dissipated this corps and but few of them could be rallied by their officers and brought to the attack. Of this corps there are some who merit well of their country, but more who covered themselves with disgrace. The defection of the Indians and of my reserve, and the loss of the services of the cavalry and mounted men, by reason of the nature of the ground on which they must act, left the forces engaged exposed to veteran and highly disciplined troops, overwhelmed by numbers and nearly surrounded, a retreat became necessary to their safety, which was accordingly made. I then made every effort to rally the troops, with a view to renew the attack on the enemy's columns on their approach to the village of Buffalo. But every effort proved ineffectual and experience proves that with militia retreat becomes a flight, and, a battle once ended, the army is dissipated. Deserted by my principal force, I fell back that night to 11 Mile Creek and was forced to leave the flourishing villages of Black Rock and Buffalo a prey to the enemy, which they have pillaged and laid in ashes. At the 11 Mile Creek I collected between 200 and 300 who remained faithful to their country; with those I preserved the best show of defence in my power, to cover the flying inhabitants and check the advance of the enemy. The enemy have gained but little plunder from the public stores. The chief loss has fallen upon individual sufferers. Eight pieces of artillery fell into the hands of the enemy, of which but one was mounted on a travelling carriage. What little remained of the public stores capable of being removed is preserved through the exertions of Captain Camp of the quartermaster's department, whose bravery is only equalled by his zeal for the public service. It is not in my power to give a particular account of our loss in killed and wounded, as the wounded were generally got off by their friends and taken to their houses, and our dead mostly buried by the enemy. But from the best information I can collect, our loss is about 30 killed and perhaps 40 wounded. In prisoners our loss is ascertained to be 69, twelve of whom are wounded. The enemy's loss must be much greater, as many were killed in their boats before landing. Their loss may reasonably be presumed in killed and wounded at not less than 200. Lieut.-Colonel Boughton of the light dragoons is among the slain. He was a good officer and a valuable citizen. I regret that it is not in my power to do justice to all who were engaged on this day. The veteran Blakeslee and his corps were pre-eminently distinguished. There were of the broken remains of other corps many officers and soldiers whose bravery and conduct merits my warmest praise, but having fought irregularly and in detachments I cannot designate them to do them that justice they deserve. The good conduct of Lieut. Seeley and Lieut. Farnum, who had charge of the artillery, was particularly noticed. The cavalry under Colonel Boughton, and mounted volunteers under Major Warren receive my thanks for their prompt obedience of orders and the valuable services rendered in the fatiguing duties of patroling, and it is a matter of regret that the nature of the ground on which we contended deprived me of that support which I might confidently expect of their bravery. To Lieut. Frazer of the United States Infantry I tender my thanks for the valuable services he rendered me as one of my staff. To my two aides de camp, Majors Hosmer and Norton, I cannot withhold my warmest thanks for their cool deliberate bravery and alacrity with which they executed my orders from the first movements of the troops in the morning to the close of the day.

I have the honor to be, Your Excellency's most obedient and humble servant,

A. HALL, Major General.

George Prevost: Proclamation

January 12, 1814

As the new year began, leaders on both sides of the Niagara frontier sought to frame the final actions of the previous year's campaign, actions that threatened to escalate the war to new levels of savagery. In a letter of January 6 to Sir George Prevost, governor and commander-in-chief of British North America, James Wilkinson disavowed the burning of Newark, casting McClure as insubordinate and his actions reckless and unrepresentative. Six days later, Prevost issued the following proclamation to His Majesty's British subjects in Canada, and on February 10, forwarded a printed copy to Wilkinson. Prevost told Wilkinson that the proclamation was "expressive of the determination, as to his future line of conduct," and that he was "happy to learn, that there was no probability, that any measures, on the part of the American government, would oblige him to depart from it."

By His Excellency Sir George Prevost, Baronet, Commander of His Majesty's Forces in North America, &c., &c., &c.

To the inhabitants of His Majesty's Provinces in North America:

A PROCLAMATION.

The complete success which has attended His Majesty's arms on the Niagara Frontier having placed in our possession the whole of the enemy's posts on that line, it became a matter of imperious duty to retaliate on America the miseries which the unfortunate inhabitants of Newark had been made to suffer on the evacuation of Fort George.

The villages of Lewiston, Black Rock and Buffalo have accordingly been burned.

At the same time that His Excellency the Commander of the Forces sincerely deprecates this mode of warfare, he trusts it will be sufficient to call the attention of every candid and impartial person, both amongst ourselves and the enemy, to the circumstances from which it has arisen to satisfy them that this departure from the established usages of war has originated with America herself, and that to her alone are justly chargeable all the awful and unhappy consequences which have hitherto flowed and are likely to result from it.

It is not necessary to advert to the conduct of the troops employed on the American coast in conjunction with His Majesty's squadron under Admiral Sir John B. Warren; since they were neither within the command nor subject to the control of His Excellency their acts cannot be ascribable to him, even if they wanted that justification which the circumstances that occasioned them so amply afford.

It will be sufficient for the present purpose, and to mark the character of the war as carried on upon the frontiers of these Provinces, to trace the line of conduct observed by His Excellency and the troops under his command since the commencement of hostilities, and to contrast it with that of the enemy.

The first invasion of Upper Canada took place in July, 1812, when the American forces under Brigadier-General Hull crossed over and took possession of Sandwich, where they began to manifest a disposition so different from a magnanimous enemy, and which they have since invariably displayed, in marking out as objects of their resentment the loyal subjects of His Majesty and in dooming their property to plunder and conflagration.

Various instances of this kind occurred, both at Sandwich and in its neighborhood, at the very period when His Majesty's standard was waving upon the fort of Michilimackinac and affording protection to the persons and property of those who had submitted to it. Within a few weeks afterwards the British flag was also hoisted on the fortress of Detroit, which, together with the whole of the Michigan territory, had surrendered to His Majesty's arms.

Had not His Excellency been actuated by sentiments far different from those which had influenced the American Government, and the persons employed by it, in the wanton acts of destruction of private property, committed during their short occupation of a part of Upper Canada, His Excellency could not have failed to have availed himself of the opportunity which the undisturbed possession of the whole of the Michigan Territory afforded him of amply retaliating for the devastating system which had been pursued at Sandwich and on the Thames.

But strictly in conformity to the views and disposition of his own Government and to that liberal and magnanimous policy which it had dictated, he chose rather to forbear an imitation of the enemy's example in the hope that such forbearance would be duly appreciated by the Government of the United States, and would produce a return to the more civilized usages of war.

The persons and property therefore of the inhabitants of Michigan Territory were respected and remained unmolested.

In the winter of the following year, when the success which attended the daring and gallant enterprise against Ogdensburg, had placed that populace and flourishing village in our possession, the generosity of the British character was again conspicuous in the scrupulous preservation of every article which could be considered as private property, such public buildings only being destroyed as were used for the accommodation of troops and for public stores.

The destruction of the defences of Ogdensburg and the dispersion of the enemy's force in that neighborhood laid open the whole of their frontier on the St. Lawrence to the incursions of His Majesty's troops, and Hamilton as well as the numerous settlements on the banks of the river might at any hour, had such been the disposition of His Majesty's Government or of those acting under it, been plundered and laid waste.

During the course of the following summer, by the fortunate result of the enterprise against Plattsburg, that town was for several hours in the complete possession of our troops, there not being a force in the neighborhood which could attempt a resistance.

Yet even then, under circumstances of strong temptation, and when the recent example of the enemy in the wanton destruction at York of private property and buildings not used for military purposes must have been fresh in the recollection of the force employed on that occasion, and would have justified a retaliation on their part, their forbearance was strongly manifested, and the directions His Excellency had given to the commander of that expedition, so scrupulously obeyed, that scarcely can another instance be shown, in which, during a state of war and under similar circumstances, an enemy so completely under the power and at the mercy of their adversaries had so little cause of complaint.

During the course of the same summer Forts Schlosser and Black Rock were surprised and taken by a part of the forces under the command of Major-General de Rottenburg, on the Niagara Frontier, at both of which places personal property was respected and the public buildings alone were destroyed.

It was certainly matter of just and reasonable expectation that the humane and liberal course of conduct pursued by His Excellency on these different occasions would have had its due weight with the American Government, and would have led it to have abstained, in the further prosecution of the war, from any act of wantonness and violence, which could only tend unnecessarily to add to its ordinary calamities, and to bring down upon their own unoffending citizens a retaliation, which, though distant, they must have known would await and certainly follow such conduct.

Undeterred, however, by His Excellency's example of moderation, or by any of the consequences to be apprehended from the adoption of such barbarous measures, the American forces at Fort George, acting, as there is every reason to believe, under the orders or with the approbation of their Government, for some time previous to the evacuation of that fortress, under various pretences, burned and destroyed the farm houses and buildings of many of the respectable and peaceable inhabitants of the neighborhood. But the full measure of this species of barbarity remained to be completed when all its horrors might be more fully and keenly felt by those who were to become the wretched victims of it.

It will be hardly credited by those who shall hereafter read it in the page of history, that in the enlightened era of the 19th century and in the inclemency of a Canadian winter, the troops of a nation calling itself civilized and Christian, had wantonly and without the shadow of a pretext, forced 400 helpless women and children to quit their dwellings and to be mournful spectators of the conflagration and total destruction of all that belonged to them.

Yet such was the fate of Newark on the 10th of December, a day which the inhabitants of Upper Canada can never forget, and the recollection of which cannot but nerve their arms when again opposed to their vindictive foe. On the night of that day the American troops under Brigadier General McClure, being about to evacuate Fort George, which they could no longer retain, by an act of inhumanity, disgraceful to themselves and to the nation to which they belong, set fire to upwards of 150 houses, composing the beautiful village of Newark, and burned them to the ground, leaving without covering or shelter those "innocent, unfortunate and distressed inhabitants" whom that officer by his proclamation had previously engaged to protect.

His Excellency would have ill considered the honor of his country and the justice due to His Majesty's injured and insulted subjects, had he permitted an act of such needless cruelty to pass unpunished, or had he failed to visit, whenever the opportunity arrived, upon the inhabitants of the neighboring American frontier the calamities thus inflicted upon those of our own.

The opportunity has occurred, and a full measure of retaliation has taken place, such as, it is hoped, will teach the enemy to respect in future the laws of war, and recall him to a sense of what is due to himself as well as to us.

In the further prosecution of the contest, to which such an extraordinary character has been given, His Excellency must be guided by the course of conduct which the enemy shall hereafter pursue. Lamenting, as His Excellency does, the necessity imposed upon him of retaliating upon the subjects of America the miseries inflicted upon the inhabitants of Newark, it is not his intention to pursue further a system of warfare so revolting to his own feelings and so little congenial to the British character unless the future measures of the enemy should compel him again to resort to it.

To those possessions of the enemy along the whole line of the frontier which have hitherto remained undisturbed, and which are now within His Excellency's reach and at the mercy of the troops under his command, His Excellency has determined to extend the same forbearance and the same freedom from rapine and plunder which they have hitherto experienced, and from this determination the future conduct of the American Government shall alone induce His Excellency to depart.

The inhabitants of these Provinces will in the meantime be prepared to resist with firmness and with courage, whatever attempts the resentment of the enemy, arising from their disgrace and their merited sufferings, may lead them to make, well assured that they will be powerfully assisted at all points by the troops under His Excellency's command, and that prompt and signal vengeance will be taken for every fresh departure of the enemy from that system of warfare which ought to subsist between enlightened and civilized nations.

Given under my hand and seal at arms at Quebec, this 12th day of January, 1814.

GEORGE PREVOST.

By His Excellency's command, E. B. BRENTON.

Henry Kent: A Winter's March

Henry Kent was the young lieutenant of His Majesty's Sloop *Fantome* when the War of 1812 began. Captured from the French in 1810, *Fantome* was commissioned in Bermuda and, under the command of John Lawrence, saw action in the North Sea and along the Portuguese coast before sailing for America in December 1812. In late 1813, after participating in raids along Chesapeake Bay, Kent volunteered for service on the Great Lakes. He joined a navy detachment of 210 men that, after sailing from Halifax, Nova Scotia, to Saint John, New Brunswick, trekked nine hundred miles overland to Kingston, Britain's major naval base on Lake Ontario. Kent's narrative of the hazardous winter journey, written at the request of his father, was published in the London *Naval Chronicle* in 1815.

Kingston, on Lake Ontario, June 20th, 1814

We left Halifax in the *Fantome*, on the 22d of January last, and arrived at St. John's (New Brunswick), on the 26th, making a passage of four days, the weather extremely bad: the brig appeared a complete mass of ice, it freezing as fast as the sea broke over us. The inhabitants of St. John's came forward in the most handsome manner in a subscription to forward us in sleighs to Frederickston, the seat of government, a distance of 80 miles. The seamen were divided into three divisions, each of 70 men, the first under Captain Collier, of the *Manly*, the second under Lieutenant Russel, and the third under myself. On the 29th of January, the first division proceeded about nine in the morning, and in the afternoon the second followed; the next morning I disembarked, the rigging of all the ships being manned, and the crews cheering us. On landing, we were received by the band of the 8th regiment, and a large concourse of people, who escorted us to the sleighs, when we set off at full speed. In eight hours we went fifty miles, and then halted for the night at a small house on the banks of the river; started again in the morning, and in the afternoon reached Frederickston, and found both divisions had halted there.—The seamen were lodged in a barrack, which was walled in, but they soon scaled the walls, and were running about the town; you may therefore judge what trouble we had to collect them again. The seamen were now divided into two divisions, the first under Captain Collier's command, the second under mine, as being the senior officer.

On the 2d of February, Captain Collier proceeded with his division in sleighs, furnished by the inhabitants at their own expense, and the day following I left with mine: I was obliged to leave one of my best seamen sick at the hospital, frost bitten, and I have since learnt he lost two of his toes. From Frederickston we continued on the ice of the river St. John, except in places where, from shoals, the ice is thrown up in heaps. The country, after leaving Frederickston, is but thinly inhabited; a settlement you may see occasionally, but never more than three houses together. I kept always in the wake of the first division, halting where they had the day before. On the third evening, at the house where I halted, I found the master of the *Thistle* a corpse, having died with intense cold. Captain Collier having made every arrangement for burying him, I put his body into a sleigh, and sent it to a village a few miles distant. On the 7th reached Presque Isle, where there is a barrack and dépôt for provisions, but no houses near it; this place is 82 miles from Frederickston. Discharged the sleighs, and began making preparations for our march, each of us being furnished with a pair of snow shoes, two pair of moccasins, a toboggan between every four men, a camp kettle to every twelve, with axes and tinder-box. As you may not know the use of those articles by their Indian names, I will endeavour to describe them: Snow shoes are of a singular shape, something like a pear, formed by a hoop, and the bottom of them netted across with the hides of some animal; they are fixed by a strap round the heel, and tied across the instep, as you do a pair of skates; they are about two feet in length, and one in breadth. Moccasins are made of buffalo's hide, sole and tops in one, roughly sewed up with twine, a strip of hide run through notches, cut round the quarters, to haul it tight on your foot. Toboggans are hand sleighs, about four feet in length, and one in breadth, made of such light wood that they do not weigh above four pounds. On these you lash your provisions and clothes, and with the bight of a rope over your shoulder, drag it with great ease on the snow. I provided myself at Halifax with a jacket, trousers, and waistcoat, lined with fine flannel, so that with those, three flannel shirts, and a linen one, three pair of stockings, and a square piece of blanket wrapped on my feet, with moccasins over all, I felt pretty warm.

At day-break, commenced lashing our provisions on the to-boggans, and at eight o'clock commenced our march. The clothes I had with me being four shirts, the same of stockings, a coat and trousers, with a great coat, and a cap to sleep in. We marched daily from fifteen to twenty-two miles, and though that appears but a little distance, yet, with the snow up to our knees, was as much as any man could do. The first night we reached two small huts, the next the same accommodation, and the third slept in the woods. On the fourth, reached the Grand Falls,* which are about forty feet in height; none of us saw them, as they were a mile distant, and all of us too fatigued to go that distance: next day reached a small French settlement on Grande Riviere. The march from here to Madawaska (an-other French settlement), was beyond any thing you can con-ceive; it blew a gale of wind from the northward, and the drift of snow was so great, it was almost impossible to discern a man a hundred yards distant: before I got half way, the men lay down, saying they could not possibly go further; I endeav-oured by every persuasion to cheer them, and succeeded in getting about one half to accompany me. We reached it about nine o'clock at night, almost fainting, a distance of 21 miles. The following morning, having sent all the midshipmen in search of the men; I was therefore obliged to halt for a day to recruit them. The next morning, being the 15th of February, renewed our march, leaving a midshipman and 12 men behind sick, chiefly frost bitten. The three following nights slept in the woods, after going each day about 15 miles on the river Mada-waska, where, finding the ice in many places broken through, I made the men take the banks of the river, but continued on

---

*Although this place is denominated the Grand Falls, the cataract is a mile distant.

the ice all the way myself. On the 18th, crossing the Lake Tamasquata: it was here we were apprehensive of being cut off by the enemy, being in the territory of the United States; however, we did not fall in with them. On the 19th, commenced our march across the Grande Portage, or neck of land between the above Lake and the river St. Lawrence; this was dreadfully fatiguing, continually marching up and down hill, and the snow upwards of five feet deep. The other division being ahead, was very serviceable to us by their treading the snow down, which made a small path just sufficient for one man to walk on, but frequently, in slipping our feet off the path, we went up to our shoulders in snow; got half way through this night, and again slept in the woods: the distance through is 38 miles. On the afternoon of the 20th reached the St. Lawrence, and found thirty carioles waiting to convey us to Riviere de Caps, a French village about three miles distant. The next day procured carioles for all the men to Kamaraska, another village 15 miles distant. On the 22d reached Riviere Oneille, a neat little village, distant from Kamaraska about 12 miles. I should mention, that from Kamaraska to Kingston is 478 miles, which we were obliged to march, as on our arrival at Quebec we had not sufficient interest to procure more sleighs than sufficient to carry our provisions, baggage, and sick. On the 24th reached St. Rocques, another village, distant 13 miles; the 25th, La Forte, 15 miles; the 26th, St. Thomas, 18 miles; the 27th, Berthier, 10 miles; and on the 28th, Point Levy, opposite Quebec, a distance of 20 miles. On the following morning launched the canoes through the broken ice, and crossed over to the city. You would have been much diverted to see the Canadians in the canoes, watching a favourable opportunity to get through the ice, and perhaps each taking a different route; some got entangled, and were not able to extricate themselves for hours; at the same time drifting up and down as the current set them. In attempting to launch one over the ice, I fell through it up to my neck, and was two hours before I could get my clothes shifted. Marched the people on board the *Æolus* and *Indian*, lying in Wolf's Cove, and then gave them leave to go on shore. The following morning the first division again proceeded on the march, and the next morning myself, with the second, followed. I forgot mentioning to you an unfortunate accident which happened to me on the second day of our march from Presque Isle: by a severe fall on the ice, I broke the bone of the fore finger of my right hand, between the knuckle and the wrist, so that for five weeks I had my hand in splints, and suspended in a sling, which I found not a little inconvenience from, and not until my arrival here did the bone unite, and then so awkwardly as to leave a very considerable lump on my hand; I have lost the use of my knuckle, but can use the finger, as you may see by my writing.

The first day of our march from Quebec, stopped for the night at St. Augustine, 15 miles distant from that city. On the 3d, at Cape Sante, 15 miles. On the 4th, at Grondines, 18 miles. On the 5th, at Baptisca, 10 miles. On the 6th, arrived at Trois Rivieres, 21 miles; this is considered the third river in Canada.— I did not halt here, but marched three miles beyond it, to avoid the trouble of collecting the people, as I knew they were too tired to walk back that distance. On the 7th, stopped at Machiche, 15 miles. On the 8th, at Masquinonge, 16 miles. On the 9th, at Berthier, 17 miles. On the 19th, at La Valtre, 15 miles. On the 11th, at Pegerrigue, 15 miles; and the next morning marched through Montreal to La Chiene, 12 miles beyond it. On passing the monument erected to the memory of the immortal Lord Nelson, halted, and gave three cheers, which much pleased the inhabitants.

From Montreal to this place we were eleven days performing a journey of 190 miles; the places where we stopped I have not noted, as we seldom found a village, but mostly scattered houses, inhabited by all nations; *viz.* English, Scotch, Dutch, American, and a few French. We passed several tremendous Rapids; the Long Son in particular, which was most awfully grand to look at. We likewise passed Chrystian's Farm, where Colonel Morrison defeated General Wilkin's army, with a mere handful of men. On the 22d of March we reached this place: the officers and seamen of the squadron were drawn out to receive us with three cheers: we were lodged in a block-house, and allowed four days to recruit. I was then appointed to the gun-boat service (as was Lieutenant Russel), under Captain Owen. In a few days I joined the *Princess Charlotte*, of 42 guns, commanded by Captain William Howe Mulcaster, as first lieutenant. The *Regent* and her were on the stocks, planked up, and their decks laying. The *Regent* is about eight feet longer than our 38-gun frigates, having fifteen ports on each side of her main-deck, and guns on her gangways, so that she carries twenty-eight long 24-pounders on her main-deck; eight 68-pound carronades, two long 18, and eighteen 32-pound carronades on her upper deck, with a complement of 550 men. The *Princess Charlotte* is about the length of a 32-gun frigate, but eighteen inches more beam, pierced for thirteen ports on her main-deck, and carrying twenty-four long 24-pounders on that deck, with two 68-pound carronades, and sixteen 32-pound carronades on her upper deck, and a complement of 330 men. The other ships are the *Wolfe* (now the *Montreal*), a ship corvette, of 20 guns, chiefly 32-pound carronades, and 120 men; the *Royal George* (now the *Niagara*), of eighteen guns, 32-pound carronades, with a long 24-pounder on a pivot abaft, as in each of these ships; her complement 120 men. Two brigs, the *Star* and *Charwell*, the former of 14, the latter of 16 guns; the largest 100, the other 90 men. Two schooners, the *Magnet* and *Netley*, of 10 guns each, and 75 men. Ten or twelve gun-boats (none of them covered over), one carrying a long 18-pounder and a 32-pound carronade; the others a 32-pound carronade each. The establishment is for three lieutenants to be on the gunboat service, each to a division of four boats, commanded by midshipmen.

From the time of my joining the *Princess Charlotte* I never quitted the ship or barracks. The interval between her launching, till we went to sea, was but eleven days, three of which were occupied in heaving down the ship, to get the cleats off her bottom. The result of our attack upon the enemy's Fort Oswego you already know.

Arthur Wellesley, Marquess of Wellington, to Henry, Earl Bathurst

As the campaign of 1814 got under way, Henry Bathurst, the British secretary of state for war and the colonies, continued to deny George Prevost's requests for significant reinforcements. Both men knew that Britain's chief military threat came not from America but from France, and that few troops could be diverted from the Continental war until after Napoleon was defeated. Yet in early 1814 the prospects for British success on the Continent looked hopeful: after the Battle of Leipzig in October 1813, an allied coalition led by Russia pushed Napoleon west of the Rhine, while in the Iberian Peninsula, Field Marshal Arthur Wellesley, Marquess (later Duke) of Wellington, pushed north toward the border with France. In the following letter, Wellington gives Bathurst advice about how to wage war on the United States, counsel informed by his experience in Spain and Portugal, where, as in America, roads were few, army transportation slow, and control of rivers essential to success.

MY DEAR LORD,   Garris, 22nd February, 1814.

I have received your Lordship's letters of the 28th January and 10th and 14th February.

In answer to the first, I have to inform your Lordship that I have turned my mind but little to American affairs; that I have but little knowledge of the topography of that country, and I have no means here of obtaining information to enable me to form an opinion on which I could at all rely.

I believe that the defence of Canada, and the co-operation of the Indians, depends upon the navigation of the lakes; and I see that both Sir G. Prevost and Commodore Barclay complain of the want of the crews of two sloops of war. Any offensive operation founded upon Canada must be preceded by the establishment of a naval superiority on the lakes.

But even if we had that superiority, I should doubt our being able to do more than secure the points on those lakes at which the Americans could have access. In such countries as America, very extensive, thinly peopled, and producing but little food in proportion to their extent, military operations by large bodies are impracticable, unless the party carrying them on has the uninterrupted use of a navigable river, or very extensive means of land transport, which such a country can rarely supply.

I conceive, therefore, that were your army larger even than the proposed augmentation would make it, you could not quit the lakes; and, indeed, you would be tied to them the more necessarily in proportion as your army would be large.

Then, as to landings upon the coast, they are liable to the same objections, though to a greater degree, than an offensive operation founded upon Canada. You may go to a certain extent, as far as a navigable river or your means of transport will enable you to subsist, provided your force is sufficiently large compared with that which the enemy will oppose to you. But I do not know where you could carry on such an operation which would be so injurious to the Americans as to force them to sue for peace, which is what one would wish to see.

The prospect in regard to America is not consoling. That power will always hang on the skirts of Great Britain, unless there should be some change in her own situation; or the state of the Spanish colonies should make an alteration, not only in America in general, but in the colonial system of the world; or our own colonies in America should grow so fast, as that, with very little assistance from the mother country, they shall be equal to their own defence.

I am quite certain that Buonaparte will begin the war again, if he can, by interfering as a neutral in our dispute with America.

I am obliged to your Lordship for the supplies of money, which are very ample.

I am very much obliged to your Lordship for the answer you have given regarding reports. There would be no end to reports if I were to send all I receive; and it would be no easy matter to make out what happened on any occasion. The best of it is, that I was on the field myself, before the action was over, and before the attack with General Byng's brigade. In the same manner, I was present in all Sir John Hope's actions; and when I am there, although I may choose to say that another commands, I suppose I command myself. I know that I am responsible, and your Lordship would not be satisfied if I did not make the report.

I am sure I always mean to do justice to the officers under my command, and I hope their friends will be convinced that I have not held back their reports in order to do them an injury.

Believe me, &c.

WELLINGTON.

The Crew of USS Essex
to the Crew of HMS Phoebe

Late in the year 1812, David Porter, captain of the U.S. frigate *Essex* (46 guns), rounded Cape Horn and brought the war to the Pacific. For more than a year he cruised those waters, destroying British whalers, taking prizes, and living off the enemy. "The valuable whale Fishery there is entirely destroyed," Porter wrote Secretary of the Navy William Jones, "and the actual injury we have done [to the British] may be estimated at two and a half millions of dollars." Porter greatly exaggerated the value of the British losses but did do enough damage to get the attention of the Admiralty, which in late 1813 dispatched a squadron of three ships to bring him to heel. In February of 1814, two of the British ships, the frigate *Phoebe* (46 or 53 guns) and the sloop *Cherub* (26 guns), caught up with *Essex*, which they found at anchor in the neutral harbor of Valparaiso, Chile. The crew of *Phoebe* blockaded the harbor and harassed Porter with taunting missives, hollered insults, and ribald songs to the tune of "Yankee Doodle." On March 9, the crew of *Essex* sent the crew of *Phoebe* the following reply.

On board the U.S. frigate *Essex*, March 9th, 1814.
The sons of liberty and commerce, on board the saucy *Essex*, whose motto is "Free Trade and Sailor's Rights," present their compliments to their oppressed brother tars, on board the ship whose motto is too tedious to mention, and hope they will put an end to all this nonsense of singing, sporting, hunting and writing, which we know less about than the use of our guns— Send the *Cherub* away, we will meet your frigate and fight you, then shake hands and be friends; and whether you take us or we take you, either will be to your advantage; as in the first case, you will not doubt, for the service you render in a cause every brave and free man detests, be turned over to Greenwich hospital or to a new ship, on your arrival to England; and if we

take you, we shall respect the rights of a sailor, hail you as brethren whom we have liberated from slavery, and place you in future beyond the reach of a press gang.

FROM THE SONS OF LIBERTY.

A Midshipman of HMS Phoebe
to the Crew of USS Essex

In reply to *Essex*'s challenge, a midshipman of *Phoebe* wrote the following verse. Porter believed the doggerel was the work of *Phoebe*'s commander, Captain Sir James Hillyar.

———————

To you, Americans, who seek redress,
For fancied wrongs from Britons you've sustained;
Hear what we Britons now to you address,
From malice free, from blasphemy unstain'd;
Think not, vain boasters, that your insidious lay,
Which calls for vengeance from the Almighty God—
Can from their duty Britons lead away,
Or path of honor which they have always trod.
No—Your vile infamy can never fail,
To excite disgust in each true Briton's heart;
Your proffered liberty cannot avail,
For virtue is the sons of Albion's crest.
Our God, our king, our country and our laws,
We proudly reverence like Britons true;
Our captain who defends such glorious cause,
Meets due respect from all his grateful crew.
When to the battle we're by duty called,
Our cause, like Britons, bravely we'll maintain;
W'ell fight like men whom fear ne'er yet appall'd,
And hope, AMERICANS! you'll do the same.
Your vile letter, which on board was brought,
We scorn to answer, tho' with malice frought;
But if, by such foul means, you think to make
Dissentions rise our loyalty to shake,
Know then we are Britons all, both stout and true,
We love our king, our country, captain too;

When honor calls, we'll glory in his name,
Acquit like men and hope you'll do the same.

Lieut. Ingraham acknowledged the above to have been written by a midshipman of the *Phoebe*, and with the approbation of com. Hillyar.

David G. Farragut: from The Life of David Glasgow Farragut, Embodying His Journal and Letters, *by Loyall Farragut*

In his *Journal of a Cruise* (1822), David Porter wrote: "Finding Captain Hillyar determined to yield none of the advantages of his superior force, and being informed there were other ships bound into the Pacific Ocean in pursuit of me, I secretly resolved to take every means of provoking him to a contest with his single ship. . . . On the 28th of March, the day after this determination was formed, the wind came on to blow fresh from the southward, when I parted my larboard cable and dragged my starboard anchor directly out to sea. Not a moment was to be lost in getting sail on the ship." When a sudden squall cracked and splintered *Essex*'s topmast, Porter was forced to retreat into a small bay and to watch helplessly as *Phoebe* closed in, with *Cherub* close behind. Porter's adopted son, twelve-year-old David G. Farragut, was aboard *Essex* that day, and several years later recorded his memories in a journal, published by his family in 1879.

During the action I was like "Paddy in the cat-harpins," a man on occasions. I performed the duties of Captain's aid, quarter-gunner, powder-boy, and in fact did everything that was required of me. I shall never forget the horrid impression made upon me at the sight of the first man I had ever seen killed. He was a boatswain's mate, and was fearfully mutilated. It staggered and sickened me at first; but they soon began to fall around me so fast that it all appeared like a dream, and produced no effect on my nerves. I can remember well, while I was standing near the Captain, just abaft the mainmast, a shot came through the waterways and glanced upward, killing four men who were standing by the side of the gun, taking the last one in the head and scattering his brains over both of us. But this awful sight did not affect me half as much as the death of the first poor fellow. I neither thought of nor noticed anything but the working of the guns.

On one occasion Midshipman Isaacs came up to the Captain and reported that a quarter-gunner named Roach had deserted his post. The only reply of the Captain, addressed to me, was, "Do your duty, sir." I seized a pistol and went in pursuit of the fellow, but did not find him. It appeared, subsequently, that when the ship was reported to be on fire he had contrived to get into the only boat that could be kept afloat, and escaped, with six others, to the shore. The most remarkable part of this affair was that Roach had always been a leading man in the ship, and, on the occasion previously mentioned, when the Phœbe seemed about to run into us, in the harbor of Valparaiso, and the boarders were called away, I distinctly remember this man standing in an exposed position on the cathead, with sleeves rolled up and cutlass in hand, ready to board, his countenance expressing eagerness for the fight: which goes to prove that personal courage is a very peculiar virtue. Roach was brave with a prospect of success, but a coward in adversity.

Soon after this, some gun-primers were wanted, and I was sent after them. In going below, while I was on the ward-room ladder, the Captain of the gun directly opposite the hatchway was struck full in the face by an eighteen-pound shot, and fell back on me. We tumbled down the hatch together. I struck on my head, and, fortunately, he fell on my hips. I say fortunately, for, as he was a man of at least two hundred pounds' weight, I would have been crushed to death if he had fallen directly across my body. I lay for some moments stunned by the blow, but soon recovered consciousness enough to rush up on deck. The Captain, seeing me covered with blood, asked if I was wounded, to which I replied, "I believe not, sir." "Then," said he, "where are the primers?" This first brought me completely to my senses, and I ran below again and carried the primers on deck. When I came up the second time I saw the Captain fall, and in my turn ran up and asked if he was wounded. He answered me almost in the same words, "I believe not, my son; but I felt a blow on the top of my head." He must have been knocked down by the windage of a passing shot, as his hat was somewhat damaged.

When my services were not required for other purposes, I

generally assisted in working a gun; would run and bring powder from the boys, and send them back for more, until the
Captain wanted me to carry a message; and this continued to
employ me during the action.

When it was determined to surrender, the Captain sent me
to ascertain if Mr. ———— had the signal-book, and, if so, to
throw it overboard. I could not find him or the book for some
time; but at last saw the latter lying on the sill of a port, and
dashed it into the sea. After the action, Mr. ———— said he was
overboard himself, trying to clear the book from some part of
the wreck where it had lodged—a very unfortunate story, as I
had seen it sink into the depths below.

Isaacs and I amused ourselves throwing overboard pistols
and other small arms, to prevent their falling into the hands of
the enemy. At length the boarding officer came on board, and,
running up to Captain Porter, asked him how he would account to somebody (I do not remember who) for allowing his
men to jump overboard, and at the same time demanded his
sword. "That, sir," replied Porter, "is reserved for your master." The Captain went on board the Phœbe, and I followed
half an hour later.

I have already remarked how soon I became accustomed to
scenes of blood and death during the action; but after the
battle had ceased, when, on going below, I saw the mangled
bodies of my shipmates, dead and dying, groaning and expiring with the most patriotic sentiments on their lips, I became
faint and sick; my sympathies were all aroused. As soon as I
recovered from the first shock, however, I hastened to assist
the surgeon in staunching and dressing the wounds of my
comrades. Among the badly wounded was one of my best
friends, Lieutenant J. G. Cowell. When I spoke to him he said,
"O Davy, I fear it is all up with me." I found that he had lost a
leg just above the knee, and the Doctor informed me that his
life might have been saved if he had consented to the amputation of the limb an hour before; but, when it was proposed to
drop another patient and attend to him, he replied, "No, Doctor, none of that; fair play is a jewel. One man's life is as dear as
another's; I would not cheat any poor fellow out of his turn."
Thus died one of the best officers and bravest men among us.

It was wonderful to find dying men, who had hardly ever attracted notice among the ship's company, uttering sentiments, with their last breath, worthy of a Washington. You might have heard in all directions, "Don't give her up, Logan!"—a sobriquet for Porter—"Hurrah for liberty!" and similar expressions. One of the crew of a bow gun told me of a singular act of heroism on the part of a young Scotchman, named Bissley, who had one leg shot off close to the groin. He used his handkerchief as a tourniquet, and said to his comrades:

"I left my own country and adopted the United States to fight for her. I hope I have this day proved myself worthy of the country of my adoption. I am no longer of any use to you or to her, so good-by!" With these words, he leaned on the sill of the port and threw himself overboard.

Many of our fine fellows bled to death for want of tourniquets. An old quarter master, named Francis Bland, was standing at the wheel when I saw a shot coming over the fore-yard, in such a direction that I thought it would strike him or me; so I told him to jump, at the same time pulling him toward me. At that instant the shot took off his right leg, and I afterward found that my coat-tail had been carried away. I helped the old fellow below, and inquired for him after the action, but he had died before he could be attended to.

I escaped without injury, except the bruises from my fall.

Lieutenant Wilmer, who had been sent forward to let go the sheet anchor, was knocked overboard by a shot. After the action his little negro boy, "Ruff," came on deck and asked me what had become of his master, and when I imparted to him the sad news he deliberately jumped into the sea and was drowned.

Mr. McKnight still lived, and with Midshipman Lyman was to go to England, or to Rio de Janeiro, to give evidence in regard to the capture of the ship. Cowell was dead, and Odenheimer was the only lieutenant left with us. Barnwell, the acting master, had been wounded in the breast, but was doing well. Isaacs, Ogden, Dusenberry, and I were all who remained of the midshipmen who were not seriously injured.

Doctors Hoffman and Montgomery escaped unhurt, although

some of their patients were killed by flying splinters while under their hands. These gentlemen exhibited great skill and nerve in their care of the wounded.

It is astonishing what powers of endurance some men possess. There was one instance of a man who swam to the shore with scarcely a square inch of his body which had not been burned, and, although he was deranged for some days, he ultimately recovered, and served with me in the West Indies. He was the same old boatswain's mate, Kingsbury, who distinguished himself off Cape Horn, for which he had been made boatswain of the Essex Junior. He accompanied Captain Downes on board in his boat, as he said, "to share the fate of his old ship." Another seaman swam ashore with sixteen or eighteen pieces of iron in his leg, scales from the muzzle of his gun. He also recovered, without losing his leg.

I went on board the Phœbe about 8 A.M. on the morning of the 29th, and was ushered into the steerage. I was so mortified at our capture that I could not refrain from tears. While in this uncomfortable state, I was aroused by hearing a young reefer call out:

"A prize! a prize! Ho, boys, a fine grunter, by Jove!"

I saw at once that he had under his arm a pet pig belonging to our ship, called "Murphy." I claimed the animal as my own.

"Ah," said he, "but you are a prisoner, and your pig also."

"We always respect private property," I replied, and, as I had seized hold of Murphy, I determined not to let go, unless "compelled by superior force." This was fun for the oldsters, who immediately sung out:

"Go it, my little Yankee! If you can thrash Shorty, you shall have your pig."

"Agreed!" said I.

A ring was formed in the open space, and at it we went. I soon found that my antagonist's pugilistic education did not come up to mine. In fact, he was no match for me, and was compelled to give up the pig. So I took master Murphy under my arm, feeling that I had, in some degree, wiped out the disgrace of our defeat.

I was sent for by Captain Hillyar to come into his cabin, where Captain Porter was, and asked to take some breakfast, when, seeing my discomfiture, he remarked in a very kind manner:

"Never mind, my little fellow, it will be your turn next, per-haps."

I said I hoped so, and left the cabin to hide my emotion.

We were all soon put on parole, and went on shore; our wounded from the ship being moved to a comfortable house hired for their accommodation. I volunteered my aid to our Surgeon as an assistant, and I never earned Uncle Sam's money so faithfully as I did during that hospital service. I rose at day-light and arranged the bandages and plasters until 8 A.M.; then, after breakfast, I went to work at my patients. I was employed thus until the 27th of April, when Captain Porter succeeded in making arrangements with Captain Hillyar for the transporta-tion of our crew to the United States in the Essex Junior. That vessel was accordingly disarmed, and we embarked in her for New York.

Andrew Jackson to John Wood

Even as Tecumseh's war against America in the Old Northwest ended at the Battle of the Thames, the war waged by the Red Stick Creeks in the Old Southwest grew in intensity. The Red Sticks, who occupied most of Alabama and part of Georgia, declared war not only on the Americans who encroached upon their land but also on those peaceful factions of the Creek Nation that were embracing American ways. Throughout 1813, Andrew Jackson led a thousand unruly Tennessee men in several successful actions against the Red Sticks. As word of Jackson's victories spread, recruitment picked up, so that by February 1814 his troops numbered four thousand, including six hundred regulars. Jackson hoped that the regulars would give "strength to my arm & quell mutiny," but certain elements of the Tennessee militia remained intractable. When one new recruit, an exhausted, hungry, ill-clad eighteen-year-old named John Wood, profanely refused to obey orders during a night watch, Jackson ordered him court-martialed. Wood was convicted of disobedience, disrespect, and mutiny, and sentenced to death by firing squad—the first soldier to be executed for a crime other than desertion since the American Revolution.

Fort Strother 14th march 1814

Genl. order,
John Woods,

You have been tried by a court martial on the charges of disobedience of orders, disrespect to your commanding officer, & mutiny; & have been found guilty of all of them. The court which found you guilty of these charges has sentenced you to suffer death by shooting; and this sentence the commanding General has thought proper, & even felt himself bound, to approve, and to order to be executed—

The offences of which you have been found guilty are such as cannot be permitted to pass unpunished in an army, but at the hazard of its ruin—

This is the second time you have violated the duties of a soldier—the second time you have been guilty of offences, the punishment of which is death. When you had been regularly mustered into the service of your country, & were marching to head Quarters, under the immediate command of Brig Genl. Roberts, you were one of those who in violation of your engagement—of all the principles of honor, & of the order of your commanding General, rose in mutiny & deserted. You were arrested, & brought back; & notwithstanding the little claim you had to mercy, your General, unwilling to inflict the severity of the law, & influenced by the hope that you would atone by your future good conduct for your past error, thought proper to grant you all a pardon. This ought to have produced a salutary impression on a mind not totally dead, to every honourable sentiment, & not perversely & obstinately bent on spreading discord, & confusion in the army. It unfortunately produced no such impression on yours. But a few weeks after you had been brought back, you have been found guilty of offences not less criminal than those for which you had been so lately pardoned & which if the law, had been rigidly enforced, would have subjected you to death. This evinces but too manifestly, an incorrigible disposition of heart—a rebelious and obstinate temper of mind, which, as it cannot be rectified, ought not to be permitted to diffuse its influence amongst others—

An army cannot exist where order & subordination are wholly disregarded—it cannot exist with much credit to itself, or service to the country which employs it, but where they are observed with the most punctilious exactness. The disobedience of orders, & the contempt of officers speedily lead to a state of disorganization, & ruin; & mutiny; which includes the others aims still more immediately at the dissolution of an army—Of all these offences you have twice been guilty; & have once been pardoned. Your General must forget what he owes to the service he is engaged in, & to the country which employs him, if by pardoning you again, he should furnish an example to sanction measures which would bring ruin on the army he commands—

This is an important crisis; in which if we all act as becomes us, every thing is to be hoped for towards the accomplishment of the objects of our government; if otherwise, every thing to be feared. How it becomes us to act, we all know, and what our punishment shall be, if we act otherwise, must be known also. The law which points out the one, prescribes the other. Between that law, & its offender, the commanding General ought not to be expected to interpose, & *will not* where there are no circumstances of alleviation. There appear to be none such in your case; & however as a man he may deplore your unhappy situation, he cannot as an officer, without infringing his duty, arrest the sentence of the court martial

Andrew Jackson
Major Genl.

Copy, attest
Joel Parrish Jr. Secratary—

Andrew Jackson to Rachel Jackson

In the middle of March 1814, Jackson learned that a thousand Red
Stick Creeks had occupied and fortified an oxbow on the Tallapoosa
River known as Tohopeka, or Horseshoe Bend. He marched to the
scene with a force of more than three thousand soldiers and Indians,
including a hundred friendly Creeks, and laid plans for an attack. On
the morning of March 27, Jackson pounded the Red Sticks' breastworks with artillery while his Indian allies swam across the river and
made off with their canoes. Deprived of their means of escape, the
Red Sticks stoically met Jackson's overwhelming frontal assault, and
in the words of one witness, the Tallapoosa became "a river of blood."
Some eight hundred Red Sticks were massacred, while Jackson sustained fewer than two hundred casualties. A day after writing the following account of the battle for his wife, Jackson proclaimed to the
people of Alabama that while the Red Sticks had yet to surrender,
"the fiends of the Tallapoosa will no longer murder Women and
Children or disturb the quiet of our borders."

Head quarters Fort Williams
April 1rst. 1814

My Dear,

I returned to this place on yesterday three oclock P.M. from
an excursion against Tohopeka, and about one hour after had
the pleasure of receiving your affectionate letter of the 22nd
ultimo—

I have the pleasure to state to you that on the 27th. march
that I attacked & have destroyed the whole combined force, of
the Newyokas, oakfuskes Hillabays, Fishponds, ocaias, and
ufalee, Tribes—The *carnage* was *dreadfull*—They had possessed themselves of one of the most military sites, I Ever saw,
which they had as strongly fortified with logs, across the neck
of a bend—I endeavoured, to levell the works with my cannon,
but in vain—The balls passed thro the works without shaking the wall—but carrying destruction to the enemy behind

it—I had sent Genl Coffee across the river, with his horse and Indians who had compleatly surrounded the bend which cut off [   ] their escape—and the cherokees Effected a landing on the extreme point of the bend with about one hundred and fifty of Genls coffees Brigade, including Capt Russles spy company—The Battle raged, about two hours, when I found those engaged in the interior of the bend, were about to be overpowered, I ordered, the charge and carried the works, by storm—after which they Indians took possessession of the river bank, and part of their works raised with brush getting into the interior of the bend—and It was dark before we finished killing them—I ordered the dead bodies of the Indians to be counted, the next morning, and exclusive of those buried in their watry grave, who were killed in the river and who after being wounded plunged into it, there were counted, five hundred and fifty seven—from the report of Genl Coffee and the officers surrounding the bend, they are of oppinion, that there could not be less than three hundred, killed in the river, who sunk and could not be counted—I have no doubt, but at least Eight hundred and fifty were slain—about twenty who had hid under the bank in the water, made their Escape in the night, one of whom was taken the next morning who gives this account, that they were all wounded from which I believe about 19 wounded Indians alone escaped—we took about three hundred and fifty prisoners, weomen & children and three warriors—What effect this will produce upon those infatuated and deluded people I cannot yet say—having destroyed at To'hope'ka, three of their principl prophets leaving but two in their nation—having tread their holy ground as the termed it, and destroyed all their chiefs & warriors on the Tallapoosee river above the big bend, it is probable they may now sue for peace should they not (If I can be supplied with provisions) I will give them, with the permission of heaven the final stroke at the hickory ground, in a few days we have lost in killed of the whites 26, and one hundred and seven wounded—amonghst the former is Major Montgomery who bravely fell on the walls, and of the latter Colo. Carroll—slightly—our friends all safe, and Jack you may say to Mrs. Caffery reallised all my expectations he fought bravely—and killed an indian—every officer and man did his duty—the 39th distinguished themselves and so did the militia, who stormed the works with them. There never was more heroism or roman courage displayed—I write in haste surrounded with a pressure of business, and a little fatigued—I will write you again before I leave this place—for the present I can only add, that I hope shortly to put an end to the war and return to your arms, kiss my little andrew for me, tell him I have a warriors bow & quiver for him—give my compliments to all friends, and cheer up the spirits of your Sister Cafferry—and receive my sincere prayers for your health & happiness untill I return—affectionately adieu—

Andrew Jackson

Robert Young to Phineas Riall

The British had planned a winter campaign on the Niagara frontier, but it was never executed. At Fort Niagara, one of their few remaining strongholds in the United States, the army was bored, aimless, and impatient for action. The commanding officer at the fort, Colonel Robert Young, could find no way to manage their restlessness or to stem the trickle of desertion from the post. In despair he wrote to his superior, Major General Phineas Riall.

—————

FORT NIAGARA, March 17th, 1814.

MY DEAR SIR,—

I am heartbroken at the general spirit of defection which has evinced itself in the regiment. I cannot divine the cause. I have indirectly employed agents to discover the source of grievance and complaint, and the full result of my inquiries are that they have incessant fatigues independent of their military duties and no comforts of any kind. In fact the men seem generally dissatisfied, and that spirit once disseminated amongst them not all the exertions and rhetoric of the officers can counterbalance. I feel my personal situation with respect to the regiment more humiliating than I have language to express. The regiment has lost its wonted character, and the more mortifying circumstance to me is that the very best men in the corps have evinced the greatest disposition to desert. I am not myself. I do not know what to say upon the occasion. I am chagrined and desponding and can only most conscientiously aver that I am ashamed and feel disgraced by associating my name with what I formerly and *proudly* designated the King's Regiment. In the name of God remove us as unworthy of retaining the Post of Honour. My confidence in the regiment is now gone, and its villainous conduct will bring my grey hairs with sorrow to the grave. It is hard, nay cruel, that after more than twenty-two years service in the regt. I should live to witness the disgrace which has been brought upon it. In despair I remain,

SECOND BATTLE OF LACOLLE MILL: LOWER CANADA, MARCH 1814

George McFeely: Diary

After his disastrous attempt on Montreal in the fall of 1813, General Wilkinson ordered his army into winter quarters at French Mills, New York. Desperate to restore his reputation, he considered many possible objectives for the spring and at last settled on taking out the British outpost at Lacolle Mill, Lower Canada, about seventy miles east of French Mills. Consisting of a heavily fortified stone mill and block-house garrisoned by 180 men, the outpost seemed an easy target for his army of four thousand. On March 27, Wilkinson's army began a two-day march to Odelltown, just south of Lacolle Mill, where they found the ground too muddy for the transport of fieldpieces; on the 30th, the day of the attack, only three of the smallest cannons could be brought within firing distance of the mill. Lieutenant Colonel George McFeely, of the 22nd U.S. Infantry Regiment, recounts Wilkinson's ill-fated artillery attack, which ended in a British defensive victory, 154 U.S. casualties, and Wilkinson's removal from command.

March 30th. The whole army was on the march, a little after sunrise. About 11 o'clock our riflemen fell in with and engaged the enemy at Odletown. The firing increased, the first brigade came up to the support of the riflemen. The second and third brigades having arrived on the field of battle and commenced to deploy into line when the British gave way and retreated to LaColle Mill. An attack was made on our right flank from a point in the woods, but they were soon dispersed by Lt. Scof-field with his company who were detached for that purpose. In this affair I saw the Congreve rocket used for the first time. The enemy threw a number which passed over our and burst in the air harmless. They might answer a good purpose for burning a town or frightening raw soldiers, but in the field they are a poor contrivance for killing men, when compared to the rifle and musket.

The road to LaColle was blocked so that our army had to counter march about a mile and took a by-road through the deep woods. The enemy harassed our front at every advantageous piece of ground. At one place they had killed two Riflemen, after this the Riflemen flanked the road. The enemy intended to make a stand on a piece of rising ground where there was a cabin. They told the woman off the cabin their intentions and she must clear out. She accordingly wrapped a blanket around each of her two little girls and one around herself and took to the woods. The Riflemen in flanking the road mistaking them for Indians fired and wounded the two girls, the one through the hip and the other through the abdomen; two balls also passed through the woman's clothing. They discovered their mistake and carried them home to their cabin. This firing in the woods at the poor woman and children alarmed the enemy, they believed they would be surrounded, hastily retreated from their ambuscade. When the main army came up I saw two dead riflemen lying at the cabin door. I stopped for a minute while the troops were filing past to ask the cause of the two dead men lying there. The poor woman was almost distracted, she informed me of the circumstances, how her little girls were wounded. One of our surgeons was dressing their wounds at the time. He said the one was only a flesh-wound and not dangerous, but the other was mortal. I asked the woman where her husband was, she said she did not know where. I asked if the British had not compelled him to take up arms and enter into their ranks to fight the Yankees, she replied, "I do not know, but as like as not they did." I proceeded on and with some difficulty I regained my place in line.

On arriving at the Mill, the enemy were soon driven in. Gen'l Smith's brigade was formed with its left resting on the road and his right extending off towards the Sorel river. General Bissell's brigade was formed on his right on the road and opposite General Smith's left extending towards the LaColle River. These two brigades formed at an angle, fronting and within two hundred yards of the Mill. General Macomb's brigade was drawn across the road in the rear of the angle and one hundred yards in rear on the front line. A battery of three or four light pieces formed in the road and forty yards in front of the angle of the front line. Two regiments were thrown across the LaColle River for the purpose of cutting off the enemy should he attempt to retreat. About an hour after the battle commenced the British sallied out of the Mill and formed under the bank of the LaColle, mounted the bank, beat the charge and advanced in column (their grenadiers in front). Our fire was reserved until within forty yards, when a tremendous volley was fired from four pieces of artillery and two thousand infantry. The whole front of the British column went down, the remainder retreated into the mill in confusion. A grenadier who was in front of the British column was taken; he was wounded in fifteen different places, and strange to say he could walk, none of his wounds were deep or dangerous.

Our artillerymen suffered severely, the guns in the evening were supplied and served by infantry. Our light guns making no impression on the enemy's works and night coming on, the army was drawn off and marched to Odletown, five miles in the rear. I was ordered down with three regiments and covered the front line while it was filing off. General Wilkinson remained on the ground until the last corps filed off.

The road to Odletown had many deep ravines, there were full of water running like a torrent; this was in consequence of the fine day and a warm south wind that blew all day. I never saw the snow melt so fast as it did this day. Our men were all wet up to the haunches and much fatigued, having been on their feet from daylight in the morning until 11 o'clock at night. Our loss was about 130 killed and wounded, all of which were brought off the ground to Odletown. The place could have easily been taken had the heavy cannon been brought up, but this was impossible without a great deal of trouble and time such was the state of the road.

During the battle two soldiers belonging to Captain Whitting's company, 23rd Regt., the one named Dexter, a youth of about sixteen, the other's name was Frank, who was a deserter from the British and enlisted in Captain Whitting's company, wandered off from their company in the woods to the left of our lines, perhaps in search of plunder. They fell in with a British picquet guard who was going down the LaColle River on the ice to join their companions in the Mill. Frank and Dexter were made prisoners and taken along. Frank was recognized by some of his old companions. They arrived at the Mill at the time the British were forming under the bank and preparing to charge our cannon and the guard was formed in the column, and Dexter and Frank were left in charge of one soldier. The column mounted the bank to charge, the British soldier with his two prisoners anxious to see the fun crawled up the bank as to creep over. Dexter observing his keeper off guard picked up his own musket that had been laying on the ground where the column had formed, fired at five paces and killed the British soldier dead, he rolled down the bank to Dexter's feet. Frank knew nothing of the matter till it was done. Dexter stripped his enemy dead of his side arms, plundered his pockets, took to his heels with his companion up under cover of the river until they had gained the woods and came in safe in the rear of our lines. Dexter came up to me much excited with British belts on and said, "Well, Colonel, I have been a prisoner and just made my escape, I killed one red coats and here is his cartridge box and belt." I asked him how dare he leave the ranks without leave, he said Captain Whitting had permitted himself to report to me. I told him I did not believe one word he said and ordered him, to fall into the ranks in his place immediately. He turned round and exclaimed, "Well, then you may ask Frank the fifer, by G_d I killed one red coat any how." I did not believe this story at the time, but afterwards hearing from Captain Whitting, Frank's story of the matter which corroborated Dexter's statement so well that I was induced to believe it to be a matter of fact.

Benjamin F. Browne: from "Papers of an old Dartmoor Prisoner"

Benjamin Frederick Browne, of Salem, Massachusetts, was nineteen years old in September 1812, when he enlisted as a surgeon's mate on the privateer *Alfred*. On April 20, 1814, he was serving on the U.S. schooner *Frolic* when the ship was captured, somewhere off the coast of Cuba, by HMS *Shelburne*. Browne was taken to Barbados and then shipped to England, where he was imprisoned for six months in Devon's notorious Dartmoor Prison. After the war he returned to Salem, opened an apothecary, and became a respected civic and political leader. An ardent Democrat, he was Salem's postmaster when in 1846 fellow party man Nathaniel Hawthorne won a political appointment at the Salem Custom House, in part thanks to Browne's recommendation. That same year, Hawthorne edited Browne's memoirs, which were then serialized anonymously under the title "Papers of an old Dartmoor Prisoner" in the *United States Magazine and Democratic Review*. In this excerpt, Browne writes of his fascination with the hardened criminals at Dartmoor.

W<small>E</small> had a gang of men at Dartmoor, called "rough allies," and they were as rascally a set of devils as ever escaped drowning, to have the chance at some future day of standing on air and pulling hemp. I know not the etymology of the word; but it was highly expressive of the qualities of those who bore it. They were rough as untamed bears, and allied together in the bonds of wickedness; for they were the very antipodes to anything savoring of morality and decency. I verily believe that three quarters of all the misery and privations we endured here, were owing to these human brutes; and I *know* that however blameable Captain Shortland may have been on the day of the massacre, he would have wanted the pretence for his conduct had it not been supplied by these graceless scoundrels. They were the most miserable, debased wretches one can possibly conceive of; the promoters of all riots and plundering expeditions; and were continually prowling about the prisons, day and night, seeking what they might steal and devour. Some one has aptly enough denominated them the Janizaries of Dartmoor; and the analogy holds that they were the terror and detestation of the orderly portion of the community.

If one of these rough allies coveted the goods of a neighboring shop-keeper, he would go round to some of his comrades, and say that the shop-keeper had sold light penny-worths of tobacco, butter or bread. Immediately the watchword of "Heave O!" would resound throughout the prison; the rough allies would assemble in force, and make a foray upon the shop-keeper, capsize his table and steal his goods; and he would deem himself lucky if he came off no worse.

I find in my diary the following entry: "1815, Feb. 13th. The market stopped in consequence of a man having escaped from the cachot, (or black hole,) where he had been confined some months. He scaled the palisades when the turnkey was off his guard, and got in among the rest of the prisoners, who refused to deliver him up when demanded by Capt. Shortland."

"Mr. ———, a shop-keeper in No. 7, was reported to have said that the man ought to be delivered up, when some rough allies assembled in great force, and demolished his stand and plundered his goods."

Such an occurrence as this was but too common. The principal leader of these wretches was an unprincipled scoundrel, who, I am happy to say, was not an American. He had been tried in the United States for piracy and murder, and defended himself, I have understood, with much ability. He was acquitted for want of evidence, though in prison he often boasted of his crime. He was an artful, plausible fellow, of a very good education, report said learned, and master of several languages and sciences, and possessing an uncommon dexterity in the use of the pen. He could counterfeit any man's handwriting, and so exactly imitate steel-plate engraving, that it was extremely difficult to distinguish between the imitation and the genuine. He was very fluent in the use of language, possessing, what sailors call *the gift of gab*, in perfection.

When he first came to the depot, he took up his residence in No. 7, where he soon set himself to work to stir up strife among the inmates. He asserted that they were cheated by the committee and the cooks, who, he said, were in the daily habit of embezzling a part of their provisions. No other charge could be so likely to excite the indignation of the captives: for the allowance was but small at most, and to abstract any portion of it from hungry maws, was the most heinous offence that could be committed. This the demagogue understood well enough, and he laid his scheme accordingly. He gathered around him all the rough allies, and deluded many right-minded, but unthinking men, of a better character, to his party; when feeling himself to be strong enough, he one day took possession of the cook-house, turned out the cooks and appointed others, and usurped the whole authority of the committee. Like the despot of former times, he was himself the state, but only for a short time; for the holy alliance of the commandant and turnkeys made an invasion of his usurped dominions, overthrew the usurper, vanquished his forces, and led the conqueror off captive to the black hole; and the committee and cooks were reinstated in office. But quietness was not restored to our community; the elements of rebellion were at work; the volcano burst forth, and the chairman of the committee, a highly respectable gentleman, of correct deportment and unassuming manners, nearly sixty years of age, was seized by the rough allies, placed under a guard of their number, and, notwithstanding his age and respectable character, they were preparing to commit further violence on his person by whipping him. But his son, who was also in the same prison, being a high-spirited young man, gathered together a number of his friends, and rescued him from the hands of these desperadoes.

Their leader was in a short time released from the cachot, but he did not come into our prison again. He went into No. 5, where he followed the business of gambling and counterfeiting. He could counterfeit the notes of the Tavistock and Plymouth banks so well, that a great many were passed to the market-people, who came to the prisons. He was also an adept at coining.

I have frequently traced the sure and rapid progress of vice in many young men, who came to the prisons with fair moral characters, and who, before gaming was generally introduced among the prisoners, passed their time in innocent amusements, or in acquiring useful knowledge. As the first step in the career of depravity, he would hover round the gaming-table, where he would soon be fleeced of all the little money he had. His clothing, piece by piece, would be "shoved up the spout," for a quarter of its value, till he was left with barely enough to cover his person, but not enough to defend him from the damps of the prison and the cold of winter. From gaming, the transition to theft was a rapid one; detection and punishment soon followed, and then farewell, a long farewell to all sense of self-esteem and moral rectitude. The once high-minded and honorable youth became a confirmed rough ally, prowling about the prisons seeking what he might be able to steal, or perhaps tending a gambling table in No. 4, a miserable slave to an ignorant negro. I had to mourn over the degradation of several youths of my own acquaintance—and, so far as I know their future history, they never recovered from it.

The term federalists was one of great opprobrium in Dartmoor, and it was the one most frequently made use of by the rough allies to give a pretext for, or to extenuate their acts of violence and plunder; and it answered quite as well, or perhaps a little better, than the charge of selling light ha'penny-worths.

These fellows would hang about the market on market-days, watching their chance to steal. Their depredations on the market-people were so frequent, that, at last, the commandant would not allow any of the captives to go out into the market-yard when the market was held, but caused them to stand in the passage-way of communication with the prisons, with the iron gate in front of them shut, so that when an article was bargained for, it was handed in between the bars of the gate, and the purchase-money passed through in the same manner. But the poor market-people were not much the better for this arrangement; the purchasers too often forgot to pay when they had received the article, but would move off with it as fast as their legs could carry them; or, as they used to term it, "Give leg-bail for security." When the market people became more cautious, and refused to deliver the goods with one hand until they had received the money in the other, the rough allies resorted to another expedient. They would carry in their hands, concealed under their outer garments, a rope coiled up, to one end of which was attached a number of fish-hooks. Watching their chance, they would throw it, as expertly as a

South American does his lasso, into the baskets containing the goods for sale; then singing out, "Heave oh!" they would run down the yard, while their comrades would cluster around the palings, to conceal them from sight, and to facilitate the passage of the plundered article through the palings; and this kind of *hooking* was generally successful.

I am sorry to say that these depredations on the English were viewed in a very different light from depredations committed on the property of each other. They were looked upon as being no concern of ours, and they were never punished. I do not think that the generality of the prisoners would have been sorry to see these men punished by the English authorities; but it was considered to be strictly their business to do it, and they could never detect the offenders. These men would insult the general and the officers all day long, quarrel and fight with each other, when they had no one else to quarrel with, and were generally as near being drunk as the state of their finances would permit them to be. In short, they were a nuisance and annoyance to every decent man in the prisons.

We were very often embargoed (as we termed it,) that is, confined to our own yards, and sometimes shut up in our prisons, in consequence of the depredations of these fellows; and in this, as in many other affairs of this life, the innocent and guilty suffer alike.

At first, the British government furnished the prisoners with clothing; and nothing could exceed the grotesqueness of appearance of an individual rigged out in this garb of captivity. It consisted of a coarse woollen jacket, dyed a bright yellow color, marked on the back with what is called the king's broad arrow, which resembles the two sides of a triangle, the point turned upward, and another straight line running from the point, equi-distant through the middle; and the letters T. O., being the initials of transport office, in staring black letters, one letter on each side of the arrow. Also, a pair of pantaloons of the same color and material, with the same marks upon them; a comical cap made of coarse woollen stuff, and a pair of woven list shoes, with wooden soles about an inch thick. I regret that I did not procure a suit of this clothing, to bring home and deposit in some museum; and I think that a Dartmoor rough ally, rigged out in his prison toggery, would form a valuable addition to a travelling menagerie, to be exhibited as a curiosity.

Very few of the prisoners would accept of this dress, preferring rather to suffer the cold and dampness of the prisons than to wear it; and at last, Mr. Beasly, the nominal agent for prisoners of war, sent down from London some clothing for the destitute.

The trade in old clothes furnished employment for a part of the prisoners, who were almost as great nuisances as the rough allies. They would go about the prisons at all times of the day, crying out, "any old clothes to sell? who wants to buy any old clothes?" They made great profits, for in a week or two after the allowance had been paid us by Mr. Beasly's clerk, many of the improvident and gambling prisoners would be destitute of money; they would then sell their clothes for a small sum; and when the time came round again to receive their money, they would buy in again the same garments, or others, at an exorbitant profit, again to sell and again to buy, according to the state of their finances. These men had the character, and I suspect justly, of being great rascals—frequently stealing the clothes they had to sell.

The situation of the prisons was a very unhealthy one, and great mortality generally prevailed among the prisoners. Situated as we were, on a mountain said to be seventeen hundred feet above the level of the sea, in a climate proverbial as is the west of England for moisture of atmosphere; poorly paid and scarcely clad; immured in gloomy stone prisons, which a ray of sun scarcely ever penetrated; without glass in the windows to guard us against the cold and dampness, and no fires allowed in the prisons, we could not be otherwise than unhealthy. The weather, except when by a mere chance it was fair, was continually drizzling. I do not believe, that in the seven months I was there, we had more than six weeks when it did not rain, and this at long intervals. I find entries in my diary where I have noted the appearance of the sun after intervals of six, ten, and in one instance, fourteen days; and these entries are not unfrequent. I think I can say, without the least particle of exaggeration, that I did not enjoy a single day of good health while at Dartmoor; and as friends, acquaintances, and townsmen were dropping away all around me, I contemplated the strong probability that I, too, should leave my bones in the prison burying-ground.

Those who were considered well, were afflicted a large portion of the time with swelled jaws and tooth-ache; so much so, that there were men in the prisons who had no other employment than to cure the tooth-ache. This they did by making a paste of bee's-wax, sulphur, and a little British oil. A small piece of this paste was put into a saucer or plate and set on fire; a small paper cone was then placed over it, and the smoke conveyed through a small hole in the point of the cone into the hollow of the acheing tooth. There was a deal of quackery about it, as they pretended to extract a worm from the tooth, and they exhibited it on the plate. This was done by putting a mustard-seed into each parcel of the paste, which getting shrivelled and parched by the heat, passed off well enough as a small worm. I can testify to the efficacy of the process; and it was probably caused by the conversion, in the act of combustion, of a portion of the sulphur into sulphuric acid.

Small pox and measles made great ravages, but the most prevailing disease was that disorder of the lungs, called by physicians, 'Peripneumonia notha.' It hewed down the prisoners in vast numbers; and, as I have already mentioned, almost the whole crew of a South American privateer were exterminated by it.

The whole number of prisoners who died at the depot was two hundred and fifty-two. The prisons were used to confine Americans in about a year, and the average number of prisoners there was under four thousand. The mortality, then, was about one in thirteen, or six or seven times the average of mortality in our New-England towns; and when it is recollected that the prisoners were generally robust men, in youth or middle life, and that, at home, comparatively few deaths take place among men of this description, it must be conceded that the mortality at Dartmoor was frightful.

Alexander Cochrane: Proclamation

On April 1, 1814, Admiral John Borlase Warren stepped down as commander of the British North American Station, headquartered at the Royal Naval dockyard in Bermuda. His successor, Vice Admiral Alexander Cochrane, was eager not only to attack America's Atlantic coast but also to disrupt the war effort in the slave states. He immediately issued a proclamation that was widely interpreted as an offer of freedom to American slaves. Scores of runaway slaves had already found sanctuary with the British, and with Cochrane's proclamation hundreds more followed their example, many serving as guides or scouts for the British or seeing combat as members of a special corps of Colonial Marines.

---

*By the Honorable Sir ALEXANDER COCHRANE, K.B.
Vice Admiral of the Red, and Commander in Chief of His
Majesty's Ships and Vessels, upon the North American Station,
&c. &c. &c.*

A PROCLAMATION.

WHEREAS it has been represented to me, that many Persons now resident in the UNITED STATES, have expressed a desire to withdraw therefrom, with a view of entering into His Majesty's Service, or of being received as Free Settlers into some of His Majesty's Colonies.

This is therefore to Give Notice,

That all those who may be disposed to emigrate from the UNITED STATES will, with their Families, be received on board of His Majesty's Ships or Vessels of War, or at the Military Posts that may be established, upon or near the Coast of the UNITED STATES, when they will have their choice of either entering into His Majesty's Sea or Land Forces, or of being sent as FREE Settlers to the British Possessions in North

America or the West Indies, where they will meet with all due encouragement.

> GIVEN *under my Hand at Bermuda, this 2nd day of April, 1814.*
> ALEXANDER COCHRANE.

By Command of the Vice Admiral,
  WILLIAM BALHETCHET.

> *GOD SAVE THE KING.*

Thomas Jefferson: from a letter to John Adams

The spring of 1814 found Napoleon backed into a corner and the British ascendant. At the Battle of Leipzig the previous October, a coalition led by Britain's Russian allies had forced the emperor to abandon his campaign east of the Rhine and retreat to France. Meanwhile, the Duke of Wellington had shattered French power in Spain and invaded France from the south. On March 31, 1814, the Russians marched into Paris and occupied the capital, forcing Napoleon to abdicate unconditionally, and on April 11 he was exiled to the Mediterranean island of Elba. For the first time in more than a decade, Europe was at peace. In America, Federalists rejoiced in the humbling of the "Anti-Christ," and some Republicans, including Thomas Jefferson, joined them. Federalists hoped that Napoleon's defeat would pave the way to a peace treaty with Great Britain, but Republicans were skeptical. The United States was now alone in the field against Great Britain, and many predicted a terrible battle for America's very existence. Jefferson, in the letter below, expected peace but hoped that America would continue to fight, if necessary, for its maritime rights.

Monticello, July 5, 1814

DEAR SIR—Since mine of Jan. 24. yours of Mar. 14. was recieved. It was not acknoleged in the short one of May 18. by Mr. Rives, the only object of that having been to enable one of our most promising young men to have the advantage of making his bow to you. I learned with great regret the serious illness mentioned in your letter: and I hope Mr. Rives will be able to tell me you are entirely restored. But our machines have now been running for 70. or 80. years, and we must expect that, worn as they are, here a pivot, there a wheel, now a pinion, next a spring, will be giving way: and however we may tinker them up for awhile, all will at length surcease motion. Our watches, with works of brass and steel, wear out within that period. Shall you and I last to see the course the seven-fold wonders of the times will take? The Attila of the age dethroned, the ruthless destroyer of 10. millions of the human race, whose thirst for blood appeared unquenchable, the great oppressor of the rights and liberties of the world, shut up within the circuit of a little island of the Mediterranean, and dwindled to the condition of an humble and degraded pensioner on the bounty of those he had most injured. How miserably, how meanly, has he closed his inflated career! What a sample of the Bathos will his history present! He should have perished on the swords of his enemies, under the walls of Paris.

'Leon piagato a morte
Sente mancar la vita,
Guarda la sua ferita,
Ne s'avilisce ancor.

Cosi fra l'ire estrema
rugge, minaccia, e freme,
Che fa tremar morendo
Tal volta il cacciator.'
    Metast Adriano.

But Bonaparte was a lion in the field only. In civil life a cold-blooded, calculating unprincipled Usurper, without a virtue, no statesman, knowing nothing of commerce, political economy, or civil government, and supplying ignorance by bold presumption. I had supposed him a great man until his entrance into the Assembly des cinq cens, 18. Brumaire (an. 8.) From that date however I set him down as a great scoundrel only. To the wonders of his rise and fall, we may add that of a Czar of Muscovy dictating, *in Paris*, laws and limits to all the successors of the Caesars, and holding even the balance in which the fortunes of this new world are suspended. I own that, while I rejoice, for the good of mankind, to the deliverance of Europe from the havoc which would have never ceased while Bonaparte should have lived in power, I see with anxiety the tyrant of the ocean remaining in vigor, and even participating in the merit of crushing his brother tyrant. While the world is thus turned up side down, on which side of it are we? All the strong reasons indeed place us on the side of peace; the interests of the continent, their friendly dispositions, and even the interests of England. Her passions alone are opposed to it. Peace would seem now to be an easy work, the causes of the war being removed. Her orders of council will no doubt be taken care of by the allied powers, and, war ceasing, her impressment of our seamen ceases of course. But I fear there is foundation for the design intimated in the public papers, of demanding a cession of our right in the fisheries. What will Massachusets say to this? I mean her majority, which must be considered as speaking, thro' the organs it has appointed itself, as the Index of it's will. She chose to sacrifice the liberty of our seafaring citizens, in which we were all interested, and with them her obligations to the Co-states; rather than war with England. Will she now sacrifice the fisheries to the same partialities? This question is interesting to her alone: for to the middle, the Southern and Western States they are of no direct concern; of no more than the culture of tobacco, rice and cotton to Massachusets. I am really at a loss to conjecture what our refractory sister will say on this occasion. I know what, as a citizen of the Union, I would say to her. 'Take this question ad referendum. It concerns you alone. If you would rather give up the fisheries than war with England, we give them up. If you had rather fight for them, we will defend your interests to the last drop of our blood, chusing rather to set a good example than follow a bad one.' And I hope she will determine to fight for them. With this however you and I shall have nothing to do; ours being truly the case wherein 'non tali auxilio, nec defensoribus istis Tempus eget.'

Henry, Earl Bathurst to George Prevost

After April 1814 the British government, now at war only with the United States, began sending waves of seasoned veterans from the Continent to North America and developing plans for a sea-and-land offensive along the Great Lakes and the Atlantic and Gulf coasts. On June 3, the secretary of state for war and the colonies communicated details of those plans to the governor-general of British North America. The offensive initially had two objectives: first, to guarantee the safety of Canada during the balance of the war, and second, to strategically occupy as much U.S. territory as possible for leverage at the eventual peace negotiations, talk of which was already in the air. But with the shift in the balance of power in their favor, many British subjects longed to punish the Americans first. "Chastise the savages," said the *Times* of London on May 24, "for such they are, in a much truer sense than the followers of Tecumseh or the Prophet."

––––––––––

Secret

Downing Street,
3rd June, 1814.

Sir,

I have already communicated to you in my despatch of the 14th of April the intention of His Majesty's Government to avail themselves of the favourable state of Affairs in Europe, in order to reinforce the Army under your command. I have now to acquaint you with the arrangements which have been made in consequence, and to point out to you the views with which His Majesty's Government have made so considerable an augmentation of the Army in Canada.

The 4th Battalion of the Royal Scots of the strength stated in the margin sailed from Spithead on the 9th ulto. direct for Quebec, and was joined at Cork by the 97th Regiment destined to relieve the Nova Scotia Fencibles at Newfoundland; which latter will immediately proceed to Quebec.

The 6th and 82nd Regiments of the strength as per margin

sailed from Bordeaux on the 15th ulto. direct for Quebec. Orders have also been given for embarking at the same port, twelve of the most effective Regiments of the Army under the Duke of Wellington together with three Companies of Artillery on the same service.

This force, which (when joined by the detachments about to proceed from this Country) will not fall far short of ten thousand infantry, will proceed in three divisions to Quebec. The first of these divisions will be embarked immediately, the second a week after the first and the third as soon as the means of Transport are collected. The last division however will arrive at Quebec long before the close of the year.

Six other Regiments have also been detached from the Gironde and the Mediterranean, four of which are destined to be employed in a direct operation against the Enemy's Coast, and the other two are intended as a reinforcement to Nova Scotia and New Brunswick; available (if circumstances appear to you to render it necessary) for the defence of Canada, or for the offensive operations on the Frontier, to which your attention will be particularly directed. It is also in contemplation at a later period of the year to make a more serious attack on some part of the Coasts of the United States; and with this view a considerable force will be collected at Cork without delay. These operations will not fail to effect a powerful diversion in your favor.

The result of this arrangement, as far as you are immediately concerned, will be to place at your disposal the Royals, The Nova Scotia Fencibles, the 6th & the 82nd Regiments amounting to three thousand one hundred and twenty seven men: and to afford you in the course of the year a further reinforcement of ten thousand British Troops.

When this force shall have been placed under your command, His Majesty's Government conceive that the Canadas will not only be protected for the time against any attack which the enemy may have the means of making, but it will enable you to commence offensive operations on the Enemy's Frontier before the close of this Campaign. At the same time it is by no means the intention of His Majesty's Government to encourage such forward movements into the Interior of the American Territory as might commit the safety of the Force placed under your command. The object of your operations will be; first, to give immediate protection: secondly, to obtain if possible ultimate security to His Majesty's Possessions in America.

The entire destruction of Sackets harbour and the Naval Establishments on Lake Erie and Lake Champlain come under the first description.

The maintenance of Fort Niagara and so much of the adjacent Territory as may be deemed necessary: and the occupation of Detroit and the Michigan Country come under the second.

If our success shall enable us to terminate the war by the retention of the Fort of Niagara, and the restoration of Detroit and the whole of the Michigan Country to the Indians, the British Frontier will be materially improved. Should there be any advanced position on that part of our frontier which extends towards Lake Champlain, the occupation of which would materially tend to the security of the Province, you will if you deem it expedient expel the Enemy from it, and occupy it by detachments of the Troops under your command, always however taking care not to expose His Majesty's Forces to being cut off by too extended a line of advance.

If you should not consider it necessary to call to your assistance the two Regiments which are to proceed in the first instance to Halifax, Sir J. Sherbroke will receive instructions to occupy so much of the District of Maine as will secure an uninterrupted intercourse between Halifax and Quebec.

In contemplation of the increased force which by this arrangement you will be under the necessity of maintaining in the Province directions have been given for shipping immediately for Quebec, provisions for ten thousand men for six months.

The Frigate which conveys this letter has also on board one hundred thousand pounds in Specie for the use of the Army under your command. An equal sum will also be embarked on board the Ship of War which may be appointed to convoy to Quebec the fleet which is expected to sail from this Country on the 10th or at the latest on the 15th instant.

I have the honor etc.,
BATHURST

Albert Gallatin to James Monroe

In July 1813, Madison sent Secretary of the Treasury Albert Gallatin to St. Petersburg to head a U.S. commission in peace talks sponsored by Tsar Alexander I. Britain, however, refused to participate in mediated talks, and in November proposed direct negotiations on its own terms. Lord Castlereagh, the British foreign secretary, arranged for peace talks eventually held in Ghent (in present-day Belgium), and Madison dispatched a strong team of negotiators to the host city. John Quincy Adams, recalled from his post as U.S. minister to Russia, headed the delegation, and was joined by Speaker of the House Henry Clay, Delaware senator James A. Bayard, Massachusetts diplomat Jonathan Russell, and Gallatin. On the eve of his departure for Ghent, Gallatin, who had been gathering intelligence in London, offered Secretary of State Monroe a sobering picture of the prospects for peace.

LONDON, 13th June, 1814.

SIR,—The armament fitted against America will enable the British, besides providing for Canada, to land at least 15 to 20,000 men on the Atlantic coast. Whether the Ministry be nevertheless disposed for peace a few weeks will determine. It may be intended to continue the war for the purpose of effecting a separation of the Union, or with a view of promoting the election of a President of the Federal party, or in the hope of imposing conditions which will curtail the territory, the fisheries, and diminish the commerce of the United States; but even with the intention of a speedy and equal peace, the pride and vindictive passions of the nation would be highly gratified by what they would consider a glorious termination of the war, by an expedition that may console them for the mortification of naval defeats, retrieve the disgrace of the campaign in the Chesapeake, and cripple the naval and commercial resources, as well as the growing manufactures, of the United States. To use their own language, they mean to inflict on America a chastisement that will teach her that war is not to be declared against Great Britain with impunity. This is a very general sentiment in the nation, and that such are the opinions and intentions of the Ministry was strongly impressed on the mind of ———— by a late conversation he had with Lord Castlereagh. Admiral Warren also told to Levett Harris, with whom he was intimate at St. Petersburg, that he was sorry to say that the instructions given to his successor on the American station were very different from those under which he had acted, and that he apprehended that very serious injury would be inflicted on America. Knowing the species of warfare practised under him, and that he was blamed for the inefficiency and not on account of the nature of his operations, you may infer what is now intended. Without pretending to correct information respecting their plan of campaign, I think it probable that Washington and New York are the places the capture of which would most gratify the enemy, and that Norfolk, Baltimore, and the collected manufacturing establishments of the Brandywine and Rhode Island are also in danger. The ostensible object everywhere will be the destruction of the public naval magazines and arsenals, and of all the shipping, whether public or private; but heavy contributions, plunder, and whatever marks a predatory warfare must be expected, unless the ultimate object be to sever the Union, demand a cession of territory, &c., in which case the permanent occupation of New York or some other important tenable point will probably be attempted instead of mere destruction. Whatever may be the object and duration of the war, America must rely on her resources alone. From Europe no assistance can, for some time, be expected. British pride begins, indeed, to produce its usual effect. Seeds of dissension are not wanting. Russia and England may, at the approaching Congress of Vienna, be at variance on important subjects, particularly as relates to the aggrandizement of Austria. But questions of maritime rights are not yet attended to, and America is generally overlooked by the European sovereigns or viewed with suspicion. Above all, there is nowhere any navy in existence; and years of peace must elapse before the means of resisting with effect the sea power of Great Britain can again be created. In a word, Europe wants peace, and neither will nor can at this time make war against Great

Britain. The friendly disposition of the Emperor of Russia, and a just view of the subject, make him sincerely desirous that peace should be restored to the United States. He may use his endeavors for that purpose; beyond that he will not go, and in that it is not probable he will succeed. I have also the most perfect conviction that, under the existing unpropitious circumstances of the world, America cannot, by a continuance of the war, compel Great Britain to yield any of the maritime points in dispute, and particularly to agree to any satisfactory arrangement on the subject of impressment, and that the most favorable terms of peace that can be expected are the status ante bellum, and a postponement of the questions of blockade, impressment, and all other points which in time of European peace are not particularly injurious; but, with firmness and perseverance, those terms, though perhaps unattainable at this moment, will ultimately be obtained, provided you can stand the shock of this campaign, and provided the people will remain and show themselves united; this nation and government will be tired of a war without object, and which must become unpopular when the passions of the day will have subsided and the country sees clearly that America asks nothing from Great Britain. It is desirable that the negotiations of Ghent, if not productive of immediate peace, should at least afford satisfactory proof of this last point. I might have adduced several facts and collateral circumstances in support of the opinions contained in this letter, but you know I would not risk them on light grounds. You may rest assured of the general hostile spirit of this nation and of its wish to inflict serious injury on the United States; that no assistance can be expected from Europe; and that no better terms of peace will be obtained than the status ante bellum, &c., as above stated. I am less positive, though I fear not mistaken, with respect to the views of the Ministry, to the object of the armament, to the failure of the Emperor's interference, and to the consequent improbability of peace, even on those terms, before the conclusion of this year's campaign.

I have the honor to be, with great respect, your obedient servant.

Stephen Popham to James Yeo

On May 5–6, 1814, James Yeo, commander of the British forces on Lake Ontario, mounted an attack on Oswego, New York, where Fort Ontario was an important way station in the supply line between New York City and the U.S. naval yard at Sackets Harbor. A British army of nine hundred men destroyed the fort but missed a large cache of naval guns, ropes, and cables—ordnance and rigging intended for the U.S. frigate *Superior*—stashed some twelve miles to the south. On the night of May 29, an American flotilla under Master Commandant Melancthon Woolsey, second-in-command at Sackets Harbor, tried to ferry the guns and cable from Oswego to the naval yard. With a powerful British squadron nearby, Woolsey hugged the shore and took refuge the following morning in Big Sandy Creek, only twenty miles from his destination, where he was joined by three hundred men from Sackets Harbor and 120 Oneida Indians. Stephen Popham, a captain of the British squadron, here describes to Commodore Yeo what happened after he discovered Woolsey's presence and, leading a flotilla of gunboats carrying two hundred men, sailed up the creek.

————————

Sacketts Harbour   June 1st. 1814

Sir

Having obtained certain information that the Enemys Boats with their Guns and stores, had taken shelter in Sandy Creek, I proceeded to that place (having ordered Captain Spilsbury to accompany me) and reached the entrance of it shortly after day light, yesterday morning. I landed accompanied by Captain Spilsbury and some of the Officers, and having reconnoitred their Position, determined on an immediate attack.

The masts of their Boats (consisting of eighteen) were plainly seen over the marsh, and from their situation did not appear to be very near the woods, and their not attempting to interrupt our entry into the Creek, led me to hope they were only protected by Militia. This circumstance, added to the very great importance of the lading of their Boats, to the equipment of their Squadron, was a strong motive for me to risk the attack, not aware that they had brought their Riflemen in their Boats, and that a body of Indians had accompanied them along the Beach—

The Boats advanced cautiously to within about a quarter of a mile of the Enemy's, when Lieut. Cox of the Royal Marines, was landed with the principal part of his men, on the left Bank: and Captain Spilsbury and Lieut. Brown, with the Cohorn and Small arm Party accompanied by Lieut. McVeagh, with a few Marines, were landed on the Right Bank: these respective Parties, advanced on the flanks of the Gun Boats (which had from their fire dispersed a Body of Indians) to a turning which opened the Enemys Boats to our view, when unfortunately the Sixty eight Pounder Carronade, on which much depended, was disabled, seeing us pulling the Boat round to bring the 24 pounder to bear, the Enemy thought we were commencing a retreat, when they advanced with their whole force, consisting of one hundred and fifty Riflemen, near two Hundred Indians, and a numerous Body of Militia and Cavalry: which soon overpowered the few men I had, their resistance was such as I could have expected from a brave and well disciplined Body, but opposed to such numbers unavailing, their officers set them an example honorable to themselves, and worthy of a better fate. Captain Spilsbury for a time checked the advance of the Enemy by the fire he kept up with the Cohorn, and his Party; and I feel much indebted to him for his conduct throughout—

Lieutenants Cox and McVeagh, who nobly supported the honor of their Corps, are I am sorry to say dangerously wounded. Mr. Hoare Master's mate of the *Montreal*, whose conduct was conspicuous throughout, is the only Officer killed; our loss in killed and wounded (mostly dangerous) is great, I send as correct a return as I can possibly get of them as well as of the Survivors—

The winding of the Creek which gave the Enemy great advantage in advancing to intercept our retreat, rendered any further perseverance unavailing, and would have subjected the men to certain death.

Lieutenants Majoribanks and Rowe, in the rear, with the small boats, did every thing in their power, and Lieut. Loveday's exertions in the *Lais* Gun Boat was such as I was much pleased with—

The exertions of the American Officers of the Rifle Corps commanded by Major Appling, in saving the lives of many of the Officers and men, whom their own men, and the Indians were devoting to Death, was conspicuous, and claim our warmest gratitude   I have the honor to be Sir &c.

Stephen Popham
Captain

N. W. Hibbard to Alvin Hunt

After all the guns, ropes, and small cables intended for *Superior* had been loaded on ox carts for transport from Sandy Creek to Sackets Harbor, one great cable remained. The size of this cable varies among the several eyewitness accounts, but it was at least one hundred yards long, as stout as "a seven-inch stove pipe," and weighed nearly five tons—too large to fit in an ox cart. After some delay, a regiment of New York militiamen volunteered to carry the cable the twenty miles to the navy yard. A long length of cable was loaded into a wagon, and the rest was shouldered by the men, about a hundred of them, marching single file. The most detailed account of this feat was left by Nathaniel Wood Hibbard, who in 1859, at the age of seventy-five, wrote the following memoir at the request of Alvin Hunt, a local historian and newspaperman in Watertown, New York.

———————

RURAL HILL, Feb. 10, 1859.

A. HUNT, Esq.:

Dear Sir:—Having been informed by my son that you wish me to send you some account of the occurrences that took place in the attack of the British on the American flotilla at Sandy Creek, and of the events which transpired immediately before and after said attack, I will do so, as nearly as I can from recollection. I think it was in the month of June, but am unable to say what day of the month, that the American flotilla entered the mouth of Big Sandy Creek. The brigade consisted, if I recollect right, of eighteen boats, under command of Commodore Woolsey, accompanied by eighty-four riflemen under command of Captain Appling—afterwards Colonel Appling. They left Oswego with nineteen boats, one of which fell off from the brigade in a fog, and was captured by the enemy, who, having the command of the lake, had been for some time watching the coast for the arrival of the American boats having on board the armament for the frigate Superior, now ready at Sackets Harbor to receive it. The enemy well knew, that if the armament arrived safe at Sackets Harbor, the superiority of the Americans on the lake would become a fixed fact; hence their anxiety to prevent the arrival of the boats and to capture the armament. The American boats arrived at their moorings on Sunday afternoon. Commodore Woolsey sent Lieut. Ridgely in a small boat to examine the coast as far up as Big Stony Creek, intending to proceed, if possible, with the flotilla to that place. Some time in the night, Lieut. Ridgely fell in with the detachment of the enemy destined for the capture of the American boats. The Lieutenant immediately put about, and about daylight reported the facts to the Commodore. Capt. Appling had, in the meantime, sent Capt. Harrington express to Col. Mitchell, then commanding at Sackets Harbor, who instantly sent Captain Harris' company of mounted dragoons and a corps of flying artillery, I believe Major McIntosh's, to reinforce Appling. They arrived at the boats in time, and were immediately drawn up in line, prepared for battle, near the boats, while Appling proceeded down the creek and secreted his riflemen behind a brush fence among the alders in the margin of the marsh. The British force, under command of Capt. Popham, R. N., entered the mouth of the creek about sunrise, and consisted of five boats, some forty marines, and something more than 200 sailors; they proceeded cautiously up the crooked channel of the creek, often discharging from a carronade six to eight pound shots, which neither scared nor hurt anybody, as no one was near them, and they only fired at such places as might conceal mischief. With their eyes fixed on the American troops at the boats, and knowing nothing of Appling, they landed their marines, who, in platoons, proudly marched up the creek by the side of the boats. When near the edge of the marsh, and within a stone's throw of Appling, the signal was given, and Appling's men poured upon them their deadly fire. In ten minutes all was over. I do not know how many were killed; I helped to lay side by side upon the grass thirteen dead of the rank and file; sixty-four were wounded, and two hundred and thirty-four taken prisoners. Of the officers I cannot give much account, as Col. Clark Allen, then commanding the 55th regiment N. Y. militia infantry, with some 300 men, were soon on the ground, and the rank and file of the prisoners were handed over to them, with orders to proceed with them to Sackets Harbor. After a most fatiguing march, we arrived at Sackets Harbor about sundown, where we lay on our arms till sundown, when we returned to Sandy Creek. There being now no means of getting the armament to Sackets Harbor, except by land, and that doubtful, as the force at Sackets Harbor was light, and the enemy having our coast under blockade, and in force sufficient to cut us all up, if they should try, Col. Allen's regiment was stationed at the Creek to guard the boats and property. Teams and carriages were hired, and commenced moving the property, and in about two weeks it was accomplished, without anything remarkable, except that a cable of 22 inches circumference, and weighing, according to my best recollection, about five tons, could not be transported safely on any carriage that could be procured. The men were clamorous for their discharge, as their spring's work was far behind the usual time, but this cable must be strictly guarded, as without it our superiority on the lake could not be acquired. The officers of the regiment held a meeting, and proposed carrying the cable by hand, and in this meeting agreed that no officer should be exempt from helping carry the cable, except the Colonel, and if the men would help carry it to the Harbor, they should be discharged. We took up the cable about noon, and arrived that night at what is now Roberts' Corners; here, during the night, perhaps one-third of our men deserted, leaving a heavy load for the remainder to carry, and every man's shoulders were bruised till they were black and blue—larger than the palm of a man's hand; but finding the bottom of an old straw-stack near, we made mattresses from it, and placed them on our shoulders, and thus shouldering the cable, arrived at the Harbor before sundown; perhaps few of the men were able to make much use of their arms for a week. When we arrived at the Harbor, we numbered just 100, all told, and received of Commodore Chauncey $2.00 each. I cannot recollect the names of the men that assisted; no officer failed to fulfill his pledge; Clark Allen was our Colonel; did not carry. Major Arnold Earl, Captains Gad Ackley, Brooks Harrington, Daniel Ellis, Oliver Scott, Lieutenants Charles Hollister and Grout Hossington, I recollect, and I also recollect Captain Jacob Wood, of revolutionary memory, carried through.

I am so much afflicted with palsy, and trembling in my right hand, that I write with much difficulty.

Respectfully yours,
N. W. HIBBARD.

N. B.—The enemy made their appearance in the creek, as I am informed, on the 28th day of May. That efficient gentleman, our former fellow-citizen, M. W. Gilbert, superintended the removal of the public property from the Creek to the Harbor.

N. W. H.

Jarvis Hanks: Memoir

In the spring of 1813, Jarvis Frary Hanks, a thirteen-year-old music pupil in Pawley, Vermont, was hired as drummer boy for the recruitment office of the 11th U.S. Infantry. The regiment promised Hanks's parents that their son would serve only as a kind of traveling mascot, playing while the recruiting sergeant canvassed for volunteers throughout upper New England, but seven months later young Hanks was carrying a rifle at Crysler's Farm. The destruction of life during battle seems to have shocked him less than did the rough justice meted out by the army to its disobedient soldiers. Hanks's memoirs, published in 1831, detail the many "awful punishments" he saw "inflicted for the crime of desertion." Within weeks of joining the army, he watched one deserter run the gauntlet between "two ranks of men, fifty in each." These men each delivered a stroke on the offender's naked back, after which "it was entirely divested of its integument and presented a spectacle to melt the heart of a stone." Later that year, he witnessed the hanging of two more offenders. In this passage, Hanks writes of the execution by firing squad on June 4, 1814, of five deserters on the orders of Winfield Scott, "the most thorough disciplinarian I ever saw."

During the time we remained at Buffalo, five men were sentenced to be publicly shot for the offense of desertion. They were dressed in white robes with white caps upon their heads, and a red target fastened over the heart. The army was drawn up into a hollow square to witness the example that was about to be made of their comrades who had proved recreant to the regulations of the service. Five graves were dug in a row, five coffins placed near them, also in a line, with distance between coffins and graves, to enable the criminals to kneel between them. About twelve men were assigned to the execution of each offender. Their guns were loaded by officers, and they were not permitted to examine them afterwards until they had fired.

All things being in readiness, the chaplain made a prayer, the caps were pulled down over the eyes of the poor culprits, and the word of command given: "Ready! Aim! Fire!" They all fell! Some into their graves, some over their coffins. One struggled faintly and the commanding officer ordered a sergeant to approach and end his misery. He obeyed by putting the muzzle of his piece within a yard of his head, and discharging it. This quieted him perfectly!

At this time one of the condemned slowly arose from his recumbent position to his knees and was assisted to his feet. His first remark was, "By G——, I thought I was dead". In consequence of his youth and the peculiar circumstances of his case, he had been reprieved, but the fact was not communicated to him, until this moment. He had anticipated execution with his comrades, and when the report of the guns took place, he fell with them, though not a ball touched him. The platoon assigned to him, had guns given to them which were not charged, or at least had nothing but powder in them.

This young soldier was only eighteen years of age and had been recently transferred to Captain Bliss's company. This officer was a cruel, tyrannical man, and the soldiers all hated him most cordially. As this youthful son of Mars was permitted to return to his quarters accompanied by many of his fellows, he remarked that he would desert again, if obliged to remain under the command of Capt. Bliss. He was soon suffered to resume his place in the company to which he originally belonged, where he was well satisfied, and exhibited no further disposition to insubordination.

William E. Horner: from "Surgical Sketches"

William E. Horner, of Warrenton, Virginia, was a medical student at the University of Pennsylvania when, in the summer of 1813, he received his commission as a surgeon's mate in the U.S. Army. He served on the Niagara frontier for five months, tending the sick and the wounded, after which he received a furlough to return to Philadelphia and complete his M.D. In June 1814 he came back to the frontier to work in the newly opened general hospital at Buffalo, near the camp of Winfield Scott. His "Surgical Sketches," published in 1853, offer a vivid record of his war years. Here he details the sufferings of two New York militiamen wounded in the American capture of Fort Erie, a vital British post on the Niagara.

The encampments of the army at Buffalo were broken up about the first day of July, 1814. Orders were issued for hospital preparations, a number of tents were left behind for future sick service, and for the sick of the regiments then on hand. The present Eagle Hotel and Rail Road Depot of Buffalo occupy the part of the city upon which the hospital was opened. The entire area allotted to it was to the west of the principal street, upon the first rise of ground there in ascending from the Creek. The space was about equal to that of the State House Square in Philadelphia, perhaps longer, in being more of an oblong.

While in the act of getting the hospital ready for service, it received a visit from General Scott, the universal favorite of the day, for his gallantry in the preceding campaign. As he rode through the hospital grounds, in his usual dashing style, with his aids, he said in passing, "Well, Doctor, but little work here as yet." "No, General, we are looking for some." "You will get it before long," was his reply, and off he careered with his staff.

His promise was sufficiently kept, as the records of that celebrated period will show. It was the first time since the declaration of war that the tactics of an open field combat were tried. Line having been regularly displayed against line, each party directed by its special inspirations of skill and valor. There was, perhaps, never a campaign in which the belligerents came to a better understanding of what they might expect in battle at each other's hands; and where the leaders, though under the excitement of a state of war, left off with more military respect for one another.

The operations commenced with the crossing of the Niagara river near its head, at Black Rock, by the American army, under the direction of Major General Brown. This was accomplished on the night of the second of July, and early the next morning, Fort Erie, nearly opposite the place of embarkation, was invested. A few scattering fires were directed from the Fort, and it surrendered in the afternoon of the third. In this affair only two or three soldiers were wounded, one in the knee, by a grape shot, and another in the head, by a buckshot.

The first one must have had his knee in a flexed position at the time of injury, judging from the course of the ball. The ball entered on the end of the right tibia, opposite its head; it did not penetrate or injure the bone, but glancing obliquely upwards, came out in the inside of the vastus internus, just above the knee.

From the nature of this wound, and the pain the patient experienced, an unfavorable result was looked for. The patient was dressed with a pledget of lint, and a bandage, on the field. The day afterwards, he was brought to the general hospital at Buffalo. I removed the first dressing, washed the wound well with soap and water, and applied a pledget of lint spread with simple cerate, and confined it with a bandage loosely applied. The use of ardent spirits, then universal, and really considered as the water of life, (aqua vitæ) was forbidden. He was ordered to live on thin soup and boiled rice, and to keep the limb undeviatingly in a straight position. On the fourth day after the injury, the pain of the limb increased, and a swelling of the joint was perceptible; the part was so extremely tender to the touch that the patient could scarcely bear the falling of the water on it from a sponge used in dressing it. A saturnine poultice was then applied; he was bled to the amount of a pint, and, in order to counteract the irritation of the wound, which had kept him sleepless since its reception, an opiate was given. On the morning of the fifth day the pain had abated in a measure, the swelling was stationary, and a small quantity of pus was perceptible on the surface of the wound. The poultice was renewed, and the opiate at night. This plan of treatment assuaged the violent pain; the sore got into a healthy condition on the tenth day. The suppuration became very copious and healthy, and the tension of the knee removed; everything was then dispensed with, except the daily washing of the sore and a dressing of cerate.

The suppuration gradually diminished, the cicatrix contracted, the knee became flexible, and, on the fortieth day after the reception of the injury, he returned to his duties in the line, in consequence of a general order for all convalescents of the hospitals, able to bear arms, to repair immediately to their respective corps.

The other patient, who was wounded in the head, was a boy of fifteen, much esteemed in his company for his gallantry and attention to his duties. He being on a scouting party, employed in exploring the adjacent country, the party was met at night in the woods by another of our scouting parties on the same business. They mistook each other for the enemy, and a firing ensued accordingly, in which one on each side was wounded, before they discovered their mistake. This boy was brought to the hospital the next day; he was in a comatose state, attended with delirium; however, when spoken to, his attention could be directed to the person who addressed him. The wound was extremely small, in consequence of being inflicted by a buckshot, was situated on the right temple, and had been closed up by the tumefaction of its edges, so that only a small bloody scab about a quarter of an inch in diameter, was visible. The temple was much swollen; he complained of great pain in the right ear and back of his head. The wound being closed, prevented the probing of it.

A poultice of bread and water (it being impossible to obtain milk,) was applied and confined by a bandage.

The patient, from his restless and painful situation, did not allow this to remain more than an hour or two; it was frequently applied, and as often displaced; it was given up the next day and the wound dressed with cerate. Third day, the appearance of the wound was not much altered, it had discharged a little blood and serum; the patient still restless, and moaning through excess of agony; his pulse was frequent and feeble. An anodyne at night. A little nourishment of soup was occasionally put into his mouth. The fourth and fifth day he was in pretty much the same situation as in the preceding, only it was more difficult to obtain his attention, the delirium and comatose state having increased. Death put an end to his sufferings on the morning of the fifth day.

On examining the head, it was found that the buckshot had passed through the temporal muscle and entered the cranium through the anterior angle of the right os parietale, just before the squamous suture, penetrated through the dura mater into the substance of the brain, and passed through the cortical part of it, not far from the right lateral verticle, and lodged above the tentorium on the same side.

Winfield Scott: from Memoirs of Lieutenant-General Scott

In March 1814, Winfield Scott, at twenty-seven, became one of the youngest brigadier generals in the history of the U.S. Army. All that spring at his encampment near Buffalo, he drilled American regulars seven hours a day, with excellent results. By early summer, other forces had arrived at camp, including regulars under Major General Jacob Brown, militia under Brigadier General Peter B. Porter, and a band of Iroquois led by Red Jacket—a combined army of more than five thousand men. On July 3, Brown crossed from Black Rock into Upper Canada, took Fort Erie, and ordered Scott to lead an advance along the Niagara River. The British, under Major General Phineas Riall, had expected such an invasion and so had built up their position at Chippawa, twenty miles north of the fort. Riall sent a detachment from Chippawa to delay Scott, who by the afternoon of the Fourth of July had nearly reached the British position, with Brown not far behind. In this excerpt from his 1864 autobiography, grandiloquently written in the third person, Scott describes the ensuing battle.

THE night had been rainy; but a bright sun cheered the invaders on the morning of the glorious Fourth of July. To seek the enemy below, Scott was early detached with his brigade—the 25th Infantry, commanded by Major T. S. Jesup; the 9th by Major H. Leavenworth, and the 11th by Major J. McNiel, together with Captain S. D. Harris's troop of light dragoons, and the light batteries under Major Hindman, of Captains N. Towson and Thomas Biddle of Scott's late regiment of artillery.

Early in the march, a little above Blackrock, a considerable body of the enemy was discovered. It proved to be a corps of observation under the command of the Marquess of Tweedale. All hearts leaped with joy at the chance of doing something worthy of the anniversary, and to cheer our desponding countrymen at home—something that might ever, on that returning day—

"Be in their flowing cups, freshly remembered."

The events of the day, however, proved most tantalizing. An eager pursuit of sixteen miles ensued. The heat and dust were scarcely bearable; but not a man flagged. All felt that immortal fame lay within reach. The enemy, however, had the start in the race by many minutes; but his escape was only insured by a number of sluggish creeks in the way, each with an ordinary bridge, and too much mud and water to be forded near its mouth. The floors of those bridges were, in succession, thrown off by the marquess, but he was never allowed time to destroy the sleepers. Taking up positions, however, to retard the relaying the planks, obliged Scott to deploy a part of his column and to open batteries. The first bridge, forced in that way, the chase was renewed, and so was the contest at two other bridges, precisely in the manner of the first and with the same results. Finally, toward sunset, the enemy were driven across the Chippewa River behind a strong *tête de pont*, where they met their main army under Major-General Riall.

This running fight, of some twelve hours, was remarkable in one circumstance: in the campaigns of the autobiographer, it was the first and only time that he ever found himself at the head of a force superior to that of the enemy in his front: their relative numbers being, on this occasion, about as four to three.

The Marquess of Tweedale, a gallant soldier, on a visit to the United States soon after peace, made several complimentary allusions to the prowess of our troops in the war, and particularly to the events of the 4th of July, 1814, on the Niagara—among them, that he could not account for the impetuosity of the Americans, in that pursuit, till a late hour, when some one called out—*it is their National Anniversary!**

The proximity of Riall reversed the strength of the antagonists, and Scott, unpursued, fell back a little more than a mile,

---

*Scott passing through London, in 1815, to Paris, met the Marquess of Tweedale in the street, when the parties kindly recognized each other. The latter was on the point of setting out for Scotland, and the former for France. Scott was assured of a welcome at Yester House, the seat of the marquess, if he should visit Scotland. This meeting soon became strangely misrepresented, on both sides of the Atlantic, to the great annoyance of the parties.

to take up a strong camp behind Street's Creek, to await the arrival of the reserve under Major-General Brown. The junction took place early in the morning of the 5th.

Brown lost no time in giving orders to prepare the materials for throwing a bridge across the Chippewa, some little distance above the village and the enemy at its mouth. (There was no travelling *ponton* with the army.) That work was put under the charge of our able engineers, McRee and Wood—the wise counsellors of the general-in-chief. This was the labor of the day. In the mean time the British militia and Indians filled the wood to our left and annoyed the pickets posted in its edge. Porter's militia were ordered to dislodge the enemy, and much skirmishing ensued between the parties.

The anniversary dinner cooked for Scott's brigade, with many extras added by him in honor of the day, happily came over from Schlosser on the 5th, and was soon despatched by officers and men, who had scarcely broken fast in thirty-odd hours.

To keep his men in breath, he had ordered a parade for grand evolutions in the cool of the afternoon. For this purpose there was below the creek, a plain extending back from the Niagara of some hundreds of yards in the broader part, and a third narrower lower down. From the dinner, without expecting a battle, though fully prepared for one, Scott marched for this field. The view below from his camp was obstructed by the brushwood that fringed the creek; but when arrived near the bridge at its mouth, he met Major-General Brown, coming in at full gallop, who, in passing, said with emphasis: *You will have a battle!* and, without halting, pushed on to the rear to put Ripley's brigade in motion—supposing that Scott was perfectly aware of the near approach of the entire British army and going out expressly to meet it. The head of his (Scott's) column had scarcely entered the bridge before it was met by a fire, at an easy distance, from nine field guns. Towson's battery quickly responded with some effect. The column of our infantry, greatly elongated by the diminution of front, to enable it to pass the narrow bridge, steadily advanced, though with some loss, and battalion after battalion when over, formed line to the left and front, under the continued fire of the enemy's battery. When Scott was seen approaching the bridge, General

Riall, who had dispersed twice his numbers the winter before, in his expedition on the American side, said: *It is nothing but a body of Buffalo militia!* But when the bridge was passed in fine style, under his heavy fire of artillery, he added with an oath: *Why, these are regulars!* The gray coats at first deceived him, which Scott was obliged to accept, there being no blue cloth in the country. (In compliment to the battle of Chippewa, our military cadets have worn gray coats ever since.) Two hostile lines were now in view of each other, but a little beyond the effective range of musketry.

It has been seen that the model American brigade, notwithstanding the excessive vigor and prowess exerted the day before, had failed in the ardent desire to engraft its name, by a decisive victory, on the great national anniversary. The same corps again confronting the enemy, but in an open field, Scott, riding rapidly along the line, threw out a few short sentences—among them, alluding to the day before, was this: *Let us make a new anniversary for ourselves!* Not finding his name in the official paper (Gazette) after his handsome services at the capture of Bastia and Calvi, early in his career, Nelson with the spirit of divination upon him, said: "Never mind; I will have a Gazette of my own." A little arrogance, near the enemy, when an officer is ready to suit the action to the word, may be pardoned by his countrymen. And it has often happened, if not always, when Fourths of July have fallen on Sundays, that Chippewa has been remembered at the celebrations of Independence on the 5th of July.

The brigade had scarcely been fully deployed, when it was perceived that it was outflanked by the enemy on the plain, besides the invisible force that had just driven Porter and the militia out of the wood. Critical manœuvring became necessary on the part of Scott; for the position and intentions of Brown, with Ripley and Porter, were, and remained entirely unknown to him till the battle was over. The enemy continuing to advance, presented a new right flank on the widened plain, leaving his right wing in the wood which Scott had caused to be confronted by Jesup's battalion, the 25th Infantry, which leaped the fence, checked, and soon pushed the enemy toward the rear. At the same time having ordered that the right wing of the consolidated battalion (9th and 22d Infantry) commanded by Leavenworth, should be thrown forward, with Towson's battery on the extreme right, close to the Niagara, Scott flew to McNiel's battalion, the 11th Infantry, now on the left, and assisted in throwing forward its left wing. The battalions of Leavenworth and McNiel thus formed, pointed to an obtuse angle in the centre of the plain, with a wide interval between them, that made up for deficiency of numbers. To fire, each party had halted more than once, at which the Americans had the more deadly aim. At an approximation to within sixty or seventy paces, the final charge (mutual) was commenced. The enemy soon came within the obliqued battalions of Leavenworth and McNiel. Towson's fire was effective from the beginning. At the last moment, blinded by thick smoke, he was about to lose his most effective discharge, when Scott, on a tall charger, perceiving that the enemy had come within the last range of the battery, caused a change that enfiladed many files of the opposing flank. The clash of bayonets, at each extremity, instantly followed, when the wings of the enemy being outflanked, and to some extent doubled upon, were mouldered away like a rope of sand. It is not in human nature that a conflict like this should last many seconds. The enemy's whole force broke in quick succession and fled, leaving the field thickly strewn with his dead and wounded. The victory was equally complete in front of Jesup. A hot pursuit was continued to within half gunshot of the batteries at Chippewa Bridge, to gather up prisoners and with good success. Returning, Scott met Major-General Brown coming out of the forest, who, with Ripley's regulars and the rallied militia of Porter, had made a wide circuit to the left, intending to get between the enemy and the Chippewa, and this might have been effected if the battle had lasted a half hour longer; but suppose that Scott in the mean time had been overwhelmed by superior numbers!

The term *charge* occurs several times above, and often in military narratives. A word to explain its professional meaning may be acceptable. General Moreau, when in America, remarked that in all his campaigns he had "never known anything approaching to a *general* conflict of bayonets;" though perhaps in all battles between infantry, a few files at a time, or small parts of opposing lines (as at Chippewa) come into the deadly rencounter.

"A *charge*, in military phrase, is said to be made, when either party stops firing, throws bayonets forward, and advances to the shock, whether the enemy receive it or fly. An actual crossing of bayonets, therefore, is not indispensable to the idea of a charge. To suppose it is, is a mistake. Another popular error is, that the parties come up to the shock in parallel lines. Such a case has rarely, if ever, occurred. Each commander always seeks by manœuvring to gain the oblique position, and, if possible, to outflank his enemy. With superior forces both advantages may easily be gained; but with inferior numbers the difficulty is extreme. The excess on the part of the enemy can only be overcome by celerity of movement, accuracy, hardihood, skill, and zeal."*

Few men now alive are old enough to recall the deep gloom, approaching to despair, which about this time oppressed the whole American people—especially the supporters of the war. The disasters on the land have been enumerated, and now the New England States were preparing to hold a convention—it met at Hartford—perhaps to secede from the Union—possibly to take up arms against it. Scott's brigade, nearly all New England men, were most indignant, and this was the subject of the second of the three pithy remarks made to them by Scott just before the final conflict at Chippewa. Calling aloud to the gallant Major Hindman, he said: "*Let us put down the federal convention by beating the enemy in front. There's nothing in the Constitution against that.*"†

History has recorded many victories on a much larger scale than that of Chippewa; but only a few that have wrought a greater change in the feelings of a nation. Everywhere bonfires blazed; bells rung out peals of joys; the big guns responded, and the pulse of Americans recovered a healthy beat.

---

*This paragraph is taken from Mansfield's life of the autobiographer, but was originally furnished (substantially) in the notes of the latter.

†The third, addressed to the 11th Infantry, at the last moment, was this: *The enemy say that Americans are good at long shot; but cannot stand the cold iron. I call upon you instantly to give the lie to the slander. Charge!*

Isaac Chauncey to Jacob Brown

After the American victory at Chippawa, Major General Brown occupied Queenston with the intent to retake Fort George. On July 13,
1814, three days after arrival, he wrote a letter to Isaac Chauncey,
commander of the U.S. Navy on Lake Ontario, then bedridden with
malaria at Sackets Harbor. "All accounts agree that the force of the
enemy in Kingston is very light," Brown began. "Meet me on the lake
shore, north of Fort George, with your fleet, and we will be able, I
have no doubt, to settle a plan of operation that will break the power
of the enemy in Upper Canada, and that in the course of a short time.
. . . I do not doubt my ability to meet the enemy in the field, and to
march in any direction over his country, your fleet carrying for me the
necessary supplies. We can threaten forts George and Niagara, and
carry Burlington Heights and York, and proceed directly to Kingston
and carry that place. . . . At all events have the politeness to let me
know what aid I am to expect from the fleet of Lake Ontario." Almost
a month later, Chauncey, now recovered and with his focus trained
on the British fleet at Kingston, replied to Brown's request for
"prompt and zealous co-operation."

Major General   U.S. Ship *Superior*
Jacob Brown   Off Kingston   10th Aug. 1814
Command'g the left Division
of the American Army &ca &ca &ca
Buffaloe

Sir

Your Letter of the 13th Ulto. was received by me on a sick
bed hardly able to hear it read and entirely unfitted to reply to
it— I however requested General Gaines to acquaint you with
my situation—the probable time of the Fleet's sailing and my
views of the extent of its cooperation with the Army.

From the tenor of Your Letter it would appear that you had
calculated much upon the cooperation of the Fleet— You cannot surely have forgotten the conversation We held on this

subject at Sacketts Harbor previous to your departure for Niagara— I then professed to feel it my duty as well as inclination to afford every assistance in my power to the Army and to cooperate with it whenever it could be done without loosing sight of this Great object for the attainment of which this fleet had been created to wit—the capture or destruction of the Enemy's fleet, but I then distinctly stated to you, that this was a primary object and would be first attempted and that you must not expect the Fleet at the head of the Lake unless that of the Enemy should induce us to follow him there.—

I will not suffer myself to believe that this conversation was misunderstood or has since been forgotten—how then shall I account for the intimation thrown out to the Public in your despatch to the Secretary of War, that you expected the Fleet to co-operate with you? was it friendly or just or honorable not only to furnish an opening for the public but thus to assist them to infer that I had pledged myself to meet you on a particular day at the head of the Lake for the purpose of co-operating and in case of disaster to your Army thus to turn their resentment from You (who are alone responsible) upon me who could not by any possibility have prevented or retarded even Your discomfiture— You well know Sir that the Fleet could not have rendered you the least Service during Your late incursion upon Upper Canada— You have not been able to approach Lake Ontario on any point nearer than Queenstown and the Enemy were then in possession of all the Country between that place and the Shores of Ontario so that I could not even communicate with You without making a circuit of 70 or 80 Miles.—

I would ask of what possible use the Fleet could have been to You either in threatning or investing Fort George when the Shallowness of the Water alone would prevent an approach with these Ships within two Miles of that Fort or Niagara.

To pretend that the Fleet could render the least assistance in Your projected capture of Burlington Heights on Your route to Kingston is Still more romantic for it is well known the Fleet could not approach within nine Miles of those Heights.

That you might find the fleet somewhat of a convenience in the transportation of Provisions and Stores for the use of the Army and an agreeable appendage to attend its marches and counter marches I am ready to believe but Sir the Secretary of the Navy has honored us with a higher destiny—we are intended to Seek and fight the Enemy's fleet—this is the great purpose of the Government in creating this fleet and I shall not be diverted in my efforts to effectuate it by any Sinister attempt to render us subordinate to or an appendage of the Army.

We have one common object in the annoyance defeat and destruction of the Enemy and I Shall always cheerfully unite with any Military Commander in the promotion of that object. I am Sir with Great consideration and respect Yr Mo. Ob. St.

I. C.

John Le Couteur: Journal

When naval support from Commodore Chauncey failed to material-ize, Brown fell back to Chippawa, knowing he would again face the army of General Riall, now reinforced by troops led by Lieutenant General Gordon Drummond. On the morning of July 25, 1814, Brown, ever on the offensive, sent Winfield Scott to seek out the enemy, who was discovered by mid-afternoon—a force sixteen hun-dred strong, on a hill at Lundy's Lane, near Niagara Falls. Scott, leading twelve hundred troops, attacked, and the battle was soon joined by Drummond and Brown. One of Drummond's soldiers was John Le Couteur, of the 104th Regiment of Foot, who left a vivid firsthand account of the confused and bloody six-hour contest, a stalemate that dragged on long into the night. More than a quarter of the six thousand combatants were killed, injured, or missing, and Scott, who sustained a severe wound to the left shoulder, was inca-pacitated for the rest of the war.

Monday, 25 July

Roused at 3 o'clock. The 89th came up last night. We received *false information* that the enemy had recrossed to the United States at Chippewa. We snatched up a breakfast near the 103rd, who were with us waiting for orders to move.

12 Noon. Moved to the Twelve-Mile Creek, where we made ourselves comfortable and got a good dinner. 4 o'clock, received pressing orders to hurry on to Lundy's Lane where the enemy were already engaged with the 89th and Glengarry. It would be difficult to describe the feelings of us young Soldiers hurrying into action, with the roar of Artillery and Musketry pealing in Our front, sometimes rattling in heavy surges, sometimes scant, as if troops pressed were retiring. The echo through the woods too as we were not marching, but running up, for our anxiety to aid our hard-pressed comrades became painful and short breathed. Some old Hero talked of "this flesh trembling at the dangers his Spirit would launch it into." I am persuaded that many of us had that feeling.

It was near 8 o'clock and getting dark as we reached the battle field. I made my usual prayers to God to grant me his protection and my life, ready though I was to lay that down for my country, at his pleasure, but hoping that no worse than a wound might befall me—nor a fall into the hands of the Savages—death we thought preferable.

They were hard at it. A staff officer placed our Companies in rear of the Centre of the 89th as we came up. Drummond finding us very much exposed to all the shots that missed the 89th, moved us on about twenty yards where there was a cross railed fence behind which he ordered us to lie down till we were wanted. It was funny and very satisfactory too to hear the balls rattling against the rails just over our heads, without hitting any of us.

An incident or two in war I must relate. As we marched up, to my utter astonishment, I saw the Captain of Artillery passing me. "What, in the name of fortune, brings you from your guns?" "Two of them were taken at the Bayonet's point and my Gunners are despatched. They made me a Prisoner, shoved me into the church above there, but as I saw a window at the other end and no one watching. I jumped out and here I am." Captain Glew of the 41st Light Company who was on the left under the crest of the hill, saw all this. When Jonathan thought He had the Guns safe, and like a raw fool had bayonetted the horses as well as what men he could catch, and fancied the centre of the battle won—bold Capt. Glew charged them with his gallant light bobs and retook our Guns, and one from the enemy. He ought to have been made a Knight Bannaret or a Major on the spot.

Another. While we were under this fire, Lieutenant Colonel Drummond was seated on his war horse like a knightly man of valour as He was exposed to a ragged fire from hundreds of brave Yankees who were pressing our brave 89th. It was an illumination of musquetry in our left front. Capt. Shore's servant, Nickerson, a short active highlander, was lying down, or on his knee often as I was peeking at the fray, when presently He stood bolt up. "Nic, Lie down!" Down He came. Presently up again. "Don't you hear the shot all around you, lie down!" "Yas Sur!" Down again. Up again in five minutes. "What's the use of my speaking to you, and your disobeying my orders—this is no place to be finding fault with a good Soldier!" "Wall Sir, do ye no see Col. Drummond sitting on that great horse, up there amongst all the balls—and sale I be laying down, sneaking whan he's exposed—Noe I wunt!" "Please yourself then!"—for I could not but admire the fellow's generous heroism!

The battle ceased in our front, while the enemy withdrew to make fresh dispositions. We were moved on, in first line, to the right of the 103rd, the Royals on our Right. Just then, a curious event in war occurred. The Glengarry light Infantry, who had been covering the extreme right, were recalled into line. Suddenly our line saw a black line rising over the hill in our front, when we poured in a rolling volley on them. Lt. Colonel Battersby in the most daring manner rode down and shouted: "We're British!" Happily the rise of the hill and the darkness favoured them, and few if any were hurt.

Immediately after this, the enemy, having reformed and obtained reinforcements, came forward in great strength continuing his efforts to take the hill till midnight. The Centre of the 89th was literally charged five times. Capt. Spunner, on seeing Lt. Latham fall, seized the King's Color which He had carried, and shouted "My boys, would you desert this color!" The fine fellows rallied to the color—but poor Spunner was killed. One heavy column, which crossed our front, I heard receive the word, "Form Subdivisions" and the officers repeating the words—into which we poured some heavy vollies till they retreated. Two officers were taken Prisoner in our front by the Americans, on being questioned, answering: "We are the Glengarry and Royals" and walking up to them. did not return.

One circumstance I have never forgot, as a lesson in war. Genl. Drummond rode up to the 103rd. "My lads *will you* charge the Americans?" He *put a question* instead of *giving the order*—they fired instead of charging.

About midnight the whole of the American army had retired, while we kept the field. As there was a rumour that General Brown was coming to renew his attack on our small but victorious army, twenty-five hundred to three thousand at most, Lieutenant Colonel Drummond made us draw all the dead horses into a line on the crest of our position and, if attacked, to kneel behind them as a breastwork, a capital one it would have proved.

I was on duty that night. What a dismal night. There were three hundred dead on the Niagara side of the hillock, and about a hundred of ours, besides several hundred wounded. The miserable badly-wounded were groaning and imploring us for water, the Indians prowling about them and scalping or plundering. Close by me lay a fine young man, the son of the American general Hull. He was mortally wounded, and I gave him some brandy and water, and wished Him to give me his watch, rings and anything He wished sent to his family. He told me much about Himself and to come to Him in the morning when He would give them to me in charge. When I got to Him, He was a beautiful Corpse, stripped stark naked, amidst a host of friends and foes.

Our Mens' heads and those of the Americans were within a few yards of each other at this spot, so close had been the deadly strife at this point—a magnificent man, a Field Officer of the Yankee army, lay close by Him. One old Yankee, who I relieved much, told me it was a judgement on Him for leaving his happy home, wife & Children. I sent an American Captain to the rear on a litter, shot through both legs.

The scene of the morning was not more pleasant than the night's horrors. We had to wait on our slaughterhouse till 11 before we got a mouthful—when a great Camp Kettle full of thick chocolate revived us surprisingly, though we devoured it among dead bodies in all directions.

Poor Moorsom of ours, the D. Assant. Adj General was killed early in the action, the last of four or five brothers killed in the Service. We had the mortification to see the smoke rising in minute column from Street's Mills, which the enemy burned in his retreat, for, although our Cavalry, Indians and light troops followed them, we were not in force sufficient to punish them farther. We accordingly moved down to Queenston. The 41st marched on to Ft. George.

William Dunlop: from "Recollections of the American War"

After Lundy's Lane, the Americans, about twenty-two hundred strong, withdrew to Fort Erie, where they enlarged the earthworks to accommodate the influx of soldiers. The British regrouped at Butler's Barracks, a fortified shantytown southwest of Fort George, well out of reach of American guns. It was the day after the battle that a twenty-one-year-old Scotsman named William Dunlop, an assistant surgeon of the 89th Regiment of Foot, began work in the makeshift hospital at Butler's Barracks. In this excerpt from his memoirs, published in 1847, he remembers his first days on the Niagara, treating "waggon after waggon" of the wounded of Lundy's Lane.

———————————

Luckily the moment we arrived at Toronto, we were informed that a gun-brig was about to sail for Niagara, on board which we were shipped. About sun-set we sailed, and the wind being fair, we arrived in the mouth of the Niagara river at daylight, and lost no time in ordering horses; and while they were getting ready, we were anxiously employed in examining and cross-examining witnesses as to the contradictory reports that were in circulation as to a battle. All we could elicit was, that there had been some fighting, for many had heard from Queenston Heights the noise both of artillery and musketry. Some said we had been defeated, and were in full retreat on Niagara; others that we had cut the enemy to pieces, and that the few that were left were busy crossing to their own side. Of course, as in most matters of rumor, both reports were partly true and partly false. We had obtained a victory, but lost severely in so doing; and the enemy, in consequence of the masterly arrangements of Major General Scott, one of the best soldiers in the American Army; (and one of the most gentlemanly men I ever met with,) had retired on Fort Erie; and a body of our troops, under Major General Conran of the Royals, had pressed hard upon them, and had he not been disabled by a wound, it is the general opinion, would have followed them into the Fort. The first of the particulars we were told by an officer who had come from the field on the spur, with the despatches, and he advised me as a friend (for we were old acquaintances) to stay where I was, and get my hospital in readiness, for, he assured me, that from the manner our Regiment had been handled, I would have quite enough to do at home without going abroad to look for adventures. Accordingly, upon inquiring where my wounded were to be put, I was shown a ruinous fabric, built of logs, called Butler's Barracks, from having been built during the revolutionary war by Butler's Rangers for their temporary accommodation. Nothing could be worse constructed for an hospital for wounded men—not that it was open to every wind that blew, for at midsummer in Canada that is rather an advantage; but there was a great want of room, so that many had to be laid on straw on the floor, and these had the best of it, for their comrades were put into berths one above another as in a transport or packet, where it was impossible to get round them to dress their wounds, and their removal gave them excrutiating pain.

In the course of the morning I had my hands full enough. Our Surgeon had gone to Scotland in a state of health which rendered recovery hopeless, and our senior assistant, naturally of a delicate constitution, and suffering under disease at the time of the action, had the last of his strength exhausted in bringing his wounded down. Waggon after waggon arrived, and before mid-day I found myself in charge of two hundred and twenty wounded, including my own Regiment, prisoners and militia, with no one to assist me but my hospital serjeant, who, luckily for me, was a man of sound sense and great experience, who made a most able second; but with all this the charge was too much for us, and many a poor fellow had to submit to amputation whose limb might have been preserved had there been only time to take reasonable care of it. But under the circumstances of the case it was necessary to convert a troublesome wound into a simple one, or to lose the patient's life from want of time to pay him proper attention.

One of the many blunders of this blundering war, was that the Staff of the Army was never where it was wanted. The Medical and Commissariat Staffs, for instance, were congregated at the head quarters at Quebec, where they were in redundancy, with nothing for them to do, while a Staff Surgeon and an Hospital Mate were all that was allowed for the Army of the Right,—men who must have been active beyond all precedent if they could keep the office business, the accounts and returns square, without even attempting to interfere with the practice; and all this at a time too, when there was hardly a regiment in the field that had its full complement of medical officers.

There is hardly on the face of the earth a less enviable situation than that of an Army Surgeon after a battle—worn out and fatigued in body and mind, surrounded by suffering, pain and misery, much of which he knows it is not in his power to heal or even to assuage. While the battle lasts these all pass unnoticed, but they come before the medical man afterwards in all their sorrow and horror, stripped of all the excitement of the "heady fight."

It would be a useful lesson to cold-blooded politicians, who calculate on a war costing so many lives and so many limbs as they would calculate on a horse costing so many pounds—or to the thoughtless at home, whom the excitement of a gazette, or the glare of an illumination, more than reconciles to the expense of a war—to witness such a scene, if only for one hour. This simple and obvious truth was suggested to my mind by the exclamation of a poor woman. I had two hundred and twenty wounded turned in upon me that morning, and among others an American farmer, who had been on the field either as a militia man or a camp follower. He was nearly sixty years of age, but of a most Herculean frame. One ball had shattered his thigh bone, and another lodged in his body, the last obviously mortal. His wife, a respectable elderly looking woman, came over under a flag of truce, and immediately repaired to the hospital, where she found her husband lying on a truss of straw, writhing in agony, for his sufferings were dreadful. Such an accumulation of misery seemed to have stunned her, for she ceased wailing, sat down on the ground, and taking her husband's head on her lap, continued long, moaning and sobbing, while the tears flowed fast down her face; she seemed for a considerable time in a state of stupor, till awakened by a groan from her unfortunate husband, she clasped her hands, and looking wildly around, exclaimed, "O that the King and the President were both here this moment to see the misery their quarrels lead to—they surely would never go to war again without a cause that they could give as a reason to God at the last day, for thus destroying the creatures that He hath made in his own image." In half an hour the poor fellow ceased to suffer.

I never underwent such fatigue as I did for the first week at Butler's Barracks. The weather was intensely hot, the flies were in myriads; and lighting on the wounds, deposited their eggs, so that maggots were bred in a few hours, producing dreadful irritation, so that long before I could go round dressing the patients, it was necessary to begin again; and as I had no assistant but my serjeant, our toil was incessant. For two days and two nights, I never sat down; when fatigued I sent my servant down to the river for a change of linen, and having dined and dressed, went back to my work quite refreshed. On the morning of the third day, however, I fell asleep on my feet, with my arm embracing the post of one of the berths. It was found impossible to awaken me, so a truss of clean straw was laid on the floor, on which I was deposited, and an hospital rug thrown over me; and there I slept soundly for five hours without ever turning.

Shadrach Byfield: from "Narrative of a Light Company Soldier's Service"

In his "Recollections," William Dunlop observed that "many a poor fellow had to submit to amputation whose limb might have been preserved had there been only time to take reasonable care of it," and this was indeed true for many of the wounded of the War of 1812. Here Shadrach Byfield, a private of the British 41st Regiment of Foot, recounts being shot in the arm during the failed British raid on Black Rock, New York—a chief supply base for Fort Erie—on August 3, 1814. Memories of the arm's amputation, and thoughts of its effect on every aspect of his life, haunt the final pages of his memoir of the war, published in 1840.

———————

We joined our regiment at Niagara, and in a short time part of the regiment, including the light company, was ordered to cross the river to Fort George, and from thence towards Fort Erie. In going up the lines we fell in with our main force. We were expecting to storm Fort Erie, when orders were given for the 41st and part of the 104th, with a rocket party under the command of Captain Perry, to cross the river below Black Rock. While on the water we heard firing in the direction of Black Rock. We landed and advanced towards it. When we were here last there was a bridge between us and the town, over a small creek, but the enemy had destroyed it, and on the inner bank they had thrown up breastworks. They commenced firing upon us, we advanced, thinking to charge, when we discovered that the bridge was gone. We instantly retreated, and remained until daylight, when a party was ordered to erect a temporary bridge across the creek, and our company and the rocket company were to cover them. We stood some time and some of our shot took effect. We saw one of the enemy fall, who was daring enough to get upon their works. About this time I received a musket ball through my left arm, below the elbow. I went into the rear. One of my comrades, seeing that I was badly wounded, cut my belts from me and let them drop. I walked to the doctor, and desired him to take my arm off. He said it might be cured without it, and ordered me down to a boat, saying that the wounded men were to cross the river and they (the doctors) would soon follow. The party failed in erecting the bridge, and retreated with loss. When on the other side of the river, the wounded were put into a house and the doctors soon came. They examined my arm, and made preparations for amputation; but after a further consultation they told me that although I was rendered unfit for further service, yet if the wound could be healed it would be better for my hand to remain on, if it was not much use to me, and that it had better be first tried. I was then sent to my regiment at Niagara.

After a few days our doctor informed me that my arm must be taken off, as mortification had taken place. I consented, and asked one of my comrades who had lately gone through a like operation: "Bill, how is it to have the arm taken off?" He replied, "Thee woo't know, when it's done." They prepared to blind me, and had men to hold me, but I told them there was no need of that. The operation was tedious and painful, but I was enabled to bear it pretty well. I had it dressed, and went to bed. They brought me some mulled wine and I drank it. I was then informed that the orderly had thrown my hand to the dung heap. I arose, went to him, and felt a disposition to strike him. My hand was taken up and a few boards nailed together for a coffin, my hand was put into it and buried on the ramparts. The stump of my arm soon healed, and three days after I was able to play a game of fives for a quart of rum; but before I left the fort a circumstance happened which I here relate. There was a sentry posted near the wood to prevent any of the men entering it, and we had to go near the sentry for water. One of the artillerymen went on pretence of fetching some water, and when the sentry's back was turned towards him he started into the wood for the purpose of deserting, and the sentry (one of the 41st) shot him. The ball entered his body and the wound proved mortal; he was brought into the barracks. His captain came into the barracks to see him. The dying man charged him with being the cause of what had happened. The captain left the room, and he died shortly after. My comrades, and the messman whom I had been serving, out of kindness and respect to me made a subscription of several pounds and gave it to me. As soon as the wounded men were somewhat recovered they were ordered from the different regiments to go on board the boats used on the river, to go to Kingston, and in going down the river we went on shore by night.

On board the boat I was in was a young man, a sailor, who had lost one of his arms near the shoulder. I felt a kind regard towards him, and we became comrades. He was going down the country to be cook on board a King's ship, the *St. Lawrence*, 110 guns; he shared with me the gratuity my friends had bestowed upon me. From Kingston we proceeded to Montreal, and from thence to Quebec. One evening after going ashore, I took a walk alone a little way into the country and came near a large neat-looking house, and seeing a lad I asked who lived there; he replied, "A three-handed man." I said "That's the very man that I want to see, as I have but one hand; if he should be disposed to give me one of his, we shall have two apiece!" The lad said that by a "three-handed man" they meant that he was wealthy.

We now had orders to go on board the *Phoenix* transport and sailed for England. We had a tolerably good passage, but was a little alarmed one night, by a sudden squall of wind. The sails backed and we were near foundering, but in a short time the vessel righted and all was well. We landed in the Isle of Wight, and marched into Newport barracks December, 1814.

After examination we were sent to Chatham by water. Having been passed by the inspecting officer there I was sent to Chelsea. I appeared before the board and was ordered nine pence per day, pension.

My feelings were much excited that day, on learning that our bugle-horn man, who was a young soldier, who had been but in one action and had lost a forearm, about the same length as mine, was rewarded with one shilling per day. I must say that I felt very much dissatisfied with nine pence, and I made applications at different times to the Honourable Commissioners of Chelsea Hospital, to augment my pension, but without success. Hearing of a field-officer, residing in the

neighbourhood of the town where I live, and that he was a
soldier's friend, I made bold to wait upon him, and requested
that he would be pleased to hear my case. He kindly conde-
scended to comply with my request, and after hearing my
statement he was of opinion that I was not remunerated for
my services and loss. He very kindly said he would represent
my case; and it was not merely a *promise*, he persevered until
he had caused an addition to be made to my pension, of three
pence per day. For which I very kindly thank him, and shall be
ever bound gratefully to acknowledge his kindness to me.
Being deprived of my trade in consequence of losing my arm
in the service and having received several very severe wounds,
it was with great difficulty I could support my wife and children in a respectable manner, my pension at that time being
only ninepence per day.

One night I dreamt that I was working at my trade; and on
awaking I related my dream to my wife and told her I could
weave. She said, "Go to sleep, there was never such a thing
known as a person having but one arm, to weave"; and on
going to sleep a second time, I had the form of an instrument
revealed to me, which would enable me to work at my trade. I
awoke my wife and told her of the circumstance. I went to a
blacksmith of the name of Court, and having drawn a design
for him on a board, he made an instrument for me, similar to
the pattern with the exception of some little alteration, which
I thought was for the best, but which, on trial, I was obliged to
alter to the shape I saw in my dream; and I am happy to say
that I have been enabled to labour for my family and keep
them comfortably, for nearly twenty years, in the employ of
Edward Cooper, Esq., clothier, Staverton Works, near Bradford, Wilts.

The above is a true and correct account, as given by Shadrach
Byfield, before me.

EDWARD COOPER.
January 1st, 1840.

BATTLE OF FORT ERIE:
UPPER CANADA, AUGUST 1814

John Le Couteur: Journal

Throughout early August the Americans, under the able leadership of Brigadier General Edmund P. Gaines, continued to strengthen their position at Fort Erie. Lieutenant General Drummond, daunted by the seeming impenetrability of the fort, first tried to force evacuation by attacking its supply bases at Black Rock and Buffalo. When that raid failed, he ordered a strike against the three American schooners anchored off the fort, capturing two and thereby depriving the Americans of artillery support from the river. On August 13, Drummond opened an effective bombardment of Fort Erie from batteries north of the post. Late the next evening, he ordered his twenty-five hundred men to execute an ambitious and doomed attack on the fort. Here John Le Couteur of the 104th describes his part in what he called "a disgraceful day for Old England!"

---

14 August

About sunset Col. Drummond told Coates & me that our Flankers were to form the Storming party with the 103rd under Col. Scott and two companies of the Royals, to move at 2 o'clock in the morning on Fort Erie by Signal from a Rocket. That the Snake Hill works were to be stormed by De Wattevilles, the King's, the 89th and 100th Light Companies at the same moment.

I shall never forget the solemn tone in which our good, kind and gallant Col. Drummond took leave of us. He told me that it was probable we should never meet again, something whispered this would be his last day. He must not impart any fears for Him in my mind because He would lead on his men as usual. I urged on Him His many escapes, to look cheerfully upon this attack, we might all meet happily—under Providence! He desired me to tell Bedel his Servant to send his Trinkets & Papers to Mrs. Drummond and took a most affectionate farewell of us both which brought tears to my eyes.

"Remember the honor of the Regiment, dear Boys, God Bless You!"

To give some idea of the fort we had to attack, I will endeavour to describe it. It was neither Badajoz or St. Sebastian, nor anything of such strength, yet it was an ugly Customer for fifteen hundred men to attack Six thousand, it was said, placed behind breastworks and ramparts, with guns and a blockhouse bristling in every direction. The fort was of irregular form, with demi-bastions that flanked the ditches. The faces were of earth, but the embrasures seemed to me to be of masonry—at any rate our fire, instead of affecting a breach, seemed to me and others to ram the earth harder.

15 August

Monday. There was a strong blockhouse in the rear of the Curtain or in the body of the place, which was full of men. The distance from the woods which afforded us cover, our point of entry, on to the plain to the ditch of the fort might be three hundred yards. About an hour before daylight, our Columns led by Cols. Drummond and Scott marched as silently as death—not a whisper—presently we got within two hundred yards we were discovered. As we heard the roll of fire to our right by the attack on Snake hill—in an instant, a blaze of musquetry and Artillery opened upon us—happily considerably too high.

We still marched at a rapid but steady pace, in a few minutes the head of the column, or rather the forlorn hope, got to the ditch, jumped in, reared the Scaling ladders and cheered us as they mounted. We increased our pace and cheered loudly, defying the fire of the enemy. I jumped with our Company into the ditch. It was slow work to get up the ladders—of which there was not one quarter enough—there were palisades to be cut away, while a galling flank fire from a Gun and musquetry annoyed us sadly. Still, on we pressed, cheering.

I had mounted the ladder, got over one palisade into an embrasure and was in the act of jumping into the place when I saw it full of combatants. Our men had carried the Fort, all but the Block house from which I heard them firing and shouting: "Come over you rascals, we're British deserters and Irish rebels" when, just then, I remember seeing a black volume rise from the earth and I lost my senses.

After I recovered them, I was lying in the ditch fifteen or twenty feet down where I had been thrown by a tremendous explosion of gunpowder which cleared the Fort of three hundred men in an Instant. The platform had been blown over and a great beam had jammed me to the earth but it was resting on the Scarp. I got from under it with ease, bruised but otherwise unhurt.

But what a horrid sight presented itself. Some three hundred men lay roasted, mangled, burned, wounded, black, hideous to view. On getting upon my legs, I trod on poor Lt. Horrens broke leg of the 103rd, which made me shudder to my marrow. In placing my hand on Captain Shore's back to steady myself from treading on some other poor mangled person, for the ditch was so crowded with bodies it was almost unavoidable, I found my hand in a mass of blood and brains—it was sickening.

But lively notions quickly followed. The explosion had caused a cessation of hostilities on both sides for a few minutes—then the Americans finding but a handful of men in the Fort, rushed to their Guns and then turned a Six pounder on the ditch in which we stood and gave us a round of grape shot. I, happily for me, had seen them preparing and had proposed to Shore to form and try to carry the Gun but it was impossible to maintain order, or to enforce obedience. So I made myself as pancake like as possible against the scarp while the grape shot flew by. Some of the men shouted: "They are going to spring another mine!" when all rushed to escape. The Yankees yelled, fired and cheered.

I turned to Shore & Major Elliot. "I will not stay to be made a Prisoner, I shall run across the Plain & take my chance—Good bye!" Away I started, bringing with me a steel-mounted scabbard which I picked up from the ditch to replace my own, burnt on picquet by accident which had obliged me to carry a naked sword for a month so that the wags had called me "bloody-minded Johnny." However, in that horrid melee, I got a memento which now hangs on my Light Infantry sabre at Belle Vue.

I dashed across the Plain under such a roar of voices, Musquetry & Artillery as I never desire to run from again. Just as I had cleared half the distance, Lt. Fallon of the 103rd Grenadiers was close before me, staggering, his sling belt caught a stump. "Oh" he exclaimed, "I am caught at last." "No, Jack, my boy," I said, "you're not caught, its a tree." "Oh Johnny, I'm so dreadfully wounded in two places, I can't get on, I'm so weak." As we spoke, a grist of grape shot scattered at our feet. We escaped, as all of us have seen a Sparrow escape from a charge of No. 4. "Never fear, place your arm over my Neck and I'll take your waist, I'll run you in and not desert you—hurrah!" And we got to our batteries safely.

After handing my wounded friend to some of his own men, I looked for some of mine. Sorrow and despair took hold of me. Forgetting where I was, I threw my sword down on the battery, weeping: "this is a disgraceful day for Old England!" I had noticed no one, it was a sort of soliloquy, an escape of feeling. Col. M said: "For shame, Mr. Le Couteur, cannot you conceal your feelings, is it not enough to meet defeat without adding despair to it before the men?" Col. P called out: "No, no, Myers, it's not that, it is the generous feeling of a young Soldier's disappointment!" and He took me kindly by the hand as I picked up my Sword.

To my confusion and regret I saw General Drummond and his Staff close to me. The General called me to Him. "Do you know anything about Yr Colonel?" I could not articulate for grief. "Killed, Sir." "Col. Scott?" "Shot thro' the head, Sir, Your Grenadiers are bringing Him in, Major Leonard & Maclauchlan wounded & Capt. Shore a prisoner." The General felt for me and said "Never mind, Cheer up. You are wanted here. Fall in any men of any regiment as they come up, to line our batteries for fear of an attack." Duty instantly set me to rights and I was actively employed cheering & ranging the men as they came in.

Our men behaved admirably, two mistakes leading to the failure. The two Cols, Scott & Drummond, went in with the forlorn hopes, or leading men, and were both killed—hence all direction ceased. Then the Blockhouse was impregnable to us—the doors below had been removed, the staircases or ladders also—so that when our men got in with a view to assault the garrison, they were shot through the loop-holed floors. It should have been destroyed by hot shot before the assault. But the explosion which we thought was designed, they declare was accidental. It cleared the Fort of three or four hundred men at a blast.

It was feaful list of hors de Combat—Killed, wounded & missing, burned or Prisoner.

Lt. Cols.	Majs.	Capts.	Subs.	Staff	Sgts.	Privates
2	1	10	21	2	64	903

—or one strong regiment put out of the way.

When calling the roll of the company on the evening of that sad day, myself and twenty-three of us out of seventy-seven all burst into tears together.

Jarvis Hanks: Memoir

The explosion of the powder magazine at Fort Erie was tremendous. It killed or incapacitated most of the assault force, turning what had been a stalemate into a decisive American victory. The British casualties were 360 killed or wounded and almost 540 captured or missing. American losses numbered only 85. In his memoir of 1831, Jarvis Hanks, the drummer boy of the U.S. 11th Infantry, speculated on the cause of the explosion and recalled the carnage he surveyed on the morning of August 15, 1814.

———————

It remains uncertain by what means the explosion took place. Many rumours were afloat, the next day, among the soldiers. We all were acquainted with the fact that there was a powder magazine under that bastion; but supposed it so secure that no accident could ignite it. Two of the most probable reports I shall record. 1st. In firing the cannon upon the 9th Regiment, our enemies pointed it down hill, which they were obliged to do, in order to do execution; for that regiment lay twenty or thirty feet below the level of the floor of the fort. In doing this, they actually forced the fire of the gun through the cracks in the floor, into the magazine beneath, & blew themselves up. 2nd. Fearing that the enemy would get into the fort, our officers previously caused a train to be laid from a distance to the magazine; and when the British had got in, in multitudes, fire was set to the train, which, in a moment caused the fatal result. It was also said that the soldier who performed this act, was, next day, offered his discharge from the army and a considerable sum of money, as a reward for his bravery.

This explosion occurred just before daylight. During the forenoon, I inspected the awful scene. I counted 196 bodies lying in the ditch and about the fort; most of them dead; some dying. Their faces and hands were burned black, many of them were horribly mutilated. Here and there were legs, arms and heads, lying, in confusion, separated, by the concussion, from the trunks to which they had long been attached. One trunk I observed, deprived of all its limbs and head.

Col. Drummond was laid under a cart. When I first saw him he was naked except his shirt. All the remainder of his clothing, his gold watch, sword, epaulettes, and money, had been plundered by some of our men. We even picked the pockets of those who were dead and dying in the ditch. In the course of the day, the soldier who got Drummond's watch, sold it to one of our officers, for a small sum compared with its real value.

A large hole was dug outside the fort, and these bodies thrown in and buried before night. The enemy was so devoid of humanity, that they fired on us, while we were engaged in this melancholy service.

Andrew Jackson: Address to the Cherokee and Creek Nations

August 5, 1814

While Horseshoe Bend brought an end to the Creek War, it remained for the United States to define the terms of peace. Secretary of War John Armstrong initially appointed Major General Thomas Pinckney and the Indian agent Benjamin Hawkins to draft a treaty with the Creeks, but leaders in the South regarded them as too sympathetic toward the Indians. They preferred Andrew Jackson, now himself a major general, and Armstrong was persuaded to name him sole commissioner. Jackson would have no qualms about implementing Armstrong's original instructions to Pinckney, which specified that the treaty "take a form altogether military, and be in the nature of a capitulation; in which case the sole authority of making and concluding the terms shall rest with you, exclusively, as commanding General." On August 5, he ordered tribal leaders to assemble at Fort Jackson, near present-day Wetumpka, Alabama, where Hawkins read out the treaty's terms in their native tongue. Only one of the leaders present was a Red Stick; the others were Creeks and Cherokee who had been allied with the United States. The severity of Jackson's terms therefore came as a profound shock. The most remarkable of the treaty's nine clauses demanded that the tribal leaders cede to the United States some twenty-three million acres of land—all the remaining Creek territory in Alabama and Georgia. To justify this, Jackson insisted that both factions of the Creeks had forfeited all right to the territory by waging war on each other—a violation, he said, of the Treaty of New York, which in 1790 established the Creek Nation as a U.S. protectorate. He further reasoned that the value of the Creeks' land was the equivalent of expenses borne by the United States to prosecute the war.

Chiefs and warriors of the Cherokee Nation, and the friendly Creeks.

Friends and Brothers,

You have fought, with the armies of the united States, against the hostile creeks; many of you have fought by my side.

I am happy to meet and shake you by the hand, and rejoice with you in the pleasing prospects of returning peace. You have shewn yourselves worthy the friendship of your father the President of the United States—in battle you have been brave—in friendship stedfast. You have given proofs, that you cannot be lead astray by the deceptions of bad men and lying Prophets, sent among you by the agents of all our enemies the British. I am charged by your father the President of the United States, to say to you chiefs and warriors, that your conduct has met with his entire approbation.

Chiefs and warriors of the creek nation who have been at war with your own nation and the United States; I am happy to meet you once more at peace with the United States and your own nation; and to call you friends and Brothers—War is a dreadful calamity—it has reduced your whole nation to misery and ruin.

Your father, the President of the United States, is rejoiced that you are again his friends; that you have found out the truth; that you have found your Prophets to be impostures—but, he laments that such bad men, with vagabonds employed by his enemies to deceive you, have ever had influence over your councils to reduce a nation like yours to such distress.

Brothers, The President of the United States, for your own good, advises you always hereafter to hear the counsel of your wise chiefs and good men; to listen to the words of your chiefs and warriors who have always held him by the hand. Had you listened to them, you would yet have been a rich, powerful and happy people. Your woods would yet have been filled with flocks, and herds of cattle—your fields with corn. Your towns and villages would not have been burned, nor your women and children wandering in the woods, exposed to starvation and cold. But you listened to Prophets and bad men; your warriors have been slain, your nation is defenceless—you are reduced to such want as to receive food from your father the President of the United States.

Friends and Brothers, You have followed the counsel of bad men, and made war on a part of your own nation and the United States. This war has cost the United States a large sum. You must yield as much of your land as will pay this sum. But it must be taken from your whole nation, in such a manner as to destroy the communication with our enemies every where.

Your brothers the friendly creeks will agree to it; for wherever we take any of their land to cut off all communication with foreign powers, we will give them land of yours to which we are intitled by conquest in the place of it.

Friends and Brothers of the whole Creek Nation, The united States will again send into your country, goods and necessaries to supply your wants; but you must keep bad men out of your nation. Have no intercourse with these enemies; they are yours. Give to the United States, the right to open roads through your country—to build store houses—and you will be able by your industry to procure supplies of every thing you want and give to us scites for fortifications, and you will be defended from your own enemies and ours.

Brothers, Your game is destroyed; you must become farmers like your brothers the americans. Your warriors must raise cattle and corn for their families—your women must raise cotton—spin, weave and clothe their husbands and children. You will then become a happy people & not before.

Brothers, The terms of peace I hold in my hand. They will ensure a lasting peace between all the red nations, and between the red nations and the United States. As soon as they shall be signed, all former enmities must cease and be forgotten. That part of your Nation which has been at war and has submitted must have the forgivness of and friendship of those who have always been at peace with us, and no person must be punished, but by the United States or the grand council of your Nation. The Prophets and bad men of your nation, and the Vagabonds from our foreign enemies must be given up to the United States, or you must destroy them yourselves. As long as *they* live, your councils will be corrupted by their words—they will try again to bring you into war, and destroy the remnant of your people.

The terms of Peace will be read to you.

Big Warrior to Benjamin Hawkins

August 6, 1814

Big Warrior was chief of the Upper Creeks at Tukabatchee, seat of the Creek national council, south of present-day Tallassee, Alabama, on the banks of the Tallapoosa. Upon his death, in 1825, *Niles' Register* described him as "a person of immense bodily powers . . . endowed with a mind as colossal as his body . . . [who had] done much towards improving the condition of his people, and had great influence over them." In 1814 he was speaker of the Creek Nation, the strongest voice among those Creeks eager to keep the peace with the United States, and Washington's closest Indian ally in its campaign against the Red Sticks. The day after hearing the terms of the Treaty of Fort Jackson, Big Warrior implored Benjamin Hawkins to seek an easement of terms and some sort of justice for the friendly Creeks. But Hawkins was powerless before Jackson, and all the Creek leaders were forced to sign the treaty on August 9, 1814, some more than once as if to underscore their subjugation. Most of the surviving Red Sticks had already joined the Seminoles in Florida to fight another day, while the friendly Creeks who accepted the new order were, in the 1830s, removed to Oklahoma, a forced migration remembered as the Trail of Tears.

Yesterday my friend gave in a speech, and now I am going to give an answer. When I asked the U. S. for help, it was agreeable to the treaty of New York. We wanted to save that, and for that we asked the U. S for assistance to save us. The friendly chiefs adhered to the treaty with the U. S—There was a convention of the four nations at the Ocheubofau council House Governor Folks son was present. The plan was to have, from this council House four roads—and all promised if anything happend amiss to try in time to prevent it, and if broken to repair it. The shedding of blood was the cause of war. The spilling blood of white people, and giving satisfaction for it, was the cause of war amongst us and nothing else. This divided us, and the opposition was for breaking the chain of friendship. I called on the Cherokees Chickasaws and Choctaws, and then the fourth brother the white people to give us help. A few of us only were sensible of those treaties which were made by our old chiefs. We were weak and they were strong who understood not the form of treaties and we asked the government for help to overpower them.

They had no great chief or speaker over them, when they began to spill blood—They seemed to be of one mind, and helped each other. When I applied to your government for help we were weak and they were strong. Great spirits came to our assistance to help us wind up our entangled affairs. When it was over we expected to settle with them, and wind it up. When I asked your government for help, a part of the nation, the principle speakers, the first of the nation—were together, when they found distresses coming on them—we thought to destroy those red sticks and save their lands It was the land I wanted to save—You say you fought for it, I wanted to save that land—Friends and brothers, White Brothers—you have fought for us—our warriors were with you, you fought and spilled your blood together—It is not yet settled and you asked for the land—You seem to impose upon us the war is not yet settled—Before we asked for help we settled how we would fulfil our promises—You talk the expence is heavy on the U. S. government we have caused expences. The expences was caused by the red sticks—Part are destroyed and the rest are on the east side of us towards Pensacola. When we have conquered these people it will be time enough to talk about settling the expence to the U. S I did not expect you would call on us for a settlement. You have called on me before the Alabama red sticks were overpowered. Brothers, when two nations ask each other for help, in cases of difficulty like overpowering a country, when they help each other, The one that asks for help will give his thanks—and ask if it is satisfactory for payment—When I have settled once with you, we both are satisfied. I look on the land as the property of the nation, and thought to pay the expence out of it. This land I asked you to fight for. Before we are done fighting you ask for a part which is like imposing upon us: it is too rash. We have our senses yet. The red sticks had none. Our government when we overpower the red sticks will hold a council. Then we will ask the government of the U. S what expence we have been to them, when they give us an accurate account of the actual expences we are able to fulfil our payment. I will now state all I know concerning the treaties from time to time. The President tells us to be honest, to settle on good terms, not to be too rash, that he wishes to see Justice done to both in their settlement. This way presented to us gives us alarm. I hope and beg the U. S to settle on easy terms. This war I made for my nation on account of the treaty with old Washington called Washingtons Treaty—He advised us for our conduct in the line of that treaty—To that arm of friendship I hold fast, which is the cause of the wars made in the nation—If I had wished to break the chain of friendship I would have listened to the hostiles—and all would have broken the treaty. It belonged to the nation and we fought for it—The President Washington Father to all us old Children Muscoga. He advised us to stand to the U. S by the treaty he made for us. He was not only a Father to Muskoga, he was father to all the children under the Sun—His talk I have in my hand. Here is a man sits along side me—Colo Hawkins he was out as his agent, he has lived among us many years, he acted in his agency and never has broke the treaty, he has seen among us children born who now have children—By his direction cloth was wove clothes made and spred over the country and then the red sticks came and destroyed all, and we have none now—you ought to consider our situation. I state what all the nation knows. I will not keep any thing secret. There is the little warrior known to colo Hawkins, when we were giving satisfaction for murders he went to the lakes to the British, he was a mischief maker, Brought a packet to the edge of the frontier. part of that increased the murders—When the British found that lying and mischief brought these people to suffer. acquainted with this they are encouraging it on the sea near to Pensacola. The red sticks have no sense they will believe it, and be encouraged as long as they can see their faces. But we a rational people are not going to Join in it, like those hostile people, who have no sense—You must not think our old Chiefs have lost their senses—In the war of the revolution the British encouraged our old Chiefs to Join in the war, and our old Chiefs had no sense in those days. When we were young we were driven to fight the U S the promises the British made our old Chiefs were lost, they did not Join it, they kept us in the Island with the U S—now the British cannot persuade us to their purposes, they have deceived us once, and cannot deceive us again. You are two great Powers if you get to fighting we will have no concern in it—Thus considering we will not concern ourselves with it we are not able to fight any nation of people, we wish to be at peace with, all nations—If they offer me arms to fight—I shall tell them they put me in danger to fight my own people born in one land.

They will force me into danger. You will never see the chiefs and warriors are boys of this council who will be forced to do things—I give this answer knowing our Father advised me not to interfere in wars, those in peace are the happiest people. He told me if any enemy attacked me on this side, he had men enough and did not want the red children to interfere. The U. S officers would not be pleased when they heard our old friends the British advised us to take arms from them. The hostiles who have got away from us are the only army to be apprehended—If the British advise us to any thing I will communicate, and not hide it from you—If they say we must fight I will tell them no.

Colonel Hawkins, I will now give you the close of my reply. I inform you that there is a part of the settlers of Tallesachee who are not here—We are apprehensive the British may persuade them to acts of mischief, at such time we will put our heads together, we will convince them we have now two brothers cherokees and creeks—when we get, Choctaws, and Chickasaws the four nations we will try to settle this line for the expences incurred by the U. S. You hurry me, and I am sorry I cannot fulfil your expectations. I beg our friend and Brother, will consider us and not scold us & be vexed. We state to you the result of our councils—we of the four nations will put our heads together to settle our difficulties, and call on the officers of the U. S to settle with us our entangled affairs I hope you will think for your red friends—This is my answer to your speech friend & Brother.

Big Warrior

Alexander Cochrane to Commanding Officers of the North American Station

During the Niagara campaign of spring 1814, American forces under Colonel John B. Campbell raided several Canadian towns along the northern shore of Lake Erie, including Patterson's Creek, Charlotte's Creek, Port Talbot, Long Point, and Dover. Though their stated objective was to destroy food stores, distilleries, and mills servicing the British military, they also looted homes and burned private property, sometimes to the cry of "Remember Black Rock and Buffalo!" Sir George Prevost was livid, and in a letter of May 27 asked Vice Admiral Cochrane, commander of British forces on the Atlantic coast, to "assist in inflicting that measure of retaliation which shall deter the enemy from a repetition of similar outrages." Cochrane responded by issuing the following orders to the commanding officers of his fleet.

————————

By the Honorable Sir A. Cochrane

Whereas by Letters from His Excellency Lt. General Sir George Prevost of the 1st & 2d of June last, it appears that the American Troops in upper Canada have committed the most wanton & unjustifiable outrages on the unoffending Inhabitants by burning their Mills & houses & by a general devastation of private property— And whereas His Excy has requested that in order to deter the Enemy from a repetition of similar outrages I would assist in inflicting measures of retalliation— You are hereby required and directed to destroy & lay waste such Towns and Districts upon the Coast as you may find assailable; you will hold Strictly in view the conduct of the American Army towards His Majesty's unoffending Canadian Subjects.

For only by carrying this retributary justice into the Country of our Enemy can we hope to make him sensible of the impolicy as well as inhumanity of the system he has adopted.

You will take every opportunity of explaining to the people how much I lament the necessity of following the rigorous example of the Commanders of the American forces   And as these Commanders must obviously have acted under instructions from the Executive Govt. of the U S whose intimate & unnatural connexion with the late Govt. of France has led them to adopt the same system of Plunder & Devastation; it is therefore to their own Govt. the unfortunate Sufferers must look for indemnification for their loss of Property.

And this order is to remain in force until I receive information from Sir Geo. Prevost that the Executive Govt. of the U.S. have come under an obligation to make full remuneration to the injured & unoffending Inhabitants of the Canadas for all the outrages their Troops have committed.

Given under my hand at Bermuda   18th. July 1814
(Sigd.) A. Cochrane

To the respective Flag Officers, Captains, and Commanding Officers upon the North American Station.

By Command of the Vice Admiral (Sigd.) Wm. Balhetchet

Secret Memo.   Bermuda   18th. July 1814

Notwithstanding my public order of this days date directing you to destroy & lay waste Such Towns & Districts of the Enemy as may be within your power, you are hereby authorized to except Such Islands & places as either from furnishing Supplies or from being likely to be hereafter occupied by us in furtherance of the object of the War in which we are engaged it may be more advantageous to ourselves to treat with a marked lenity & forbearance— And if in any descent you Shall be enabled to take Such a position as to threaten the Inhabitants with the destruction of their property, you are hereby authorized to levy upon them contributions in Return for your forbearance (& in proportion to the value of the private property thus Spared) But you will not by this, understand that the Magazines belonging to the Government or their harbors, or their Shipping are to be included in Such arrangements,   These together with their Contents are in all cases to be taken away or destroyed—

(Signed) A. Cochrane—

To, Cockburn, Milne   Griffith   Hotham   Jackson—Skene —Pym, Nash   Sir T Cochrane, Percy

Robert Rowley to Owsley Rowley

In March 1814, Robert Rowley, captain of the British frigate *Melpomene* (38 guns), set sail with three hundred troops from the dockyard at Chatham, England, for the North American Station. "We are to meet Sir Alexr. Cochrane at Bermuda," Rowley wrote to his cousin Owsley Rowley, Lord Lieutenant of Huntingdonshire, "there to join an expedition formed—and what part of the Coast of America we start for from thence I know not—but I hope to God we shall be successful and lessen the dignity, and the pomp, of a misjudged and impolitic people." By early July, Rowley and *Melpomene* were in Chesapeake Bay, part of an extensive campaign of naval harassment led by Rear Admiral George Cockburn. In the following letter of August 10 to his cousin, Rowley describes his part in British actions in the bay, including encounters with the "Chesapeake Bay Flotilla," a squadron of U.S. Navy barges and gunboats under the command of Joshua Barney, who, as a commander of privateers and as a U.S. Navy officer, was a hero in both of America's wars with Great Britain.

My dear Sir,

From Bermuda I address'd you detailing particulars of our passage—and willing you should know our further movements I avail myself of the Jasseurs going from hence to Halifax, taking with her under Convoy the Spoils of our active operations here. We entered the heads of the Chesapeake on the 11th. Ulto. and on the 15th. joined our most active Gallant and admirable Admiral Cockburn up the Patuxent whither he had been to drive Commodore Barneys flotilla away. On the 17th. a division of our force took place—leaving 1 in the River Patuxent. The Severn Captain Nourse Brune another Trooper, Etna Bomb, and Manly Brig. The Admiral in the Albion, Loire, Regulus, and ourselves compos'd this Squadron. On the 18th we proceeded up this River, and at midnight of the 18th. we assembled in our boats under orders of Captn Browne of the Loire, Captn Ramsay of Regulus taking charge of first division, myself of the 2nd. At dawn of day we landed 7 miles up a

Creek, and by six we were in quiet possession of the Town of
St. Leonards having taken it by surprize. We here took 80
Hhds. of Tobacco, some flour, Military Clothing, several stand
of Arms. The inhabitants being peaceable we did not fire any
of their houses. The Ladies declared we were very civil and
vastly polite—and by ten that night we were all on board again.
Our force consists about 800 Marines & with the blue Jackets
about 1500. But the latter are so wild we do not let them land
unless absolutely to storm a field piece which they do in great
style sword in hand. They desire no better fun. On the 20th
we met resistance & took up a position for the night had two
men killed two wounded and an attempt to poison some of us
by putting Arsenic in some Whiskey laid out for Jack to take.
We burnt and destroyed Houses, Corn and every thing in our
route, for which we are termed in the American papers a Merciless Enemy, Savages. These are foul Epithets but they come
from a dastardly Yankee. They say also they have ascertained
we have Cavalry—fools that they are. Our Cavalry consisted of
Admiral Cockburn, Capt. Browne of Loire, myself occy.
mounted & the Major Commanding. We returned on the
night 21st. 23rd we were off again. The enemy showed themselves on a plain—but the moment our bayonets were seen &
Bugle sounded to advance they fled. Our skirmishers are fine
light troops. 'Tis astonishing with what rapidity & precision
they advance. We here destroyed several vessels that had been
run ashore on our approach   brought off two light ones.
Purchased live stock from a man who had not quitted his
property which is an inviolable rule with Admiral Cockburn.
Any person who stays by his property and does not drive his
stock away he affords protection & purchases from him at the
market price—but if they run away & stock driven off—then
we hunt for stock, drive it down to the boats & take it off as
plunder & fire their houses. Our next trip 26th destroyed 7
vessels brought off 22 Hd of oxen, 60 sheep. On 30th. we
went 20 miles up the Wicomico River, there took possession
of the Town of Chaptico—where some Ladies who had heard
of our good behaviour at Leonards Town remained—and sang
and played on the Piano. We took from thence 70 Hhds of
tobacco, some flour, & military stores but preserved their
houses   purchased from them stock and various articles of

provisions. The men all fled, but the Ladies remained to see the wonderful Admrl. Cockburn and the British folks. On the 1st. we moved down again, and on the 3rd. we met the warmest resistance up the Yeocomico River. Field pieces opened on us just at day light, the Admiral far advanced. They fired some excellent shot. However it did not dismay our boats but caused them to pull in with greater rapidity. The boats grounded the troops were out in an instant though up to their hips in the water and galling 'fire' away we dashed. We saw them tackle their horses to the field pieces, but to no avail. The Admiral & skirmishers came up with them 8 miles off. They fled in all directions & we brought off the field piece in fine triumph. All this done between 6 A.M. & noon. At 1 P.M. we observed a body of Cavalry collected and infantry drawn up on a hill above the town of Kinsale. We got into our boats again pulled up directly for them, when at two they opened their fire, our boats & schooners with Guns returned a sharp fire and the Marines landed. They fled. Here we killed 8. Saw a quantity of blood evidently from wounded carried off. This village was immediately fired their breastworks & battery destroyed, burnt 3 schooners brought off four and 67 Hds of Tobacco, some flour. On the 6th in the Evg. we saw about 1000 Collect at the mouth of the River Coan throwing up breastworks: although the following morning was Sunday the Admiral made a dash. They kept up a brisk fire at our boats but retreated. We destroyed their batteries but coud not come up with 4 field pieces—being obliged to keep the whole body together. However we fired their houses brought off 20 Hhds of Tobacco, 3 schooners. Since which Sir Peter Parker in the Menelaus, and the Hebrus have joined—informing the Admiral of the Commander in Chiefs intention of joining us immediately. Arrangements are making for his reception. He brings an additional force of 5,000 men—when I suppose some grand attack will be meditated. They must soon begin, for the sickly season is advancing fast. Next month all operations must cease. Thank God we have not a sick man on board. The few in the Surgeon's list are from accidents, from Bayonets, Thorns, not a Case of fever, nor have we buried a man since we left England. None of ours have been killed or wounded. I have one officer & man hurt. There was an explosion in my launch made all hands jump overboard   two alone were hurt thank God. To night or tomorrow we attack the Town of St. Mary's. I expect resistance will be made as I think they are in force—but unless very superior they cannot stand the valour of our little Army, such unanimity exists between the Red & Blue, and so gallantly led by our Admiral. I am now become Head Quarter Ship, having on board Col. Malcolm. Recd. him yesterday. I will create additional expense, but I hope this month will clear £150 from Agents Debt if tobacco arrives safe at Halifax. Agents have been liberal—which will never escape my memory. I almost fear you will be tired of my long history which might have been compressed in one half the space—but you will I trust forgive me. The warfare is a strange one and a most harrassing one to the Enemy as well as to ourselves, for it is intensely Hot. Thermometer from 79 to 89 in the shade at intervals—to move in the heat of the day double quick time in chace of an Enemy Carrying a musket, & days provision is trying to the Constitution. I have had two attacks of Cholera Mortis—two or three doses of Calomel have removed it—but it produces such immediate debility. Admiral would not let me go this last attack but must have a touch at St. Mary's. I have quite an establishment on board—a very nice little Charger taken at Nomini where they fired at us briskly. A Mule & Cow I have also. The Charger was saddled when taken so that I have him ready for the field. We are about to take possession of the Island of St. Georges at the mouth of a river of that name near the Entrance of the Potowmac when we shall land our troops and water the squadron. I shall land my Rosinante & go through Equestrian Evolutions. He is rather too much for me I fear. He has a vast deal of blood & I keep him too well. He gave me a precious kick the other day. Sailors spoil him. What think you Sir of the Naval Captain mounted as a Dragoon. After this long, viz my role, allow me to inquire after Mrs. Rowley & all your truly amiable family. I shall have a new subject to converse on whenever fortune, good fortune, allows me to pay my respects to you as to her. However, I must acknowledge I do not wish to quit these shores until the war is at an End, and that we have brought America to a right & proper understanding. Her declaration was unwarrantable & unjust in the extreme. The Federalists are gaining ground—the Cry for peace is resounded where they dare open their lips. The [   ] Virginians are Democrats. It is them we have been opposed to. Something 'Ere long must take place, there will be a division in the States no doubt their papers are filled with Bombast, and unjust illiberal sentiments and Cowardly abuse. I must now close. Pray offer to Mrs. Rowley, David and every individual of your excellent & amiable family my warmest regards. I have had no time to collect roots yet. May I beg you to remember me with respect to all those I am acquainted with in Huntingdonshire—particularly the "Ommission" family—the Duberlys. I will have some Botanical history for Miss Duberly when next we meet. With every feeling of High respect & grateful regards believe me ever your obliged & faithful.

By the same conveyance I address'd you before I wrote Mr. Hay determining not to lose sight of his friendship. We are here very happy the Captains more like brothers than anything else our minds well employ'd by the Energetic movements of our Admiral. All Ennui all Hypochrondiac complaints are here banished but one spirit prevails that is a thirst after Glory an anxious wish to meet the Enemy even upon more than equal terms. God bless you my dear Sir and all your treasures, an amiable & interesting family & believe me in sincerity & truth *Your faithful and grateful Captain*, Robert Rowley.

James Scott: from Recollections
of a Naval Life

In his *Recollections* of 1834, Lieutenant James Scott of the Royal Navy wrote that the British raids on the Patuxent River "were carried on for the express purpose of misleading the enemy as to the true and ultimate point of attack, harassing the troops, and destroying the different depôts of military stores collected in Virginia and Maryland . . . intended for the protection of the capital." The attacks, Scott argued, "had the effect of dampening the spirit of the militia, and of shewing them how completely they were in our power." When Alexander Cochrane arrived in the Chesapeake on August 14, Rear Admiral George Cockburn, encouraged by the success of these actions, urged that now was the moment for a psychologically devastating strike on a demoralized and poorly defended Washington, D.C. In this excerpt from his memoirs, Scott recounts the first leg of the British troops' march on Washington, beginning with the landing of forty-five hundred men under newly-arrived Major General Robert Ross at Benedict, Maryland, forty miles southeast of the capital.

———

On the 20th the whole of the troops were landed, including the battalion of marines; and Rear-admiral Cockburn, with the boats of the squadron and the smaller tenders, accompanied by the marines of the ships, began to ascend the Patuxent, keeping on the right flank of our army.* I accompanied the Rear-admiral in my old post as his aid-de-camp. On the 21st we reached Lower Marlborough, where General

———

*The American forces are thus enumerated as ready to meet the attack on Washington.

"Without saying any thing that can be useful to the enemy, the following may be useful to our friends:—

"The Baltimore City Brigade consists of one full regiment of artillery, (besides the marine artillery, two hundred strong,) with from seventy to ninety

Ross and the Rear-admiral met. After a rest of some hours
the army was again put in motion for Nottingham, while the
Rear-admiral pushed on with the boats for the same destination. Here we got sight, for the first time, of some of the enemy's cavalry, who opened out a fire upon our leading boats,
but went off at a rapid pace on discovering the advance of our
troops. The last-named town was made the head-quarters for
the night, and the tenders and boats anchored off it. As soon
as day dawned, army and navy were in motion. On reaching
Pig Point the marines of the squadron were landed, under
the command of the senior officer, Captain Robyns, for the
purpose of routing out any of the enemy's troops that might
be stationed on the banks for the protection of the enemy's
flotilla, some of whose mast-heads were seen above the Point.
The river had now dwindled to a small stream. As we advanced,

---

pieces of cannon on travelling carriages; one company of horse artillery, one
regiment of cavalry, one battalion of riflemen, and five regiments of infantry,
found with all needful munitions, and the greater part well disciplined. Adjacent
to the city a body of hardy fellows from the interior, 2000 strong, is encamped.
A camp of 3000 militia is to be immediately formed at Bladensburg. The district
of Columbia has about 2000 men well organized; militia, artillerymen, riflemen,
and infantry, and the regular force, marines, &c. at that place amount to ——
men. The 36th and 2nd battalion of the 38th United States Infantry, with the
force under Commodore Barney, —— strong, in the neighbourhood. Arrangements have been made to call out 5000 Pennsylvanians at a moment's notice, and
through the indefatigable exertions of General Winder, who receives all possible
assistance from the Government, this force can be directly collected at any required point between the two places. We cannot be attacked suddenly; we must
have several days' notice of a force likely to make an impression; and though *Mr.
Madison's capital* may be threatened, or the destruction of Baltimore talked of,
we guess they will not be burned at present. Besides these, the militia of our
own neighbourhood, of Baltimore, Harford, and Anne Arundel counties, &c.
would swell the entire force to an amount needful for any emergency, and we
have powder and ball, muskets, and prepared ammunition enough (if properly
managed), to kill all the Englishmen in or coming to America."—Nile's Register, vol. vi. page 408.

"GENERAL ORDERS.
"Adjutant-General's Office, Head-Quarters, Military District No. 10,
Washington City, August 20, 1813.
"Soldiers! the enemy threaten the capital of your country, and are now
pressing towards it with a force which will require every man to do his duty,

Commodore Barney's broad pendant was discovered flying on board the Scorpion, and the whole of the gunboats in a line above her, with their ensigns and pendants fluttering in the breeze. Here, then, was the boasted flotilla; we had brought them to bay, and in a few minutes we should see what they were made of. The Admiral, dashing on in his gig, led the attack. On closing with the Commodore, the silence of his guns, and a smoke issuing from the sloop, at once made known what was to follow: the order to lie on their oars was immediately given to the boats, and in a few minutes the Scorpion, like the venomous insect she was named after, unable to wound her enemies, turned the sting of death upon herself, and exploding, blew stars, stripes, broad pendant and herself, into a thousand atoms. Each of her consorts went off in a like manner, nearly in succession, the last of which, being

---

without regard to sacrifices and privations. The zeal and promptitude evinced by those in the field, with the reinforcements which are rapidly pressing to your aid, afford the fairest promise that the enemy will receive the just chastisement of his temerity. Besides those legally called to the honourable and glorious task of defending from insult and devastation the capital of your country, hallowed by the venerated name of Washington, thousands, animated by the warmest zeal for the honour, liberty, and independence of their country, will voluntarily flock to its standard, and teach our haughty foe that freemen are never unprepared to expel from their soil the insolent foot of the invader.

"Let no man allow his private opinion, his prejudices, or caprices in favour of this or that particular arm or weapon of annoyance, be a pretended excuse for deserting his post, but seizing on those which can be furnished him, or he can command himself, resolutely encounter the enemy, and prove that the bravery of freemen fighting for their families, their liberty, their country, can render every weapon formidable.

"Let obedience and alacrity in discharge of the duties required, however irksome or painful, prove their title to the appellation of defenders of their country.

"By Order of the General Commanding,
"R. G. HITE."

Nile's Register, vol. vi. page 441.

"To the Citizens of Washington.

"The whole body of the militia of this district having marched to meet the enemy," &c.

In giving these extracts, I merely wish to show that the enemy were perfectly prepared to receive us.

the magazine-vessel, almost cracked the drums of our ears.* It was a grand sight; one vast column of flame appeared to ascend and lose itself in the clouds; from the summit of the evanescent flash issued a black floating mass of smoke, which, quickly unfolding itself in curling wreaths, gradually but quickly obscured the heavens from our view. Out of the seventeen vessels composing Commodore Barney's force, one alone escaped the conflagration, which fell into our hands. The American chief preferred abandoning his charge, to the risk of trying the fortune of war at close quarters. Thirteen merchant vessels were found lying above the flotilla; some were burned, and the others sent to Pig Point. The banks of the river abreast the merchant vessels were very high, and studded with bushes. The Rear-admiral had landed me from his gig for the purpose of reconnoitring; I had attained the highest ridge, and was passing some bushes, when a shot whizzed past my ear from the opposite side of the bush. Nobody was visible, but the Admiral calling out, "He is below you, S——, he is below you," I jumped down, and found myself within arm's-length of an American seaman. His second hostile attempt upon me was defeated by my securing his sword-arm. Seeing him completely in my power, Admiral Cockburn called out, "Do not hurt him, S——, do not hurt him;" and the fellow himself loosing the grasp of his weapon and calling for quarter at the same time, he was saved from acquaintance with an excellent piece of cold steel.

I delivered him over to the coxswain of the gig, who had jumped overboard quick as lightning to my succour, and

---

*Extract of a letter from Commodore Barney to Mr. Pleasants, dated Baltimore, Oct. 30th, 1814.

"For it is well known, when orders were given to blow up the flotilla, that the enemy were firing upon them from forty barges with cannon and rockets. So far from being able to get 'farther up the river,' as was said, the vessels were aground, and blown up in that situation; and as to having time to save the baggage, so contrary is it to truth, that several of the men were taken prisoners in the act of destroying the flotilla."—Nile's Register, vol. vii. page 142.

It is well known to every officer and man who accompanied the Admiral, that not a single shot or rocket was fired at the flotilla. This is error the first of Commodore Barney.

arrived by my side just as I had disarmed my adversary. The coxswain, conceiving that firing at me through the hedge was by no means according to the laws of fair play, displayed his anger by laying hold of his prisoner, and, flinging him to the bottom of the slope, exclaimed, "I'll learn you, you beggar, to fire at my officer." It now appeared that several of the crew were stationed along the bank, who opened out a fire on the Rear-admiral's gig; in a few minutes, however, we made them all prisoners.

Having secured all the prizes off Pig Point to load them with part of the immense stores of tobacco found there, the Admiral, early in the morning of the 23rd, landed at Mount Calvert, and proceeded to Upper Marlborough to meet Major-general Ross. I accompanied him, and being mounted upon good horses, we soon reached head-quarters, where measures were decided upon for immediately attacking Washington. I was despatched to the Commander-in-chief with the news of the flotilla's destruction, and the intended descent upon the capital. I had also to request that supplies might be ready to meet us on our retreat by either of the roads that might eventually be fixed upon. Rear-admiral Cockburn directed me to hasten back with all possible speed to Upper Marlborough, where a rear-guard would be left till my return, and with them I was to proceed on to the ground on which the army intended to bivouac for the night. The Rear-admiral's gig conveyed me with rapidity to Sir Alexander Cochrane, whom I found on board one of the advanced frigates. The captain of the fleet was with him in the cabin when I delivered the information and message with which I was charged.

A long discussion ensued: the junior officer, appearing to think the attempt was too rash, stated his opinion to that effect; and finally an order was penned for the Rear-admiral, (intended of course as a guidance to General Ross also,) and handed over to me with directions to proceed without a moment's loss of time to head-quarters.

Before I took my departure, I was desired by the Commander-in-chief to open the letter, tear off the blank half-sheet, and make myself master of its contents; so that in case of falling in with any enemy, before I could reach Upper Marlborough, (not an improbable event, as I had to traverse some distance by myself,) and any chance existed of being made a prisoner, I was to devour it, or do anything to secure it from falling into the hands of the enemy; but that, should I destroy it under any such impression, and still effect a junction with Rear-admiral Cockburn, I was so to note its purport as to be enabled to communicate the contents to him. I carefully perused and reperused the despatch, and retaining only the written part of the sheet, I quitted the Commander-in-chief. The orders contained in that letter were to the following effect:—That under all circumstances the Rear-admiral had already effected more than England could have expected with the small force under his orders; that he was on no account to proceed one mile farther, but, upon the receipt of that order, the army was immediately to return to Benedict to re-embark; that the ulterior and principal objects of the expedition would be risked by an attempt upon the capital with such inadequate means;—and concluded with a reiteration of the orders to return immediately.

It was late before I reached Marlborough, and the commanding officer of the rear-guard immediately set forward. It was very dark, and we had some difficulty in finding our way; before we had proceeded far, we fell in with some of the enemy's cavalry, who however galloped off without making any attempt to molest us. I was right glad when the bivouac fires of our friends appeared in sight, having for some time previous strongly suspected that we were not in the right road. The army had taken up a position on rather elevated ground, in the centre of which, in a shepherd's hut, the General and Admiral had fixed their quarters. I did not reach the spot till two o'clock in the morning; I found both of them stretched out on their cloaks, enjoying the rest which the severe fatigues of the preceding day must have rendered so grateful. My arrival broke in upon their slumbers, and I delivered my open packet to the Admiral; he read it, and handed it over to General Ross.

It is not surprising that the latter, who had been so lately accustomed to the regular warfare carried on in the Peninsula, should have felt diffident in having with so small a force advanced thus far into an enemy's country, or that that diffidence should be increased upon the receipt of such a document as I have detailed. Having perused it, he remarked that there was now no other alternative than to return. "No," replied the Admiral, "we cannot do that; we are too far advanced to think of a retreat: let us take a turn outside, and talk the matter over." Both officers left the hut. The general's aid-de-camp, the quarter-master-general, and myself, were at a short distance, and could not avoid occasionally hearing what passed as they walked to and fro in earnest conversation. "If we proceed," said our energetic commander, "I'll pledge every thing that is dear to me as an officer that we shall succeed. If we return without striking a blow, it will be worse than a defeat—it will bring a stain upon our arms. I know their force—the militia, however great their numbers, will not—cannot stand against your disciplined troops. It is too late," continued the Admiral—"we ought not to have advanced—there is now no choice left us. We must go on."*

The consultation lasted till the eastern sky became tinged with the blush of day. The General had been apparently much excited, and at this moment, striking his hand against his forehead, he exclaimed, "Well, be it so, we will proceed." Calling his suite to him he quickly gave his orders, which they as quickly conveyed to the different commanding officers, while I rode off with the Admiral's to the naval brigade. By some means a report had flown throughout our little army that a retrograde movement was in contemplation, and a proportionate sense of disappointment had crept through its ranks. They were standing to their arms when the orders to move forward arrived. A low murmuring burst of enthusiasm involuntarily escaped from the lips of the officers and men, sufficiently indicative of the spirit that animated the hearts of the gallant band. In less than five minutes the whole army were in full march for the capital of the United States.

In our progress, the two senior officers, with their suites, were more than once fired at by ambushed riflemen. Three or four of these gentlemen were suddenly discovered above us on a high bank, secured by a paling. The acting quarter-master-

---

*The Admiral's advice was ably seconded by Lieutenant Evans, (the present Member for Westminster,) the acting Quarter-master-general, an officer whose skill and gallantry were powerfully displayed throughout the Washington business, and subsequent battle at Baltimore.

general, who was at a short distance in the rear, was the first to observe them, mounted the bank by the slope leading up to their hiding-place, clapped his spurs into the flanks of his charger, and gallantly taking the pales, leaped into the thick of them the moment they had fired upon us: they instantly threw away their rifles and scampered into the brushwood adjoining. I think it highly probable that this decisive step prevented that deadly aim they would have deliberately taken, had they not seen the officer in full career approaching them.

The oppressive heat of the day was severely felt by the men; they were however refreshed by a considerable halt, and about noon we arrived at the heights above Bladensburg, from which the whole American army were discovered drawn up strongly posted in two lines on the opposite side of the river, and their artillery so placed as to enfilade the bridge which we were obliged to cross before we could come to close quarters with them. The road led directly through their position from the bridge. In addition to the heavy artillery on the upper height, a block-house and field-pieces on the lower range defended the passage across. The enemy had tried the range of their guns, had been practising for some hours the previous day, and with some justice believed themselves secure against any attack. I accompanied the advance to the foot of the bridge, where we halted. The whole of the American artillery now opened out upon the advanced guard, and caused a fearful destruction among our brave fellows; the survivors were instantly ordered to fall back behind the adjoining houses out of the line of fire. This movement was no sooner perceived by the enemy than a deafening round of cheers ran along their lines. A gallant soldier of the 85th, a Scotchman, whose arm had been shattered by a round-shot, and which was still dangling by a fibre to the stump, was seating himself on the steps of a house as the clamorous shout was rending the air: he coolly exclaimed, "Dinna halloo, my fine lads, you're no' yet out of the wood: wait a wee bit, wait a wee, wie your skirling." I cannot forget the poor sufferer, and deeply regret that I have never seen or heard of him since.

Few minutes elapsed before the 85th regiment and the flank companies, headed by Colonel Thornton, moved up and wheeling round appeared on the bridge. This was the signal for recommencing with their great guns, accompanied by roars of musketry; round, grape, and small shot came like a hailstorm. The Colonel dashed forward, followed by his gallant regiment, in a manner that elicited enthusiastic applause from the General and his companion the Rear-admiral, who crossed at the same time. The intrepid Colonel was within a few paces of the field-pieces and block-house, when his horse was knocked from under him by a round shot. As the noble animal sank to the ground, his gallant rider alighted upon the road, and drawing his sabre, still kept the advance, leading on his men in a style of devoted and chivalrous bravery that may be equalled but never surpassed. The field-pieces and block-house were instantly taken possession of, and the 85th continued their sweeping career. Arrived on the crest of the first hill, the fire of the whole of the enemy's artillery, directed to this spot, made sad ravages among our soldiers. Colonel Thornton was one of the first to fall severely wounded; he was removed to the side of the road, when a shower of grape added to his sufferings; his jacket was literally torn with shot, nor do I think on inspection it would have been deemed possible for the wearer to have survived such a shower. Lieutenant-colonel Wood, on assuming the command of the regiment, was almost immediately badly wounded.

The road thus enfiladed, the General directed the troops* to move off to the right and left through the woods, and advance under their friendly cover towards the enemy's position. Our men, as they came up, consisting of the 44th and the flank companies of the 4th and 21st, were despatched to the right and left. The enemy's first line soon gave way at the point of the British bayonet, and retired in great confusion on their second; the action became general throughout the line. The Rear-admiral had kept the road and ascended the second height, and there he remained mounted on his white charger, his conspicuous gold-laced hat and epaulettes fully exposed within one hundred and thirty or forty yards of his foes, directing the fire of some rockets of the marine artillery, who had

---

*By the American account, as given in Wilkinson's Memoirs, it appears that the force opposed to Colonel Brookes's brigade (consisting of seven hundred and fifty men) amounted to four thousand, and sixteen pieces of artillery.

made their way to this advanced position. I was standing beside him (for Jonathan had, I guess, very discourteously unhorsed me by one of his round-shot on mounting the first hill); the fire was so heavy that I could not avoid saying, "I trust, Sir, you will not unnecessarily expose yourself, for, however much the enemy may suffer, they will regard your death as ample compensation." I made this remark in the hope that it would have induced him to move half a dozen steps to the right, where he would have been in some degree protected by a small stone quarry or excavation in the side of the road, which situation would have been equally efficient for his purpose. "Poh! poh! nonsense!" was the only reply, whilst he was eagerly watching a couple of rockets that were on the point of being discharged by Lieutenant Laurence, of the marine artillery, assisted by Mr. J. McDaniel, of the Tonnant. The fiery missiles went directly into the enemy's ranks, creating a fearful gap, and a much more fearful panic in the immediate vicinity— "Capital!" he exclaimed, "excellent!" and at the same moment Mr. McDaniel fell severely wounded. The gallant young man was soothed by the praises of his Admiral, and an assurance that he should be promoted for his good conduct: he recovered, and received his commission immediately. While speaking to the wounded master's mate, and giving directions for his removal, a musket-shot passed between the Admiral's leg and the flap of his saddle, cutting the stirrup leather in two, without doing any injury to him or the horse. He dismounted, and I was endeavouring to lash the broken parts together with a piece of twine, assisted by a marine, when a round-shot came over the saddle and dismissed my assistant to the other world.

Our gallant fellows had now got on the flanks of the enemy, and advancing in front at the same time with the bayonet, a general rout took place, the enemy abandoning great part of their artillery, every one appearing to think only of his own safety. As our troops advanced, so did the Admiral. I was about rejoining my chief, after conveying some orders to the marine artillery with the rockets, when I stumbled upon an American officer among the bushes, close to their principal battery. He was severely wounded in the leg, and requested me to remain by him, announcing himself as Commodore Barney. I assured him that he had nothing to fear in his state from our people, as he himself was, no doubt, aware. He related to me the following anecdote on the spot. A corporal of the 85th was the first who came upon him, to whom he offered his watch and a well-lined purse, if he would agree to the same request he had just made to me: the noble fellow refused both, saying, his wounded situation was a sufficient protection from his countrymen, and that he might remain easy on that score; for himself, as long as firing was going on in front, he could not remain in the rear: and he left his fallen foe in admiration of his disinterested conduct. Great pains were taken by the Rear-admiral to find out this worthy son of Mars, but ineffectually; the probability is, that he fell in the ardour of pursuit. I left the Commodore, informing him that I would report his condition to the Admiral, who would doubtless visit him. In a few minutes I conducted the latter and General Ross to the wounded officer, who, on perceiving the Admiral, began the conversation: "Well, Admiral, you have got hold of me at last."—"Do not let us speak on that subject, Commodore; I regret to see you in this state. I hope you are not seriously hurt."—"Quite enough to prevent my giving you any trouble for some time." A conversation now took place: it seemed as if the wounded prisoner and the captured officers around him doubted the sanity of their auditory nerves, as the Admiral proceeded to tender the Commodore his liberty on parole, with the selection of any of his officers upon the same terms, to see him safely conveyed to the abode he might fix upon. The offer was delivered in a manner at once so soothing to his pride, and grateful to his feelings, that he thankfully accepted the conditions. The arrival of an English surgeon finished the interview, and committing him to his care, the Admiral and General took their leave. The Commodore evidently had expected that his adversary would have gloried over his reversed fortunes, but he knew him not. It made a deep impression on his mind, and induced him, on his recovery, to proceed in a flag of truce down the Chesapeake, for the purpose of returning his thanks in person to Rear-admiral Cockburn. The Albion was absent at the time, and he made his appearance on board the Dragon; he expressed his disappointment to Captain Barrie in these words—"It was not you I wished to see, Captain Barrie, but that gallant and noble fellow your Admiral, Cockburn."

When the officers selected to accompany Commodore Barney had, with himself, pledged their parole, he entered more freely into conversation with the Admiral. Among other questions the latter inquired what force had been opposed to us; to which he replied, from the number that had joined that morning, he supposed there could not have been less than ten thousand men, adding, "If I had had five hundred such brave fellows as yours in this position, I could have defied ten thousand of the best troops in the world."* It seems that the President, "whose martial appearance gladdened every countenance and encouraged every heart,"† was on the field at the commencement of the action, but on the first shot had hastened back to Washington, doubtless to hurry on the preparations for feasting his victorious generals, to whom he had somewhat prematurely given invitations.‡

---

*"In a short time I observed a British soldier, and had him called, and directed him to seek an officer; in a few minutes an officer came, and on learning who I was, brought General Ross and Admiral Cockburn to me. These officers behaved to me with the most marked attention, respect, and politeness, had a surgeon brought and my wound dressed immediately. After a few minutes' conversation, the General informed me (after paying me a handsome compliment,) that I was paroled, and at liberty to proceed to Bladensburg or Washington. * * * During the stay of the enemy at Bladensburg, I received every marked attention possible from the officers of the army and navy." Extract from Commodore Joshua Barney's official letter to the Honourable William Jones, Secretary of the Navy.—Brannan's Official Letters, page 407.

†Wilkinson's Memorandum, vol. i. page 766.

‡An American writer, in speaking of Mr. Madison on the field of battle, says—

"Not all the allurements of fame, not all the obligations of duty, nor the solemn invocations of honour, could exite a spark of courage: * * * * * * * * and at the very first shot the trembling coward with a faltering voice exclaimed, "Come, General Armstrong, come, Colonel Munro, let us go, and leave it to the commanding General."

BATTLE OF BLADENSBURG:
MARYLAND, AUGUST 1814

Joshua Barney to William Jones

When they learned of the British landing at Benedict, Secretary of War Armstrong and Secretary of the Navy Jones assumed that the expedition's target was the strategically important port of Baltimore, not the small though symbolically significant city of Washington, D.C. Armstrong had put William H. Winder in charge of defense of the capital, but the newly appointed brigadier general's preparations were haphazard and indecisive. ("The shameful neglect of the administration to provide an adequate defence of the capital," one Federalist newspaper editorialized, "is a just cause of loud complaint among all parties.") Jones, meanwhile, had belatedly ordered Joshua Barney and his Chesapeake Bay flotillamen, their fleet scuttled in the Patuxent River, to join him, and most of the rest of Madison's cabinet, at Long Old Fields, and then to hasten to Bladensburg, where some seven thousand Americans, mostly militia, massed in a desperate bid to repel the invaders.

FARM AT ELK RIDGE, *August* 29, 1814.

SIR:

This is the first moment I have had it in my power to make a report of the proceedings of the forces under my command, since I had the honor of seeing you at the camp at the "Old Fields." On the afternoon of that day, we were informed that the enemy was advancing upon us. The army was put under arms, and our positions taken; my forces on the right, flanked by the two battalions of the 36th and 38th, where we remained some hours; the enemy did not make his appearance. A little before sunset, General Winder came to me, and recommended that the heavy artillery should be withdrawn, with the exception of one twelve pounder to cover the retreat. We took up our line of march; and, in the night, entered Washington, by the Eastern Branch bridge. I marched my men, &c. to the Marine barracks, and took up quarters for the night; myself sleeping at Commodore Tingey's, in the navy yard. About two o'clock General Winder came to my quarters; and we made some arrangements for the morning. In the morning I received a note from General Winder, and waited upon him: he requested me to take command, and place my artillery to defend the passage of the bridge, on the Eastern Branch, as the enemy was approaching the city in that direction. I immediately put my guns in position, leaving the marines and the rest of my men at the barracks, to wait further orders. I was in this situation when I had the honor to meet you, with the President and Heads of Departments; when it was determined I should draw off my guns and men, and proceed towards Bladensburg, which was immediately put into execution; on our way, I was informed the enemy was within a mile of Bladensburg; we hurried on. The day was hot; and my men very much crippled from the severe marches we had experienced the days before; many of them being without shoes; which I had replaced that morning. I preceded the men; and when I arrived at the line, which separates the District from Maryland, the battle began. I sent an officer back to hurry on my men; they came up in a *trot*; we took our position on the rising ground; put the pieces in battery; posted the marines, under Captain Miller; and the flotilla men, who were to act as infantry, under their own officers, on my right, to support the pieces; and waited the approach of the enemy. During this period the engagement continued, and the enemy advancing; our own army retreating before them, apparently in much disorder. At length the enemy made his appearance on the main road, in force, and in front of my battery, and on seeing us, made a halt. I reserved our fire. In a few minutes the enemy again advanced, when I ordered an eighteen pounder to be fired, which completely cleared the road; shortly after, a second and a third attempt was made, by the enemy, to come forward, but all were destroyed. They then crossed over into an open field, and attempted to flank our right; he was there met by three twelve pounders, the marines under Captain Miller, and my men, acting as infantry; and again was totally cut up. By this time not a vestige of the American army remained, except a body of five or six hundred, posted on a height, on my right, from whom I expected much support, from their fine situation.

The enemy from this period never appeared, in force, in front of us; they pushed forward their sharp shooters; one of which

shot my horse under me; who fell dead between two of my
guns. The enemy, who had been kept in check by our fire, for
nearly half an hour, now began to out-flank us on the right: our
guns were turned that way; he pushed up the hill, about two or
three hundred, towards the corps of Americans stationed as
above described; who, to my great mortification, made no resistance, giving a fire or two, and retired. In this situation we had
the whole army of the enemy to contend with. Our ammunition
was expended; and, unfortunately, the drivers of my ammunition wagons had gone off in the general panic. At this time, I
received a severe wound in my thigh; Captain Miller was
wounded; Sailingmaster Warner killed; Acting Sailingmaster
Martin killed; and Sailingmaster Martin wounded; but, to the
honor of my officers and men, as fast as their companions and
messmates fell at the guns, they were instantly replaced from the
infantry.

Finding the enemy now completely in our rear, and no
means of defence, I gave orders to my officers and men to retire. Three of my officers assisted me to get off a short distance,
but the great loss of blood occasioned such a weakness that I
was compelled to lie down. I requested my officers to leave
me, which they obstinately refused; but, upon being *ordered*,
they obeyed; one only remained. In a short time I observed a
British soldier, and had him called, and directed him to seek an
officer; in a few minutes an officer came, and, on learning who
I was, brought General Ross and Admiral Cockburn to me.
Those officers behaved to me with the most marked attention,
respect, and politeness, had a surgeon brought, and my wound
dressed immediately. After a few minutes' conversation, the
General informed me (after paying me a handsome compliment) that I was paroled, and at liberty to proceed to Washington or Bladensburg; as, also, Mr. Huffington, who had
remained with me, offering me every assistance in his power,
giving orders for a litter to be brought, in which I was carried
to Bladensburg. Captain Wainwright, first Captain to Admiral
Cochrane, remained with me, and behaved to me as if I was a
brother. During the stay of the enemy at Bladensburg, I received every marked attention possible from the officers of the
navy and army.

My wound is deep, but I flatter myself not dangerous: the

ball is not yet extracted. I fondly hope a few weeks will restore me to health, and that an exchange will take place, that I may resume my command, or any other that you and the President may think proper to honor me with.

Yours, respectfully,
JOSHUA BARNEY.

Hon. W. JONES.

Dolley Madison to
Lucy Payne Washington Todd

As the British advanced on Washington, residents and government employees fled in every available conveyance. The President nearly crossed the eastern branch of the Potomac (the Anacostia River) and met the approaching enemy head-on before he was luckily intercepted by General Winder, who provided him, Armstrong, Monroe, and other government officials with a U.S. Army escort that led them away from the field. First Lady Dolley Madison remained at the Executive Mansion to oversee the removal of executive records, a task badly hampered by shorthandedness and lack of transportation. As she recorded in this letter to her sister, she also saved several White House treasures, including Gilbert Stuart's full-length oil of President Washington—a five-by-eight-foot replica of the iconic Lansdowne Portrait—now in the East Room of the White House. Dolley Madison reluctantly left the President's house on the evening of August 23 and met her husband two nights later at Wiley's Tavern, in Fairfax County, Virginia.

Dear Sister   Tuesday Augt. 23d. 1814.
    My husband left me yesterday morng. to join Gen. Winder. He enquired anxiously whether I had courage, or firmness to remain in the President's house until his return, on the morrow, or succeeding day, and on my assurance that I had no fear but for him and the success of our army, he left me, beseeching me to take care of myself, and of the cabinet papers, public and private. I have since recd. two despatches from him, written with a pencil; the last is alarming, because he desires I should be ready at a moment's warning to enter my carriage and leave the city; that the enemy seemed stronger than had been reported and that it might happen that they would reach the city, with intention to destroy it. . . . I am accordingly ready; I have pressed as many cabinet papers into trunks as to fill one carriage; our private property must be sacrificed, as it is impossible to procure wagons for its transportation. I am

determined not to go myself until I see Mr Madison safe, and he can accompany me, as I hear of much hostility towards him, . . . disaffection stalks around us. . . . My friends and acquaintances are all gone; Even Col. C with his hundred men, who were stationed as a guard in the enclosure . . . French John (a faithful domestic,) with his usual activity and resolution, offers to spike the cannon at the gate, and to lay a train of powder which would blow up the British, should they enter the house. To the last proposition I positively object, without being able, however, to make him understand why all advantages in war may not be taken.

Wednesday morng., twelve o'clock. Since sunrise I have been turning my spy glass in every direction and watching with unwearied anxiety, hoping to discern the approach of my dear husband and his friends, but, alas, I can descry only groups of military wandering in all directions, as if there was a lack of arms, or of spirit to fight for their own firesides!

Three O'clock. Will you believe it, my Sister? We have had a battle or skirmish near Bladensburg, and I am still here within sound of the cannon! Mr. Madison comes not; may God protect him! Two messengers covered with dust, come to bid me fly; but I wait for him. . . . At this late hour a wagon has been procured, I have had it filled with the plate and most valuable portable articles belonging to the house; whether it will reach its destination; the Bank of Maryland, or fall into the hands of British soldiery, events must determine.

Our kind friend, Mr. Carroll, has come to hasten my departure, and is in a very bad humor with me because I insist on waiting until the large picture of Gen. Washington is secured, and it requires to be unscrewed from the wall. This process was found too tedious for these perilous moments; I have ordered the frame to be broken, and the canvass taken out it is done, and the precious portrait placed in the hands of two gentlemen of New York, for safe keeping. And now, dear sister, I must leave this house, or the retreating army will make me a prisoner in it, by filling up the road I am directed to take. When I shall again write you, or where I shall be tomorrow, I cannot tell!!

Paul Jennings: from A Colored Man's Reminiscences of James Madison

In 1799, Paul Jennings was born a slave at Montpelier, the Madison family estate in Orange, Virginia. He served James Madison as a footman and moved to Washington when Madison assumed the presidency, eventually becoming his personal servant. In a memoir published in 1865, Jennings remembered the events of August 24, 1814, when, at the age of fifteen, he was an eyewitness to the British invasion of the capital.

———————

After the war had been going on for a couple of years, the people of Washington began to be alarmed for the safety of the city, as the British held Chesapeake Bay with a powerful fleet and army. Every thing seemed to be left to General Armstrong, then Secretary of war, who ridiculed the idea that there was any danger. But, in August, 1814, the enemy had got so near, there could be no doubt of their intentions. Great alarm existed, and some feeble preparations for defence were made. Com. Barney's flotilla was stripped of men, who were placed in battery, at Bladensburg, where they fought splendidly. A large part of his men were tall, strapping negroes, mixed with white sailors and marines. Mr. Madison reviewed them just before the fight, and asked Com. Barney if his "negroes would not run on the approach of the British?" "No sir," said Barney, "they don't know how to run; they will die by their guns first." They fought till a large part of them were killed or wounded; and Barney himself wounded and taken prisoner. One or two of these negroes are still living here.

Well, on the 24th of August, sure enough, the British reached Bladensburg, and the fight began between 11 and 12. Even that very morning General Armstrong assured Mrs. Madison there was no danger. The President, with General Armstrong, General Winder, Colonel Monroe, Richard Rush, Mr. Graham, Tench Ringgold, and Mr. Duvall, rode out on horseback to Bladensburg to see how things looked. Mrs. Madison ordered dinner to be ready at 3, as usual; I set the table myself, and brought up the ale, cider, and wine, and placed them in the coolers, as all the Cabinet and several military gentlemen and strangers were expected. While waiting, at just about 3, as Sukey, the house-servant, was lolling out of a chamber window, James Smith, a free colored man who had accompanied Mr. Madison to Bladensburg, gallopped up to the house, waving his hat, and cried out, "Clear out, clear out! General Armstrong has ordered a retreat!" All then was confusion. Mrs. Madison ordered her carriage, and passing through the dining-room, caught up what silver she could crowd into her old-fashioned reticule, and then jumped into the chariot with her servant girl Sukey, and Daniel Carroll, who took charge of them; Jo. Bolin drove them over to Georgetown Heights; the British were expected in a few minutes. Mr. Cutts, her brother-in-law, sent me to a stable on 14th street, for his carriage. People were running in every direction. John Freeman (the colored butler) drove off in the coachee with his wife, child, and servant; also a feather bed lashed on behind the coachee, which was all the furniture saved, except part of the silver and the portrait of Washington (of which I will tell you by-and-by).

I will here mention that although the British were expected every minute, they did not arrive for some hours; in the mean time, a rabble, taking advantage of the confusion, ran all over the White House, and stole lots of silver and whatever they could lay their hands on.

About sundown I walked over to the Georgetown ferry, and found the President and all hands (the gentlemen named before, who acted as a sort of body-guard for him) waiting for the boat. It soon returned, and we all crossed over, and passed up the road about a mile; they then left us servants to wander about. In a short time several wagons from Bladensburg, drawn by Barney's artillery horses, passed up the road, having crossed the Long Bridge before it was set on fire. As we were cutting up some pranks a white wagoner ordered us away, and told his boy Tommy to reach out his gun, and he would shoot us. I told him "he had better have used it at Bladensburg." Just then we came up with Mr. Madison and his friends, who had been wandering about for some hours, consulting what to do. I walked on to a Methodist minister's, and in the evening, while he was at prayer, I heard a tremendous explosion, and, rushing out, saw that the public buildings, navy yard, ropewalks, &c., were on fire.

Mrs. Madison slept that night at Mrs. Love's, two or three miles over the river. After leaving that place she called in at a house, and went up stairs. The lady of the house learning who she was, became furious, and went to the stairs and screamed out, "Miss Madison! if that's you, come down and go out! Your husband has got mine out fighting, and d—— you, you shan't stay in my house; so get out!" Mrs. Madison complied, and went to Mrs. Minor's, a few miles further, where she stayed a day or two, and then returned to Washington, where she found Mr. Madison at her brother-in-law's, Richard Cutts, on F street. All the facts about Mrs. M. I learned from her servant Sukey. We moved into the house of Colonel John B. Taylor, corner of 18th street and New York Avenue, where we lived till the news of peace arrived.

———

It has often been stated in print, that when Mrs. Madison escaped from the White House, she cut out from the frame the large portrait of Washington (now in one of the parlors there), and carried it off. This is totally false. She had no time for doing it. It would have required a ladder to get it down. All she carried off was the silver in her reticule, as the British were thought to be but a few squares off, and were expected every moment. John Susé (a Frenchman, then door-keeper, and still living) and Magraw, the President's gardener, took it down and sent it off on a wagon, with some large silver urns and such other valuables as could be hastily got hold of. When the British did arrive, they ate up the very dinner, and drank the wines, &c., that I had prepared for the President's party.

George R. Gleig: *from* The Campaigns of the British Army at Washington and New Orleans, 1814–15

Among Major General Ross's junior officers was Captain George R. Gleig, an eighteen-year-old Scotsman who, in 1813, had suspended his divinity studies at Oxford to fight in Spain under Wellington. After the peace with France, he and many of his comrades in the 85th Light Infantry sailed to Bermuda, and from there to the Chesapeake: "Thus, like a snowball, we had gathered as went on, and from having set out a mere handful of soldiers, were now an army, formidable as well from its numbers as its discipline." Gleig's remarkably vivid memoirs of the war in America, based upon his journals of the period, were published in 1821.

The hour of noon was approaching, when a heavy cloud of dust, apparently not more than two or three miles distant, attracted our attention. From whence it originated there was little difficulty in guessing, nor did many minutes expire before surmise was changed into certainty; for on turning a sudden angle in the road, and passing a small plantation, which obstructed the vision towards the left, the British and American armies became visible to one another. The position occupied by the latter was one of great strength, and commanding attitude. They were drawn up in three lines upon the brow of a hill, having their front and left flank covered by a branch of the Potomac, and their right resting upon a thick wood and a deep ravine. This river, which may be about the breadth of the Isis at Oxford, flowed between the heights occupied by the American forces, and the little town of Bladensburg. Across it was thrown a narrow bridge, extending from the chief street in that town to the continuation of the road, which passed through the very centre of their position; and its right bank (the bank above which they were drawn up) was covered with a narrow stripe of willows and larch trees, whilst the left was altogether bare, low, and exposed. Such was the general aspect of their position as at the first glance it presented itself; of which I must endeavour to give a more detailed account, that my description of the battle may be in some degree intelligible.

I have said that the right bank of the Potomac was covered with a narrow stripe of willow and larch trees. Here the Americans had stationed strong bodies of riflemen, who, in skirmishing order, covered the whole front of their army. Behind this plantation, again, the fields were open and clear, intersected, at certain distances, by rows of high and strong palings. About the middle of the ascent, and in the rear of one of these rows, stood the first line, composed entirely of infantry; at a proper interval from this, and in a similar situation, stood the second line; while the third, or reserve, was posted within the skirts of a wood, which crowned the heights. The artillery, again, of which they had twenty pieces in the field, was thus arranged: on the high road, and commanding the bridge, stood two heavy guns; and four more, two on each side of the road, swept partly in the same direction, and partly down the whole of the slope into the streets of Bladensburg. The rest were scattered, with no great judgment, along the second line of infantry, occupying different spaces between the right of one regiment and the left of another; whilst the cavalry showed itself in one mass, within a stubble field, near the extreme left of the position. Such was the nature of the ground which they occupied, and the formidable posture in which they waited our approach; amounting, by their own account, to nine thousand men, a number exactly doubling that of the force which was to attack them.

In the mean time, our column continued to advance in the same order which it had hitherto preserved. The road having conducted us for about two miles in a direction parallel with the river, and of consequence with the enemy's line, suddenly turned, and led directly towards the town of Bladensburg. Being of course ignorant whether this town might not be filled with American troops, the main body paused here till the advanced guard should reconnoitre. The result proved that no opposition was intended in that quarter, and that the whole of the enemy's army had been withdrawn to the opposite side of the stream, whereupon the column was again put in motion, and in a short time arrived in the streets of Bladensburg, and within range of the American artillery. Immediately on our reaching this point, several of their guns opened upon us, and kept up a quick and well-directed cannonade, from which, as we were again commanded to halt, the men were directed to shelter themselves as much as possible behind the houses. The object of this halt, it was conjectured, was to give the General an opportunity of examining the American line, and of trying the depth of the river; because at present there appeared to be but one practicable mode of attack, by crossing the bridge, and taking the enemy directly in front. To do so, however, exposed as the bridge was, must be attended with bloody consequences, nor could the delay of a few minutes produce any mischief which the discovery of a ford would not amply compensate.

But in this conjecture we were altogether mistaken; for without allowing time to the column to close its ranks, or to be joined by such of the many stragglers as were now hurrying, as fast as weariness would permit, to regain their places, the order to halt was countermanded, and the word given to attack; and we immediately pushed on at double quick time, towards the head of the bridge. While we were moving along the street, a continued fire was kept up, with some execution, from those guns which stood to the left of the road; but it was not till the bridge was covered with our people that the two-gun battery upon the road itself began to play.—Then, indeed, it also opened, and with tremendous effect; for at the first discharge almost an entire company was swept down; but whether it was that the guns had been previously laid with measured exactness, or that the nerves of the gunners became afterwards unsteady, the succeeding discharges were much less fatal. The riflemen likewise began to gall us from the wooded bank, with a running fire of musketry; and it was not without trampling upon many of their dead and dying comrades, that the light brigade established itself on the opposite side of the stream.

When once there, however, everything else appeared easy. Wheeling off to the right and left of the road, they dashed into the thicket, and quickly cleared it of the American skirmishers; who, falling back with precipitation upon the first line, threw it into disorder before it had fired a shot. The consequence was, that our troops had scarcely shown themselves when the whole of that line gave way, and fled in the greatest confusion, leaving the two guns upon the road in possession of the victors.

But here it must be confessed that the light brigade was guilty of imprudence. Instead of pausing till the rest of the army came up, the soldiers lightened themselves by throwing away their knapsacks and haversacks; and extending their ranks so as to show an equal front with the enemy, pushed on to the attack of the second line.—The Americans, however, saw their weakness, and stood firm, and having the whole of their artillery, with the exception of the pieces captured on the road, and the greater part of their infantry in this line, they first checked the ardour of the assailants by a heavy fire, and then, in their turn, advanced to recover the ground which was lost. Against this charge, the extended order of the British troops would not permit them to offer an effectual resistance, and they were accordingly borne back to the very thicket upon the river's brink; where they maintained themselves with determined obstinacy, repelling all attempts to drive them through it; and frequently following, to within a short distance of the cannon's mouth, such parts of the enemy's line as gave way.

In this state the action continued till the second brigade had likewise crossed, and formed upon the right bank of the river; when the 44th regiment moving to the right, and driving in the skirmishers, debouched upon the left flank of the Americans, and completely turned it. In that quarter, therefore, the battle was won; because the raw militia-men, who were stationed there as being the least assailable point, when once broken could not be rallied. But on their right, the enemy still kept their ground with much resolution; nor was it till the arrival of the 4th Regiment, and the advance of the British forces in firm array to the charge, that they began to waver. Then, indeed, seeing their left in full flight, and the 44th getting in their rear, they lost all order, and dispersed, leaving clouds of riflemen to cover their retreat; and hastened to conceal themselves in the woods, where it would have been madness to follow them. The rout was now general throughout the line. The reserve, which ought to have supported the main body, fled as soon as those in its front began to give way; and the cavalry, instead of charging the British troops, now scattered in pursuit, turned their horses' heads and galloped off, leaving them in undisputed possession of the field, and of ten out of the twenty pieces of artillery.

This battle, by which the fate of the American capital was decided, began about one o'clock in the afternoon, and lasted till four. The loss on the part of the English was severe, since, out of two-thirds of the army, which were engaged, upwards of five hundred men were killed and wounded; and what rendered it doubly severe was, that among these were numbered several officers of rank and distinction. Colonel Thornton who commanded the light brigade, Lieutenant Colonel Wood commanding the 85th Regiment, and Major Brown who led the advanced guard, were all severely wounded; and General Ross himself had a horse shot under him. On the side of the Americans the slaughter was not so great. Being in possession of a strong position, they were of course less exposed in defending, than the others in storming it; and had they conducted themselves with coolness, and resolution, it is not conceivable how the battle could have been won. But the fact is, that, with the exception of a party of sailors from the gun boats, under the command of Commodore Barney, no troops could behave worse than they did. The skirmishers were driven in as soon as attacked, the first line gave way without offering the slightest resistance, and the left of the main body was broken within half an hour after it was seriously engaged. Of the sailors, however, it would be injustice not to speak in the terms which their conduct merits. They were employed as gunners, and not only did they serve their guns with a quickness and precision which astonished their assailants, but they stood till some of them were actually bayoneted, with fuzes in their hands; nor was it till their leader was wounded and taken, and they saw themselves deserted on all sides by the soldiers, that they quitted the field. With respect to the British army, again, no line of distinction can be drawn. All did their duty, and none more gallantly than the rest; and though the brunt of the affair fell upon the light brigade, this was owing chiefly to the circumstances of its being at the head of the column, and perhaps, also, in some degree, to its own rash impetuosity. The artillery, indeed, could do little; being unable to show itself in presence of a force so superior; but the six-pounder was nevertheless brought into action, and a corps of rockets proved of striking utility.

Our troops being worn down from fatigue, and of course as ignorant of the country, as the Americans were the reverse, the pursuit could not be continued to any distance. Neither was it attended with much slaughter. Diving into the recesses of the forests, and covering themselves with riflemen, the enemy were quickly beyond our reach; and having no cavalry to scour even the high road, ten of the lightest of their guns were carried off in the flight. The defeat, however, was absolute, and the army which had been collected for the defence of Washington, was scattered beyond the possibility of, at least, an immediate reunion; and as the distance from Bladensburg to that city does not exceed four miles, there appeared to be no further obstacle in the way to prevent its immediate capture.

AN opportunity so favourable was not endangered by any needless delay. While the two brigades which had been engaged remained upon the field to recover their order, the third, which had formed the reserve, and was consequently unbroken, took the lead, and pushed forward at a rapid rate towards Washington.

As it was not the intention of the British Government to attempt permanent conquests in this part of America; and as the General was well aware that, with a handful of men, he could not pretend to establish himself, for any length of time, in an enemy's capital, he determined to lay it under contribution, and to return quietly to the shipping. Nor was there anything unworthy of the character of a British officer in this determination. By all the customs of war, whatever public property may chance to be in a captured town, becomes, confessedly, the just spoil of the conqueror; and in thus proposing to accept a certain sum of money in lieu of that property, he was showing mercy, rather than severity, to the vanquished. It is true, that if they chose to reject his terms, he and his army would be deprived of their booty, because, without some more convenient mode of transporting it than we possessed, even the portable part of the property itself could not be removed. But, on the other hand, there was no difficulty in destroying it;

and thus, though we should gain nothing, the American Government would lose probably to a much greater amount than if they had agreed to purchase its preservation by the money demanded.

Such being the intention of General Ross, he did not march the troops immediately into the city, but halted them upon a plain in its immediate vicinity, whilst a flag of truce was sent forward with terms. But whatever his proposal might have been, it was not so much as heard; for scarcely had the party bearing the flag entered the street, when it was fired upon from the windows of one of the houses, and the horse of the General himself, who accompanied it, killed. The indignation excited by this act throughout all ranks and classes of men in the army, was such as the nature of the case could not fail to occasion. Every thought of accommodation was instantly laid aside; the troops advanced forthwith into the town, and having first put to the sword all who were found in the house from which the shots were fired, and reduced it to ashes, they proceeded, without a moment's delay, to burn and destroy every thing in the most distant degree connected with Government. In this general devastation were included the Senate-house, the President's palace, an extensive dock-yard and arsenal, barracks for two or three thousand men, several large store-houses filled with naval and military stores, some hundreds of cannon of different descriptions, and nearly twenty thousand stand of small arms. There were also two or three public rope-walks which shared the same fate, a fine frigate pierced for sixty guns, and just ready to be launched, several gun brigs and armed schooners, with a variety of gun boats and small craft. The powder magazines were set on fire, and exploded with a tremendous crash, throwing down many houses in their vicinity, partly by pieces of the walls striking them, and partly by the concussion of the air; whilst quantities of shot, shell, and hand-grenades, which could not otherwise be rendered useless, were cast into the river. In destroying the cannon, a method was adopted, which I had never before witnessed, and which, as it was both effectual and expeditious, I cannot avoid relating. One gun of rather a small calibre was pitched upon as the executioner of the rest; and being loaded with ball, and turned to the muzzles of the others, it was fired, and thus beat out their breechings. Many, however, not being mounted, could not be thus dealt with; these were spiked, and having their trunnions knocked off, were afterwards cast into the bed of the river.

All this was as it should be, and had the arm of vengeance been extended no further, there would not have been room given for so much as a whisper of disapprobation. But, unfortunately, it did not stop here; a noble library, several printing offices, and all the national archives were likewise committed to the flames, which, though no doubt the property of Government, might better have been spared. It is not, however, my intention to join the outcry, which was raised at the time, against what the Americans and their admirers were pleased to term a line of conduct at once barbarous and unprofitable. On the contrary, I conceive that too much praise cannot be given to the forbearance and humanity of the British troops who, irritated as they had every right to be, spared, as far as possible, all private property, neither plundering nor destroying a single house in the place, except that from which the General's horse had been killed.

Whilst the third brigade was thus employed, the rest of the army, having recalled its stragglers, and removed the wounded into Bladensburg, began its march towards Washington. Though the battle came to a close by four o'clock, the sun had set before the different regiments were in a condition to move, consequently this short journey was performed in the dark. The work of destruction had also begun in the city, before they quitted their ground; and the blazing of houses, ships, and stores, the report of exploding magazines, and the crash of falling roofs, informed them, as they proceeded, of what was going forward. It would be difficult to conceive a finer spectacle than that which presented itself as they approached the town. The sky was brilliantly illumined by the different conflagrations; and a dark red light was thrown upon the road, sufficient to permit each man to view distinctly his comrade's face. Except the burning of St. Sebastian's, I do not recollect to have witnessed, at any period of my life, a scene more striking or more sublime.

Having advanced as far as the plain, where the reserve had previously paused, the first and second brigades halted; and, forming into close column, passed the night in bivouac. At first, this was agreeable enough, because the air was mild, and weariness made up for what was wanting in comfort. But towards morning, a violent storm of rain, accompanied with thunder and lightning, came on, which disturbed the rest of all who were exposed to it. Yet, in spite of the inconvenience arising from the shower, I cannot say that I felt disposed to grumble at the interruption, for it appeared that what I had before considered as superlatively sublime, still wanted this to render it complete. The flashes of lightning vied in brilliancy with the flames which burst from the roofs of burning houses, whilst the thunder drowned, for a time, the noise of crumbling walls, and was only interrupted by the occasional roar of cannon, and of large depôts of gunpowder, as they one by one exploded.

I need scarcely observe, that the consternation of the inhabitants was complete, and that to them this was a night of terror. So confident had they been of the success of their troops, that few of them had dreamt of quitting their houses, or abandoning the city; nor was it till the fugitives from the battle began to rush in, filling every place as they came with dismay, that the President himself thought of providing for his safety. That gentleman, as I was credibly informed, had gone forth in the morning with the army, and had continued among his troops till the British forces began to make their appearance. Whether the sight of his enemies cooled his courage or not, I cannot say, but, according to my informant, no sooner was the glittering of our arms discernible, than he began to discover that his presence was more wanted in the senate than in the field; and having ridden through the ranks, and exhorted every man to do his duty, he hurried back to his own house, that he might prepare a feast for the entertainment of his officers, when they should return victorious. For the truth of these details I will not be answerable; but this much I know, that the feast was actually prepared, though, instead of being devoured by American officers, it went to satisfy the less delicate appetites of a party of English soldiers. When the detachment, sent out to destroy Mr. Maddison's house, entered his dining parlour, they found a dinner table spread, and covers laid for forty guests. Several kinds of wine, in handsome cut-glass decanters, were cooling on the sideboard; plate-holders stood by the fire-place, filled with dishes and plates; knives, forks and spoons, were arranged for immediate use; everything in short was ready for the entertainment of a ceremonious party. Such were the arrangements in the dining-room, whilst in the kitchen were others answerable to them in every respect. Spits, loaded with joints of various sorts, turned before the fire; pots, saucepans, and other culinary utensils, stood upon the grate; and all the other requisites for an elegant and substantial repast, were in the exact state which indicated that they had been lately and precipitately abandoned.

The reader will easily believe, that these preparations were beheld, by a party of hungry soldiers, with no indifferent eye. An elegant dinner, even though considerably over-dressed, was a luxury to which few of them, at least for some time back, had been accustomed; and which, after the dangers and fatigues of the day, appeared peculiarly inviting. They sat down to it, therefore, not indeed in the most orderly manner, but with countenances which would not have disgraced a party of aldermen at a civic feast; and having satisfied their appetites with fewer complaints than would have probably escaped their rival *gourmands*, and partaken pretty freely of the wines, they finished by setting fire to the house which had so liberally entertained them.

I have said that, to the inhabitants of Washington, this was a night of terror and dismay. From whatever cause the confidence arose, certain it is, that they expected anything rather than the arrival among them of a British army; and their consternation was proportionate to their previous feeling of security, when an event, so little anticipated, actually came to pass. The first impulse naturally prompted them to fly, and the streets were speedily crowded with soldiers and senators, men, women, and children, horses, carriages, and carts loaded with household furniture, all hastening towards a wooden bridge which crosses the Potomac. The confusion thus occasioned was terrible, and the crowd upon the bridge was such as to endanger its giving way. But Mr. Maddison, as is affirmed, having escaped among the first, was no sooner safe on the opposite bank of the river, than he gave orders that the bridge should be broken down; which being obeyed, the rest were obliged to return, and to trust to the clemency of the victors.

In this manner was the night passed by both parties; and at daybreak next morning, the light brigade moved into the city, whilst the reserve fell back to a height, about half a mile in the rear. Little, however, now remained to be done, because everything marked out for destruction was already consumed. Of the senate-house, the President's palace, the barracks, the dock-yard, &c., nothing could be seen, except heaps of smoking ruins; and even the bridge, a noble structure upwards of a mile in length, was almost entirely demolished. There was, therefore, no further occasion to scatter the troops, and they were accordingly kept together as much as possible on the Capitol Hill.

Mary Stockton Hunter
to Susan Stockton Cuthbert

Meeting with the President at Long Old Fields prior to the Battle of
Bladensburg, Secretary of the Navy Jones had impressed upon him
and the rest of the cabinet present the Washington Navy Yard's importance to the British, not only for its stores and provisions but also
for the vessels docked there—two gunboats, three barges, a schooner,
and two new ships nearing completion, the sloop *Argus* and the frigate *Columbia*. He had argued that if the British seized the yard, they
would gain the only strategic target that Washington offered them,
and, by adding the 18-gun *Argus* and 44-gun *Columbia* to their fleet,
would "greatly extend the field of [their] plunder and devastation."
In light of this possibility, the President agreed that should the British
take possession of the city, the Navy Yard must be destroyed. And so,
at two in the morning on August 25, the stores, provisions, *Argus*,
and *Columbia* were set ablaze. Mary S. Hunter, whose husband Andrew was a chaplain stationed in the yard, described the great conflagration to her sister.

Washington City Aug. 30th, 1814

My dear Sister,
 You will doubtless wish to hear how we have passed through
the perils to which we have been lately exposed by an invading
foe, whether our lives have been spared or our habitations have
escaped the devouring flames. With respect to both these
events we have been highly favoured. We are all in good health
and our house unmolested. But our fears and troubles for
some time past have been almost beyond description. The
British army commanded by Genll Ross, and the seamen by
Admll Cockburn had been advancing upon us for more than
two weeks, and as we supposed were not likely to be stopped
or prevented from ravaging our city, and destroying our property to the extent of their wishes. To crown this scene of affliction on Wednesday last the 24th of the month we heard in the

morning that the enemy were on their march near Bladensburgh and that our militia were on their way to meet them.
My husband and myself concluded that it would be prudent to
take our children and servants out of the way and place them a
few miles off till the storm should be ended. I myself concluded
to stay in our house with our house-keeper and one black servant, and my husband took away the children and other servants. About the middle of the day we heard a severe
cannonading in the direction of Bladensburgh and some hours
after we saw our men running in great numbers in a disorderly
manner. And in the evening, perhaps at sunsetting, I will leave
you to conjecture what our feelings must have been when we
saw the British flag flying on Capitol-Hill, and the rockets
brandished for the destruction of our Capitol and for what
other property we knew not.

In a few minutes a grum looking officer rode up to our door
and asked me where my husband was. I informed him he was
not at home. He asked me when he went abroad. I told him
this morning. What induced him, he said, to go abroad just at
this time. I then looked him fully in the face and very deliberately told him that my husband was gone to take a family of
young children from witnessing such a horrid scene. He asked
when my husband was expected home. I told him that I had
expected him this evening; but that under existing circumstances I hardly thought he would be home. This put a stop to
all further interrogatories. I then asked him to go to the sideboard and help himself to any refreshments that were agreeable to him. And while he was regaling himself I asked in my
turn what they were going to do; whether to burn the City
generally, or confine themselves to the public buildings? He
said that would depend on circumstances. Where no resistance was made private property would be safe; especially to
those who remained in their houses. But that every house
where resistance was made or in which arms should be found
would be fired. He then told us that Genll Ross's horse had
been shot under him from Galatin's house and that it was
burnt. After graciously assuring us that we need be under
no apprehensions—that their troops were under the strictest
discipline—that none dared to come into our houses without
permission. Soon after I went across the street to a neighbour's

house from whence I could have a better view of the Capitol. At this house a number of the officers were taking some refreshment, and seeing us alarmed they said everything that could be said to quiet us. I told them I had seen many B. officers who were gentlemen, and that I could not bring myself to be afraid. I mentioned that a quantity of powder had been deposited in the Capitol and that I was apprehensive when the fire reached it, it might injure the inhabitants—they said it would be immediately removed, and that the Capitol would not be blown up. They talked of burning the Washington Bank, but were informed that it was private property and that it must destroy a great deal of individual property if it should be burnt—under these considerations they spared it. They mentioned that it was a painful service to them—that they were disposed to do all in their power to mitigate the distress of the citizens against whom they had no enmity. That their war was with the government and not with the people. All this relieved our fears concerning the city and ourselves. But a most awful scene was yet to follow. Our important Navy-Yard was yet to be destroyed by our own hands—the most suicidal act ever committed. No pen can describe the apalling sound that our ears heard, and the sight that our eyes saw. We could see everything from the upper part of our house as plainly as if we had been in the Yard. All the vessels of war on fire—the immense quantity of dry timber, together with the houses and stores in flames produced an almost meridian brightness. You never saw a drawing room so brilliantly lighted as the whole city was that night. Few thought of going to bed—they spent the night in gazing on the fires, and lamenting the disgrace of the city. The british never went near the navy-yard till next morning. On the morning of the 25th we were introduced to a number of officers among whom was Admiral Cockburn who said he admired the American Ladies—they made excellent wives and good mothers; but they were very much prejudiced against him—that his friend Jo. Gales had told so many lies about him that he was afraid he should never be a favorite. But he said he had paid him by scattering his types—that he had left a line to desire him to publish it in his next paper. He inquired of me and all the ladies present in a very particular manner if they had sustained any injury—if any of the soldiers had come into our houses, or taken any thing from us. He intreated us if any thing of that nature occurred that we would immediately complain, and they should be punished. I began to think ourselves happy, when a most alarming storm of wind and rain came on which blew down and unroofed many houses. This storm we believe hurried the army off. They were in danger of being separated from their shipping.

Yours affectionately
M. H.

George R. Gleig: *from* The Campaigns of the British Army at Washington and New Orleans, 1814–15

The fires set by both the British and the U.S. Navy burned through the night of August 24–25, lighting up the sky for miles around. The morning revealed the charred and roofless shells of most of Washington's public buildings, including the White House, the Capitol, the Treasury, and the offices of the War and State departments. The post office and patent office were spared, as were most private buildings, though Admiral Cockburn personally oversaw the destruction of the pressroom of the *National Intelligencer*, the administration organ that had published so many articles insulting to him and the dignity of His Majesty's forces. In this excerpt from his memoirs, George Gleig concludes his detailed and triumphal account of the British occupation of Washington.

———————

I have stated above that our troops were this day kept as much together as possible upon the Capitol Hill. But it was not alone on account of the completion of their destructive labours that this was done. A powerful army of Americans already began to show themselves upon some heights, at the distance of two or three miles from the city; and as they sent out detachments of horse even to the very suburbs, for the purpose of watching our motions, it would have been unsafe to permit more straggling than was absolutely necessary. The army which we had overthrown the day before, though defeated, was far from annihilated; it had by this time recovered its panic, began to concentrate itself in our front, and presented quite as formidable an appearance as ever. We learnt, also, that it was joined by a considerable force from the back settlements, which had arrived too late to take part in the action, and the report was, that both combined, amounted to nearly twelve thousand men.

Whether or not it was their intention to attack, I cannot pretend to say, because it was noon before they showed themselves; and soon after, when something like a movement could be discerned in their ranks, the sky grew suddenly dark, and the most tremendous hurricane ever remembered by the oldest inhabitant in the place, came on. Of the prodigious force of the wind, it is impossible for one, who was not an eye-witness to its effects, to form a conception. Roofs of houses were torn off by it, and whirled into the air like sheets of paper; whilst the rain which accompanied it resembled the rushing of a mighty cataract, rather than the dropping of a shower. The darkness was as great as if the sun had long set, and the last remains of twilight had come on, occasionally relieved by flashes of vivid lightning streaming through it; which, together with the noise of the wind and the thunder, the crash of falling buildings, and the tearing of roofs as they were stript from the walls, produced the most appalling effect I ever have, and probably ever shall, witness. The storm lasted for nearly two hours without intermission; during which time, many of the houses spared by us were blown down; and thirty of our men, besides several of the inhabitants, buried beneath their ruins. Our column was as completely dispersed as if it had received a total defeat; some of the men flying for shelter behind walls and buildings, and others falling flat upon the ground, to prevent themselves from being carried away by the tempest; nay, such was the violence of the wind, that two pieces of light cannon, which stood upon the eminence, were fairly lifted from the ground, and borne several yards to the rear.

WHEN the hurricane had blown over, the camp of the Americans appeared to be in as great a state of confusion as our own; nor could either party recover themselves sufficiently, during the rest of the day, to try the fortune of a battle. Of this General Ross did not fail to take advantage. He had already attained all that he could hope, and perhaps more than he originally expected to attain; consequently, to risk another action, would only be to spill blood for no purpose. Whatever might be the issue of the contest, he could derive from it no advantage. If he were victorious, it would not do away with the necessity which existed of evacuating Washington; if defeated, his ruin was certain. To avoid fighting was, therefore, his object, and perhaps he owed its accomplishment to the fortunate occurrence of the storm. Be that, however, as it may, a retreat was resolved upon; and we now only waited for night, to put the resolution into practice.

There was, however, one difficulty to be surmounted in this proceeding. Of the wounded, many were so ill, as to preclude all possibility of their removal, and to leave them in the hands of an enemy whom we had beaten, was rather a mortifying anticipation. But for this there was no help; and it now only remained to make the best arrangements for their comfort, and to secure for them, as far as could be done, civil treatment from the Americans.

It chanced that, among other prisoners taken at Bladensburg, was Commodore Barney, an American officer of much gallantry and high sense of honour. Being himself wounded, he was the more likely to feel for those who were in a similar condition, and having received the kindest treatment from our medical attendants, as long as he continued under their hands, he became, without solicitation, the friend of his fellow-sufferers. To him, as well as to the other prisoners, was given his parole, and to his care were our wounded, in a peculiar manner, intrusted,—a trust which he received with the utmost willingness, and discharged with the most praiseworthy exactness. Among other stipulations, it was agreed that such of our people as were left behind, should be considered as prisoners of war, and should be restored to us, as soon as they were able to travel; and that, as soon as they reached the ships, the Commodore and his countrymen would, in exchange, be released from their engagements.

As soon as these arrangements were completed, and darkness had come on, the third brigade, which was posted in the rear of our army, began to withdraw. Then followed the guns, afterwards the second, and last of all the light brigade, exactly reversing the order which had been maintained during the advance. Instead of an advanced guard, this last now furnished a party to cover the retreat, and the whole procession was closed by the mounted drivers.

It being a matter of great importance to deceive the enemy, and to prevent pursuit, the rear of the column did not quit its ground upon the Capitol till a late hour. During the day, an order had been issued that none of the inhabitants should be seen in the streets after eight o'clock; and as fear renders most men obedient, the order was punctually attended to. All the horses belonging to different officers were removed to drag the guns, no one being allowed to ride, lest a neigh, or even the trampling of hoofs, should excite suspicion. The fires were trimmed, and made to blaze brightly; fuel enough was left to keep them so for some hours; and finally, about half past nine o'clock, the troops formed in marching order, and moved off in the most profound silence. Not a word was spoken, nor a single individual permitted to step one inch out of his place, by which means they passed along the streets perfectly unnoticed, and cleared the town without any alarm being given. Our pace, it will be imagined, was none of the most tardy, consequently it was not long before we reached the ground which had been occupied by the other brigades. Here we found a second line of fires blazing in the same manner as those deserted by ourselves; and the same precautions, in every respect, adopted, to induce a belief that our army was still quiet.—Beyond these, again, we found two or three solitary fires, placed in such order as to re-semble those of a chain of piquets. In a word, the deception was so well managed, that even we ourselves were at first doubtful whether the rest of the troops had fallen back.

When we reached the ground where yesterday's battle had been fought, the moon rose, and exhibited a spectacle by no means enlivening.—The dead were still unburied, and lay about in every direction, completely naked. They had been stripped even of their shirts, and having been exposed in this state to the violent rain in the morning, they appeared to be bleached to a most unnatural degree of whiteness. The heat and rain together had likewise affected them in a different manner; and the smell which rose upon the night air was horrible.

There is something, in such a scene as this, extremely hum-bling, and repugnant to the feelings of human nature. During the agitation of a battle, it is nothing to see men fall in hun-dreds by your side. You may look at them, perhaps, for an instant, but you do so almost without being yourself aware of it, so completely are your thoughts carried away by the excita-tion of the moment, and the shouts of your companions.—But when you come to view the dead in an hour of calmness, stripped as they generally are, you cannot help remembering how frail may have been the covering which saved yourself from being the loathsome thing on which you are now gazing.—For myself, I confess that these reflections rose within my mind on the present occasion; and if any one should say, that, similarly situated, they would not rise in his, I should give him no credit for a superior degree of courage, though I might be inclined to despise him for his want of the common feelings of a reasonable being.

In Bladensburg, the brigade halted for an hour, while those men who had thrown away their knapsacks endeavoured to recover them. During this interval, I strolled up to a house which had been converted into an hospital, and paid a hasty visit to the wounded. I found them in great pain, and some of them deeply affected at the thought of being abandoned by their comrades, and left to the mercy of their enemies. Yet, in their apprehension of evil treatment from the Americans, the event proved that they had done injustice to that people; who were found to possess at least one generous trait in their character, namely, that of behaving kindly and attentively to their prisoners.

As soon as the stragglers had returned to their ranks, we again moved on, continuing to march without once stopping to rest, during the whole of the night. Of the fatigue of a night march none but those who have experienced it can form the smallest conception. Oppressed with the most intolerable drowsiness, we were absolutely dozing upon our legs; and if any check at the head of the column caused a momentary delay, the road was instantly covered with men fast asleep. It is generally acknowledged, that no inclination is so difficult to resist as the inclination to sleep; but when you are compelled not only to bear up against that, but to struggle also with weariness, and to walk at the same time, it is scarcely possible to hold out long. By seven o'clock in the morning, it was found absolutely necessary to pause, because numbers had already fallen behind, and numbers more were ready to follow their example; when throwing ourselves upon the ground, almost in the same order in which we had marched, in less than five minutes there was not a single unclosed eye throughout the whole brigade. Piquets were of course stationed, and sentinels placed, to whom no rest was granted, but, except these, the entire army resembled a heap of dead bodies on a field of battle, rather than living men.

In this situation we remained till noon, when we were again roused to continue the retreat. Though the sun was oppressively powerful, we moved on without resting till dark, when having arrived at our old position near Marlborough, we halted for the night. During this day's march, we were joined by numbers of negro slaves, who implored us to take them along with us, offering to serve either as soldiers or sailors, if we would but give them their liberty; but as General Ross persisted in protecting private property of every description, few of them were fortunate enough to obtain their wishes.

We had now proceeded a distance of thirty-five miles, and began to consider ourselves beyond the danger of pursuit. The remainder of the retreat was accordingly conducted with more leisure; our next march carrying us no farther than to Nottingham, where we remained during an entire day, for the purpose of resting the troops. It cannot, however, be said, that this resting-time was spent in idleness. A gun-brig, with a number of ships' launches, and long-boats, had made their way up the stream, and were at anchor opposite to the town. On board the former were carried such of the wounded as had been able to travel, whilst the latter were loaded with flour and tobacco, the only spoil which we found it practicable to bring off.

———

The wounded, the artillery, and plunder, being all embarked on the 28th, at daybreak on the 29th we took the direction of St. Benedict's, where we arrived, without any adventure, at a late hour in the evening. Here we again occupied the ground of which we had taken possession on first landing, passing the night in perfect quiet; and next day, the boats of the fleet being ready to receive us, the regiments, one by one, marched down to the beach. We found the shore covered with sailors from the different ships of war, who welcomed our arrival with loud cheers; and having contrived to bring up a larger flotilla than had been employed in the disembarkation, they removed us within a few hours, and without the occurrence of any accident to our respective vessels.

Such is a plain impartial account of the inroad upon Washington, an affair than which the whole war produced none more brilliant or more daring. In whatever light we may regard it, whether we look to the amount of difficulties which it behoved him to overcome, the inadequacy of the force which he commanded, or the distance which he was called upon to march, in the midst of a hostile population, and through deep and trackless forests, we cannot deny to General Ross the praise which is his due, of having planned and successfully accomplished an expedition, which none but a sagacious mind could have devised, and none but a gallant spirit carried into execution. Among the many important transactions which then occupied the public attention, the campaign at Washington was, I believe, but little spoken of; and even now, it is overwhelmed in the recollections of the all-engrossing Waterloo; but the time will probably come, when he, who at the head of four thousand men, penetrated upwards of sixty miles into an enemy's country; overthrew an army more than double his own in point of numbers; took possession of the capital of a great nation, and having held it as long as it suited his own purposes to hold it, returned again in triumph to his fleet, will be ranked, as he deserves to be ranked, among the number of those who have most successfully contributed to elevate Great Britain to the height of military glory on which she now stands.

Thomas Boyle: Proclamation

Thomas Boyle, of Marblehead, Massachusetts, boarded a merchant ship at the age of ten and spent much of the next forty years at sea. In June 1812, he was commissioned to command the U.S. sloop *Comet* as a privateer, and in three cruises between then and March 1814, he and *Comet*'s fourteen guns prowled the West Indies and the coast of Brazil, taking some thirty prizes. In July 1814, Boyle became part owner and commander of *Chasseur* (16 guns), a swift and graceful clipper that *Niles' Register* would later call "the most beautiful vessel that ever floated on the ocean." *Chasseur* cleared New York on July 24 and charted her course to the coast of Great Britain to harass the enemy's merchant fleet. After capturing the first of this cruise's eighteen prizes, Boyle released the vessel, sending it back to port with a mock proclamation of blockade, which he ordered be hung on the front door of Lloyd's of London, Britain's foremost maritime insurance company. Americans had long complained of Britain's use of so-called paper blockades; here, at last, was a fitting riposte. The resulting publicity served to magnify the success of Boyle and other American privateers, provoking the London *Morning Chronicle* to grouse: "That the whole coast of Ireland, from Wexford round by Cape Clear to Carrickfergus, should [be] under the unresisted domination of a few petty 'fly-by-nights' from the blockaded ports of the United States is a grievance equally intolerable and disgraceful."

PROCLAMATION
issued by
Thomas Boyle, Esq.
COMMANDER of the CHASSEUR, &c.

WHEREAS it has become customary with the Admirals of Great Britain commanding the small forces on the coast of the United States, particularly with Sir John Borlaise Warren and Sir Alexander Cochrane, to declare all the coast of the said

United States in a state of strict and rigorous blockade without possessing the power to justify such a declaration, or stationing an adequate force to maintain said blockade,

I do therefore, by virtue of the *Power* and *Authority* in me vested (possessing sufficient force) declare all the *Ports*, *Harbours*, *Bays*, *Creeks*, *Rivers*, *Inlets*, *Outlets*, *Islands* and *Sea Coasts* of the *United Kingdom* of *Great Britain* and *Ireland* in a state of strict and rigorous *Blockade*.

And I do further declare, that I consider the force under my command adequate to maintain strictly, rigorously and effectually the said blockade.

And I do hereby require the respective officers, whether Captains, Commanders or Commanding Officers under my command, employed or to be employed on the coasts of England, Ireland and Scotland, to pay strict attention to this my *PROCLAMATION*.

And I do hereby caution and forbid the *SHIPS* and *VESSELS* of all and every *Nation* in *Amity* and *Peace* with the United States from entering or attempting to enter, or coming or attempting to come out of any of the said *Ports*, *Harbours*, *Bays*, *Creeks*, *Rivers*, *Inlets*, *Outlets*, *Islands* and *Sea Coasts*, under any pretence whatsoever.

And that NO PERSON may plead IGNORANCE of this my *Proclamation* I have ordered the same to be made public in *England*.

Given under my hand on board the *Chasseur*.

.   THOMAS BOYLE.

By command of the Commanding Officer.
                              J. J. STANBURY, *Sec'y.*

Philip Reed to Benjamin Chambers

The British success at Washington emboldened Vice Admiral Cochrane to plan an all-out, punishing attack on the neighboring metropolis of Baltimore, a hotbed of anti-British sentiment and the home port of many American privateers. As both a diversionary tactic and a preemptive strike on the Maryland militia, Cochrane ordered one of his ablest young captains, Sir Peter Parker, to lead an attack on Maryland's Eastern Shore where he learned that the 21st Regiment of Maryland militia was camped at Chestertown. Lieutenant Colonel Philip Reed, a veteran of the War of Independence and a former U.S. senator, was in charge of 175 men there when, just before sunrise on August 31, Parker and more than two hundred British seamen and marines approached from the west via Fairlee Creek. In this, his official report to his commanding officer, Brigadier General Benjamin Chambers, Reed describes what happened when he marched his troops to meet the British in a field west of camp, where his lifelong knowledge of the local terrain was used to decisive advantage.

Camp at Belle Air, 3d Sept. 1814.

Sir—

I avail myself of the first moment I have been able to seize from incessant labor, to inform you that about half past 11 o'clock, on the night of the 30th ult. I received information that the barges of the enemy, then lying off Waltham's farm were moving in shore. I concluded their object was to land and burn the houses, &c. at Waltham's and made the necessary arrangements to prevent them, and to be prepared for an opportunity which I had sought for several days to strike the enemy. During our march to the point threatened, it was discovered that the blow was aimed at our camp. Orders were immediately given to the quarter master, to remove the camp and baggage, and to the troops to countermarch, pass the road by the right of our camp and form on the rising ground about three hundred paces in the rear—the right towards Caulk's house, and the left retiring on the road, the artillery in the centre, supported by the infantry on the right and left. I directed capt. Wickes and his second lieutenant Beck, with a part of the rifle company to be formed, so as to cover the road by which the enemy marched, and with this section I determined to post myself, leaving the line to be formed under the direction of major Wickes and capt. Chambers.

The head of the enemy's column soon presented itself and received the fire of our advance party, at seventy paces distance, and, being pressed by numbers vastly superior, I repaired to my post in the line; having ordered the riflemen to return and form on the right of the line. The fire now became general along the whole line, and was sustained by our troops with the most determined valor. The enemy pressed our front; foiled in this he threw himself on our left flank, which was occupied by capt. Chambers's company. Here too his efforts were equally unavailing. His fire had nearly ceased, when I was informed that in some parts of our line the cartridges were entirely expended, nor did any of the boxes contain more than a very few rounds, although each man brought about twenty into the field.— The artillery cartridges were entirely expended. Under these circumstances I ordered the line to fall back to a convenient spot where a part of the line was fortified, when the few remaining cartridges were distributed amongst a part of the line, which was again brought into the field, where it remained for a considerable time, the night preventing a pursuit. The artillery and infantry for whom there were no cartridges were ordered to this place. The enemy having made every effort in his power, although apprized of our having fallen back, manifested no disposition to follow us up, but retreated about the time our ammunition was exhausted.

When it is recollected that very few of our officers or men had ever heard the whistling of a ball; that the force of the enemy, as the most accurate information enables us to estimate, was double ours; that it was commanded by *sir Peter Parker* of the *Menelaus*, one of the most distinguished officers in the British navy, and composed (as their officers admitted in a subsequent conversation,) of as fine men as could be selected from the British service, I feel fully justified in the assertion, that the gallantry of the officers and men engaged on this occasion, could not be excelled by any troops. The officers and men performed their duty. It is however but an act of justice to notice those officers who seemed to display more than a common degree of gallantry. Major Wickes and captain Chambers were conspicuous— captain Wickes and his lieutenant Beck of the rifle corps, lieutenant Eunick and ensign Shriven of captain Chambers' company exerted themselves, as did captain Hynson and his lieutenant Grant, capt. Ussleton of the brigade artillery and his lieutenants Reed and Brown— Lieut. Tilghman who commanded the guns of the volunteer artillery, in the absence of captain Hands who is in ill health and from home, was conspicuous for his gallantry, his ensign Thomas also manifested much firmness.

I am indebted to captain Wilson of the cavalry, who was with me, for his exertions, and also to adjutant Hynson, who displayed much zeal and firmness throughout— To Dr. Blake, Dr. Gordon and to Isaac Spencer, Esq. who were accidentally in camp, I am indebted for their assistance in reconnoitering the enemy on his advance.

You will be surprised, sir, when I inform you that in an engagement of so long continuance in an open field, when the moon shone brilliantly on the rising ground occupied by our troops, while the shade of the neighboring woods, under the protection of which the enemy fought, gave us but an indistinct view of any thing but the flash of his guns; that under the disparity of numbers against us, and the advantage of regular discipline on the side of the enemy, we had not one man killed, and only one serjeant, one corporal, and one private wounded, and those slightly. The enemy left one midshipman and eight men dead on the field, and nine wounded; six of whom died in the coarse of a few hours. *Sir Peter Parker* was amongst the slain—he was mortally wounded with a buck-shot, and died before he reached the barges, to which he was conveyed by his men. The enemy's force, consisting of marines and musqueteers, was in part armed with boarding pikes, swords, and pistols, no doubt intended for our tents, as orders had been given by sir Peter not to fire—many of these arms, with rockets, muskets, &c. have fallen into our hands, found by the picket guard under ensign Shriven, which was posted on the battle ground for the remainder of the night—nothing but the want of ammunition saved the enemy from destruction.

Attached are the names of the wounded; and, as an act of justice to those concerned, I inclose you a list of the names of every officer and soldier engaged in the affair— certain information from the enemy assures us, that his total loss in killed and wounded was forty-two or forty-three, including two wounded lieutenants. I am, sir, your most obedient humble servant,

PHIL. REED,
Lieut. Col. commandant

Benjamin Chambers, brigadier-general,
6th brigade Maryland militia.

Names of the wounded of capt. Chambers' company. John Magnor, sergeant, slightly, in the thigh.— Philip Crane, corporal, a ball between the tendons and the bone of the thigh near the knee.

Of captain Page's company.—John Glanville, a private, in the arm.

George Gordon, Lord Byron: "Elegiac Stanzas on the Death of Sir Peter Parker, Bart."

Sir Peter Parker, 2nd Baronet, served the Royal Navy from the age of thirteen, first under his grandfather, Admiral Peter Parker, and then under Lord Nelson. In 1805, when he was not yet twenty, he commanded HMS *Weazel* at the Battle of Trafalgar, and for his conduct during that decisive victory was promoted to captain. After 1810 he was master of the frigate *Menelaus*, which, in early 1814, was ordered to Bermuda by Cochrane and from there to Chesapeake Bay. A promising career ended abruptly when Parker's femoral artery was severed by gunshot during the Battle of Caulk's Field, and he was killed. His sister, Margaret, the boyhood sweetheart of Lord Byron, requested, on behalf of her family, the following verse from the celebrated poet. "I have just been writing some elegiac stanzas on the death of Sir P. Parker," wrote Byron to his friend and future biographer, Thomas Moore, on October 6, 1814. "He was my first cousin"—the son of Byron's paternal aunt Augusta—"but [we] never met since boyhood. . . . I am as sorry for him as one could be for one I never saw since I was a child; but should not have wept melodiously, except at the request of friends." The elegy was published in the London *Morning Chronicle* of October 7, and Byron included it in his collection *Hebrew Melodies* (1815).

ELEGIAC STANZAS ON THE DEATH OF SIR PETER PARKER, BART.

There is a tear for all that die,
    A mourner o'er the humblest grave;
But nations swell the funeral cry,
    And Triumph weeps above the brave.

For them is Sorrow's purest sigh
    O'er Ocean's heaving bosom sent:

In vain their bones unburied lie,
   All earth becomes their monument!

A tomb is theirs on every page,
   An epitaph on every tongue:
The present hours, the future age,
   For them bewail, to them belong.

For them the voice of festal mirth
   Grows hush'd, *their name* the only sound;
While deep Remembrance pours to Worth
   The goblet's tributary round.

A theme to crowds that knew them not,
   Lamented by admiring foes,
Who would not share their glorious lot?
   Who would not die the death they chose?

And, gallant Parker! thus enshrined
   Thy life, thy fall, thy fame shall be;
And early valour, glowing, find
   A model in thy memory.

But there are breasts that bleed with thee
   In woe, that glory cannot quell;
And shuddering hear of victory,
   Where one so dear, so dauntless, fell.

Where shall they turn to mourn thee less?
   When cease to hear thy cherish'd name?
Time cannot teach forgetfulness,
   While Grief's full heart is fed by Fame.

Alas! for them, though not for thee,
   They cannot choose but weep the more;
Deep for the dead the grief must be,
   Who ne'er gave cause to mourn before.

Isaac Munroe to a Friend in Boston

September 17, 1814

The British assault on Baltimore was initially led by Major General Ross, who on September 12 was killed in a skirmish with American troops about seven miles outside the city. Ross's command immediately passed to Colonel Arthur Brooke, who prudently decided not to attack Baltimore until he had secured the necessary naval support from Cochrane. It was the admiral's plan to soften up the American lines with artillery fire from Baltimore Harbor, but first he had to silence the guns of Fort McHenry, a star-shaped fort at the entrance of the harbor defended by a thousand men under Major George Armistead. On September 13–14, Cochrane's fleet fired more than fifteen hundred rounds at the fort—both traditional shells and the fearsome new Congreve rockets—about four hundred of which found their target. Among McHenry's volunteer defenders was Isaac Munroe, founding editor of the *Baltimore Patriot*, publication of which was suspended during the time of the assault. He sent this account of the defense of Fort McHenry to "his Friend in Boston," most likely David Everett, editor of the *Yankee*, a Republican newspaper in Boston, who published it on September 30.

I will give you an account of the approach of the enemy before this place, so far as it came under my own observation.

On Saturday last and the day previous, we had intelligence that the enemy had collected all his force, to the amount of 47 sail, and were proceeding down the bay, consequently we were led to hope we should have a little rest from our incessant labors, in preparing to resist them.

On Saturday-noon Major Armistead, the commander of Fort McHenry, permitted Chief Justice Nicholson who commands a volunteer corps of 80 men, to march to town, holding ourselves in readiness to return the instant he thought prudent to call. As it turned out, while we were marching to town, the enemy tacked about and just at dusk, were seen under a press of sail, with a fair wind, approaching the town. Their movements were closely watched at the Fort, and at half past 9 o'clock, Judge Nicholson received orders to repair to the Fort with his men. We were all immediately rallied at the Fort before 12, although the rain poured down in torrents.

On our arrival we found the matches burning, the furnaces heated and vomiting red shot, and every thing ready for a gallant defense. At this time the enemy had arrived as far up as North Point, 12 miles below the Fort. We remained at our post til day-light at which time the enemy remained at the same place, some at anchor, and others under steady sail, laying off and on. They continued this kind of movement all day on Sunday.

During the preceding night, and the forepart of Monday, they were hastily employed in landing their troops, but all was quiet on the part of the Naval operation against the Fort, til Tuesday morning at which time they had advanced to within two and a half miles of the Fort, arranged in elegant order, all at anchor, forming a half circle, with four bomb vessels and a rocket ship, which was harmless indeed.

These, I am sure, were not intended as an attack upon us, but fired a signal to inform their land troops of their readiness of co-operation. Immediately after their discharges, two of the head small frigates opened upon us, but finding their shot not reaching us, they ceased and advanced up a little nearer.

The moment they had taken their position, Major Armistead mounted the parapet and ordered a battery of 24 pounders to be opened upon them and immediately after, a battery of 42's followed, and then the whole Fort let drive at them. We could see the shot strike the frigates in several instances, when every heart was gladdened, and we gave three cheers, the music playing Yankee Doodle. Upon this the frigates stood off, and in five minutes, all lay just out of reach of our shot. The bomb vessels advanced a little and commenced a tremendous bombardment, which lasted all day and all night, with hardly a moments intermission.

Finding our shot would not reach them, the cannonading, which was sublime and enliving, was ordered to be closed. We then resorted to our mortars, and fired six or eight, but sorrowful to relate, they like our shot fell short, owing to their chambers not being so deep, and were reduced to the dreadful alternative, of facing by far the most tremendous bombardment ever known this enemy, without any means of returning it—upwards of 1500 bombs having fallen in and about the Fort. Fortunately little damage was done.

In our company we had six severely wounded, and two killed. Serjeant Clemm, a young man of most amiable character, gentlemanly manners and real courage, was killed by my side; a bomb bursting over our heads a piece of the size of a dollar, two inches thick, passed through his body in a diagonal direction from his navel, and went into the ground upwards of two feet. It was dug up immediately after, and is preserved by his friends.

Instantly before this, a bomb struck the bastion, then in charge of Lieut. Clagett, our 3rd, which killed him upon the spot, wounded four men, dismounted a 24 pounder, broke the carriage wheel and did considerable damage. This happened on my right, about 25 paces distant. In the whole, we had seven killed in the Fort, and 15 wounded.

From 12 to 1 o'clock in the night, the enemy slackened a little; during which time, a picked party of marines towed up, in a silent manner, a bomb vessel, which got almost in rear of our Fort, unobserved by the look-outs on account of the extreme darkness of the night. After choosing her position, she began on our right, in high stile.

Capt. Evans and Nicholson, were instantly ordered to open their batteries of 24's with grape and cannister, which was immediately followed by Fort Covington, a tight little place one and a half miles above us. The enemy likewise poured in their cannister and grape, but in less than 5 minutes was silenced, and we heard no more of them from that quarter, but the bombardment was kept up from their old position, with intensified fury, til dawn of day, when they appeared to be disposed to decline the unprofitable conflict.

At this time our morning gun was fired, the flag hoisted, Yankee Doodle played, and we all appeared in full view of a formidable and mortified enemy, who calculated upon our surrender in 20 minutes after the commencement of the action.

Francis Scott Key:
"Defence of Fort M'Henry"

On September 3, 1814, Francis Scott Key, a thirty-five-year-old Georgetown attorney, and Colonel John Stuart Skinner, a U.S. prisoner-of-war exchange officer, boarded HMS *Tonnant*, Cochrane's flagship, then at anchor in the Patapsco River near Baltimore. President Madison had dispatched the pair to negotiate the freedom of Key's friend Dr. William Beanes, a leading citizen of Upper Marlboro, Maryland, who had been taken prisoner for arresting British stragglers following the burning of Washington. Their mission was successful, but because they had become privy to British war intelligence, the three Americans were detained until after the attack on Baltimore. On the night of September 13–14, they watched the bomb-and-rocket assault on Fort McHenry from the deck of their truce ship, and Key, an amateur poet moved by the spectacle, began to compose the opening verse of a song, taking his melody from an English drinking tune popular since the 1760s. "Defence of Fort M'Henry," later retitled "The Star-Spangled Banner," quickly became one of America's best-loved patriotic songs, and in 1931 Congress made it the national anthem. The text below is that of its first printing, as a Baltimore handbill, on September 17, 1814.

DEFENCE OF FORT M'HENRY.

The annexed song was composed under the following circumstances—A gentleman had left Baltimore, in a flag of truce for the purpose of getting released from the British fleet, a friend of his who had been captured at Marlborough.—He went as far as the mouth of the Patuxent and was not permitted to return lest the intended attack on Baltimore should be disclosed. He was therefore brought up the Bay to the mouth of the Patapsco, where the flag vessel was kept under the guns of a frigate, and he was compelled to witness the bombardment of Fort M'Henry, which the Admiral had boasted that he would carry in a few hours, and that the city must fall. He watched the flag at the Fort through the whole day with an anxiety that can be better felt than described, until the night prevented him from seeing it. In the night he watched the bomb shells, and at early dawn his eye was again greeted by the proudly waving flag of his country.

Tune—Anachreon in Heaven.

O! say can you see by the dawn's early light,
　What so proudly we hailed at the twilight's last gleaming,
Whose broad stripes and bright stars through the perilous
　　fight,
　O'er the ramparts we watch'd, were so gallantly streaming?
And the Rockets' red glare, the Bombs bursting in air,
Gave proof through the night that our Flag was still there;
　　O! say does that star-spangled Banner yet wave,
　　O'er the Land of the free, and the home of the brave?

On the shore dimly seen through the mists of the deep,
　Where the foe's haughty host in dread silence reposes,
What is that which the breeze, o'er the towering steep,
　As it fitfully blows, half conceals, half discloses?
Now it catches the gleam of the morning's first beam,
In full glory reflected now shines in the stream,
　　'Tis the star spangled banner, O! long may it wave
　　O'er the land of the free, and the home of the brave.

And where is that band who so vauntingly swore
　That the havoc of war and the battle's confusion,
A home and a country, shall leave us no more?
　Their blood has washed out their foul footsteps pollution;
No refuge could save the hireling and slave,
From the terror of flight or the gloom of the grave,
　　And the star-spangled banner in triumph doth wave,
　　O'er the land of the Free, and the Home of the Brave.

O! thus be it ever when freemen shall stand,
　Between their lov'd home, and the war's desolation,
Blest with vict'ry and peace, may the Heav'n rescued land,

Praise the Power that hath made and preserv'd us a nation!
Then conquer we must, when our cause it is just,
And this be our motto—"In God is our Trust;"
    And the star-spangled Banner in triumph shall wave,
    O'er the Land of the Free and the Home of the Brave.

Roger B. Taney to Charles Howard

Roger B. Taney, a leading Maryland Federalist during the War of 1812 and, from 1836 to 1864, the fifth chief justice of the U.S. Supreme Court, was married to Anne Phoebe Charlton Key, the sister of Francis Scott Key. In a letter of 1856, Taney gave an account of the origins of "The Star-Spangled Banner" to the lawyer Charles Howard, who in 1825 had married Key's daughter, Elizabeth. The letter was printed as part of the hagiographic *Memoir of Roger Brooke Taney*, by Samuel Tyler, LL.D., of the Maryland Bar, published in Baltimore in 1872. In that book Tyler called "The Star-Spangled Banner" "the song of Maryland Federalism, which became the song of the nation because of its patriotism and its origin in the midst of battle." The song "will live in the American heart," Tyler predicted, "until the stars fall from the national flag."

WASHINGTON, D.C., March 12, 1856.

MY DEAR SIR:—I promised some time ago to give you an account of the incidents in the life of Mr. F. S. Key which led him to write "The Star-Spangled Banner," and of the circumstances under which it was written. The song has become a national one, and will, I think, from its great merit, continue to be so, especially in Maryland; and everything that concerns its author must be a matter of interest to his children and descendants. And I proceed to fulfil my promise with the more pleasure, because, while the song shows his genius and taste as a poet, the incidents connected with it, and the circumstances under which it was written, will show his character and worth as a man. The scene he describes, and the warm spirit of patriotism which breathes in the song, were not the offspring of mere fancy or poetic imagination. He describes what he actually saw. And he tells us what he felt while witnessing the conflict, and what he felt when the battle was over and the victory won by his countrymen. Every word came warm from his heart, and for that reason, even more than for its poetical merit, it never fails to find a response in the hearts of those who listen to it.

You will remember that in 1814, when the song was written, I resided in Frederick and Mr. Key in George Town. You will also recollect that soon after the British troops retired from Washington, a squadron of the enemy's ships made their way up the Potomac, and appeared before Alexandria, which was compelled to capitulate; and the squadron remained there some days, plundering the town of tobacco and whatever else they wanted. It was rumored and believed in Frederick, that a marauding attack of the same character would be made on Washington and George Town before the ships left the river. Mr. Key's family was in George Town. He would not, and indeed could not, with honor, leave the place while it was threatened by the enemy; for he was a volunteer in the Light Artillery, commanded by Major Peter, which was composed of citizens of the District of Columbia, who had uniformed themselves and offered their services to the Government, and who had been employed in active service from the time the British fleet appeared in the Patuxent preparatory to the movement upon Washington. And Mrs. Key refused to leave home while Mr. Key was thus daily exposed to danger. Believing, as we did, that an attack would probably be made on George Town, we became very anxious about the situation of his family. For if the attack was made, Mr. Key would be with the troops engaged in the defence; and as it was impossible to foresee what would be the issue of the conflict, his family, by remaining in George Town, might be placed in great and useless peril. When I speak of *we*, I mean Mr. Key's father and mother and Mrs. Taney and myself. But it was agreed among us that I should go to George Town and try to persuade Mrs. Key to come away with her children, and stay with me or with Mr. Key's father until the danger was over. When I reached George Town, I found the English ships still at Alexandria, and a body of militia encamped in Washington, which had been assembled to defend the city. But it was then believed, from information received, that no attack would be made by the enemy on Washington or George Town; and preparations were making, on our part, to annoy them by batteries on shore, when they descended the river. The knowledge of the preparations probably hastened their departure; and the second or third day after my arrival, the ships were seen moving down the Potomac.

On the evening of the day that the enemy disappeared, Mr. Richard West arrived at Mr. Key's, and told him that after the British army passed through Upper Marlbro on their return to their ships, and had encamped some miles below the town, a detachment was sent back, which entered Dr. Beanes's house about midnight, compelled him to rise from his bed, and hurried him off to the British camp, hardly allowing him time to put his clothes on; that he was treated with great harshness, and closely guarded; and that as soon as his friends were apprised of his situation, they hastened to the head-quarters of the English army to solicit his release; but it was peremptorily refused, and they were not even permitted to see him; and that he had been carried as a prisoner on board the fleet. And finding their own efforts unavailing, and alarmed for his safety, his friends in and about Marlbro thought it advisable that Mr. West should hasten to George Town, and request Mr. Key to obtain the sanction of the Government to his going on board the admiral's ship, under a flag of truce, and endeavoring to procure the release of Dr. Beanes before the fleet sailed. It was then lying at the mouth of the Potomac, and its destination was not at that time known with certainty. Dr. Beanes, as perhaps you know, was the leading physician in Upper Marlbro, and an accomplished scholar and gentleman. He was highly respected by all who knew him; was the family physician of Mr. West, and the intimate friend of Mr. Key. He occupied one of the best houses in Upper Marlbro, and lived very handsomely; and his house was selected for the quarters of Admiral Cockburn, and some of the principal officers of the army, when the British troops encamped at Marlbro on their march to Washington. These officers were, of course, furnished with everything that the house could offer; and they, in return, treated him with much courtesy, and placed guards around his grounds and out-houses, to prevent depredations by their troops.

But on the return of the army to the ships, after the main body had passed through the town, stragglers, who had left the ranks to plunder, or from some other motive, made their appearance from time to time, singly or in small squads; and

Dr. Beanes put himself at the head of a small body of citizens to pursue and make prisoners of them. Information of this proceeding was, by some means or other, conveyed to the English camp; and the detachment of which I have spoken was sent back to release the prisoners and seize Dr. Beanes. They did not seem to regard him, and certainly did not treat him, as a prisoner of war, but as one who had deceived, and broken his faith to them.

Mr. Key readily agreed to undertake the mission in his favor, and the President promptly gave his sanction to it. Orders were immediately issued to the vessel usually employed as a cartel, in the communications with the fleet in the Chesapeake, to be made ready without delay; and Mr. John S. Skinner, who was agent for the Government for flags of truce and exchange of prisoners, and who was well known as such to the officers of the fleet, was directed to accompany Mr. Key. And as soon as the arrangements were made, he hastened to Baltimore, where the vessel was to embark; and Mrs. Key and the children went with me to Frederick, and thence to his father's on Pipe Creek, where she remained until he returned.

We heard nothing from him until the enemy retreated from Baltimore, which, as well as I can now recollect, was a week or ten days after he left us; and we were becoming uneasy about him, when, to our great joy, he made his appearance at my house, on his way to join his family.

He told me that he found the British fleet at the mouth of the Potomac, preparing for the expedition against Baltimore. He was courteously received by Admiral Cochrane and the officers of the army, as well as of the navy. But when he made known his business, his application was received so coldly that he feared it would fail. General Ross and Admiral Cockburn— who accompanied the expedition to Washington—particularly the latter, spoke of Dr. Beanes in very harsh terms, and seemed at first not disposed to release him. It however happened, fortunately, that Mr. Skinner carried letters from the wounded British officers left at Bladensburg; and in these letters to their friends on board the fleet they all spoke of the humanity and kindness with which they had been treated after they had fallen into our hands. And after a good deal of conversation, and strong representations from Mr. Key as to the character and standing of Dr. Beanes, and of the deep interest which the community in which he lived took in his fate, General Ross said that Dr. Beanes deserved much more punishment than he had received; but that he felt himself bound to make a return for the kindness which had been shown to his wounded officers, whom he had been compelled to leave at Bladensburg, and upon that ground, and that only, he would release him. But Mr. Key was at the same time informed that neither he, nor any one else, would be permitted to leave the fleet for some days, and must be detained until the attack on Baltimore, which was then about to be made, was over. But he was assured that they would make him and Mr. Skinner as comfortable as possible while they detained them. Admiral Cochrane, with whom they dined on the day of their arrival, apologized for not accommodating them in his own ship, saying that it was crowded already with officers of the army; but that they would be well taken care of in the frigate *Surprise*, commanded by his son, Sir Thomas Cochrane. And to this frigate, they were accordingly transferred.

Mr. Key had an interview with Dr. Beanes before General Ross consented to release him. I do not recollect whether he was on board of the admiral's ship, or the *Surprise*, but I believe it was the former. He found him in the forward part of the ship, among the sailors and soldiers; he had not had a change of clothes from the time he was seized; was constantly treated with indignity by those around him, and no officer would speak to him. He was treated as a culprit, and not as a prisoner of war. And this harsh and humiliating treatment continued until he was placed on board of the cartel.

Something must have passed, when the officers were quartered at his house on the march to Washington, which, in the judgment of General Ross, bound him not to take up arms against the English forces until the troops had re-embarked. It is impossible, on any other grounds, to account for the manner in which he was spoken of and treated. But whatever General Ross and the other officers might have thought, I am quite sure that Dr. Beanes did not think he was in any way pledged to abstain from active hostilities against the public enemy. And when he made prisoners of the stragglers, he did not consider himself as a prisoner on parole, nor suppose himself to be violating any obligation he had incurred. For he was a gentleman of untainted character and a nice sense of honor, and incapable of doing anything that could have justified such treatment. Mr. Key imputed the ill usage he received to the influence of Admiral Cockburn, who, it is still remembered, while he commanded in the Chesapeake, carried on hostilities in a vindictive temper, assailing and plundering defenceless villages, or countenancing such proceedings by those under his command.

Mr. Key and Mr. Skinner continued on board of the *Surprise*, where they were very kindly treated by Sir Thomas Cochrane, until the fleet reached the Patapsco, and preparations were making for landing the troops. Admiral Cochrane then shifted his flag to the frigate, in order that he might be able to move farther up the river and superintend in person the attack by water on the fort; and Mr. Key and Mr. Skinner were then sent on board their own vessel, with a guard of sailors or marines, to prevent them from landing. They were permitted to take Dr. Beanes with them; and they thought themselves fortunate in being anchored in a position which enabled them to see distinctly the flag of Fort McHenry from the deck of the vessel. He proceeded then, with much animation, to describe the scene on the night of the bombardment. He and Mr. Skinner remained on deck during the night, watching every shell from the moment it was fired until it fell, listening with breathless interest to hear if an explosion followed. While the bombardment continued, it was sufficient proof that the fort had not surrendered. But it suddenly ceased some time before day, and, as they had no communication with any of the enemy's ships, they did not know whether the fort had surrendered or the attack had been abandoned. They paced the deck for the residue of the night in painful suspense, watching with intense anxiety for the return of day, and looking every few minutes at their watches to see how long they must wait for it; and as soon as it dawned, and before it was light enough to see objects at a distance, their glasses were turned to the fort, uncertain whether they should see the Stars and Stripes or the flag of the enemy. At length the light came, and they saw that "our flag was still there." And, as the day advanced, they discovered, from the movements of the boats between the shore and the fleet, that the troops had been roughly handled, and that many wounded men were carried to the ships. At length he was informed that the attack on Baltimore had failed, and the British army was re-embarking, and that he and Mr. Skinner and Dr. Beanes would be permitted to leave them, and go where they pleased, as soon as the troops were on board and the fleet ready to sail.

He then told me that, under the excitement of the time, he had written the song, and handed me a printed copy of "The Star-Spangled Banner." When I had read it, and expressed my admiration, I asked him how he found time, in the scenes he had been passing through, to compose such a song? He said he commenced it on the deck of their vessel, in the fervor of the moment, when he saw the enemy hastily retreating to their ships, and looked at the flag he had watched for so anxiously as the morning opened; that he had written some lines, or brief notes, that would aid him in calling them to mind, upon the back of a letter which he happened to have in his pocket; and for some of the lines, as he proceeded, he was obliged to rely altogether on his memory; and that he finished it in the boat on his way to the shore, and wrote it out, as it now stands, at the hotel on the night he reached Baltimore, and immediately after he arrived. He said that, on the next morning, he took it to Judge Nicholson, to ask him what he thought of it; that he was so much pleased with it that he immediately sent it to a printer, and directed copies to be struck off in handbill form; and that he, Mr. Key, believed it to have been favorably received by the Baltimore public.

Judge Nicholson and Mr. Key, you know, were nearly connected by marriage, Mrs. Key and Mrs. Nicholson being sisters. The Judge was a man of cultivated taste; had, at one time, been distinguished among the leading men in Congress, and was, at the period of which I am speaking, the Chief Justice of the Baltimore-Court, and one of the Judges of the Court of Appeals of Maryland. Notwithstanding his judicial character, which exempted him from military service, he accepted the command of a volunteer company of artillery; and when the enemy approached, and an attack on the fort was expected, he and his company offered their services to the Government to assist in the defence. They were accepted, and formed a part of the garrison during the bombardment. The Judge had been relieved from duty, and returned to his family, only the night before Mr. Key showed him his song; and you may easily imagine the feelings with which, at such a moment, he read it and gave it to the public. It was, no doubt, as Mr. Key modestly expressed it, favorably received. In less than an hour after it was placed in the hands of the printer, it was all over town, and hailed with enthusiasm, and took its place at once as a national song.

I have made this account of "The Star-Spangled Banner" longer than I intended, and find that I have introduced incidents and persons outside of the subject I originally contemplated. But I have felt a melancholy pleasure in recalling events connected in any degree with the life of one with whom I was so long and so closely united in friendship and affection, and whom I so much admired for his brilliant genius, and loved for his many virtues. I am sure, however, that neither you, nor any of his children or descendants, will think the account I have given too long.

With great regard, dear sir,
Your friend truly,
R. B. TANEY.

CHARLES HOWARD, ESQ.

William Dunlop: from "Recollections of the American War"

The Royal Navy's failure to capture Fort McHenry scuttled Colonel Brooke's plans to attack Baltimore and marked the end of hostilities in the Chesapeake. Meanwhile, on the Niagara frontier, the British maintained their siege of Fort Erie, the last American possession on the Canadian side of the river. Throughout the summer of 1814, both sides deployed picket guards of riflemen or light infantry in the no-man's-land between the fort and the British lines in an effort to ambush, fatigue, and demoralize each other. In his memoir of 1847, William Dunlop, the assistant surgeon of the 89th Regiment of Foot, wrote of that long summer's war of attrition, a deadly game played by individual soldiers living by their talents and their wits.

During the whole time we lay before Fort Erie, bush-skirmishing was an every day's occurrence, and though the numbers lost in each of these affairs may seem but trifling, yet the aggregate of men put *hors de combat* in a force so small as ours became very serious in the long run. They generally commenced with some accidental rencontre of videttes—their firing brought out the piquet, then the brigade on duty, and then, not unfrequently, the brigade next for duty. I think, on a fair average of three months, I enjoyed this amusement about three times a week.

Excepting only a melée of cavalry, a bush skirmish is the only aspect in which modern warfare appears in anything picturesque. Look at all attempts at painting a modern battle, and unless the painter takes such a distance as to render every thing indistinct, you have nothing but a series of stiff, hard, regular, straight lines, that might represent a mathematical diagram in uniform. Not so with light infantry in a wood. There a man ceases to be merely a part of a machine, or a point in a long line. Both his personal safety and his efficiency depend on his own knowledge and tact. To stand straight upright and be shot at is no part of his duty; his great object is to annoy the enemy, and keep himself safe; and so far was this carried by the tacticians of the Prussian school, that in a German Contingent, which served on this continent during the revolutionary war, a yager has been flogged for *getting himself wounded*.

Perhaps there can be no military scene more fit for the pencil than a body of light infantry awaiting an attack. The variety of attitude necessary to obtain cover—the breathless silence—the men attentive by eye and ear—every glance (furtively lowered) directed to the point—some kneeling, some lying down, and some standing straight behind a tree—the officer with his silver whistle in his hand, ready to give the signal to commence firing, and the bugle boy looking earnestly in his officer's face waiting for the next order. This is worth painting, which cannot, by any one having a decent regard for truth, be said of the bas reliefs that we see on the tombs of heroes, of a line of men marching in step, each with his bayonet levelled at precisely the same angle, in a manner that would draw forth the enthusiastic approbation of the shade of Sir David Dundas, but which no effort of the genius of sculptor or painter could even render more tolerable, than a well executed representation of the same quantity of park pales.

This species of warfare necessarily draws forth the individual talent of the soldier. I once saw a soldier of the 32nd take two American sentries prisoners, by placing his cap and great coat on a bush, and while they were busy firing at his image and superscription, he fetch'd a circuit, got behind them, waited till both of their firelocks were discharged, and then drove them before him into the picquet guard.

The Glengarry Regiment being provincials, possessed many excellent shots. They were not armed with the rifle, but with what I greatly prefer to that arm, the double sighted light infantry musket. A rifle is by no means suited for a day's fighting; when it gets foul from repeated firing it is difficult even to hammer the ball down, and the same foulness which clogs the barrel must injure the precision of the ball. The well made smooth barrel on the contrary, is to a certain degree scoured by every discharge, and can stand sixty rounds without the necessity of cleaning. Nor is it in the precision of its aim for any useful purpose inferior to the rifle, that is to say in the hands of a man who knows how to use it. I have seen a Sergeant of the Glengarries who would allow you to pick out a musket from any of the corps, and let him load it, when he would knock the head off a pigeon on the top of the highest tree in the forest.

In the British Army one would suppose that the only use of a musket was understood to be that it could carry a bayonet at the end of it. The quantity of powder allowed to be expended in teaching the men the use of their principal weapon is fifteen rounds per annum. Now, suppose such a limitation was placed on sportsmen, is it possible to conceive that on the twelfth of August, or the first of September, there could be found one man who could bring down a grouse or a partridge? No; the officers in command of corps should have an unlimited power in the expenditure of ammunition, and should only be made answerable for their Regiment being efficient in their practice when called into the field.

In this regiment there were a father and three sons, American U. E. Loyalists, all of them crack shots. In a covering party one day the father and one of the sons were sentries on the same point. An American rifleman *dropped* a man to his left, but in so doing exposed himself, and almost as a matter of course, was instantly dropped in his turn by the unerring aim of the father. The enemy were at that moment being driven in, so the old man of course (for it was a ceremony seldom neglected,) went up to rifle his victim. On examining his features he discovered that it was his own brother. Under any circumstances this would have horrified most men, but a Yankee has much of the stoic in him, and is seldom deprived of his equanimity. He took possession of his valuables, consisting of an old silver watch and a clasp knife, his rifle and appointments, coolly remarking, that it "served him right for fighting for the rebels, when all the rest of his family fought for King George." It appeared that during the revolutionary war his father and all his sons had taken arms in the King's cause, save this one, who had joined the Americans. They had never met him from that period till the present moment; but such is the virulence of political rancour, that it can overcome all the ties of nature.

With all our hardships and privations there was no where to be met with a merrier set of fellows than in the camp before

Fort Erie. One of the chief promoters of this was worthy Billy R. of the King's, who, to all the qualifications of a most accomplished soldier, added all the lightheartedness and wit of an Irishman.

There was in the camp an old thorn, up which a wild vine had climbed, and then descended in long branches to the ground, forming a natural bower impervious to the rays of the sun. The root of this tree was Billy's favourite seat (for he was too much of the Falstaff build to be more peripatetic than was absolutely necessary) and no sooner was he seated than a group of officers was established around him, and to these he would tell funny stories and crack jokes by the hour together. He was appointed to the command of the Incorporated Militia, and a more judicious selection could not have been made, not only on account of his military talents, but his invincible good temper and good humour, which endeared him to the men, and made them take a pleasure and a pride in obeying his orders and attending to his instructions. Some idea may be formed of his talents in this way, when I state that in the course of a very few months, he rendered a body of raw lads from the plough-tail as efficient a corps as any in the field.

Towards the end of the business, when his men were acting as light infantry, he was knocked off his horse by a ball, which struck him in the forehead and came out over the ear. This would have knocked the life out of most men, but it did not knock the wit out of Billy. He was raised and placed in a blanket, his eyes still fixed on his men, who he saw were pushing on in a way to expose themselves. "Stop till I spake to the boys," said he to the men, who were carrying him off the field; "Boys!" shouted he, "I have only one remark to make, and that is, that a stump or a log will stand a leaden bullet better than the best of yees, and therefore give them the honor to be your front rank men." Poor Billy survived this severe wound many years, but at last its effects began to tell. He became paralytic of the lower extremities, and had to be carried from place to place; but his wit and good humour never forsook him. He died in the Isle of Wight in 1827, on his way to Canada to draw his land.

One day, when relieved from piquet, I announced to Col. P., who commanded our brigade, that I had discovered a short way through the woods to the camp, and accordingly I led the way, he and Captain F., of the Glengarries, following. By some fatality I mistook the path, and took a wrong turn, so that instead of finding the camp we came right on the top of an American piquet, which opened fire upon us at about fifty yards distance. Being used to this we were behind trees in a moment, and the next were scampering in different directions at greater or less angles from the enemy. It may well be supposed I did not wait on our brigadier, during the time we were off duty, to receive thanks for my services as a guide, nor when we did go on duty again was I at all anxious to obtrude myself upon him; indeed I kept as far from him as I could, but in going his rounds at daylight he came up with me seated by a piquet fire at the extreme left of the line. He saluted me most graciously, alluded to our late exploit as a good joke, and asked me to breakfast with him. "Ho, ho," thinks I, "he has forgotten it all, and I'm forgiven—this is as it should be." Lounging about after breakfast, and talking over indifferent matters, a sputtering fire began a little to our left, and the Colonel ordering a look out on the right, proceeded, followed by me, to the scene of action. We soon saw that this was the point of attack, so he sent me to order up the reserve. This done I rejoined him, and found him standing coolly giving his orders in the middle of a whistling of bullets, far too thick to be pleasant. I stood by his side for some minutes, thankful that none of these missiles had a billet on us, when on a sudden I felt a severe sharp pain from my brow to the back of my head at the same moment the Colonel exclaimed; "By G—d! you are shot through the head." I sunk upon one knee, and taking off my forage cap felt along my head for blood, but none was to be found. "It is only a graze," said I. "Colonel, is there any mark?" "Yes," said he, "there is a red mark, but not from a ball, it came from my switch. You gave me a d——l of a fright the other day—now I have given you one, so we are quits."

Weeks passed at this kind of warfare, that served no purpose to the parties except to harass one another, and mutually to thin our ranks.

Jarvis Hanks: Memoir

Still recovering from a thigh wound suffered at Lundy's Lane, Major General Brown resumed command at Fort Erie on September 2. Though advised by his aides to abandon the fort, he was determined to dislodge the British siege guns. Short on manpower, he sent a plea across the river for reinforcements, asking Governor Tompkins to mobilize the New York militia. One of his aides, General Eleazar W. Ripley, was skeptical: "No Military man who has known the Conduct of the Militia of this frontier, even on their own ground, should hold a post & hazard an army on this side [of] the straits by relying on them." Three thousand volunteers soon assembled at Buffalo, and with some cajoling from militia Brigadier General Peter B. Porter most were persuaded to cross to the fort on September 9 and 10. On September 16, confronting a shortage of ammunition and debilitating conditions exacerbated by seemingly endless rain, a dispirited Lieutenant General Gordon Drummond decided to call off the siege. But before this order could be carried out, Brown, concluding that his men "would prefer to die in the blaze of their own glory, than live dishonoured by Captivity or Defeat," directed twelve hundred of Porter's volunteers and eight hundred regulars under Lieutenant Colonel James Miller to launch a strike. Recounted here by Jarvis Hanks, the attack rescued the reputation of the militia while effectively bringing to a close the bloody but strategically inconsequential struggle for control of the Niagara frontier.

On the 17th of September, "the *sortie*" of Fort Erie was performed. "Sortie", I believe, means to attack an enemy who are besieging a fort or town. It was a rainy, dark day and probably they did not expect us to call on them just at that time. We passed through a deep ravine, which lay between them and us, and came within a few rods of them before they discovered our approach. A few men were left in the fort and the cannonading was continued with little abatement. When we came upon them, they seemed to be thunderstruck, and surrendered at pleasure. Their main army however, were two miles from that place in their tents. Without firing a musket we took thirteen Commissioned officers, 400 soldiers and spiked all their cannon, and cut to pieces their wheels, and blew up their powder magazine; after which we precipitately returned by the way we came. When I say we did not fire a musket, I mean not after we came up to the batteries. Previously, however, there was quite a little engagement, with their picket guards and several of our officers and men killed, among the former of whom was Capt. Hale who commanded the company to which I was attached.

In a very few days after this, the enemy withdrew, to Chippawa, and we soon evacuated the fort and crossed over to Black rock, and marched to Sackets Harbor, into winter quarters.

Thomas Macdonough to William Jones

As the peace talks at Ghent got under way, the British felt the need to seize and hold a significant area of American territory to be used as a chip at the negotiating table. Their target was Plattsburgh, New York, on Lake Champlain, which was twenty miles south of the border and defended by thirty-four hundred mostly untested regulars and a growing number of militia. Sir George Prevost, commander-in-chief of British North America, marched eight thousand troops from Montreal to the outskirts of the town, but before launching an attack he awaited the outcome of a naval encounter on the lake. The British had won control of Lake Champlain in June 1813, when they captured the U.S. warships *Eagle* and *Growler*. Since then both sides had been building more ships on the lake, and by September 1814 they were evenly matched. The British squadron was headed by the frigate *Confiance* (37 guns), the flagship of Captain George Downie, and supported by *Linnet*, *Chub*, *Finch*, and twelve gunboats. The American squadron was headed by the corvette *Saratoga* (26 guns), the flagship of Master Commandant Thomas Macdonough, and supported by *Eagle*, *Ticonderoga*, *Preble*, and ten gunboats. On the morning of September 11, the Americans were anchored east of Plattsburgh, out of reach of British shore cannon, when the British rounded Cumberland Head to attack. As a result of the engagement that followed, which Macdonough describes here for Secretary of the Navy Jones, Prevost abandoned his offensive, leaving Plattsburgh unmolested and his reputation a shambles.

U.S. Ship *Saratoga*
Plattsburgh Bay   Sept. 13th. 1814.

Sir,

I have the honor to give you the particulars of the action which took place on the 11th. Inst. on this Lake.—

For several days the Enemy were on their way to Plattsburgh by Land and water, and it being well understood that an attack would be made at the same time by their land & naval forces, I determined to await at anchor the approach of the latter.—

At 8 A.M. the look out boat announced the approach of the Enemy.— At 9 he anchor'd in a line ahead at about 300 yards distance from my line.— His Ship opposed to the *Saratoga*— his Brig to the *Eagle*, Capt Robt. Henly—his Gallies, thirteen in number, to the Schooner, Sloop, and a division of our Gallies.— One of his Sloops assisting their Ship & Brig—the other assisting their Gallies. Our remaining Gallies with the *Saratoga* and *Eagle*.—

In this situation the whole force, on both sides, became engaged—the *Saratoga* suffering much from the heavy fire of the *Confiance*.— I could perceive at the same time, however, that our fire was very destructive to her.— The *Ticonderoga*, Lt. Commt. Cassin, gallantly sustained her full share of the Action.— At ½ past 10 the *Eagle*, not able to bring her Guns to bear, cut her Cable and anchor'd in a more eligible position, between my ship and the *Ticonderoga*, where she very much annoyed the Enemy, but unfortunately leaving me exposed to the galling fire from the Enemy's Brig.—

Our Guns on the starboard side, being nearly all dismounted, or not manageable, a Stern anchor was let go, the bower Cable cut, and the ship winded with a fresh broadside on the Enemys Ship, which soon after surrendered.— Our broadside was then sprung to bear on the Brig, which surrendered in about fifteen minutes after.—

The Sloop that was opposed to the *Eagle* had struck some time before and drifted down the line—the Sloop which was with their Gallies having struck also.— Three of their Gallies are said to be sunk, the others pulled off.— Our Gallies were about obeying with alacrity the signal to follow them, when all the Vessels were reported to me to be in a sinking state— it then became necessary to annul the signal to the Gallies, and order their men now to the Pumps.—

I could only look at the Enemy's gallies going off in a shatter'd condition, for there was not a Mast in either squadron that could stand to make sail on; the lower rigging, being nearly all shot away, hung down as though it had been just placed over the mast heads.—

The *Saratoga* had Fifty five round Shot in her Hull—the *Confiance* One hundred & five.— The Enemy's shot passed principally just over our heads, as there were not 20 whole hammocks in the nettings at the close of the action, which lasted without intermission Two hours & twenty minutes.—

The absence and sickness of Lt. Raymond Perry left me without the services of that excellent Officer—much ought fairly to be attributed to him for his great care and attention in disciplining the Ships crew, as her first Lieutenant.— His place was filled by a gallant young Officer Lt. Peter Gamble, who I regret to inform you, was killed early in the action.—

Acting Lt. Vallette worked the 1st. & 2nd. divisions of Guns with able effect.— Sailing Master Brum's attention to the Springs, and in the execution of the order to Wind the Ship, and occasionally at the Guns, meets with my entire approbation,— also Capt. Youngs comm'g the acting marines, who took his men to the Guns.—

Mr. Beale, Purser, was of great service at the Guns, and in carrying my Orders throughout the Ship, with midshipman Montgomery.—

Master's Mate, Joshua Justin, had command of the 3rd division—his conduct during the action was that of a brave and correct Officer.— Midshipmen Monteath, Graham, Williamson, Platt, Thwing, and Act'g Mids: Baldwin, all behaved well, and gave evidence of their making valuable Officers.

The *Saratoga* was twice set on fire by hot Shot from the Enemy's Ship.—

I close, Sir, this communication with feelings of gratitude for the able support I received from every officer and man attached to the Squadron which I have the honor to command.— I have the honor to be with great respect, Sir, Yr Mot. obt. St.

T. Macdonough

P.S. accompanying this is a list of Killed & wounded, a list of Prisoners & a precise statement of both forces engaged—Also letters from Capt Henly & Lt. Commt. Cassin.—

T. Macdonough

Thomas Jefferson to Samuel H. Smith

In April 1800, Congress appropriated five thousand dollars for the creation of a library of legislative reference works "necessary to its deliberations." The Library of Congress, housed in the Capitol and developed under the direction of President Jefferson, consisted of three thousand volumes when it and the rest of the building were burned by the British. When Jefferson, struggling with personal debt, learned of the loss of the library, he wrote a letter to Samuel H. Smith, former editor of Washington's *National Intelligencer*, proposing that the government purchase his own collection, the largest personal library in the nation, as a replacement. After much bickering and a party-line vote—Federalists were concerned both about the outlay and about the utility of certain esoteric volumes—Congress acquired the library of 6,487 volumes for the sum of $23,950. In a letter of May 8, 1815, Jefferson congratulated Smith on the sale, adding that "an interesting treasure is added to your city, now become the depository of unquestionably the choicest collection of books in the U.S., and I hope it will not be without some general effect on the literature of our country."

Monticello, September 21, 1814

DEAR SIR,—I learn from the newspapers that the Vandalism of our enemy has triumphed at Washington over science as well as the arts, by the destruction of the public library with the noble edifice in which it was deposited. Of this transaction, as of that of Copenhagen, the world will entertain but one sentiment. They will see a nation suddenly withdrawn from a great war, full armed and full handed, taking advantage of another whom they had recently forced into it, unarmed, and unprepared, to indulge themselves in acts of barbarism which do not belong to a civilized age. When Van Ghent destroyed their shipping at Chatham, and De Ruyter rode triumphantly up the Thames, he might in like manner, by the acknowledgment of their own historians, have forced all their ships up to London bridge, and there have burnt them, the tower, and city, had these examples been then set.

London, when thus menaced, was near a thousand years old, Washington is but in its teens.

I presume it will be among the early objects of Congress to re-commence their collection. This will be difficult while the war continues, and intercourse with Europe is attended with so much risk. You know my collection, its condition and extent. I have been fifty years making it, and have spared no pains, opportunity or expense, to make it what it is. While residing in Paris, I devoted every afternoon I was disengaged, for a summer or two, in examining all the principal bookstores, turning over every book with my own hand, and putting by everything which related to America, and indeed whatever was rare and valuable in every science. Besides this, I had standing orders during the whole time I was in Europe, on its principal book-marts, particularly Amsterdam, Frankfort, Madrid and London, for such works relating to America as could not be found in Paris. So that in that department particularly, such a collection was made as probably can never again be effected, because it is hardly probable that the same opportunities, the same time, industry, perseverance and expense, with some knowledge of the bibliography of the subject, would again happen to be in concurrence. During the same period, and after my return to America, I was led to procure, also, whatever related to the duties of those in the high concerns of the nation. So that the collection, which I suppose is of between nine and ten thousand volumes, while it includes what is chiefly valuable in science and literature generally, extends more particularly to whatever belongs to the American statesman. In the diplomatic and parliamentary branches, it is particularly full. It is long since I have been sensible it ought not to continue private property, and had provided that at my death, Congress should have the refusal of it at their own price. But the loss they have now incurred, makes the present the proper moment for their accommodation, without regard to the small remnant of time and the barren use of my enjoying it. I ask of your friendship, therefore, to make for me the tender of it to the library committee of Congress, not knowing myself of whom the committee consists. I enclose you the catalogue, which will enable them to judge of its contents. Nearly the whole are well bound, abundance of them elegantly, and of the choicest editions existing. They may be valued by persons named by themselves, and the payment made convenient to the public. It may be, for instance, in such annual instalments as the law of Congress has left at their disposal, or in stock of any of their late loans, or of any loan they may institute at this session, so as to spare the present calls of our country, and await its days of peace and prosperity. They may enter, nevertheless, into immediate use of it, as eighteen or twenty wagons would place it in Washington in a single trip of a fortnight. I should be willing indeed, to retain a few of the books, to amuse the time I have yet to pass, which might be valued with the rest, but not included in the sum of valuation until they should be restored at my death, which I would carefully provide for, so that the whole library as it stands in the catalogue at this moment should be theirs without any garbling. Those I should like to retain would be chiefly classical and mathematical. Some few in other branches, and particularly one of the five encyclopedias in the catalogue. But this, if not acceptable, would not be urged. I must add, that I have not revised the library since I came home to live, so that it is probable some of the books may be missing, except in the chapters of Law and Divinity, which have been revised and stand exactly as in the catalogue. The return of the catalogue will of course be needed, whether the tender be accepted or not. I do not know that it contains any branch of science which Congress would wish to exclude from their collection; there is, in fact, no subject to which a member of Congress may not have occasion to refer. But such a wish would not correspond with my views of preventing its dismemberment. My desire is either to place it in their hands entire, or to preserve it so here. I am engaged in making an alphabetical index of the author's names, to be annexed to the catalogue, which I will forward to you as soon as completed. Any agreement you shall be so good as to take the trouble of entering into with the committee, I hereby confirm. Accept the assurance of my great esteem and respect.

Samuel C. Reid to the New-York Mercantile Advertiser

In 1814, thirty-year-old Samuel C. Reid, a sailor since the age of eleven, was captain of the Baltimore clipper *General Armstrong*, a 7- or 9-gun privateer brig with a crew of ninety. On April 19, 1814, this underdog captured the British merchantman *Fanny* (18 guns) off the coast of Ireland, but her most famous exploit came five months later in the Azores, while anchored in the neutral Portuguese harbor of Fayal. In the early evening of September 26, a trio of British warships—the third-rate *Plantagenet* (74 guns), the frigate *Rota* (38 guns), and the sloop *Carnation* (18 guns)—entered the harbor while en route to Jamaica, where they were to join the fleet amassing for an assault on New Orleans. The squadron anchored provocatively close to the American ship, and Reid moved her nearer to shore. Later that evening, *Carnation* released four boats full of armed men that rapidly closed in on *General Armstrong*, and Reid, after issuing repeated warnings to back off, opened fire. His account of the ensuing battle, a Pyrrhic victory for the British, was published in New York's leading newspaper, the *Mercantile Advertiser*, on December 15, 1814. For delaying the British squadron's arrival in Jamaica by at least a week, Reid was retrospectively hailed as a hero of the Battle of New Orleans.

Fayal, 4th October, 1814.

With infinite regret I am constrained to say it has eventually fallen to my lot to state to you the loss and total destruction of the private armed brig Gen. Armstrong, late under my command.

We sailed from Sandy Hook on the evening of the 9th ult. and about midnight fell in close aboard of a razee and ship of the line. They pursued till next day noon, when they thought proper to give over chase. On the 11th, after a nine hour's chase, boarded the private armed schr. Perry, John Colman, 6 days from Philadelphia; had thrown over all his guns. On the following day fell in with an enemy's gun brig; exchanged a few shots with, and left him. On the 24th, boarded a Spanish brig and schooner, and a Portuguese ship, all from the Havanna. On the 26th following, came too in Fayal Roads, for the purpose of filling water; called on the American Consul, who very politely ordered our water immediately sent off, it being our intention to proceed to sea early the next day. At 5 P.M. I went on board, the consul and some other gentlemen in company. I asked some questions concerning enemy's cruizers, and was told there had been none at these Islands for several weeks; when about dusk, while we were conversing the British brig Carnation suddenly hove in sight close under the N. E. head of the harbour, within gunshot when first discovered. The idea of getting under way was instantly suggested; but finding the enemy's brig had the advantage of a breeze and but little wind with us, it was thought doubtful if we should be able to get to sea without hazarding an action. I questioned the Consul to know if in his opinion the enemy would regard the neutrality of the port? He gave me to understand I might make myself perfectly easy, assuring me at the same time they would never molest us while at anchor. But no sooner did the enemy's brig understand from the pilot-boat who we were, when she immediately hauled close in and let go her anchor within pistol shot of us. At the same moment the Plantagenet, and frigate Rota, hove in sight, to whom the Carnation instantly made signal, and a constant interchange took place for some time. The result was the Carnation proceeded to throw out all her boats; despatched one on board the commodore, and appeared otherwise to be making unusual exertions. From these circumstances I began to suspect their real intentions. The moon was near its full, which enabled us to observe them very minutely; and I now determined to haul in nearer the shore. Accordingly, after clearing for action we got under way, and began to sweep in. The moment this was observed by the enemy's brig, she instantly cut her cable, made sail, and despatched four boats in pursuit of us. Being now about 8 P.M. as soon as we saw the boats approaching, we let go our anchor, got springs on our cable, and prepared to receive them. I hailed them repeatedly as they drew near, but they felt no inclination to reply. Sure of their game, they only pulled up with the greater speed. I observed the boats were well manned, and apparently as well armed; and as soon as they had cleverly got alongside, we opened our fire, which was as soon returned; but meeting with rather a warmer reception than they had probably been aware of, they soon cried out for quarters, and hauled off. In this skirmish I had one man killed and my first lieutenant wounded. The enemy's loss must have been upwards of twenty killed and wounded.

They had now repaired to their ships to prepare for a more formidable attack. We, in the interim, having taken the hint, prepared to haul close in to the beach, where we moored head and stern within half pistol shot of the castle. This done, we again prepared in the best possible manner for their second reception. About 9 P.M. we observed the enemy's brig towing in a large fleet of boats. They soon after left the brig and took their stations in three divisions, under covert of a small reef of rocks, within about musket shot of us. Here they continued manœuvring for some time, the brig still keeping under way to act with the boats, should we at any time attempt our escape.

The shore was lined with the inhabitants, waiting the expected attack; and from the brightness of the moon, they had a most favourable view of the scene. The governor, with most of the first people of the place, stood by and saw the whole affair.

At length about midnight, we observed the boats in motion, (our crew having laid at their quarters during the whole of this interval.) They came on in one direct line, keeping in close order; and we plainly counted twelve boats.——As soon as they came within proper distance we opened our fire, which was warmly returned from the enemy's carronades and small arms. The discharge from our Long Tom rather staggered them; but soon recovering, they gave three cheers, and came on most spiritedly. In a moment they succeeded in gaining our bow and starboard quarter, and the word was *Board*. Our great guns now becoming useless, we attacked them sword in hand, together with our pikes, pistols, and musketry, from which our lads poured on them a most destructive fire. The enemy made frequent and repeated attempts to gain our decks, but were repulsed at all times, and at all points, with the greatest slaughter.——About the middle of the action I received intelligence of the death of my second Lieutenant; and soon after of the third Lieutenant being badly wounded. From this and other causes, I found our fire had much slackened on the forecastle; and, fearful of the event, I instantly rallied the whole of our after division, who had been bravely defending and now had succeeded in beating the boats off the quarters.—They gave a shout, rushed forward, opened a fresh fire, and soon after decided the conflict, which terminated in the total defeat of the enemy, and the loss of many of their boats: two of which, belonging to the Rota, we took possession of, literally loaded with their own dead. Seventeen only escaped from them both, who had swam to the shore. In another boat under our quarter, commanded by one of the Lieutenants of the Plantagenet, all were killed saving four. This I have from the Lieutenant himself, who further told me that he jumped overboard to save his own life.

The duration of this action was about 40 minutes. Our deck was now found in much confusion, our Long Tom dismounted, and several of our carriages broken; many of our crew having left the vessel, and others disabled. Under these circumstances, however, we succeeded in getting Long Tom in his birth, and the decks cleared in some sort for a fresh action, should the enemy attack us again before daylight.— About 3 A.M. I received a message from the American Consul, requesting to see me on shore, where he informed me the Governor had sent a note to Captain Lloyd, begging him to desist from further hostilities. To which Captain Lloyd sent for answer, that he was now determined to have the privateer at the risk of knocking down the whole town; and that if the Governor suffered the Americans to injure the privateer in any manner, he should consider the place an enemy's port, and treat it accordingly. Finding this to be the case, I considered all hopes of saving our vessel to be at an end. I therefore went on board, and ordered all our wounded and dead to be taken on shore, and the crew to save their effects as fast as possible.—Soon after this it became daylight, when the enemy's brig stood close in, and commenced a heavy fire on us with all her force. After several broadsides she hauled off, having received a shot in her hull, her rigging much cut, and her foretopmast wounded; (of this I was informed by the

British Consul.) She soon after came in again, and anchored close to the privateer. I then ordered the Armstrong to be scuttled, to prevent the enemy from getting her off. She was soon after boarded by the enemy's boats, and set on fire, which soon completed her destruction.

They have destroyed a number of houses in the town, and murdered some of the inhabitants.

By what I have been able to learn from the British Consul and officers of the fleet, it appears there were about 400 officers and men in the last attack by the boats, of which 120 were killed and about 130 wounded.——Captain Lloyd, I am told by the British Consul, is badly wounded in the leg; a jury of Surgeons had been held, who gave as their opinion that amputation would be necessary to insure his life. Tis said, however, that the wound was occasioned by an *Ox treading on him*. The fleet has remained here about a week, during which they have been principally employed in burying their dead, and taking care of their wounded.

Three days after the action they were joined by the ship Thais and brig Calypso (two sloops of war) who were immediately taken into requisition by Captain Lloyd, to take home the wounded men.—The Calypso sailed for England with part of the wounded, on the 2d instant, among whom was the first Lieutenant of the Plantagenet. The Thais sails this evening with the remainder. Capt. Lloyd's fleet, sailed to day, supposed for the West-Indies.

The loss on our part, I am happy to say is comparatively trifling; two killed and seven wounded. With regard to my officers in general I feel the greatest satisfaction in saying they one and all fought with the most determined bravery, and to whom I feel highly indebted for their officer-like conduct during the short period we were together; their exertions and bravery deserved a better fate.

I here insert for your inspection, a list of the killed and wounded.

KILLED.

Mr. Alexander O. Williams, 2d Lieut. by a musket ball in the forehead, died instantly; Burton Lloyd, Seaman, do. through the heart, do.

WOUNDED.

Fredk. A. Worth, 1st Lieut. in the right side,
Robert Johnson, 3d do. left knee,
Bazilla Hammond, Qr. Master, left arm,
John Piner, Seaman, knee,
Wm. Castle, do. arm,
Nicholas Scalsan, do. arm and leg,
John Harrison, do. hands and face, by the explosion
of a gun.

It gives me much pleasure to announce to you that our wounded are all in a fair way of recovery, through the unremitted care and attention of our worthy surgeon.

Mr. Dabney, our Consul, is a gentleman possessing every feeling of humanity, and to whom the utmost gratitude is due from us for his great care of the sick and wounded, and his polite attention to my officers and myself.

Mr. Williams was a most deserving and promising officer. His country, in him, has lost one of its brightest ornaments; and his death must be sadly lamented by all who knew his worth.

Accompanied with this you will find a copy of my Protest, together with copies of letters written by Mr. Dabney to the governor of Fayal, our Minister at Rio Janeiro, and our Secretary of State. These letters will develope more fully the circumstances of this unfortunate affar.

We expect to sail to morrow in a Portuguese brig for Amelia Island, which takes the whole of our crew; till when, I remain gentleman, your very obedient humble servant.

SAM. C. REID.

Benjamin F. Browne: from "Papers of an old Dartmoor Prisoner"

The American sailor Benjamin Browne, who took an anthropologist's interest in the folkways of Dartmoor Prison, here continues the story of his six months' incarceration with an account of the prisoners' attempts at self-government.

———————————

THE government of the prisons was essentially democratical; that is, the interior police, and all matters relating to our intercourse with each other, were under the control of a committee chosen by the captives from among themselves. I know not whether they were chosen by ballot, viva voce, or how, nor to what extent the right of suffrage was exercised; for, although I was present when government was first instituted in No. 7 prison, I do not recollect being called upon to vote, nor of having witnessed the election; nor do I find any other reference to it in my diary, than that such and such persons were elected committee-men. The committee had the appointment of the cooks, sweepers, crier, &c.; but these persons were paid by the British government.—There were several cooks to each prison, who were paid three pence a day each; and the cook's office was one which seemed to be eagerly desired, for these members of the *kitchen cabinet* had an opportunity of getting a good belly-full every day, and perhaps some other perquisites; —there are candle-ends and cheese-parings in all offices. They, however, held their offices by a frail tenure; for it was as true at Dartmoor, in the nineteenth century, as it was two centuries before, that "he has a habitation giddy and unsure who builds it on the fickle multitude." They were often suspected of skimming the coppers, putting the fat into their own pockets, and abstracting it from our hungry maws; and whether the charge were true or not, it was a convenient one to get up, by some aspirant for the office of cook to the sovereign people of Dartmoor.

The sweepers had the duty of sweeping the prisons out every morning in fair weather; but when the weather was so bad that the prisoners could not be turned out into the yards, their duty was confined to sweeping the alleys. The prisoners were turned out every morning early, while two turnkeys stood at the door, to count them as they passed out; and the same precaution was taken when they were turned in at night, to ascertain if the whole number were present; but I suspect, however, they might report to the principal, that they were not very accurate in counting; and the prisoners used to take a malicious pleasure in perplexing them as much as they could.

The crier's duty was to make proclamation of all things interesting to the prisoners to know—new orders, items of news, goods lost and found, articles to sell, &c. This they did by sound of bell. It was also their duty to attend to the selection of jurors, when any one was to be tried, and to officiate as constables at the trials. The selection of jurors was made by the committee, who wrote the names of such persons as they judged to be qualified; and the crier went round to each man, who made a mark against the names of the twelve individuals he preferred. The twelve having the most marks against their names were notified to serve as jurors on that trial; and this process was repeated on the next occasion, those who had previously served, being exempted.

These trials were for offences against public order and against property. Offences against morals were not very strictly inquired into, unless they involved a crime against property; and in this case the inquiry was strict, and the punishment, on conviction, tremendously severe in many cases. I have known an individual, convicted of stealing, tied up to a post and whipped with a cat-o'-nine-tails so severely, that he was obliged to be carried to the hospital; and another who was whipped almost as severely for a gross want of cleanliness. The trials were conducted with a good deal of order and decorum in an odd way. They were held in the upper story of each prison in a place set apart for the use of the committee, and were open to the public, as all trials should be. The committee acted as judges, and were seated together, with very grave and sagacious looks.

These "potent, grave and reverend seignors," no doubt, felt all the dignity and consequence attached to their high functions. It was rather a grotesque sight, at first, to see judges with tarpaulin hats, short jackets, or in shirt sleeves and duck trowsers—to see jurymen in the same habiliments—and lawyers squirting tobacco juice out of one corner of their mouths, in the midst of an eloquent harangue; one hand inforcing by action the power of their rhetoric, while the other was employed in hitching up their trowsers.

The indictments, the pleas, the demurrers, and sur-rejoinders, were not very technical, and were all made *viva voce*; for special pleading was unknown.

There were a number of these sailor-lawyers in the prisons, and they were generally very adroit in the management of their cases. They did not conform very strictly to any known rules, but ranged pretty much at random—they were generally very fluent with their blarney; and it was no small treat to hear some of the cleverest of them. There were no monopoly bar-rules there, but every one was free to practise, who felt himself moved to the vocation, and could get clients.

The committee, too, had the appointment of the barbers, of whom there were several to each prison. I do not know whether these knights of the razor were paid in the same manner as the cooks and sweepers, or whether they were paid by those who availed themselves of their services. For myself, a barber was, then, a useless artizan, my beard (it is now stiff and wiry, to the great annoyance of my worthy razor driver,) had hardly begun to sprout.

It was the committee's duty, likewise, to receive the provisions from the contractors every day; to stand between these grasping gentlemen and the captives, to see that the latter had fair-play, that the provisions were of good quality and sufficient weight. They were furnished with a copy of the contracts, and had the power of rejecting what they did not approve, subject to the further action, on appeal, of the commandant of the depot.

There was, also, another committee called, "The Committee of Correspondence," and these had charge of all matters of correspondence with the agent in London. I do not know who elected them, but they had the full confidence of the prisoners, and were worthy and proper men.

No. 4, or the negro-prison, was an exception to the demo-cratical form of government; this was under a regal, or rather despotic form. A tall, powerful black man, known among the prisoners as "Big Dick," or "King Dick," from being president of the committee, had contrived to depose his brethren in of-fice and to usurp the sovereign sway, and he ruled the poor blacks with as arbitrary an authority as any other despot could. He was nearly seven feet tall and proportionally large, was of a muscular and athletic make, of a commanding aspect, shrewd mind, and an expert boxer. These qualities rendered him very formidable to the poor beings with whom he was surrounded, and contributed altogether to his gaining the sway over them, and very much to its continuance. But one great means of his continuing in power was, I think, the countenance he derived from the white prisoners. They very early perceived the advan-tage to their own quiet which grew out of Dick's authority; for, in all cases of conflict between whites and blacks, he invari-ably took the part of the former. I have seen it stated, that the inhabitants of this prison were pre-eminent in Dartmoor for their wickedness and disorder. My own observation did not confirm this statement. I believe that these blacks were, to say the least, as orderly and correct in their deportment, and as moral as their more intelligent white neighbors. Indeed I know, that many of the most respectable prisoners preferred to mess in No. 4, on account of the superior order of that prison. It derived, at first, a bad character from its gaming tables; but the keepers were as often whites as blacks; and after a few months, when gaming became general in all the prisons, we could reproach the blacks with nothing that they could not retort on us with interest.

There was much secret murmuring and dissatisfaction among the subjects of King Richard, and one or two conspira-cies to dethrone him; but he, by means of his spies, had knowl-edge of the treason. Thereupon he went to the neighbors, and told them of their purposes, and further said, that he would give them fair play; they must come out, one at a time, and try a match at boxing with him; and if either of them could con-quer him, he would give up his power to the conqueror; but if no one could, and he ever heard of their rebelling against him again, he would flog them within an inch of their lives. The result was, that he flogged them all, and never heard of any more conspiracies.

Instead of a diadem, Dick usually wore a shaggy bear-skin cap, and for a sceptre, he carried a powerful club in his hand when he went the rounds of his prison; and many of his subjects had a *feeling* sense of his royal grace and condescension, in the love-pats with which he honored them. He dubbed his knights by a blow on the head, instead of the shoulder; and instead of rising up after the blow was inflicted, they were very apt to fall down; but this probably arose from the defective education of the monarch. He probably had not read the ancient or modern writers on chivalry; they were to him sealed-books, for, I believe, he could not read at all. His valiant knights, from a modest and becoming sense of their own unworthiness, seemed as anxious to avoid the honor, as some reverend clergymen in our own time and country have been to eschew the collegiate dignity of a D. D.

The monarch sometimes so far descended from the regal dignity as to throw away the cares of state for a time, and teach a boxing-school in the cock-loft of No. 4. His pupils were mostly white men; for Dick did not care to teach any of his own subjects an art which might prove dangerous to his power.

Dick understood one part of the art of governing as well as any potentate or power that ever existed—that is, the art of levying contributions in a way to cheat the generality of his subjects into a belief that they contributed but little, if anything, to the support of government; for the monarch levied contributions on the shop-keepers, who, in turn, were obliged to collect it of their customers, but in a way that their customers did not wot of. I have heard a story of a master of a merchant vessel, who, returning from a foreign voyage, was settling his account of disbursements with his owner. One item in the account particularly displeased the worthy citizen, and that was a charge for jack-ass hire. He struck it out of his allowance, and sent the master on another voyage to the same port. On settling again, the objectionable item did not appear. "Oh! Captain," said the owner, "I like this; here is no charge for jack-ass hire." The captain, turning on his heel, murmured, aside, "But it is *there*, though you don't see it." The reader, I have no doubt, will make the application of this story, and agree with me, that many men, besides this wise ship-owner and the poor blacks at Dartmoor, pay for jack-ass hire, though they *don't see it.*

Dick understood another kingly art too, very well, for he was a monopolist, and engrossed the sale of beer within his prison; and as too many of his living subjects imitated the example of their more enlightened white brethren, in "taking an enemy into their mouths to steal away their brains," he found it very profitable— the sale of this commodity giving the vender cent. per cent. profit. Dick did not descend so low as to tend the tap himself, but kept a shopman for that purpose. He had probably little knowledge of the monopolies of any of his fellow-sovereigns; but he had an ex- ample nearer home; for the sale of beer was monopolized by the committee in three of the white prisons. The pretence in these, as elsewhere, was, that it was for the public good, and that the profits were expended for the equal benefit of all the inmates of those prisons; and this may have been the case, but then it must have cost a good deal to maintain government there; for, though the revenue must have been large, I never heard of any distribution of the surplus. We managed this thing more wisely and honestly in No. 7 prison; for there, the doctrine of free trade prevailed, and the sale of every thing was left free for any one to engage in who had the means and the inclination to do so. In fact, we were troubled very little with governmental legislation of any kind in No. 7; for both rulers and ruled seemed to understand that the prevailing error of all systems of government is, that the people are governed too much. Every body in No. 7 was left free to do pretty much as he pleased, if he did not molest his neighbor's person and property, and I do not know that we did not fare as well for it.

Like other monarchs, Dick had his parasites and flatterers; and, though as he engrossed nearly all the functions of the state in his own proper person, he had few or no offices of honor or emolument to bestow upon them; yet, I dare say, they reaped, in some way or other, substantial fruits of his royal bounty.

He kept two white lads continually about his person, whom he took care to select for their comely looks, and to keep them handsomely clad. We denominated them his secretaries, but I rather think that the office of secretary was nearly a sinecure, as

I never saw or heard of any state documents within his realm. His orders, like those of other African potentates, were given *viva voce*, and all the proceedings of state and justice within his dominions were of the most simple and summary nature. Their duties, as secretaries, were probably to collect his beer-score, to keep account of his money, and to collect the contributions from the shop-keepers.

He sometimes punished gross instances of drunkenness very severely; and it used to excite my youthful wonder, for, as beer was the favorite potation, the inebriating draught must, in most cases, have been drawn from the royal fountain; but I have for a long time ceased to wonder at it, for I perceive, (or think I perceive,) that the tendency of a good deal of government craft is to tempt men to the commission of crime, and then to punish them on detection. It was said that his royal majesty was sometimes in the habit of indulging his own bibulous appetite to a crapulous degree—but then he had the monarch's privilege;

> 'What in the captain's but a choleric word,
> Is in the soldier rank blasphemy.'

After the peace, Dick was well known, in Boston and vicinity, as a teacher of pugilistics.

Timothy Pickering to Caleb Strong

On August 8, 1814, at the first meeting of the British and American peace commissioners in Ghent, the official British protocol, as recorded by the American envoys, outlined four subjects to which discussion "would be likely to turn":

1. The forcible seizure of mariners on board of merchant vessels, and the claim of allegiance, of his Britannic majesty, upon all native-born subjects of Great Britain.

2. The Indian allies of Great Britain to be included in the pacification, and a boundary to be settled between the dominions of the Indians and those of the United States. Both parts of this point are considered by the British government as a sine qua non to the conclusion of the treaty.

3. The revision of the boundary line between the territories of the United States and those of Great Britain, adjoining them in North America.

4. The fisheries—respecting which the British government will not allow the people of the United States the privilege of landing and drying fish within the territorial jurisdiction of Great Britain, without an equivalent.

The American commissioners' report on the deliberation of these subjects was submitted to Congress by President Madison on October 10. Timothy Pickering, a representative of Massachusetts in the U.S. House, wrote to Governor Strong about the significance of this report to the future of their state and of the Federalist Party.

CITY OF WASHINGTON, Oct. 12, 1814.

DEAR SIR,—Yesterday I enclosed to you copies of the letters and papers from our Commissioners at Ghent, stating their communications with the British Commissioners on the subject of peace, and intimated my intention to follow them with some remarks.

When read in the House (and they were read but once), considerable excitement was produced among some on the right as well as on the wrong side of that body. I thought the few observations then made premature; and that it had been better to wait until we could deliberately read the documents ourselves. I confess, at the same time, that the demands of the British did not surprise me or rouse any resentment; for they seemed to be the natural result of the war, waged as it was on such unsufficient grounds (if the ostensible had been, what they were not, the real excuses of the war), and under such peculiar circumstances, when not the fate of Britain only, but of the whole civilized world, was at stake. I have uniformly thought that Great Britain might justly demand some indemnity for the injuries actually done her, and the fatal mischief manifestly intended against her, by this base, unjust, and unnatural war. But yet she asks not any indemnity: security will satisfy her, and to that she is entitled.

1. I presume no Federalist has doubted that Great Britain could insist, as she does, on the right to take by force her natural-born subjects from our merchant vessels on the high seas. I also presume that now the President has yielded that point; although the maintaining of it, when no other pretence for continuing the war existed, has cost many millions of money, and the sacrifice of many thousand lives.

2. To comprehend the Indians, her allies, in the pacification was the indispensable duty of Great Britain; and to secure for them a permanent boundary was in itself an act of benevolence, though doubtless an interested policy strongly influenced the demand. And how will the United States be affected, should the demand be admitted? Had the just and humane system towards the Indians, formed under the administration of Washington, but which, you will recollect, was vehemently oppugned by the then opposition, been pursued subsequently to the year 1800, we should have had no Indian war; but since that time the North-western Indians have been pressed and constrained to relinquish vast tracts of their hunting-grounds, which are as necessary to them as farms to their white neighbors, by treaty upon treaty,—many of them, I have no doubt, unfairly conducted,—until their resentments were roused, and, by Governor Harrison's incursion and attack at Tippecanoe, a war enkindled.

Now, to secure peace and their property to those Indians,

and fix their attachment to their powerful ally, Great Britain demands for them a permanent boundary line, over which neither nation shall pass to purchase the Indian lands. These, no doubt, are the lands which fall within the limits of the United States by the treaty of peace of 1783. In effect, then, the demand of Great Britain amounts to this, and to no more: That, as the United States have now the right of pre-emption (and that is all they have) in respect to those lands, they should relinquish it to the Indians, who are the right owners and possessors of the soil; and the two powers are to guarantee the same to the Indians, and to stipulate that neither shall purchase any of them. In conversation, the British Commissioners said the Indians might sell to a third person or power; but this is omitted in their written note, and ought not to be admitted on our part in a treaty. Let those lands remain (according to the idea suggested by the British Commissioners) a wilderness, and so a perpetual barrier in that quarter between the British territories and ours. And as this proposition, particularly as to boundary, was to be subject to modifications, unquestionably such parts of the Indian territories as had been already purchased and settled would have been excepted and reserved without that boundary. Should any unseated tracts be then comprehended, they must have been the subjects of speculation, and not improbably the very objects of those irritating treaties and the real causes of the Indian war. To such tracts, no exception need be made. Should the United States have sold and received the consideration for them, the money may be refunded.

In a political point of view, this relinquishment of our preemption right to the Indians might be really desirable. It is this wild spirit which has scattered our citizens in the wilderness, and exposed them to destruction; because, so dispersed, they are unequal to their own protection, and by their collisions with the Indians are always endangering our peace. From all that I have heard (and I have sought for information), I entertain no doubt that the Indian war on the Ohio frontiers was produced by the injustice of our own people towards the Indians.

You know that the Western lands were early pledged for the redemption of the sacred debt of the Revolution. They have yielded about eight millions of dollars; while the expenditures in that region in the two years of this war have, I doubt not, risen to double that sum,—probably to much more. That pledge, then, to the public creditors is gone. It would have been good economy in the United States if they had given away all those lands to the settlers, solely on condition that they should defend themselves.

That it was not necessary to coerce (I do not mean by military force, but by the irresistible influence of superior power impending, and seen to be always ready to fall upon them and crush them),—that it was not necessary to coerce the Indians to sell their lands in that region to make room for settlers, is perfectly evident from this single fact, that, in the direct tax imposed in 1813, a greater sum was assessed on non-residents' lands in the State of Ohio than on the lands of all the inhabitants of that State, although they send six members to Congress! In like manner, a large portion (I do not remember how much) of the direct tax in Kentucky was imposed on the lands of non-residents.

As Indian lands were not wanted to make room for settlers, why have they been so eagerly grasped? For two reasons: to give opportunity for the speculations of men in office and their friends; and to furnish occasion to erect more territorial governments, with a train of officers and dependants, to extend executive patronage and gain partisans to the cause of the dominant party.

3. The proposition that the United States should have no naval force on the Lakes, nor fortresses on their borders, I was prepared for, and on the very ground taken by the British Commissioners. It is, I believe, more than a year since, in conversation with some of my friends, I remarked that it would be happy for both countries if they could agree never to have either armed vessels or military posts on their whole interior frontiers washed by the Great Lakes and their connecting waters. But I added (having contemplated the subject), Great Britain cannot agree to this; for her Canadian Provinces are weak from their small population, and the United States are strong, which in case of future hostilities would enable them to overrun the Canadas before they could prepare for their defence. And can we think it unreasonable in Great Britain to ask for this security? Should not we do it, were our relative situation like hers?

It is to be noted, however, that this proposition is not a *sine qua non*; it is a fair subject of negotiation, and doubtless may be modified in a manner mutually satisfactory. For instance, it may be agreed that neither shall have any armed vessels on the Lakes, while each may maintain its fortresses on the land. If there were to be no stipulation of the kind demanded, it would be good policy on the part of the United States to haul up their armed vessels, and never to repair them; such only of the smaller ones being excepted as, being for ever dismantled of arms, should be useful as trading vessels on those waters. Peace once restored, such a period would probably elapse before another war would arise that three or four or half a dozen sets of armed vessels might be built and rot before they would be wanted for defence or offence. And surely we shall have need enough of economy to save so great an expense as even that of the annual repairs of the vessels now in existence.

4. The only remaining proposition respects the fisheries and the cession of land in the north-east corner of Maine, to enable Great Britain to open a road of its own by which to communicate between Halifax and New Brunswick and Quebec.

The declaration relative to the fisheries was precisely what was expected by myself and my intelligent friends with whom I conversed on the subject before I left home. We did not believe that Great Britain would attempt to deprive us of the Bank fisheries in the open sea; while we supposed she would deny us the fisheries in the bays and coasts of her own dominions, of which she would conceive herself the sovereign. But the latter she is ready to yield for an equivalent. Now, Great Britain well knows that Massachusetts is almost exclusively interested in the cod-fisheries; and it is through her territories that she wants a road between Quebec and New Brunswick and Nova Scotia,—not a right of passage merely, but the land itself, to have the road in the fullest property. And this, I imagine, is the equivalent she contemplates for yielding a right to the fisheries in question.

Not knowing the quality of the lands in Maine of which Great Britain wants a cession, and the proposition being too indefinite to enable me to judge how far down the line between Maine and New Brunswick it may be needful for the road to cross, I should be happy to receive information on the subject. A road from Halifax round the head of the Bay of Fundy, and thence directly to Quebec, would appear to take off but a small portion of Maine; and if the road for New Brunswick were to run northerly until it fell in with the Halifax road, before it crossed the line of Maine, it would seem that the contemplated cession would not cover a very large tract of land.

These papers having been committed to the Committee for Foreign Affairs, and there being in one portion of that committee at least as much of zeal as of prudence and knowledge, I look for an inflammatory report. Perhaps this may not be acted upon before I receive your sentiments upon the subject; and I hope your public duties may not be such as to deny you time to favor me with an answer.

For several years past, I have heard the expression from sound and discreet Federalists of the Middle and Southern States, "We look to New England for salvation." I pray God that New England may not now be wanting to herself and to her brethren, the most valuable members of our great political society. The dominant party have brought the United States to the brink of ruin, and treated us, not as equals, but as their field-laborers, bound to toil for, as if to compensate, them for the trouble of ruling over us with rods of iron. I am weary and indignant at this servitude, and unwilling longer to submit to it. Yet without some extraordinary effort, some act becoming the high spirit of freemen, such as our predecessors would have approved, I see not but our chains are to be riveted for ever; as, abandoned by the general government, except for taxing us, we must defend ourselves, so we ought to secure and hold fast the revenues indispensable to maintain the force necessary for our protection against the foreign enemy, and the still greater evil in prospect,—domestic tyranny.

Thomas Jefferson to James Madison

On the day that the President submitted the peace commissioners' report to Congress, he also sent a copy to Jefferson. "The British sine qua non," Madison summarized in a cover note, "excluded us from fishing within the soverignty attached to her shores, and from using these in curing fish—required a Cession of as much of Maine as wd remove the obstruction to a *direct* communication between Quebec & Halifax, confirmed to her the Passamaquoddy Islands as always hers of right—included in the pacification the Indian Allies, with a boundary for them . . . agst the U.S. mutually guaranteed, and the Indians restrained from selling their lands to either party, but free to sell them to a *third* party—prohibited the U.S. from having an armed force on the Lakes or forts on their shores, the British prohibited as to neither—and substituted for the present N.W. limit of the U.S. a line running direct from the W. end of L. Superior to the Mississippi, with a right of G. B. to the navigation of this river. Our ministers were all present & in perfect harmony of opinion on the arrogance of such demands." He concluded that, barring "a sudden change in the B. Cabinet," peace negotiations were likely to break down and the war to continue. Jefferson replied five days later.

Monticello Oct. 15, 1814

DEAR SIR,

I thank you for the information of your letter of the 10th. it gives at length a fixed character to our prospects. the war undertaken, on both sides, to settle the questions of impressment & the Orders of Council, now that these are done away by events, is declared by Great Britain to have changed it's object, and to have become a war of Conquest, to be waged until she conquers from us our fisheries, the province of Maine, the lakes, states & territories North of the Ohio, and the Navigation of the Missisipi; in other words, till she reduces us to unconditional submission. on our part then we ought to propose, as a counterchange of object, the establishment of the meridian of the mouth of the Sorel Northwardly as the Western boundary of all her possessions. two measures will enable us to effect it, and, without these, we cannot even defend ourselves. 1. to organize the militia into classes, as you have recommended in your message; abolishing by a Declaratory law the doubts which abstract scruples in some, and cowardice & treachery in others have conjured up about passing imaginary lines, & limiting, at the same time, their services to the *contiguous* provinces of the enemy. the 2d is the Ways and Means. you have seen my ideas on this subject; and I shall add nothing but a rectification of what either I have ill expressed, or you have misapprehended. if I have used any expression restraining the emissions of Treasury notes to a *sufficient* medium, as your letter seems to imply, I have done it inadvertently, and under the impression then possessing me, that the war would be very short. a *sufficient* medium would not, on the principles of any writer, exceed 30. Millions of Dollars, & on those of some not 10. Millions. our experience has proved it may be run up to 2. or 300.M. without more than doubling what would be the prices of things under a *sufficient* medium, or say a Metallic one, which would always keep itself at the *sufficient* point: and if the rise to this term, and descent from it, be gradual, it would not produce sensible revolutions in private fortunes. I shall be able to explain my views more definitely by the use of numbers. suppose we require, to carry on the war, an annual loan of 20.M. then I propose that in the 1st year you shall lay a tax of 2.M. and emit 20.M. of Treasury notes, of a size proper for circulation, & bearing no interest, to the redemption of which the proceeds of that tax shall be inviolably pledged & applied by recalling annually their amount of the identical bills funded on them. the 2d year lay another tax of 2.M., and emit 20.M. more. the 3d. year the same, and so on, until you reach the Maximum of taxes which ought to be imposed. let me suppose this Maximum to be 1.D. a head, or 10.M. of Dollars; merely as an exemplification more familiar than would be the Algebraical symbols *x*. or *y*. you would reach this in 5. years. the 6th year then, still emit 20.M. of treasury notes, and continue all the taxes 2. years longer. the 7th year 20.M. more & continue the whole taxes another two years; and so on. Observe, that altho' you emit 20.M. a year, you call in 10.M. and consequently add but 10.M. annually to the circulation. it would be in 30. years then, primâ facie, that you would reach the present circulation of 300.M. or the ultimate term to which we might adventure. but observe also that in that time we shall have become 30.M. of people, to whom 300.M. of D. would be no more than 100.M. to us now, which sum would probably not have raised prices more than 50. p.c. on what may be deemed the standard or Metallic prices. this increased population and consumption, while it would be increasing the proceeds of the redemption-tax, and lessening the balance annually thrown into circulation, would also absorb, without saturation, more of the surplus medium, and enable us to push the same process to a much higher term, to one which we might safely call indefinite, because extending so far beyond the limits, either in time or expence, of any supposable war. all we should have to do would be, when the war should be ended, to leave the gradual extinction of these notes to the operation of the taxes pledged for their redemption, not to suffer a dollar of paper to be emitted either by public or private authority, but let the metallic medium flow back into the channels of circulation, and occupy them until another war should oblige us to recur for it's support, to the same resource, & the same process on the circulating medium.

The citizens of a country like ours, will never have unemployed capital. too many enterprises are open, offering high profits, to permit them to lend their capitals on a regular and moderate interest. they are too enterprising and sanguine themselves not to believe they can do better with it. I never did believe you could have gone beyond a 1st or at most a 2d loan: not from a want of confidence in the public faith, which is perfectly sound, but from a want of disposable funds in individuals. the circulating fund is the only one we can ever command with certainty. it is sufficient for all our wants; and the impossibility of even defending the country without it's aid as a borrowing fund, renders it indispensable that the nation should take and keep it in their own hands, as their exclusive resource.

I have trespassed on your time so far for explanation only: I will do it no further than by adding the assurances of my affectionate & respectful attachment.

TH: JEFFERSON

A tabular statement of the amount of emissions taxes, redemptions, and balances left in circulation, every year, on the plan above sketched.

Years.	Emissions.	Taxes & Redemptions.	Bal. in circulation at end of year.
1815	20 millions	2 millions	18 millions.
1816	20　″	4　″	34　″
1817	20　″	6　″	48　″
1818	20　″	8　″	60　″
1819	20　″	10　″	70　″
1820	20　″	10　″	80　″
1821	20　″	10　″	90　″
	140		

Suppose the war to terminate here, to wit, at the end of 7d. years, then the reduction will proceed as follows:

Years.	Taxes & Redemptions.	Bal. in cir. at end of year.
1822	10 millions	80 millions
1823	10　″	70　″
1824	10　″	60　″
1825	10　″	50　″
1826	10　″	40　″
1827	10　″	30　″
1828	10　″	20　″
1829	10　″	10　″
1830	10　″	0　″
	140	

Charles Willing Hare to Harrison Gray Otis

By the fall of 1814, it was clear that the United States was facing a crisis. As Great Britain aggressively built up forces in Canada and in the Caribbean and stalled the peace talks at Ghent, Washington keenly felt the lack of men, money, and strategies with which to continue fighting the war; in November the situation would become so dire that the federal government would default on the national debt. Questions of how to raise troops and money preoccupied Congress, but partisan and sectional divisions made consensus difficult. In New England, where opposition to the war had always been strongest, state and local governments continued to defy orders from the War Department, and now Madison, in reprisal, refused to fund the militias of the worst offenders—Massachusetts, Rhode Island, and Connecticut. Gouverneur Morris, a prominent Federalist in New York City, spoke for many in his party when he declared that "a union of the commercial states to take care of themselves, leaving the War, its expenses, and its debts to those choice spirits so ready to declare and so eager to carry it on, seems to be now the only rational course." On October 1, Charles Willing Hare, a leader among Pennsylvania Federalists, wrote to Harrison Gray Otis, the most effective legislator in Massachusetts, about the need to call a constitutional convention to rescue the country.

Philadelphia Oct 1, 1814

My dear Sir,

The threatening aspect of our public affairs, has deterred me from carrying my plans with regard to a voyage to Europe into execution, nor shall I now leave this country, until the storms which threaten us shall have dissipated. I have not yet entirely surrendered the opinion that peace will grow out of the pending negociations, yet the prospect has become so much clouded, as to make it perhaps a duty, to stay until the struggle shall have been terminated.

In the event of a breach of the Negociations and a probable continuance of the War, I am very desirous to possess early information of the course of measures which may be resolved on in New England, since the system to be pursued here must be almost entirely dependent on it, and since the prospect of a change in this State, tho' it may not extensively shew itself, at the ensuing elections, is believed to be more favorable than it has been at any time since the first election of Mr Jefferson.

You will have seen Campbells Reports and the wretched State of the finances. This Report makes it evident beyond all doubt that the war operations of the Government, cannot be long conducted, without the emission of a paper currency, and a heavy taxation on an impoverished people among whom industry ceases to yield the Means of bearing taxation. This taken in connexion with other considerations, which are beginning to obtain influence on the senses as well as the reason, must I think in a few Months produce a strong popular disposition for a much more rapid change of Men & Measures, than can be effected through the medium of the elections. The Manner then in which you will avail yourselves of this disposition, to save our misguided country, becomes a subject of the first importance. By means of resignation it will not I fear be effected without the application of force. A rupture of the Union, is the worst evil which could assail us, except a submission to the present order of things. And the idea of a reversion of authority to the people, by means of committees of safety, tho' it may become necessary to realize it, is dreadful in theory, and may be ruinous in practice. Is there then any course left, but that of calling a convention with power to decide on peace & war, & to make such modifications of our existing political arrangements, as shall reconcile jarring interests, secure the observance of a wise commercial policy, and establish on a sure foundation, the durability of the Union. The boldness of such a step may create objections to it, and the federalists accustomed to dread innovation, may be particularly startled at it, but if peace shall not be immediately concluded, can a less vigorous measure save us from utter destruction? Can the present organisation of the Ministerial party be in any other manner broken up. And while that organisation continues is it not evident, that every effort on our part to produce a change must be fruitless? I am aware that it will be objected that the requisite number of States cannot be induced to accede to such a measure, and I admit it is probable, that if proposed by a single State, it would not be agreed to, but I think that if a meeting of deputies from the New England States should recommend the proceeding, and the recommendation were followed up with vigour by all your Legislatures, the impulse (seconded as it would be by the danger of a separation, and the growing discontent) would prevail in all the States north of the Potomac & in the State of Ohio, if not elsewhere. I perceive no ill which could attend such an effort whether it succeed or fail. If it should succeed, the current which may enable it to do so, would be favourable to a far better organisation of the government than now exists. If it should fail, it will have put you in an attitude not the least engaging to the democrats, and will have opened views to the party in power which will teach them more strongly the danger of persisting in their system than they yet appear to feel. No man of common sense can doubt, that two years longer continuance of the War will ruin our country. Its commerce credit industry and reputation are already gone, and the paper system will revolutionise its property more than confiscation or the axe could do. Tho' in six months you should have with you a majority of the people, you may not in two years have a majority in the two houses of Congress. And possibly within that time new deceptions may produce new errours. There is no doubt Madison will hold his place to the last gasp. You will be unwilling to resort to force or to disunite. What then can you do but appeal to the Sovereign authority of the people, and in what shape can this be done so free from inconvenience, as in that of a constitutional call for a convention?

I will be much obliged my dear Sir, by your attention to these suggestions, & a full & confidential communication to me of your opinions in regard to them. Should you approve them and think they may be acted on, I will aid the efforts as far as may be in my power, and will at once endeavour to turn the attention of our Newspapers in that direction.

I pray you to present my most respectful compliments to Mrs Otis and your family and to give my most affectionate remembrance to Harry & remain with high respect

Your friend & Servt.
C. W. HARE.

John C. Sherbrooke to Henry, Earl Bathurst

Since arriving in Halifax in the autumn of 1811 to assume his duties as lieutenant governor of Nova Scotia and commander of British forces in the Maritime Provinces, Lieutenant General John C. Sherbrooke had maintained a delicate balance, rebuilding defensive fortifications and reorganizing provincial militia while avoiding any acts likely to provoke the Americans. After war came, he issued a proclamation that bordered on a declaration of neutrality, directing his people not to molest American coastal traders and pledging to respect the property and persons of peaceably inclined U.S. citizens. He also liberally authorized special licenses allowing Yankee merchants to trade at Halifax and elsewhere, bringing in much needed provisions for British garrisons. All this changed in June 1814, when Sherbrooke was ordered to attack the District of Maine (then a part of Massachusetts) and to occupy that portion "which at present intercepts the communication between Halifax and Quebec." A career soldier who had been Wellington's second in Spain, he successfully landed twenty-five hundred troops at Castine, and in the face of little resistance the British occupied the coast from Castine to Eastport, offering the local population full commercial privileges if they took a loyalty oath to the Crown. Here Sherbrooke, back in Halifax, relates to Lord Bathurst a secret communication from an agent of the Massachusetts governor, one rife with portents of an American civil war.

Halifax 20th: Novr: 1814

Duplicate.
Secret and
Confidential

My Lord:

A Gentleman who is a most respectable Inhabitant of the Country lying between the Penobscot and the Boundary Line of New Brunswick And who was a Member of the House of Representatives of the State of Massachusetts having lately been allowed to go from Castine to Boston informed M Genl.

Gosselin on his return that He had a Communication of importance to make to me which induced the Majr: General to grant him leave to come to this place.

On receiving this Gentleman (who was personally known both to Admiral Griffith & Myself at Castine) He stated that the business which he came here upon was of a very delicate nature And that he felt awkwardly situated from having no Credentials to shew, As he did not think it prudent to carry any written documents about him lest they should be discovered. He then said that He was Commissioned by the Executive of Massachusets to Communicate with me on some very important points which I desired him to Commit to writing And which I have now the honor to submit for Your Lordships Consideration neither Admiral Griffith nor Myself conceiving Ourselves Competent to discuss a subject of this magnitude without having received an especial authority so to do.

From the respectable Character of this Person & other Circumstances, Admiral Griffith & Myself have no doubt of his having been Commissioned to make the enclosed proposals on the part of the Government of Massachusets: It therefore now rests with Your Lordship to receive them or not as You may think proper under the peculiar Circumstances of the Case.

It seems the New England States are very apprehensive that If Great Britain should conclude a Peace with the general Government their interests would be sacrificed—And as the President has refused to repay the expences already incurred by the Northern Commonwealths for the purposes of defence, the Executive of Massachusets has resolved to withold all pecuniary Aid from the General Government And to apply the Amount of the Taxes raised to the defence of their own Frontier, And It is supposed that the other New England States will adopt the same line of Conduct at the Congress appointed to meet at Hartford on the 15th: of next Month to which Connecticut & Long Island have already Nominated their Delegates, But as the Legislatures of New Hampshire & Vermont are not now in Session theirs have not yet been appointed.

Notwitstanding the Custom which prevails of Calling these the "*Federal States*" It is right Your Lordship should be informed that there is a very strong democratic Party in each of these Commonwealths And as they will in the event of any attempt being made to seperate New England from the Union most probably be assisted by the General Government in resisting this Measure, It appears that the Federal Party wishes to ascertain at this early period whether Great Britain would under these Circumstances afford them Military assistance to effect their purpose should they stand in need of it.

Whether the British Government shall deem it expedient to comply with this request or not for the present, Your Lordship will I think see the good policy of sending more Troops out here immediately, to be in readiness either to oppose the Levies now raising in New England should they be inclined to act hostilely towards us, Or to assist them If the contrary policy be pursued in seperating themselves from the Union & in forming a Government of their Own.

In this state of things the importance of Our having taken possession of Castine & the territory Contiguous to it will I doubt not strike Your Lordship forcibly, As from thence Whenever the necessary arrangements are made We can supply the Federallists with everything they can require Should it be the policy of Britain to assist them in seperating from the Union, Or If Affairs take a contrary turn We have at the Penobscot a Frontier much more easy to be defended than the Old One was, Whenever a sufficient Force arrives for that purpose.

Altho' I shall be extremely happy to attend to any Instructions I may receive from Your Lordship relative to the Communication I am now transmitting And to act in any way you may be pleased to direct Yet I feel it my duty to state to Your Lordship candidly that I am unacquainted with & quite a stranger to diplomatic business—And as the subtlety of the New Englanders will require a most able Negociator to treat with them I presume to recommend that Your Lordship should under some feigned pretence send a person out here who is in Your Confidence, Well skilled in the finesse of diplomacy & thoroughly acquainted with the British Interests in this part of the World to be in readiness to take advantage of Circumstances as they occur, & taking care to conceal for the present the real purpose for which such person has been sent out.

I shall await Your Lordships Answer to this Communication

with great anxiety As It involves in its Consequences events of Considerable importance And I mean not to interfere with the Politics of the New England States in any way until I am honoured with further instructions unless Circumstances should produce an open rupture between them & the Government of the United States sooner than is expected, in which Case I shall think it my duty to afford all the assistance I am able to the former As We are actually at War with the latter.

I have the honor to be with great respect My Lord
Your Lordship's
Very Obedient and
Most humble Servant
J. C. SHERBROOKE

The Rt. Honble
The Earl Bathurst
&c &c &c

Duplicate.

This Paper the object of which is to prepare the way for Peace & Friendship between Great Britain and such States as may hereafter be disposed to pursue in good faith, a course of measures calculated to produce that desirable object, is submitted & received under the fullest pledge of Confidence,—that should any thing occur to prevent the accomplishment of that object, the Parties & Persons directly or indirectly concerned, and who may be implicated thereby, shall in no case be exposed while any evil consequences may result therefrom.

The State of Massachusets has been actuated by a strong desire not only to prevent the declaration of War by the united States against great Britain, but since that declaration has been made to embrace the earliest opportunity to bring the War to a close: Such circumstances have hitherto existed as have rendered inexpedient, a direct & decisive effort to accomplish that desirable object: If however the British Goverment does in fact entertain such Sentiments and Views, as the Goverments of New England have attributed to it, the period is now probably near, when the War may be brought to a Conclusion,—mutually advantageous to Great Britain, and to those who may concur in producing that Event.

With a View to meet the occasion, the Goverment of Massachusetts at its late Session, has appointed delegates to assemble at Hartford, in Connecticut on the 15th of December 1814, And there to meet such Delegates from the other New England States, as may be by then appointed for the purpose contemplated in the appointment of those by Massachusetts:—The States of Connecticut and Rhode Island, have already acceded to the principle of the proposed Convention, and appointed their Delegates accordingly. It is confidently expected that as soon as Expedient the other two New England States, will not for a moment hesitate to adopt the same measure.

The Ostensible objects for which this Convention is to be organized, will fully appear from the resolve of the Legislature of Massachusetts for the appointment of Delegates, by which it will be seen, that a prominent subject for deliberation is to be that of providing for the common defence and Welfare of the States represented in that Body, whose defence is neglected by the Goverment of the United States, whilst that Goverment exacts from these States the Means of Defence existing within their respective Territories, to employ them in making foreign conquest, explicitly refusing at the same time to reimburse to a State the Expences it may incur in providing for its own defence. For the purpose of providing for defence, it is contemplated that the States convened will among other things devise the necessary measures for taking into their own hands the Revenues of all kinds accruing to the general Goverment within their respective Territories, with a view to appropriate those Revenues to their own immediate and joint defence.

It will require no great degree of prescience, to forsee that this measure forced upon those States by the conduct of the general Goverment, and the law of self preservation, will necessarily lead to collision between that Goverment and these States, and also that the credit of that Goverment already greatly impaired, and always founded principally on the basis of Northern revenue, must entirely fail.

One other great subject for consideration in the Convention will probably be, the establishment in due time of a goverment for the States present, and such as may acceed afterwards, calculated to insure the pursuit of such regular and legitimate policy, as may afford security to foreign as well as domestic relations, and prevent as far as may be, a recurrence of that vascillating policy, as almost necessarily results from a Goverment entirely and immediately directed and controuled by popular caprice.

For the purpose of being prepared to operate in such manner as future exigencies may require, the Legislature of Massachusetts has authorized his Excellency the Governor to levy an Army of 10,000 regular Troops, and probably a similar measure will be adopted by the other States acceding to the Convention, according to their ability.

It will be apparent, that situated as the States must be that accede to the Convention, they will not be disposed to carry on the War longer than until it can be terminated consistently with their interest and their honor, and it will be equally apparent, that it is in the highest degree important, they should as early as possible be able to know, what is to be the relation that is to exist between them and the British Goverment. The distance between the two Countries is so great and the importance of the question growing out of this novel state of things, should it exist to the full extent contemplated, so weighty as respects those States, that it will not excite astonishment, that the earliest opportunity has been taken even before the subject is matured, to obtain such an answer as to satisfy the States in regard to the views of the British Goverment towards them. The liberal views of the Executive part of the Goverment of Massachusetts, under whose auspices this communication is made, will it is confidently presumed be fully reciprocated.

It will be understood that the object of this communication is to ascertain whether Negociation will under existing circumstances be agreeable to the British Goverment. If so, to pave the way to it, and to prepare as expeditiously as is consistent for its conclusion. The Convention not having yet been in Session, and their views not being yet certainly known, but only presumed upon (though as is believed with good reason) no precise proposition can with propriety at this time be made. Still however the views of those under whose patronage this communication is made, may perhaps afford evidence sufficiently satisfactory at this stage of what will be the eventual determination of the Convention, more especially when the importance of Massachusetts among the Northern States is considered. They extend decisively to peace and friendship upon such principles of reciprocity, as shall be calculated in any event of peace or War, to promote as far as possible, the interests of both Countries; How far there can be aid afforded directly by the States in the event of an European War, appears questionable, so long as her Colonies remain unmolested. Should those Colonies on the Continent be attacked, the States would not hesitate it is believed, to assist in the defence of them, under stipulation offensive and Defensive so far as relates to this Continent.

It is not to be concealed, that possibly, though not probably, the democracy of some one, perhaps more of the state Goverments, influenced and countenanced, by the Executive of the United States, may overcome in an Election, the best exertions of well disposed people. It will be necessary to know whether in an event of that kind, any competent Military force, can be certainly relied on, to be provided by great Britain, in aid of the present authorities of the States, or of such Goverment as may grow out of measures now in operation. This is a point of great importance, as events may turn. At the same time it must be understood that provided the force of the States is competent to preserve peace and order, prudential motives arising from the tenderness and apprehension of many at seeing British Troops in the Country, will urge strongly and conclusively against their being employed.

The Goverment of Massachusetts has observed with no small degree of satisfaction the wise and prudent course of conduct pursued by the officers commanding the Military and Naval forces of His Majesty in this quarter. It becomes however necessary to state, and it is done with extreme regret, that the order of the Admiral permitting or ordering depredations on our Coasts, has had the most painful effects on the Politics of the Eastern States, and certainly with very little benefit, perhaps none, in any point of view, to the British Interests. Indeed it is a measure pregnant with the most serious consequences to both Countries. The levying of Contributions has excited a great degree of feeling and alarm, and has undoubtedly produced a war spirit in some limited degree, where it did not exist before. It would seem that no good can possibly result from pursuing that course of warfare in the North, and certainly much evil must result from it. In almost every instance the Sufferers being Men of some property are well disposed;

Such proceedings will alienate extensively the friendly affections of good people, while the property obtained in such cases will be no object in a national point of view. If compensation can be made voluntarily in some delicate way, vast good would result from it, and to a degree that would perhaps many times counter-ballance the evil already experienced. If indeed the preservation of the good feelings of the people of this and the adjoining States towards Great Britain, be thought an object of any importance, depredation must cease on our Shore. If that mode of Warfare be thought advisable, it must operate altogether on the South. Punishment will then be brought Home to the Doors of the guilty. In that Country the British Goverment and people have no affections to lose.

There is, it is believed little room to doubt, that if these States be left unmolested, they will soon be able to establish a system of order and power, that will paralyze the Authority of the United States, and crush the baneful Democracy of the Country. The measures now ripening by means of the Convention, will soon afford a more decisive and important view of the ultimate measures proper to be taken by the British Goverment.

The Duke of Wellington to the Earl of Liverpool

On July 5, 1814, the Duke of Wellington was appointed His Majesty's Ambassador Extraordinary and Plenipotentiary to the Court of His Most Christian Majesty Louis XVIII of France. His tenure in this post, like the restored Bourbon king's first stint on the throne, would be brief and tumultuous. Upon his return to Paris in April, Louis had been greeted with relief and some affection by war-weary French *citoyens*, but by November the bloom was beginning to fade, and Napoleon's officer corps was growing increasingly disaffected, a prospect to cheer the former emperor in his exile on Elba. Amid the growing civil unrest, Wellington took a moment to offer the British prime minister his candid thoughts on the prospects for the war with America and on the impracticality of the ministry's demand for a peace based on *uti possidetis*, which would allow each side to retain whatever territory it possessed at the war's end.

MY DEAR LORD,   Paris, 9th Nov., 1814.

The messenger for England was despatched so immediately after I received your letter of the 4th, that I had not time to write to you upon many of the points which occurred to me upon it.

My safety here depends upon the King's; and although I hear every day of the discontents and of their probable result, and I have reason to believe, from a communication I have had with the Duc d'Orléans, that Blacas is inclined to give more credit to both than he has ever acknowledged to me, and that I don't see what means the King has of resisting the brisk attack of a few hundred officers determined to risk everything, I can scarcely bring my mind to give credit to so infamous a design. It is impossible, however, to conceive the distress in which individuals of all descriptions are. The only remedy is the revival of Buonaparte's system of war and plunder; and it is evident that that remedy cannot be adopted during the reign of the Bourbons. I am quite certain that the population of the country, and even of Paris, is favourable to the Bourbons.

The discontented and dangerous class are the reduced officers and employés civiles, particularly those returned from being prisoners of war; and of those the worst, especially in hatred to the English, are those who have been prisoners in England.

I am quite clear, however, that if you remove me from hence, it must be to employ me elsewhere. You cannot, in my opinion, at this moment decide upon sending me to America. In case of the occurrence of anything in Europe, there is nobody but myself in whom either yourselves or the country, or your Allies, would feel any confidence; and yet, for a great length of time, whoever you employ would have to operate upon a system which would be approved only because he who should carry it on would possess the public confidence.

If, therefore, you persist in thinking you ought to remove me from hence, you had better avail yourself of the pretence of the court martial, leaving all my establishments, &c., here; and the duration of my absence might easily be drawn on till the period at which you might see whether you could or not send me to America.

I have already told you and Lord Bathurst that I feel no objection to going to America, though I don't promise to myself much success there. I believe there are troops enough there for the defence of Canada for ever, and even for the accomplishment of any reasonable offensive plan that could be formed from the Canadian frontier. I am quite sure that all the American armies of which I have ever read would not beat out of a field of battle the troops that went from Bordeaux last summer, if common precautions and care were taken of them.

That which appears to me to be wanting in America is not a General, or General officers and troops, but a naval superiority on the Lakes. Till that superiority is acquired, it is impossible, according to my notion, to maintain an army in such a situation as to keep the enemy out of the whole frontier, much less to make any conquest from the enemy, which, with those superior means, might, with reasonable hopes of success, be undertaken. I may be wrong in this opinion, but I think the whole history of the war proves its truth; and I suspect that you will find that Prevost will justify his misfortunes, which, by the bye, I am quite certain are not what the Americans have represented them to be, by stating that the navy were defeated, and even if he had taken Fort Moreau he must have retired. The question is, whether we can acquire this naval superiority on the Lakes. If we can't, I shall do you but little good in America; and I shall go there only to prove the truth of Prevost's defence, and to sign a peace which might as well be signed now. There will always, however, remain this advantage, that the confidence which I have acquired will reconcile both the army and people in England to terms of which they would not now approve.

In regard to your present negotiations, I confess that I think you have no right from the state of the war to demand any concession of territory from America. Considering every thing, it is my opinion that the war has been a most successful one, and highly honourable to the British arms; but from particular circumstances, such as the want of the naval superiority on the Lakes, you have not been able to carry it into the enemy's territory, notwithstanding your military success, and now undoubted military superiority, and have not even cleared your own territory of the enemy on the point of attack. You cannot then, on any principle of equality in negotiation, claim a cession of territory excepting in exchange for other advantages which you have in your power.

I put out of the question the possession taken by Sir John Sherbrooke between the Penobscot and Passamaquoddy Bay. It is evidently only temporary, and till a larger force will drive away the few companies he has left there; and an officer might as well claim the sovereignty of the ground on which his piquets stand, or over which his patrols pass.

Then if this reasoning be true, why stipulate for the uti possidetis? You can get no territory; indeed the state of your military operations, however creditable, does not entitle you to demand any; and you only afford the Americans a popular and creditable ground which, I believe, their government are looking for, not to break off the negotiations, but to avoid to make peace. If you had territory, as I hope you soon will have New Orleans, I should prefer to insist upon the cession of that province as a separate article than upon the uti possidetis as a principle of negotiation.

I am sure you will excuse the liberty I take in giving you my opinion on this subject, on which government intend to employ me; but I do so only that we may thoroughly understand each other before I undertake the concern.

Believe me, &c.,

WELLINGTON.

Daniel Webster: *"Speech on the Conscription Bill"*

December 9, 1814

The Thirteenth Congress assembled for its third and final session on September 19, Madison having called it to convene earlier than usual to deal with the "great and weighty matters" confronting the nation. With the Capitol in ruins, the legislators commandeered the Patent Office, one of the few undamaged government buildings in town, which a young Federalist congressman from New Hampshire named Daniel Webster found "confined, inconvenient, and unwholesome." While the administration scrambled to reconstitute the cabinet after the resignations of the war, treasury, and navy secretaries—Secretary of State Monroe continued to do double duty, having stepped in to head the war department—its Republican supporters in Congress were divided over the monetary and military measures required to confront the crisis, most of which ran counter to the party's small-government orthodoxy. At the same time, British occupation of American territory led some Federalists to question their continued opposition to the war. Into this cauldron Monroe presented yet another plan for an invasion of Canada, estimating in an October 17 report to Congress that a hundred thousand men would be needed to prosecute the war in 1815. To reach that number, Monroe proposed a conscription plan that called for dividing all eligible males into classes of a hundred men each and requiring each class to furnish four recruits. A modified version of this plan passed the Senate, and debate turned to the House, where Webster rose to the floor to deliver the following speech.

————————

MR. CHAIRMAN: After the best reflection which I have been able to bestow on the subject of the bill before you, I am of opinion that its principles are not warranted by any provision of the Constitution. It appears to me to partake of the nature of those other propositions for military measures which this session, so fertile in inventions, has produced. It is of the same class with the plan of the Secretary of War; with the bill reported to this House by its own Committee for filling the ranks of the regular army, by classifying the free male population of the United States; and with the resolution recently introduced by an honorable gentleman from Pennsylvania (Mr. Ingersoll), and which now lies on your table, carrying the principle of compulsory service in the regular army to its utmost extent.

This bill indeed is less undisguised in its object, and less direct in its means, than some of the measures proposed. It is an attempt to exercise the power of forcing the free men of this country into the ranks of an army, for the general purposes of war, under color of a military service. To this end it commences with a classification which is no way connected with the general organization of the militia, nor, to my apprehension, included within any of the powers which Congress possesses over them. All the authority which this Government has over the militia, until actually called into its service, is to enact laws for their organization and discipline. This power it has exercised. It now possesses the further power of calling into its service any portion of the militia of the States, in the particular exigencies for which the Constitution provides, and of governing them during the continuance of such service. Here its authority ceases. The classification of the whole body of the militia, according to the provisions of this bill, is not a measure which respects either their general organization or their discipline. It is a distinct system, introduced for new purposes, and not connected with any power which the Constitution has conferred on Congress.

But, sir, there is another consideration. The services of the men to be raised under this act are not limited to those cases in which alone this Government is entitled to the aid of the militia of the States. These cases are particularly stated in the Constitution, "to repel invasion, suppress insurrection, or execute the laws." But this bill has no limitation in this respect. The usual mode of legislating on the subject is abandoned. The only section which would have confined the service of the militia, proposed to be raised, within the United States has been stricken out; and if the President should not march them into the Provinces of England at the north, or of Spain at the south, it will not be because he is prohibited by any provision in this act.

This, sir, is a bill for calling out the militia, not according to its existing organization, but by draft from new created classes;—not merely for the purpose of "repelling invasion, suppressing insurrection, or executing the laws," but for the general objects of war—for defending ourselves, or invading others, as may be thought expedient;—not for a sudden emergency, or for a short time, but for long stated periods; for two years, if the proposition of the Senate should finally prevail; for one year, if the amendment of the House should be adopted. What is this, sir, but raising a standing army out of the militia by draft, and to be recruited by draft, in like manner, as often as occasion may require?

This bill, then, is not different in principle from the other bills, plans, and resolutions which I have mentioned. The present discussion is properly and necessarily common to them all. It is a discussion, sir, of the last importance. That measures of this nature should be debated at all, in the councils of a free government, is cause of dismay. The question is nothing less than whether the most essential rights of personal liberty shall be surrendered, and despotism embraced in its worst form.

I have risen, on this occasion, with anxious and painful emotions, to add my admonition to what has been said by others. Admonition and remonstrance, I am aware, are not acceptable strains. They are duties of unpleasant performance. But they are, in my judgment, the duties which the condition of a falling State imposes. They are duties which sink deep in his conscience, who believes it probable that they may be the last services which he may be able to render to the Government of his country. On the issue of this discussion, I believe the fate of this Government may rest. Its duration is incompatible, in my opinion, with the existence of the measures in contemplation. A crisis has at last arrived, to which the course of things has long tended, and which may be decisive upon the happiness of present and of future generations. If there be anything important in the concerns of men, the considerations which fill the present hour are important. I am anxious, above all things, to stand acquitted before God and my own conscience, and in the public judgment, of all participations in the counsels which have brought us to our present condition and which now threaten the dissolution of the Government. When the present generation of men shall be swept away, and that this Government ever existed shall be matter of history only, I desire that it may be known that you have not proceeded in your course unadmonished and unforewarned. Let it then be known, that there were those who would have stopped you, in the career of your measures, and held you back, as by the skirts of your garments, from the precipice over which you are plunging and drawing after you the Government of your country.

I had hoped, sir, at an early period of the session, to find gentlemen in another temper. I trusted that the existing state of things would have impressed on the minds of those who decide national measures, the necessity of some reform in the administration of affairs. If it was not to have been expected that gentlemen would be convinced by argument, it was still not unreasonable to hope that they would listen to the solemn preaching of events. If no previous reasoning could satisfy them, that the favorite plans of Government would fail, they might yet be expected to regard the fact, when it happened, and to yield to the lesson which it taught. Although they had, last year, given no credit to those who predicted the failure of the campaign against Canada, yet they had seen that failure. Although they then treated as idle all doubts of the success of the loan, they had seen the failure of that loan. Although they then held in derision all fears for the public credit, and the national faith, they had yet seen the public credit destroyed, and the national faith violated and disgraced. They had seen much more than was predicted; for no man had foretold that our means of defence would be so far exhausted in foreign invasion, as to leave the place of our own deliberations insecure, and that we should this day be legislating in view of the crumbling monuments of our national disgrace. No one had anticipated that this city would have fallen before a handful of troops, and that British generals and British admirals would have taken their airings along the Pennsylvania Avenue, while the Government was in full flight, just awaked perhaps from one of its profound meditations on the plan of a conscription for the conquest of Canada. These events, sir, with the present state of things, and the threatening aspect of what is future, should have brought us to a pause. They might have reasonably been expected to induce Congress to review its own measures, and to exercise its great duty of inquiry relative to the conduct of others. If this was too high a pitch of virtue for the multitude of party men, it was at least to have been expected from gentlemen of influence and character, who ought to be supposed to value something higher than mere party attachment, and to act from motives somewhat nobler than a mere regard to party consistency. All that we have yet suffered will be found light and trifling in comparison with what is before us, if the Government shall learn nothing from experience but to despise it, and shall grow more and more desperate in its measures, as it grows more and more desperate in its affairs.

It is time for Congress to examine and decide for itself. It has taken things on trust long enough. It has followed executive recommendation, till there remains no hope of finding safety in that path. What is there, sir, that makes it the duty of this people now to grant new confidence to the administration, and to surrender their most important rights to its discretion? On what merits of its own does it rest this extraordinary claim? When it calls thus loudly for the treasure and the lives of the people, what pledge does it offer that it will not waste all in the same preposterous pursuits which have hitherto engaged it? In the failure of all past promises, do we see any assurance of future performance? Are we to measure out our confidence in proportion to our disgrace and now at last to grant away everything, because all that we have heretofore granted has been wasted or misapplied? What is there in our condition that bespeaks a wise or an able government? What is the evidence that the protection of the country is the object principally regarded? In every quarter that protection has been more or less abandoned to the States. That every town on the coast is not now in possession of the enemy, or in ashes, is owing to the vigilance and exertions of the States themselves, and to no protection granted to them by those on whom the whole duty of their protection rested.

Or shall we look to the acquisition of the professed objects of the war, and there find grounds for approbation and confidence. The professed objects of the war are abandoned in all due form. The contest for sailors' rights is turned into a negotiation about boundaries and military roads, and the highest hope entertained by any man of the issue, is that we may be able to get out of the war without a cession of territory.

Look, sir, to the finances of the country. What a picture do they exhibit of the wisdom and prudence and foresight of Government. "The revenue of a State," says a profound writer, "is the State." If we are to judge of the condition of the country by the condition of its revenues, what is the result? A wise government sinks deep the fountain of its revenues—not only till it can touch the first springs, and slake the present thirst of the treasury, but till lasting sources are opened, too abundant to be exhausted by demand, too deep to be affected by heats and droughts. What, sir, is our present supply, and what our provision for the future resource? I forbear to speak of the present condition of the treasury; and as to public credit, the last reliance of government, I use the language of government itself only, when I say it does not exist. This is a state of things calling for the soberest counsels, and yet it seems to meet only the wildest speculations. Nothing is talked of but banks, and a circulating paper medium, and exchequer notes, and the thousand other contrivances which ingenuity, vexed and goaded by the direst necessity, can devise, with the vain hope of giving value to mere paper. All these things are not revenue, nor do they produce it. They are the effect of a productive commerce, and a well ordered system of finance, and in their operation may be favorable to both, but are not the cause of either. In other times these facilities existed. Bank paper and government paper circulated because both rested on substantial capital or solid credit. Without these they will not circulate, nor is there a device more shallow or more mischievous, than to pour forth new floods of paper without credit as a remedy for the evils which paper without credit has already created. As was intimated the other day by my honorable friend from North Carolina (Mr. Gaston) this is an attempt to act over again the farce of the Assignats of France. Indeed, sir, our politicians appear to have but one school. They learn everything of modern France; with this variety only, that for examples of revenue they go to the Revolution, when her revenue was in the worst state possible, while their model for military force is sought after in her imperial era, when her military was organized on principles the most arbitrary and abominable.

Let us examine the nature and extent of the power which is assumed by the various military measures before us. In the present want of men and money, the Secretary of War has proposed to Congress a military conscription. For the conquest of Canada, the people will not enlist; and if they would, the treasury is exhausted, and they could not be paid. Conscription is chosen as the most promising instrument, both of overcoming reluctance to the service, and of subduing the difficulties which arise from the deficiencies of the exchequer. The administration asserts the right to fill the ranks of the regular army by compulsion. It contends that it may now take one out of every twenty-five men, and any part, or the whole of the rest, whenever its occasions require. Persons thus taken by force, and put into an army, may be compelled to serve there during the war, or for life. They may be put on any service, at home or abroad, for defence or for invasion, according to the will and pleasure of the Government. This power does not grow out of any invasion of the country, or even out of a state of war. It belongs to government at all times, in peace as well as in war, and it is to be exercised under all circumstances, according to its mere discretion. This, sir, is the amount of the principle contended for by the Secretary of War.

Is this, sir, consistent with the character of a free government? Is this civil liberty? Is this the real character of our Constitution? No, sir, indeed it is not. The Constitution is libelled, foully libelled. The people of this country have not established for themselves such a fabric of despotism. They have not purchased at a vast expense of their own treasure and their own blood a Magna Charta to be slaves. Where is it written in the Constitution, in what article or section is it contained, that you may take children from their parents, and parents from their children, and compel them to fight the battles of any war in which the folly or the wickedness of government may engage it? Under what concealment has this power lain hidden which now for the first time comes forth, with a tremendous and baleful aspect, to trample down and destroy the dearest rights of personal liberty? Who will show me any constitutional injunction which makes it the duty of the American people to surrender everything valuable in life, and even life itself, not when the safety of their country and its liberties may demand the sacrifice, but whenever the purposes of an ambitious and mischievous government may require it? Sir, I almost disdain to go to quotations and references to prove that such an abominable doctrine has no foundation in the Constitution of the country. It is enough to know that that instrument was intended as the basis of a free government, and that the power contended for is incompatible with any notion of personal liberty. An attempt to maintain this doctrine upon the provisions of the Constitution is an exercise of perverse ingenuity to extract slavery from the substance of a free government. It is an attempt to show, by proof and argument, that we ourselves are subjects of despotism, and that we have a right to chains and bondage, firmly secured to us and our children by the provisions of our government. It has been the labor of other men, at other times, to mitigate and reform the powers of government by construction; to support the rights of personal security by every species of favorable and benign interpretation, and thus to infuse a free spirit into governments not friendly in their general structure and formation to public liberty.

The supporters of the measures before us act on the opposite principle. It is their task to raise arbitrary powers, by construction, out of a plain written charter of National Liberty. It is their pleasing duty to free us of the delusion, which we have fondly cherished, that we are the subjects of a mild, free, and limited government, and to demonstrate, and to demonstrate by a regular chain of premises and conclusions, that government possesses over us a power more tyrannical, more arbitrary, more dangerous, more allied to blood and murder, more full of every form of mischief, more productive of every sort and degree of misery than has been exercised by any civilized government, with a single exception, in modern times.

The Secretary of War has favored us with an argument on the constitutionality of this power. Those who lament that such doctrines should be supported by the opinion of a high officer of government, may a little abate their regret, when they remember that the same officer, in his last letter of instructions to our ministers abroad, maintained the contrary. In that letter he declares, that even the impressment of seamen, for which many more plausible reasons may be given than for the impressment of soldiers, is repugnant to our Constitution. It might therefore be a sufficient answer to his argument, in the present case, to quote against it the sentiments of its own author, and to place the two opinions before the House, in a state of irreconcilable conflict. Further comment on either might then be properly forborne, until he should be pleased to inform us which he retracted, and to which he adhered. But the importance of the subject may justify a further consideration of the arguments.

Congress having, by the Constitution, a power to raise armies, the secretary contends that no restraint is to be imposed on the exercise of this power, except such as is expressly stated in the written letter of the instrument. In other words, that Congress may execute its powers, by any means it chooses, unless such means are particularly prohibited. But the general nature and object of the Constitution impose as rigid a restriction on the means of exercising power as could be done by the most explicit injunctions. It is the first principle applicable to such a case, that no construction shall be admitted which impairs the general nature and character of the instrument. A free constitution of government is to be construed upon free principles, and every branch of its provisions is to receive such an interpretation as is full of its general spirit. No means are to be taken by implication which would strike us absurdly if expressed. And what would have been more absurd than for this Constitution to have said that to secure the great blessings of liberty it gave to government an uncontrolled power of military conscription? Yet such is the absurdity which it is made to exhibit, under the commentary of the Secretary of War.

But it is said that it might happen that an army could not be raised by voluntary enlistment, in which case the power to raise armies would be granted in vain, unless they might be raised by compulsion. If this reasoning could prove anything, it would equally show, that whenever the legitimate power of the Constitution should be so badly administered as to cease to answer the great ends intended by them, such new powers may be assumed or usurped, as any existing administration may deem expedient. This is the result of his own reasoning, to which the secretary does not profess to go. But it is a true result. For if it is to be assumed, that all powers were granted, which might by possibility become necessary, and that government itself is the judge of this possible necessity, then the powers of government are precisely what it chooses they should be. Apply the same reasoning to any other power granted to Congress, and test its accuracy by the result. Congress has power to borrow money. How is it to exercise this power? Is it confined to voluntary loans? There is no express limitation to that effect, and, in the language of the secretary, it might happen, indeed it has happened, that persons could not be found willing to lend. Money might be borrowed then in any other mode. In other words, Congress might resort to a *forced* loan. It might take the money of any man by force, and give him in exchange exchequer notes or certificates of stock. Would this be quite constitutional, sir? It is entirely within the reasoning of the secretary, and it is a result of his argument, outraging the rights of individuals in a far less degree than the practical consequences which he himself draws from it. A compulsory loan is not to be compared, in point of enormity, with a compulsory military service.

If the Secretary of War has proved the right of Congress to enact a law enforcing a draft of men out of the militia into the regular army, he will at any time be able to prove, quite as clearly, that Congress has power to create a Dictator. The arguments which have helped him in one case, will equally aid him in the other, the same reason of a supposed or possible state necessity, which is urged now, may be repeated then, with equal pertinency and effect.

Sir, in granting Congress the power to raise armies, the people have granted all the means which are ordinary and usual, and which are consistent with the liberties and security of the people themselves, and they have granted no others. To talk about the unlimited power of the Government over the means to execute its authority, is to hold a language which is true only in regard to despotism. The tyranny of arbitrary governments consists as much in its means as in its ends; and it would be a ridiculous and absurd constitution which should be less cautious to guard against abuses in the one case than in the other. All the means and instruments which a free government exercises, as well as the ends and objects which it pursues, are to partake of its own essential character, and to be conformed to its genuine spirit. A free government with arbitrary means to administer it is a contradiction; a free government without adequate provision for personal security is an absurdity; a free government, with an uncontrolled power of military conscription, is a solecism, at once the most ridiculous and abominable that ever entered into the head of man.

Sir, I invite the supporters of the measures before you to look to their actual operation. Let the men who have so often pledged their own fortunes and their own lives to the support of this war, look to the wanton sacrifice which they are about to make of their lives and fortunes. They may talk as they will about substitutes, and compensations, and exemptions. It must come to the draft at last. If the Government cannot hire men voluntarily to fight its battles, neither can individuals. If the war should continue, there will be no escape, and every man's fate and every man's life will come to depend on the issue of the military draft. Who shall describe to you the horror which your orders of conscription shall create in the once happy villages of this country? Who shall describe the distress and anguish which they will spread over those hills and valleys, where men have heretofore been accustomed to labor, and to rest in security and happiness. Anticipate the scene, sir, when the class shall assemble to stand its draft, and to throw the dice for blood. What a group of wives and mothers and sisters, of helpless age and helpless infancy, shall gather round the theatre of this horrible lottery, as if the stroke of death were to fall from heaven before their eyes on a father, a brother, a son, or a husband. And in a majority of cases, sir, it will be the stroke of death. Under present prospects of the continuance of the war, not one half of them on whom your conscription shall fall will ever return to tell the tale of their sufferings. They will perish of disease and pestilence, or they will leave their bones to whiten in fields beyond the frontier. Does the lot fall on the father of a family? His children, already orphans, shall see his face no more. When they behold him for the last time, they shall see him lashed and fettered, and dragged away from his own threshold, like a felon and an outlaw. Does it fall on a son, the hope and the staff of aged parents? That hope shall fail them. On that staff they shall lean no longer. They shall not enjoy the happiness of dying before their children. They shall totter to their grave, bereft of their offspring and unwept by any who inherit their blood. Does it fall on a husband? The eyes which watch his parting steps may swim in tears forever. She is a wife no longer. There is no relation so tender or so sacred that by these accursed measures you do not propose to violate it. There is no happiness so perfect that you do not propose to destroy it. Into the paradise of domestic life you enter, not indeed by temptations and sorceries, but by open force and violence.

But this father, or this son, or this husband goes to the camp. With whom do you associate him? With those only who are sober and virtuous and respectable like himself? No, sir. But you propose to find him companions in the worst men of the worst sort. Another bill lies on your table offering a bounty to deserters from your enemy. Whatever is most infamous in his ranks you propose to make your own. You address your-selves to those who will hear you advise them to perjury and treason. All who are ready to set heaven and earth at defiance at the same time, to violate their oaths and run the hazard of capital punishment, and none others, will yield to your solici-tations. And these are they whom you are allowing to join your ranks, by holding out to them inducements and bounties with one hand, while with the other you are driving thither the honest and worthy members of your own community, under the lash and scourge of conscription. In the line of your army, with the true levelling of despotism, you propose a promiscu-ous mixture of the worthy and the worthless, the virtuous and the profligate; the husbandman, the merchant, the mechanic of your own country, with the beings whom war selects from the excess of European population, who possess neither inter-est, feeling, nor character in common with your own people, and who have no other recommendation to your notice than their propensity to crimes.

Nor is it, sir, for the defence of his own house and home, that he who is the subject of military draft is to perform the task allotted to him. You will put him upon a service equally foreign to his interests and abhorrent to his feelings. With his aid you are to push your purposes of conquest. The battles which he is to fight are the battles of invasion,—battles which he detests perhaps and abhors, less from the danger and the death that gather over them, and the blood with which they drench the plain, than from the principles in which they have their origin. Fresh from the peaceful pursuits of life, and yet a soldier but in name, he is to be opposed to veteran troops, hardened under every scene, inured to every privation, and disciplined in every service. If, sir, in this strife he fall—if, while ready to obey every rightful command of government, he is forced from his home against right, not to contend for the defence of his country, but to prosecute a miserable and detestable project of invasion, and in that strife he fall, 'tis murder. It may stalk above the cognizance of human law, but in the sight of Heaven it is murder; and though millions of years may roll away, while his ashes and yours lie mingled together in the earth, the day will yet come when his spirit and the spirits of his children must be met at the bar of omnipotent justice. May God, in his compassion, shield me from any participation in the enormity of this guilt.

I would ask, sir, whether the supporters of these measures have well weighed the difficulties of their undertaking. Have they considered whether it will be found easy to execute laws which bear such marks of despotism on their front, and which will be so productive of every sort and degree of misery in their execution? For one, sir, I hesitate not to say that they cannot be executed. No law professedly passed for the purpose of compelling a service in the regular army, nor any law which, under color of military draft, shall compel men to serve in the army, not for the emergencies mentioned in the Constitution, but for long periods, and for the general objects of war, can be carried into effect. In my opinion it ought not to be carried into effect. The operation of measures thus unconstitutional and illegal ought to be prevented by a resort to other measures which are both constitutional and legal. It will be the solemn duty of the State Governments to protect their own authority over their own militia, and to interpose between their citizens and arbitrary power. These are among the objects for which the State Governments exist; and their highest obligations bind them to the preservation of their own rights and the liberties of their people. I express these sentiments here, sir, because I shall express them to my constituents. Both they and myself live under a constitution which teaches us that "the doctrine of non-resistance against arbitrary power and oppression is absurd, slavish, and destructive of the good and happiness of mankind."

With the same earnestness with which I now exhort you to forbear from these measures, I shall exhort them to exercise their unquestionable right of providing for the security of their own liberties.

In my opinion, sir, the sentiments of the free population of this country are greatly mistaken here. The nation is not yet in a temper to submit to conscription. The people have too fresh and strong a feeling of the blessings of civil liberty to be willing thus to surrender it. You may talk to them as much as you please, of the victory and glory to be obtained in the enemy's provinces; they will hold those objects in light estimation if the means be a forced military service. You may sing to them the song of Canada Conquest in all its variety, but they will not be charmed out of the remembrance of their substantial interests and true happiness. Similar pretences, they know, are the grave in which the liberties of other nations have been buried, and they will take warning.

Laws, sir, of this nature can create nothing but opposition. If you scatter them abroad, like the fabled serpents' teeth, they will spring up into armed men. A military force cannot be raised in this manner, but by the means of a military force. If administration has found that it cannot form an army without conscription, it will find, if it venture on these experiments, that it cannot enforce conscription without an army. The Government was not constituted for such purposes. Framed in the spirit of liberty, and in the love of peace, it has no powers which render it able to enforce such laws. The attempt, if we rashly make it, will fail; and having already thrown away our peace, we may thereby throw away our government.

Allusions have been made, sir, to the state of things in New England, and, as usual, she has been charged with an intention to dissolve the Union. The charge is unfounded. She is much too wise to entertain such purposes. She has had too much experience, and has too strong a recollection of the blessings which the Union is capable of producing under a just administration of government. It is her greatest fear, that the course at present pursued will destroy it, by destroying every principle, every interest, every sentiment, and every feeling which have hitherto contributed to uphold it. Those who cry out that the Union is in danger are themselves the authors of that danger.

They put its existence to hazard by measures of violence, which it is not capable of enduring. They talk of dangerous designs against government, when they are overthrowing the fabric from its foundations. They alone, sir, are friends to the union of the States, who endeavor to maintain the principles of civil liberty in the country, and to preserve the spirit in which the Union was framed.

Treaty of Peace and Amity between His Britannic Majesty and the United States of America, Concluded at Ghent, December 24, 1814

Madison had seized the opportunity presented by the British terms, particularly the provision for an Indian buffer state, to drive a wedge into the opposition. He publicized his envoys' dispatches from Ghent as well as the instructions they had received just before the negotiations commenced to drop impressment as a condition—proof, as he saw it, of how reasonable his administration was and how intransigent the British were. "Mr. Madison has acted most scandalously," declared Lord Liverpool when he learned of this gambit, accusing the administration of a breach of protocol unprecedented "on the part of any civilized government." But by November, when he received Wellington's advice from Paris, the prime minister was softening. Having allowed the peace talks to stall in vain hope of good news from Ross at Baltimore and Prevost at Plattsburgh, and confronted with mounting hostility in the British press to continued war taxes, he wrote on November 18 to Castlereagh, leading the British delegation at the Congress of Vienna, that "I think we have determined, if all other points can be satisfactorily settled, not to continue the war for the purpose of obtaining or securing any acquisition of territory." With the stumbling blocks of impressment and territorial concessions removed, the delegations at Ghent reconvened on December 1, and within the month the envoys were able to resolve the remaining points of contention either by resort to status quo ante bellum—restoring, for example, the Indians to their 1811 boundaries—or, as with such issues as open access to the Mississippi and the Canadian fisheries, by ignoring them altogether in the final text of the treaty.

His Britannic Majesty and the United States of America, desirous of terminating the war which has unhappily subsisted between the two countries, and of restoring, upon principles of perfect reciprocity, peace, friendship, and good understanding between them, have for that purpose appointed their respective plenipotentiaries; that is to say, His Britannic Majesty, on his part, has appointed the right honorable James Lord Gambier, late admiral of the white, now admiral of the red squadron of His Majesty's fleet, Henry Goulburn, Esquire, a member of the Imperial Parliament, and Under Secretary of State, and William Adams, Esquire, doctor of civil laws: and the President of the United States, by and with the advice and consent of the Senate thereof, has appointed John Quincy Adams, James A. Bayard, Henry Clay, Jonathan Russell, and Albert Gallatin, citizens of the United States, who, after a reciprocal communication of their respective full powers, have agreed upon the following articles:

ARTICLE I. There shall be a firm and universal peace between His Britannic Majesty and the United States, and between their respective countries, territories, cities, towns, and people of every degree, without exception of places or persons. All hostilities, both by sea and land, shall cease as soon as this treaty shall have been ratified by both parties, as hereinafter mentioned. All territory, places, and possessions whatsoever taken by either party from the other during the war, or which may be taken after the signing of this treaty, excepting only the islands hereinafter mentioned, shall be restored without delay, and without causing any destruction or carrying away any of the artillery or other public property originally captured in the said forts or places, and which shall remain therein upon the exchange of the ratifications of this treaty, or any slaves or other private property. And all archives, records, deeds, and papers, either of a public nature or belonging to private persons, which in the course of the war may have fallen into the hands of the officers of either party, shall be, as far as may be practicable, forthwith restored and delivered to the proper authorities and persons to whom they respectively belong. Such of the islands in the bay of Passamaquoddy as are claimed by both parties shall remain in the possession of the party in whose occupation they may be at the time of the exchange of the ratifications of this treaty, until the decision respecting the title to the said islands shall have been made, in conformity with the fourth article of this treaty. No disposition made by this treaty, as to such possession of the islands and territories claimed by both parties, shall in any manner whatever be construed to affect the right of either.

ART. 2. Immediately after the ratifications of this treaty by both parties, as hereinafter mentioned, orders shall be sent to the armies, squadrons, officers, subjects, and citizens of the two Powers to cease from all hostilities; and to prevent all causes of complaint which might arise on account of the prizes which may be taken at sea after the said ratifications of this treaty, it is reciprocally agreed that all vessels and effects which may be taken after the space of twelve days from the said ratifications, upon all parts of the coast of North America, from the latitude of twenty-three degrees north to the latitude of fifty degrees north, and as far eastward in the Atlantic ocean as the thirty-sixth degree of west longitude from the meridian of Greenwich, shall be restored on each side; that the time shall be thirty days in all other parts of the Atlantic ocean north of the equinoctial line or equator, and the same time for the British and Irish channels, for the Gulf of Mexico, and all parts of the West Indies; forty days for the North seas, for the Baltic, and for all parts of the Mediterranean; sixty days for the Atlantic ocean south of the equator as far as the latitude of the Cape of Good Hope; ninety days for every part of the world south of the equator; and one hundred and twenty days for all other parts of the world, without exception.

ART. 3. All prisoners of war taken on either side, as well by land as by sea, shall be restored as soon as practicable after the ratifications of this treaty, as hereinafter mentioned, on their paying the debts which they may have contracted during their captivity. The two contracting parties respectively engage to discharge, in specie, the advances which may have been made by the other for the sustenance and maintenance of such prisoners.

ART. 4. Whereas it was stipulated by the second article in the treaty of peace of one thousand seven hundred and eighty-three between His Britannic Majesty and the United States of America, that the boundary of the United States should comprehend all islands within twenty leagues of any part of the shores of the United States, and lying between lines to be drawn due east from the points where the aforesaid boundaries between Nova Scotia on the one part, and East Florida on the other, shall respectively touch the bay of Fundy and the Atlantic ocean, excepting such islands as now are, or heretofore have been, within the limits of Nova Scotia; and whereas several islands in the bay of Passamaquoddy, which is part of the bay of Fundy, and the island of Grand Manan, in the said bay of Fundy, are claimed by the United States as being comprehended within their aforesaid boundaries, which said islands are claimed as belonging to His Britannic Majesty, as having been at the time of, and previous to, the aforesaid treaty of one thousand seven hundred and eighty-three within the limits of the province of Nova Scotia: in order, therefore, finally to decide upon these claims, it is agreed that they shall be referred to two commissioners, to be appointed in the following manner, viz: One commissioner shall be appointed by His Britannic Majesty, and one by the President of the United States, by and with the advice and consent of the Senate thereof; and the said two commissioners so appointed shall be sworn impartially to examine and decide upon the said claims according to such evidence as shall be laid before them, on the part of His Britannic Majesty and of the United States, respectively. The said commissioners shall meet at St. Andrew's, in the province of New Brunswick, and shall have power to adjourn to such other place or places as they shall think fit. The said commissioners shall, by a declaration or report under their hands and seals, decide to which of the two contracting parties the several islands aforesaid do respectively belong, in conformity with the true intent of the said treaty of peace of one thousand seven hundred and eighty-three; and if the said commissioners shall agree in their decision, both parties shall consider such decision as final and conclusive. It is further agreed, that in the event of the two commissioners differing upon all or any of the matters so referred to them, or in the event of both or either of the said commissioners refusing, or declining, or wilfully omitting to act as such, they shall make, jointly or separately, a report or reports, as well to the Government of His Britannic Majesty as to that of the United States, stating in detail the points on which they differ, and the grounds upon which their respective opinions have been formed, or the grounds upon which they, or either of them, have so refused, declined, or omitted to act. And His Britannic Majesty and the Government of the United States hereby agree to refer the report or reports of the said commissioners to some friendly Sovereign or State, to be then named for that purpose, and who shall be requested to decide on the differences which may be stated in the said report or reports, or upon the report of one commissioner, together with the grounds upon which the other commissioner shall have refused, declined, or omitted to act, as the case may be; and if the commissioner so refusing, declining, or omitting to act, shall also wilfully omit to state the grounds upon which he has so done, in such manner that the said statement may be referred to such friendly sovereign or state, together with the report of such other commissioner, then such sovereign or state shall decide *ex parte* upon the said report alone. And His Britannic Majesty and the Government of the United States engage to consider the decision of some friendly Power or state to be such and conclusive on all the matters so referred.

ART. 5. Whereas neither that point of the highlands lying due north from the source of the river St. Croix, and designated in the former treaty of peace between the two Powers as the northwest angle of Nova Scotia, nor the northwesternmost head of Connecticut river, has yet been ascertained; and whereas that part of the boundary line between the dominions of the two Powers which extends from the source of the river St. Croix, directly north, to the above-mentioned northwest angle of Nova Scotia; thence along the said highlands which divide those rivers that empty themselves into the river St. Lawrence from those which fall into the Atlantic ocean, to the northwesternmost head of Connecticut river; thence down along the middle of that river to the forty-fifth degree of north latitude; thence by a line due west on said latitude, until it strikes the river Iroquois or Cataraguy, which has not yet been surveyed: it is agreed that, for these several purposes, two commissioners shall be appointed, sworn, and authorized to act exactly in the manner directed with respect to those mentioned in the next preceding article, unless otherwise specified in the present article. The said commissioners shall meet at St. Andrew's, in the province of New Brunswick, and shall have power to adjourn to such other place or places as they shall think fit. The said commissioners shall have power to ascertain

and determine the points above mentioned, in conformity
with the provisions of the said treaty of peace of one thousand
seven hundred and eighty-three, and shall cause the boundary
aforesaid, from the source of the river St. Croix to the river
Iroquois or Cataraguy, to be surveyed and marked according
to the said provisions. The said commissioners shall make a
map of the said boundary, and annex to it a declaration under
their hands and seals, certifying it to be the true map of the
said boundary, and particularizing the latitude and longitude
of the northwest angle of Nova Scotia, of the northwesternmost head of Connecticut river, and of such other points of
the said boundary as they may deem proper; and both parties
agree to consider such map and declaration as finally and conclusively fixing the said boundary. And in the event of the said
two commissioners differing, or both or either of them refusing, or declining, or wilfully omitting to act, such reports,
declarations, or statements shall be made by them, or either of
them, and such reference to a friendly Sovereign or State shall
be made in all respects as in the latter part of the fourth article
is contained, and in as full a manner as if the same was herein
repeated.

ART. 6. Whereas, by the former treaty of peace, that portion
of the boundary of the United States from the point where the
forty-fifth degree of north latitude strikes the river Iroquois
or Cataraguy to the Lake Superior was declared to be "along
the middle of said river into Lake Ontario; through the middle of said lake, until it strikes the communication by water
between that lake and Lake Erie; thence along the middle of
said communication into Lake Erie, through the middle of said
lake, until it arrives at the water communication into the Lake
Huron; thence through the middle of said lake, to the water
communication between that lake and Lake Superior:" and
whereas doubts have arisen what was the middle of the said
river, lakes, and water communications, and whether certain
islands lying in the same were within the dominions of His
Britannic Majesty or of the United States: in order, therefore,
finally to decide these doubts, they shall be referred to two
commissioners to be appointed, sworn, and authorized to act
exactly in the manner directed with respect to those mentioned

in the next preceding article, unless otherwise specified in this present article. The said commissioners shall meet in the first instance at Albany, in the State of New York, and shall have power to adjourn to such other place or places as they shall think fit. The said commissioners shall, by a report or declaration under their hands and seals, designate the boundary through the said river, lakes, and water communications, and decide to which of the two contracting parties the several islands lying within the said river, lakes, and water communications do respectively belong, in conformity with the true intent of the said treaty of one thousand seven hundred and eighty-three; and both parties agree to consider such designation and decision as final and conclusive. And in the event of the said two commissioners differing, or both or either of them refusing, declining, or wilfully omitting to act, such reports, declarations, or statements shall be made by them, or either of them, and such reference to a friendly Sovereign or State shall be made in all respects as in the latter part of the fourth article is contained, and in as full a manner as if the same was herein repeated.

ART. 7. It is further agreed that the said two last mentioned commissioners, after they shall have executed the duties assigned to them in the preceding article, shall be, and they are hereby, authorized upon their oaths impartially to fix and determine, according to the true intent of the said treaty of peace of one thousand seven hundred and eighty-three, that part of the boundary between the dominions of the two Powers, which extends from the water communication between Lake Huron, and Lake Superior, to the most northwestern point of the Lake of the Woods, to decide to which of the two parties the several islands lying in the lakes, water communications, and rivers, forming the said boundary, do respectively belong, in conformity with the true intent of the said treaty of peace of one thousand seven hundred and eighty-three, and to cause such parts of the said boundary as require it to be surveyed and marked. The said commissioners shall, by a report or declaration under their hands and seals, designate the boundary aforesaid, state their decision on the points thus referred to them, and particularize the latitude and longitude of the most northwestern point of the Lake of the Woods, and of such other parts of the said boundary as they may deem proper; and both parties agree to consider such designation and decision as final and conclusive. And in the event of the said two commissioners differing, or both or either of them refusing, declining, or wilfully omitting to act, such reports, declarations, or statements shall be made by them, or either of them, and such reference to a friendly Sovereign or State shall be made in all respects as in the latter part of the fourth article is contained, and in as full a manner as if the same was herein repeated.

ART. 8. The several Boards of two commissioners mentioned in the four preceding articles shall respectively have power to appoint a secretary, and to employ such surveyors or other persons as they shall judge necessary. Duplicates of all their respective reports, declarations, statements, and decisions, and of their accounts, and of the journal of their proceedings, shall be delivered by them to the agents of His Britannic Majesty, and to the agents of the United States, who may be respectively appointed and authorized to manage the business on behalf of their respective Governments. The said commissioners shall be respectively paid in such manner as shall be agreed between the two contracting parties, such agreement being to be settled at the time of the exchange of the ratifications of this treaty; and all other expenses attending the said commission shall be defrayed equally by the two parties. And in the case of death, sickness, resignation, or necessary absence, the place of every such commissioner respectively shall be supplied in the same manner as such commissioner was first appointed; and the new commissioner shall take the same oath or affirmation, and do the same duties. It is further agreed between the two contracting parties, that in case any of the islands mentioned in any of the preceding articles, which were in the possession of one of the parties prior to the commencement of the present war between the two countries, should, by the decision of any of the boards of commissioners aforesaid, or of the Sovereign or State so referred to, as in the four next preceding articles contained, fall within the dominions of the other party, all grants of land made previous to the commencement of the war by the party having had such possession shall be as valid as if such island or islands had, by such decision or decisions, been adjudged to be within the dominions of the party having had such possession.

ART. 9. The United States of America engage to put an end, immediately after the ratification of the present treaty, to hostilities with all the tribes or nations of Indians with whom they may be at war at the time of such ratification, and forthwith to restore to such tribes or nations, respectively, all the possessions, rights, and privileges which they may have enjoyed, or been entitled to, in one thousand eight hundred and eleven, previous to such hostilities: provided always, that such tribes or nations shall agree to desist from all hostilities against the United States of America, their citizens and subjects, upon the ratification of the present treaty being notified to such tribes or nations, and shall so desist accordingly. And His Britannic Majesty engages, on his part, to put an end, immediately after the ratification of the present treaty, to hostilities with all the tribes or nations of Indians with whom he may be at war at the time of such ratification, and forthwith to restore to such tribes or nations, respectively, all the possessions, rights, and privileges, which they may have enjoyed, or been entitled to, in one thousand eight hundred and eleven, previous to such hostilities: provided always, that such tribes or nations shall agree to desist from all hostilities against His Britannic Majesty and his subjects, upon the ratification of the present treaty being notified to such tribes or nations, and shall so desist accordingly.

ART. 10. Whereas the traffic in slaves is irreconcilable with the principles of humanity and justice; and whereas both his Majesty and the United States are desirous of continuing their efforts to promote its entire abolition, it is hereby agreed that both the contracting parties shall use their best endeavors to accomplish so desirable an object.

ART. 11. This treaty, when the same shall have been ratified on both sides, without alteration by either of the contracting parties, and the ratifications mutually exchanged, shall be binding on both parties, and the ratifications shall be exchanged at Washington in the space of four months from this day, or sooner if practicable.

In faith whereof, we, the respective plenipotentiaries, have signed this treaty, and have hereunto affixed our seals.

Done, in triplicate, at Ghent, the twenty-fourth day of December, one thousand eight hundred and fourteen.

> GAMBIER.
> HENRY GOULBURN.
> WILLIAM ADAMS.
> JOHN QUINCY ADAMS.
> J. A. BAYARD.
> HENRY CLAY.
> JONATHAN RUSSELL.
> ALBERT GALLATIN.

Albert Gallatin to James Monroe

Though the terms of the final treaty represented a major retreat on the part of the British from their opening position, all but one of the U.S. commissioners nonetheless felt apologetic about it. (The lone exception was James A. Bayard, the only Federalist in the delegation.) Writing to his wife, Louisa Catherine, the night before the signing ceremony, John Quincy Adams confessed that he viewed the treaty more as "an unlimited armistice than a peace," one "hardly less difficult to preserve than it was to obtain." To his mother, Abigail, he was only slightly more sanguine, observing, "We have abandoned no essential right, and if we have left everything open for future controversy, we have at least secured to our country the power, at her own option to extinguish the War." Writing to James Monroe the day after the treaty was signed, Henry Clay admitted that "the terms of the instrument are undoubtedly not such as our country expected at the commencement of the war," but he insisted that when evaluated in light of "the actual condition of things, so far as it is known to us, they cannot be pronounced very unfavorable. We lose no territory, I think no honor." In his own Christmas Day letter to the secretary of state, Albert Gallatin offered a more detailed appraisal of the final terms, one especially attentive to the prevailing American concern: territorial integrity.

GHENT, December 25, 1814.

SIR,—The treaty of peace we signed yesterday with the British ministers is, in my opinion, as favorable as could be expected under existing circumstances, so far as they were known to us. The attitude taken by the State of Massachusetts, and the appearances in some of the neighboring States, had a most unfavorable effect. Of the probable result of the congress at Vienna we had no correct information. The views of all the European powers were precisely known from day to day to the British Ministry. From neither of them did we in any shape receive any intimation of their intentions, of the general prospect of Europe, or of the interest they took in our contest with

Great Britain. I have some reason to believe that all of them were desirous that it might continue. They did not intend to assist us; they appeared indifferent about our difficulties; but they rejoiced at anything which might occupy and eventually weaken our enemy. The manner in which the campaign has terminated, the evidence afforded by its events of our ability to resist alone the now very formidable military power of England, and our having been able, without any foreign assistance, and after she had made such an effort, to obtain peace on equal terms, will raise our character and consequence in Europe. This, joined with the naval victories and the belief that we alone can fight the English on their element, will make us to be courted as much as we have been neglected by foreign governments. As to the people of Europe, public opinion was most decidedly in our favor. I anticipate a settlement with Spain on our own terms, and the immediate chastisement of the Algerines. Permit me to suggest the propriety of despatching a squadron for that purpose without losing a single moment. I have little to add to our public despatch on the subject of the terms of the treaty. I really think that there is nothing but nominal in the Indian article as adopted. With respect to precedents, you will find two, though neither is altogether in point, viz.: the article of the Treaty of Utrecht, and the latter part of the article of our treaty with Spain. You know that there was no alternative between breaking off the negotiations and accepting the article, and that we accepted it only as provisional and subject to your approbation or rejection. The exception of Moose Island from the general restoration of territory is the only point on which it is possible that we might have obtained an alteration if we had adhered to our opposition to it. The British government had long fluctuated on the question of peace: a favorable account from Vienna, the report of some success in the Gulf of Mexico, or any other incident, *might* produce a change in their disposition; they had already, after the question had been referred to them, declared that they could not consent to a relinquishment of that point. We thought it too hazardous to risk the peace on the question of the temporary possession of that small island, since the question of title was fully reserved, and it was therefore no cession of territory. On the subject of the fisheries within the jurisdiction of Great Britain, we have certainly done all that could be done. If, according to the construction of the treaty of 1783, which we assumed, the right was not abrogated by the war, it remains entire, since we most explicitly refused to renounce it directly or indirectly. In that case it is only an unsettled subject of difference between the two countries. If the right must be considered as abrogated by the war, we cannot regain it without an equivalent. We had none to give but the recognition of their right to navigate the Mississippi, and we offered it on this last supposition. This right is also lost to them, and in a general point of view we have certainly lost nothing. But we have done all that was practicable in support of the right to those fisheries, 1, by the ground we assumed respecting the construction of the treaty of 1783; 2, by the offer to recognize the British right to the navigation of the Mississippi; 3, by refusing to accept from Great Britain both her implied renunciation to the right of that navigation and the convenient boundary of 49 degrees for the whole extent of our and her territories west of the Lake of the Woods, rather than to make an implied renunciation on our own part to the right of America to those particular fisheries. I believe that Great Britain is very desirous of obtaining the northern part of Maine, say from about 47 north latitude to the northern extremity of that district as claimed by us. They hope that the river which empties into Bay des Chaleurs, in the Gulf of St. Lawrence, has its source so far west as to intervene between the head-waters of the river St. John and those of the streams emptying into the river St. Lawrence: so that the line north from the source of the river St. Croix will first strike the heights of land which divide the waters emptying into the Atlantic Ocean (river St. John's) from those emptying into the Gulf of St. Lawrence (River des Chaleurs), and afterwards the heights of land which divide the waters emptying into the Gulf of St. Lawrence (River des Chaleurs) from those emptying into the river St. Lawrence; but that the said line never can, in the words of the treaty, strike any spot of land actually dividing the waters emptying into the Atlantic Ocean from those which fall into the river St. Lawrence. Such will be the foundation of their disputing our claim to the northern part of that territory; but, feeling that it is not very solid, I am apt to think that they will be disposed to offer the whole of Passamaquoddy Bay and the disputed fisheries as an equivalent for this portion of northern territory, which they want in order to connect New Brunswick and Quebec. This may account for their tenacity with respect to the temporary possession of Moose Island, and for their refusing to accept the recognition of their right to the navigation of the Mississippi, provided they recognized ours to the fisheries. That northern territory is of no importance to us, and belongs to the United States, and not to Massachusetts, which has not the shadow of a claim to any land north of 45 to the eastward of the Penobscot River, as you may easily convince yourself of by recurring to her charters.

I have the honor to be, with respect, &c.

ALBERT GALLATIN.

The Hon. the Secretary of State
of the United States, Washington.

The Earl of Liverpool to George Canning

While the British and American commissioners were negotiating at Ghent, the future of Europe was being charted at the Congress of Vienna. There Viscount Castlereagh, the British foreign secretary, faced a legion of challenges, not least the ambitions of Tsar Alexander I of Russia who, like subsequent invaders from the east, was reluctant to relinquish the leverage he had gained when his armies marched across Poland and into the heart of the Continent. While Castlereagh sought to forge a united front against Alexander, the Tsar and the foreign ministers of the other European powers looked to the war in America as a welcome distraction that diminished Britain's power and influence. The Viscount was therefore quite heartened when informed by Liverpool of the final peace treaty, calling it a "most auspicious and seasonable event" and congratulating the prime minister on at last "being released from the millstone of an American war." Liverpool also shared the news with Castlereagh's bitter rival, George Canning, who had himself been foreign secretary from 1807 to 1809 and who was now ambassador to Portugal.

Fife House, 28th Dec., 1814.

MY DEAR CANNING,

I have received your private letters of the 9th inst. I am sorry to find that you should have been visited at Lisbon by a fit of the gout. As a warm climate has, however, generally been found to be the most effectual remedy for this disorder, I trust the next packet will bring us an account of your entire recovery.

You will hear by this conveyance of the restoration of peace between this country and the United States of America. The general nature of the terms is accurately stated in the public papers. I will endeavour to send you a copy of the treaty by the next packet.

You know how anxious I was that we should get out of this war as soon as we could do so with honour. This anxiety was increased by communications which I had (after you left London) with the Duke of Wellington. He had agreed to take the command of the army in the ensuing campaign, if the war should continue; but he was particularly solicitous for peace, being fully satisfied that there was no vulnerable point of importance belonging to the United States which we could hope to take and hold except New Orleans, and this settlement is one of the most unhealthy in any part of America.

We might certainly land in different parts of their coast, and destroy some of their towns, or put them under contribution; but in the present state of the public mind in America it would be in vain to expect any permanent good effects from operations of this nature.

The continuance of the war for the purpose of obtaining a better frontier for Canada would, I am persuaded, have been found impracticable; for when that question came to be argued, it would be stated, and stated with truth, that no additional frontier which you could possibly expect to obtain would materially add to the security of Canada.

The weakness of Canada consists in this: that the United States possess 7,500,000 people; the two Canadas not more than 300,000. That the government of the United States have access to Canada at all times of the year, whereas Great Britain is excluded from such access for nearly six months. As long as we have the larger and better army we shall be able to defend the country, notwithstanding all these disadvantages; but the frontier must in any case be of such prodigious extent that it never could be made, as frontier, defensible against the means which the Americans might bring against it.

In addition to these considerations, we could not overlook the clamour which has been raised against the property-tax, and the difficulties we shall certainly have in continuing it for one year, to discharge the arrears of the war.

From all I have heard, I do not believe it would have been possible to have continued it for the purpose of carrying on an American war, even though the negotiation had turned upon points on which persons were more generally agreed than on the question of Canadian boundary.

The question therefore was whether, under all these circumstances, it was not better to conclude the peace at the present moment, before the impatience of the country on the subject had been manifested at public meetings or by motions in Parliament, provided we could conclude it by obliging the American Commissioners to waive all stipulations whatever on the subject of maritime rights, by fulfilling our engagements to the Indians who were abandoned in the Treaty of 1783, and by declining to revive in favour of the United States any of the commercial advantages which they enjoyed under former treaties. As far as I have any means of judging, our decision is generally approved.

I wrote to Bristol and Liverpool the night the treaty arrived. I have had a most satisfactory answer this morning from Bristol, both respecting the peace and the terms of it. I shall probably hear from your friend Gladstone by the post on Friday.

The negotiations at Vienna are not proceeding in the way we could wish. Not that I think there is any chance of their leading to hostilities, but a great deal of irritation will, I fear, remain; and this consideration itself was deserving of some weight in deciding the question of peace with America.

Fortunately for us the fate of the Low Countries was decided by a secret article in the Treaty of Paris. We are not apprehensive therefore of any serious difficulty on this point.

The question likewise respecting the annexation of Genoa, under certain conditions, to the King of Sardinia's dominions, has been arranged to the satisfaction of all parties, even to that of the representative of the state of Genoa at Vienna.

The negotiations respecting Switzerland are likewise in a favourable course, and all might therefore have ended smoothly and well (except, perhaps, the very difficult question of Naples) if it had not been for the extravagant pretensions of the Emperor of Russia regarding Poland. On this subject we have only a distant and contingent interest, and we must endeavour to prevent the differences respecting it leading to a renewal of war on the Continent. It is a curious circumstance that all the Russians are against the Emperor. He does not even venture to trust them with the correspondence which passes through Prince Czartoriski, who at present holds no official situation under him.

I am persuaded, from all I hear, that the Emperor of Russia will never be able to carry his own views and promises respecting Poland into execution. The Russians never will submit to the Polish provinces (which have been incorporated with Russia) being severed again from the Russian Empire and reunited to the Duchy of

Warsaw for the purpose of forming a kingdom of Poland. They will not be reconciled to it on the plea of the Sovereign being their own Emperor. Nay, some say that they would prefer the alternative (if Poland is to be reconstructed) that it should be reconstructed under an independent Sovereign.

If the Emperor of Russia cannot carry into effect the expectations he has held out to the Poles in this respect, they will be grievously disappointed, and he will not have accomplished the purpose of making them faithful and attached subjects. In short, in whatever way the affairs of Poland can now be settled, they will afford ample ground for war and confusion hereafter.

I think of going to Bath for a fortnight about the beginning of next week. We must look forward to a very active session. I have not seen for several years so much party animosity as appeared during the three weeks of November whilst Parliament was sitting.

A great struggle will probably take place on the Property-Tax. I hope we shall be able to carry it for a year: in which case, if peace continues, substitutes may be found, though none in my judgment so equal and just; but many of the persons who have been praising the tax for the last ten years as the greatest discovery in finance, are now the most loud in disapproving and objecting to the continuance of it.

I send you a copy of the treaty with America, a few copies of which, for the sake of convenience, have been printed at the private press in the Foreign Office. As the treaty cannot, however, properly be published until the ratifications of it are exchanged, I shall be obliged to you if you will not let this copy go out of your own hands.

I shall be most happy to hear that Mrs. Canning and your family are well, and have not suffered in consequence of the passage, and particularly how the climate agrees with your eldest son, and whether you think he gains ground in consequence of it.

Believe me, yours, &c.

LIVERPOOL.

George R. Gleig: *from* The Campaigns of the British Army at Washington and New Orleans, 1814–15

The signing of the Treaty of Ghent did not bring about an immediate truce, for two reasons. The first was purely practical: even by the fastest ship it usually took six weeks for news to cross the Atlantic. The second was procedural: having three times entered into treaties with the United States only to have the President or the Senate demand changes before ratification (in 1794, 1803, and 1806), the British government this time stipulated that hostilities would cease only when both sides had ratified the agreement. Anthony Baker, the secretary to the British delegation, sped a copy to London, where the prince regent ratified it on December 27, but it and the American copy would not reach New York until February 11, 1815. So the fighting would continue. Alexander Cochrane had early identified the Chesapeake and New Orleans as the places "where the Americans are most vulnerable." Having menaced the former throughout the spring and summer of 1814, in autumn he turned his attention toward the latter. Initially conceived as a way of taking pressure off Canada, the expedition against New Orleans took on greater strategic significance as the peace talks at Ghent got underway. General Ross, who was supposed to lead it, had been instructed "to obtain command of the embouchure [mouth] of the Mississippi, so as to deprive the back settlements of America of their communication with the sea." On November 26, Cochrane's armada of more than sixty vessels sailed from the expedition's staging site at Jamaica, carrying an invasion force ten thousand strong under Major General John Keane, who assumed temporary command after Ross's death. Among its ranks was Captain George Gleig.

New Orleans is a town of some note, containing from twenty to thirty thousand inhabitants. It stands upon the eastern bank of the Mississippi, in 30° north latitude, and about 110 miles from the Gulf of Mexico. Though in itself unfortified, it is difficult to conceive a place capable of presenting greater obstacles to an invader; and at the same time more conveniently situated with respect to trade. Built upon a narrow neck of land, which is confined on one side by the river, and on the other by impassable morasses, its means of defence require little explanation; and as these morasses extend to the distance of only a few miles, and are succeeded by Lake Pontchartrain, which again communicates through Lake Borgne* with the sea, its peculiar commercial advantages must be equally apparent. It is by means of the former of these Lakes, indeed, that intercourse is maintained between the city and the northern parts of West Florida, of which it is the capital; a narrow creek, called, in the language of the country, a Bayo or Bayouke, navigable for vessels drawing less than six feet water, running up through the marsh, and ending within two miles of the town. The name of this creek is the Bayouke of St. John, and its entrance is defended by works of considerable strength.

But to exhibit its advantages in a more distinct point of view, it will be necessary to say a few words respecting that mighty river upon which it stands. The Mississippi, (a corruption of the word Mechasippi, signifying, in the language of the natives, "the father of rivers,") is allowed to be inferior, in point of size and general navigability, to few streams in the world. According to the Sioux Indians, it takes its rise from a large swamp, and is increased by many rivers emptying themselves into its course as far as the fall of St. Anthony, which, by their account, is upwards of seven hundred leagues from its source. But this fall, which is formed by a rock thrown across the channel, of about twelve feet perpendicular height, is known to be eight hundred leagues from the sea; and therefore the whole course of the Mississippi, from its spring to its mouth, may be computed at little short of 5000 miles.

Below the fall of St. Anthony, again, the Mississippi is joined by a number of rivers considerable in point of size, and leading out of almost every part of the continent of America. These

---

*These are, properly speaking, one and the same lake. From the entrance, however, as far as Ship Island, is called by the inhabitants Lake Borgne, whilst all above that point goes under the name of Lake Pontchartrain. They are both extremely shallow, varying from 12 to 6 feet in depth.

are the St. Pierre, which comes from the west; St. Croix, from the east; the Moingona, which is said to run 150 leagues from the west, and forms a junction about 250 below the fall; and the Illinois, which rises near the Lake Michigan, 200 leagues east of the Mississippi.

But by far the most important of these auxiliary streams is the Missouri, the source of which is as little known as that of the Father of Rivers himself. It has been followed by traders upwards of 400 leagues, who traffic with the tribes which dwell upon its banks, and obtain an immense return for European goods. The mouth of this river is five leagues below that of the Illinois, and is supposed to be 800 from its source, which, judging from the flow of its waters, lies in a north-west direction from the Mississippi. It is remarkable enough, that the waters of this river are black and muddy, and prevail over those of the Mississippi, which, running with a clear and gentle stream till it meets with this addition, becomes from that time both dark and rapid.

The next river of note is the Ohio, which, taking its rise near Lake Erie, runs from the north-east to the south-west, and joins the Mississippi about seventy leagues below the Missouri. Besides this, there are the St. Francis, an inconsiderable stream, and the Arkansas, which is said to originate in the same latitude with Santa Fé in New Mexico, and which, holding its course nearly 300 leagues, falls in about 200 above New Orleans. Sixty leagues below the Arkansas, comes the Yazous from the north-east; and about fifty-eight nearer to the city is the Rouge, so called from the colour of its waters, which are of a reddish dye, and tinge those of the Mississippi at the time of the floods. Its source is in New Mexico, and after running about 200 leagues it is joined by the Noir thirty miles above the place where it empties itself into the Mississippi.

Of all these rivers, there is none which will not answer the purposes of commerce, at least to a very considerable extent; and as they join the Mississippi above New Orleans, it is evident that this city may be considered as the general mart of the whole. Whatever nation, therefore, chances to possess this place, possesses in reality the command of a greater extent of country than is included within the boundary line of the whole United States; since from every direction are goods, the produce of East, West, North, and South America, sent down by the Mississippi to the Gulf. But were New Orleans properly supplied with fortifications, it is evident that no vessels could pass without the leave of its governor; and therefore is it that I consider that city as of greater importance to the American government, than any other within the compass of their territories.

———————

Such are the advantages of New Orleans; and now it is only fair that I should state its disadvantages: these are owing solely to the climate. From the swamps with which it is surrounded, there arise, during the summer months, exhalations extremely fatal to the health of its inhabitants. For some months of the year, indeed, so deadly are the effects of the atmosphere, that the garrison is withdrawn, and most of the families retire from their houses to more genial spots, leaving the town as much deserted as if it had been visited by a pestilence. Yet, in spite of these precautions, agues and intermittent fevers abound here at all times. Nor is it wonderful that the case should be so; for independent of the vile air which the vicinity of so many putrid swamps occasions, this country is more liable than perhaps any other to sudden and severe changes of temperature. A night of keen frost, sufficiently powerful to produce ice a quarter of an inch in thickness, frequently follows a day of intense heat; whilst heavy rains and bright sunshine often succeed each other several times in the course of a few hours. But these changes, as may be supposed, occur only during the winter; the summer being one continued series of intolerable heat and deadly fog.

Of all these circumstances, the conductors of the present expedition were not ignorant. To reduce the forts which command the navigation of the river, was regarded as a task too difficult to be attempted; and for any ships to pass without their reduction, seemed impossible. Trusting, therefore, that the object of the enterprize was unknown to the Americans, Sir Alexander Cochrane and General Keane determined to effect a landing somewhere on the banks of the Lake; and pushing directly on, to take possession of the town, before any effectual preparation could be made for its defence. With this view the troops were removed from the larger into the lighter vessels, and these, under convoy of such gun-brigs as the shallowness of the water would float, began on the 13th to enter Lake Borgne. But we had not proceeded far, when it was apparent that the Americans were well acquainted with our intentions, and ready to receive us.

Thomas ap Catesby Jones to Daniel T. Patterson

How had the British lost the element of surprise? Their complicated invasion plan had begun in August with the establishment of forward bases in Spanish West Florida, at Pensacola and on the Apalachicola River. From there, they launched an unsuccessful attack in mid-September on Fort Bowyer, which guarded the entrance to Mobile Bay. This foray signaled to Andrew Jackson—in command of the region after his humbling of the Creeks—that the British had a larger operation planned for the Gulf coast. His first action, on November 7, was to dislodge the British from Pensacola—warnings from Washington not to risk war with Spain arrived too late to deter him—and there he was informed by a merchant fresh from Jamaica that New Orleans was the British target. Jackson raced his troops to the Crescent City, arriving there on December 1 to find its defenses weak. Further intelligence came when local pirates revealed that the British had sought to line them up as allies. While Jackson hastily mobilized defenses on land, responsibility for protecting the many water approaches fell to Master Commandant Daniel Todd Patterson. To Lake Borgne, an inlet of the Gulf that guarded the crucial approach of Bayou Bienvenu, Patterson dispatched Thomas ap Catesby Jones, who with 175 men on just five gunboats and two small schooners (carrying 23 guns in all) would confront a British force of forty barges bearing 42 guns and one thousand men.

New Orleans, 12th *March*, 1815.

SIR,

Having sufficiently recovered my strength, I do myself the honour of reporting to you the particulars of the capture of the division of United States' gun-boats late under my command.

On the 12th December, 1814, the enemy's fleet off Ship island increased to such a force as to render it no longer safe or prudent for me to continue on that part of the lakes with the small force which I commanded. I therefore determined to gain a station near the Malhereux islands as soon as possible, which situation would better enable me to oppose a further penetration of the enemy up the lakes, and at the same time afford me an opportunity of retreating to the Petite Coquilles if necessary.

At 10, A.M. on the 13th I discovered a large flotilla of barges had left the fleet, (shaping their course towards the Pass Christian) which I supposed to be a disembarkation of troops intended to land at that place. About 2, P.M. the enemy's flotilla having gained the Pass Christian, and continuing their course to the westward, convinced me that an attack on the gun-boats was designed. At this time the water in the lakes was uncommonly low, owing to the westerly wind which had prevailed for a number of days previous, and which still continued from the same quarter. Nos. 156, 162 and 163, although in the best channel, were in 12 or 18 inches less water than their draught. Every effort was made to get them afloat by throwing overboard all articles of weight that could be dispensed with. At 3 30, the flood-tide had commenced; got under weigh, making the best of my way towards the Petite Coquilles. At 3 45, the enemy despatched three boats to cut out the schooner Seahorse, which had been sent into the bay St. Louis that morning to assist in the removal of the public stores, which I had previously ordered. There finding a removal impracticable, I ordered preparations to be made for their destruction, least they should fall into the enemy's hands. A few discharges of grape-shot from the Seahorse compelled the three boats, which had attacked her, to retire out of reach of her gun, until they were joined by four others, when the attack was recommenced by the seven boats. Mr. Johnson having chosen an advantageous position near the two six-pounders mounted on the bank, maintained a sharp action for near 30 minutes, when the enemy hauled off, having one boat apparently much injured, and with the loss of several men killed and wounded. At 7 30, an explosion at the bay, and soon after a large fire, induced me to believe the Seahorse was blown up and the public storehouse set on fire, which has proved to be the fact.

About 1 A.M. on the 14th, the wind having entirely died away, and our vessels become unmanageable, came to anchor in the west end of Malheureux island's passage. At daylight next morning, still a perfect calm, the enemy's flotilla was about nine miles from us at anchor, but soon got in motion and rapidly advanced on us. The want of wind, and the strong ebb-tide which was setting through the pass, left me but one alternative; which was, to put myself in the most advantageous position, to give the enemy as warm a reception as possible. The commanders were all called on board and made acquainted with my intentions, and the position which each vessel was to take, the whole to form a close line abreast across the channel, anchored by the stern with springs on the cable, &c. &c. Thus we remained anxiously awaiting an attack from the advancing foe, whose force I now clearly distinguished to be composed of forty-two heavy lanches and gun-barges, with three light gigs, manned with upwards of one thousand men and officers. About 9 30, the Alligator (tender) which was to the southward and eastward, and endeavouring to join the division, was captured by several of the enemy's barges, when the whole flotilla came to, with their grampnels a little out of reach of our shot, apparently making arrangements for the attack—At 10 30, the enemy weighed, forming a line abreast in open order, and steering direct for our line, which was unfortunately in some degree broken by the force of the current, driving Nos. 156 and 163 about one hundred yards in advance. As soon as the enemy came within reach of our shot, a deliberate fire from our long guns was opened upon him, but without much effect, the objects being of so small a size. At 10 minutes before 11, the enemy opened a fire from the whole of his line, when the action became general and destructive on both sides. About 11 49, the advance boats of the enemy, three in number, attempted to board No. 156, but were repulsed with the loss of nearly every officer killed or wounded, and two boats sunk.— A second attempt to board was then made by four other boats, which shared almost a similar fate. At this moment I received a severe wound in my left shoulder, which compelled me to quit the deck, leaving it in charge of Mr. George Parker, master's-mate, who gallantly defended the vessel until he was severely wounded, when the enemy, by his superior number, succeeded in gaining possession of the deck about 10 minutes past 12 o'clock. The enemy immediately turned the guns of his prize on the other gun-boats, and fired several shot previous to striking the American colours. The action continued with un-abating severity until 40 minutes past 12 o'clock, when it terminated with the surrender of No. 23, all the other vessels having previously fallen into the hands of the enemy.

In this unequal contest our loss in killed and wounded has been trifling, compared to that of the enemy.

Enclosed you will receive a list of the killed and wounded, and a correct statement of the force which I had the honour to command at the commencement of the action, together with an estimate of the force I had to contend against, as acknowledged by the enemy, which will enable you to decide how far the honour of our country's flag has been supported in this conflict.

I have the honour to be, &c.

(Signed)   THOMAS AP CATESBY JONES.

Harrison Gray Otis and Fellow Delegates from New England: Report and Resolutions of the Hartford Convention

January 6, 1815

Even as a major confrontation loomed in New Orleans, the political opposition to the war entered a dramatic new phase fifteen hundred miles away, in Hartford, Connecticut. The War of 1812 had been a partisan affair from the start, and throughout its course Federalists in Congress had maintained an extraordinary level of cohesion born of the shared conviction that the war had been launched for cynical political purposes. "I regard the war, as a war of party, & not of the Country," Rufus King had said in 1812. Though Federalists everywhere were opposed to the war, those in New England were the most strident, and only there were they able to use the machinery of state and local government to obstruct the war effort, especially by resisting federal demands to mobilize and direct militia. On October 5, 1814, Massachusetts governor Caleb Strong addressed a special session of the state legislature convened to deal with the British invasion of Maine and the administration's refusal to reimburse the state for the costs of its defense. From this session came a call for a convention—a time-honored American custom in times of trouble—where representatives of the New England states could air their grievances. Connecticut and Rhode Island answered Massachusetts's call, as did delegates from three counties in New Hampshire and Vermont, and from December 15 to January 5 the convention met in secret in the Old State House in Hartford. Its final report, principally authored by Harrison Gray Otis of Boston, offered a series of proposals to address not only the crisis at hand, but also the very structures of government that had enabled the Republicans to dominate national politics since 1801.

The delegates from the legislatures of the states of Massachusetts, Connecticut, and Rhode-Island, and from the counties of Grafton and Cheshire in the state of New-Hampshire and the county of

Windham in the state of Vermont, assembled in convention, beg leave to report the following result of their conference.

The convention is deeply impressed with a sense of the arduous nature of the commission which they were appointed to execute, of devising the means of defence against dangers, and of relief from oppressions proceeding from the acts of their own government, without violating constitutional principles, or disappointing the hopes of a suffering and injured people. To prescribe patience and firmness to those who are already exhausted by distress, is sometimes to drive them to despair, and the progress towards reform by the regular road, is irksome to those whose imaginations discern, and whose feelings prompt, to a shorter course. But when abuses, reduced to a system, and accumulated through a course of years, have pervaded every department of government, and spread corruption through every region of the state; when these are clothed with the forms of law, and enforced by an executive whose will is their source, no summary means of relief can be applied without recourse to direct and open resistance. This experiment, even when justifiable, cannot fail to be painful to the good citizen; and the success of the effort will be no security against the danger of the example. Precedents of resistance to the worst administration, are eagerly seized by those who are naturally hostile to the best. Necessity alone can sanction a resort to this measure; and it should never be extended in duration or degree beyond the exigency, until the people, not merely in the fervour of sudden excitement, but after full deliberation, are determined to change the constitution.

It is a truth, not to be concealed, that a sentiment prevails to no inconsiderable extent, that administration have given such constructions to that instrument, and practised so many abuses under colour of its authority, that the time for a change is at hand. Those who so believe, regard the evils which surround them as intrinsic and incurable defects in the constitution. They yield to a persuasion, that no change, at any time, or on any occasion, can aggravate the misery of their country. This opinion may ultimately prove to be correct. But as the evidence on which it rests is not yet conclusive, and as measures adopted upon the assumption of its certainty might be irrevocable, some general considerations are submitted, in the hope of reconciling all to a course of moderation and firmness, which may save them from the regret incident to sudden decisions, probably avert the evil, or at least insure consolation and success in the last resort.

The constitution of the United States, under the auspices of a wise and virtuous administration, proved itself competent to all the objects of national prosperity comprehended in the views of its framers. No parallel can be found in history, of a transition so rapid as that of the United States from the lowest depression to the highest felicity—from the condition of weak and disjointed republics, to that of a great, united, and prosperous nation.

Although this high state of public happiness has undergone a miserable and afflicting reverse, through the prevalence of a weak and profligate policy, yet the evils and afflictions which have thus been induced upon the country, are not peculiar to any form of government. The lust and caprice of power, the corruption of patronage, the oppression of the weaker interests of the community by the stronger, heavy taxes, wasteful expenditures, and unjust and ruinous wars, are the natural offspring of bad administrations, in all ages and countries. It was indeed to be hoped, that the rulers of these states would not make such disastrous haste to involve their infancy in the embarrassments of old and rotten institutions. Yet all this have they done; and their conduct calls loudly for their dismission and disgrace. But to attempt upon every abuse of power to change the constitution, would be to perpetuate the evils of revolution.

Again, the experiment of the powers of the constitution to regain its vigour, and of the people to recover from their delusions, has been hitherto made under the greatest possible disadvantages arising from the state of the world. The fierce passions which have convulsed the nations of Europe, have passed the ocean, and finding their way to the bosoms of our citizens, have afforded to administration the means of perverting public opinion, in respect to our foreign relations, so as to acquire its aid in the indulgence of their animosities, and the increase of their adherents. Further, a reformation of public opinion, resulting from dear-bought experience, in the southern Atlantic states, at least, is not to be despaired of. They will have felt, that the eastern states cannot be made exclusively the victims of a capricious and impassioned policy. They will have seen that the great and essential interests of the people are common to the south and to the east. They will realize the fatal errors of a system which seeks revenge for commercial injuries in the sacrifice of commerce, and aggravates by needless wars, to an immeasurable extent, the injuries it professes to redress. They may discard the influence of visionary theorists, and recognize the benefits of a practical policy. Indications of this desirable revolution of opinion, among our brethren in those states, are already manifested. While a hope remains of its ultimate completion, its progress should not be retarded or stopped, by exciting fears which must check these favourable tendencies, and frustrate the efforts of the wisest and best men in those states, to accelerate this propitious change.

Finally, if the Union be destined to dissolution, by reason of the multiplied abuses of bad administrations, it should, if possible, be the work of peaceable times, and deliberate consent. Some new form of confederacy should be substituted among those states which shall intend to maintain a federal relation to each other. Events may prove that the causes of our calamities are deep and permanent. They may be found to proceed, not merely from the blindness of prejudice, pride of opinion, violence of party spirit, or the confusion of the times; but they may be traced to implacable combinations of individuals, or of states, to monopolize power and office, and to trample without remorse upon the rights and interests of commercial sections of the Union. Whenever it shall appear that these causes are radical and permanent, a separation, by equitable arrangement, will be preferable to an alliance by constraint, among nominal friends, but real enemies, inflamed by mutual hatred and jealousy, and inviting, by intestine divisions, contempt and aggression from abroad. But a severance of the Union by one or more states, against the will of the rest, and especially in a time of war, can be justified only by absolute necessity. These are among the principal objections against precipitate measures tending to disunite the states, and when examined in connection with the farewell address of the Father of his country, they must, it is believed, be deemed conclusive.

Under these impressions, the convention have proceeded to confer and deliberate upon the alarming state of public affairs, especially as affecting the interests of the people who have appointed them for this purpose, and they are naturally led to a consideration, in the first place, of the dangers and grievances which menace an immediate or speedy pressure, with a view of suggesting means of present relief; in the next place, of such as are of a more remote and general description, in the hope of attaining future security.

Among the subjects of complaint and apprehension, which might be comprised under the former of these propositions, the attention of the convention has been occupied with the claims and pretensions advanced, and the authority exercised over the militia, by the executive and legislative departments of the national government. Also, upon the destitution of the means of defence in which the eastern states are left; while at the same time they are doomed to heavy requisitions of men and money for national objects.

The authority of the national government over the militia is derived from those clauses in the constitution which give power to Congress "to provide for calling forth the militia to execute the laws of the Union, suppress insurrections and repel invasions;"—Also "to provide for organizing, arming, and disciplining the militia, and for governing such parts of them as may be employed in the service of the United States, reserving to the states respectively the appointment of the officers, and the authority of training the militia according to the discipline prescribed by Congress." Again, "the President shall be commander in chief of the army and navy of the United States, and of the militia of the several states, *when called into the actual service of the United States.*" In these specified cases only, has the national government any power over the militia; and it follows conclusively, that for all general and ordinary purposes, this power belongs to the states respectively, and to them alone. It is not only with regret, but with astonishment, the convention perceive that under colour of an authority conferred with such plain and precise limitations, a power is arrogated by the executive government, and in some instances sanctioned by the two houses of congress, of control over the militia, which if conceded will render nugatory the rightful authority of the individual states over that class of men, and by placing at the disposal of the national government the lives and services of the great body of the people, enable it at pleasure to destroy their liberties, and erect a military despotism on the ruins.

The last inquiry, what course of conduct ought to be adopted by the aggrieved states, is in a high degree momentous. When a great and brave people shall feel themselves deserted by their government, and reduced to the necessity either of submission to a foreign enemy, or of appropriating to their own use those means of defence which are indispensable to self-preservation, they cannot consent to wait passive spectators of approaching ruin, which it is in their power to avert, and to resign the last remnant of their industrious earnings to be dissipated in support of measures destructive of the best interests of the nation.

This convention will not trust themselves to express their conviction of the catastrophe to which such a state of things inevitably tends. Conscious of their high responsibility to God and their country, solicitous for the continuance of the Union, as well as the sovereignty of the states, unwilling to furnish obstacles to peace—resolute never to submit to a foreign enemy, and confiding in the Divine care and protection, they will, until the last hope shall be extinguished, endeavor to avert such consequences.

With this view they suggest an arrangement, which may at once be consistent with the honour and interest of the national government, and the security of these states. This it will not be difficult to conclude, if that government should be so disposed. By the terms of it these states might be allowed to assume their own defence, by the militia or other troops. A reasonable portion, also, of the taxes raised in each state might be paid into its treasury, and credited to the United States, but to be appropriated to the defence of such state, to be accounted for with the United States. No doubt is entertained that by such an arrangement, this portion of the country could be defended with greater effect, and in a mode more consistent with economy, and the public convenience, than any which has been practised.

Should an application for these purposes, made to Congress by the state legislatures, be attended with success, and should peace upon just terms appear to be unattainable, the people would stand together for the common defence, until a change of administration, or of disposition in the enemy, should facilitate the occurrence of that auspicious event. It would be inexpedient for this Convention to diminish the hope of a successful issue to such an application, by recommending, upon supposition of a contrary event, ulterior proceedings. Nor is it indeed within their province. In a state of things so solemn and trying as may then arise, the legislatures of the states, or conventions of the whole people, or delegates appointed by them for the express purpose in another Convention, must act as such urgent circumstances may then require.

But the duty incumbent on this Convention will not have been performed, without exhibiting some general view of such measures as they deem essential to secure the nation against a relapse into difficulties and dangers, should they, by the blessing of Providence, escape from their present condition, without absolute ruin. To this end a concise retrospect of the state of this nation under the advantages of a wise administration, contrasted with the miserable abyss into which it is plunged by the profligacy and folly of political theorists, will lead to some practical conclusions. On this subject, it will be recollected, that the immediate influence of the Federal Constitution upon its first adoption, and for twelve succeeding years, upon the prosperity and happiness of the nation, seemed to countenance a belief in the transcendency of its perfection over all other human institutions. In the catalogue of blessings which have fallen to the lot of the most favoured nations, none could be enumerated from which our country was excluded—a free Constitution, administered by great and incorruptible statesmen, realized the fondest hopes of liberty and independence—The progress of agriculture was stimulated by the certainty of value in the harvest—and commerce, after traversing every sea, returned with the riches of every clime. A revenue, secured by a sense of honour, collected without oppression, and paid without murmurs, melted away the national debt; and the chief concern of the public creditor arose from its too rapid diminution. The wars and commotions of the European nations, and their interruptions of the commercial intercourse afforded to those who had not promoted, but who would have rejoiced to alleviate their calamities, a fair and golden opportunity, by combining themselves to lay a broad foundation for national wealth. Although occasional vexations to commerce arose from the furious collisions of the powers at war, yet the great and good men of that time conformed to the force of circumstances which they could not control, and preserved their country in security from the tempests which overwhelmed the old world, and threw the wreck of their fortunes on these shores. Respect abroad, prosperity at home, wise laws made by honoured legislators, and prompt obedience yielded by a contented people, had silenced the enemies of republican institutions. The arts flourished—the sciences were cultivated—the comforts and conveniences of life were universally diffused—and nothing remained for succeeding administrations but to reap the advantages and cherish the resources flowing from the policy of their predecessors.

But no sooner was a new administration established in the hands of the party opposed to the Washington policy, than a fixed determination was perceived and avowed of changing a system which had already produced these substantial fruits. The consequences of this change, for a few years after its commencement, were not sufficient to counteract the prodigious impulse towards prosperity, which had been given to the nation. But a steady perseverance in the new plans of administration, at length developed their weakness and deformity, but not until a majority of the people had been deceived by flattery, and inflamed by passion, into blindness to their defects. Under the withering influence of this new system, the declension of the nation has been uniform and rapid. The richest advantages for securing the great objects of the constitution have been wantonly rejected. While Europe reposes from the convulsions that had shaken down her ancient institutions, she beholds with amazement this remote country, once so happy and so envied, involved in a ruinous war, and excluded from intercourse with the rest of the world.

To investigate and explain the means whereby this fatal reverse has been effected, would require a voluminous discussion. Nothing more can be attempted in this report than a general allusion to the principal outlines of the policy which has produced this vicissitude. Among these may be enumerated—

First.—A deliberate and extensive system for effecting a

combination among certain states, by exciting local jealousies and ambition, so as to secure to popular leaders in one section of the Union, the controul of public affairs in perpetual succession. To which primary object most other characteristics of the system may be reconciled.

Secondly.—The political intolerance displayed and avowed in excluding from office men of unexceptionable merit, for want of adherence to the executive creed.

Thirdly.—The infraction of the judiciary authority and rights, by depriving judges of their offices in violation of the constitution.

Fourthly.—The abolition of existing taxes, requisite to prepare the country for those changes to which nations are always exposed, with a view to the acquisition of popular favour.

Fifthly.—The influence of patronage in the distribution of offices, which in these states has been almost invariably made among men the least entitled to such distinction, and who have sold themselves as ready instruments for distracting public opinion, and encouraging administration to hold in contempt the wishes and remonstrances of a people thus apparently divided.

Sixthly.—The admission of new states into the Union formed at pleasure in the western region, has destroyed the balance of power which existed among the original States, and deeply affected their interest.

Seventhly.—The easy admission of naturalized foreigners, to places of trust, honour or profit, operating as an inducement to the malcontent subjects of the old world to come to these States, in quest of executive patronage, and to repay it by an abject devotion to executive measures.

Eighthly.—Hostility to Great Britain, and partiality to the late government of France, adopted as coincident with popular prejudice, and subservient to the main object, party power. Connected with these must be ranked erroneous and distorted estimates of the power and resources of those nations, of the probable results of their controversies, and of our political relations to them respectively.

Lastly and principally.—A visionary and superficial theory in regard to commerce, accompanied by a real hatred but a feigned regard to its interests, and a ruinous perseverance in efforts to render it an instrument of coercion and war.

But it is not conceivable that the obliquity of any administration could, in so short a period, have so nearly consummated the work of national ruin, unless favoured by defects in the constitution.

To enumerate all the improvements of which that instrument is susceptible, and to propose such amendments as might render it in all respects perfect, would be a task which this convention has not thought proper to assume. They have confined their attention to such as experience has demonstrated to be essential, and even among these, some are considered entitled to a more serious attention than others. They are suggested without any intentional disrespect to other states, and are meant to be such as all shall find an interest in promoting. Their object is to strengthen, and if possible to perpetuate, the union of the states, by removing the grounds of existing jealousies, and providing for a fair and equal representation, and a limitation of powers, which have been misused.

The first amendment proposed, relates to the apportionment of representatives among the slave holding states. This cannot be claimed as a right. Those states are entitled to the slave representation, by a constitutional compact. It is therefore merely a subject of agreement, which should be conducted upon principles of mutual interest and accommodation, and upon which no sensibility on either side should be permitted to exist. It has proved unjust and unequal in its operation. Had this effect been foreseen, the privilege would probably not have been demanded; certainly not conceded. Its tendency in future will be adverse to that harmony and mutual confidence which are more conducive to the happiness and prosperity of every confederated state, than a mere preponderance of power, the prolific source of jealousies and controversy, can be to any one of them. The time may therefore arrive, when a sense of magnanimity and justice will reconcile those states to acquiesce in a revision of this article, especially as a fair equivalent would result to them in the apportionment of taxes.

The next amendment relates to the admission of new states into the Union.

This amendment is deemed to be highly important, and in fact indispensable. In proposing it, it is not intended to recognize the right of Congress to admit new states without the original limits of the United States, nor is any idea entertained of disturbing the tranquillity of any state already admitted into the Union. The object is merely to restrain the constitutional power of Congress in admitting new states. At the adoption of the constitution, a certain balance of power among the original parties was considered to exist, and there was at that time, and yet is among those parties, a strong affinity between their great and general interests.—By the admission of these states that balance has been materially affected, and unless the practice be modified, must ultimately be destroyed. The southern states will first avail themselves of their new confederates to govern the east, and finally the western states, multiplied in number, and augmented in population, will control the interests of the whole. Thus for the sake of present power, the southern states will be common sufferers with the east, in the loss of permanent advantages. None of the old states can find an interest in creating prematurely an overwhelming western influence, which may hereafter discern (as it has heretofore) benefits to be derived to them by wars and commercial restrictions.

The next amendments proposed by the convention, relate to the powers of Congress, in relation to embargo and the interdiction of commerce.

Whatever theories upon the subject of commerce have hitherto divided the opinions of statesmen, experience has at last shown that it is a vital interest in the United States, and that its success is essential to the encouragement of agriculture and manufactures, and to the wealth, finances, defence, and liberty of the nation. Its welfare can never interfere with the other great interests of the state, but must promote and uphold them. Still those who are immediately concerned in the prosecution of commerce, will of necessity be always a minority of the nation. They are, however, best qualified to manage and direct its course by the advantages of experience, and the sense of interest. But they are entirely unable to protect themselves against the sudden and injudicious decisions of bare majorities, and the mistaken or oppressive projects of those who are not actively concerned in its pursuits. Of consequence, this interest is always exposed to be harassed, interrupted, and entirely destroyed, upon pretence of securing other interests. Had the merchants of this nation been permitted by their own government to pursue an innocent and lawful commerce, how different would have been the state of the treasury and of public credit! How short-sighted and miserable is the policy which has annihilated this order of men, and doomed their ships to rot in the docks, their capital to waste unemployed, and their affections to be alienated from the government which was formed to protect them! What security for an ample and unfailing revenue can ever be had, comparable to that which once was realized in the good faith, punctuality, and sense of honour, which attached the mercantile class to the interests of the government! Without commerce, where can be found the aliment for a navy; and without a navy, what is to constitute the defence, and ornament, and glory of this nation! No union can be durably cemented, in which every great interest does not find itself reasonably secured against the encroachment and combinations of other interests. When, therefore, the past system of embargoes and commercial restrictions shall have been reviewed—when the fluctuation and inconsistency of public measures, betraying a want of information as well as feeling in the majority, shall have been considered, the reasonableness of some restrictions upon the power of a bare majority to repeat these oppressions, will appear to be obvious.

The next amendment proposes to restrict the power of making offensive war. In the consideration of this amendment, it is not necessary to inquire into the justice of the present war. But one sentiment now exists in relation to its expediency, and regret for its declaration is nearly universal. No indemnity can ever be attained for this terrible calamity, and its only palliation must be found in obstacles to its future recurrence. Rarely can the state of this country call for or justify offensive war. The genius of our institutions is unfavourable to its successful prosecution; the felicity of our situation exempts us from its necessity. In this case, as in the former, those more immediately exposed to its fatal effects are a minority of the nation. The commercial towns, the shores of our seas and rivers, contain the population whose vital interests are most vulnerable by a foreign enemy. Agriculture, indeed, must feel at last, but this appeal to its sensibility comes too late. Again, the immense population which has swarmed into the west, remote from immediate danger, and which is constantly augmenting, will not be averse from the occasional disturbances of the Atlantic states. Thus interest may not unfrequently combine with passion and intrigue, to plunge the nation into needless wars, and compel it to become a military, rather than a happy and flourishing people. These considerations, which it would be easy to augment, call loudly for the limitation proposed in the amendment.

Another amendment, subordinate in importance, but still in a high degree expedient, relates to the exclusion of foreigners hereafter arriving in the United States from the capacity of holding offices of trust, honour, or profit.

That the stock of population already in these states is amply sufficient to render this nation in due time sufficiently great and powerful, is not a controvertible question. Nor will it be seriously pretended, that the national deficiency in wisdom, arts, science, arms, or virtue, needs to be replenished from foreign countries. Still, it is agreed, that a liberal policy should offer the rights of hospitality, and the choice of settlement, to those who are disposed to visit the country. But why admit to a participation in the government aliens who were no parties to the compact—who are ignorant of the nature of our institutions, and have no stake in the welfare of the country but what is recent and transitory? It is surely a privilege sufficient, to admit them after due probation to become citizens, for all but political purposes. To extend it beyond these limits, is to encourage foreigners to come to these states as candidates for preferment. The Convention forbear to express their opinion upon the inauspicious effects which have already resulted to the honour and peace of this nation, from this misplaced and indiscriminate liberality.

The last amendment respects the limitation of the office of President to a single constitutional term, and his eligibility from the same state two terms in succession.

Upon this topic it is superfluous to dilate. The love of power is a principle in the human heart which too often impels to the use of all practicable means to prolong its duration. The office of President has charms and attractions which operate as powerful incentives to this passion. The first and most natural exertion of a vast patronage is directed towards the security of a new election. The interest of the country, the welfare of the people, even honest fame and respect for the opinion of posterity, are secondary considerations. All the engines of intrigue, all the means of corruption are likely to be employed for this object. A President whose political career is limited to a single election, may find no other interest than will be promoted by making it glorious to himself, and beneficial to his country. But the hope of re-election is prolific of temptations, under which these magnanimous motives are deprived of their principal force. The repeated election of the President of the United States from any one state, affords inducements and means for intrigues, which tend to create an undue local influence, and to establish the domination of particular states. The justice, therefore, of securing to every state a fair and equal chance for the election of this officer from its own citizens is apparent, and this object will be essentially promoted by preventing an election from the same state twice in succession.

Such is the general view which this Convention has thought proper to submit, of the situation of these states, of their dangers and their duties. Most of the subjects which it embraces have separately received an ample and luminous investigation, by the great and able assertors of the rights of their country, in the national legislature; and nothing more could be attempted on this occasion than a digest of general principles, and of recommendations suited to the present state of public affairs. The peculiar difficulty and delicacy of performing even this undertaking, will be appreciated by all who think seriously upon the crisis. Negotiations for peace are at this hour supposed to be pending, the issue of which must be deeply interesting to all. No measures should be adopted which might unfavourably affect that issue; none which should embarrass the administration, if their professed desire for peace is sincere; and none which on supposition of their insincerity, should afford them pretexts for prolonging the war, or relieving themselves from the responsibility of a dishonourable peace. It is also devoutly to be wished, that an occasion may be afforded to all friends of the country, of all parties, and in all places, to pause and consider the awful state to which pernicious counsels and blind passions have brought this people. The number of those who perceive, and who are ready to retrace errors, must, it is believed, be yet sufficient to redeem the nation. It is necessary to rally and unite them by the assurance that no hostility to the constitution is meditated, and to obtain their aid in placing it under guardians who alone can save it from destruction. Should this fortunate change be effected, the hope of happiness and honour may once more dispel the surrounding gloom. Our nation may yet be great, our union durable. But should this prospect be utterly hopeless, the time will not have been lost which shall have ripened a general sentiment of the necessity of more mighty efforts to rescue from ruin, at least some portion of our beloved country.

THEREFORE RESOLVED,

That it be and hereby is recommended to the legislatures of the several states represented in this Convention, to adopt all such measures as may be necessary effectually to protect the citizens of said states from the operation and effects of all acts which have been or may be passed by the Congress of the United States, which shall contain provisions, subjecting the militia or other citizens to forcible drafts, conscriptions, or impressments, not authorised by the constitution of the United States.

Resolved, That it be and hereby is recommended to the said Legislatures, to authorize an immediate and earnest application to be made to the government of the United States, requesting their consent to some arrangement, whereby the said states may, separately or in concert, be empowered to assume upon themselves the defence of their territory against the enemy; and a reasonable portion of the taxes, collected within said States, may be paid into the respective treasuries thereof, and appropriated to the payment of the balance due said states, and to the future defence of the same. The amount so paid into the said treasuries to be credited, and the disbursements made as aforesaid to be charged to the United States.

Resolved, That it be, and hereby is, recommended to the legislatures of the aforesaid states, to pass laws (where it has not already been done) authorizing the governors or commanders-in-chief of their militia to make detachments from the same, or to form voluntary corps, as shall be most convenient and conformable to their constitutions, and to cause the same to be well armed, equipped, and disciplined, and held in readiness for service; and upon the request of the governor of either of the other states to employ the whole of such detachment or corps, as well as the regular forces of the state, or such part thereof as may be required and can be spared consistently with the safety of the state, in assisting the state, making such request to repel any invasion thereof which shall be made or attempted by the public enemy.

Resolved, That the following amendments of the constitution of the United States be recommended to the states represented as aforesaid, to be proposed by them for adoption by the state legislatures, and in such cases as may be deemed expedient by a convention chosen by the people of each state.

And it is further recommended, that the said states shall persevere in their efforts to obtain such amendments, until the same shall be effected.

First. Representatives and direct taxes shall be apportioned among the several states which may be included within this Union, according to their respective numbers of free persons, including those bound to serve for a term of years, and excluding Indians not taxed, and all other persons.

Second. No new state shall be admitted into the Union by Congress, in virtue of the power granted by the constitution, without the concurrence of two thirds of both houses.

Third. Congress shall not have power to lay any embargo on the ships or vessels of the citizens of the United States, in the ports or harbours thereof, for more than sixty days.

Fourth. Congress shall not have power, without the concurrence of two thirds of both houses, to interdict the commercial intercourse between the United States and any foreign nation, or the dependencies thereof.

Fifth. Congress shall not make or declare war, or authorize acts of hostility against any foreign nation, without the concurrence of two thirds of both houses, except such acts of hostility be in defence of the territories of the United States when actually invaded.

Sixth. No person who shall hereafter be naturalized, shall be eligible as a member of the senate or house of representatives of the United States, nor capable of holding any civil office under the authority of the United States.

Seventh. The same person shall not be elected president of the United States a second time; nor shall the president be elected from the same state two terms in succession.

Resolved, That if the application of these states to the government of the United States, recommended in a foregoing resolution, should be unsuccessful, and peace should not be concluded, and the defence of these states should be neglected, as it has been since the commencement of the war, it will, in the opinion of this convention, be expedient for the legislatures of the several states to appoint delegates to another convention, to meet at Boston in the state of Massachusetts, on the third Thursday of June next, with such powers and instructions as the exigency of a crisis so momentous may require.

Resolved, That the Hon. George Cabot, the Hon. Chauncey Goodrich, and the Hon. Daniel Lyman, or any two of them, be authorized to call another meeting of this convention, to be holden in Boston, at any time before new delegates shall be chosen, as recommended in the above resolution, if in their judgment the situation of the country shall urgently require it.

GEORGE CABOT,
NATHAN DANE,
WILLIAM PRESCOTT,
HARRISON GRAY OTIS,
TIMOTHY BIGELOW,
JOSHUA THOMAS,
SAMUEL SUMNER WILDE,
JOSEPH LYMAN,
STEPHEN LONGFELLOW, Jun.
DANIEL WALDO,
HODIJAH BAYLIES,
GEORGE BLISS.
} *Massachusetts.*

CHAUNCEY GOODRICH,
JOHN TREADWELL,
JAMES HILLHOUSE,
ZEPHANIAH SWIFT,
NATHANIEL SMITH,
CALVIN GODDARD,
ROGER MINOT SHERMAN.
} *Connecticut.*

Daniel Lyman,
Samuel Ward,
Edward Manton,
Benjamin Hazard,
} *Rhode-Island.*

Benjamin West,
Mills Olcott.
} *N. Hampshire.*

William Hall, Jun.   *Vermont.*

Harry Smith: from Autobiography

January 7–8, 1815

After suffering costly delays trying to navigate the shallow waters of Lake Borgne in heavy barges, the British forces completed their landing on December 23, establishing their headquarters at the plantation of Jacques Villeré, eight miles below New Orleans on the Mississippi. That night, determined to engage the enemy as far away from the city as possible and supported by two American warships on the river, Jackson led eighteen hundred men in a nighttime attack that ended with the British suffering 275 casualties, the Americans 215. More British forces landed over the next two days, including Major General Sir Edward Pakenham, the Duke of Wellington's brother-in-law and a veteran of the Peninsular War, who finally arrived to assume command. His army now totaled four thousand men, well more than Jackson's, and yet, save for one abortive attack on December 28, Pakenham did not seek to press his advantage, preferring instead to wait on artillery laboriously brought up from Cochrane's ships. These delays enabled Jackson to establish a formidable line of defense below the city along the edge of a canal connecting a cypress swamp on the east and the Mississippi on the west, and a less well-defended battery on the far side of the river. Assistant Adjutant-General Harry Smith had traveled with Pakenham, and he developed a great affection for his commander, one that magnified his sense of foreboding about the battle to come. Just before the fateful engagement, Pakenham dispatched Smith to the rear, to the headquarters of Major General Sir John Lambert, who had just arrived with a brigade of reserve troops.

The night of the 7th January, the rivulet (or bayou, as then called) was reported dammed, and the boats above the dam ready for the banks of the Mississippi to be cut. The water within the banks was higher than the level of the water in the bayou, consequently so much water must be let into the bayou as to provide for the level. In the meanwhile, the enemy had not been asleep. They had been apprised of our operations to establish ourselves on the right bank; they had landed the guns from the second ship (which we ought to have destroyed), and were respectably in possession of that which we must turn them out of. Sir Edward Pakenham went to inspect the bayou, the boats, etc. I heard him say to the engineer, "Are you satisfied the dam will bear the weight of water which will be upon it when the banks of the river are cut?" He said, "Perfectly." "I should be far more so if a second dam was constructed." The engineer was positive. After dark the banks were cut, the dam went as Sir Edward seemed to anticipate, and the delay in repairing it prevented the boats being got into the river in time for the troops under Colonel Thornton of the 85th to reach their ground and make a simultaneous attack with the main body, according to the plan arranged. Sir John Lambert's Brigade, the *élite* 7th Fusiliers and 43rd, were in reserve. Sir Edward said, "Those fellows would storm anything, but, indeed, so will the others, and when we are in New Orleans, I can depend upon Lambert's Reserve." We were all formed in three columns about 6000 British soldiers and some sailors: a column under Colonel Renny of the 21st were destined to proceed on the banks of the river and right of the enemy, and carry a powerful battery which enfiladed the whole position: General Keane's Brigade was to assail the enemy's right-central position: General Gibbs's Brigade to attack well upon the enemy's left: General Lambert's Brigade to be in reserve nearer Gibbs's Brigade than Keane's.

About half an hour before daylight, while I was with General Lambert's column, standing ready, Sir Edward Pakenham sent for me. I was soon with him. He was greatly agitated. "Smith, most Commanders-in-Chief have many difficulties to contend with, but surely none like mine. The dam, as you heard me say it would, gave way, and Thornton's people will be of no use whatever to the general attack." I said, "So impressed have you ever been, so obvious is it in every military point of view, we should possess the right bank of the river, and thus enfilade and divert the attention of the enemy; there is still time before daylight to retire the columns now. We are under the enemy's fire so soon as discovered." He says, "This may be, but I have twice deferred the attack. We are strong in numbers now comparatively. It will cost more men, and the assault must be

made." I again urged delay. While we were talking, the streaks
of daylight began to appear, although the morning was dull,
close, and heavy, the clouds almost touching the ground. He
said, "Smith, order the rocket to be fired." I again ventured to
plead the cause of delay. He said, and very justly, "It is now too
late: the columns would be visible to the enemy before they
could move out of fire, and would lose more men than it is to
be hoped they will in the attack. Fire the rocket, I say, and go
to Lambert." This was done. I had reached Lambert just as the
stillness of death and anticipation (for I really believe the
enemy was aware of our proximity to their position) was broken by the firing of the rocket. The rocket was hardly in the air
before a rush of our troops was met by the most murderous
and destructive fire of all arms ever poured upon column. Sir
Edward Pakenham galloped past me with all his Staff, saying,
"That's a terrific fire, Lambert." I knew nothing of my General
then, except that he was a most gentlemanlike, amiable fellow,
and I had seen him lead his Brigade at Toulouse in the order of
a review of his Household Troops in Hyde Park.* I said, "In
twenty-five minutes, General, you will command the Army. Sir
Edward Pakenham will be wounded and incapable, or killed.
The troops do not get on a step. He will be at the head of the
first Brigade he comes to, and what I say will occur." A few
seconds verified my words. Tylden came wildly up to tell the
melancholy truth, saying, "Sir Edward Pakenham is killed. You
command the Army, and your Brigade must move on immediately." I said, "If Sir Edward Pakenham is killed, Sir John
Lambert commands, and will judge of what is to be done." I
saw the attack had irretrievably failed. The troops were beat
back, and going at a tolerable pace too; so much so, I thought
the enemy had made a sortie in pursuit, as so overpowering a
superiority of numbers would have induced the French to do.
"May I order your Brigade, sir, to form line to cover a most
irregular retreat, to apply no other term to it, until you see
what has actually occurred to the attacking columns?" He as-
sented, and sent me and other Staff Officers in different directions to ascertain our condition. It was (summed up in few

---

*Sir J. Lambert was always in the Guards, and prided himself on being Ad-
jutant of the Grenadier Guards, as his eldest son now is.—H.G.S. (1844).

words) that every attack had failed; the Commander-in-Chief and General Gibbs and Colonel Renny killed; General Keane, most severely wounded; and the columns literally destroyed. The column for the right bank were seen to be still in their boats, and not the slightest impression had been made on the enemy.

Never since Buenos Ayres had I witnessed a reverse, and the sight to our eyes, which had looked on victory so often, was appalling indeed. Lambert desired me, and every Staff Officer he could get hold of, to go and reform the troops, no very easy matter in some cases. However, far to the rear, they (or, rather, what were left) were formed up, Sir John meanwhile wondering whether, under all the circumstances, he ought to attack. He very judiciously saw that was impossible, and he withdrew the troops from under a most murderous fire of round shot. Soon after this we heard the attack on the right bank, which succeeded easily enough. The extent of our loss was ascertained: one-third.

A Kentucky Soldier's Account
of the Battle of New Orleans

The Battle of New Orleans was the most lopsided of the war. Paken-ham was one of some two thousand British casualties on the day, against perhaps seventy total for the Americans. "[T]he vast disparity of loss," observed the *National Intelligencer*, "would stagger credu-lity itself, were it not confirmed by a whole army of witnesses." One of those witnesses was the anonymous Kentucky rifleman who left this account, first published by the Louisiana Historical Society in 1926.

Col. Smiley, from Bardstown, was the first one who gave us orders to fire from our part of the line; and then, I reckon, there was a pretty considerable noise. There were also brass pieces on our right, the noisest kind of varmints, that began blaring away as hard as they could, while the heavy iron can-non, toward the river, and some thousands of small arms, joined in the chorus and made the ground shake under our feet. Directly after the firing began, Capt. Patterson, I think he was from Knox County, Kentucky, but an Irishman born, came running along. He jumped upon the brestwork and stooping a moment to look through the darkness as well as he could, he shouted with a broad North of Ireland brogue, "shoot low, boys! shoot low! rake them—rake them! They're comin' on their all fours!"

The official report said that the action lasted two hours and five minutes, but it did not seem half that length of time to me. It was so dark that little could be seen, until just about the time the battle ceased. The morning had dawned to be sure, but the smoke was so thick that every thing seemed to be covered up in it. Our men did not seem to apprehend any danger, but would load and fire as fast as they could, talking, swearing, and joking all the time. All ranks and sections were soon broken up. After the first shot, every one loaded and banged away on his own hook. Henry Spillman did not load and fire quite so often as some of the rest, but every time he did fire he would go up to the brestwork, look over until he could see something to shoot at, and then take deliberate aim and crack away. Lieut. Ashby was as busy as a nailor and it was evident that, the River Raisin was uppermost in his mind all the time. He kept dashing about and every now and then he would call out, with an oath, "We'll pay you now for the River Raisin! We'll give you something to remember the River Raisin!" When the British had come up to the opposite side of the brestwork, having no gun, he picked up an empty barrel and flung it at them. Then finding an iron bar, he jumped up on the works and hove that at them.

At one time I noticed, a little on our right, a curious kind of a chap named Ambrose Odd, one of Captain Higdon's company, and known among the men by the nickname of "Sukey," standing cooly on the top of the brestworks and peering into the darkness for something to shoot at. The balls were whistling around him and over our heads, as thick as hail, and Col. Slaughter coming along, ordered him to come down. The Colonel told him there was policy in war, and that he was exposing himself too much. Sukey turned around, holding up the flap of his old broad brimmed hat with one hand, to see who was speaking to him, and replied: "Oh! never mind Colonel—here's Sukey—I don't want to waste my powder, and I'd like to know how I can shoot until I see something?" Pretty soon after, Sukey got his eye on a red coat, and, no doubt, made a hole through it, for he took deliberate aim, fired and then coolly came down to load again.

During the action, a number of the Tennessee men got mixed with ours. One of them was killed about five or six yards from where I stood. I did not know his name. A ball passed through his head and he fell against Ensign Weller. I always thought, as did many others who were standing near, that he must have been accidentally shot by some of our own men. From the range of the British balls, they could hardly have passed over the brestwork without passing over our heads, unless we were standing very close to the works, which were a little over brest high, and five or six feet wide on the top. This man was standing a little back and rather behind Weller. After the battle, I could not see that any of the balls had struck the oak tree lower than ten or twelve feet from the ground. Above that height it was thickly peppered. This was the only man killed near where I was stationed.

It was near the close of the firing. About the time that I observed three or four men carrying his body away or directly after, there was a white flag raised on the opposite side of the brestwork and the firing ceased.

The white flag, before mentioned, was raised about ten or twelve feet from where I stood, close to the brestwork and a little to the right. It was a white handkerchief, or something of the kind, on a sword or stick. It was waved several times, and as soon as it was perceived, we ceased firing. Just then the wind got up a little and blew the smoke off, so that we could see the field. It then appeared that the flag had been raised by a British Officer wearing epaulets. It was told he was a Major. He stepped over the brestwork and came into our lines. Among the Tennesseeans who had got mixed with us during the fight, there was a little fellow whose name I do not know; but he was a cadaverous looking chap and went by that of Paleface. As the British Officer came in, Paleface demanded his sword. He hesitated about giving it to him, probably thinking it was derogatory to his dignity, to surrender to a private all over begrimed with dust and powder and that some Officer should show him the courtesy to receive it. Just at that moment, Col. Smiley came up and cried, with a harsh oath, "Give it up—give it up to him in a minute!" The British Officer quickly handed his weapon to Paleface, holding it in both hands and making a very polite bow.

A good many others came in just about the same time. Among them I noticed a very neatly dressed young man, standing on the edge of the brestwork, and offering his hand, as if for some one to assist him. He appeared to be about nineteen or twenty years old, and, as I should judge from his appearance, was an Irishman. He held his musket in one hand, while he was offering the other. I took hold of his musket and set it down, and then giving him my hand, he jumped down quite lightly. As soon as he got down, he began trying to take off his cartouch box, and then I noticed a red spot of blood on his clean white under jacket. I asked him if he was wounded, he said that he was and he feared pretty badly. While he was trying to disengage his accounterments, Capt. Farmer came up, and said to him, "Let me help you my man!" The Captain and myself then assisted him to take them off. He begged us not to take his canteen, which contained his water. We told him we did not wish to take anything but what was in his way and cumbersome to him. Just then one of the Tennesseeans, who had run down to the river, as soon as the firing had ceased, for water, came along with some in a tin coffee-pot. The wounded man observed him, asked if he would please give him a drop. "O! Yes," said the Tenneessean, "I will treat you to anything I've got." The young man took the coffee-pot and swallowed two or three mouthfuls out of the spout. He then handed back the pot, and in an instant we observed him sinking backward. We eased him down against the side of a tent, when he gave two or three gasps and was dead. He had been shot through the breast.

On the opposite side of the brestwork there was a ditch about ten feet wide, made by the excavation of the earth, of which the work was formed. In it, was about a foot or eighteen inches of water, and to make it the more difficult of passage, a quantity of thornbush had been cut and thrown into it. In this ditch a number of British soldiers were found at the close under the brestwork, as a shelter from our fire. These, of course, came in and surrendered.

When the smoke had cleared away and we could obtain a fair view of the field, it looked, at the first glance, like a sea of blood. It was not blood itself which gave it this appearance but the red coats in which the British soldiers were dressed. Straight out before our position, for about the width of space which we supposed had been occupied by the British column, the field was entirely covered with prostrate bodies. In some places they were laying in piles of several, one on the top of the other. On either side, there was an interval more thinly sprinkled with the slain; and then two other dense rows, one near the levee and the other towards the swamp. About two hundred yards off, directly in front of our position, lay a dark dapple gray horse, which we understood had been Packenham's.

Something about half way between the body of the horse and our brestwork there was a very large pile of dead, and at this spot, as I was afterward told, Packenham had been killed; his horse having staggered off to a considerable distance before he fell. I have no doubt that I could . . . have walked on the bodies from the edge of the ditch to where the horse was laying, without touching the ground. I did not notice any other horse on the field.

When we first got a fair view of the field in our front, individuals could be seen in every possible attitude. Some laying quite dead, others mortally wounded, pitching and tumbling about in the agonies of death. Some had their heads shot off, some their legs, some their arms. Some were laughing, some crying, some groaning, and some screaming. There was every variety of sight and sound. Among those that were on the ground, however, there were some that were neither dead nor wounded. A great many had thrown themselves down behind piles of slain, for protection. As the firing ceased, these men were every now and then jumping up and either running off or coming in and giving themselves up.

Among those that were running off, we observed one stout looking fellow, in a red coat, who would every now and then stop and display some gestures toward us, that were rather the opposite of complimentary. Perhaps fifty guns were fired at him, but as he was a good way off, without effect. "Hurra, Paleface! load quick and give him a shot. The infernal rascal is patting his butt at us!" Sure enough, Paleface rammed home his bullet, and taking a long sight, he let drive. The fellow, by this time, was from two to three hundred yards off, and somewhat to the left of Packenham's horse. Paleface said as he drew sight on him and then run it along up his back until the sight was lost over his head, to allow for the sinking of the ball in so great a distance, and then let go. As soon as the gun cracked, the fellow was seen to stagger. He ran forward a few steps, and then pitched down on his head, and moved no more. As soon as he fell, George Huffman, a big stout Dutchman, belonging to our Company, asked the Captain if he might go and see where Paleface hit him. The Captain said he didn't care and George jumping from the brestwork over the ditch, ran over the dead and wounded until he came to the place where the fellow was lying. George rolled the body over until he could see the face and then turning round to us, shouted at the top of his voice, "Mine Gott! he is a nagar!" He was a mulatto and he was quite dead. Paleface's ball had entered between the shoulders and passed out through his breast. George, as he came back, brought three or four muskets which he had picked up. By this time, our men were running out in all directions, picking up muskets and sometimes watches and other plunder. One man who had got a little too far out on the field was fired at from the British brestwork and wounded in the arm. He came running back a good deal faster than he had gone out. He was not much hurt but pretty well scared.

Harry Smith: from Autobiography

As the smoke from the furious thirty-minute battle cleared, Harry Smith walked among the battered troops to assess their morale. He was present later when General Lambert convened an impromptu council of war, and an admiral responsible for supplying the invasion force with provisions suggested that "the troops must attack or the whole will be starved." "Kill plenty more, Admiral," Smith tartly replied, "fewer rations will be required." He then vigorously argued for calling off the assault on New Orleans and securing the army's safe withdrawal. General Lambert agreed, but first he had a grim mission for his adjutant.

Late in the afternoon I was sent to the enemy with a flag of truce, and a letter to General Jackson, with a request to be allowed to bury the dead and bring in the wounded lying between our respective positions. The Americans were not accustomed to the civility of war, like our old *associates* the French, and I was a long time before I could induce them to receive me. They fired on me with cannon and musketry, which excited my choler somewhat, for a round shot tore away the ground under my right foot, which it would have been a bore indeed to have lost under such circumstances. However, they did receive me at last, and the reply from General Jackson was a very courteous one.

After the delivery of the reply to General Lambert, I was again sent out with a fatigue party—a pretty large one too—with entrenching tools to bury the dead, and some surgeons to examine and bring off the wounded. I was received by a rough fellow—a Colonel Butler, Jackson's Adjutant-General. He had a drawn sword, and no scabbard. I soon saw the man I had to deal with. I outrode the surgeon, and I apologized for keeping him waiting; so he said, "Why now, I calculate as your doctors are tired; they have plenty to do to-day." There was an awful spectacle of dead, dying, and wounded around us. "*Do?*" says I, "why this is nothing to us Wellington fellows! The next brush we have with you, you shall see how a Brigade of the Peninsular army (arrived yesterday) will serve you fellows out with the bayonet. They will lie piled on one another like round shot, if they will only stand." "Well, I calculate you must get at 'em first." "But," says I, "what do you carry a drawn sword for?" "Because I reckon a scabbard of no use so long as one of you Britishers is on our soil. We don't wish to shoot you, but we must, if you molest our property; we have thrown away the scabbard."

By this time our surgeon had arrived. There were some awful wounds from cannon shot, and I dug an immense hole, and threw nearly two hundred bodies into it. To the credit of the Americans not an article of clothing had been taken from our dead except the shoes. Every body was straightened, and the great toes tied together with a piece of string. A more appalling spectacle cannot well be conceived than this common grave, the bodies hurled in as fast as we could bring them. The Colonel, Butler, was very sulky if I tried to get near the works. This scene was not more than about eighty yards away from them, and, had our fellows rushed on, they would not have lost one half, and victory would have been ours. I may safely say there was not a vital part of man in which I did not observe a mortal wound, in many bodies there were three or four such; some were without heads; there were others, poor fellows, whom I recognized. In this part of America there were many Spaniards and Frenchmen. Several soldiers and officers gathered round me, and I addressed them in their own language. Colonel Butler became furious, but I would not desist for the moment, and said, "The next time we meet, Colonel, I hope to receive you to bury your dead." "Well, I calculate you have been on that duty to-day," he said. God only knows I had, with a heavy heart. It was apparently light enough before him, but the effort was a violent one.

At night it was General Lambert's intention to withdraw his line more out of cannon shot, for we were on a perfect plain, not a mound as cover, and I and D'Este (His Royal Highness, as I used to call him) were sent to bring back Blakeney's Brigade. Blakeney was as anxious a soldier in the dark as he was noble and gallant when he saw his enemy. He would fain induce me to believe I did not know my road. I got all right, though, with the aid of D'Este, who, if the war had lasted, would have made as able a soldier as his ancestor George the Second. I did not regard myself, though, as Marlborough, who was little employed on any retiring duty.

That night I lay down in my cloak, in General Lambert's room, at twelve o'clock, so done that all care or thought was banished in sleep. Before daylight I awoke to the horror of the loss of the man I so loved, admired, and esteemed, and to the feelings of a soldier under such melancholy circumstances. Those feelings could be but momentary. It was my duty to jump on my horse and see what was going on at our post, which I did, after returning Almighty God thanks. Thence to the hospital to render the Inspector whatever aid he required in orderlies, etc. Robb deserved and received the highest encomiums for the arrangements, which secured every care to our wounded.

In returning from the outposts, I met General Lambert. Upon my assuring him everything was perfectly quiet, he said, "I will now ride to the hospital." "I was just going there, sir, and will ride with you." The General said, "You must have been pretty well done last night, for I did not see you when I lay down." "Yes, I had a long day, but we Light Division fellows are used to it." "Smith, that most amiable man and cool and collected soldier, Secretary Wylly, will take home the dispatches of the melancholy disaster, and of the loss of his General and patron, and I offer for your acceptance my Military Secretaryship." I laughed, and said, "Me, sir! I write the most illegible and detestable scrawl in the world." "You can, therefore," he mildly said, "the more readily decipher mine. Poor Pakenham was much attached to you, and strongly recommended you to me." I had borne up well on my loss before, but I now burst into a flood of tears, with—"God rest his gallant soul." From that moment to the present, dear General Lambert has ever treated me as one of his own family. Our lamented General's remains were put in a cask of spirits and taken home by his Military Secretary, Wylly, who sailed in a few days with dispatches of no ordinary character—a record of lamentable disaster, and anything but honour to our military fame.

Andrew Jackson to James Monroe

To the defense of New Orleans, Andrew Jackson had brought the tireless energy and ruthless single-mindedness that would make him the dominant personality of his age. Some two weeks after his arrival there he had proclaimed martial law, commandeering men and supplies as needed and jailing anyone who would dissent. "Those who are not for us," he threatened, "are against us, and will be dealt with accordingly." But in the end, the severity of his command over soldiers and civilians alike would do little to tarnish his popular reputation. For at the Battle of New Orleans, which he describes in this official report to the secretary of war (which quickly found its way into the newspapers), he had shown that Americans could defeat the most seasoned troops in the British army. No one yet knew that the greatest U.S. victory of the war had been won after the peace treaty was already signed.

Head Quarters, 7th Military District,
Camp, 4 miles below New Orleans, January 13th, 1815

SIR—At such a crisis, I conceive it my duty to keep you constantly advised of my situation.

On the 10th inst. I forwarded you an account of the bold attempt made by the enemy on the morning of the 8th to take possession of my works by storm, and of the severe repulse which he met with. That report having been sent by the mail which crosses the lake, may possibly have miscarried; for which reason, I think it the more necessary briefly to repeat the substance of it.

Early on the morning of the 8th, the enemy having been actively employed the two preceding days in making preparation for a storm, advanced in two strong columns on my right and left. They were received, however, with a firmness which it seems they little expected, and which defeated all their hopes. My men, undisturbed by their approach, which indeed they had long anxiously wished for, opened upon them a fire so deliberate and certain, as rendered their scaling ladders and facines, as well as their more direct implements of warfare, perfectly useless. For upwards of an hour it was continued, with a briskness of which there have been but few instances, perhaps, in any country. In justice to the enemy it must be said, they withstood it as long as could be expected from the most determined bravery. At length, however, when all prospect of success became hopeless, they fled in confusion from the field, leaving it covered with their dead and wounded. Their loss was immense. I had at first computed it at 1500; but it is since ascertained to have been much greater. Upon information, which is believed to be correct, col. Haynes, the inspector general, reports it to be in total 2600. His report I enclose you. My loss was inconsiderable, being only 7* killed and 6 wounded. Such a disproportion in loss, when we consider the number and the kind of troops engaged, must, I know, excite astonishment, and may not everywhere be fully credited; yet I am perfectly satisfied that the account is not exaggerated on the one part, nor underrated on the other.

The enemy having hastily quitted a post which they had gained possession of, on the other side of the river, and we having immediately returned to it, both armies at present occupy their former positions. Whether after the severe losses he has sustained, he is preparing to return to his shipping, or to make still mightier efforts to attain his first object, I do not pretend to determine. It becomes me to act as though the latter were his intention. One thing, however, seems certain, that if he still calculates on effecting what he has hitherto been unable to accomplish, he must expect considerable reinforcements; as the force with which he landed must undoubtedly be diminished by at least 3000. Besides the loss which he sustained on the night of the 23d ult. which is estimated at 400, he cannot have suffered less between that period and the morning of the 8th inst. than 3000—having, within that time, been repulsed in two general attempts to drive us from our position, and there having been continual cannonading and skirmishing, during the whole of it. Yet he is still able to shew a very formidable force.

---

*This was in the action on the line—afterwards a skirmishing was kept up in which a few more of our men was lost.

There is little doubt that the commanding general, sir Edward Packenham, was killed in the action of the 8th, and that major generals Keane and Gibbs were badly wounded.

Whenever a more leisure moment shall occur, I will take the liberty to make and forward you a more circumstantial account of the several actions, and particularly that of the 8th, in doing which my chief motive will be to render justice to those brave men I have the honor to command, and who have so remarkably distinguished themselves.

I have the honor to be, most respectfully, your obedient servant,

ANDREW JACKSON,
Maj. gen. commanding

Thomas Jefferson to Marquis de Lafayette

On January 2, 1815, Henry Clay's personal secretary boarded the ship *Favorite* in London with the U.S. copy of the Treaty of Ghent. Prevented from sailing directly to Washington by bad weather, *Favorite* docked in New York at around 8:00 P.M. on February 11. From there the news spread in all directions. It greeted the delegation from the New England states dispatched to Washington to seek federal funds for defense while it was en route, as did the first reports of Jackson's triumph at New Orleans. The timing was devastating for the Federalists, enabling their opponents to portray the Hartford Convention as defeatist and unpatriotic: "The grievance deputies from Massachusetts & Connecticutt," jeered Winfield Scott from Baltimore, have "afforded a fine Subject of jest & merriment to men of all parties." In the following letter to his old friend Lafayette, Jefferson joins the chorus of scorn and offers his appraisal of the war just concluded.

Monticello, February 14, 1815

MY DEAR FRIEND,—Your letter of August the 14th has been received and read again, and again, with extraordinary pleasure. It is the first glimpse which has been furnished me of the interior workings of the late unexpected but fortunate revolution of your country. The newspapers told us only that the great beast was fallen; but what part in this the patriots acted, and what the egotists, whether the former slept while the latter were awake to their own interests only, the hireling scribblers of the English press said little and knew less. I see now the mortifying alternative under which the patriot there is placed, of being either silent, or disgraced by an association in opposition with the remains of Bonapartism. A full measure of liberty is not now perhaps to be expected by your nation, nor am I confident they are prepared to preserve it. More than a generation will be requisite, under the administration of reasonable laws favoring the progress of knowledge in the general mass of the people, and their habituation to an independent security of person and property, before they will be capable of estimating the value of freedom, and the necessity of a sacred adherence to the principles on which it rests for preservation. Instead of that liberty which takes root and growth in the progress of reason, if recovered by mere force or accident, it becomes, with an unprepared people, a tyranny still, of the many, the few, or the one. Possibly you may remember, at the date of the *jeu de paume*, how earnestly I urged yourself and the patriots of my acquaintance, to enter then into a compact with the king, securing freedom of religion, freedom of the press, trial by jury, *habeas corpus*, and a national legislature, all of which it was known he would then yield, to go home, and let these work on the amelioration of the condition of the people, until they should have rendered them capable of more, when occasions would not fail to arise for communicating to them more. This was as much as I then thought them able to bear, soberly and usefully for themselves. You thought otherwise, and that the dose might still be larger. And I found you were right; for subsequent events proved they were equal to the constitution of 1791. Unfortunately, some of the most honest and enlightened of our patriotic friends, (but closet politicians merely, unpractised in the knowledge of man,) thought more could still be obtained and borne. They did not weigh the hazards of a transition from one form of government to another, the value of what they had already rescued from those hazards, and might hold in security if they pleased, nor the imprudence of giving up the certainty of such a degree of liberty, under a limited monarch, for the uncertainty of a little more under the form of a republic. You differed from them. You were for stopping there, and for securing the constitution which the National Assembly had obtained. Here, too, you were right; and from this fatal error of the republicans, from their separation from yourself and the constitutionalists, in their councils, flowed all the subsequent sufferings and crimes of the French nation. The hazards of a second change fell upon them by the way. The foreigner gained time to anarchise by gold the government he could not overthrow by arms, to crush in their own councils the genuine republicans, by the fraternal embraces of exaggerated and hired pretenders, and to turn the machine of Jacobinism from the change to the destruction of

order; and, in the end, the limited monarchy they had secured
was exchanged for the unprincipled and bloody tyranny of
Robespierre, and the equally unprincipled and maniac tyranny
of Bonaparte. You are now rid of him, and I sincerely wish you
may continue so. But this may depend on the wisdom and
moderation of the restored dynasty. It is for them now to read
a lesson in the fatal errors of the republicans; to be contented
with a certain portion of power, secured by formal compact
with the nation, rather than, grasping at more, hazard all upon
uncertainty, and risk meeting the fate of their predecessor, or a
renewal of their own exile. We are just informed, too, of an
example which merits, if true, their most profound contemplation. The gazettes say that Ferdinand of Spain is dethroned, and his father re-established on the basis of their
new constitution. This order of magistrates must, therefore,
see, that although the attempts at reformation have not succeeded in their whole length, and some secession from the ultimate point has taken place, yet that men have by no means
fallen back to their former passiveness, but on the contrary,
that a sense of their rights, and a restlessness to obtain them,
remain deeply impressed on every mind, and, if not quieted by
reasonable relaxations of power, will break out like a volcano
on the first occasion, and overwhelm everything again in its
way. I always thought the present king an honest and moderate man; and having no issue, he is under a motive the less for
yielding to personal considerations. I cannot, therefore, but
hope, that the patriots in and out of your legislature, acting in
phalanx, but temperately and wisely, pressing unremittingly
the principles omitted in the late capitulation of the king, and
watching the occasions which the course of events will create,
may get those principles engrafted into it, and sanctioned by
the solemnity of a national act.

  With us the affairs of war have taken the most favorable turn
which was to be expected. Our thirty years of peace had taken
off, or superannuated, all our revolutionary officers of experience and grade; and our first draught in the lottery of untried
characters had been most unfortunate. The delivery of the fort
and army of Detroit by the traitor Hull; the disgrace at Queenstown, under Van Rensellaer; the massacre at Frenchtown
under Winchester; and surrender of Boerstler in an open field

to one-third of his own numbers, were the inauspicious beginnings of the first year of our warfare. The second witnessed but
the single miscarriage occasioned by the disagreement of
Wilkinson and Hampton, mentioned in my letter to you of
November the 30th, 1813, while it gave us the capture of York
by Dearborne and Pike; the capture of Fort George by Dearborne also; the capture of Proctor's army on the Thames by
Harrison, Shelby and Johnson, and that of the whole British
fleet on Lake Erie by Perry. The third year has been a continued series of victories, to-wit: of Brown and Scott at Chippewa,
of the same at Niagara; of Gaines over Drummond at Fort
Erie; that of Brown over Drummond at the same place; the
capture of another fleet on Lake Champlain by M'Donough;
the entire defeat of their army under Prevost, on the same day,
by M'Comb, and recently their defeats at New Orleans by
Jackson, Coffee and Carroll, with the loss of four thousand
men out of nine thousand and six hundred, with their two
Generals, Packingham and Gibbs killed, and a third, Keane,
wounded, mortally, as is said.

This series of successes has been tarnished only by the conflagration at Washington, a *coup de main* differing from that at
Richmond, which you remember, in the revolutionary war, in
the circumstance only, that we had, in that case, but forty-eight
hours' notice that an enemy had arrived within our capes;
whereas, at Washington, there was abundant previous notice.
The force designated by the President was double of what was
necessary; but failed, as is the general opinion, through the
insubordination of Armstrong, who would never believe the
attack intended until it was actually made, and the sluggishness
of Winder before the occasion, and his indecision during it.
Still, in the end, the transaction has helped rather than hurt us,
by arousing the general indignation of our country, and by
marking to the world of Europe the Vandalism and brutal
character of the English government. It has merely served to
immortalize their infamy. And add further, that through the
whole period of the war, we have beaten them single-handed
at sea, and so thoroughly established our superiority over them
with equal force, that they retire from that kind of contest, and
never suffer their frigates to cruize singly. The Endymion
would never have engaged the frigate President, but knowing

herself backed by three frigates and a razee, who, though
somewhat slower sailers, would get up before she could be
taken. The disclosure to the world of the fatal secret that they
can be beaten at sea with an equal force, the evidence furnished
by the military operations of the last year that experience is
rearing us officers who, when our means shall be fully under
way, will plant our standard on the walls of Quebec and Halifax, their recent and signal disaster at New Orleans, and the
evaporation of their hopes from the Hartford convention, will
probably raise a clamor in the British nation, which will force
their ministry into peace. I say *force* them, because, willingly,
they would never be at peace. The British ministers find in a
state of war rather than of peace, by riding the various contractors, and receiving *douceurs* on the vast expenditures of the war
supplies, that they recruit their broken fortunes, or make new
ones, and therefore will not make peace as long as by any delusions they can keep the temper of the nation up to the war
point. They found some hopes on the state of our finances. It is
true that the excess of our banking institutions, and their present discredit, have shut us out from the best source of credit we
could ever command with certainty. But the foundations of
credit still remain to us, and need but skill which experience will
soon produce, to marshal them into an order which may carry
us through any length of war. But they have hoped more in
their Hartford convention. Their fears of republican France
being now done away, they are directed to republican America,
and they are playing the same game for disorganization here,
which they played in your country. The Marats, the Dantons
and Robespierres of Massachusetts are in the same pay, under
the same orders, and making the same efforts to anarchise us,
that their prototypes in France did there.

I do not say that all who met at Hartford were under the
same motives of money, nor were those of France. Some of
them are Outs, and wish to be Inns; some the mere dupes of
the agitators, or of their own party passions, while the Marat-
ists alone are in the real secret; but they have very different
materials to work on. The yeomanry of the United States are
not the *canaille* of Paris. We might safely give them leave to go
through the United States recruiting their ranks, and I am
satisfied they could not raise one single regiment (gambling

merchants and silk-stocking clerks excepted) who would support them in any effort to separate from the Union. The cement of this Union is in the heart-blood of every American. I do not believe there is on earth a government established on so immovable a basis. Let them, in any State, even in Massachusetts itself, raise the standard of separation, and its citizens will rise in mass, and do justice themselves on their own incendiaries. If they could have induced the government to some effort of suppression, or even to enter into discussion with them, it would have given them some importance, have brought them into some notice. But they have not been able to make themselves even a subject of conversation, either of public or private societies. A silent contempt has been the sole notice they excite; consoled, indeed, some of them, by the *palpable* favors of Philip. Have then no fears for us, my friend. The grounds of these exist only in English newspapers, credited or endowed by the Castlereaghs or the Cannings, or some other such models of pure and uncorrupted virtue. Their military heroes, by land and sea, may sink our oyster boats, rob our hen roosts, burn our negro huts, and run off. But a campaign or two more will relieve them from further trouble or expense in defending their American possessions.

You once gave me a copy of the journal of your campaign in Virginia, in 1781, which I must have lent to some one of the undertakers to write the history of the revolutionary war, and forgot to reclaim. I conclude this, because it is no longer among my papers, which I have very diligently searched for it, but in vain. An author of real ability is now writing that part of the history of Virginia. He does it in my neighborhood, and I lay open to him all my papers. But I possess none, nor has he any, which can enable him to do justice to your faithful and able services in that campaign. If you could be so good as to send me another copy, by the very first vessel bound to any port in the United States, it might be here in time; for although he expects to begin to print within a month or two, yet you know the delays of these undertakings. At any rate it might be got in as a supplement. The old Count Rochambeau gave me also his *memoire* of the operations at York, which is gone in the same way, and I have no means of applying to his family for it. Perhaps you could render them as well as us, the service of procuring another copy.

I learn, with real sorrow, the deaths of Monsieur and Madame de Tessé. They made an interesting part in the idle reveries in which I have sometimes indulged myself, of seeing all my friends of Paris once more, for a month or two; a thing impossible, which, however, I never permitted myself to despair of. The regrets, however, of seventy-three at the loss of friends, may be the less, as the time is shorter within which we are to meet again, according to the creed of our education.

This letter will be handed you by Mr. Ticknor, a young gentleman of Boston, of great erudition, indefatigable industry, and preparation for a life of distinction in his own country. He passed a few days with me here, brought high recommendations from Mr. Adams and others, and appeared in every respect to merit them. He is well worthy of those attentions which you so kindly bestow on our countrymen, and for those he may receive I shall join him in acknowledging personal obligations.

I salute you with assurances of my constant and affectionate friendship and respect.

P. S. February 26th. My letter had not yet been sealed, when I received news of our peace. I am glad of it, and especially that we closed our war with the eclat of the action at New Orleans. But I consider it as an armistice only, because no security is provided against the impressment of our seamen. While this is unsettled we are in hostility of mind with England, although actual deeds of arms may be suspended by a truce. If she thinks the exercise of this outrage is worth eternal war, eternal war it must be, or extermination of the one or the other party. The first act of impressment she commits on an American, will be answered by reprisal, or by a declaration of war here; and the interval must be merely a state of preparation for it. In this we have much to do, in further fortifying our seaport towns, providing military stores, classing and disciplining our militia, arranging our financial system, and above all, pushing our domestic manufactures, which have taken such root as never again can be shaken. Once more, God bless you.

TH. JEFFERSON

James Madison: Special Message to Congress

The President presented the Treaty of Ghent to the Senate for ratification on February 15, and the next day it voted unanimously (35–0) to approve it. Madison signed the instrument of ratification later that same day, and this formally ended the war. The following day at 11:00 P.M., Monroe and Anthony Baker exchanged ratifications, which brought the treaty into force. Federalists celebrated the end of the war, and when they read the terms of the treaty they felt vindicated. Its failure to even mention the maritime rights that had been cited as the principal cause of the war seemed to confirm their belief in the conflict's futility, and they cheerfully expected to reap the benefits from the exposure of the administration's folly. But at least one of their number was not so optimistic. James Robertson of Philadelphia correctly predicted the Republicans' strategy: they would ignore the issues that had so animated them in the summer of 1812 and portray the conflict as "a war on our part of pure self defence against the designs of the British to reduce us again to subjection." He concluded that "the President will only have to call it a glorious peace, and the party here will echo it."

Washington, February 18, 1815.
To the Senate and House of Representatives of the United States:
I lay before Congress copies of the treaty of peace and amity between the United States and His Britannic Majesty, which was signed by the commissioners of both parties at Ghent on the 24th of December, 1814, and the ratifications of which have been duly exchanged.

While performing this act I congratulate you and our constituents upon an event which is highly honorable to the nation, and terminates with peculiar felicity a campaign signalized by the most brilliant successes.

The late war, although reluctantly declared by Congress, had become a necessary resort to assert the rights and independence of the nation. It has been waged with a success which is the natural result of the wisdom of the legislative councils, of the patriotism of the people, of the public spirit of the militia, and of the valor of the military and naval forces of the country. Peace, at all times a blessing, is peculiarly welcome, therefore, at a period when the causes for the war have ceased to operate, when the Government has demonstrated the efficiency of its powers of defense, and when the nation can review its conduct without regret and without reproach.

I recommend to your care and beneficence the gallant men whose achievements in every department of the military service, on the land and on the water, have so essentially contributed to the honor of the American name and to the restoration of peace. The feelings of conscious patriotism and worth will animate such men under every change of fortune and pursuit, but their country performs a duty to itself when it bestows those testimonials of approbation and applause which are at once the reward and the incentive to great actions.

The reduction of the public expenditures to the demands of a peace establishment will doubtless engage the immediate attention of Congress. There are, however, important considerations which forbid a sudden and general revocation of the measures that have been produced by the war. Experience has taught us that neither the pacific dispositions of the American people nor the pacific character of their political institutions can altogether exempt them from that strife which appears beyond the ordinary lot of nations to be incident to the actual period of the world, and the same faithful monitor demonstrates that a certain degree of preparation for war is not only indispensable to avert disasters in the onset, but affords also the best security for the continuance of peace. The wisdom of Congress will therefore, I am confident, provide for the maintenance of an adequate regular force; for the gradual advancement of the naval establishment; for improving all the means of harbor defense; for adding discipline to the distinguished bravery of the militia, and for cultivating the military art in its essential branches, under the liberal patronage of Government.

The resources of our country were at all times competent to the attainment of every national object, but they will now be enriched and invigorated by the activity which peace will introduce into all the scenes of domestic enterprise and labor. The provision that has been made for the public creditors during the present session of Congress must have a decisive effect in the establishment of the public credit both at home and abroad. The reviving interests of commerce will claim the legislative attention at the earliest opportunity, and such regulations will, I trust, be seasonably devised as shall secure to the United States their just proportion of the navigation of the world. The most liberal policy toward other nations, if met by corresponding dispositions, will in this respect be found the most beneficial policy toward ourselves. But there is no subject that can enter with greater force and merit into the deliberations of Congress than a consideration of the means to preserve and promote the manufactures which have sprung into existence and attained an unparalleled maturity throughout the United States during the period of the European wars. This source of national independence and wealth I anxiously recommend, therefore, to the prompt and constant guardianship of Congress.

The termination of the legislative sessions will soon separate you, fellow-citizens, from each other, and restore you to your constituents. I pray you to bear with you the expressions of my sanguine hope that the peace which has been just declared, will not only be the foundation of the most friendly intercourse between the United States and Great Britain, but that it will also be productive of happiness and harmony in every section of our beloved country. The influence of your precepts and example must be every where powerful; and while we accord in grateful acknowledgments for the protection which Providence has bestowed upon us, let us never cease to inculcate obedience to the laws, and fidelity to the union, as constituting the palladium of the national independence and prosperity.

National Aegis: *"The Peace"*

February 22, 1815

The President's exultant tone was indeed echoed by Republican orators and editors across the country, and collectively they shaped a narrative of the war and its meaning that would prove durable. "Never did a country occupy more lofty ground," said Supreme Court justice Joseph Story; "we have stood the contest, single-handed, against the conqueror of Europe." For the *National Advocate* of New York, "this second war of independence has been illustrated by more splendid achievements than the war of the revolution." Not surprisingly, the *National Intelligencer* singled out the administration for special praise, asserting that it "has succeeded in asserting the principles of God and nature against the encroachments of human ambition and tyranny." The Worcester *National Aegis*, a Republican voice in the wilderness of Federalist Massachusetts, would not be outdone.

THE WAR IS OVER—The return of Peace cheers every heart, brightens every eye and raises from every tongue a song of DELIVERANCE and TRIUMPH. Yes, *we have triumphed*—let snarling malcontents say what they will, *we have gloriously triumphed!* We have wiped away our disgrace. We have retrieved our honour. We have exalted our character. We present to the world the noble spectacle of a young but brave people, who, feeling their rights trampled upon, their remonstrance derided and their forbearance despised, drew the sword against the haughty Oppressor, and have not sheathed it, till he has severely felt its keenness and the strength of the arm which wielded it.

We shall not repeat arguments to prove that the war was just and proper in its origin. Very few real republicans can have ever doubted its justice—its expediency—its necessity. It was *just*, because we had been injured, and could neither obtain reparation for the past nor security for the future. It was *expedient*, because that time appeared to be the crisis when we had the fairest chance to bring the aggressor to terms, while he was pressed with danger at home. It was indeed *absolutely neces-sary*, because to have submitted longer would have been to lie down in utter disgrace, and the surrender of our rights would have been followed by the surrender of our liberties. We felt proud of our country at its commencement. We felt prouder as its progress manifested our resolution and ability to sustain the unequal contest—and we now exult in its happy conclusion. Out ship of state has survived the storm, and directed by a steady and helmsman, has, with the blessing of God, reached the haven of safety.

We are luckily extricated from the War, says the discontented oppositionist, but what have we gained by it? What object have we accomplished? What is our return for the blood and trea-sure we have expended? The answer is ready—*We have preserved our honour*—which would have been irretrievably forfeited had we brooked the insults and injuries heaped upon us. With na-tions as with individuals, honour should be dearer than life or any earthly interest. It should be considered as their *chief good*, without which plenty and prosperity would be worthless and insipid, and with which poverty and adversity might not only admit of consolation but of happiness. Such were once the maxims and feelings of patriots. When their national honour was touched, they did not stop to count the cost like the calcu-lating politicians of the present day. They spurned every insult, they resisted every aggression, fearless of the consequences and trusting their cause to Heaven. Money was not their God. If their country needed it, their whole property was at its dis-posal. There was no danger of publick bankruptcy. How do such examples soar above the pitiful, sordid, craving policy so predominant in these times!

We have accomplished the main objects of the War. The Orders in Council were rescinded soon after its commencement. This to be sure was not a consequence of the war, but it removed one of its chief causes and one of the principle objects of an adjustment. The Impressment of our Seamen, of course, ceases *in practice*, since the pacification of Europe. The pretended *right* of searching our vessels for their own seamen is not relin-quished by the British, neither is it recognized by us. It is quite certain that the government would not have been justified in continuing the war for an abstract question, when it ceased to have any practical operation. Should the practice be resumed, then may we resume an attitude of hostility.

We have finished the War with great glory and much to our honour in the view of the world. The courage and heroism of *America* in declaring war, were conspicuous to all *Europe*. Prejudice and misrepresentation for a while obscured our real motives, and led the nations who were enslaved by France or threatened with immediate subjugation, to look upon us as the allies of their oppressor. These clouds have long since cleared away; our independence of French influence had been made manifest; our conduct was viewed in its true light; and the best wishes of continental Europe have accompanied us in the struggle. The firmness with which we supported the shock, when, by a sudden and wonderful revolution, we were left to contend single-handed against the mighty power of Britain— the constancy we have exhibited during the tremendous and appalling conflict—our undaunted perseverance in resisting the extravagant pretensions of the enemy and refusing to yield one inch of territory or one tittle of our rights, by which we have at last secured an honourable peace—the splendid successes of our arms by sea and land, which have mortified British pride and chastised their presumption—and especially the triumphant termination of the last campaign, which closes the war with glory to *America* and disgrace to *England*—*all these things will tell well in history.* They will shine with lustre before the eyes of all nations. They will exalt their estimation of the American character to the highest respect and admiration. Above all, they will furnish an impressive lesson to Great Britain, teaching her, that this free and brave people will not submit to the violation of their rights, and that they are strong enough to vindicate them. She has suffered too severely in this war soon to provoke another. This is what we have gained by the war, in addition to the acquisition of experience; and in our humble opinion it is worth all it has cost us. The millions we have spent are but trash compared with the independence we have secured. A few years of peace and commerce will amply repay us and fill our empty treasury to overflowing. The loss of lives we regret as deeply as any one—they are a necessary sacrifice to the publick defence, the inevitable consequence of war. Let the memories of those who have fallen be respected and their families generously provided for.

We have concluded a Peace upon honourable terms. Great Britain has abandoned her unreasonable demands, her unrighteous schemes of aggrandizement. We are restored to all our possessions and to an unshackled commerce. The privilege of curing our fish on the shores of *Newfoundland* and of trading to the British parts in the *East Indies* is now withheld from us. But we could claim neither of them as a right and we have abundant means of retaliating if Britain pursues a system of exclusion. We are put into a better condition than *status quo ante bellum*, for the *Orders in Council* have ceased and the *Impressment of Seamen* is relinquished!

The Republican Party have the greatest reason for joy and gratulation. They may look back with self-satisfaction upon the course which they have pursued, and by steadily adhering to which, they have alone saved the country at the hazard of their own preponderance. They disinterestedly incurred and sustained the sole responsibility of the war. They conducted it not only without federal aid but in spite of federal opposition. They stemmed the current of faction. They, in general, supported the government with fidelity. They have carried the country through a sea of difficulties in safety, and have placed her destiny upon a solid foundation. During all the embarrassments which have surrounded them, they have preserved the confidence of the people. Federalists may now take a final adieu of that power and place they fancied they had in near prospect. If their opposition was in vain during the tremendous troubles and distresses of war, what will it avail them in the sunshine of peace? With their present principles and the memory of their former conduct, they will always remain a minority.

George Prevost: General Order

After the failure to take New Orleans, the British expeditionary force turned again to Mobile, and on February 11 five thousand men under General Lambert forced the surrender of Fort Bowyer. This was the last major land action of the war, for before the British could move on to occupy Mobile itself, news of the peace came, and they withdrew. Though a handful of skirmishes with Indians and naval encounters would follow, the war was over. In British Canada, as in America, it was pronounced a success. Despite Jefferson's prediction in August 1812 that the U.S. conquest of Canada would be a "mere matter of marching," the British had retained their North American possessions, and the assistance of the Canadians themselves, both Anglophone and Francophone, had played a role. But for George Prevost the war would end in disgrace, his failure at Plattsburgh overshadowing his otherwise able tenure. On March 2, 1815, a day after learning of the Treaty of Ghent, he was removed from office and summoned to London, there to face charges of misconduct lodged by Sir James Yeo. As he took his leave, he offered the following appraisal of the war in his final general orders, issued through Edward Baynes, his adjutant.

Adjutant General's Office,
Head-Quarters, Quebec, 3d April, 1815.

GENERAL ORDERS.

His Excellency the Commander of the forces announces to the army serving in British North America, that he has received the commands of His Royal Highness the Prince Regent to return to England.

In taking leave of an army he had the honor to command from the commencement of hostilities with the United States to the termination of the war, His Excellency has great satisfaction in expressing his entire approbation and acknowledging the sense he entertains of the zeal, courage and discipline that has been so eminently displayed by this portion of his Majesty's troops.

It has fallen to the lot of this army to struggle through an arduous and unequal contest, remote from succour, and deprived of many advantages experienced in the more cultivated countries of Europe; yet his Excellency has witnessed with pride and admiration, the firmness, intrepidity, and patient endurance of fatigue and privations, which have marked the character of the army of Canada. Under all these circumstances, valour and discipline have prevailed, and although local considerations and limited means have circumscribed the war principally to a defensive system, it has, notwithstanding, been ennobled by numerous brilliant exploits, which will adorn the page of future history. At Detroit and at the River Raisin, two entire armies with their commanding generals were captured, and greatly superior armies were repulsed. The several battles of Queenstown, Stoney Creek, Chateauguay, Chrystler's, La Cole, Lundy's Lane, near the Falls of Niagara, and the subsequent operations on that frontier, will ever immortalize the heroes who were on those occasions afforded the opportunity of distinguishing themselves. The capture of Michilimackinac, Ogdensburg, Oswego and Niagara by assault, are trophies of the prowess of British arms. The names of the respective officers who led his Majesty's troops to these several achievements are already known to the world, and will be transmitted by the faithful historian with glory to a grateful posterity.

In viewing past events, it is with exultation his Excellency reflects on the complete success which has crowned the valour, exertions, and perseverance of this gallant army, by terminating each successive campaign in the defeat and discomfiture of all the enemy's plans, in which the utmost energies of the government of the United States had been exhausted in vain efforts to accomplish his avowed object, the conquest of these Provinces.

Lieut. Gen. Sir John C. Sherbrooke, and the army under his immediate orders, are entitled to the highest praise for the bravery and promptness displayed in the occupation of a large District of the enemy's territory, and his Excellency request the Lieut. General will accept his thanks for the cordial assistance he has at all times afforded him.

To Lieut. General Sir Gordon Drummond, on whom the

command of the Canadas devolves, his Excellency's best thanks are due, for his unwearied exertions and support under circumstances of peculiar difficulty: To the general officers, general staff, and officers and soldiers, his Excellency feels himself highly indebted, and duly appreciates their respective merits. To Major General Baynes the adjutant general, and Maj. Gen. Sir Sidney Beckwith, the quarter master general, and to the officers of his personal staff, his Excellency's thanks are also due, for the judgment, alacrity and zeal evinced in the discharge of their several duties.

His Excellency has every reason to be satisfied with the conduct and exertions of the public departments of this army, and he feels it an act of justice to express particularly his approbation of the very efficient manner in which the commissariat has been conducted under the zealous and judicious arrangements of Commissary-general Robinson.

His Excellency will have peculiar gratification in representing his Royal Highness the Prince Regent, the services and talents of the officers of this army, to the honourable survivors of which, Lieut. Gen. Sir George Prevost offers the heartfelt tribute of his warmest thanks.

(Signed)   EDWARD BAYNES
Adjutant General North America

THE DARTMOOR MASSACRE:
DEVON, ENGLAND, APRIL 1815

Lewis Peter Clover: from "Reminiscences of a Dartmoor Prisoner"

Over the course of the war there were roughly twenty thousand American prisoners of war, most of them privateersmen. As internees found their way home after the war ended, reports of harsh conditions began to appear in print. "The return of our people from British prisons," observed *Niles' Register*, "have filled the newspapers with tales of horror." Perhaps the most notorious of the British prisons was Dartmoor, a damp and dreary place on the moors of Devon in southwest England. By 1815 it housed some five thousand Americans, including Lewis Peter Clover who, on January 17, 1814, was arrested aboard the merchantman *Union*, which had been detained by a British naval vessel off Calcutta. He was incarcerated at Dartmoor from October 21, 1814, to July 1, 1815, and here, in a memoir published in *The Knickerbocker Magazine* nearly thirty years later, he offers an account of the terrible events of April 6, 1815.

———————

At length, about the middle of March, intelligence was received of the ratification of peace; and although the joy was as great as when the *news* was first heard, it was not manifested with the same outward appearances, for the want of means, the money having been nearly all spent on the former occasion. From this time forward the captives were not so strictly guarded: the yards were thrown open in common through the day, and they were permitted to take such exercise and engage in such amusements as were consistent, until arrangements could be made for their return home.

One morning, at the usual time of serving out the provisions, it was announced that there was no bread, and that ship-biscuit must be substituted. This met with decided opposition; the prisoners were determined not to be imposed upon by the contractors and agents, nor to allow them to palm upon them the damaged remnant of ship's bread which they

had on hand, in lieu of the usual kind. They were informed
that there was no other, and that they must take that or none.
They remained without bread all that day, but toward night
they grew restless. At night-fall they became 'like a raging
tempest.' From some cause, which I never heard accounted
for, the prison doors had been left open, and the inmates had
free access to the yards, where a great number had assembled,
giving vent to their feelings in curses loud and deep. All at
once, and as with one mind, they made a rush toward the
market-square, where the provision stores were situated. In an
instant the ponderous gates and massive iron barriers were
prostrated: then seizing the bread, which had probably lain
there during the whole day, they quietly returned to the prisons, and suffered themselves to be locked in as usual. They
then divided the bread, and partook of their scanty fare, the
only food which had passed their lips for the space of thirty-six
hours or more. I never before or since saw the old proverb realized, that 'Hunger will break through stone walls;' in this
case it was literally breaking through walls of iron. If the prisoners had been desirous of escaping, they certainly had at that
time a fair opportunity; for I did not hear of the slightest resistance being made to them by any one; and another and a less
effort would have put them in possession of the arms. It was
said that Captain SHORTLAND was absent at the time; I think
this very probable, for if he had been present blood would
have been shed. It was reported that on his return, learning
what had taken place, he became frantic with rage. I have no
doubt of it; for threats which were then uttered were terribly
fulfilled but a few weeks afterward.

   Time wore tediously on, appearing tenfold longer in proportion to the growing impatience of confinement, which seemed
so uselessly prolonged. As the season advanced, the weather
became more temperate; and the sun seemed to coquet with the
earth, in occasional glimpses through the thick veil of fog which
enveloped that dreary waste; and the prisoners embraced the
opportunity of enjoying her smiles. At this time they were allowed to do pretty much as they pleased; indeed, they were
scarcely considered as prisoners, being only confined at night,
and having the free scope of the yards during the day. They

appeared merely to be kept together, until arrangements could be made for their embarkation for the United States.

On the sixth day of April, 1815, the sun broke forth with unusual splendor. A warm, gentle breeze dispersed the heavy pall of vapor which had enveloped the place during the winter; and it appeared as though all nature smiled, to make glad the heart of the poor captive. All that day the yard was thronged, and faces were lighted up with joy, hope, and peace, that had long been worn and furrowed with care. The sick and feeble came forth to enjoy the air; the hale and the strong were there; the youth of fourteen, and the gray-headed man of sixty, were there; some amusing themselves at various games: some wrestling, some walking, and meditating upon their homes, wives, children, and friends, whom they hoped soon to see, after a separation of many years. Tears filled their eyes, and sobs choked their utterance, as they conversed together upon their anticipated happiness. The day was spent as in a happy dream.

Late in the afternoon, a small party was engaged in a game of ball, in the upper part of the yards of prisons Nos. 5, 6, and 7, and near the wall separating them from the soldiers' quarters. During their play, the ball was sometimes knocked over the wall, which was as often thrown back by some one of the guard who was not then on duty. At length, becoming tired of returning the ball, the amusement was at an end. They then threatened, if the ball was not returned, that they would break through and get it. Receiving no answer, they proceeded at once to put their threat into execution; and with their knives soon succeeded in making a small breach. By this time it was nearly dark, and most of the prisoners had retired to their quarters, it being about their usual supper time: a few remained in the lower part of the yard, walking and conversing together, enjoying the tranquillity of the evening; and some dozen or two continued around the hole which had been made in the wall.

I was within the building, standing by a window, when a person who had just come in, observed, 'There will be trouble soon, caused by that break in the wall.' This was the first intimation conveyed of the occurrence; myself and a large majority of the prisoners were totally ignorant of it up to this time. While conversing, we heard the report of fire-arms, and looking out, we beheld the walls lined with soldiers, and down in the yard, saw the prisoners closely pursued by a platoon of soldiers at a charge speed, led on by Shortland. All was now in the utmost confusion. It was discovered that the monster Shortland, in order to 'make surety doubly sure,' had unobserved closed all the doors but one, of each prison. The long-threatened storm had now burst upon them in all its fury. On the first alarm, many of those within rushed out to learn the cause, by which means the only entrance was for a time blocked up; and those outside, finding escape cut off at the closed doors, hastened to that which was open, closely pursued by the soldiers, who used their bayonets without mercy; they suffered severely at the same time from a cross-fire from those stationed on the walls. The scene now baffled description. The fugitives, in their haste to get under shelter, were met by those coming out, by which means they were for a time exposed in a body to the balls and bayonets of Shortland and his mercenaries. At length they all got in, dragging with them at the same time several of the killed and wounded of their comrades. The door was then closed and secured, and Shortland and his heroes retired.

It would be impossible to give a correct description of the scene which now presented itself. On the floor opposite where I messed lay a handsome youth, of about fifteen years of age, stiff, and cold as marble, pierced through the heart by a bayonet. A few yards farther on, lay another: a ball had entered his forehead, and passed out at the back of his head. I examined the spot the next morning, and saw part of his brains which had been dashed against the wall nearly opposite the prison door. Among the wounded, who were brought in by their comrades, was one with a wound in the shoulder; another with his thigh broken; another had a most miraculous escape with his life; a musket ball had passed through his mouth from side to side, taking out nearly the whole of his teeth. I saw him after he had got well: he could take no food except with a spoon. It was several days before the full extent of the mischief was known, when it was ascertained that the amount was seven killed, and fifty wounded, some of them severely. The accompanying engraving will afford a correct idea of the several prisons, and the scene which I have endeavored to describe:

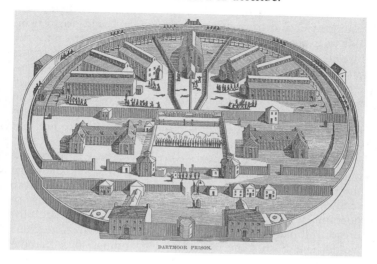

DARTMOOR PRISON.

No language can depict the deep, burning feeling of hatred and indignation which now broke forth in bitter execrations from the survivors. If they could have obtained arms of any kind, dreadful would have been the retaliation! In about an hour a litter was sent in, and the dead and wounded were taken to the Hospital. Not an eye was closed that night. Some gave vent to their feelings by threats and exclamations, others brooded over their wrongs in silence. Alas! who can tell what a day may bring forth! Who could have believed that a morning of so fair a promise would close in blood and sorrow? Who could have imagined that a body of unarmed men, in time of peace, in charge of 'one of the most enlightened and christian nations on the earth,' would be most foully and cowardly butchered in cold blood? Would that this were the only blot upon the history of that arrogant nation; that 'champion of the civil and religious liberty of the world!' When this brutal transaction became rumored abroad, it was scarcely believed for a time; but when it was confirmed, astonishment at the atrocity of the deed bewildered the minds of the people, and they exclaimed, 'Can such things be!' To allay the public excitement, and attempt a justification of their proceedings, a court of inquiry was called; and Mr. CHARLES KING was appointed to act in behalf of the Americans. He was then a very young man, and from want of experience, could not reasonably be expected to be as competent as an older person for the investigation of so grave and important a transaction. It was easy to forsee the result, surrounded as he was by old and interested veterans in intrigue and diplomacy. Capt. Shortland was acquitted, on the ground, first, that he was justifiable, in consequence of an attempt on the part of the prisoners to break out; secondly, that he did not give the order to fire, and therefore was not guilty.

The idea that the prisoners wished to escape, was preposterous. They had no inducement to do so, as they well knew that they were merely waiting for arrangements to be completed to send them home. If it had been their wish, they had a fair opportunity about a fortnight before, when they seized upon the bread. If it had been their intention, at the present time, there would have been some mutual understanding, some preconcerted plan; instead of which, the breaking of the wall was known only to the few who were foolishly engaged in it; the great body of the prisoners being at the time within the prisons, with the exception of the few who were conversing and walking at the lower end of the yard, all of whom knew nothing of the affair; and beside all this, the whole difficulty originated in the yard enclosing Nos. 5, 6, and 7 prisons; the inmates of the other four knowing nothing of the transaction, until they were assailed by the soldiers, and made to suffer equally with the others. As to the supposition that the soldiers commenced firing without orders, who does not know that the strict discipline enforced in the military of Great-Britain, at all times, forbade for an instant such an absurd idea? Indeed, had the soldiers been possessed of the demoniac spirit of their leader, the havoc would have been threefold greater than it was; for it was evident that they must have generally fired very low, or over their heads, to have caused so many wounded and so few killed.

It would be difficult to account for the motive which actuated Capt. Shortland, in his conduct toward the prisoners, unless it was from his having been many years in the British navy, and having belonged to the class termed the 'old school;' possessing all the coarse brutality of that early period of the English service; tyrannical and overbearing to those under his command, and servile to his superiors. There is but little doubt that the repeated reverses of his countrymen on their favorite element, the ocean, and the finale of the contest in the decisive victory at New-Orleans, rankled in his bosom; and the affair of the bread, and the breach in the wall, served him as a pretext for his unnecessary and brutal act.

John Quincy Adams to William Eustis

The timing of the peace at Ghent had been fortunate for the Liverpool ministry. Had the war continued into 1815, it was likely that the Duke of Wellington and a significant number of troops would have been dispatched to North America. Instead, they were close at hand when, on March 20, Napoleon returned from his exile on Elba to roil Europe once more. Wellington, who had replaced Castlereagh at Vienna, would assume command of seventy-three thousand men in the allied campaign that led to Bonaparte's final defeat at Waterloo on June 18, and brought about the restoration once more of Louis XVIII to the French throne. This, coupled with the final resolutions of the Congress of Vienna, would usher in a period of relative quietude in Europe. Surveying the state of affairs from his vantage point as American minister to Great Britain, though, John Quincy Adams everywhere saw signs of conflict to come. His letter to William Eustis, formerly the secretary of war and now U.S. minister to the Netherlands, reveals the enduring legacy of Anglophobia that the War of 1812 would leave in its wake.

Boston House, Ealing. 31. August 1815.

Dear Sir.

Your favours of the 25.th instant were left at my Office in London, by Mr Langdon whom I had hoped to have the pleasure of seeing here, where I have taken my Summer, and perhaps my winter residence—It is seven miles out of London, and had the name, by which I date, before I took it.—Mr. Langdon is so much pressed for time, that he cannot at present come out—If he comes back here, I hope to be more fortunate. He does me the favour to take this Letter.

The Newspapers give us accounts from France almost every day, and some of our Countrymen are coming from that Country, almost every week—As the allied Sovereigns came to an agreement together, in the distributions at Vienna, I see no reason for doubting that they will agree equally well upon the distributions of the present day—Now probably as then the

706

principal difficulty will be to make up the Russian portion— But as to France the case is plain enough, though there has been some mincing in stating it, France is a conquest and as a conquest will be treated.

I am sorely disappointed at the "gratuitous compliment," to the Dey of Algiers—Will it always be our destiny to end with shame, what we begin with glory?—Never was there such an opportunity for putting down those Pirates, as we have had— The work was half-done, and instead of completing it we restore to the reptile the very sting we had extracted from him—And what will the Peace be worth, when he has got back his ships and men?—A snare to the unwary!

Mr Changuion has been here, and is gone home—I had not the pleasure of seeing him, but he speaks well of our Country, and of the reception and treatment which he met with there— I see no occasion for us to be more solicitous for a new commercial Treaty with the Netherlands, than their Government —The old Treaty as recognized by both Governments will do no harm—I know not that it will do much good—I am surprized to hear that they have no Commerce—though it is evident the policy of their great Ally will be to allow them as little of that as possible.

The present price at London, of all our six percent Stocks, the Interest of which is payable in the United States is 90—The Hague never was and never will be a place of Commerce—And even at Amsterdam you will find great difficulty in disposing of any American securities. The price there always depends upon that of the London market, combined with the course of Exchange—The Exchange between this Country and Holland is about 5 per Cent below par, though an Exchange of paper for specie. Before the Battle of Waterloo it was 20 per Cent below par.

I have received dispatches from our government of 21 July— The horizon between the two Hemispheres is yet dark, and what is worse, darkening. The British naval commanders, in defiance of the Treaty of Ghent, have carried away from the United States all the slaves they had taken—There was no certainty that Michillimakinac had been restored—The Agents and Traders were instigating the Indians in the North, and a British officer posted in Florida was doing the same thing with the Creeks—Our Fishing Vessels had been turned away, and warned to twenty leagues from the Coast—The British Packet had been seized at New-York for an attempt to smuggle goods—At the same time the cabinet here have determined to increase their naval Armaments on the Lakes of Canada—and the Ministerial Gazettes are marked with strong symptoms of hostility—The language held here is temperate, and full of conciliatory professions—But when the affairs of France shall be settled to their satisfaction (which I think will be soon) I expect a change of tone—It is said they have met with some new difficulties in India, where there is a call for additional troops from Europe—This too I presume will come to nothing.—The fleet however is reducing to a Peace Establishment.

Mr Everett was good enough to send me a copy of the new Constitution for the Netherlands—Paper Constitutions are something in the United States; but they are something like the Baltimore Schooners, which they say, European sailors cannot manage to navigate.

Mr Pederson has just embarked at Liverpool for Philadelphia —He goes out as Minister from his Danish Majesty to the United States.

I am, Dear Sir, very faithfully yours
John Quincy Adams.

His Excellency., W. Eustis.
Minister Plenipotentiary from the United States
of America. The Hague.

James Madison: Seventh Annual Message to Congress

Although his opponents called the War of 1812 "Mr. Madison's War," the President was often unable to impose his will on its course. His cautious nature and deferential leadership style allowed backbiting and incompetence to reign unchallenged among cabinet members and military officers, and made it difficult for him to secure vital legislation from Congress. Even Republicans criticized his leadership. "Our President," said John C. Calhoun in 1812, "has not . . . those commanding talents, which are necessary to control those about him." In 1814 a Pennsylvania congressman noted that Madison's "spirit and capacity for a crisis of war are very generally called in question." Much of this criticism was forgotten after February 1815, however, when the news from Hartford, New Orleans, and Ghent converged into a happy denouement for the President, one that laid the groundwork for the period of national unity to come. "Notwithstanding a thousand faults and blunders," John Adams would concede, "his Administration has acquired more glory, and established more Union than all three Predecessors, Washington, Adams, and Jefferson put together." Here, almost a year after Ghent, the President surveys the bright prospects ahead, and proposes a program that, in its creative fusion of traditionally Republican and Federalist positions, suggests the extent to which the experience of war had transformed the young republic.

Washington, December 5, 1815.
Fellow-Citizens of the Senate and of the House of Representatives:

I have the satisfaction on our present meeting of being able to communicate to you the successful termination of the war which had been commenced against the United States by the Regency of Algiers. The squadron in advance on that service, under Commodore Decatur, lost not a moment after its arrival in the Mediterranean in seeking the naval force of the enemy then cruising in that sea, and succeeded in capturing two of his ships, one of them the principal ship, commanded by the Algerine admiral. The high character of the American commander was brilliantly sustained on that occasion which brought his own ship into close action with that of his adversary, as was the accustomed gallantry of all the officers and men actually engaged. Having prepared the way by this demonstration of American skill and prowess, he hastened to the port of Algiers, where peace was promptly yielded to his victorious force. In the terms stipulated the rights and honor of the United States were particularly consulted by a perpetual relinquishment on the part of the Dey of all pretensions to tribute from them. The impressions which have thus been made, strengthened as they will have been by subsequent transactions with the Regencies of Tunis and of Tripoli by the appearance of the larger force which followed under Commodore Bainbridge, the chief in command of the expedition, and by the judicious precautionary arrangements left by him in that quarter, afford a reasonable prospect of future security for the valuable portion of our commerce which passes within reach of the Barbary cruisers.

It is another source of satisfaction that the treaty of peace with Great Britain has been succeeded by a convention on the subject of commerce concluded by the plenipotentiaries of the two countries. In this result a disposition is manifested on the part of that nation corresponding with the disposition of the United States, which it may be hoped will be improved into liberal arrangements on other subjects on which the parties have mutual interests, or which might endanger their future harmony. Congress will decide on the expediency of promoting such a sequel by giving effect to the measure of confining the American navigation to American seamen—a measure which, at the same time that it might have that conciliatory tendency, would have the further advantage of increasing the independence of our navigation and the resources for our maritime defence.

In conformity with the articles in the treaty of Ghent relating to the Indians, as well as with a view to the tranquillity of our western and northwestern frontiers, measures were taken to establish an immediate peace with the several tribes who had been engaged in hostilities against the United States. Such of them as were invited to Detroit acceded readily to a renewal of the former treaties of friendship. Of the other tribes who were invited to a station on the Mississippi the greater number have also accepted the peace offered to them. The residue, consisting of the more distant tribes or parts of tribes, remain to be brought over by further explanations, or by such other means as may be adapted to the dispositions they may finally disclose.

The Indian tribes within and bordering on the southern frontier, whom a cruel war on their part had compelled us to chastise into peace, have latterly shown a restlessness which has called for preparatory measures for repressing it, and for protecting the commissioners engaged in carrying the terms of the peace into execution.

The execution of the act fixing the military peace establishment has been attended with difficulties which even now can only be overcome by legislative aid. The selection of officers, the payment and discharge of the troops enlisted for the war, the payment of the retained troops and their reunion from detached and distant stations, the collection and security of the public property in the Quartermaster, Commissary, and Ordnance departments, and the constant medical assistance required in hospitals and garrisons rendered a complete execution of the act impracticable on the 1st of May, the period more immediately contemplated. As soon, however, as circumstances would permit, and as far as it has been practicable consistently with the public interests, the reduction of the Army has been accomplished; but the appropriations for its pay and for other branches of the military service having proved inadequate, the earliest attention to that subject will be necessary; and the expediency of continuing upon the peace establishment the staff officers who have hitherto been provisionally retained is also recommended to the consideration of Congress.

In the performance of the Executive duty upon this occasion there has not been wanting a just sensibility to the merits of the American Army during the late war; but the obvious policy and design in fixing an efficient military peace establishment did not afford an opportunity to distinguish the aged and infirm on account of their past services nor the wounded and disabled on account of their present sufferings. The extent of the reduction, indeed, unavoidably involved the exclusion of many meritorious officers of every rank from the service of their country; and so equal as well as so numerous were the claims to attention that a decision by the standard of comparative merit could seldom be attained. Judged, however, in candor by a general standard of positive merit, the Army register will, it is believed, do honor to the establishment, while the case of those officers whose names are not included in it devolves with the strongest interest upon the legislative authority for such provision as shall be deemed the best calculated to give support and solace to the veteran and the invalid, to display the beneficence as well as the justice of the Government, and to inspire a martial zeal for the public service upon every future emergency.

Although the embarrassments arising from the want of an uniform national currency have not been diminished since the adjournment of Congress, great satisfaction has been derived in contemplating the revival of the public credit and the efficiency of the public resources. The receipts into the Treasury from the various branches of revenue during the nine months ending on the 30th of September last have been estimated at $12,500,000; the issues of Treasury notes of every denomination during the same period amounted to the sum of $14,000,000, and there was also obtained upon loan during the same period a sum of $9,000,000, of which the sum of $6,000,000 was subscribed in cash and the sum of $3,000,000 in Treasury notes. With these means, added to the sum of $1,500,000, being the balance of money in the Treasury on the 1st day of January, there has been paid between the 1st of January and the 1st of October on account of the appropriations of the preceding and of the present year (exclusively of the amount of the Treasury notes subscribed to the loan and of the amount redeemed in the payment of duties and taxes) the aggregate sum of $33,500,000, leaving a balance then in the Treasury estimated at the sum of $3,000,000. Independent, however, of the arrearages due for military services and supplies, it is presumed that a further sum of $5,000,000, including the interest on the public debt payable on the 1st of January next, will be demanded at the Treasury to complete the expenditures of the present year, and for which the existing ways and means will sufficiently provide.

The national debt, as it was ascertained on the 1st of October last, amounted in the whole to the sum of $120,000,000, consisting of the unredeemed balance of the debt contracted before the late war ($39,000,000), the amount of the funded debt contracted in consequence of the war ($64,000,000), and the amount of the unfunded and floating debt, including the various issues of Treasury notes, $17,000,000, which is in a gradual course of payment. There will probably be some addition to the public debt upon the liquidation of various claims which are depending, and a conciliatory disposition on the part of Congress may lead honorably and advantageously to an equitable arrangement of the militia expenses incurred by the several States without the previous sanction or authority of the Government of the United States; but when it is considered that the new as well as the old portion of the debt has been contracted in the assertion of the national rights and independence, and when it is recollected that the public expenditures, not being exclusively bestowed upon subjects of a transient nature, will long be visible in the number and equipments of the American Navy, in the military works for the defense of our harbors and our frontiers, and in the supplies of our arsenals and magazines the amount will bear a gratifying comparison with the objects which have been attained, as well as with the resources of the country.

The arrangements of the finances with a view to the receipts and expenditures of a permanent peace establishment will necessarily enter into the deliberations of Congress during the present session. It is true that the improved condition of the public revenue will not only afford the means of maintaining the faith of the Government with its creditors inviolate, and of prosecuting successfully the measures of the most liberal policy, but will also justify an immediate alleviation of the burdens imposed by the necessities of the war. It is, however, essential to every modification of the finances that the benefits of an uniform national currency should be restored to the community. The absence of the precious metals will, it is believed, be a temporary evil, but until they can again be rendered the general medium of exchange it devolves on the wisdom of Congress to provide a substitute which shall equally engage the confidence and accommodate the wants of the citizens throughout the Union. If the operation of the State banks can not produce this result, the probable operation of a national bank will merit consideration; and if neither of these expedients be deemed effectual it may become necessary to ascertain the terms upon which the notes of the Government (no longer required as an instrument of credit) shall be issued upon motives of general policy as a common medium of circulation.

Notwithstanding the security for future repose which the United States ought to find in their love of peace and their constant respect for the rights of other nations, the character of the times particularly inculcates the lesson that, whether to prevent or repel danger, we ought not to be unprepared for it. This consideration will sufficiently recommend to Congress a liberal provision for the immediate extension and gradual completion of the works of defense, both fixed and floating, on our maritime frontier, and an adequate provision for guarding our inland frontier against dangers to which certain portions of it may continue to be exposed.

As an improvement in our military establishment, it will deserve the consideration of Congress whether a corps of invalids might not be so organized and employed as at once to aid in the support of meritorious individuals excluded by age or infirmities from the existing establishment, and to procure to the public the benefit of their stationary services and of their exemplary discipline. I recommend also an enlargement of the Military Academy already established, and the establishment of others in other sections of the Union; and I can not press too much on the attention of Congress such a classification and organization of the militia as will most effectually render it the safeguard of a free state. If experience has shewn in the recent splendid achievements of militia the value of this resource for the public defense, it has shewn also the importance of that skill in the use of arms and that familiarity with the essential rules of discipline which can not be expected from the regulations now in force. With this subject is intimately connected the necessity of accommodating the laws in every respect to the great object of enabling the political authority of the Union to employ promptly and effectually the physical power of the Union in the cases designated by the Constitution.

The signal services which have been rendered by our Navy and the capacities it has developed for successful co-operation in the national defense will give to that portion of the public force its full value in the eyes of Congress, at an epoch which calls for the constant vigilance of all governments. To preserve the ships now in a sound state, to complete those already contemplated, to provide amply the imperishable materials for prompt augmentations, and to improve the existing arrangements into more advantageous establishments for the construction, the repairs, and the security of vessels of war is dictated by the soundest policy.

In adjusting the duties on imports to the object of revenue the influence of the tariff on manufactures will necessarily present itself for consideration. However wise the theory may be which leaves to the sagacity and interest of individuals the application of their industry and resources, there are in this as in other cases exceptions to the general rule. Besides the condition which the theory itself implies of a reciprocal adoption by other nations, experience teaches that so many circumstances must concur in introducing and maturing manufacturing establishments, especially of the more complicated kinds, that a country may remain long without them, although sufficiently advanced and in some respects even peculiarly fitted for carrying them on with success. Under circumstances giving a powerful impulse to manufacturing industry it has made among us a progress and exhibited an efficiency which justify the belief that with a protection not more than is due to the enterprising citizens whose interests are now at stake it will become at an early day not only safe against occasional competitions from abroad, but a source of domestic wealth and even of external commerce. In selecting the branches more especially entitled to the public patronage a preference is obviously claimed by such as will relieve the United States from a dependence on foreign supplies ever subject to casual failures, for articles necessary for the public defense or connected with the primary wants of individuals. It will be an additional recommendation of particular manufactures where the materials for them are extensively drawn from our agriculture, and consequently impart and insure to that great fund of national prosperity and independence an encouragement which can not fail to be rewarded.

Among the means of advancing the public interest the occasion is a proper one for recalling the attention of Congress to the great importance of establishing throughout our country the roads and canals which can best be executed under the national authority. No objects within the circle of political economy so richly repay the expense bestowed on them; there are none the utility of which is more universally ascertained and acknowledged; none that do more honor to the governments whose wise and enlarged patriotism duly appreciates them. Nor is there any country which presents a field where nature invites more the art of man to complete her own work for his accommodation and benefit. These considerations are strengthened, moreover, by the political effect of these facilities for intercommunication in bringing and binding more closely together the various parts of our extended confederacy. Whilst the States individually, with a laudable enterprise and emulation, avail themselves of their local advantages by new roads, by navigable canals, and by improving the streams susceptible of navigation, the General Government is the more urged to similar undertakings, requiring a national jurisdiction and national means, by the prospect of thus systematically completing so inestimable a work; and it is a happy reflection that any defect of constitutional authority which may be encountered can be supplied in a mode which the Constitution itself has providently pointed out.

The present is a favorable season also for bringing again into view the establishment of a national seminary of learning within the District of Columbia, and with means drawn from the property therein, subject to the authority of the General Government. Such an institution claims the patronage of Congress as a monument of their solicitude for the advancement of knowledge, without which the blessings of liberty can not be fully enjoyed or long preserved; as a model instructive in the formation of other seminaries; as a nursery of enlightened preceptors, and as a central resort of youth and genius from every part of their country, diffusing on their return examples of those national feelings, those liberal sentiments, and those congenial manners which contribute cement to our Union and strength to the great political fabric of which that is the foundation.

In closing this communication I ought not to repress a sensibility, in which you will unite, to the happy lot of our country and to the goodness of a superintending Providence, to which we are indebted for it. Whilst other portions of mankind are laboring under the distresses of war or struggling with adversity in other forms, the United States are in the tranquil enjoyment of prosperous and honorable peace. In reviewing the scenes through which it has been attained we can rejoice in the proofs given that our political institutions, founded in human rights and framed for their preservation, are equal to the severest trials of war as well as adapted to the ordinary periods of repose. As fruits of this experience and of the reputation acquired by the American arms on the land and on the water, the nation finds itself possessed of a growing respect abroad and of a just confidence in itself, which are among the best pledges for its peaceful career. Under other aspects of our country the strongest features of its flourishing condition are seen in a population rapidly increasing on a territory as productive as it is extensive; in a general industry and fertile ingenuity which find their ample rewards, and in an affluent revenue which admits a reduction of the public burdens without withdrawing the means of sustaining the public credit, of gradually discharging the public debt, of providing for the necessary defensive and precautionary establishments, and of patronizing in every authorized mode undertakings conducive to the aggregate wealth and individual comfort of our citizens.

It remains for the guardians of the public welfare to persevere in that justice and good will toward other nations which invite a return of these sentiments toward the United States; to cherish institutions which guarantee their safety and their liberties, civil and religious; and to combine with a liberal system of foreign commerce an improvement of the national advantages and a protection and extension of the independent resources of our highly favored and happy country.

In all measures having such objects my faithful co-operation will be afforded.

CHRONOLOGY

BIOGRAPHICAL NOTES

NOTE ON THE TEXTS

NOTES

INDEX

Chronology, 1811–1815

On November 4, the first session of the Twelfth Congress, subsequently known as the War Congress, convenes in Washington. The following day President James Madison delivers his opening address, calling for the nation to be put "into an armor and an attitude demanded by the crisis." On November 7, Governor William Henry Harrison of the Indiana Territory, having marched a small army into Shawnee country as a show of force, sustains heavy casualties in the Battle of Tippecanoe but drives off the attacking Indians. The next day he burns Prophet's Town, center of an emerging Indian confederacy, and the food supplies there. This marks the beginning of an Indian war in the Old Northwest that will blend into the War of 1812 seven months later.

On November 12, the United States and Great Britain agree to settle the *Chesapeake* affair, which has been a festering sore in Anglo-American relations since 1807, when a British warship fired on the American warship and removed four deserters from the Royal Navy. But other issues between the two nations, most notably the British Orders-in-Council, which restrict American trade with the European continent, and impressment, which is the practice of removing seamen from American merchant ships and forcing them to serve in the Royal Navy, remain unresolved. Hence, between December 24 and April 10 of the following year, Congress, spurred on by the new Speaker of the House, Henry Clay, and other War Hawks, adopts a series of war preparations.

On March 9, President Madison submits documents to Congress showing that British officials in Canada sent John Henry to New England in 1809 as a spy. The administration hopes that this will increase support for war by showing the perfidy of the British and the disloyalty of New England Federalists, but the papers implicate no American, and the Federalists are infuriated, especially after learning that the administration has paid $50,000 for the documents.

On April 4, Congress adopts a ninety-day embargo, prohibiting American ships from leaving port, and follows up ten days later with a ninety-day non-exportation law, prohibiting all exports, even in foreign ships. Although the War Hawks see these measures as a preliminary to war, other Republicans support them as coercive measures and hope that the loss of trade will force the British to make concessions that will avert war. Congress now bides its time until the USS *Hornet* (carrying 20 guns) returns from Europe with the latest news. The ship arrives in New York Harbor on May 19, and the dispatches it carries reach Washington three days later. But these papers present no evidence that the British government has softened its position. On May 27, Britain's minister in Washington offers the United States a share of the British license trade with the Continent. Although in practice this amounts to a partial suspension of the Orders-in-Council, the administration has no interest in sanctioning any trade under British licenses and summarily rejects the proposal.

On June 1, President Madison submits a war message to Congress in secret session. The House passes a bill declaring war against Britain on June 4, but the Senate does not concur until June 17. The vote in both houses is divided: 79 to 49 in the House and 19 to 13 in the Senate. Some Republicans and all of the Federalists vote against the measure. Madison signs the war bill into law on June 18, and the following day issues a proclamation announcing that a state of war now exists with Great Britain.

On June 16, British officials in London announce a plan to suspend the Orders-in-Council, and on June 23 the entire system is scrapped. The news of the British repeal reaches Quebec on July 30 and Boston on August 4. On August 9, Major General Henry Dearborn of the U.S. Army and Governor-General George Prevost of Canada sign an armistice, but this is cancelled by the United States on September 8 because the impressment issue remains unresolved. Reluctant to sanction hostilities, the British government does not authorize general reprisals against the United States until October 13.

From June 22 to August 4, Baltimore is rocked by a series of vicious and deadly riots that target the *Federal Republican* newspaper, Federalist opponents of the war, and free blacks in the city. This drives Federalists everywhere deeper into opposition.

In anticipation of war, the War Department on April 9 had ordered Brigadier General William Hull to march a large force (the Northwestern Army) from Ohio to the Detroit frontier in Michigan, but his progress is slow because he has to construct a road through Ohio's Black Swamp. On the Maumee River, Hull charters the ship *Cuyahoga* to carry his baggage, papers, and medical supplies to Detroit. Officials at Fort Amherstburg, the major British post in the western province of Upper Canada, who have learned of the declaration of war seize this vessel on July 2 when it reaches the Detroit River and from the papers on board learn of Hull's impending arrival. Hull himself learns of the declaration of war on July 2 and reaches the Detroit River three days later. He invades Upper Canada on July 12 and issues a proclamation promising to liberate the province.

Desultory fighting ensues from July 16 to July 26 on the Canard River, but Hull refuses to assault Fort Amherstburg until carriages he has ordered constructed for his field guns are complete. The British capture Fort Mackinac on July 17, and Hull, fearing that he will be overrun by Indians from the north, withdraws from Canada on August 7. He attempts to keep his supply lines open to Ohio by sending detachments south, but they are defeated at Brownstown on August 5 (by an Indian force under the Shawnee leader Tecumseh) and at Maguaga on August 9 (by an Anglo-Indian force). Hull orders Fort Dearborn in present-day Chicago evacuated, and the departing soldiers and civilians are attacked on August 15 in what becomes known as the Fort Dearborn Massacre. When Major General Isaac Brock, who heads an Anglo-Indian force on the Detroit River, demands Hull's surrender, the American commander, who fears an Indian massacre if he resists, complies on August 16, and the British take possession of Detroit.

With the British now in the ascendant in the Old Northwest, their Indian allies become more aggressive, besieging (unsuccessfully) Fort Harrison in Indiana Territory from September 4 to 16, Fort Madison in present-day Iowa from September 5 to 8, and Fort Wayne in Indiana Territory from September 5 to 12. Meanwhile, Harrison is given a major general's commission and begins rebuilding the Northwestern Army and accumulating supplies for a counteroffensive. All he can accomplish by year's end, however, is the burning of several native villages and the defeat of Indians in the Battle of the Mississinewa River in Indiana Territory on December 17–18.

The campaign on the Niagara front gets off to a promising start for the Americans on October 9 with the capture of two British brigs in the Niagara River, *Detroit* (carrying 6 guns) and *Caledonia* (3 guns). Four days later, however, an American invasion at Queenston Heights ends in disaster when the commanding officer, Major General Stephen Van Rensselaer of the New York militia, cannot persuade his volunteers to cross the river to reinforce the advance party of regulars and militia that has established a position on the Canadian side. An Anglo-Indian force headed by Major General Isaac Brock and Mohawk leader John Norton defeats the American force in a counterattack, although Brock, the hero of Detroit and arguably Britain's best general in Canada, is killed. Brigadier General Alexander Smyth succeeds Van Rensselaer in command, but other than issuing a blustery proclamation on November 17 threatening to annex Upper Canada, he achieves nothing of consequence.

Farther east the results are equally disappointing for the United States. Although a British attack on Ogdensburg, New York, fails on October 4, Major General Henry Dearborn, who is supposed to launch a major offensive against Montreal, has no taste for campaigning and does not cross into Lower Canada until November 19. His militia forces refuse to cross the border, and after a detachment from his army fights the inconclusive First Battle of Lacolle Mill on November 20, Dearborn abandons the campaign. On November 23, he withdraws to American territory and goes into winter quarters.

American failure on the Canadian frontier is to some extent offset by success at sea. In the first action of the war, on June 23, a naval squadron headed by the USS *President* (54) pursues and clashes with HMS *Belvidera* (42) in the North Atlantic, but the British ship escapes. From July 16 to 19 a British squadron from Halifax chases the USS *Constitution* (55 guns) in the eastern Atlantic, but in a remarkable display of seamanship the American frigate escapes. On August 13 the USS *Essex* (46) captures HMS *Alert* (18) in the North Atlantic; on August 19 *Constitution* (55) defeats HMS *Guerrière* (49) in the North Atlantic; on October 18, the USS *Wasp* (18) defeats HMS *Frolic* (22) in the North Atlantic; on October 25, the USS *United States* (56) captures HMS *Macedonian* (49) in the North Atlantic; and on December 29, *Constitution* (now carrying 54 guns) defeats HMS *Java* (49) off the coast of Brazil.

British successes at sea are less impressive. On July 16 a British squadron captures the USS *Nautilus* (14) in the North Atlantic; on October 18, HMS *Poictiers* (80) captures *Wasp* (18) in the North Atlantic; and on November 22, HMS *Southampton* (41) captures the USS *Vixen* (14) in the North Atlantic. These naval engagements are of little strategic consequence, but they boost sagging American morale and anger and perplex the British.

1813   In mid-January, Brigadier General James Winchester exceeds his instructions from Harrison and leads an American force into Michigan Territory to protect settlers on the River Raisin. After a preliminary skirmish on January 18, Winchester is defeated four days later by an Anglo-Indian force under the command of Colonel Henry Procter and surrenders his entire force. The following day, drunken Indians kill some thirty of the American prisoners of war in what is remembered as the River Raisin Massacre.

On May 1, the British and their Indian allies lay siege to Fort Meigs in Ohio. On May 5, an American relief force under Brigadier General Green Clay sustains heavy casualties in the Battle of Fort Meigs, and Indians massacre some of the American prisoners of war. But the fort holds out, and the siege is lifted on May 9. A second Anglo-Indian siege of Fort Meigs lasting from July 21 to 28 also fails, as does a British attack on August 1–2 against another American outpost in Ohio, Fort Stephenson. This marks the end of British offensive operations in the region. On September 10, Master Commandant Oliver H. Perry defeats a British squadron on Lake Erie under Commander Robert H. Barclay. Perry's after-action report to Harrison—"We have met the enemy, and they are ours"—adds to his reputation. Loss of control over Lake Erie, vital for resupplying British troops and Indians on the Detroit River, forces Major General Procter to retreat eastward into Upper Canada. Harrison catches up with retreating British and their Indian allies at Moraviantown and defeats them in the Battle of the Thames on October 5. Although Procter escapes with a few of his soldiers, the rest are captured, and Tecumseh is killed. The following day Kentucky volunteers take the famous Indian's clothing and pieces of his skin as souvenirs. With the Americans triumphant in the Old Northwest, many of the Indian tribes who have fought alongside the British make peace with the United States.

To the east, on April 27, the U.S. launches a successful amphibious operation against York (now Toronto), the provincial capital of Upper Canada, located on the north shore of Lake Ontario. But the Americans suffer significant losses when the retreating British blow up their magazine. Among those killed is Brigadier General Zebulon Pike. The Americans retaliate by looting and burning the public buildings. The U.S. launches a second successful raid on York on July 31.

On May 27, American forces mount a second successful expedition, this time against Fort George at the mouth of the Niagara River. The capture of this post forces the British to evacuate their positions all along the river the following day. The British retaliate on May 29 at the other end of Lake Ontario by assaulting Sackets Harbor, the American naval base on the lake, but they withdraw before doing any material damage. The American position on the Niagara River deteriorates when two forces sent west from Fort George are defeated, one in the Battle of Stoney Creek on June 5–6 and the other in the Battle of Beaver Dams on June 24. The first British victory leads to the capture of two American generals, William Winder and John Chandler, and the second is facilitated by Laura Secord, who has made a twenty-mile trek on June 22–23 through rough country to warn of the impending attack. After these defeats, American troops are confined to Fort George, and the British and their Indian allies mount a loose siege.

The American force at Fort George is gradually depleted in the summer and fall of 1813 as regulars are sent east and militia enlistments expire. By December, the commanding officer, Brigadier General George McClure of the New York militia, concludes that the post can no longer be held. On December 10, he evacuates the fort and orders the nearby village of Newark burned. Lieutenant General Gordon Drummond, who is now in command of the British on this front, responds by dispatching a force across the river that, in a surprise night attack on December 19, captures Fort Niagara. In retaliation for the destruction of Newark, the nearby towns of Lewiston, Youngstown, and Manchester are burned on December 19–21 and those of Black Rock and Buffalo on December 30. Thus, by the end of the year the British control the forts on both sides of the Niagara River, and American settlements all along this front are in ruins.

Farther east, on February 22, a British force attacks and occupies Ogdensburg. Although the British soon withdraw, the town remains ungarrisoned for the rest of the war and thus poses no threat to the British supply line on the St. Lawrence River. The Niagara front has been denuded of American troops to prepare for a major two-pronged campaign against Montreal: Major General James Wilkinson advances on the Canadian city by traveling down the St. Lawrence River from Sackets Harbor, while Major General Wade Hampton approaches Montreal overland from Plattsburgh, on Lake Champlain. Hampton is defeated on October 26 in the Battle of Châteauguay by a force of French Canadians and Indians under the command of Lieutenant Colonel Charles de Salaberry, while a detachment from Wilkinson's army is beaten on November 11 in the Battle of Crysler's Farm. This effectively ends the campaign.

Meanwhile an Indian war erupts in the Old Southwest against the Creeks. The Creeks are already in the midst of a civil war that pits militants, known as Red Sticks, who are determined to resist American encroachments, against accommodationists. On July 27, about eighty miles north of Pensacola, militia from the Mississippi Territory attack a Red Stick party that has purchased supplies in Spanish Florida. Known as the Battle of Burnt Corn, this marks the beginning of the Creek War. Red Sticks retaliate by attacking Fort Mims in present-day Alabama on August 30, killing 250 soldiers and civilians.

Major General Andrew Jackson raises a force in Tennessee to respond and defeats the Red Sticks in the Battle of Tallushatchee on November 3 and the Battle of Talladega six days later. Although the Creeks living in the Hillabee towns are now interested in peace, Major General John Cocke is unaware of this and kills many of them on November 18 in the Hillabee Massacre. The Creeks suffer additional losses at the hands of a force under Major General John Floyd in the Battle of Autosee on November 29. Jackson's victory in the Battle of the Holy Ground on December 23 leaves the Creek forces still further depleted, although Jackson has to pause to rebuild his own army.

The British in 1813 make good use of their navy after increasing its presence in American waters. Having established an informal blockade of the south Atlantic coast between Charleston, South Carolina, and Spanish Florida the previous fall, they now extend that blockade. On February 6, they proclaim a blockade of the Delaware and Chesapeake Bays; on May 26, the blockade is expanded to include all the major ports in the middle and southern states; and on November 16, Long Island Sound and remaining ports in middle and southern states are added to the list. The blockade sharply curtails domestic and foreign trade, taking a huge toll on the economy and government revenue.

The British also launch a series of amphibious raids in the Chesapeake in the hope of drawing off U.S. troops from Canada and bringing the war home to Americans. Although an attack on Norfolk, Virginia—where the USS *Constellation* is docked—fails in the Battle of Craney Island on June 22, the British overrun and burn many other towns and settlements in the Chesapeake, and on June 25, at Hampton, Virginia, French units in the British army commit a host of atrocities. Thereafter, "Hampton" becomes a byword for the British way of war in the Chesapeake, just as "River Raisin" and "Fort Mims" are rallying cries in the West.

The United States continues to enjoy some success on the high seas in 1813. On February 24, the USS *Hornet* (20) defeats HMS *Peacock* (20) off the coast of Guiana; on August 5 the privateer *Decatur* (7) captures HMS *Dominica* (16) near Bermuda; on September 5 the USS *Enterprise* (16) defeats HMS *Boxer* (14) off the coast of Maine; and on September 23 the USS *President* (54) captures HMS *Highflyer* (5) in the eastern Atlantic. But the balance at sea is clearly shifting in favor of the Mistress of the Seas. On January 17, HMS *Narcissus* (38) captures the USS *Viper* (16) in the Caribbean; on June 1 HMS *Shannon* (52) defeats the USS *Chesapeake* (50) off the coast of Massachusetts; and on August 14, HMS *Pelican* (21) defeats USS *Argus* (20) off the coast of Wales in the Irish Sea. American captain James Lawrence is killed in the *Shannon-Chesapeake* engagement, but his dying words—"Don't give up the ship"—become the motto of the U.S. Navy.

1814   While preparing for the campaigning season in 1814, American officials have to take into account the changing situation in Europe. Ever since his retreat from Russia in the fall of 1812, Napoleon has been on the defensive. News reaches the United States at the end of 1813 that the allies have defeated Napoleon in the Battle of Leipzig in mid-October, and thereafter they tighten the noose on France. The allies enter Paris on March 31, and on April 11 Napoleon abdicates and is soon exiled to the Mediterranean island of Elba. For the first time in a decade, Europe is at peace, and Great Britain is now free to devote greater resources to the American war.

Jackson renews his campaign in the Old Southwest against the Red Sticks in January, inflicting severe blows on the Creeks in battles at Emuckfau Creek on the 22nd and Enitachopco Creek on the 24th. The Creeks also sustain heavy casualties at the hands of an army commanded by General Floyd in the Battle of Calabee Creek on January 27. After pausing yet again to rebuild his army, Jackson defeats the Red Sticks in the climatic one-sided Battle of Horseshoe Bend on March 27–28. On August 9, Jackson imposes the Treaty of Fort Jackson on the Creeks, forcing friend and foe alike to agree to surrender over twenty million acres, which is more than half of the Creek lands. This huge landgrab produces consternation in Washington but is welcome news in the West.

Although the United States remains dominant in the Old Northwest, the two sides continue to mount raids against each other, the Americans using their control of the Detroit River and Lake Erie to good effect and the British using Fort Mackinac as a base and relying heavily on their remaining Indian allies. On May 14–15, Colonel John B. Campbell leads an American raid against Dover and nearby settlements on the north shore of Lake Erie and burns many of the buildings there, and on May 20 Port Talbot is the target of a similar raid. The British compel the surrender of Prairie du Chien on July 20 after a three-day siege. In the hope of ending British influence in the region, the United States mounts an assault under the command of Major George Croghan on Fort Mackinac on August 4, but the attack fails. The U.S. destroys Britain's remaining ship on Lake Huron, the *Nancy* (4 guns), in the Battle of Nottawasaga River on August 14, but the British regain control of the lake when a force under Lieutenant Miller Worlsey captures the USS *Tigress* (1) on September 3 and the USS *Scorpion* (2) three days later. The final campaign in the Old Northwest is Brigadier General Duncan McArthur's extended raid from Detroit into Upper Canada mounted from October 22 to November 17. McArthur destroys a great many mills during the raid, but the only engagement is the Battle of Malcolm's Mills on November 6 in which the casualties on both sides are slight.

The United States launches its most ambitious campaign of the year on the Niagara frontier, hoping to drive the British completely out of this part of Upper Canada. On July 3, Major General Jacob Brown crosses the river and compels the surrender of the lightly garrisoned post of Fort Erie. An American force under Brigadier General Winfield Scott marches north from Fort Erie and defeats a British force under Major General Phineas Riall in the Battle of Chippawa on July 5. When the Americans push farther north, the bloody but inconclusive Battle of Lundy's Lane follows on July 25. All four senior officers, Brown and Scott on the American side, and Drummond and Riall on the British side, are wounded in this battle, and Riall is captured. Afterwards, the Americans withdraw to Fort Erie.

A British force is dispatched to the American side of the Niagara River in the hope of destroying a supply base there but is defeated on August 3 in the Battle of Conjocta Creek. The British capture two American schooners, *Somers* (2) and *Ohio* (1), in a surprise attack on August 12, thus depriving the Americans at Fort Erie of naval protection. Drummond mounts a complicated night attack on Fort Erie on August 15, but the results are disastrous for the British, who suffer greatly when their troops at the south end of the fort are driven off and a magazine explosion takes a heavy toll on the assault force at the north end. On September 17, Brown orders a sortie from Fort Erie to silence several batteries of guns that have been pounding the post, and this attack is largely successful although at great cost to both sides. In the final engagement of the campaign, the Battle of Cook's Mills on October 19, an American force drives off the British and destroys a small stockpile of grain. The U.S. blows up Fort Erie on November 5 and withdraws to the American side of the river. The campaign has burnished the reputation of the U.S. Army but achieved little of strategic significance.

Farther east, Major General James Wilkinson makes a halfhearted foray into Canada but withdraws after an inconclusive action, the Second Battle of Lacolle Mill, on March 30. In this theater, it is mainly the British who are on the offensive. On May 5–6, the British mount an amphibious assault on Oswego, an essential way station on the supply line from New York City to Sackets Harbor. Although the village is captured and the British carry off some guns and naval stores, they miss a much larger cache of vital naval supplies some twelve miles upriver at Oswego Falls. On May 30 a detachment from the British squadron on Lake Ontario is defeated in the Battle of Sandy Creek after pursuing an American flotilla of boats up the creek in the hope of capturing the naval stores the flotilla is ferrying from Oswego to Sackets Harbor. To avoid being targeted by the British squadron again, most of the stores are transported overland to Sackets Harbor in wagons. A huge cable weighing nearly five tons is moved partly in a wagon and partly on the shoulders of a New York militia regiment.

On August 31, the British launch one of their biggest operations of the war, invading New York from Montreal with some ten thousand men under the command of Sir George Prevost. On September 11, Prevost's troops are on the verge of overrunning the American defenses at Plattsburgh when Master Commandant Thomas Macdonough defeats a British squadron on Lake Champlain under the command of Captain George Downey. Downey is killed in the engagement. Because his lines of supply and retreat are now vulnerable, Prevost orders his army to withdraw to Lower Canada, much to the disgust of many of his officers and men.

For the first time in the war, the British in 1814 target Federalist New England. On April 25, the blockade of the American coast is extended to New England. The British also target two Connecticut coastal towns, attacking Pettipaug Point on April 7 and Stonington on August 9–11. On August 28, Nantucket, facing starvation, declares its neutrality in the war. In exchange for surrendering its public stores and supplying the Royal Navy, Nantucket is permitted to fish in nearby waters and trade with the mainland. On July 11, the British capture Fort Sullivan and occupy Moose Island on the border between Maine and New Brunswick, and then from September 1 to 11, they occupy a hundred miles of the coast of Maine, from Eastport to Castine. Before retreating, Americans on September 3 burn the USS *Adams* at Hampden to prevent it from falling to the enemy. The coast of Maine remains in British hands for the rest of the war. On October 8, the United States prohibits all trade with Block Island, which has been openly supplying the Royal Navy with food and other supplies as well as intelligence.

The British also step up their raids in the Chesapeake. On April 2, Vice Admiral Alexander Cochrane issues a proclamation inviting slaves to join the British forces or resettle in British territories. Several thousand seek refuge with the British, some serving as guides and others enlisting in a special corps of Colonial Marines. This raises the specter of a slave revolt and forces the use of local militia to ensure domestic security. A flotilla of gunboats under the command of Captain Joshua Barney harasses British ships and boats in the Chesapeake and engages in several battles, including two in St. Leonard's Creek on June 8–10 and June 26. On August 22, however, with his flotilla in danger of being captured, Barney orders it blown up.

On August 24, a British force under Major General Robert Ross defeats an American force under Brigadier General William Winder in the Battle of Bladensburg, opening the road to Washington. On August 24–25, the British occupy the capital city and burn the public buildings. On August 29, a British squadron that has sailed up the Potomac River compels Alexandria to surrender its public stores and maritime property. A British force sent to the Eastern Shore is defeated in the Battle of Caulk's Field on August 31, and Sir Peter Parker, the naval captain in command, is killed. His cousin, Lord Byron, memorializes him in a poem.

The British next target Baltimore. En route, a British force sustains heavy casualties in the Battle of North Point on September 12, and the commanding officer, Major General Ross, is killed. The British troops, now under the command of Colonel Arthur Brooke, advance to the outskirts of Baltimore but see that it is heavily fortified; the Royal Navy is asked to soften the lines with naval fire. In order to get close enough to do the job, a British squadron must first silence the guns of Fort McHenry, a coastal fortification that protects the harbor. British bomb and rocket ships pummel Fort McHenry for some twenty-five hours on September 13–14 but fail to achieve their objective. On the morning of September 14, Francis Scott Key is so moved by the sight of the American flag still flying over Fort McHenry that he writes "The Star-Spangled Banner." By this time, the British land forces have already withdrawn, and thus Baltimore is spared.

Another British force threatens the Gulf coast. On September 15, a British squadron fails to capture Fort Bowyer in the Battle of Mobile Bay. The following day a U.S. force destroys the base of the Baratarian pirates on Grand Isle in Barataria Bay. On November 7, a U.S. force under Andrew Jackson occupies Spanish Pensacola to deny it to the British, and there Jackson gains intelligence that the British target in the region is New Orleans, to which he quickly proceeds. On December 14, a flotilla of British ship boats defeats a flotilla of American gunboats in the Battle of Lake Borgne. Two days later, Jackson proclaims martial law in New Orleans. Jackson engages a large and growing British force that threatens New Orleans, first in the Battle of Villeré's Plantation (also known as the Night Engagement) on December 23 and then in an action known as the British Reconnaissance in Force on December 28. As the year ends, the British are planning a major attack on Jackson's defenses at New Orleans.

Although the balance at sea still favors the British, American warships and privateers continue to make a good showing. On February 14, the USS *Constitution* (52) captures HMS *Pictou* (14) in the Caribbean; on April 29, the USS *Peacock* (22) defeats HMS *Epervier* (18) in the Caribbean; and the USS *Wasp* (22), operating in the North Atlantic, defeats HMS *Reindeer* (19) on June 28 and HMS *Avon* (20) on September 1. On August 27, Captain Thomas Boyle of the privateer *Chasseur* (16) proclaims a mock blockade of Great Britain and Ireland; on September 26–27, a squadron of British boats is mauled in an attack on the privateer *General Armstrong* (9) in the Azores; and on October 11, another squadron of British boats suffers a similar fate when it attacks the becalmed privateer *Prince-de-Neufchatel* (17) near Nantucket. But in the Pacific, after cruising freely against British whalers for months, the USS *Essex* (46) is defeated on March 28 by HMS *Phoebe* (46 or 53) and HMS *Cherub* (26) in Chilean waters; on April 20, HMS *Orpheus* (36) captures the USS *Frolic* (22) in the Caribbean; and on July 12, HMS *Medway* (80) captures the USS *Syren* (16) off the coast of South Africa.

While the British step up the military pressure on the United States, domestic developments undermine the republic's ability to wage war. In August treasury officials are unable to fill a national loan and public credit collapses. At the same time, banks outside of New England suspend specie payment, making it impossible for the administration to shift funds from one bank to another. Troops and contractors go unpaid, and in November the U.S. Treasury defaults on its debt. Federalist New England threatens to nullify a minor enlistment law and a proposed conscription law, and there is talk of secession. The Hartford Convention meets from December 15 to January 5 to protest the war and a decade of Republican policies.

Representatives of the United States and Great Britain meet in Ghent (in present-day Belgium) to try to hammer out a settlement that will end the war. By the time of their first meeting on August 8, the United States has dropped its demand for an end to impressment, but between August 8 and 19 the British lay down their own terms for peace: territorial concessions in northern Maine and modern-day Minnesota, the American demilitarization of the Great Lakes, the establishment of an Indian state in the Old Northwest, and an end to American fishing privileges in Canadian waters. The U.S. delegation adamantly rejects these demands. It also rejects a scaled-back British demand on October 21 to make peace on the basis of *uti possidetis*, meaning that each side will keep whatever enemy territory it holds. The two sides sign the Treaty of Ghent on December 24, which provides for returning to the status quo ante bellum. The British ratify the treaty on December 27.

1815   On January 1, Jackson engages the British for the third time at New Orleans in the Battle of Rodriguez Canal. The following day, HMS *Favorite* (18) departs from London with the American copy of the Treaty of Ghent and the British instrument of ratification. On January 8, Jackson wins a one-sided victory over the British in their fourth clash, the Battle of New Orleans. The British sustain two thousand casualties, Jackson only seventy. Among the British dead are Major General Edward Pakenham, the commanding officer and the Duke of Wellington's brother-in-law. From January 9 to 18, the British bombard Fort St. Philip on the Mississippi River but are unable to compel its submission. On January 10, the British occupy Cumberland Island in Georgia; three days later they attack and capture the American stronghold on the island at Point Peter. On January 15, a British squadron captures the USS

President (52) in the eastern Atlantic. On February 8, the British besiege Fort Bowyer; the fort falls on the 11th.

HMS *Favorite* reaches New York City on February 11. The documents it has brought arrive in Washington three days later. On February 16, the U.S. Senate unanimously approves the treaty, and later that day the President signs all documents. This completes the ratification process and marks an end to the war. Representatives of both nations immediately send out orders to cease hostilities. Instruments of ratification are exchanged the following day, and with this the terms of the treaty become binding.

Because of slow communication, desultory fighting continues. On February 20, the USS *Constitution* (52) defeats HMS *Cyane* (33) and HMS *Levant* (21) off the Atlantic coast of North Africa. On February 21, on Jackson's orders, six militiamen are executed in Mobile for leaving camp earlier in the campaign. On February 26, the privateer *Chasseur* (15) defeats HMS *St. Lawrence* (13) in the Caribbean. On March 13, official news of peace reaches New Orleans, and Jackson lifts martial law. On March 23, the USS *Hornet* (20) defeats HMS *Penguin* (19) near Tristan da Cunha in the South Atlantic. News of peace reaches Quebec on March 1, London on March 28.

On April 6, a number of unruly American prisoners of war, eager to be repatriated, are killed in the Dartmoor Massacre in England. On May 24, a small American force near St. Louis fights the Battle of the Sinkhole against Indians. On June 30, the USS *Peacock* (22) defeats the East India cruiser *Nautilus* (14) in the Indian Ocean. This is the last military engagement of the War of 1812, although the last hostile Indians do not agree to peace until 1817.

Biographical Notes

John Quincy Adams (July 11, 1767–February 23, 1848) Born in Braintree, Massachusetts, the first child of John Adams, a lawyer then emerging as a leader in the patriot cause, and Abigail (Smith) Adams. In 1778 he accompanied his father on a diplomatic mission to France and attended school in Paris until their return to America the following year. Sailing again to Europe, he served as private secretary to Francis Dana, American minister to Russia, 1781–82, before rejoining his father in the Netherlands and traveling with him to England after the signing of the Treaty of Paris in September 1783. He graduated from Harvard College in 1787, and began to practice law in 1790 in Newburyport, Massachusetts. In a series of pseudonymous contributions to the Boston *Columbian Centinel*, begun as a rejoinder to Thomas Paine's celebration of the French Revolution in *The Rights of Man*, Adams launched a conservative attack on the Francophilic secretary of state Thomas Jefferson and the controversial Genet diplomatic mission from Revolutionary France, among other targets; these essays hastened the rise of factionalism in the new republic. In May 1794, he was appointed minister to the Netherlands by George Washington, and he sailed in September, bringing younger brother and newly minted lawyer Thomas Boylston Adams as his secretary. In 1797 he married Louisa Catherine Johnson, an Englishwoman, in London; they had four children. Following his father's election as president, he was appointed minister to Prussia, serving until 1801, when his father lost his bid for reelection to Jefferson. Elected to the Senate in 1803, he resigned in 1808 after being repudiated by fellow Massachusetts Federalists for supporting Jefferson's Embargo Act of 1807. Named the first Boylston Professor of Rhetoric and Oratory at Harvard in 1805, he published his *Lectures on Rhetoric and Oratory* in 1810. Adams resumed his diplomatic career in 1809 when James Madison appointed him minister to Russia. As leader of the American peace commissioners, he helped negotiate the Treaty of Ghent (signed December 24, 1814), which brought an end to the War of 1812; he subsequently served as minister to Great Britain, 1815–16. As secretary of state under James Monroe, 1817–25, he supported Andrew Jackson's invasion of Florida, negotiated Spain's cession of Florida and the abandonment of its claims in the Pacific Northwest, secured an agreement with Great Britain on the U.S.-Canadian border, and played a major role in the formulation of the Monroe Doctrine. In the four-way presidential contest of 1824, he ran second to Andrew Jackson in the electoral vote, no candidate receiving a majority; the election was decided by the House of Representatives, which elected Adams the sixth president of the United States with the support of fellow candidate Henry Clay (whom Adams then appointed secretary of state). His presidency, 1825–29, was clouded by bitter party conflict among Jacksonians, Democratic Republicans, and Adams-Clay National Republicans, and he was defeated decisively by Jackson in the presidential election of 1828. He was elected to Congress as an independent in 1830 and served until his death. As a congressman, he opposed the extension of slavery and the annexation of Texas and waged a long, ultimately successful campaign (1836–44) to overturn the "gag rule" that prevented congressional debate of antislavery petitions. In 1841 he successfully defended African mutineers of the slave ship *Amistad* before the Supreme Court. He suffered a stroke during a session of Congress and was carried to the Speaker's Room, where he died two days later. His last words are said to have been "This is the end of the earth—I am content."

William Atherton (January 10, 1793–September 17, 1863) At the outbreak of the War of 1812, he enrolled as a private in the 1st Volunteer Rifle Regiment of Kentucky, mustering at Georgetown on August 12, 1812, and returning finally to his home in Shelbyville on June 20, 1814. He recounted his wartime experiences of privation and captivity in *Narrative of the Suffering & Defeat of the North-Western Army, under General Winchester*, privately printed in Frankfort in 1842. Buried in Greencastle City Cemetery, Putnam County, Indiana, next to his wife, Mary, his gravestone indicates that he had been a minister.

Charles Ball (c. 1781–a. 1837) Born into slavery in Calvert County, Maryland, the grandson of an African man who had been brought to Maryland sometime around 1730. He was separated from his mother as a small child and with his siblings sold at a public auction. Working with Isaac Fisher, a lawyer in Lewiston, Pennsylvania, he fashioned a memoir, later published as *Slavery in the United States: A Narrative of the Life and Adventures of Charles Ball* in New York in 1837; it was part of "The Cabinet of Freedom," a series of abolitionist books and pamphlets edited by William Jay, George Bush, and Gerrit Smith and produced and distributed by New York bookseller John S. Taylor. On the book's title page Ball is described as "A black man, who lived forty years in Maryland, South Carolina and Georgia, as a slave, under various masters, and was one year in the navy with Commodore Barney, during the late war"; his narrative as "an account of the manners and usages of the planters and slaveholders of the South—a description of the condition and treatment of the slaves, with observations upon the state of morals amongst the cotton planters, and the perils and sufferings of a fugitive slave, who twice escaped from the cotton country."

Joshua Barney (July 6, 1759–December 1, 1818) Born in Baltimore, Maryland, and at the age of twelve apprenticed to his brother-in-law, who was captain of a small ship engaged in the transatlantic trade. He served with distinction in the Revolutionary War, first as master's mate of the Continental sloop *Hornet* (taking part in the capture of New Providence in the West Indies), later as lieutenant on the sloops *Wasp* and *Sachem*. Three times captured by the British during the war, he was twice exchanged and the third time escaped from Mill Prison, near Plymouth, England, after nearly a year in confinement. In 1782, he was reunited in Philadelphia with his wife Anne, whom he had married before his third capture in 1780, and given command of the Pennsylvania ship *Hyder-Ally*, a small vessel of sixteen six-pound cannons and 110 men. On April 8, he engaged and defeated the twenty-gun *General Monk*, a British vessel patrolling off of Cape May, New Jersey, in an action that James Fenimore Cooper, in his *History of the Navy*, concluded "has been justly deemed one of the most brilliant that ever occurred under the American flag." He continued in the service of Congress until May 1784, when the American navy was effectively disbanded, and then spent a decade engaged in various commercial measures. In 1794, as captain of the merchant vessel *Cincinnatus*, he transported James Monroe to his post as American minister to France, there coming to the attention of the French minister of marine. After completing his commercial duties, he accepted commission in the French navy, serving as captain and *chef de division* (commodore), 1796–1802. He commanded numerous successful privateering enterprises in the first two years of the War of 1812, before being engaged by Secretary of the Navy William Jones in July 1814 to command a flotilla of barges and other vessels to defend Chesapeake Bay against British invasion, which for some weeks deterred small attacks but which was no match for the full British squadron. Barney blew up his flotilla to keep it out of enemy hands and marched five hundred flotillamen to Bladensburg, Maryland, to meet the British force advancing on the nation's capital. Their ammunition depleted, his men were forced to retreat, having offered the only effective American resistance during the Battle of Bladensburg; Barney was wounded and captured. Died in Pittsburgh, Pennsylvania, from complications related to his war wound.

Henry Bathurst, 3rd Earl Bathurst (May 22, 1762–July 27, 1834) Born at the Bathurst family estate in Cirencester Park, Gloucestershire, England, son of the 2nd Earl, also named Henry, who had served as Lord High Chancellor and Lord President of the Privy

Council. He was educated at Eton and Christ Church, Oxford. As Lord Apsley, he was member of Parliament for Cirencester from 1783 to 1794 when, upon the death of his father, he succeeded to the earldom. A moderate Tory, he held a number of important positions: lord of the admiralty, 1783–89; lord of the treasury, 1789–91; commissioner of the board of control, 1793–1802; master of the mint, 1804–6; and president of the board of trade, a cabinet post, 1807–12. In 1812, he joined Lord Liverpool's ministry as secretary of state for war and the colonies, remaining in that post until 1827. With the prime minister and foreign secretary, Castlereagh, he oversaw imperial strategy during the latter campaigns of the Napoleonic Wars and the War of 1812. Committed to a policy focused on the Continent, he strongly supported Wellington's campaign in the Iberian Peninsula, while approving George Prevost's defensive strategy for British North America. Only with the end of major fighting in Europe did he commit some twenty thousand reinforcements to Canada. He later served as lord president of the council in the government of the Duke of Wellington, 1828–32. Died in London.

Thomas Hart Benton (March 14, 1782–April 10, 1858) Born in Harts Mill, near Hillsboro (today Hillsborough), North Carolina, the son of Jesse Benton, a wealthy landowner who died in 1790, and Ann (Gooch) Benton. After some informal education and an interrupted stint studying law at the University of North Carolina, he moved to Tennessee to manage a large family claim near Nashville. He was admitted to the bar in Nashville in 1806 and served in the Tennessee Senate, 1809–11, where he attracted the attention of Andrew Jackson; in 1812, dreaming of military glory, he became an aide-de-camp to Jackson in the Tennessee militia. A tavern brawl between Benton and Jackson in September 1813 resulted in a gunfight in which Jackson was seriously wounded by Benton's brother Jesse. Alienated from Jackson, Benton accepted a commission as a lieutenant colonel of the 39th U.S. Infantry, 1813–15. At the end of the war, he moved to St. Louis to practice law. In the second of two duels with Charles Lucas, U.S. attorney in Missouri, he killed his opponent, an act that would tarnish his reputation and which he would lament on his deathbed. He edited the *Missouri Enquirer*, 1818–20. He married Elizabeth Preston in 1821; they had five children. Upon the admission of Missouri into the Union, he was elected to the U.S. Senate as a Democratic Republican (later as a Democrat), serving from 1821 to 1851, with important positions on military affairs, foreign relations, and Indian affairs committees. He reconciled with Jackson in the wake of the 1824 presidential election and later was the author of the resolution to expunge from the Senate Journal a resolution of censure on President Andrew

Jackson for his controversial bank veto. Benton was defeated for reelection after opposing the Compromise of 1850 as too favorable to
proslavery interests. He served in the Thirty-third Congress, 1853–55,
but was defeated for reelection because of his opposition to the Kansas-
Nebraska Act; he was also defeated in the 1856 Missouri gubernatorial
election. Died in Washington, D.C.

Big Warrior (c. 1760–March 8, 1825) Thought to have been born in
Tukabatchee, a Creek settlement on the Tallapoosa River in present-
day Alabama, he was signatory to treaties between the Creek Nation
and the United States at Colerain, Ohio (June 29, 1796), and Fort
Wilkinson (June 16, 1802). It is not known exactly when he became
Speaker of the Upper Creeks, but he may have already been the effective leader of his people when he resisted the appeal of Tecumseh,
who visited Tukabatchee in the fall of 1811, to join in his confederation against the Americans. He had certainly assumed that role by
1813 when the split between pro- and anti-war factions among the
Upper Creeks threatened his leadership and led him to construct a
fort at Tukabatchee to defend himself and his pro-American peace
faction against the larger pro-war Red Stick Creeks. The siege of this
fort was lifted only by the intervention of a force of two hundred
warriors from Coweta, to where Big Warrior and his people then removed. He remained loyal to the Americans throughout the War of
1812, and was a reluctant signatory to treaties ceding Creek lands to
the United States at Fort Jackson (August 9, 1814), the Creek Agency
(on the Flint River, in Georgia, January 22, 1818), and Indian Springs
(also in Georgia, January 8, 1821). Died in Washington, D.C., on an
embassy to the federal government.

Blackbird (Jean-Baptiste Assiginack, c. 1768–November 3, 1866) An
Ottawa Indian thought to have been born at Arbre Croche (present-
day Harbor Springs, Michigan) and to have been a student at the
French Sulpician school at Lac-des-Deux-Montagnes in Lower Canada, and there converted to Catholicism. He may have participated in
the British capture of Michilimackinac (Mackinac Island) in 1812. In
July 1813, now chief of a band of Ottawas allied with the British, he
led warriors in a series of skirmishes against American forces; the band
was later accused of torturing and killing Lieutenant Joseph C. Eldridge of the 13th U.S. Infantry, whom they had taken prisoner. In
the ensuing controversy, American leaders implored their British
counterparts to admonish Blackbird, and in an effort to curb such
atrocities the British offered the Ottawa chief a bounty of five dollars
for each American prisoner turned over to them alive. Citing the
many American depredations of his lands and people, Blackbird was
unmoved. After the war, he served as an interpreter for the Indian

Department at Drummond Island, then part of Upper Canada, and later at Penetanguishene, to where the British garrison had removed after Drummond Island was transferred to the United States. At Penetanguishene, and later at nearby Coldwater, where the Indian Department sought to encourage fixed agricultural settlement, he led many Indians to Catholicism through preaching and catechizing. With the failure of the Coldwater experiment, in 1836 he moved with his people to Manitoulin Island in Lake Huron, there to establish at Manitowaning a new model settlement further removed from contact with the white population. Internal tensions between Ottawas and Ojibwas undermined the experiment, and the island was opened to white settlement in 1861. Died at Manitowaning.

Black Hawk (Makataimeshekiakiak, c. 1767–October 3, 1838) A Sauk Indian thought to have been born in the seasonal village of Saukenuk, on the Rock River, in present-day Rock Island, Illinois. He early established a reputation as an effective warrior, leading many successful raids against Osages, Cherokees, and other tribes and becoming the war leader of the Sauks at Saukenuk. Opposed to ceding Indian lands, he rejected the terms of the 1804 Treaty of St. Louis, concluded when four Sauks and a Fox were induced to transfer all Sauk lands in present-day Illinois, Wisconsin, and Missouri to the United States, represented by William Henry Harrison, governor of the Louisiana and Indiana Territories, in exchange for goods valued at $2,234.50 and a small annual annuity, also in goods, and he led skirmishes against American efforts to militarize the territory. With the coming of the War of 1812, he proved a valuable ally to the British, recruiting and leading Indian warriors from several tribes. He participated in or was present at several actions during the war's early campaigns, including attacks on Fort Meigs and Fort Stephenson and possibly the Battle of the Thames (Moraviantown), but disappointed by the lack of success (and plunder) and repulsed by the high mortality rates associated with the Anglo-American fighting style, he returned with his men to Saukenuk, where he found that a rival, Keokuk, had supplanted him as the tribe's war chief. Toward the end of the war Black Hawk rejoined the fight against the U.S. and saw action at the Battles of Campbell's Island, Credit Island, and the Sinkhole in 1814 and 1815 (a series of skirmishes along the Mississippi River north of St. Louis). On May 13, 1816, he signed a peace treaty between the Sauk and the United States, unaware, he would later insist, that it reaffirmed the terms of the 1804 treaty and called for the removal of his people west of the Mississippi River. In 1832, in an effort to reclaim ancestral lands and to find refuge from the Sioux, his people's traditional enemies to the west, he led a band of some fifteen hundred men, women, and children back across the river, only to be repulsed in a series of one-sided engagements with territorial militias and U.S. regulars that became known as the Black Hawk War. On August 27, 1832, three and a half weeks after a decisive encounter at Bad Axe (near present-day Victory, Wisconsin), where 150 of his people were massacred as they attempted to recross the Mississippi, he surrendered to federal forces at Prairie du Chien. Held prisoner in Missouri for eight months, he was then brought with other Indian leaders to Fort Monroe in Virginia, and then to Washington, D.C., to meet with President Andrew Jackson. From there the prisoners were led on a tour throughout the country to be exhibited to curious crowds. During the summer of 1833, he recounted his life to Antoine LeClaire, an army interpreter, whose text was edited by Rock Island journalist John B. Patterson and published in 1834 as *Life of Ma-ka-tai-me-she-kia-kiak or Black Hawk*, among the first published autobiographies of an American Indian. Upon release, he returned to Sauk settlements in what is today southeast Iowa, where he died.

Thomas Verchères de Boucherville (Thomas-René-Verchères Boucher de Boucherville, December 21, 1784–December 13, 1857) Born in Boucherville, Lower Canada, son of René-Amable Boucher, a prominent landowner (seigneur of Boucherville) and military officer who had served in both French and British Canadian forces, and Madeleine Raimbault de Saint-Blaint, heiress to the seigneury of Verchères. He studied at the Sulpician Collège Saint-Raphaël in Montreal, 1792–99, without completing a degree, and served as clerk for a fur trading company, 1803–4, embarking on a winter expedition far to the west (to present-day Manitoba). He was employed in 1804 by Laurent Quetton de Saint-Georges, a trader of general merchandise in Upper Canada with stores in York (Toronto) and Newark (Niagara-on-the-Lake), and, two years later, was established by his employer with £2,500 in merchandise in a new branch in Amherstburg, in western Upper Canada; he purchased the store outright in 1808. In 1811, he rescued $58,000 worth of goods belonging to his former employer that had been impounded by U.S. customs officials in Lewiston, New York, under terms of the American Non-Intercourse Act of 1809. With the coming of the War of 1812, he served as a volunteer on the Detroit frontier, and prospered in wartime trading at Amherstburg, until defeat of the British fleet on Lake Erie in September 1813 forced him to flee to Montreal. Returning to Boucherville, he served as captain (adjutant) in the local militia. After attempts to re-establish stores at Amherstburg and Boucherville, he retired from trade in 1816, becoming justice of the peace and a major in the militia. In 1819, he married Josephine Proulx of Montreal; they had five children. He inherited title to family lands in the 1820s. In 1847, he wrote for his children an account of his experiences in the fur trade and in the war. Died at Boucherville.

Thomas Boyle (June 29, 1775–October 12, 1825) Born in Marblehead, Massachusetts, he was said to have his first command of a ship at age sixteen. He married Mary Gross in Baltimore, Maryland, in 1794. In July 1812, he took command at Baltimore of the fourteen-gun privateer *Comet*, capturing four vessels valued at more than $400,000 during a four-month tour in the West Indies. A second tour, to the Brazilian coast in the winter of 1812, was somewhat less successful, though he was able to slip *Comet* through the British blockade of Chesapeake Bay and return safely to Baltimore. In April 1813 he accepted a post as sailing master in the U.S. Navy, protecting intercoastal commerce on the bay. He put to sea again in *Comet* in October 1813, and in a six-month cruise of the West Indies captured multiple prizes. He returned to the U.S. in March 1814 and took command and partial ownership of the privateer *Chasseur*, a fast ship known as the "Pride of Baltimore." He embarked from New York in July on a three-month tour of the British Isles, capturing a score of prizes, issuing a cheeky proclamation of blockade, and almost single-handedly causing insurance rates for British merchants plying the Irish Sea to soar. From December 1814 to March 1815, he undertook in *Chasseur* a fifth and final cruise of the war, to the West Indies, where he captured the British naval schooner *St. Lawrence* among other mercantile prizes. He is thought to have returned to the merchant service after the war, and to have engaged in privateering during the wars of independence in Spanish America. He died at sea and was eulogized in the *U.S. Gazette* (Philadelphia) of October 21, 1825, as "one of the oldest & most respectable ship masters out of the port of Baltimore; possessing a generous disposition, & a nobleness of mind, blending the polished gentleman with that of the sailor made him the favorite of all who knew him."

Philip B. V. Broke (September 9, 1776–January 2, 1841) Born Philip Bowes Vere Broke at Broke Hall, Nacton, England, approximately seventy miles northeast of London, eldest son of Philip Bowes Broke and Elizabeth (Beaumont) Broke. He entered the Royal Navy Academy at Portsmouth in 1788, becoming a midshipman four years later. In 1797, as third lieutenant of HMS *Southampton*, he was present at the Battle of Cape St. Vincent, a major English naval victory over Spain. He rose to captain in 1801. In 1802, he married Sarah Louisa Middleton; they had eleven children. He assumed command of the frigate *Shannon* on August 31, 1806, and instituted a rigorous training program to improve the ship's standard of gunnery. In August 1811, he was ordered to join Vice Admiral Herbert Sawyer's squadron at Halifax, Nova Scotia, from there to harass French and later American shipping in the western Atlantic. Having patrolled off Boston for some months, on June 1, 1813, *Shannon* spied the U.S. frigate *Chesapeake* under sail in the harbor, and Broke issued a written challenge to her captain, James Lawrence: "As the *Chesapeake* appears now ready for Sea, I request that you will do me the favor to meet the *Shannon* with her, Ship to Ship, to try the fortune of our respective Flags." The challenge did not reach Lawrence, who had in any case already determined to engage *Shannon*. In the brief but furious battle that ensued, Broke was badly injured by a blow on the head suffered during hand-to-hand combat, but *Shannon* was victorious, capturing *Chesapeake* and providing a significant fillip for the British, who had suffered a series of shocking naval reversals early in the war. While he recovered at the naval station in Halifax, an account of the battle, written in his name, was widely circulated, and for his feat he was made a baronet on September 25. He resumed command of *Shannon* and sailed to England in October. Troubled by his injury, he left active service and retired to Broke Hall. He was knighted on January 3, 1815, and promoted to rear admiral on July 22, 1830. He died in London while undergoing an operation to repair damage sustained in the 1813 battle. Buried at St. Martin's Church, Nacton.

Benjamin F. Browne (July 14, 1793–November 23, 1873) Born Benjamin Frederick Browne in Salem, Massachusetts, son of Benjamin and Mary (Andrew) Browne. He was apprenticed to E. S. Lang, an apothecary, in 1807, completing his term in 1812, just as war hindered the commerce of the port and his ability to pursue his trade. He shipped as a surgeon's assistant on the privateer *Alfred* in September 1812, returning to Portsmouth, New Hampshire, in January 1813. He embarked later that year on the privateer *Frolic*, this time as captain's clerk, purser, and sergeant of marines, responsible for drilling new recruits in techniques of seizing and boarding another vessel. On January 25, 1814, after *Frolic* was captured by HMS *Heron*, he was brought as a prisoner with the rest of the crew to Barbados and, in August 1814, to England, and there marched from Plymouth to Dartmoor, where he was imprisoned until May 1, 1815. He then returned to Salem and to the apothecary trade, establishing his own store in 1823. In 1825 he married Sally Bott; they had five children. Active as civic leader, mason, militia commander, volunteer fireman, and antiquarian, he was twice elected to the Massachusetts legislature, as representative in 1831 and senator in 1843, and he was postmaster of Salem, 1845–49. With the assistance of fellow Democrat Nathaniel Hawthorne, he published anonymous memoirs of war and imprisonment, "Papers of an old Dartmoor Prisoner, Edited by

Nathaniel Hawthorne," in the *United States Magazine and Democratic Review* in 1846. He retired from business in 1860 and died in Salem thirteen years later.

Shadrach Byfield (September 16, 1789–before 1851) Born in Woolley, Wiltshire, England. Trained as a weaver, he enlisted in the British army in 1807, serving in British North America in the 41st Regiment of Foot. He saw action at Detroit, Frenchtown, Fort Stephenson, Moraviantown (Battle of the Thames), Fort Niagara, Lundy's Lane, and, finally, at Black Rock, where he lost his left arm to a musket ball. He returned to England and a meager army pension, and privately printed a memoir, *A Narrative of a Light Company Soldier's Service in the Forty-first Regiment of Foot (1807–1814)*, in 1841. His date of death is unknown, though in the 1851 census of Woolley his wife, Sarah, is listed as a widow and a pauper.

George Gordon, Lord Byron (January 22, 1788–April 19, 1824) Born in London, his father, John "Mad Jack" Byron, was a profligate sea captain who had been disinherited by his family and who died in 1791; his mother, Catherine (Gordon) Byron, was one of three surviving daughters of George Gordon, twelfth laird of Gight, Aberdeenshire, Scotland. He succeeded to the family title when he was ten. Educated at Harrow and Trinity College, Cambridge, where he received an M.A. in 1808, he began writing poetry while still in his teens. With the publication of such works as *English Bards and Scotch Reviewers* (1809) and *Childe Harold's Pilgrimage* (1812) he was by 1812 among the most celebrated poets in England. In 1814, he wrote "Elegiac Stanzas on the Death of Sir Peter Parker, BART." about his cousin, who was killed at the Battle of Caulk's Field, in Maryland. Byron pursued many love affairs, including with his half-sister Augusta. He married Annabella Milbanke in 1815; in 1816 the couple separated amidst much scandal. Hounded by accusations of insanity and incest, he left England for good in 1816. He lived for a time in Switzerland but most of his remaining life was spent in Italy, occasionally in the company of Percy Bysshe Shelley and his wife Mary. Considered among the foremost poets of the English Romantic movement, he is best remembered for numerous excellent short lyrics (including "She Walks in Beauty") and for the ambitious epic *Don Juan* (1819–24). Died of fever while in Greece supporting the movement for independence from the Ottoman Empire.

John C. Calhoun (March 18, 1782–March 31, 1850) Born John Caldwell Calhoun in the South Carolina backcountry, near Mount Carmel, the son of Patrick Calhoun, a farmer who served in the state legislature, and Martha (Caldwell) Calhoun. He was schooled by a tutor in Georgia until his father's death in 1796 forced him to return to the family farm. Four years later, with the support of an older brother, he left to study at Yale College, graduating in 1804. He was admitted to the South Carolina bar in 1807 and after gaining attention for a vigorous speech in defense of American maritime rights in the wake of the *Chesapeake-Leopard* Affair (June 1807, when the USS *Chesapeake* was fired upon and four of its crew were seized by the HMS *Leopard*), he was elected to the South Carolina legislature, serving 1808–9. He married Floride Bonneau Colhoun, the daughter of a cousin, in 1811; they had ten children. That same year he was elected to Congress as a Democratic Republican, quickly becoming a leading figure among the young "War Hawks" in the House, a group that included Speaker Henry Clay of Kentucky, who appointed Calhoun to the important Committee on Foreign Relations. He was soon its acting chairman, and in that role he was the principal author of the June 3, 1812, committee report that called for war with Great Britain. (Secretary of State James Monroe is thought to have collaborated with Calhoun and other committee members on the report.) Though the course of the war would bear out none of the sanguine forecasts he offered in the report and elsewhere, upon learning of the conclusion of peace at Ghent he could pronounce: "To all practical purposes, we have attained complete success." He was secretary of war in the cabinet of James Monroe, 1817–25. Elected vice president in 1824 after being nominated on both the John Quincy Adams and Andrew Jackson tickets, he was reelected in 1828 on the Jackson ticket. Much exercised over the issue of the federal tariff, Calhoun abandoned the staunch nationalism that had characterized his early political philosophy and articulated the doctrine of nullification, which held that states had the right to nullify federal acts they deemed unconstitutional, even to secede in the absence of any other redress. He parted with Jackson over the issue, and resigned as vice president on December 28, 1832, after being elected to the Senate, where he served until his resignation in 1843. There, on February 6, 1837, he delivered a speech entitled "Slavery a Positive Good," which signaled a major escalation in the sectional debate over slavery. He was briefly secretary of state in the cabinet of John Tyler, 1844–45, before being elected again to the Senate, serving from November 26, 1845, until his death, from tuberculosis, in Washington, D.C. His political philosophy was given formal expression in two works, *A Disquisition on Government* and the unfinished *Discourse on the Constitution and Government of the United States*, published together in a posthumous edition in 1851.

William Ellery Channing (April 7, 1780–October 2, 1842) Born in Newport, Rhode Island, son of William Channing, a lawyer and public official, and Lucy (Ellery) Channing, daughter of William

Ellery, a signer of the Declaration of Independence. After his father's death in 1792, he was sent to Harvard, living at Cambridge with the family of his uncle Francis Dana, the chief justice of Massachusetts. During his senior year, he "*found for what I was made*," a life in the ministry. Upon graduation in 1798 he tutored the family of David Meade Randolph in Richmond, Virginia, for a year and a half before returning to Newport to continue his studies in theology. In 1802 he assumed an academic position at Harvard, and, on June 1, 1803, was ordained and installed as minister of the Federal Street (later Arlington Street) Church in Boston, where he would remain until his death. He married Ruth Gibbs, a cousin, in 1814, and they had four children. His preaching focused on the practical application of Christian morality, downplaying key tenets of the orthodox Calvinist doctrine of his forebears and emphasizing the goodness of God, the perfectibility of man, and the freedom of the will. On two public fast days in the summer of 1812, he delivered passionate sermons in protest of the Madison administration and the U.S. declaration of war. By 1815, thanks to his widely published sermons, he was becoming a central figure in the splintering of the New England churches into orthodox (Congregationalist) and liberal (soon to be called Unitarian) camps. Though he resisted this sectarianism at first—"I desire to escape the narrow walls of a particular church, and to live under the open sky"—he was soon the acknowledged leader of New England Unitarianism, propounding its essential elements in influential sermons like "Unitarian Christianity" (1819), "The Moral Argument Against Calvinism" (1820), and "Likeness to God" (1828), and through the *Christian Register*, the official organ of the American Unitarian Association (founded 1825). His teachings exercised considerable influence over some of the major New England writers of the age, and his *The Importance and Means of a National Literature* (1830) is a call for literary independence from the Old World. In later years he became an outspoken opponent of slavery, though, as founder of the Massachusetts Peace Society (1838), he was opposed to militancy in all forms, including that of some in the abolitionist movement. Died in Bennington, Vermont. The pedestal of a statue erected in his honor in 1903 in the Boston Public Garden reads: "He breathed into theology a humane spirit and proclaimed anew the divinity of man. He preached with spiritual power and led a great advance toward the Christian ideals."

Cyrenius Chapin (February 7, 1769–February 20, 1838) Born in Bernardston, Massachusetts, son of Captain Caleb Chapin, an officer in the Revolutionary War. He studied medicine with his brother, Dr. Caleb Chapin, and practiced for several years in Vermont and in

Oneida County, New York. He married Sylvia Burnham, also of Bernardston, in 1793, and moved to Buffalo in 1801, establishing a practice and opening the town's first apothecary. A Federalist who supported the war, in 1812 he raised a company of mounted volunteers and was successively commissioned captain, major, and lieutenant colonel. His company, known as "the Forty Thieves" because of its numerous successful cross-border raids into Canada, was among the American forces that on May 25, 1813, captured Fort George, in Niagara. It later formed the vanguard of Colonel Charles Boerstler's June 23 infantry expedition against a British outpost approximately eighteen miles southwest of Fort George. The American force was ambushed by Indians at Beaver Dams and forced to surrender, but on July 12, while being transported by boat to Kingston, Chapin and twenty-eight of his men overpowered their sixteen guards and brought them to Fort George as prisoners. On December 20, 1813, at Buffalo, Brigadier General George McClure of the New York militia, who viewed Chapin as a rival for leadership of the New York volunteers, had him arrested for treason and mutiny, declaring that "there is not a greater rascal [who] exists than Chapin, and he is supported by a pack of *tories* and enemies to our Government." Chapin was rescued by armed supporters, and McClure was forced to flee the town. On December 30, Chapin led a spirited defense of Black Rock and Buffalo against British assault before being taken prisoner and brought to Montreal, where he was held for nine months. Returning to Buffalo, he was appointed surgeon of the military hospital. He returned to practice after the war, and was named first president of the Erie County Medical Society in 1821. Died in Buffalo.

Isaac Chauncey (February 20, 1772–January 27, 1840) Born in Black Rock, Fairfield County, Connecticut, son of Wolcott and Ann (Brown) Chauncey. As first lieutenant of the newly built U.S. frigate *President* (appointed June 11, 1799), he saw limited action in the Quasi-War with France. On USS *John Adams*, he served two tours to the North African coast during the First Barbary War, 1802–4, earning distinction during the American attack on Tripoli in August 1804. Promoted to captain in 1806, he took command of the New York Navy Yard the following year, where he was stationed until the outbreak of war in 1812, when he was put in charge of U.S. naval forces on Lakes Ontario and Erie. He established headquarters at Sackets Harbor, New York, in October 1812, assuming direct command of operations on Lake Ontario and placing Commodore Oliver H. Perry in charge of the fleet on Lake Erie. Throughout 1813, his forces cooperated with the U.S. Army in successful joint operations against York (Toronto) on April 24 and Fort George, in Niagara, on May 27, but avoided direct confrontation with the British Lake Ontario fleet commanded by Sir James Yeo. His base having been attacked while assisting in the capture of Fort George, he grew cautious about deploying his forces in support of army operations and concentrated instead on building more ships to secure naval preponderance on the lake. Under his command, Sackets Harbor became the country's largest naval station. Illness and interservice jealousy compromised his leadership at critical moments during the 1814 campaign season, inviting criticism from Washington and elsewhere. In the summer of 1815, he was ordered to shut down the base at Sackets Harbor and remove to Portsmouth, New Hampshire, there to assume command of USS *Washington*, which served as flagship of the Mediterranean squadron, 1816–18. Along with American consul William Shaler, he negotiated a treaty with the Dey of Algiers in December 1816. He spent the remainder of his career alternately as commandant of the New York naval station (1819–20, 1825–34) and as a member of the navy's board of commissioners in Washington, D.C. (1820–24, 1833–40, president 1837–40). Died in Washington.

Henry Clay (April 12, 1777–June 29, 1852) Born in Hanover County, Virginia, son of John Clay, a Baptist minister and farmer, and Elizabeth (Hudson) Clay. When, at fifteen, his family moved to Kentucky, Clay was left at Richmond, where he clerked for George Wythe, judge in Virginia's High Court of Chancery. He was admitted to the bar in 1797 and began practicing law in Lexington, Kentucky. In 1799 he married Lucretia Hart, daughter of a wealthy Lexington merchant; they had eleven children. In 1803 he was elected to the Kentucky House of Representatives, becoming Speaker in 1808. His service in the state legislature was interrupted by two appointments (1806–7 and 1810–11) to fill the remainder of unexpired terms in the U.S. Senate. In 1809 he fought a duel with Humphrey Marshall in which both men were wounded. (A second duel, in 1826 with U.S. senator John Randolph, was bloodless.) A staunch advocate of war against Britain, he was elected to the U.S. House of Representatives and served as its Speaker from March 1811 to January 1814. As Speaker, he interpreted the rules, used committee assignments, and controlled debate to keep the war movement on track, though he was only partly successful in preserving party unity. Resigning to join the peace commission sent to negotiate the Treaty of Ghent, he remained in Europe after the treaty was signed on December 24, 1814, to negotiate a commerce treaty with Great Britain. He was again Speaker of the House, 1815–21 and 1823–25. In his second stint as Speaker, he engineered passage of a series of infrastructure and tariff measures collectively known as "the American System." Finishing fourth in the 1824 presidential election, he supported John

Quincy Adams when the election was decided in the House of Representatives, and then became secretary of state in the Adams administration, 1825–29, an appointment some criticized as quid pro quo for swinging the election. Elected to the Senate as a National Republican in 1831, he served until his resignation in 1842. He ran unsuccessfully for president against Andrew Jackson as the National Republican candidate in 1832 and against James Polk as the Whig candidate in 1844. Elected once more to the Senate as a Whig in 1849, he served there until his death, from tuberculosis, in Washington, D.C.

Lewis (or Louis) Peter Clover (December 16, 1790–January 21, 1879) Born near Morristown, New Jersey, the son of a farmer, he ran away to sea at age sixteen. Taken prisoner on January 17, 1814, when his ship, the merchantman *Union*, was captured by a British naval vessel off Calcutta, he was incarcerated at Dartmoor Prison, in Devon, England, from October 21, 1814, to July 1, 1815. There he witnessed, on April 6, 1815, the infamous Dartmoor Massacre, when British guards fired upon a group of prisoners, killing six and wounding sixty. He returned to New York, trained as a wood framer and engraver, married Bridget Murphy in 1816, and set up a picture shop in lower Manhattan in 1825. In 1844 he serialized "Reminiscences of a Dartmoor Prisoner" in four issues of the *Knickerbocker* magazine, and in recognition of his wartime sacrifice, he was awarded a minor post in the New York customs office in 1845, but was removed for a party appointment in 1849. In 1852, he led an effort to organize New York City's surviving prisoners of war from the War of 1812 to petition for government assistance. He died in Brooklyn, New York, and was eulogized in the January 23, 1879, edition of the *Brooklyn Union-Argus* as "The Last Survivor."

A. W. Cochran (c. 1792–July 11, 1849) Born Andrew William Cochran in Windsor, Nova Scotia, son of the Reverend William Cochran, editor of *The Nova Scotia Magazine* and president of King's College, Windsor, and Rebecca (Cuppaidge) Cochran. He studied classics and law at King's before interrupting his studies in 1811 to accept the post of assistant to the governor-general of British North America, Sir George Prevost. In July 1813 he became deputy judge advocate of militia staff and, in November 1814, acting deputy judge advocate of the army staff. Admitted to the bar in June 1817, he built a private practice in Quebec City while also serving as clerk of the Prerogative Court through 1826 and holding a variety of other civil service positions. In 1818 he married Houstoun Thomson; they had seven children. He was a member of the Legislative Council for Lower Canada, 1827–39, after which he resumed private law practice. His wife having died in 1837, he married Magdalen Kerr in 1843. Died in Sillery, Lower Canada.

Alexander Cochrane (April 23, 1758–January 26, 1832) Born Alexander Forrester Inglis Cochrane, a younger son of Thomas Cochrane, the eighth Earl of Dundonald (Scotland). He embarked early on a naval career, achieving the rank of lieutenant by 1778, and during the American War of Independence, he was wounded in action against the French at Martinique in 1780, and later stationed out of the British base at New York City. (A brother, Charles, was killed at the Battle of Yorktown.) In 1788, he married the widow Maria (Shaw) Wheate; they had five children. In the war against revolutionary France, he participated as captain of HMS *Ajax* in the capture of Alexandria, Egypt, in 1801. He retired from the navy after the Peace of Amiens, serving as a member of Parliament, 1803–5. He returned to active duty in 1805, as rear admiral, and was placed in command of the Leeward Islands naval station, conducting operations aboard HMS *Northumberland* against French and Spanish forces, including at the Battle of San Domingo, February 6, 1806, where he was nearly killed. His courage under fire earned him the thanks of Parliament and a knighthood. He later led expeditions against Danish and French colonies in the Caribbean, for which service he was appointed governor and commander-in-chief of Guadeloupe, 1810–13. Named vice admiral and commander of the Royal Navy's North American station in 1814, with headquarters at Bermuda, he implemented more aggressive policies against the United States, such as imposing a general blockade of all American ports (including in Federalist New England) and providing naval support for expeditions against Baltimore and Washington. He also issued a proclamation, presumably targeting American slaves, promising to all interested Americans a "choice of either entering into His Majesty's Sea or Land Forces, or being sent as FREE Settlers, to the British Possessions in North America or the West Indies." In December 1814, he transported ten thousand soldiers and sailors in support of Major General Sir Edward Pakenham's unsuccessful assault on New Orleans, inviting criticism from the Duke of Wellington (Pakenham's brother-in-law and former commander) for his role in conceiving and planning the expedition. He returned to England in 1815, was promoted to admiral in 1819, and was named commander-in-chief of Plymouth naval station, 1821–24. Died in Paris, visiting his daughter, Anna-Maria, Lady Trowbridge.

James Fenimore Cooper (September 15, 1789–September 14, 1851) Born James Cooper in Burlington, New Jersey, twelfth of thirteen children of William and Elizabeth (Fenimore) Cooper. In 1790, his family moved to Lake Ostego, in upstate New York, where his father, a Federalist, had acquired a large tract of land and established a wilderness settlement, Cooperstown. He studied at Yale College, 1803–5, but was inattentive and prankish and was expelled in his junior year. He sailed to Europe aboard the merchant vessel *Stirling*, 1806–7, and on this voyage he met apprentice seaman Edward R. "Ned" Myers. He joined the U.S. Navy in 1808, and was posted to Lake Ontario to apprehend smugglers violating the U.S. embargo. His father died in 1809, leaving him a large but contested estate; the subsequent deaths of his older brothers left Cooper with burdensome family responsibilities and substantial personal debt, which was aggravated by the economic disruption and depression brought on by the War of 1812. He married Susan Augusta De Lancey, of Mamaroneck, New York, in January 1811, and resigned his commission; the first of their seven children was born in September. He purchased a farm near Cooperstown, which he renamed Fenimore, hoping to establish permanent residence there, but removed with his growing family to De Lancey land in Westchester County, New York, in 1818, in order to pursue ventures that might address his financial difficulties. He purchased a stake in, and frequently sailed on, a whaling ship in 1819, but to no great profit. He published his first novel, *Precaution*, in 1820, and began to write reviews. A second novel, *The Spy*, appeared in 1821 and he moved his family to New York City in 1822. His literary reputation grew with publication of *The Pioneers* (1823)—the first of five novels featuring the character Natty Bumppo (collectively known as the Leatherstocking Tales)—*The Pilot* (1824), *The Last of the Mohicans* (1826, when he formally added Fenimore to his name), *The Prairie* (1827), and *The Red Rover* (1828). In 1826, at the height of his popularity, he sailed with his family to Europe, there to stay for seven years, living mostly in Paris. He published *Notions of the Americans*, a critical assessment of the American character, in 1829. He returned to a chilly reception in New York City in 1833, and in 1834 purchased and moved to the family seat, Ostego Hall, in Cooperstown, where litigious behavior brought him afoul of the local populace. He published a bitter and condescending *Letter to His Countrymen* in 1834, increasing his unpopularity. Later works include *History of the Navy* (1839), *The Pathfinder* (1840) and *The Deerslayer* (1841), the last of the Leatherstocking Tales, and *Ned Myers; or, A Life Before the Mast* (1843), his biography of the seaman he met on his first ocean voyage. More admired in Europe than in America, the bulk of Cooper's income from publications was from international sales. Died at Ostego Hall.

George Croghan (November 15, 1791–January 8, 1849) Born at Locust Grove, an estate near Louisville, Kentucky, son of William and

Lucy (Clark) Croghan (pronounced "Crawn"). His father was an Irishman and veteran of the Continental Army, his mother a sister of William Clark, of the Lewis and Clark Expedition, and George Rogers Clark, a brigadier general who had commanded American forces in the Old Northwest during the Revolutionary War and who spent the last years of his life, 1809–18, at Locust Grove. Croghan studied at the College of William and Mary, graduating in 1810, and studied law briefly before serving as volunteer aide-de-camp in William Henry Harrison's mostly militia expedition against Prophet's Town, November 1811; Harrison later recommended him for appointment as captain in the U.S. Army and placed him in command of Fort Stephenson in northern Ohio. In defiance of Harrison's subsequent order to abandon Fort Stephenson, Croghan successfully defended it against an assault by British and Indian forces on August 2, 1813, repulsing what was the last British offensive of the war in the Northwest and scoring a major morale boost for the American war effort. He was brevetted lieutenant colonel in recognition of his victory. In the summer of 1814, he participated in a failed attack on the British post on Mackinac Island. He resigned from the army in 1816 and traveled to New York where he met and married Serena Livingston, of the prominent New York clan; they had seven children. He moved his family to New Orleans in 1824, where he served as postmaster. Named inspector general of the army the following year, he served in that post until 1845. He was awarded a gold medal by Congress in 1835 for his defense of Fort Stephenson. Often in debt due to gambling, he narrowly escaped a court-martial for repeatedly seeking double payment of wages. He left New Orleans to fight in the Mexican-American War, contracting cholera in Monterrey, Mexico. Died in New Orleans.

Daniel Curtis (?–d. Winter 1833/34) Born in New Hampshire, he moved to Michigan Territory and taught school in Detroit before enlisting in 1st U.S. Infantry Regiment in 1812. He married Eliza Whistler, sister of William Whistler, a second lieutenant in the 1st Regiment. Posted first to Fort Detroit and then, in June, to Fort Wayne, in the Indiana Territory, he was present for siege there, as second lieutenant, September 5–12. He was the temporary commandant at Fort Wayne from February to May 1817. Promoted to captain in 1820, he was later reposted to Fort Detroit and then to Fort Howard, on the Fox River near Green Bay. Discharged from the army in 1823, he opened a school at Prairie du Chien, Michigan Territory (present-day Wisconsin), where he died.

Elias Darnell (c. 1789–1861) The eighth child of Isaac and Stacia (McDonald) Darnell, the place and exact date of Darnell's birth are unknown, as is the date of his marriage to Elizabeth Grant. Enlisting

as a private in the Kentucky militia on August 15, 1812, he served in
the regiment of Lieutenant Colonel William Lewis and was among
the American forces under the direction of Major General James
Winchester at the Battle of Frenchtown, January 22, 1813; he was held
by Indians after the Americans surrendered to the British. Escaping
from his Indian captors, he fled to the British at Amherstburg and
from there was marched with other prisoners 250 miles through cold
and snow to Fort George, on the New York border, and paroled on
February 10. Upon returning home he wrote a journal of his experience, which, along with short narratives by two other men who were
taken captive by Indians, was published in Philadelphia in 1854 as
*Journal Containing an Accurate and Interesting Account of the Hard-
ships, Sufferings, Battles, Defeat, and Captivity of those Heroic Kentucky
Volunteers and Regulars Commanded by General Winchester, in the
Years 1812–13.* Place and exact date of death unknown.

William Dunlop (November 19, 1792–June 29, 1848) Born in Greenock, Scotland, third son of Alexander Dunlop, a banker, and Janet
(Graham) Dunlop. Educated first at Greenock, he later pursued
medical studies at the University of Glasgow and in London. He
joined the army in December 1812, and was appointed assistant surgeon to the 89th Regiment of Foot on February 4, 1813. Posted to
Upper Canada, he treated wounded soldiers in battles at Crysler's
Farm, Lundy's Lane, and Fort Erie. He retired on half pay on January
25, 1817, and traveled to India, working as a journalist and editor in
Calcutta and hunting tigers, becoming known thereafter as "Tiger"
Dunlop. He returned to Scotland in 1820, writing and lecturing
about India, before moving to London in 1824, where he established
a newspaper, the *Telescope*, which he ran for a year. In 1826, he was
contracted by the Canada Company, a colonization enterprise established by Scottish novelist John Galt, to serve as warden of the woods
and forests, inspecting lands, building roads, and managing the allo-
cation and use of land and timber. He established his home, Gairbraid,
near Goderich, in Upper Canada, where the Maitland River flows
into Lake Huron. An outsized personality, he engaged in newspaper
skirmishes with critics of company policy, displaying a lively and
caustic wit. As "A Backwoodsman," he wrote a humorous promo-
tional tract, *Statistical Sketches of Upper Canada*, published in London
in 1832. He was resident general superintendent of the million-acre
Huron Tract, the company's principal holding, 1833–38, resigning
when he was criticized for commandeering company supplies in his
capacity as militia leader during the rebellion against Crown authority
in Upper Canada. He represented Huron County for two terms in
the legislative assembly of the newly united Province of Canada

(comprising Upper and Lower Canada), 1842–46. He did not seek reelection in 1846, instead accepting appointment as superintendent of the Lachine Canal, in Montreal. There, in 1847, he published "Recollections of the American War" in the magazine *Literary Garland*. Died in Montreal.

David G. Farragut (July 5, 1801–August 14, 1870) Born James Glasgow Farragut at Campbell's Station, near Knoxville, Tennessee, second son of George and Elizabeth (Shine) Farragut. His father was Minorcan (born Jordi Farragut, when the Spanish island was a British possession); he fought in the Revolutionary War and in 1807 became an officer in the U.S. Navy. Stationed in New Orleans, George Farragut met a fellow naval officer, David Porter Sr., who in 1808 was cared for in his last illness in the Farragut home. Elizabeth Farragut died shortly thereafter. In gratitude to the Farragut family, David Porter Jr., also a naval officer, offered to adopt young James and sponsor his naval career, which offer George Farragut accepted. (By 1814, if not earlier, James's name was changed to David, presumably in Porter's honor.) James was educated in Washington, D.C., and Chester, Pennsylvania (Porter's home), and on December 17, 1810, not yet ten, he was appointed midshipman in the navy. During the War of 1812, he was posted to the frigate *Essex*, under Porter's command, seeing action in both the Atlantic and the Pacific, and even commanding a prize ship, the *Alexander Barclay*, at age twelve. Captured with the rest of the *Essex* crew at Valparaiso, Chile, March 28, 1814, he was released on parole until exchanged in November of that year. He then served several tours in the Mediterranean, 1815–20, receiving sporadic formal education at ports of call. (Eventually he learned to speak French, Italian, Spanish, and Arabic.) Promoted to lieutenant in 1822, he was posted to the West Indies and Gulf of Mexico, again under Porter's overall command, to combat pirates. On September 24, 1823, he married Susan C. Marchant of Norfolk, Virginia, which would be his home until 1861; Susan Farragut died on December 27, 1840. On December 26, 1843, he married Virginia Loyall, also of Norfolk, with whom he had one surviving son. Promoted to commander in 1841, he was assigned inconsequential blockade duty during the Mexican-American War, and then posted as inspector of ordnance in Norfolk and Washington, D.C. In 1854, he established Mare Island Navy Yard at Vallejo, California, serving as its commander until 1858, having been promoted to captain in 1855. He was in Norfolk when, on April 17, 1861, the Virginia Convention voted to secede from the Union. Loyal to the United States, he promptly moved with family to Hastings-on-Hudson, New York, to await orders from the navy. On January 9, 1862, he was appointed to command of the

West Gulf Blockading Squadron, with orders to capture New Orleans, which he accomplished in April 1862, a signal victory that Congress recognized by creating, on July 16, 1862, the rank of rear admiral for him. He won another important victory at the Battle of Mobile Bay, August 5, 1864, when Union forces under his command captured the Confederacy's last major port on the Gulf of Mexico (and where he famously declared "Damn the torpedoes!"). Promoted to vice admiral in 1864 and admiral in 1866, he remained on active duty until his death, in Portsmouth, New Hampshire.

Patrick Finan (fl. 1812–28) An Irishman, though place and date of birth unknown. All that is known about Finan is derived from his memoir, *Journal of a Voyage to Quebec, in the Year 1825, with Recollections of Canada, during the Late American War, in the Years 1812–13*, published in Ireland in 1828. A somewhat digressive work, it suggests that Finan had had some classical education, was possessed of a pious sensibility, and was supportive of temperance and other reforms but strongly opposed to the institution of marriage. It recounts the following details: he sailed to Canada with his mother and siblings in August 1812 to live near his father, a British officer posted at Kingston, Upper Canada: "I was a very young boy at the time." At La Chien, nine miles south of Montreal, he encountered his father's regiment escorting U.S. general William Hull and his forces captured at Detroit to Montreal. Shortly after, he witnessed a skirmish with American forces along the St. Lawrence River. He was settled at Kingston until February 1813, when his father's regiment was ordered to York (Toronto). There, on April 25, he witnessed an attack by American forces, and the explosion of a munitions storehouse. He fled with his family and retreating British forces to Kingston, where he witnessed and was "deeply affected" by the execution of a deserter. He later attended school in Montreal and left Canada around 1815. He departed from Ireland aboard the *Lord Wellington* for a second journey to Canada on April 19, 1825, to inspect lands ("concessions") he had purchased there, embarking on the return voyage to Ireland on July 19. He lived at Newry, in Ulster. Place and date of death unknown.

Cornelius Flummerfelt (Plomerfelt) Place and date of birth unknown. A private in the 1st Flank Company of the 3rd York (Upper Canada) militia and the recipient of a general service medal for action seen at Fort Detroit, he is thought to have composed "The Bold Canadian," a panegyric for the Canadian militiaman, returning from the Detroit campaign. Place and date of death unknown.

Philip Freneau (January 2, 1752–December 18, 1832) Born in New York City and raised in Monmouth County, New Jersey, son of Pierre

Fresneau (old spelling), a wine merchant, and Agnes (Watson) Fresneau. Educated by tutors as a youth, he graduated from the College of New Jersey (now Princeton) in 1771; at his college commencement, a classmate, Hugh Henry Brackenridge, read from *The Rising Glory of America*, a patriotic poem on which the two had collaborated. After graduating he taught school briefly before traveling to the West Indies where he spent two years as secretary to a planter on St. Croix. Volunteering for military service in 1778, he was captured by a British man-of-war in the Caribbean and imprisoned, later recounting his ordeal in a long poem, "The British Prison-Ship" (1781). During the 1780s, he worked as a postal clerk in Philadelphia and captained a merchant ship in the Caribbean. He published *The Poems of Philip Freneau, Written Chiefly during the Late War* in 1786 and *The Miscellaneous Works of Mr. Philip Freneau* in 1788. In 1790 he married Eleanor Forman (they had four children) and became the editor of the New York *Daily Advertiser*. The next year, at the instigation of James Madison, another college classmate of Freneau's, Secretary of State Thomas Jefferson offered Freneau a government clerkship to entice him to Philadelphia to found and edit the *National Gazette*, which became the organ of the emerging anti-administration republican faction. (George Washington would refer to him as "that rascal Freneau.") Later he edited small New York and New Jersey newspapers and until 1804 occasionally worked as a captain of merchant vessels. His *Poems Written between the Years 1768 & 1794* was published in 1795; *Poems Written and Published during the American Revolutionary War* appeared in 1809. He is best remembered today for such lyrics as "The Indian Burying Ground" and "The Wild Honey Suckle." Died in a blizzard near his New Jersey farm.

Albert Gallatin (January 29, 1761–August 12, 1849) Born Abraham Alfonse Albert Gallatin in Geneva, Switzerland, the son of Jean Gallatin, a prosperous merchant of a distinguished family, and Sophie Albertine (Rolaz) Gallatin; he was orphaned at age nine. Graduating from the Academy of Geneva in 1779, he declined an offer (arranged by a family member) of a commission in the Hessian army, then mobilizing mercenary corps to suppress the American rebellion, deciding instead to emigrate to the United States in 1780. After brief stays in Boston, teaching French at Harvard College, and in eastern Maine, he moved in 1784 to recently founded Fayette County in southwestern Pennsylvania where he acquired a large tract of land he called Friendship Hill. He married Sophia Allegre in the 1789; she died a few months later. He was a delegate to the 1789–90 convention to revise Pennsylvania's constitution and a member of the state House of Representatives, 1790–92. Elected by that body to the U.S. Senate in

February 1793, he took his seat in the Third Congress in December; amid much controversy, his election was invalidated by the Federalist majority in the Senate in February 1794 on the ground that he had not been a U.S. citizen for nine years. He married Hannah Nicholson in 1793; they had three children. He was elected to the U.S. House of Representatives, serving 1795–1801; upon James Madison's retirement from the House in 1797, he assumed leadership of the body's Republican faction. Appointed secretary of treasury by President Thomas Jefferson, and reappointed by President James Madison, he held the office from 1801 to 1814. In the absence of a national bank, which the Republican majority had allowed to expire in 1811, he was forced to finance the War of 1812 with a variety of measures, including direct taxes and innovative bond issues. Fatigued by his duties at Treasury, he resigned to join fellow commissioners John Quincy Adams, Henry Clay, J. A. Bayard, and John Russell in negotiations with the British to end the conflict, signing the Treaty of Ghent on December 24, 1814. He traveled to Geneva and Paris in 1815, before returning to England to negotiate, along with Adams and Clay, a commercial treaty with Great Britain. Declining to resume his post at Treasury, he served as American minister to France for Presidents Madison and Monroe, 1815–23. Upon his return to America he was nominated by the Republican congressional caucus for vice president on William H. Crawford's ticket, though he later removed his name from consideration. He retired to Friendship Hill, but was induced to accept appointment as minister to the Court of St. James (Great Britain), 1826–27. Thereafter he settled in New York City, where he became president of the National Bank of New York (1831–39) and in 1831 was one of the founders and first president of the council of the University of the City of New York (NYU). Died in Astoria, New York.

George R. Gleig (April 20, 1796–July 9, 1888) Born George Robert Gleig in Stirling, Scotland, the third, and only surviving, son of the Reverend George Gleig, bishop of Brechin and Primus of the Scottish Episcopal Church. He was educated at Glasgow University and at Balliol College, Oxford, leaving in 1813 to join a volunteer regiment passing through Oxford bound for service in the Peninsular campaign. He was soon commissioned in the 85th Regiment of Light Infantry, and saw fighting in Portugal, Spain, and France, 1813–14. As a captain, he was wounded three times in action in America, 1814–15, participating in the burning of Washington and the unsuccessful assault on New Orleans. He returned to Oxford, completing a B.A. in 1818 and an M.A. in 1821. He married in 1819, took holy orders in 1820, and eventually was established as rector at Ivy Church (today Ivychurch), in Kent, in 1822. He later served as chaplain of Chelsea

Hospital, 1834–44; chaplain general of the army, 1844–75; and inspector general of military schools, 1846–57. In 1848, he became a prebendary of St. Paul's Cathedral, serving for the remainder of his life. He was the author of numerous works, including military memoirs *The Campaigns of the British Army at Washington and New Orleans, 1814–1815* (1821), and *The Subaltern* (1825), about his service on the Continent. Died at Stratfield Turgis, in Hampshire, England.

Amos Hall (November 21, 1761–December 28, 1827) Born in Guilford, Connecticut, son of Captain Stephen Hall and Abigail (Sexton) Hall; he was a fifer in his father's regiment during the Revolutionary War. He married Phoebe Coe in 1790; they had nine children. The couple moved to upstate New York, where Hall helped found the town of West Bloomfield. He became a leading citizen in the Finger Lakes region, and, as U.S. deputy marshal, he administered the first federal census for the district in 1790. Later a Federalist state assemblyman in 1798, and state senator, 1809–13, during the War of 1812 he served as deputy to George McClure, commander of New York militia on the Niagara frontier. He assumed command himself on December 25, 1813, when the unpopular McClure was forced to step down. As major general, he led raw and disorganized militia units in an unsuccessful defense of Buffalo, December 30, 1813. He was replaced by congressman-turned-general Peter B. Porter. Died in West Bloomfield.

Jarvis Hanks (September 24, 1799–June 27, 1853) Born Jarvis Frary Hanks in Pittsford, Ostego County, New York, son of Joseph and Anna (Frary) Hanks; raised in Pawlet, Vermont. At age ten, he was sent to live in a neighboring town to learn to play the drum. In 1813, he was recruited into the U.S. Army as a drummer, over the objection of his distraught mother, who said she would rather have seen him "decently buried than in the army." Despite the army's promise that he would serve only as a recruitment tool, he saw action at Crysler's Farm, Chippawa, Lundy's Lane, and Fort Erie. Discharged on May 23, 1815, he moved to Wheeling, (West) Virginia, in 1817, working as a painter of signs and furniture. Wishing to become a portrait painter, he traveled to Philadelphia to seek formal instruction, without success. In 1823, he married Charlotte Garber (they had seven children) and moved to Ohio, eventually settling in Cleveland, where he opened a portrait, sign, and ornamental painting shop and became active in Masonry. He moved again to New York City in 1827, prospering as a sign painter and enjoying several exhibits of his portraiture at the National Academy of Design. He renounced his Masonic vows in 1829, and became an outspoken opponent of the secretive society. In 1836, he returned with his family to Cleveland, becoming a leading local artist and supporting various cultural and reform causes, especially the introduction of music instruction into public school curricula. Died in Cleveland.

Charles Willing Hare (April 23, 1778–April 15, 1827) Born at Westover, Virginia, eldest surviving son of Robert and Margaret (Willing) Hare, who were then visiting family in Virginia. He was admitted to the bar in 1799, and was a prominent lawyer in Philadelphia, serving also in the lower house of the Pennsylvania assembly. He married Anne Emlen in 1801; they had six children. He was a leader among Philadelphia Federalists, serving as secretary of the party's corresponding committee; in the presidential elections of 1808 and 1812, he sought to foster greater coordination among Federalist parties in the various states, laying the groundwork for the national political conventions of the future. In 1813 he helped found the Washington Benevolent Society, and on February 22, Washington's birthday, he delivered its inaugural oration, later published. In an October 1, 1814, letter to Harrison Gray Otis of Massachusetts he called for a convention of representatives from the New England states to address what he perceived to be the existential threat represented by the war policies of the Madison administration. On March 20, 1817, he was named professor of law at the University of Philadelphia, the first at the school in almost two decades, but was said to have "lost his reason" a year later. He was declared *non compos mentis* and his estate was authorized for sale by the Pennsylvania General Assembly on April 14, 1827, the day before he died, in Philadelphia.

Nathaniel Hawthorne (July 4, 1804–May 19, 1864) Born in Salem, Massachusetts, son of Nathaniel and Elizabeth (Manning) Hathorne. His father, a ship's captain, died of fever in Surinam when Hawthorne was four; with his mother and sisters, he lived with relatives thereafter. Educated at home for a number of years following a schoolyard injury, he attended Bowdoin College (1821–25), where he began his first novel, *Fanshawe* (1828). He then focused on writing short fiction, eventually collected in *Twice-Told Tales* (1837). He worked at customhouses in Boston, 1839–41, before joining the utopian community at Brook Farm in April 1841; he left after eight months and later published *The Blithedale Romance* (1852), a novel based on the experience. He married Sophia Peabody in 1842; they had three children. The couple settled in Concord, Massachusetts, where they became acquainted with Ralph Waldo Emerson, Henry David Thoreau, and their circle; the story collection *Mosses from an Old Manse* (1846) was written in Concord. He was employed at the Salem Custom House, 1846–49. In 1846, he facilitated publication of "Papers of an old Dartmoor Prisoner, Edited by Nathaniel Hawthorne," the anonymous memoirs of his friend and fellow Salem Democrat, Benjamin F.

Browne, in the *United States Magazine and Democratic Review*. He explored New England's Puritan past in the novels *The Scarlet Letter* (1850) and *The House of the Seven Gables* (1851). The author of the official biography for the presidential campaign of Bowdoin friend Franklin Pierce, he was appointed American consul at Liverpool after Pierce's election in 1852; he kept extensive notebooks of his travels in England, France, and Italy. His last completed novel, *The Marble Faun*, was published in 1860, the year he returned to America. Died in Plymouth, New Hampshire.

Nathan Heald (September 24, 1775–April 27, 1832) Born in New Ipswich, New Hampshire. A captain in the U.S. 1st Regiment of Infantry, he was transferred in 1810 from Fort Wayne, in Indiana Territory, to Fort Dearborn (present-day Chicago), then traveled back to Fort Wayne in 1811 to marry Rebecca Wells, niece of Captain William Wells, returning with her to Fort Dearborn. At the outbreak of the War of 1812, the fort was well provisioned and manned by fifty-four regulars and twelve militia; nine women and eighteen children were also in the fort. Nevertheless, on August 9, 1812, he received orders from General William Hull to evacuate the post and fall back to Fort Wayne, Dearborn having been deemed untenable in the wake of the British capture of Fort Michilimackinac, well to the north, in the vital straits between Lake Michigan and Lake Huron. Captain Wells and approximately thirty Miami Indians were dispatched to Fort Dearborn to provide tactical support for withdrawal, which commenced on August 15. The Miamis promptly fled the scene, leaving the American column exposed to attack by some five hundred hostile Indians, mostly Potawatomis. In less than half an hour, most of the column was dead—many after having sought to surrender—in what became known as the Fort Dearborn Massacre. Fatalities included Captain Wells, twenty-six regulars, all the militia, and two women and twelve children. Nathan and Rebecca Heald, both wounded, were taken by canoe north to the British fort on Mackinac Island (formerly Fort Michilimackinac), where they were turned over to the commander. From there they were transported to Buffalo, and returned across the border, a journey of two months and twelve hundred miles from Fort Dearborn. Promoted to major, Heald was discharged for disability in 1814, and awarded a pension of twenty dollars a month. The Healds lived in Fort Wayne, Indiana Territory, until 1817, when they moved to O'Fallon, Missouri Territory, and purchased Fort Zumwalt and its land. Died at Fort Zumwalt.

N. W. Hibbard (October 30, 1786–May 1, 1867) Born Nathaniel Wood Hibbard in Rutland Vermont, son of Ithamar Hibbard, a Congregational minister, and Hannah (Wood) Hibbard. By 1812 he was living in Jefferson County, New York, where he was listed on the militia rolls as an ensign. In 1814, he was present at the Battle of Sandy Creek and participated in the hauling of a large cable from Sandy Creek to Sackets Harbor, which he described in a letter of 1859, his only known written record. He was listed in the militia rolls of 1815 as captain of the 55th regiment, again from Jefferson County. He was living in Rural Hill, New York, when he wrote the letter recollecting his wartime experience, which reveals that he had at least one child. According to one source, he died in Hebbardsville, near Athens, Ohio.

William E. Horner (June 3, 1793–March 13, 1853) Born William Edmonds Horner in Warrenton, Fauquier County, Virginia, son of William and Mary (Edmonds) Horner. He was educated in the academy of the Reverend Charles O'Neill, a classicist, first in Warrenton and later in Dumfries, Virginia. In 1809 he began the study of medicine in the home of John Spence of Dumfries, who had had medical training in Edinburgh, while also attending sessions at the University of Pennsylvania. In July 1813, before completing his training, he was commissioned a surgeon's mate in the hospital department of the U.S. Army, and dispatched to the Niagara frontier of New York. There, he treated soldiers wounded at Chippawa, Bridgewater, Black Rock, and Fort Erie. On furlough during the following winter, he returned to Philadelphia and completed his medical studies—his thesis was entitled "Gunshot Wounds"—graduating from the University of Pennsylvania in April 1814; he returned to the New York frontier, and an army hospital in Buffalo, in June. Resigning his commission on March 13, 1815, he returned home to practice medicine in Warrenton before moving to Philadelphia in December, where he was hired by Caspar Wistar, anatomy professor at the university, to prepare dissections for his classes. By 1819, Horner was an adjunct professor of anatomy at the university, and in 1831 he became department chair. The following year he also assumed duties as the dean of the medical school, remaining in that position until 1852. He married Elizabeth Welsh in Philadelphia in 1820; they had ten children. He was the author of numerous medical texts and articles, including the multipart "Surgical Sketches: A Military Hospital at Buffalo, New York, in the year 1814," which was published in the journal *The Medical Examiner and Record of Medical Science* shortly before his death.

Eber D. Howe (June 9, 1798–November 10, 1885) Born Eber Dudley Howe, at Clifton Park, in Saratoga County, New York, son of Samuel William Howe and Mabel (Dudley) Howe, who moved to Ovid, in Seneca County, New York, in 1804 and then to the Niagara District in Upper Canada by 1811. He witnessed fighting along the Niagara front, 1812–13, and enlisted in the New York militia at Batavia, in

Genesee County, in 1814. After the war he commenced a newspaper career, working at the *Buffalo Gazette*, the *Chautauqua Gazette* (Fredonia, New York), and the *Erie Gazette* (Erie, Pennsylvania), before cofounding and publishing the *Cleveland Herald* (1819–21). He moved to Painesville, Ohio, in the spring of 1822, and founded and published the *Painesville Telegraph*, 1822–35, which featured numerous editorials against slavery and Mormonism. He married Sophia Hull of Clarence, New York, in 1823; they had six children. In 1834, after his wife and sister converted to Mormonism, he published *Mormonism Unvailed*, advancing what became known as the Spalding–Rigdon theory, which posited that the Book of Mormon was plagiarized by Joseph Smith Jr. and Sidney Rigdon from a manuscript work of fiction by Solomon Spalding. He sold his newspaper to his younger brother in 1835 and moved to Concord, Ohio, in 1838, where he later partnered with his son-in-law in a woolen manufacturing business. His *Autobiography and Recollections of a Pioneer Printer* was published in Painesville in 1878. Died at Concord.

William Hull (June 24, 1753–November 29, 1825) Born in Derby, Connecticut, son of Captain Joseph and Eliza (Clark) Hull. He graduated from Yale College in 1772, studied law at Litchfield, Connecticut, and was admitted to the bar in 1775. As captain, he led the Derby militia company to join the American army laying siege to Boston in April 1775. He subsequently saw action at several major battles of the Revolutionary War, including White Plains, Trenton, Princeton, Saratoga, Monmouth, and Stony Point, concluding his service with the rank of lieutenant colonel. He married Sarah Fuller, of Newton, Massachusetts, in 1781; they had ten children, and also adopted Isaac Hull, William's nephew, who would later command the USS *Constitution*. After the war, he established a law practice in Newton, and helped organize the Society of the Cincinnati, a veterans' organization. He also played a role in the suppression of Shays' Rebellion in 1787. Elected to the Massachusetts Senate in 1798, he was a strong supporter of Jefferson and the Democratic Republican Party. Appointed by President Jefferson the first governor of the newly organized Michigan Territory, he held that office from 1805 to 1813. As governor, he engineered numerous land concessions from Indian tribes, increasing hostility and discontent among them. As war seemed imminent in the spring of 1812, and though he was still recovering from a stroke suffered the year before, he devised a strategy for conquering Upper Canada and eagerly sought command. In Washington for consultation in early April, he was appointed by President Madison Brigadier General in command of a "North Western Army," which he raised in the following weeks; it consisted mostly of twelve hundred Ohio volunteers and eight hundred regulars of the 4th U.S. Infantry. Slow-moving and riven by internal squabbles, the American force was a reflection of its overcautious general, whose leadership was compromised by age, corpulence, and the residual effects of his stroke. It reached Fort Detroit on July 5, and crossed into Canada on July 12, Hull issuing a proclamation encouraging Canadians to remain passive as his army effected their liberation. Though possessing superior numbers to the British forces defending his target, Fort Amherstburg, Hull delayed, growing increasingly concerned with his long supply line to Ohio, which was targeted by small British and Indian forces. Fearing exposure of his force to Indian attacks in the wake of the British capture of Fort Michilimackinac, he abandoned his offensive on August 8, and withdrew to Fort Detroit, where he grew increasingly unstable and, on August 16, surrendered his army and fortifications without firing a shot. British general Isaac Brock allowed the Ohio militiamen to return home, but sent Hull and 582 regulars to Quebec as prisoners. Paroled and returned to the United States, Hull faced a court-martial in 1814 for neglect of duty, cowardice, and treason. Convicted of the first two charges, he was condemned to death, the only U.S. general officer ever so sentenced. President Madison approved the sentence, but issued a reprieve in recognition of Hull's service in the Revolution. Hull returned to Newton, where he wrote two defenses of his conduct at Detroit: *Defence of Brig. Gen. Wm. Hull* (1814) and *Memoirs of the Campaign of the Northwestern Army of the United States: A.D. 1812* (1824). Died in Newton.

Mary Stockton Hunter (April 17, 1761–March 18, 1846) Born Mary Stockton, at Morven, her family's estate in Princeton, New Jersey, daughter of Richard Stockton, a judge of the court of common pleas, member of the Second Continental Congress, and signer of the Declaration of Independence, and Annis Williams (Boudinot) Stockton, a poet. In 1794 she married forty-two-year-old Andrew Hunter, a Presbyterian minister and schoolteacher from Trenton who later became a professor of mathematics and astronomy at the College of New Jersey (Princeton), where he was also a trustee; they had five children. In 1810, her husband was commissioned a chaplain in the U.S. Navy and stationed at the naval yard in Washington; he remained at that post, training midshipmen in mathematics and navigation, until his death, on February 24, 1823. In her husband's will, Hunter was bequeathed an annuity and shares in the Trenton-Delaware Bridge and Princeton and Kingston Branch Turnpike. Died in Princeton.

James Inderwick (fl. 1808–15) Place and date of birth unknown. He graduated from Columbia College in 1808, and registered as a medical student at Columbia for the following academic year, though he seems to have completed his studies elsewhere. He was house surgeon at the New York Hospital from February 1812 to February 1813. By May 1813 he was attached to USS *Argus*, a brig with a crew of 142, which sailed from New York on June 18, carrying the new American minister to France, William H. Crawford, to his post. Commissioned by the navy on July 24, he was just the nineteenth surgeon on the naval rolls to that date. On August 14, he was captured with the rest of the crew of the *Argus* after a fierce engagement with HMS *Pelican* in St. George's Channel, near Pembrokeshire, Wales, and imprisoned in England. He was listed in 1815 as surgeon of USS *Eperveir*, which was assigned to the Mediterranean squadron of Commodore Stephen Decatur, deployed to stop harassment of American shipping by the Dey of Algiers. Upon the conclusion of a treaty with the dey, *Eperveir* was dispatched to bring a copy of the treaty to the United States. After sailing through the Straits of Gibraltar on July 14, 1815, the ship was never heard from again. Inderwick had maintained a journal during his 1813 tour of duty, which was found in the papers of the New York Hospital and presented to the New York Public Library, which published it in 1917.

Washington Irving (April 3, 1783–November 28, 1859) Born in New York City, son of William Irving, a successful merchant, and Sarah (Sanders) Irving; they had emigrated from Great Britain in 1763. Unlike his older brothers, he did not attend Columbia College but clerked in the offices of three leading New York attorneys (1799–1804). In 1802, he began publishing letters under the pseudonym "Jonathan Oldstyle, Gent." in the *Morning Chronicle*, edited by his brother Peter, to generally favorable notice. Having traveled to Europe, 1804–6, he was admitted to the New York bar upon his return. He published satiric sketches, many critical of Jeffersonian policies, in *Salmagundi: or, The Whim-Whams and Opinions of Launcelot Langstaff, Esq. and Others* (twenty numbers, 1807–8). The satirical *A History of New York,* published in 1809, confirmed Irving's local literary celebrity. He traveled to Washington, D.C., in 1811 to lobby Congress for the interests of New York merchants, including his brothers (who inherited their father's business), adversely affected by the Non-Importation Act. As editor of *Analectic Magazine*, 1813–15, he wrote essays, biographical sketches of naval heroes, and literary criticism. His patriotism aroused by the British burning of Washington in 1814, he became aide-de-camp to Governor Daniel Tompkins of New York, with the rank of colonel, and served on the Canadian frontier without seeing action. He traveled to England in 1815 in an effort to revive the family trading business, and remained in Europe for the next seventeen years. *The Sketch Book of Geoffrey Crayon, Gent.*, which includes "The Legend of Sleepy Hollow" and "Rip Van Winkle," was published first in New York and then in London (1819–20); enthusiastic reviews on both sides of the Atlantic established him as the first American man of letters with an international reputation. Subsequent works published during his years in Europe include *Bracebridge Hall* (1822), *Tales of a Traveller* (1824), and *Tales of the Alhambra* (1832). He returned to America in 1832 to a grand welcome and embarked on an extensive tour of the American West, including the newly established Indian Territory (Oklahoma). The journey inspired a trio of "western" books: *A Tour on the Prairies* (1835), *Astoria* (1836), and *The Adventures of Captain Bonneville* (1837). In 1835, he purchased a house on ten acres fronting the Hudson in Tarrytown, New York, naming the estate Sunnyside. Appointed minister to Spain by President John Tyler, he held that post from 1842 to 1845. He returned to America in 1846 and published numerous works, including *Mahomet and his Successors* (2 vols., 1849–50) and *The Life of George Washington* (5 vols., 1855–59). Died at Sunnyside.

Andrew Jackson (March 15, 1767–June 8, 1845) Born in the Waxhaw Settlement, South Carolina, the son of Andrew and Elizabeth (Hutchinson) Jackson, Scots-Irish immigrants. Acting as a courier during the Revolutionary War, he was wounded by a British officer in 1781. Admitted to the bar in North Carolina in 1787, he moved to Nashville in 1788. He married Rachel Donelson Robards in 1791. (A second wedding ceremony was performed in 1794, after it was revealed that Rachel Donelson's divorce from Lewis Robards had not been finalized.) After attending the Tennessee constitutional convention in 1796, he served in the U.S. House of Representatives, 1796–97, and in the Senate, 1797–98, and was a judge of the Tennessee Superior Court, 1798–1804. He killed Charles Dickson in a duel in 1806 and was wounded in a gunfight with Jesse and Thomas Hart Benton in 1813. As major general of the Tennessee militia, he led a decisive campaign against the Creek Indians, 1813–14, that resulted in the Treaty of Fort Jackson, which abrogated Indian title to large parts of Alabama and Georgia. Appointed a major general in the U.S. Army in recognition of this campaign, he repulsed the British invasion force at the Battle of New Orleans in January 1815. Eager to dislodge Spanish authority there, he invaded Florida in 1818, ostensibly in pursuit of Seminole Indians, inviting official criticism but reinforcing his popular image as an Indian fighter. He served as governor of Florida Territory in 1821 and resigned from the army. Once again he served a partial term in the Senate, 1823–25. Though he won a plurality of the electoral vote in the 1824 presidential election, he lost in the House of Representatives to John Quincy Adams. He defeated Adams convincingly in 1828 and served as the seventh president of the United States, 1829–33. As president he advocated for and signed the Indian Removal Act of 1830, which resulted in the forced migration to the west of some forty-five thousand Indians of various tribes. During the constitutional crisis stemming from resistance in South Carolina to a federal tariff bill, he denied the claim that states may nullify acts of Congress and vowed to use troops to enforce the law. He replaced Vice President John C. Calhoun, a South Carolinian and advocate of nullification, with Martin Van Buren of New York and won reelection in 1832 by defeating Henry Clay. Died at the Hermitage, his estate near Nashville.

Thomas Jefferson (April 13, 1743–July 4, 1826) Born in Goochland (now Albemarle) County, Virginia, son of Peter Jefferson, a landowner and surveyor, and Jane (Randolph) Jefferson, of the prominent Virginia clan. Educated at the College of William and Mary and admitted to the Virginia bar in 1767, he served in the Virginia House of Burgesses, 1769–74. He married Martha Wayles Skelton in 1772; they had six children before Martha died in 1782, only two surviving infancy. (Evidence suggests that he later had at least five children with his slave Sally Hemings, half-sister of his deceased wife.) Active in the patriot cause, he published *A Summary View of the Rights of British America* in 1774 and was a delegate to the Continental Congress, 1775–76, where he drafted the Declaration of Independence. During the Revolutionary War he served in the Virginia assembly, 1776–79; as governor of Virginia, 1779–81; and as a delegate to the Continental Congress, 1783–84. He replaced Benjamin Franklin as American minister to France, 1785–89, establishing his residence in Paris, and there had printed a private edition of *Notes on the State of Virginia* in 1785. He was appointed secretary of state by George Washington and held office from March 1790 until December 1793, during which time political alignments in Congress began to take on the character of parties, with Jefferson widely viewed as leader of the opposition to the Federalist policies of the Washington administration. The "Republican" candidate for president in 1796, he finished second in the electoral voting to John Adams and served as vice president, 1797–1801. He drafted the Kentucky Resolutions opposing the Alien and Sedition Acts in 1798. In the electoral ballot of 1800 he tied with fellow Republican Aaron Burr and was elected president by the House of Representatives; he won reelection in 1804, defeating Federalist candidate Charles Cotesworth Pinckney, and served as the third president of the United States, 1801–9. In response to wartime restrictions on trade with Europe, he advocated for and signed the Non-Importation

Act (1806) and the Embargo Act (1807), measures that severely curtailed American overseas trade in a largely vain effort to exert economic pressure on Britain and France. He carried on an extensive
correspondence in post-presidential retirement, including with his
longtime ally and presidential successor, James Madison, about the
course of diplomacy, politics, and war. In 1814, in the wake of the
British sack of Washington, and in the face of mounting personal
debts, he sold his library to the federal government; it became the
foundation of a revived Library of Congress. In 1817, he completed
plans for the University of Virginia, which was formally chartered by
the Virginia Assembly two years later; he served as the university's
first rector. Died at Monticello, his estate near Charlottesville.

Francis Jeffrey (October 23, 1773–January 26, 1850) Born in Edinburgh, Scotland, son of George Jeffrey, a court clerk and a high Tory,
and Henrietta Louden. He was educated at the Universities of
Glasgow and Edinburgh, attended Queen's College, Oxford, 1791–92,
and was admitted to the Scottish bar in 1794. In need of a reliable
income after having married Catherine Wilson in 1801, and finding
that his Whig politics hindered his advancement in the legal profession, he founded in October 1802 the quarterly *Edinburgh Review*
with Sydney Smith and Henry Brougham; he soon became its principal editor. Evincing Jeffrey's signature wit and reformist politics, the
Review became one of the most important magazines of its age, a
platform for such prominent writers as Thomas Carlyle, William
Hazlitt, John Stuart Mill, and Thomas Babington Macaulay and a
crucial catalyst in the development of modern criticism. In 1805, his
wife and his only child died. The next year, in London, he found
himself in a duel with the poet Thomas Moore, whose *Epistles, Odes,
and Other Poems* had been subjected to criticism in the *Review*, in
part for its extravagant anti-Americanism; the police interrupted the
duel, and the combatants were soon cordial friends, with Moore even
contributing to the *Review*; the episode, satirized by Byron in *English
Bards and Scotch Reviewers*, and other instances of his pro-American
bent, served to endear Jeffrey to American readers. In Edinburgh in
1810 he met a vacationing Charlotte Wilkes, daughter of the president
of the Bank of New York and great-niece of the English radical (and
American hero) John Wilkes (whose sister had married Jeffrey's uncle,
a resident of Boston, Massachusetts), and quickly proposed marriage.
With much difficulty, he traveled to America during the War of 1812
and the couple was wed in New York in October 1813. In the following weeks they toured the Atlantic seaboard, his reputation having
preceded him, and in Washington Jeffrey had a series of interviews
with Secretary of State James Monroe and President James Madison

in which he pointedly, if good-naturedly, defended British policies. He and his new wife returned to England on an American cartel ship in January 1814. Even as he continued to edit the *Review*, which he did until June 1829, he pursued his legal career, which grew with his literary reputation. With a new Whig government in 1830 he became lord advocate, and he was twice elected to Parliament. In 1834 he was elevated to the bench as Lord Jeffrey. Died in Edinburgh.

Paul Jennings (1799–1874) Much of what is known about Paul Jennings is derived from his brief memoir, *A Colored Man's Reminiscences of James Madison*, first published in 1863. It featured a preface by John Brooks Russell, a clerk in the pension office in the Department of the Interior, which began: "Among the laborers at the Department of Interior is an intelligent colored man, Paul Jennings, who was born a slave on President Madison's estate, in Montpelier, Va, in 1799. His reputed father was Benj. Jennings, an English trader there; his mother, a slave of Mr. Madison, and the granddaughter of an Indian." His mother's name is not known, nor is it known when and under what circumstances he learned to read and write. When James Madison assumed the presidency in 1809, Jennings, still a boy, traveled with the Madison household as a footman and page whose duties included serving as messenger, dining room servant, and assistant to the coachman, among other roles. He had already arranged the place settings for dinner on August 24, 1814, when British forces occupied Washington and set fire to numerous government buildings, including the President's House, from which he helped to rescue a large Gilbert Stuart portrait of George Washington. In 1817 Jennings returned with the Madisons to Montpelier where in 1820 he became the former president's body servant, attending to his daily wardrobe and toilet, and accompanying him on his travels: "I was always with Mr. Madison till he died." In 1822, he married Fanny Gordon, a slave on a nearby plantation; though not sanctioned by Virginia law, the union was consented to by Madison and Charles Howard, Gordon's master; the couple had five children, who became Howard's property. Dolley Madison elected to return to Washington after her husband's death in 1836, bringing Jennings with her and separating him from his family, a situation that became even more worrisome when Fanny died in 1844, the same year Dolley Madison sold Montpelier and many of its slaves in an attempt to rescue her son and herself from debt. In Washington, still struggling to meet expenses resulting from her lavish social calendar, Mrs. Madison rented Jennings to President James Polk, and he resumed many of the White House duties he had performed decades earlier. Finally, through a complex arrangement involving Daniel Webster, Jennings was able to secure his freedom; he worked for Webster for several years to repay the portion of the purchase price that the Massachusetts senator had advanced. Jennings became an important member of the free black community in the northwest section of Washington; he is believed to have been one of the principal organizers of the so-called Pearl Affair of 1848, an effort, ultimately unsuccessful, to transport seventy-seven fugitive slaves (including one owned by Dolley Madison) north from Washington aboard the schooner *Pearl*, the largest-scale slave escape ever attempted in America. In 1849 he married Desdemona Brooks, a free woman of color living in Alexandria, Virginia; they had no children, though, like Jennings, she had five children from a previous union. In 1851, he left Webster's employ and with his recommendation secured a job as a laborer in the Pension Office, where he would work for fifteen years. In the 1860s Jennings purchased two adjoining properties in Washington, where he resided with several of his children, who had been manumitted in the 1850s; three of his sons fought in the Union army in the Civil War. Desdemona Jennings died sometime after 1860; he married Amelia Dorsey in 1870. Died in Washington.

Thomas ap Catesby Jones (April 24, 1790–May 30, 1858) Born at Hickory Hill, his maternal grandfather's estate on Virginia's Northern Neck, son of ("ap" in Welsh) Major Catesby Jones and Lettice Corbin (Turberville) Jones. After his father's death in 1800, he and his older brother Roger were sent to the College of William and Mary and then the following year to Richmond, to live with their uncle, Merriweather Jones, who in 1805 secured a midshipman's warrant for Thomas in the U.S. Navy. He remained in Richmond until 1807, when he was ordered to Norfolk, before in the spring of 1808 being transferred to New Orleans, there to join a gunboat flotilla confronting pirates, smugglers, privateers, and illegal slave traders seeking entry to the port. He became a lieutenant on May 24, 1812. On September 16, 1814, under Commodore Daniel Todd Patterson, he participated in a raid on a pirate encampment in Barataria Bay, south of New Orleans. There, according to Patterson, "Jones particularly distinguished himself by boarding one of the schooners which had been fired and extinguishing the fire after it had made great progress." Later that year, on December 14, he commanded five gunboats, two small schooners—twenty-three guns in all—and some 175 men who attempted to prevent a British squadron of forty barges, bearing forty-two cannons, from entering Lake Borgne and landing a thousand men. Overwhelmed, the small American fleet succumbed to the weight of the attack after two hours but delayed British operations long enough to allow Andrew Jackson to better organize his defense of the city; Jones was wounded in the action and held prisoner on Bermuda until February 1815, when he was exchanged. He then served in the Mediterranean squadron for three years, before being posted to the Washington Navy Yard as inspector of ordinance. During this time he had become a master commandant, and in 1823 he married Mary Walker Carter; they had four children. In 1825, he embarked on the first of three tours in command of the Pacific squadron, establishing diplomatic relations with Tahiti and the Sandwich (Hawaiian) Islands, and challenging British claims on the latter. After another stint at the Washington Navy Yard (1831–36), now as a captain, he was appointed to head the South Seas Surveying and Exploring Expedition but resigned before it was launched. In 1842, he again resumed command of the Pacific squadron, and on October 19 of that year took possession of Monterey, capital of the Mexican territory Alta California, mistakenly thinking war had begun between the U.S. and Mexico; he was subsequently relieved of command. In 1844, during his third and final tour, he was accused of using military funds for "an improper and unauthorized" purpose and was suspended for five years, half without pay. He retired to his farm in Fairfax County, Virginia, outside Washington, where he died.

Henry Kent (fl. 1800–1824) Born in Glasgow, youngest son of John Kent, Esq., a purser in the Royal Navy and steward of the naval hospital in Plymouth. He entered the navy as a first class volunteer in 1800, achieving the rank of midshipman in 1804. On March 14, 1811, he was awarded the rank of lieutenant, serving under Captain John Lawrence on HMS *Fantome*, a sloop that sailed as part of the North Sea fleet until joining the British squadron operating in the Chesapeake Bay. He was commended for actions on the Elk River in Maryland, April–May 1813. In January of the following year, he sailed on *Fantome* from Halifax, Nova Scotia, to New Brunswick, and then led a detachment of seamen and marines overland from Saint John to Kingston, Upper Canada, a harsh winter's journey of three months and nearly a thousand miles. Kent later forwarded his account of this remarkable feat, dated June 20 in Kingston, to his father at the Plymouth naval station, who submitted it on October 22, 1814, to the editor of *The Naval Chronicle*, where it was published in 1815. Kent was later made first lieutenant of HMS *Princess Charlotte*, which he commanded in the attack on Oswego, New York, May 5–6, 1814. In June, he was placed in command of a division of the British squadron on Lake Ontario, and was later charged with establishing and serving as first superintendent of a naval depot at Penetanguishene, a remote outpost on Lake Huron. Illness forced him to relinquish that post, and eventually to return to Britain in 1822, with the rank of commander. He married Eliza Grant of London in 1824. Date and place of death are unknown.

Francis Scott Key (August 1, 1779–January 11, 1843) Born at Terra Rubra, his family's estate in Frederick (now Carroll) County, Maryland, son of Captain John Ross Key, a lawyer and judge and veteran of the Revolutionary War, and Ann Phoebe (Charlton) Key. He graduated from St. John's College, Annapolis, in 1796 and studied law, opening a practice at Fredericktown, Maryland, in 1801. He married Mary Tayloe Lloyd in 1802; they had eleven children. His practice moved to Georgetown, in the District of Columbia, where he partnered with his uncle, future congressman Philip Barton Key. In 1814, during the British withdrawal from Washington, he was asked to intervene in the plight of Dr. William Beanes, an American physician held prisoner aboard a British ship; after arranging Beanes's release, Key witnessed the British bombardment of Baltimore. In response to the sight, with the dawn of September 14, of the American flag still flying over Fort McHenry, he composed "The Star-Spangled Banner." Published (as "Defence of Fort M'Henry") in the *Baltimore American* on September 21, the poem achieved immediate nationwide popularity. He later practiced extensively in federal courts, and in 1832 defended Congressman Sam Houston during his trial in the U.S. House of Representatives, after Houston was accused of assaulting another congressman. As U.S. attorney for the District of Columbia, 1833–41, he prosecuted Richard Lawrence for the attempted assassination of President Andrew Jackson in 1835. Died in Baltimore. His poetry was collected posthumously in *Poems of the Late Francis S. Key, Esq.* (1857).

John Le Couteur (October 21, 1794–December 24, 1875) Born on the island of Jersey, in the English Channel, the son of John Le Couteur, a captain at the time of his son's birth, but later a lieutenant general. He attended the Royal Military College at High Wycombe in Buckinghamshire for three years before joining the 96th Regiment of Foot as an ensign. In November 1811 he transferred to the 104th Regiment, which was stationed in New Brunswick in British North America, arriving in the summer of 1812. When in response to rising tensions with the United States the 104th was redeployed, he marched with his regiment overland to Kingston, in Upper Canada, February 21–April 12, 1813. There he participated in the assault on the main American base on Lake Ontario at Sackets Harbor, New York, May 29, and in the blockade of Fort George (July–October), a Canadian post that American forces had captured on May 24. He also saw action in the following year's campaign at the Battle of Lundy's Lane,

July 25, 1814, and the siege of Fort Erie, August–September, and in many skirmishes. Promoted to captain in 1817, he retired on half pay and returned to Jersey, where he married Harriet Janvrin; they had five children. He wrote several books on agriculture, and held a number of official posts. He was awarded the honorary rank of lieutenant colonel in 1858 and a knighthood in 1872. Died in Jersey.

Robert Jenkinson, 2nd Earl of Liverpool (June 7, 1770–December 4, 1828) Born Robert Banks Jenkinson in London, the son of Charles Jenkinson, an advisor to King George III who was made the 1st Earl of Liverpool in 1796, and Amelia (Watts) Jenkinson. He was educated at the Charterhouse School in Surrey and at Christ Church, Oxford, receiving his M.A. in 1790. Entering the House of Commons that same year, he became a leading Tory, serving as a member of the Board of Control for India (1793–96), master of the Royal Mint (1799–1801), foreign secretary (1801–4), home secretary (1804–6, 1807–9), and secretary of state for war and the colonies (1809–12), in which capacity he maintained a hard line in the face of American protests over British trade regulations (the Orders-in-Council): "a concession once made will never be retracted." In 1795, he married Lady Theodosia Louisa Hervey; they had no children. He was elevated to the House of Lords, as Lord Hawkesbury, in 1803, and became the 2nd Earl of Liverpool upon his father's death in 1808. After the assassination of Prime Minister Spencer Perceval on May 11, 1812, Lord Liverpool was asked to form a government. He was prime minister from June 8, 1812, to April 9, 1827, a long tenure during which he oversaw Britain's conduct of the War of 1812, the latter Napoleonic Wars, and the Congress of Vienna, and hewed to a conservative, sometimes repressive course amid social protests and economic recession. Shortly after it was installed, his government, viewed by most as a fragile coalition lacking a popular mandate, agreed to suspend the Orders-in-Council in an effort to assuage public opinion, especially among northern manufacturing interests suffering from the diminution in trade with America. He later closely oversaw the peace negotiations at Ghent, which he at first sought to delay but which, after British forces suffered setbacks at Baltimore and Plattsburgh, he brought to a speedy close by reducing British demands to status quo ante. In 1822, a year after the death of his first wife, he married Lady Mary Chester; they had no children. He suffered the first of a series of strokes on April 9, 1827, and asked to be relieved of the premiership. Died at Coombe House, near Kingston-upon-Thames, Surrey.

Robert Lucas (April 1, 1781–February 7, 1853) Born at Mecklenburg, Virginia (now Shepherdstown, West Virginia), son of William Lucas, a soldier in the Revolutionary War, and Susannah (Barnes) Lucas.

Educated at home and trained as a surveyor, around 1800 he moved with his family to the Scioto Valley, in the section of Northwest Territory that would in 1803 become the state of Ohio. There he served as surveyor, justice of the peace, and officer in the militia, and was elected to the Ohio House of Representatives in 1808. He married Elizabeth Brown in 1810; they had one child before Elizabeth's death in 1812. A successful recruiter, he rose to brigadier general of the 2nd Brigade of the 2nd Division of the Ohio militia, though he sought a commission in the regular army, which he finally secured in April 1812 (a captaincy). Shortly after, responding to the call to raise volunteers for General William Hull's planned invasion of Upper Canada, he resigned his commission and, to encourage enlistments from the men in his militia brigade, joined the volunteer company as a private. He was present at Fort Detroit when Hull surrendered it and his army, a mixture of regulars and volunteers, to the British. Though he was singled out for capture by the British, Lucas escaped and incognito he was repatriated with the rest of the Ohio militia, whom the British allowed to return home. He kept a journal of the campaign, from the volunteers' assembly at Dayton, Ohio, on April 27, 1812, to his return to his home in Portsmouth, Ohio, on September 4, 1812; it was widely publicized and used as evidence at Hull's court-martial, raising Lucas's profile. He married Friendly Ashley Sumner in 1816; they had seven children. He later was major general of the Ohio militia, a member of both houses of the Ohio General Assembly, a presidential elector in 1820 (for James Monroe) and in 1828 (for Andrew Jackson), and, in 1832, chairman of the Democratic Party's first national convention, in Baltimore, before serving two terms as governor of Ohio, 1832–1836. In 1838, he was appointed by President Martin Van Buren governor and superintendent of Indian affairs for the newly created territory of Iowa, serving until 1841. He retired to Plum Grove, his estate in Iowa City, where he died.

Thomas Macdonough (December 31, 1783–November 10, 1825) Born Thomas McDonough Jr. at The Trapp, his family's estate in New Castle County, Delaware, son of Major Thomas McDonough, a physician and veteran of the Revolutionary War, and Mary (Vance) McDonough. On February 5, 1800, he entered the U.S. Navy as a midshipman, having for reasons unknown changed the spelling of his surname to Macdonough. He sailed that year on USS *Ganges*, and saw action in the Quasi-War with France, his ship capturing three French vessels on a cruise of the West Indies, May–September. The following year he was in the Mediterranean aboard USS *Constellation* and participated in actions associated with the First Barbary War, including, aboard USS *Enterprise*, a daring raid on Tripoli, February 6,

1804, and was awarded promotion to lieutenant in 1805. In 1806 he was ordered to Middletown, Connecticut, for three months to assist Captain Isaac Hull in the construction of gunboats; there he met Lucy Ann Shaler, whom he would marry in 1812 and with whom he would have nine children. He shipped as first lieutenant of USS *Wasp*, 1807–8, enforcing the Jefferson administration's embargo. On a two-year furlough he made voyages to the East Indies as captain of a merchantman before returning to active duty in 1812 amid rising tensions and eventually assumed command of the navy's Lake Champlain fleet, charged with maintaining tenuous U.S. naval superiority on the lake. By the summer of 1813, he built or obtained a fleet of thirteen vessels, which, as master commandant, he led from his flagship *Saratoga*. On September 11, his fleet won a decisive victory at the Battle of Lake Champlain, destroying or capturing the British fleet and thereby prompting British general Sir George Prevost to abandon his ground attack on Plattsburgh and retreat to Canada. Hailed as "the hero of Lake Champlain" for his impressive tactical victory, he was promoted to captain and awarded a medal by Congress. After the war, he was commander of the naval yard at Portsmouth, New Hampshire, 1815–18, and sailed again as part of the Mediterranean squadron, 1818, before returning to New York and assuming command of the still-under-construction USS *Ohio*, 1818–23. Though ill with tuberculosis, he returned once more to the Mediterranean in 1824, this time aboard USS *Constitution* as commander of the American squadron. Illness forced him to relinquish command on October 14, 1825, and embark for America; he died at sea, near Gibraltar. Buried in Middletown.

Dolley Madison (May 20, 1768–July 12, 1849) Born Dolley Payne in Guilford County, North Carolina, to Quaker parents who moved in 1769 to Virginia and in 1783 to Philadelphia, where her father, John Payne, operated a small business supplying laundry starch. In 1790, she married John Todd, a lawyer; they had two children before Todd and the younger child died in the Philadelphia yellow fever epidemic of 1793. In 1794, she married James Madison, then a congressman from Virginia; they had no children. The Madisons lived in Philadelphia until her husband retired in 1797, when they moved to the Madison family plantation, Montpelier, in Orange County, Virginia. She moved to Washington, D.C., in 1801, where her husband served as secretary of state in the Jefferson administrations (1801–9); during this time she often acted as hostess in the White House of the widower Jefferson. She was First Lady of the United States, 1809–17, and was famously said to have refused to leave the Executive Mansion before Gilbert Stuart's portrait of George Washington was removed to safety during the British assault on the capital in August 1814. (Her slave, Paul Jennings, recalled that she was more concerned with rescuing the White House silver.) She retired with her husband to Montpelier in 1817. After her husband's death in 1836, confronted by considerable personal debt as well as obligations stemming from the dissolute lifestyle of her surviving son, John Payne Todd, she decided to sell Montpelier and many of the estate's slaves (without their consent, in contravention of her husband's last wishes). In 1844 she moved permanently to Washington, where, in increasing financial distress, she died.

James Madison (March 16, 1751–June 28, 1836) Born in King George County, Virginia, son of James Madison, a planter, and Nelly (Conway) Madison, and raised at Montpelier, the family's plantation in Orange County, Virginia. Graduating from the College of New Jersey (now Princeton) in 1771, he was a member of the Orange County committee of safety in 1774 and a delegate to the Virginia convention of May 1776 that framed a new state government and instructed delegates to the Continental Congress to vote for independence. Elected to the Virginia House of Delegates in October 1776, he spent the war years as a member of the Virginia council of state, 1778–80, and a delegate to the Continental Congress, 1779–83. Returning to the Virginia House of Delegates, 1784–87, he attended the Annapolis Convention of September 1786, which issued a call for a convention of states to form a new plan of government for the United States. He was subsequently a delegate both to the last Continental Congress and to the Constitutional Convention in Philadelphia in 1787, where he drafted the Virginia plan. He wrote the *Federalist* papers (with Alexander Hamilton and John Jay) to promote the Constitution's ratification and was a member of the Virginia ratifying convention of June 1788. After ratification, he served in the U.S. House of Representatives, 1789–97, increasingly functioning as leader of the chamber's Republican faction. He married Dolley Payne Todd in 1794; they had no children together, though she had a son from her first marriage. In collaboration with Vice President Thomas Jefferson, he drafted the Virginia Resolutions opposing the Alien and Sedition Acts in 1798. He was appointed secretary of state by Jefferson in 1801 and held office until 1809. Madison survived intraparty challenges from James Monroe and Vice President George Clinton, and won the electoral vote to become the fourth president of the United States, 1809–17. Divisions among Republicans continued after his inauguration, making it difficult for him to fill his cabinet and chart a legislative agenda. Confronted by the economic fallout from Jeffersonian trade restrictions, rising tensions over the refusal of European belligerents to recognize U.S. neutral rights, and pressure from Western interests who held the British responsible for fomenting Indian resistance to U.S. expansion, he led the nation into the War of 1812, which Federalist critics derided as "Mr. Madison's War." Though his administration of the war and its financing was much criticized, he was the beneficiary of good fortune in the manner of its resolution, and he retired with factionalism on the wane. Madison succeeded Jefferson as rector of the University of Virginia in 1826 and attended the Virginia constitutional convention in Richmond, 1829–30. Died at Montpelier.

George McFeely (July 20, 1781–January 19, 1854) Born in South Middleton Township in Cumberland County, Pennsylvania, son of John and Elizabeth McFeely. Commissioned lieutenant colonel of the 22nd U.S. Infantry Regiment on July 6, 1812, he was placed in charge of recruiting at the army barracks in Carlisle, Pennsylvania. He marched two hundred men of the regiment to New York's Niagara frontier, where on November 14 he took command of Fort Niagara; he then oversaw the defense of the garrison when it was bombarded by the British from Fort George, across the Niagara River in Upper Canada, a week later. After the entire 22nd Regiment gathered at Fort Niagara in early 1813, McFeely led a detachment of the advance guard, commanded by Colonel Winfield Scott, which captured Fort George, May 27. Stationed in the Lake Champlain region, January–June 1814, he saw action at the Second Battle of Lacolle Mill, March 30. He was based for a time in Burlington, Vermont, where opposition to the war, and smuggling, were rampant; when he arrested two American citizens on suspicion of serving as guides to British raiders and they were later released by McFeely's superior, General Alexander Macomb, he was promptly sued for false arrest. Reassigned to the Niagara front as colonel of the 25th Infantry Regiment, having been promoted retroactively to April 1814, he commanded at Fort George and Black Rock, and saw action at the capture of Fort Erie, July 3. He returned to Carlisle in 1815, where he married Margaret McKean in 1819; they had seven children. He became an educator, serving as director of Carlisle's common schools. He died in Carlisle and was eulogized in the January 26, 1854, edition of *The American Volunteer*, the local paper: "Col. McFeely was a man of enlarged views and multiform experience. . . . In his political views he was a republican of the Jeffersonian school, stern, decided, unyielding, and vigorous. He had great confidence in man's capacity for self-government and believed in the gradual improvement and perfectability of the human race."

James Monroe (April 28, 1758–July 4, 1831) Born in Westmoreland County, Virginia, the son of Spence Monroe, a planter and carpenter, and Elizabeth (Jones) Monroe. He attended the College of William and Mary from 1774 to 1776, leaving to serve as a lieutenant in the 3rd Virginia Regiment in the Continental Army. During the Revolutionary War, he participated in the Battles of Harlem Heights, White Plains, Trenton (where he was wounded), Brandywine, Germantown, and Monmouth, rising to the rank of major; in 1780 he was appointed military commissioner of Virginia, with the rank of lieutenant colonel. After studying law under Governor Thomas Jefferson, 1780–81, he passed the bar in 1782 and entered the Virginia legislature the same year, before becoming a delegate from Virginia to the Continental Congress, 1783–86. He married Elizabeth Kortright in 1786; they had three children. He attended the Annapolis Convention of September 1786, which issued a call for a convention of states to form a new plan of government for the United States, and was a delegate to the Virginia ratifying convention of 1788, where he opposed ratification of the Constitution. He was a U.S. senator, 1790–94; minister plenipotentiary to France, 1794–96; governor of Virginia, 1799–1802; and minister plenipotentiary to France, Spain, and Great Britain, 1803. In April of that year, he assisted Robert R. Livingston, American minister to France, in the conclusion of the treaty of cession of Louisiana from France. Amid rising tensions as European belligerents refused to recognize U.S. neutral rights, he was minister to the Court of St. James (Great Britain), 1803–7. With U.S. special envoy William Pinkney he negotiated the Monroe-Pinkney Treaty with the British, which (to Monroe's great frustration) President Jefferson withheld from the Senate because it did not resolve the matter of impressment. Offended, Monroe returned to Virginia, where he mounted a half-hearted challenge to James Madison, the party choice for the presidency in 1808. He was elected to the Virginia legislature in 1810, and became governor of Virginia in January 1811, resigning in November 1811 to become secretary of state under Madison, serving until 1817. He also served as secretary of war from August 1814 to March 1815, personally supervising the defense of Washington in 1814. He continued the Virginia dynasty as the fifth president of the United States, 1817–25, and presided at the Virginia constitutional convention in 1829. Died in New York City.

Isaac Munroe (1785–December 22, 1859) Born near Boston, Massachusetts, and trained as a printer. As one-half of the firm of Everett & Munroe (later Munroe & French), he founded on March 3, 1809, the *Boston Patriot*, a semiweekly newspaper; by 1811 the masthead described him as "Printer to the State" of Massachusetts. For its first three years the paper regularly published letters from John Adams in which the former president offered extensive glosses on his correspondence from his time in office; the firm published these letters in book form as well. In 1812 he and partner Ebenezer French were lured to Baltimore, Maryland, by the leaders of the city's Republican faction, who wanted them to establish a pro-administration newspaper; on December 28 of that year, they launched the *Baltimore Patriot and Evening Advertiser*. In 1813 Munroe joined Captain Joseph H. Nicholson's Company of Baltimore Fencibles, a group of "gentleman volunteers" who helped to garrison Baltimore's Fort McHenry. Publication was suspended as the British Chesapeake squadron threatened Baltimore, and he was at Fort McHenry, September 13–14, 1814, when it was bombarded by British forces. Resuming publication on September 20, the *Baltimore Patriot* published "Defence of Fort McHenry," the poem by Francis Scott Key that became, as "The Star-Spangled Banner," the U.S. national anthem. Died in Baltimore, leaving a widow but no children.

Hezekiah Niles (October 10, 1777–April 2, 1839) Born at Jefferis Ford (East Bradford), in Chester County, Pennsylvania, son of Hezekiah and Mary (Way) Niles, Quakers who at the time of his birth were fleeing the British army that had just occupied Wilmington, Delaware, where they had been living. Little is known about his education, but he may have attended the Friends School in Wilmington. In 1794, he was apprenticed to Philadelphia printer and bookseller Benjamin Johnson, serving until 1798, when Johnson's business failed and Niles returned to Wilmington, where he opened a printing business with Vincent Bonsal. He married Ann Ogden; they had twelve children. Bonsal & Niles collapsed in 1799, leaving Niles with $25,000 in debt. In 1805, he published a literary magazine, *The Apollo or Delaware Weekly Magazine*, which lasted six months. He then moved to Baltimore, Maryland, and established the *Evening Post*, which he published until 1811, the year he issued a prospectus for a new periodical, *The Weekly Register*, a sixteen-page paper in which he proposed "to write for and speak to people—not the learned and wealthy . . . but the free laboring people struggling to get a little forward in the world." It distilled political news from papers around the country, reproduced speeches and state documents, and sought to present "magnanimous disputation." Soon renamed *Niles' Weekly Register*, the patriotic, staunchly pro-war paper had over three thousand subscribers within a year, and reached a national circulation of over ten thousand by 1818. Initially reflecting Niles' Jeffersonian sympathies, the nominally nonpartisan *Register* later advocated for nationalist policies—protectionism, internal improvements—that became known as "the American system" associated with the Whig Party. Declining health forced him to turn the *Register* over to his son William Ogden Niles in 1836. Died at Wilmington.

William B. Northcutt (January 19, 1790–a. 1866) Born William Brooks Northcutt in Fauquier County, Virginia, oldest son of Benjamin Northcutt, a distiller, and Winnie (Brooks) Northcutt. The family moved to Kentucky in 1797 and settled eventually in Harrison County, where, in 1800, his mother died as the result of a spider bite. He had no formal education and was granted his "freedom"—that is, his father relinquished any claim on his labor—when he turned twenty. He moved to Bourbon County where he worked in a distillery until, in the summer of 1812, he signed a yearlong enlistment in Captain William Garrard's company of mounted volunteers, "The Bourbon Blues," which was attached to Major James V. Ball's 2nd Regiment of U.S. Light Dragoons, a part of General William Henry Harrison's Army of the Northwest. Present at the siege of Fort Wayne, September 9–12, and the Battle of Mississinewa River, December 17–18, he returned to Kentucky on furlough in January 1813 to purchase a new horse, having lost his mount in the campaign. In a second season of campaigning along the Northwestern frontier, he participated in a skirmish on the Sandusky River in Ohio, July 31, and witnessed the Battle of Fort Stephenson, August 1–2. In October 1813, he returned to Kentucky to his job at the distillery and to farming. He married Joanna Hill, of Bourbon County, on May 20, 1814, and established a homestead and a distillery; the couple had thirteen children. Later he moved to Campbell County, Kentucky, where he established a farm and where, in 1832, he was appointed justice of the peace, serving until 1838. He continued to muster for militia duty until he was forty-five, and when he was seventy-six he composed, or compiled from preexisting diaries, a memoir of his life, focusing especially on his service in the War of 1812. Place and date of death unknown.

Harrison Gray Otis (October 8, 1765–October 28, 1848) Born in Boston, Massachusetts, the son of Samuel Allyne Otis, a merchant and speculator and scion of the influential Otis clan, and Elizabeth (Gray) Otis; he was named for his maternal grandfather, who had served as treasurer of the province of Massachusetts Bay before becoming a Loyalist refugee in the American Revolution. Educated at Harvard, he graduated first in his class in 1783. After securing a master's degree at Harvard, he was admitted to the Boston bar in 1786; that same year he commanded a volunteer infantry company formed to suppress Shays' Rebellion, but did not see action. He married Sally Foster in 1790; they had eleven children. He was elected to the Massachusetts legislature in 1794. An eloquent advocate for Federalist policies, he was twice appointed U.S. district attorney for Massachusetts (by President Washington, 1796–97, and by President Adams, 1801–2), and won election to Congress, 1797–1801. He reentered the Massachusetts legislature in 1802, serving in the House of Representatives, 1802–5 and 1813–14 (as Speaker 1803–5), and in the state Senate, 1805–13 and 1814–17 (as president 1805–6 and 1808–11). He was the principal organizer of and a Massachusetts delegate to the anti-war Hartford Convection, December 15, 1814–January 5, 1815, whose final report he drafted. On January 31, 1815, he was dispatched to Washington by Caleb Strong, governor of Massachusetts, to negotiate for federal revenues for the state's defense, but en route he learned of the Treaty of Ghent and his mission, like the Hartford Convention itself, was rendered moot, subjecting him to considerable ridicule and scorn; he published spirited defenses of the Hartford Convention in *Letters Developing the Character and Views of the Hartford Convention* (1820) and *Otis' Letters in Defense of the Hartford Convention and the People of Massachusetts* (1824). He was a U.S. senator, 1817–22, and Federalist nominee for Massachusetts governor in 1823, losing to Republican William Eustis, a defeat that signaled the final demise of the Federalist Party in the state that had been its bastion. From 1829 to 1832 he was the mayor of Boston, where he died, one of the richest men in New England.

"P." (**Richard E. Parker**) (December 27, 1783–September 10, 1840) Born Richard Elliott Parker at Rock Spring, his family's estate in Westmoreland County, Virginia, son of Captain William Harwar Parker and Mary (Sturman) Parker. He attended Washington College (now Washington and Lee University), 1800–3, and then studied law with his grandfather, Judge Richard Parker, and was admitted to the bar in 1804. He represented Westmoreland County in the Virginia House of Delegates, 1807–9, and was an officer in the Virginia militia. He married Elizabeth Foushee, daughter of the first mayor of Richmond; they had six children who survived to adulthood. On August 1, 1812, he was appointed lieutenant colonel and later colonel of the 111th Regiment, composed of militia from Virginia's Northern Neck. He was present at Hampton, Virginia, when British forces attacked the town and, writing under the pseudonym "P," is believed to be the author of the account of atrocities committed there that appeared in the *Richmond Enquirer*. After the war, he returned to practice in Westmoreland County, and later served as judge of the General Court of Virginia, 1817–36, and judge of the Frederick County Court of Law and Chancery, 1831–36, before being elected on December 12, 1836, to fill a vacant U.S. Senate seat. A Jacksonian Democrat, he served until March 13, 1837, resigning to become a judge of the Virginia Supreme Court of Appeals. Died at Soldier's Retreat, his estate near Snickersville (now Bluemont), Virginia.

Joseph Penley Jr. (August 22, 1792–May 17, 1865) Born in Freeport, Maine (then a district of Massachusetts), son of Joseph Penley, an Englishman who, according to one account, had been pressed into the Royal Navy and had escaped from his ship when it was cruising off the Maine coast, and Ester (Fogg) Penley, whose family had sheltered the escaped seaman. In October 1812, he was living with his father in Pejepscot (now Danville), Maine, and responded to a call to volunteer for one year's service in the U.S. Army. Stationed first at Portland, Maine, his company marched overland to Burlington, Vermont, in April 1813, and then to Champlain, New York, where he volunteered as a marine to serve aboard the American sloop *Growler*, of the Lake Champlain fleet. On June 3, 1813, when *Growler* strayed too far down the Richelieu River, the northern outlet of the lake, she was captured by the British. He was held for six months aboard HMS *Malabar*, a floating prison in the St. Lawrence River. He was then placed aboard a vessel to be transferred to Dartmoor Prison, in England, but the voyage was interrupted when the ship was damaged, and redirected to Halifax, Nova Scotia, where he spent another six months imprisoned on Melville Island. He married Louvina Monk in 1815; they had thirteen children. He wrote a memoir, published anonymously as *A Narrative: A Short and Thrilling Narrative of a Few of the Scenes and Incidents That Occurred in the Sanguinary and Cruel War of 1812–'14, Between England and the United States* in Norway, Maine, in 1853. In it, he reveals that he had lost his hearing shortly after the war. Died in Freeport.

Israel Pickens (January 30, 1780–April 24, 1827) Born near Concord, in Mecklenburg (now Cabarrus) County, North Carolina, son of Samuel Pickens, a soldier in the Revolutionary War, and Jane (Carrigan) Pickens. He graduated in 1802 from Jefferson College in Canonsburg, Pennsylvania (now Washington & Jefferson College, in Washington, Pennsylvania), and returned to North Carolina, where he studied law and was admitted to the bar, later serving in the North Carolina Senate, 1808–9. He was a member of the U.S. House of Representatives, 1811–17, where he was a consistent supporter of administration policies during the War of 1812. He married Martha Orilla in 1814; they had four children. Registrar of the land office at St. Stephens, in the new territory of Alabama, 1817–21, he was the first president of the Tombeckbee Bank of St. Stephens, 1818, and represented Washington County, Alabama, in the state's constitutional convention in 1819. He was the third governor of Alabama, serving two terms, 1821–25; much of his administration was occupied with debates over the establishment of a banking system for the fledgling state. His wife died in 1823, shortly after his reelection.

After the death of Henry H. Chambers, U.S. senator from Alabama, he was appointed to fill the vacant seat, serving February to November 1826, when complications from tuberculosis forced him to resign. He traveled to Cuba to restore his health, but died there, at Matanzas.

Timothy Pickering (July 17, 1745–January 29, 1829) Born in Salem, Massachusetts, to Timothy Pickering, of a prominent provincial family, and Mary (Wingate) Pickering. Educated at Harvard, he graduated in 1763, returned to Salem to clerk in the office of the register of deeds for Essex County, and was admitted to the bar in 1768. An early supporter of the patriot cause, he was commissioned a lieutenant in the Essex County militia and promoted to colonel of the 1st Regiment of the county militia in 1774. The next year, as revolution erupted, he published *An Easy Plan of Discipline for a Militia*, widely consulted by American armies. He married Rebecca White in 1776; they had ten children. Impressed by Pickering's manual, General Washington appointed him adjutant general of the Continental Army, and he was active in the New York and New Jersey campaigns of 1776 and 1777, and later served as the army's quartermaster general, 1780–83. He pursued business in Philadelphia after the war, but soon resettled to Pennsylvania's Wyoming Valley, charged by the state government with organizing county administration in a region subject to disputed claims by settlers from Pennsylvania and Connecticut. He represented the resulting county of Luzerne in the Pennsylvania state convention that ratified the U.S. Constitution, 1787. He was commissioned by President Washington to treat with Seneca Indians in 1790, the first of many such diplomatic missions to various tribes in following years, including the negotiation of the Treaty of Canandaigua with the Iroquois in 1794. Washington appointed him postmaster general, 1791–94, and then secretary of war, in January 1795. In August of the same year, Washington named him to replace Edmund Randolph, who had been forced to resign as secretary of state. Retained as secretary of state by President John Adams, he became a leading voice for aggressive countermeasures against France; he was dismissed in 1800, when Adams elected to pursue a conciliatory course. He retired to Wyoming Valley, then returned to Essex County, Massachusetts. As U.S. senator from Massachusetts, 1803–11, he was a vocal opponent of Jeffersonian policies. Defeated for reelection in 1811, he served on the executive council of Massachusetts, 1812–13, before becoming a member of the U.S. House of Representatives, 1813–17, where he vigorously opposed the war measures of the Republican majority. He retired in 1817, though in 1820 he made a final, unsuccessful bid to return to Congress. Died in Salem.

Stephen Popham (1780–February 25, 1842) Place and exact date of birth unknown. He entered the British navy as a midshipman on board HMS *Formidable*, March 12, 1795, and was promoted to lieutenant in 1801 and commander in 1811. Dispatched to British North America, he arrived in Quebec in 1813. Stationed first in Montreal, in April 1814 he was given command of HMS *Niagara*, and participated in, and was wounded during, the capture of Oswego, New York, and the destruction of its garrison, Fort Ontario, May 5–6, 1814. On detached duty from the Lake Ontario fleet, he led a flotilla into Sandy Creek in pursuit of American supplies and encountered strong resistance; at the Battle of Sandy Creek (May 30, 1814), his force of two hundred men suffered more than seventy casualties before surrendering, a loss of manpower that curtailed subsequent British offensives on the lake. Held first at Sackets Harbor, he is thought to have spent the rest of the war in captivity in Massachusetts. He was promoted to post captain, September 29, 1814, apparently in absentia. Died at Rhudlan, St. Asaph, England.

George Prevost (May 19, 1767–January 5, 1816) Born in Hackensack, New Jersey, son of French-speaking Swiss Protestants. His father, Augustine Prevost, had joined the British army, been wounded at the siege of Quebec (1759), and was stationed in New Jersey as a lieutenant colonel of the 60th Regiment of Foot at the time of his son's birth; his mother, Nanette (Grand) Prevost, was the daughter of a wealthy Dutch banker. Sent to England and the Continent for schooling, he was commissioned as an ensign in his father's regiment in May 1779. He secured promotions during service in other regiments, and returned to the 60th in 1790 as a major. He married Catherine Anne Phipps, at Gibraltar, in 1789; they had five children. In the war against revolutionary France, he saw action in the West Indies, and was awarded command, as lieutenant colonel, at St. Vincent, 1794–95, before being wounded and returned to England, where he became an inspecting field officer. Promoted to brigadier general in March 1798, he served as lieutenant governor of St. Lucia (1798–1802) and governor of Dominica (1803–5) before returning to England, as major general, to command the Portsmouth naval base. In 1805 he was also made a baronet. As lieutenant governor of Nova Scotia, 1808–11, he reorganized the province's defenses, conciliated the provincial assembly, and effectively encouraged trade with (and disaffection among) New Englanders chafing under President Jefferson's embargo. On October 21, 1811, amid mounting Anglo-American tensions, he was commissioned governor-in-chief of British North America and, as lieutenant general, commander of all British forces in North America, which at that time numbered some fifty-six hundred regular troops, supplemented by militia drawn from a population—French Canadians in Lower Canada, recent immigrants from the United States in Upper Canada—whose loyalty was not a given. Fearing war, he made significant overtures to French Canadian leaders, both civil and clerical, to ensure their support, rankling many in the Anglophone hierarchy. In 1812, he appointed Isaac Brock to command in Upper Canada, ordering a defensive policy predicated on control of Lake Erie. With the repeal of British Orders-in-Council, a major casus belli, he negotiated in August 1812 a cease-fire, but it was rebuffed by Washington. American forces launched invasions of both Upper and Lower Canada and in both cases were turned back, and at the conclusion of the first year of campaigning he could report that there were no American troops on Canadian soil. In 1813, he coordinated the defense of the lakes with Sir James Yeo, who reported directly to the Admiralty. In September 1814, reinforced by fifteen thousand troops from Europe after the defeat of Napoleon, he undertook an offensive campaign into New York's Lake Champlain region, targeting the town of Plattsburgh, but turned back when British naval forces on the lake were defeated, a decision that drew considerable criticism and led many, the Duke of Wellington among them, to urge his recall. On March 2, 1815, a day after learning of the Treaty of Ghent, he was removed from office and summoned to London, there to face charges of misconduct lodged by Yeo. In poor health, he requested a military court-martial to vindicate his conduct at Plattsburgh, but died, in London, before it could convene.

Robert Purdy (May 17, 1757–March 25, 1831) Born in Cumberland County, Pennsylvania. He served in the Revolutionary War and in 1779 married Elizabeth Phillips; they had two children. By the time of the declaration of the War of 1812, he lived in Tennessee. On August 26, 1812, he was appointed colonel of the U.S. Army's 4th Regiment of Infantry. In that capacity, he participated in the American army's two-pronged assault on Montreal, planned for October 1813. When, on October 25, the army led by Major General Wade Hampton met stiff and entrenched resistance at the Châteauguay River, southwest of Montreal, Purdy was ordered to lead a thousand men in a nighttime flanking movement to seize the ford behind the entrenched French Canadian and British troops. Because of poor reconnaissance and inept guides, his force became lost in a swamp, traveling twenty-five miles but making only five miles of forward progress. When, the next morning, having finally neared their target, Purdy's exhausted force came under steady sniper fire, it fell back in panic. A captain in Purdy's regiment reported that "officers deserted their posts & their commands fled from the scene of action, threw away their arms &

swam the river." After it regrouped, the American invasion force still enjoyed a numerical advantage over the Canadian defenders at Châteauguay, but nevertheless turned back, its morale shattered. After the war, Purdy served as U.S. marshal for the western district of Tennessee, 1819–31, and was based in Nashville, where he died.

Josiah Quincy (February 4, 1772–July 1, 1864) Born in Boston, Massachusetts, the son of Boston lawyer and patriot Josiah Quincy Jr., who had served as co-counsel with John Adams in the defense of British soldiers involved in the "Boston Massacre" of 1770 and who died in 1775, and Abigail (Phillips) Quincy. Educated at Phillips Academy, Andover (a member of the first class at the school founded by his mother's cousin Samuel Phillips in 1778) and at Harvard, he graduated first in his class in 1790. After securing a master's degree at Harvard, he was admitted to the Boston bar in 1793. He married Eliza Susan Morton of New York in 1794; they had seven children. After an unsuccessful bid for Congress in 1800, he served in the Massachusetts Senate, 1804–5. As a member of the U.S. House of Representatives, 1805–13, he opposed the Jefferson administration and the House Republican majority on numerous issues, including the embargo, the admission of Louisiana as a state, and the declaration of war in 1812. In the war debate, he articulated a critique of British policy at odds with many other Federalists, earning criticism from both sides: "My fate is odd. By some I am thought such a raving Federalist as to be shrewdly suspected of being one of [alleged British agent John] Henry's confidants; by others that I am so strongly hostile to the British that I am in danger of turning Democrat. The truth is, that there is an intermediate ground for an American politician to stand upon. That I seek, and when I think I have found it I shall not hesitate to defend it, let who will shake or wonder, condemn or applaud." He returned to the Massachusetts Senate in 1813, serving until 1820. He was Speaker of the Massachusetts House of Representatives, 1821–22, before resigning to become judge in Boston's municipal court. From 1823 to 1829 he served as the second mayor of the city of Boston, which had incorporated itself as a city in 1822, and was later the sixteenth president of Harvard University, 1829–45. He published numerous books in his retirement, including memoirs of his father and of John Quincy Adams. Though voting for Whig and Republican candidates later in life, he identified himself as a Federalist as late as 1861. Died in Boston.

Red Jacket (c. 1758–January 20, 1830) Born in the Finger Lakes region of New York; in keeping with the matrilineal customs of Iroquois society, he inherited his clan and tribal identity from his mother, Ahweyneyohn ("Drooping Flower"), a member of the Wolf Clan of the

Seneca Nation; his father, Thadahwahnyeh, was a member of the Turtle Clan of the Cayuga Nation. He was named Otetiani ("Always Ready") at age ten, perhaps for his eagerness to serve as a messenger throughout the Iroquois confederacy. (He early displayed a great facility with language and memory.) He fought against the Americans during the Revolutionary War, 1777–80, though rumors of cowardice in battle dogged him for the remainder of his life. For his services as an envoy during the war, British officials at Fort Niagara awarded the first of the many red jackets with which he would become identified. Around the same time he was given the name Sagoyewatha ("He Who Keeps Them Awake"), likely a reference to the oratorical skills for which he was increasingly known. In the wake of the Revolution, he settled along Buffalo Creek near Lake Erie, where he negotiated with Timothy Pickering and other American envoys, 1790–91, who pressed for land concessions. In 1792, he led a delegation to Philadelphia and there met with President George Washington, who presented him with a silver medal, which he would wear prominently in all subsequent likenesses. Committed to the retention of Indian lands and ways, he represented the Six Nations of the Iroquois in meetings with Ohio Indians and with British and American emissaries. He negotiated the treaty between the United States and the Six Nations signed at Canandaigua in 1794, and reluctantly agreed to the sale of a large portion of Seneca land at Genesco in 1797; even with these concessions, the Seneca retained the largest reservations of any other Iroquois still resident in the territory of the United States. Later he defended Seneca religious beliefs in speeches to missionaries Jacob Cram, 1805, and John Alexander, 1811; both were published and widely reprinted. In 1810, he led a delegation to Washington to air grievances, especially about settlers and missionaries encroaching on Indian lands, and to warn of the increasing bellicosity of the western tribes and their British allies. With the coming of the War of 1812, he advocated strict neutrality for his people, who had suffered much from divided loyalties during the Revolution, but once again Iroquois would fight on both sides. Throughout the war, he was primarily concerned with defense and retention of tribal lands; contrary to his reputation, some accounts suggest that he fought bravely at Fort George and Chippawa. After the war, he became a leader of the Seneca "Pagan Party" opposed to Christian missionary activity and further land sales. He met President John Quincy Adams in 1828 and President Andrew Jackson in 1829. According to some sources, he had married twice, and had thirteen children, all of whom predeceased him. Died at Buffalo Creek.

Philip Reed (1760–November 2, 1829) Born near Chesterton, in Kent County, Maryland. He was a captain in the Continental Army in the Revolutionary War, seeing action at the Battles of Stony Point and Camden, and later a member of the Maryland House of Delegates, 1787; sheriff of Kent County, 1791–94; and member of the Maryland executive council, 1805–6. He was married twice, first to Hasanah Hertford (d. 1802), with whom he had two children, and then to Mary Medford (d. 1820), with whom he had two more. In 1806 he was elected to the U.S. Senate as a Democratic Republican to fill a vacant seat, and was reelected that same year to serve a full term, 1807–13. During the War of 1812, he served in the 21st Regiment of the Maryland militia, led his men to victory at the Battle of Caulk's Field, August 31, 1814, and was made a brigadier general. A member of the U.S. House of Representatives in the Fifteenth Congress, 1817–19, he lost his bid for reelection, though he did regain his seat for part of the Seventeenth Congress, 1822–23. He died at Huntingtonfield, his residence in Kent County, Maryland. "The death of such a man is a loss to the nation," noted the November 17, 1829, edition of the *Republican Star, or, Eastern Shore General Advertiser*.

Samuel C. Reid (August 25, 1783–January 28, 1861) Born Samuel Chester Reid at Norwich, Connecticut, the son of Lieutenant John Reid, a British naval officer who defected to the American cause after being captured patrolling off New London in 1778, during the Revolutionary War, and Rebecca (Chester) Reid of Norwich. He went to sea at age eleven aboard a merchant vessel that was captured by a French privateer and spent six months imprisoned on Guadeloupe. Upon his release he joined the U.S. Navy as midshipman aboard USS *Baltimore*, and later returned to commerce as commander, at age twenty, of the New York brig *Merchant*. He married Mary Jennings in 1813; they had eight children. In the waning months of the War of 1812, he commanded the privateer *General Armstrong* (90 men, 7 or 9 guns), sailing out of New York on September 9, 1814, and arriving at the neutral port of Fayal in the Azores on September 26. That same day, three British warships entered Fayal en route to Jamaica, where naval forces were massing for an assault on New Orleans. As evening approached, and in violation of the port's neutrality, one of the British vessels dispatched four armed boats toward *General Armstrong*, which Reid had positioned under a Portuguese fort. Reid issued several warnings before unleashing a close-range barrage that killed several of the attackers. A second assault at midnight, this time by twelve boats carrying hundreds of men, was again turned back, with scores of British killed and wounded. Finally, realizing he was overmatched, Reid scuttled his ship and went ashore, where his crew was afforded protection by the island's governor and eventually repatriated aboard a Portuguese merchant brig. The delay in the transit of the British squadron caused by the Battle of Fayal, as it became known, was thought instrumental in the successful American defense of New Orleans. Reid was celebrated upon his return to America, receiving a sword from the New York State Assembly. He was subsequently for many years the harbormaster of New York, implementing numerous improvements in the pilot-boat service and publishing an updated signal code for American vessels. He also is credited with devising, in 1818, the present thirteen-stripe design of the American flag. In 1843, he was honored with a pension as a sailing master in the U.S. Navy. He died in New York City. Only in 1882 did Congress finally settle a long-standing suit for damages arising out of the action at Fayal, awarding Samuel Chester Reid Jr. a sum of $70,739.

John Richardson (October 4, 1796–May 12, 1852) Born at or near Fort George, in the Niagara region of Upper Canada, son of Robert Richardson, a Scotsman who served as a surgeon in the British army, and Madelaine (Askin) Richardson, of Queenston, Upper Canada. His family moved to Amherstburg, on the Detroit River in the western part of the province, and in July 1812, a month after the U.S. declaration of war, he joined the British 41st Regiment of Foot (infantry) as a volunteer; he observed both Major General Isaac Brock, the British commander at Amherstburg, and Tecumseh, a Shawnee chief who led Indians from several tribes allied with the British. He participated in the siege of Fort Meigs, May 1813, and the Battle of the Thames (Moraviantown, October 5, 1813), where he was captured. Imprisoned in Kentucky, he was released in July 1814, and was commissioned into the 8th (or King's) Regiment of Foot in August, and deployed to Europe in June 1815, arriving too late for the Battle of Waterloo. Promoted to lieutenant, he remained in the army until the fall of 1818, serving mostly in the Caribbean. He retired on half pay and lived in London and Paris, where, in 1825, he married Jane Marsh. His first experiment in writing, a memoir of his wartime service called "A Canadian Campaign," was serialized in 1826–27 in London's *New Monthly Magazine and Literary Journal*. He followed it with an epic poem, *Tecumseh; or, The Warrior of the West*, in 1828. *Écarté; or, The Salons of Paris*, the first of his many novels, appeared the next year; *Wacousta; or, The Prophecy* (1832), a historical novel about Pontiac's Rebellion, established his modest literary reputation. His first wife having died, he married Maria Caroline Drayson in 1832. In 1835, he joined a British auxiliary legion raised for service in Spain during the First Carlist War and later wrote a series of critical exposés about the campaign, which had ended for him in 1836 when he was wounded in battle, promoted to major, and awarded a military knighthood. In the spring of 1838 he was hired by the *Times* of London to report on the rebellions then occurring in his native Canada, though he was soon dismissed when his politics deviated from those of his Tory editors. In 1840, *The Canadian Brothers; or, The Prophecy Fulfilled*, which dramatized his experiences in the War of 1812, was published in Montreal; a sequel of sorts to *Wacousta*, it was not as successful. He twice attempted to establish a literary magazine in Montreal during the 1840s, each lasting a little more than a year. In 1842 he published *War of 1812*, but his hopes that the historical account would become a standard text in Canadian schools were disappointed. Later in the decade, he served as a police superintendent, lost his second wife (in August 1845), and established a newspaper in Montreal, before moving to New York City in 1849 to pursue his literary ambitions, with little success. He died there, his fortunes having reached "a very low ebb."

Robert Rowley (August 15, 1784–July 31, 1834) Born in Somerset, England, son of George and Elizabeth (Horsley) Rowley. He entered the Royal Navy as a youth and, according to his obituary in the *Hampshire Telegraph*, "was constantly employed from 1800 till the peace of 1815." Through the intervention of his cousin, Owsley Rowley, lord lieutenant of Huntingdonshire, he was promoted from lieutenant to commander in 1812. In March 1814, now captain of the British frigate *Melpomene*, he carried three hundred marines to join the forces reinforcing the British war effort in North America. By summer, he was cruising in Chesapeake Bay, part of a fleet commanded by Rear Admiral Sir George Cockburn, and participated in the attacks on Washington and Baltimore. He married Eliza Munro Rose of Grenada, in the West Indies; they had three children. After the war he was captain of HMS *Egeria*, patrolling the fishing grounds off Newfoundland, and flag captain with Rear Admiral Robert Plampin's Irish squadron, based in Cork. Died in Kent, England. A series of letters to his cousin Owsley detailing his wartime experiences was discovered in 1984.

James Scott (June 18, 1790–March 2, 1872) Born in London. In August 1803, he entered the Royal Navy as a "volunteer-per-order," a kind of apprentice, and shipped aboard HMS *Phaeton*, captained by George Cockburn. He became a midshipman the following year. Aboard HMS *Blanche*, in July 1806, he participated in the capture of the French frigate *Guerrière* (later, as HMS *Guerrière*, sunk by USS *Constitution* in the War of 1812). He was promoted to lieutenant in 1809. In the following years he saw action throughout the Atlantic, from the West Indies to the coast of Africa, before being assigned, early in 1813 and aboard HMS *Marlborough*, to the North America station, where he joined the task force commanded by Rear Admiral

Sir George Cockburn, his former captain. He led numerous raids on American shipping and coastal assets throughout the spring and summer of 1814, and served as Cockburn's aide-de-camp at the Battle of Bladensburg and in the assaults on Washington and Baltimore. For his service in the Chesapeake, he was promoted to commander, October 1814. He married Caroline Ann Donovan in 1819; they had at least three children. Promoted to captain in 1828, he served as flag captain to Admiral Cockburn on the North America, West India, and Pacific stations. He published *Recollections of a Naval Life* (three volumes) in London in 1834, in large measure, his introduction suggests, to set the record straight about the conduct of British forces in the War of 1812. In command of HMS *Samarang*, he participated in naval actions off China associated with the First Opium War (1839–42). For this service, he was nominated for a knighthood in 1841; one was finally awarded in 1862. He was promoted to admiral in 1865. Died at Cheltenham, England.

Winfield Scott (June 13, 1786–May 29, 1866) Born at Laurel Branch, his family's estate in Dinwiddie County, Virginia, the son of William Scott, a farmer and a captain in the Revolutionary War who died in 1792, and Ann (Mason) Scott. He studied at the College of William and Mary, but did not graduate, leaving to study law in Petersburg, Virginia (he witnessed the trial for treason of Aaron Burr in nearby Richmond in 1807). Stirred by the *Chesapeake-Leopard* Affair in the summer of 1807, when the USS *Chesapeake* was fired upon and four of its crew were seized by HMS *Leopard*, he enlisted as a corporal in a cavalry troop of the Virginia militia. He sought (from President Thomas Jefferson personally) and secured a commission as captain in the U.S. Army in 1808, and was posted to New Orleans, where he soon ran afoul of his commander, General James Wilkinson, who he indiscreetly suggested should have been tried for treason in place of Burr. Reprimanded and placed on forced leave, he returned to active duty in the fall of 1811 and with the declaration of war imminent, in the spring of 1812 he was promoted to the rank of lieutenant colonel and ordered to raise a regiment in Philadelphia. In September he was dispatched to the Niagara front, reporting to Brigadier General Alexander Smyth on October 4. He fought with distinction at Queenston (October 13) before being captured and exchanged. Later he planned and led a successful attack on Fort George, in Canada, in May 1813, and was promoted to brigadier general in March 1814. He again distinguished himself at Chippawa (July 5, 1814) and Lundy's Lane (July 25) where he was severely wounded, ending his active service in the war. He then established headquarters at Baltimore, and oversaw the postwar reduction of the army. He married Maria

Mayo in 1817; they had six children. Subsequently he commanded troops in South Carolina during the nullification crisis, 1832–33; organized removal of Cherokees from the southeastern United States, 1838; and helped settle the Anglo-American dispute over the Maine border with Canada, 1838–39. He was commissioned major general in 1841, and named general-in-chief of the U.S. Army. During the Mexican-American War, he commanded the expedition that landed at Vera Cruz and captured Mexico City in 1847. Nominated for president by the Whig Party in 1852, he was defeated by Democrat Franklin Pierce. He helped settle the Anglo-American border dispute over Puget Sound in 1859. Before retiring on November 1, 1861, he advised President Abraham Lincoln on Union strategy in the Civil War. Died at West Point, New York.

Laura Ingersoll Secord (September 13, 1775–October 17, 1868) Born Laura Ingersoll in Great Barrington, Massachusetts, eldest daughter of Thomas Ingersoll, a captain in the Revolutionary War, and Elizabeth (Dewey) Ingersoll, who died in 1784. In 1795, her father moved with his third wife and family to Upper Canada where he received a township grant and established a farm; he ran a tavern in Queenston until his township, Oxford-upon-the-Thames (Ingersoll, Ontario), was surveyed. Two years later, Laura married James Secord, a merchant in Queenston and the son of American Loyalists; they had seven children. When her husband was called up for militia duty and wounded at the Battle of Queenston (October 13, 1812), Secord rescued him from the battlefield and nursed him at home. The following summer, on June 21, 1813, she learned, probably by listening to American officers dining at her house, that the Americans intended to attack a British outpost at Beaver Dams (approximately twelve miles away) and to capture its commander, Lieutenant James FitzGibbon. Her husband disabled, Secord left early the next morning to warn FitzGibbon, avoiding the main road and traveling an indirect route through fields and woods; after a trek of nearly twenty miles, she came that evening upon a group of Indians, and convinced them to take her to FitzGibbon. Two days later, on June 24, four hundred Indians ambushed the American force approaching Beaver Dams, and FitzGibbon persuaded the American commander to surrender. No mention was made of Secord's intelligence in official reports. James Secord was later accorded a pension, and in 1828 he was appointed registrar of the Niagara Surrogate Court, becoming a judge in 1833. In 1835 he became the customs collector at Chippawa. He died in 1841, leaving Laura without reliable income. She opened a school and sought government relief, both without much success. Only in 1860, during a visit to Canada by the Prince of Wales, did her extraordinary service in the War of 1812 become known, when the prince granted her a £100 reward in response to a memorial she had submitted to him describing her twenty-mile trek. Her story, already becoming the stuff of legend, was popularized by William F. Coffin in his book *1812, The War and its Moral* (1864), the first of many accounts of the woman who became a Canadian national hero. Died at Chippawa.

John C. Sherbrooke (baptized April 29, 1764–February 14, 1830) Born John Coape Sherbrooke in Arnold, Nottinghamshire, son of William Sherbrooke, a landowner, and Sarah (Coape) Sherbrooke. Entering the army at sixteen, he was a captain before he was twenty and was stationed with the 33rd Regiment of Foot in Nova Scotia, 1784–85. Returning to England in 1786, he would see action, and be several times promoted, in the war with revolutionary France. In April 1796, now a lieutenant colonel, he sailed with his regiment to India, where he took part in the Mysore War of 1799. Ill health forced his return to England and a reserve position at half pay in 1800. In 1805, he was promoted to major general and placed in command of the Sicilian Regiment, stationed at Palermo as a check on French maneuvers in the Mediterranean; a fellow officer there described him as a "short, square, hardy little man, with a countenance that told at once the determined fortitude of his nature." Transferring in 1809 to the 68th Foot, he served as Arthur Wellesley's second in the Peninsular campaign and for his efforts there he was awarded a knighthood before his health again forced his return to England in 1810. In the summer of 1811 he was promoted to full lieutenant general and appointed lieutenant governor of Nova Scotia. He married Katherine Pyndar in August 1811, and sailed with her and her sister to Halifax in September. During the War of 1812, he deftly managed to bolster Nova Scotia's limited defenses and foster friendly and mutually lucrative relations with Federalist New England, whose traders received special licenses to carry on wartime trade with the Maritimes. This posture was terminated in 1814, when the British government determined to wage the war more aggressively; that summer, to put pressure on the U.S., Sherbrooke landed a British force at Castine, at the mouth of the Penobscot River, and established control over the sparsely populated eastern section of the province of Maine (then part of Massachusetts). The occupation of Down East Maine, which lasted eight months, proved a useful point of leverage in peace negotiations and generated customs revenues that helped found Dalhousie University in Halifax. In April 1816 Sherbrooke was commissioned governor-in-chief of all of British North America; in Quebec, as he had at Halifax, he sought to implement policies to conciliate the French

Canadian population, even establishing a close friendship with Bishop Joseph-Octave Plessis that helped to bridge political divides. His brief but effective term ended in February 1818 when he suffered a severe stroke and resigned. Died in Calverton, Nottinghamshire.

Harry Smith (June 28, 1787–October 12, 1860) Born Henry George Wakelyn Smith in Whittlesey, Cambridgeshire, the son of John Smith and Eleanor (Moore) Smith. "Every pains was taken with my education which my father could afford" before he joined the army in May 1805, as a second lieutenant in the 95th Rifle Regiment. He was made full lieutenant later that summer and saw action in South America, distinguishing himself at the Battle of Montevideo in February 1807. He fought with the 95th in Portugal, Spain, and France from August 1808 to April 1814; in Spain, in 1812, he gained the rank of captain and married fourteen-year-old Juana Maria de Los Dolores de León, who had sought protection from British forces after her family's property had been destroyed in the fighting; she would travel with Smith for the remainder of the campaign. With the defeat of Napoleon in the spring of 1814, Smith volunteered for service in North America and was present at the Battle of Bladensburg and the burning of Washington, before returning to England briefly, where he was reunited with his wife (who had not traveled with him to America) and enjoyed an audience with the Prince Regent and a dinner at Lord Bathurst's. He then joined Sir Edward Pakenham's ill-fated expedition against New Orleans, and after Pakenham's death was appointed secretary to the new commander, Sir John Lambert, who elected to withdraw British forces. He returned to England in time to muster (his wife with him, as she would be for most of his subsequent deployments) for Napoleon's final defeat at Waterloo, where he was a brigade major. After serving in various posts in England and Jamaica, he was transferred in 1828 to the Cape Colony at the southern tip of Africa where he became chief of staff to Benjamin d'Urban, the colony's governor, and participated in the Cape Frontier War of 1834–35, one of a series of imperialist conflicts known as the Xhosa Wars, after the indigenous people who resisted European colonists. In June 1840 the Smiths left Cape Town for Calcutta, where he assumed the rank of adjutant general. After the Battle of Maharajpore (December 1843), he was awarded a knighthood, and he achieved lasting fame for his charge at the Battle of Aliwal (January 1846), becoming baronet of the Aliwal on the Sutlej. He was promoted to major general in November 1846. The next year he and Lady Smith returned to South Africa; as governor and high commissioner he promptly annexed a large swath of territory held by Dutch Boers and defeated a Boer force at Boomplaats (August 1848). Further annexations provoked another war with the Xhosa in 1850. His mishandling of the costly Cape Frontier War of 1850–53 resulted in his being recalled in March 1852 to Britain, where he held various military posts until his death, in 1860, at London. His memoirs were published posthumously in 1901, in part because of interest in South Africa generated by the long siege of the British imperial outpost at Ladysmith, Natal (October 1899 to February 1900), during the Second Boer War.

Moses Smith (1783–October 4, 1870) Place of birth unknown. He joined the crew of the USS *Constitution* in 1811, sailing to France and the Netherlands, and surviving both storms and shipboard contagions. On August 19, 1812, two months after the U.S. declared war on Great Britain, *Constitution*, under Captain Isaac Hull, encountered HMS *Guerrière* off the coast of Nova Scotia and defeated her in an intense thirty-five-minute battle; relatively unscathed, *Constitution* earned the nickname "Old Ironsides." Smith was part of the ship's gunnery crew, responsible for sponging out cannons between firings. After Hull resigned his command to join the naval board, Smith transferred in December 1812 to USS *Adams*, then joined his former lieutenant from *Constitution* on the gunboat *Scorpion*, and was promoted to quartermaster, before deciding to return to *Adams*. Eluding the British blockade of the Chesapeake, *Adams*, under Captain Charles Morris, sailed from Washington on January 18, 1814, and cruised in the North Atlantic and off the British Isles, capturing five prizes. Returning homeward in the late summer of 1814, she ran aground off the coast of Maine (then a district of Massachusetts) and was brought damaged to Hampden where she was scuttled so as not to fall to pursuing British forces. On land, Morris led Smith and the rest of the crew during a brief skirmish with British forces on September 3, 1814. Smith published a memoir, *Naval Scenes in the Last War; or, Three Years on Board the Frigate Constitution, and the Adams; Including the Capture of the Guerriere. Being the True Narrative of Moses Smith, a Survivor of the "Old Ironsides" Crew*, in Boston in 1846. Celebrating the bravery and skill of American seamen, it conveys his conviction that the War of 1812 was a "struggle for our rights." He married Cecelia Donahue in 1849. Died in Quincy, Massachusetts. On January 13, 1879, his widow was granted a government pension based on his four-year service in the navy.

Alexander Smyth (1765–April 17, 1830) Born on the island of Rathlin, off the north coast of Ireland, son of the Reverend Adam Smyth; he was brought to America in 1775 when his father became rector of an Anglican parish at Fincastle in Botetourt County, Virginia. Educated at home, he read law, was appointed deputy clerk of Botetourt County in 1785 and admitted to the bar in 1789, opening a practice in

Abingdon, Virginia. He married Nancy Binkley of Wythe County, Virginia, in 1791; they had four children. A Republican, he was a member of the Virginia House of Delegates, 1792, 1796, 1801–2, and 1804–8, and served in the state Senate, 1808–9. He received a presidential commission as colonel of the Southwest Virginia Rifle Regiment in July 1808. Highly esteemed by President James Madison, he was appointed inspector general of the U.S. Army, with the rank of brigadier general, in July 1812, and he promptly published a new field manual for the army. Having requested and been granted command of a brigade in the projected invasion of Canada, he traveled to the Niagara frontier, where he soon came into conflict with Major General Stephen Van Rensselaer, overall commander of American forces in the region, who had his headquarters at Lewiston, and whose authority, as a militia commander, Smyth refused to acknowledge. Instead he set up his own headquarters at Buffalo, and failed to support Van Rensselaer's October 13, 1812, assault on Queenston, which was turned back, resulting in Van Rensselaer's resignation. Smyth then assumed command of all American forces in the region on October 24, and issued confident predictions of a swift conquest of Canada. After much delay, he launched two attempts to cross the Niagara River into Upper Canada, on November 28 and December 1, each undone by poor logistics and insufficient coordination. When a subordinate, Brigadier General Peter B. Porter of the New York militia, accused him of cowardice in the *Buffalo Gazette* (December 8), Smyth challenged him to a duel, which was conducted on Grand Isle, with no bloodshed. Shortly thereafter he was granted permission to visit his family in Virginia; before his leave expired he was removed from the army by an act of Congress. He petitioned Congress to be restored, so that he might "die, if Heaven wills it, in the defence of his country," but the matter was tabled. After the war, he spent the remainder of his life as a member either of the Virginia House of Delegates, 1816–17 and 1826–27, or of the U.S. House of Representatives, 1817–25 and 1827–30. Died in Washington.

John Strachan (April 12, 1778–November 1, 1867) Born in Aberdeen, Scotland, sixth child of John Strachan, a quarry overseer, and Elizabeth (Findlayson) Strachan, Presbyterians who hoped to establish their son as a minister. Educated at the Aberdeen Grammar School and graduating from King's College, Aberdeen, in 1797, he taught school near St. Andrews before accepting a position to teach in Upper Canada, traveling in 1799 via New York (with which he was not favorably impressed) to Kingston, on Lake Ontario; there he resided in the home of Loyalist émigré Richard Cartwright, tutoring Cartwright's children and continuing his own studies in divinity with the resident Anglican clergyman, John Stuart. He presented himself for ordination in the Church of England, and was made a deacon in May 1803. He was assigned to Cornwall, close upon New York on the St. Lawrence River, and ordained a priest in June 1804. Remaining at Cornwall until 1812, he built a small but strong congregation in a community dominated by recent emigrants from the United States, mostly Presbyterians, Methodists, Lutherans, and Catholics. He also established a private academy to educate the sons of wealthy and established families from throughout Upper and Lower Canada. He married Ann Wood McGill, of Cornwall, in 1807; they had nine children. In 1811, he received an honorary Doctor of Divinity from the University of Aberdeen. When John Stuart died later that year, Strachan hoped to return to Kingston to succeed him, but instead he was named rector of York (later Toronto), capital of Upper Canada, as well as chaplain of the garrison and provincial Legislative Council there. He arrived with his family in June 1812, as war commenced. An ardent patriot and staunch conservative, he scorned the leveling tendencies of democracy, both in the United States and in Upper Canada, and issued strong and detailed opinions about the British war effort. He founded the Loyal and Patriotic Society of Upper Canada in December 1812, raising funds for disabled militiamen and their families, and twice led negotiations with commanders of American forces attacking York, winning the admiration of his countrymen. He joined the provincial government after the war, serving on the Executive Council, 1817–35. Arguing that the interests of the Anglican establishment were underrepresented in the Legislative Council, he secured appointment to its upper house, serving from 1820 to 1841, when the provinces of Upper and Lower Canada were administratively united (a reorganization he opposed as harmful to the interests of the established church). Devoting much of his career to the promotion of education, he wrote influential white papers and helped to establish McGill University (named after benefactor James McGill, Ann Strachan's brother-in-law by her first marriage) and the University of King's College (later the University of Toronto), serving as the first president of the latter. He began a long tenure as the first Bishop of Toronto in 1839, consenting only in 1866, at the age of eighty-eight, to the appointment of a bishop coadjutor to relieve him of some of his duties. Died in Toronto, and buried at St. James Cathedral.

Caleb Strong (January 9, 1745–November 7, 1819) Born in Northampton, Massachusetts, the son of Caleb Strong, a prosperous tanner, and Phebe (Lyman) Strong. He graduated from Harvard in 1764, became a practicing attorney in 1772, and was a selectman in Northampton and a member of the local committees of correspondence and safety during the Revolutionary War. He married Sarah Hooker in 1777; they had nine children. A member of the Massachusetts Provincial Congress, 1776–78, and the first state Senate under the Massachusetts constitution, 1780–88, he was elected to the Continental Congress in 1780 but did not serve. He was a founding member of the American Academy of Arts and Sciences, 1780, and a delegate to the Constitutional Convention of 1787. Elected to a four-year term in the Senate in the first U.S. Congress in 1789, and re-elected in 1793, he served until resigning in 1796. He was elected to eleven one-year terms as governor of Massachusetts, 1800–7 and 1812–16, prevailing as a Federalist even as the state was increasingly supportive of Jeffersonian candidates at the national level. Strongly opposed to the War of 1812, he announced a public fast a week after it was declared. Believing that only he as governor was authorized to summon the state militia to action, he refused during the summer of 1812 to accede to calls from the secretary of war and from the U.S. commanders in the field to activate the Massachusetts militia, though in August he did direct a small force into federal service in the protection of Maine's eastern frontier. When he again activated the militia on the Maine frontier in 1814, Secretary of War James Monroe refused to reimburse the state for the costs of the deployment. He declined renomination in 1816 and retired to Northampton, where he died.

Roger B. Taney (March 17, 1777–October 12, 1864) Born in Calvert County, Maryland, second son of Michael Taney, a plantation owner, and Monica (Brooke) Taney, also of a landed Maryland family. He graduated from Dickinson College in 1795, read law at Annapolis, and began practicing in 1799. He married Anne Key, sister of Francis Scott Key, in 1806; they had seven children. After a brief stint in the Maryland House of Delegates, 1799–1800, he returned to private practice in Frederick, also directing the branch of the state bank there. He broke with the Federalist leadership of Maryland, and nationally, over the War of 1812, which he supported. In August 1814, his estate, Taney Place, was looted and destroyed by British troops en route to Washington. He led pro-war Federalists in the Maryland Senate, 1816–21, during which time he also began manumitting his slaves. In 1823 he moved to Baltimore, where he greatly expanded his practice, before becoming attorney general of Maryland, 1827–31. With the demise of the Federalist Party he became a Democrat, and supported Andrew Jackson in the elections of 1824 and 1828, serving in the Jackson administration as attorney general, 1831–33. He drafted Jackson's veto message when Congress renewed the charter of the Second

Bank of the United States in 1832 and was appointed secretary of the treasury, 1833–34, when the incumbent, William J. Duane, refused to carry out Jackson's order to withdraw federal deposits from the bank subsequent to the veto; Taney promptly complied with the presidential directive. Appointed chief justice of the U.S. Supreme Court by Jackson, he served 1836–64. He wrote the opinion of the Court in the *Dred Scott* case, 1857, which declared that Congress cannot exclude slavery from federal territories and that African Americans cannot be U.S. citizens. While sitting as a circuit judge in Maryland, he ruled in *Ex parte Merryman* (1861) that President Lincoln lacked the authority to suspend the writ of habeas corpus; he dissented in the *Prize Cases* (1863), in which the Court upheld the legality of the blockade proclamation issued by Lincoln in April 1861. Died in Washington, D.C.

Tecumseh (March 1768–October 5, 1813) A Shawnee Indian thought to have been born at Chillicothe, a Shawnee village on the Mad River, near present-day Dayton, Ohio. His mother, Methotaske, may have been a Creek. His father, Pucksinwa, a chief of the Kispoko band of the tribe, was killed at the Battle of Point Pleasant (October 10, 1774), when Virginia militia commanded by the colony's royal governor fought Shawnee and Mingo Indians at the confluence of the Ohio and Kanawha Rivers, in present-day West Virginia; this and other battles during the Revolutionary War resulted in the loss to the Shawnees of their traditional hunting lands along the Ohio River, as codified in the Treaty of Greenville (August 3, 1795). With other Shawnees opposed to the treaty, Tecumseh, now a chief, removed to the west, settling, with the permission of Potawatomi and Kickapoo already resident there, along the Wabash River in present-day Indiana. Later, in 1808, he established with his brother Tenskwatawa (also called the Prophet) a village that became known as Prophet's Town; located at the confluence of the Wabash and Tippecanoe Rivers, it was a center of cultural and religious revival and political experimentation, where an increasingly militant Tecumseh sought to forge a confederation of Indian tribes based on opposition to further cession of land to American settlers (as for example in the Treaty of Fort Wayne, 1809, a transfer of three million acres that William Henry Harrison, governor of the newly created Indiana Territory, had engineered through the use of alcohol and bribery). In the fall of 1811, Tecumseh traveled to Tennessee, Georgia, and Mississippi Territory to enlist southern tribes, especially the Creek, in his confederacy. While he was away, Harrison led a force of a thousand regulars and militia to Prophet's Town, ostensibly seeking redress for recent attacks on American settlements; the army was a short distance from Prophet's Town when, on November 7, 1811, some six or seven hundred Indians encouraged by Tenskwatawa surprised Harrison's force, only to be turned back (the Battle of Tippecanoe); Harrison ordered Prophet's Town burned the next day. Upon his return, Tecumseh rallied his forces and with the outbreak of the War of 1812 entered into an alliance with the British. The force of his fearsome reputation, as much as of his arms, helped secure the American surrender of Fort Detroit in August 1812; he was offered, but declined, a sash and the rank of brevet brigadier general by the British in recognition. In the campaign of 1813, he led Indian forces at unsuccessful sieges of Fort Meigs and Fort Stephenson, exhorting his British allies to remain on the offensive. He was bitterly disappointed when the British, with the loss of naval control of Lake Erie, elected to retreat into Upper Canada via the Thames River, pursued by an American force led by Harrison. On October 5, 1813, the British made a stand fifty miles east of Detroit, near the Indian village of Moraviantown (Battle of the Thames), and there Tecumseh was killed, allegedly by Kentucky militia leader and congressman Richard M. Johnson. His body was mutilated and pieces were taken as trophies; one Kentucky veteran recalled that he helped skin the corpse "and brot Two pieces of his yellow hide home with me to my Mother & Sweet Harts."

Stephen Van Rensselaer (November 1, 1764–January 26, 1839) Born in New York City, first son of Stephen Van Rensselaer II, ninth patroon of Rensselaerswyck, and Catherine (Livingston) Van Rensselaer, daughter of Philip Livingston, a signer of the Declaration of Independence. He inherited title to a vast estate when his father died in 1769, and took possession of the manor house in Albany in 1785. Educated under the care of his maternal grandfather, he graduated from Harvard College in 1782. He married Margaret Schuyler, daughter of Revolutionary War general Philip Schuyler, in 1783; they had three children before Margaret's death in 1801. A Federalist, he was a member of the New York Assembly, 1789–90, and the New York Senate, 1791–95. He was lieutenant governor of New York, 1795–1801. He ran unsuccessfully for governor in 1801, losing to George Clinton. He married Cornelia Patterson, daughter of William Patterson, former governor of New Jersey; they had nine children. An early advocate of a canal linking the Hudson and the Great Lakes, he served on the New York canal commission, 1810–39. Though lacking any military experience, he was appointed a major general in the New York militia, and called upon by Governor Daniel D. Tompkins to raise and command forces on New York's northern frontier at the outbreak of the War of 1812. He established his headquarters at Lewiston, where he commanded some six thousand volunteers. Plagued by poor relations with the regular army command on the Niagara frontier, especially

Brigadier General Alexander Smyth, he led his militia on a poorly planned and costly attack on Queenston, Upper Canada, on October 13, 1812, losing some one thousand men. He then resigned his post and returned to Albany. Renominated for governor the following spring, he was defeated by Tompkins. He served in Congress, 1822–29, where he cast the decisive vote for the New York delegation when the House elected John Quincy Adams president on February 9, 1825. In 1824, he established a school at Albany for the "application of science to the common purposes of life," later Rensselaer Polytechnic Institute. Retired from politics in 1829, he was chancellor of the University of the State of New York, 1835–39. Died at Rensselaerswyck.

Daniel Webster (January 18, 1782–October 24, 1852) Born in Salisbury, New Hampshire, son of Ebenezer Webster, a landowner and captain in the militia during the Revolutionary War, and Abigail (Eastman) Webster. Attending various schools as a child, he graduated from Dartmouth College in 1801, was admitted to the bar in 1805, and began to practice law in Portsmouth, New Hampshire, in 1807. He married Grace Fletcher in 1809; they had five children, all but one of whom predeceased him. Alarmed by what he called the "contagion of democracy" evident in the rise of Jeffersonian republicanism, and a staunch opponent of Jefferson's embargo, he authored numerous influential pamphlets and orations in opposition. After the "Rockingham Memorial," a speech against the War of 1812 delivered at a Federalist meeting in Rockingham, New Hampshire, in August 1812, he was nominated for Congress and elected the following November. Serving from 1813 to 1817, he was throughout the war a vocal critic of administration policies and a stalwart champion of the rights of the minority opposition party. Midway through his second term he moved to Boston, in preparation for turning his focus from politics to law. He appeared before the U.S. Supreme Court in numerous cases, including the Dartmouth College case, *McCulloch v. Maryland*, and *Gibbons v. Ogden*. He was a delegate to the convention that revised the Massachusetts state constitution, 1820–21, and cemented his reputation as a public orator with his bicentennial address at Plymouth, Massachusetts, on December 22, 1820. He was returned to Congress in 1823 and served until 1827, when he was elected to the U.S. Senate. After the death of his wife in January 1828, he married Caroline Le Roy, of New York, in 1829; they had no children. In the Senate he confronted the doctrine of nullification in famous speeches in response to Robert Young Hayne in 1830. Webster was one of three Whig candidates for the presidency in 1836; he won the electoral votes of only his home state of Massachusetts. Declining to stand for reelection to the Senate in 1840, he became secretary of state in the cabinets of William Henry Harrison and John Tyler, 1841–43. He negotiated the Webster-Ashburton Treaty of 1842, which resolved numerous outstanding disputes related to the border between the U.S. and British North America. Elected once more to the Senate as a Whig, he served from 1845 to 1850, vocal in his opposition to the annexation of Texas, war with Mexico, and the extension of slavery ("a great moral and political evil"), and steadfast and eloquent in his defense of the federal Union. Delivering a famous speech in support of the Compromise of 1850, he insisted that he spoke "not as a Massachusetts man, nor as a Northern man, but as an American." He served a second stint as secretary of state, in the cabinet of Millard Fillmore, from July 1850 until his death in Marshfield, Massachusetts.

Arthur Wellesley (Wesley), 1st Duke of Wellington (May 1, 1769– September 14, 1852) Born in Dublin into the Anglo-Irish aristocracy, the fourth son of Garret Wesley, the first Earl of Mornington, and Anne (Hill) Wesley, daughter of the first Viscount Dungannon. (He signed himself Arthur Wesley until 1798.) Educated at Eton, 1781–84, and thereafter by private tutors, he received a commission, purchased by his brother, as an ensign in the British 73rd Regiment of Foot in May 1787, transferring in short order to other regiments in Dublin (as a lieutenant) and serving as aide-de-camp to the lord lieutenant of Ireland, 1787–93. A member of the Irish Parliament, 1790–97, he purchased appointment as major of the 33rd Regiment of Foot in April 1793, became a lieutenant colonel in September, and that month saw his first military action, in the Netherlands, in the war against revolutionary France. Promoted to colonel in May 1796, he sailed to India with his regiment, arriving in Calcutta in February 1797; there he served as advisor to his brother, Richard, Lord Mornington, governor-general of India (1798–1805). He fought with distinction in the Fourth Anglo-Mysore War, 1798–99, and, having been promoted to the rank of major general, in the Second Anglo-Maratha War, 1803–5. He was awarded a knighthood in 1804 before returning to England in 1805. Married Catherine "Kitty" Pakenham in Dublin in 1806; they had two children. A Tory, he served as a member of Parliament (1806–7) and in the Portland administration as chief secretary for Ireland (1807–9), becoming a member of the Privy Council. He returned to active service in 1807 and in 1808, as a lieutenant general, led a force of nine thousand in a campaign against French forces in the Iberian Peninsula. He achieved numerous victories during the six-year Peninsular War, driving the French from Spain and removing Joseph Bonaparte from the Spanish throne; in recognition, he was named Earl and then Marquess of Wellington in 1812, and the 1st Duke of Wellington on May 11, 1814. With Napoleon removed from power, many of the veteran officers and soldiers under his command, including his brother-in-law Sir Edward "Ned" Pakenham, were transferred to service in the war in North America, about which he was several times asked for strategic advice. Later that year he was named ambassador to France and, in February 1815, head of the British delegation to the Congress of Vienna. After Napoleon returned to power in France in the spring, he left Vienna to command seventy-three thousand men in the allied campaign that brought about the French emperor's final defeat, at Waterloo, in present-day Belgium, on June 18, 1815. He was named to various posts, including, in 1827, commander-in-chief of the British army, before resigning to become prime minister, 1828–30. He led a Tory administration that sought to prevent passage of what became, after his government lost a vote of no confidence, the Reform Act of 1832. He served briefly as interim prime minister in 1834, then, under Robert Peel, as foreign secretary, 1834–35, and was later reappointed commander-in-chief of the British army, in 1842. Died in Walmer, in Kent, and buried at St. Paul's Cathedral.

Jared Willson (Wilson) (May 23, 1786–April 8, 1851) Born in Stockbridge, Massachusetts. Graduating from the University of Vermont and settling in Canandaigua in Ontario County, New York, in 1811, he studied law before joining the New York militia as a lieutenant with the outbreak of hostilities in 1812, serving in what he called the "Battallion of Rifle-men." He was taken prisoner at the Battle of Queenston Heights, October 13, 1812, and released on parole a week later. After the war, he was a successful lawyer in Ontario County. Died at Canandaigua.

Robert Young (fl. 1783–1815) Place and date of birth unknown. A career officer in the British army, he received his first commission, as ensign, in the 83rd Regiment of Foot in 1783. In 1790, he was appointed lieutenant in the 8th (or King's) Regiment of Foot, and achieved the rank of captain in 1793. He saw action in Flanders in the war against revolutionary France and in the West Indies as part of a British expedition against the Spanish colonies, before being promoted to major in 1797. Again in action in Egypt and the Mediterranean, he was promoted to lieutenant colonel in 1809. He served as colonel in Canada during the War of 1812, commanding the 1st Battalion of the 8th Regiment. On May 28, 1813, he led the right flank of the expedition against the U.S. base at Sackets Harbor. In the spring of 1814, he commanded the detachment occupying Fort Niagara, in New York. Subsequently he was promoted to major general on June 4, 1814, and died the following year, though it is not known where.

Note on the Texts

This volume collects nineteenth-century writing about the War of 1812, bringing together public and private letters, newspaper editorials and magazine articles, memoranda, speeches, sermons, narratives, journal and diary entries, proclamations and declarations, messages, broadsides, poems, songs, and excerpts from memoirs written by participants and observers and dealing with events in the period from June 1812 to December 1815. Most of these documents were not written for publication, and many of them existed only in manuscript form during the lifetimes of the persons who wrote them. The texts in this volume are taken from the best printed sources available. Where there is more than one printed source for a document, the text printed in this volume is taken from the source that seems to contain the fewest editorial alterations in the spelling, capitalization, paragraphing, and punctuation of the document.

The present volume prints texts as they appear in the sources listed below, but with a few alterations in editorial procedure. The bracketed conjectural readings of editors, in cases where original manuscripts or printed texts were damaged or illegible, are accepted without brackets in this volume when those readings seem to be the only possible ones; but when they do not, or when the editor made no conjecture, the missing word or words are indicated by a bracketed two-em space, i.e., [　　]. In cases where an obvious misspelling or typographical error in a manuscript was marked by earlier editors with "[*sic*]," the present volume omits the "[*sic*]" and corrects the typographical error or slip of the pen. Bracketed editorial insertions used in the source texts to identify persons or places, expand contractions and abbreviations, and clarify meaning have been deleted in this volume. In instances where canceled, but still legible, words were printed in the source texts with lines through the deleted material, this volume omits the canceled words. In certain instances where the source edition, for reasons of space or to avoid repetition, has deleted the valedictions of letters, they have been restored in this volume.

The following is a list of the documents included in this volume, in the order of their appearance, giving the source of each text:

James Madison: War Message to Congress, June 1, 1812. *The Papers of James Madison: Presidential Series*, Vol. 4, ed. J. C. A. Stagg, Ellen J. Barber, Anne Mandeville Colony, Jeanne Kerr Cross, Martha J.

King, Susan Holbrook Purdue, and Jewel L. Spangler (Charlottes-ville: University of Virginia Press, 1999), 432–38. Copyright © 1999 by the Rector and Visitors of the University of Virginia. Reprinted with permission of the University of Virginia Press.

U.S. House of Representatives, Committee on Foreign Relations: Re-port on the Causes and Reasons for War, June 3, 1812. *The Papers of John C. Calhoun*, Vol. 1, ed. Robert L. Meriwether (Columbia: University of South Carolina Press, 1959), 109–22. Copyright © 1959 by the South Carolina Archives Department.

Thomas Jefferson to James Madison, May 30, 1812. *The Papers of James Madison: Presidential Series*, Vol. 4, ed. J. C. A. Stagg et al. (Char-lottesville: University of Virginia Press, 1999), 426. Copyright © 1999 by the Rector and Visitors of the University of Virginia. Re-printed with permission of the University of Virginia Press.

Andrew Jackson to Willie Blount, June 5, 1812. *The Papers of An-drew Jackson*, Vol. 2, ed. Harold D. Moser and Sharon Macpherson (Knoxville: University of Tennessee Press, 1985), 301–2. Copyright © 1984 by University of Tennessee Press/Knoxville.

Tecumseh: Message from the Confederate Nations to Their Brit-ish Allies and Huron Brothers, June 8, 1812, translated from the Shawnee language by Esidore Chaine. *Select British Documents of the Canadian War of 1812*, Vol. 1, ed. William Wood. Publications of the Champlain Society, Vol. 13 (Toronto: The Champlain Society, 1920), 312–14.

James Monroe to John Taylor, June 13, 1812. *The Writings of James Monroe*, Vol. 5, ed. Stanislaus Murray Hamilton (New York: G. P. Putnam's Sons, 1901), 205–12.

James Madison: Proclamation of War, June 19, 1812. *The Papers of James Madison: Presidential Series*, Vol. 4, ed. J. C. A. Stagg et al. (Charlottesville: University of Virginia Press, 1999), 489–90. Copyright © 1999 by the Rector and Visitors of the University of Virginia. Reprinted with permission of the University of Virginia Press.

Hezekiah Niles: "War against England." *The Weekly Register*, 2:43 (June 27, 1812), 283–85.

Thomas Jefferson to James Madison, June 29, 1812. *The Papers of James Madison: Presidential Series*, Vol. 4, ed. J. C. A. Stagg et al. (Char-lottesville: University of Virginia Press, 1999), 519–20. Copyright © 1999 by the Rector and Visitors of the University of Virginia. Re-printed with permission of the University of Virginia Press.

Thirty-four Members of the U.S. House of Representatives: from "An Address of the Minority to Their Constituents," late June 1812. *Annals of Congress (The Debates and Proceedings in the Congress of the United States)*, 12th Congress, 1st Session (Washington, D.C.: Gales & Seaton, 1853), Appendix, 2196–99, 2219–21.

Maryland House of Delegates, Committee of Grievances and Courts of Justice: Report on the Baltimore Riots. *Report of the Committee of Grievances and Courts of Justice of the House of Delegates of Maryland, on the Subject of the Recent Mobs and Riots in the City of Baltimore, together with the Depositions Taken before the Committee* (Annapolis: Jonas Green, 1813), 1–12.

Israel Pickens: Circular Letter to His Constituents in North Carolina, July 4, 1812. *Circular Letters of Congressmen to Their Constituents, 1789–1829*, Vol. 2, ed. Noble E. Cunningham Jr. (Chapel Hill: The University of North Carolina Press, 1978), 793–94. Copyright © 1978 by The University of North Carolina Press. Reprinted with permission of the Publisher.

William Ellery Channing: *A Sermon, Preached in Boston, July 23, 1812, the Day of the Publick Fast, Appointed by the Executive of the Legislature of the Commonwealth of Massachusetts, in Consequence of the Declaration of War Against Great Britain* (Boston: Greenough and Stebbins, 1812).

William Hull: Proclamation, July 13, 1812. *Select British Documents of the Canadian War of 1812*, Vol. 1, ed. William Wood. Publications of the Champlain Society, Vol. 13 (Toronto: The Champlain Society, 1920), 355–57.

Isaac Brock: Proclamation, July 22, 1812. *Select British Documents of the Canadian War of 1812*, Vol. 1, ed. William Wood. Publications of the Champlain Society, Vol. 13 (Toronto: The Champlain Society, 1920), 371–74.

Thomas Verchères de Boucherville: Journal, July–August 1812. "Journal of Thomas Verchères de Boucherville," translated from the French by L. Oughtred Woltz, revised by Milo Milton Quaife, in *War on the Detroit*, ed. M. M. Quaife (Chicago: R. R. Donnelley & Sons, 1940), 81–84, 84–87, 88–93, 95–105.

Nathan Heald to Thomas H. Cushing, October 23, 1812. Milo Milton Quaife, *Chicago and the Old Northwest, 1673–1835: A Study of the Evolution of the Northwestern Frontier, Together with a History of Fort Dearborn* (Chicago: The University of Chicago Press, 1913), 406–8.

Caleb Strong to William Eustis, August 5, 1812. *American State Papers: Military Affairs*, Vol. 1, ed. Walter Lowrie and Matthew St. Clair Clarke (Washington, D.C.: Gales & Seaton, 1832), 323.

James Madison to Thomas Jefferson, August 17, 1812. *The Papers of James Madison: Presidential Series*, Vol. 5, ed. J. C. A. Stagg, Ellen J. Barber, Anne Mandeville Colony, Martha J. King, Angela Kreider, and Jewel L. Spangler (Charlottesville: University of Virginia Press,

2004), 165–66. Copyright © 2004 by the Rector and Visitors of the University of Virginia. Reprinted with permission of the University of Virginia Press.

Robert Lucas: Journal, August 16, 1812. *The Robert Lucas Journal of the War of 1812, during the Campaign under General William Hull*, ed. John C. Parish (Iowa City: The State Historical Society of Iowa, 1906), 63–68.

Cornelius Flummerfelt: "The Bold Canadian." James H. Coyne, "'The Bold Canadian': A Ballad of the War of 1812," *Papers and Records of the Ontario Historical Society* 23 (1926), 238–39.

Moses Smith: from *Naval Scenes in the Last War; or, Three Years on Board the Frigate "Constitution," and the "Adams"; including The Capture of the "Guerriere"; Being the True Narrative of Moses Smith, a Survivor of the "Old Ironsides" Crew* (Boston: Gleason's Publishing Hall, 1846), 30–36.

New-York City Committee of Correspondence: from *Address, of the Committee of the City of New-York, Acting Under the Authority of the General Committee of Correspondence of the State of New-York in Support of the Nomination of The Hon. De Witt Clinton, to the Presidency of the United States, at the Ensuing Election* (New York: Pelsue & Gould, 1812), 14–28.

James Madison: Address to the Delegations of Several Indian Nations, August 22, 1812. *The Papers of James Madison: Presidential Series*, Vol. 5, ed. J. C. A. Stagg et al. (Charlottesville: University of Virginia Press, 2004), 175–77. Copyright © 2004 by the Rector and Visitors of the University of Virginia. Reprinted with permission of the University of Virginia Press.

Stephen Van Rensselaer to Daniel D. Tompkins, August 31, 1812. Solomon Van Rensselaer, *Narrative of the Affair of Queenstown: In the War of 1812* (New York: Leavitt, Lord & Co., 1836), Appendix I, 34–36.

Daniel Curtis to Jacob Kingsbury, September 21, 1812. "Recent Documentary Acquisitions to the Indiana Historical Society Library Relating to Fort Wayne," ed. Howard H. Peckham, *Indiana Magazine of History* 44:4 (December 1948), 412–18. Reprinted with permission of the Trustees of Indiana University

A. W. Cochran: from a letter to Rebecca Cochran, September 13, 1812. *Select British Documents of the Canadian War of 1812*, Vol. 1, ed. William Charles Henry Wood. Publications of the Champlain Society, Vol. 13 (Toronto: The Champlain Society, 1920), 521–22.

John Strachan to John Richardson, September 30, 1812. *The John Strachan Letter Book: 1812–1834*, ed. George W. Spragge (Toronto: The Ontario Historical Society, 1946), 15–17. Copyright © 1946 by The Ontario Historical Society.

George McFeely: Diary, October 12–16, 1812. *The War of 1812 in Person: Fifteen Accounts by United States Army Regulars, Volunteers, and Militiamen*, ed. John C. Fredriksen (Jefferson, N.C.: McFarland & Co., 2010), 6–7. Copyright © 2010 by John C. Fredriksen.

Jared Willson to Alvan Stewart, November 9, 1812. Jared Willson, "A Rifleman of Queenston: Experiences of Jared Willson, 'Prisoner of War,' as Narrated to a Friend," ed. Frank H. Severance, *Publications of the Buffalo Historical Society* 9 (1906), 373–76.

John Strachan to William Wilberforce, November 1, 1812. *The John Strachan Letter Book: 1812–1834*, ed. George W. Spragge (Toronto: The Ontario Historical Society, 1946), 21–23. Copyright © 1946 by The Ontario Historical Society.

Alexander Smyth: Proclamation, November 10, 1812. *The Documentary History of the Campaigns upon the Niagara Frontier*, Vol. 4, ed. E. A. Cruikshank (Welland, Ont.: Lundy's Lane Historical Society, 1899), 193–94.

William Atherton: from *Narrative of the Suffering & Defeat of the North-Western Army, under General Winchester* (Frankfort, Ky.: Printed for the Author by J. G. Hodges, 1842), 5, 6–7, 7–10, 11–15, 16, 17–19, 24–28, 29–31, 31–32.

William B. Northcutt: Diary, December 16–25, 1812. "War of 1812 Diary of William B. Northcutt," ed. G. Glenn Clift, *Register of the Kentucky State Historical Society* 56:3 (July 1958), 256–66.

Elias Darnell: Journal, January 17–26, 1813. Elias Darnell, *A Journal: Containing an Accurate and Interesting Account of the Hardships, Sufferings, Battles, Defeat, and Captivity of Those Heroic Kentucky Volunteers and Regulars, Commanded by General Winchester, in the Years 1812–13* (Philadelphia: Lippincott, Grambo & Co., 1854), 46–69.

James Madison: Second Inaugural Address, March 4, 1813. *James Madison: Writings*, ed. Jack N. Rakove (New York: The Library of America, 1999), 693–96.

Henry, Earl Bathurst to Sir Thomas Sidney Beckwith, March 20, 1813. *The Naval War of 1812: A Documentary History*, Vol. 2, ed. William S. Dudley (Washington, D.C.: Naval Historical Center, Department of the Navy, 1992), 325–26.

Patrick Finan: from "Recollections of Canada." *Journal of a Voyage to Quebec in the Year 1825; with Recollections of Canada, during the Late American War, in the Years 1812–13* (Newry, Ireland: Alexander Peacock, 1828), 282–93.

John Richardson: from "A Canadian Campaign." John Richardson, "A Canadian Campaign, by a British Officer," *The New Monthly Magazine and Literary Journal* 19.74 (February 1827), 166–70.

Thomas Jefferson to Madame de Staël, May 24, 1813. *Thomas Jefferson: Writings*, ed. Merrill D. Peterson (New York: The Library of America, 1984), 1271–77.

George McFeely: Diary, May 27, 1813. *The War of 1812 in Person: Fifteen Accounts by United States Army Regulars, Volunteers, and Militiamen*, ed. John C. Fredriksen (Jefferson, N.C.: McFarland & Co., 2010), 18–22. Copyright © 2010 by John C. Fredriksen.

John Couteur: Journal, May 27–29, 1813. *Merry Hearts Make Light Days: The War of 1812 Journal of Lieutenant John Le Couteur, 104th Foot*, ed. Donald E. Graves (Montreal: Robin Brass Studio, 2012), 113–18. Copyright © 1993, 2012 by Donald E. Graves.

Joseph Penley Jr.: from *A Narrative: A Short and Thrilling Narrative of a Few of the Scenes and Incidents That Occurred in the Sanguinary and Cruel War of 1812–'14, Between England and the United States*, published anonymously (Norway, Me.: Printed for the Author by the Norway Advertiser Press, 1853), 22–32, 35–36, 47–48.

Philip B. V. Broke to John Borlase Warren, June 6, 1813. *The Naval War of 1812: A Documentary History*, Vol. 2, ed. William S. Dudley (Washington, D.C.: Naval Historical Center, Department of the Navy, 1992), 129, 132.

John C. Calhoun to James Macbride, June 23, 1813. *The Papers of John C. Calhoun*, Vol. 1, ed. Robert L. Meriwether (Columbia: University of South Carolina Press, 1959), 177–78. Copyright © 1959 by the South Carolina Archives Department.

Laura Ingersoll Secord: Incident at Beaver Dams, June 22–23, 1813. "History of the War Between Great Britain and the United States of America—Chapter IX," *The Anglo-American Magazine* 3:5 (November 1853), 467.

John Le Couteur: Journal, June 24, 1813. *Merry Hearts Make Light Days: The War of 1812 Journal of Lieutenant John Le Couteur, 104th Foot*, ed. Donald E. Graves (Montreal: Robin Brass Studio, 2012), 127–30. Copyright © 1993, 2012 by Donald E. Graves.

James Monroe to Thomas Jefferson, June 28, 1813. *The Writings of James Monroe*, Vol. 5, ed. Stanislaus Murray Hamilton (New York: G. P. Putnam's Sons, 1901), 271–73.

"P." (Richard E. Parker) to the *Richmond Enquirer*, July 16, 1813. *American State Papers: Military Affairs*, Vol. 1, ed. Walter Lowrie and Matthew St. Clair Clarke (Washington, D.C.: Gales & Seaton, 1832), 380–81.

Blackbird: Message from the Ottawa Nation to William Claus, July 15, 1813, translated from the Ottawa language by William Claus. "'As Long as the Powder Burnt, to Kill and Scalp': An Ottawa Chief Talks Plain to the White Man, 15 July 1813," ed. Donald E. Graves,

War of 1812 Magazine, 1:1 (January 2006), www.napoleon-series .org/military/Warof1812/2006/Issue1/c_blackbird.html.

William B. Northcutt: Diary, July 31, 1813. "War of 1812 Diary of William B. Northcutt," ed. G. Glenn Clift, *Register of the Kentucky State Historical Society*, 56:4 (October 1958), 331–33.

George Croghan to William Henry Harrison, August 5, 1813. *Messages and Letters of William Henry Harrison*, Vol. 2, ed. Logan Esarey (Indianapolis: Indiana Historical Commission, 1922), 514–16.

Black Hawk: from *Life of Ma-ka-tai-me-she-kia-kiak or Black Hawk . . . Dictated by Himself*, translated from the Sauk language by Antoine LeClair and edited by J. B. Patterson (Boston, 1834), 47.

James Fenimore Cooper: from *Ned Myers; or, A Life Before the Mast*. *Ned Myers; or, A Life Before the Mast* (New Edition), by James Fenimore Cooper (New York: Stringer & Townsend, 1856), 67–75.

James Inderwick: Journal, August 14–21, 1813. "Cruise of the U.S. Brig *Argus* in 1813: Journal of Surgeon James Inderwick," ed. Victor Hugo Paltsits, *Bulletin of the New York Public Library* 21:6 (June 1917), 400–5.

Thomas Hart Benton: Broadside, September 10, 1813. *The Papers of Andrew Jackson*, Vol. 2, ed. Harold D. Moser and Sharon Macpherson (Knoxville: University of Tennessee Press, 1985), 425–27. Copyright © 1984 by University of Tennessee Press/Knoxville.

Philip Freneau: "The Battle of Lake Erie." *The Poems of Philip Freneau, Poet of the American Revolution*, Vol. 3, ed. Fred Lewis Pattee (Princeton, N.J.: Princeton University Library, 1907), 315–18.

Washington Irving: "Biographical Memoir of Commodore Perry," *The Analectic Magazine*, 2 (December 1813), 494–510.

Tecumseh: Speech to Henry Procter, September 18, 1813, translated from the Shawnee language by Esidore Chaine. *Messages and Letters of William Henry Harrison*, Vol. 2, ed. Logan Esarey (Indianapolis: Indiana Historical Commission, 1922), 541–43.

John Richardson: from *Richardson's War of 1812, with Notes and a Life of the Author*, ed. Alexander Clark Hamilton (Toronto: Historical Publishing Company, 1902), 206–14.

William Henry Harrison: Proclamation, October 16, 1813. *Messages and Letters of William Henry Harrison*, Vol. 2, ed. Logan Esarey (Indianapolis: Indiana Historical Commission, 1922), 579.

Red Jacket: Message to Erastus Granger, October 21, 1813, translated, from the Iroquois, by Jasper Parrish. William Ketchum, *An Authentic and Comprehensive History of Buffalo*, Vol. 2 (Buffalo, N.Y.: Rockwell, Baker & Hill, 1865), 433–34.

John Le Couteur to Philip Bouton, October 24, 1813. *Merry Hearts Make Light Days: The War of 1812 Journal of Lieutenant John Le*

Couteur, 104th Foot, ed. Donald E. Graves (Montreal: Robin Brass Studio, 2012), 147–49. Copyright © 1993, 2012 by Donald E. Graves.

Robert Purdy to James Wilkinson, November 1813. *American State Papers: Military Affairs*, Vol. 1, ed. Walter Lowrie and Matthew St. Clair Clarke (Washington, D.C.: Gales & Seaton, 1832), 479–80.

Charles Ball: from *Slavery in the United States: A Narrative of the Life and Adventures of Charles Ball, a Black Man* (New York: John S. Taylor, 1837), 469–80.

James Scott: from *Recollections of a Naval Life* (London: Richard Bentley, 1834), 189–97.

Francis Jeffrey: A Conversation with James Madison, November 18, 1813. *The Papers of James Madison: Presidential Series*, Vol. 7, ed. Angela Kreider, J. C. A. Stagg, Mary Parke Johnson, Anne Mandeville Colony, and Katharine E. Harbury (Charlottesville: University of Virginia Press, 2012), 46–49. Copyright © 2012 by the Rector and Visitors of the University of Virginia. Reprinted with permission of the University of Virginia Press.

Henry Clay to Thomas Bodley, December 18, 1813. *The Papers of Henry Clay*, Vol. 1, ed. James F. Hopkins with Mary W. M. Hargreaves (Lexington: University Press of Kentucky, 1959), 841–42. Copyright © 1959 by University Press of Kentucky.

Cyrenius Chapin to the *Buffalo Gazette*, June 13, 1814. *The Documentary History of the Campaigns upon the Niagara Frontier*, Vol. 9, ed. E. A. Cruikshank (Welland, Ont.: Lundy's Lane Historical Society, 1908), 120–22.

Eber D. Howe: from "Recollections of a Pioneer Printer," ed. Frank H. Severance, *Publications of the Buffalo Historical Society* 9 (1906), 385–89.

Amos Hall to Daniel D. Tompkins, January 6, 1814. *The Documentary History of the Campaigns upon the Niagara Frontier*, Vol. 9, ed. E. A. Cruikshank (Welland, Ont.: Lundy's Lane Historical Society, 1908), 92–97.

George Prevost: Proclamation, January 12, 1814. *The Documentary History of the Campaigns upon the Niagara Frontier*, Vol. 9, ed. E. A. Cruikshank (Welland, Ont.: Lundy's Lane Historical Society, 1908), 112–16.

Henry Kent: A Winter's March. "Extraordinary March of Lieutenant Henry Kent, from St. John's, New Brunswick, to Kingston, in Upper Canada, being a distance of 900 Miles, in the depth of Winter," *The Naval Chronicle*, Vol. 33 (February 1815), 123–27.

Arthur Wellesley, Marquess of Wellington, to Henry, Earl Bathurst, February 22, 1814. *The Dispatches of Field Marshal the Duke of*

Wellington, during His Various Campaigns, Vol. 11, ed. John Gurwood (London: John Murray, 1838), 525.

The Crew of USS *Essex* to the Crew of HMS *Phoebe*, March 9, 1814. *The Naval War of 1812*, Vol. 3, ed. Michael J. Crawford (Washington, D.C.: Naval Historical Center, Department of the Navy, 2003), 721.

A Midshipman of HMS *Phoebe* to the Crew of USS *Essex*, March 10, 1814. *The Naval War of 1812*, Vol. 3, ed. Michael J. Crawford (Washington, D.C.: Naval Historical Center, Department of the Navy, 2003), 722.

David G. Farragut: from Loyall Farragut, *The Life of David Glasgow Farragut, First Admiral of the United States Navy, Embodying His Journal and Letters* (New York: D. Appleton & Co., 1879), 40–45.

Andrew Jackson to John Wood, March 14, 1814. *The Papers of Andrew Jackson*, Vol. 3, ed. Harold D. Moser, David R. Hoth, Sharon MacPherson, and John H. Reinbold (Knoxville: University of Tennessee Press, 1991), 48–49. Copyright © 1991 by University of Tennessee Press/Knoxville.

Andrew Jackson to Rachel Jackson, April 1, 1814. *The Papers of Andrew Jackson*, Vol. 3, ed. Harold D. Moser et al. (Knoxville: University of Tennessee Press, 1991), 54–55. Copyright © 1991 by University of Tennessee Press/Knoxville.

Robert Young to Phineas Riall, March 17, 1814. *The Documentary History of the Campaigns upon the Niagara Frontier*, Vol. 4, ed. E. A. Cruikshank (Welland, Ont.: Lundy's Lane Historical Society, 1899), 239–40.

George McFeely: Diary, March 30, 1814. *The War of 1812 in Person: Fifteen Accounts by United States Army Regulars, Volunteers, and Militiamen*, ed. John C. Fredriksen (Jefferson, N.C.: McFarland & Co., 2010), 29–31, 33. Copyright © 2010 by John C. Fredriksen.

Benjamin F. Browne: from "Papers of an old Dartmoor Prisoner, edited by Nathaniel Hawthorne." *The United States Magazine and Democratic Review*, Vol. 18, Series No. 96 (June 1846), 457–60.

Alexander Cochrane, Proclamation, April 2, 1814. *The Naval War of 1812*, Vol. 3, ed. Michael J. Crawford (Washington, D.C.: Naval Historical Center, Department of the Navy, 2003), 60.

Thomas Jefferson: from a letter to John Adams, July 5, 1814. *The Adams-Jefferson Letters: The Complete Correspondence Between Thomas Jefferson and Abigail and John Adams*, ed. Lester J. Cappon (Chapel Hill: The University of North Carolina Press, 1959), 458–61. Copyright © 1959 by The University of North Carolina Press. Reprinted with permission of the publisher.

Henry, Earl Bathurst to George Prevost, June 3, 1814. J. Mackay Hitsman, *The Incredible War of 1812: A Military History* (Toronto: University of Toronto Press, 1965), 249–51. Updated edition edited by Donald E. Graves, et al. (Montreal: Rubin Brass Studio, Inc., 1999). Copyright © 1999 by Donald E. Graves.

Albert Gallatin to James Monroe, June 13, 1814. *The Writings of Albert Gallatin*, Vol. 1, ed. Henry Adams (Philadelphia: J. B. Lippincott, 1879), 627–29.

Stephen Popham to James Yeo, June 1, 1814. *The Naval War of 1812*, Vol. 3, ed. Michael J. Crawford (Washington, D.C.: Naval Historical Center, Department of the Navy, 2003), 509–10.

N. W. Hibbard to Alvin Hunt, February 10, 1859. N. W. Hibbard, "A Participant's Recollection of the Battle of Big Sandy Creek," *Transactions of the Jefferson County Historical Society* 3 (1895), 29–31.

Jarvis Hanks: Memoir. *Soldiers of 1814: American Enlisted Men's Memoirs of the Niagara Campaign*, ed. Donald E. Graves (Youngstown, N.Y.: Old Fort Niagara Association, 1995), 31–32. Copyright © 1995 by Donald E. Graves.

William E. Horner: from "Surgical Sketches: A Medical Hospital at Buffalo, New York, in the Year 1814," *The Medical Examiner, and Record of Medical Science*, New Series 16, No. 96 (December 1852), 761–64.

Winfield Scott: from *Memoirs of Lieut.-General Scott, LL.D.*, Vol. 1 (New York: Sheldon & Company, 1864), 124–34.

Isaac Chauncey to Jacob Brown, August 10, 1814. *The Naval War of 1812*, Vol. 3, ed. Michael J. Crawford (Washington, D.C.: Naval Historical Center, Department of the Navy, 2003), 584–85.

John Le Couteur: Journal, July 25, 1814. *Merry Hearts Make Light Days: The War of 1812 Journal of Lieutenant John Le Couteur, 104th Foot*, ed. Donald E. Graves (Montreal: Robin Brass Studio, 2012), 174–77. Copyright © 1993, 2012 by Donald E. Graves.

William Dunlop: from "Recollections of the American War," *The Literary Garland*, New Series 5 (August 1847), 352–53.

Shadrach Byfield: from "A Narrative of a Light Company Soldier's Service, in the Forty-first Regiment of Foot, 1807–1814," ed. William Abbatt, *The Magazine of History, with Notes and Queries*, Extra Number 11 (1910), 90–92, 92–93, 93–95.

John Le Couteur: Journal, August 14–15, 1814. *Merry Hearts Make Light Days: The War of 1812 Journal of Lieutenant John Le Couteur, 104th Foot*, ed. Donald E. Graves (Montreal: Robin Brass Studio, 2012), 187–91. Copyright © 1993, 2012 by Donald E. Graves.

Jarvis Hanks: Memoir, August 16, 1814. *Soldiers of 1814: American Enlisted Men's Memoirs of the Niagara Campaign*, ed. Donald E.

Graves (Youngstown, N.Y.: Old Fort Niagara Association, 1995), 39–40. Copyright © 1995 by Donald E. Graves.

Andrew Jackson: Address to the Cherokee and Creek Nations, August 5, 1814. *The Papers of Andrew Jackson*, Vol. 3, ed. Harold D. Moser et al. (Knoxville: University of Tennessee Press, 1991), 103–4. Copyright © 1991 by University of Tennessee Press/ Knoxville.

Big Warrior to Benjamin Hawkins, August 6, 1814. *The Papers of Andrew Jackson*, Vol. 3, ed. Harold D. Moser et al. (Knoxville: University of Tennessee Press, 1991), 106–8. Copyright © 1991 by University of Tennessee Press/Knoxville.

Alexander Cochrane to Commanding Officers of the North American Station, July 18, 1814. *The Naval War of 1812*, Vol. 3, ed. Michael J. Crawford (Washington, D.C.: Naval Historical Center, Department of the Navy, 2003), 140–41.

Robert Rowley to Owsley Rowley, August 10, 1814. "Captain Robert Rowley Helps to Burn Washington, D.C.," ed. Peter Rowley, *Maryland Historical Magazine* 82:3 (Fall 1987), 243–47.

James Scott: from *Recollections of a Naval Life*, Vol. 3 (London: Richard Bentley, 1834), 274–93.

Joshua Barney to William Jones, August 29, 1814. *American State Papers: Military Affairs*, Vol. 1, ed. Walter Lowrie and Matthew St. Clair Clarke (Washington, D.C.: Gales & Seaton, 1832), 579–80.

Dolley Madison to Lucy Payne Washington Todd, August 23, 1814. *The Selected Letters of Dolley Payne Madison*, ed. David B. Mattern and Holly C. Shulman (Charlottesville: University of Virginia Press, 2003), 193–94. Copyright © 2003 by the Rector and Visitors of the University of Virginia.

Paul Jennings: from *A Colored Man's Reminiscences of James Madison* (Brooklyn: George C. Beadle, 1865), 9–13, 14–15.

George R. Gleig: from *The Campaigns of the British Army at Washington and New Orleans, in the Years 1814–1815*, Fourth Edition, Corrected and Revised (London: John Murray, 1836), 118–137.

Mary Stockton Hunter to Susan Stockton Cuthbert, August 30, 1814. "The Burning of Washington, D.C.," *The New-York Historical Society Quarterly Bulletin* 8:3 (October 1924), 80–83.

George R. Gleig: from *The Campaigns of the British Army at Washington and New Orleans, in the Years 1814–1815*, Fourth Edition, Corrected and Revised (London: John Murray, 1836), 140–50, 151–52.

Thomas Boyle: Proclamation. Manuscript I.D. MS1846, War of 1812 Collection (1794–1816), Special Collections Department, Maryland Historical Society, Baltimore. http://www.mdhs.org/digitalimage /proclamation-issued-thomas-boyle.

Philip Reed to Benjamin Chambers, September 3, 1814. *The Naval War of 1812*, Vol. 3, ed. Michael J. Crawford (Washington, D.C.: Naval Historical Center, Department of the Navy, 2003), 235–37.

George Gordon, Lord Byron: "Elegiac Stanzas on the Death of Sir Peter Parker, bart," October 7, 1814. *The Poetical Works of Lord Byron, Complete*, New Edition (London: John Murray, 1867), 183–84.

Isaac Monroe to a Friend in Boston, September 17, 1814. Isaac Monroe, "'Yankee Doodle Played': A Letter from Baltimore, 1814," ed. Scott S. Sheads, *Maryland Historical Magazine* 76:4 (Winter 1981), 380–82.

Francis Scott Key: "Defence of Fort M'Henry." Broadside printed in Baltimore, c. September 17, 1814. Special Collections Department (Broadsides), Maryland Historical Society, Baltimore. http://www.mdhs.org/digitalimage/defence-sic-fort-mhenry.

Roger B. Taney to Charles Howard, March 12, 1856. Samuel Tyler, *Memoir of Roger Brooke Taney, LL.D., Chief Justice of the Supreme Court of the United States* (Baltimore: John Murphy, 1872), 109–19.

William Dunlop: from "Recollections of the American War," *The Literary Garland*, New Series 5:8 (August 1847), 356–58.

Jarvis Hanks: Memoir, September 17, 1814. *Soldiers of 1814: American Enlisted Men's Memoirs of the Niagara Campaign*, ed. Donald E. Graves (Youngstown, N.Y.: Old Fort Niagara Association, 1995), 43, 45. Copyright © 1995 by Donald E. Graves.

Thomas Macdonough to William Jones, September 13, 1814. *The Naval War of 1812*, Vol. 3, ed. Michael J. Crawford (Washington, D.C.: Naval Historical Center, Department of the Navy, 2003), 614–15.

Thomas Jefferson to Samuel H. Smith, September 21, 1814. *Thomas Jefferson: Writings*, ed. Merrill D. Peterson (New York: The Library of America, 1984), 1353–55.

Samuel C. Reid to the *New-York Mercantile Advertiser*, October 4, 1814. *A Collection of Sundry Publications, and Other Documents, in Relation to the Attack Made during the Late War upon the Private Armed Brig "General Armstrong," of New-York, Commanded by S. C. Reid, on the Night of the 26th of September, 1814, at the Island of Fayal, by His Britannic Majesty's ships "Plantagenet" Seventy-Four, "Rota" Frigate, and "Carnation" Sloop of War* (New York: John Gray, 1833), 8–13.

Benjamin F. Browne: from "Papers of an old Dartmoor Prisoner, edited by Nathaniel Hawthorne." *The United States Magazine and Democratic Review*, Vol. 18, Series No. 93 (March 1846), 209–12.

Timothy Pickering to Caleb Strong, October 12, 1814. *Documents Relating to New-England Federalism, 1800–1815*, ed. Henry Adams (Boston: Little, Brown, 1877), 394–98.

Thomas Jefferson to James Madison, October 15, 1814. *The Papers of Thomas Jefferson*, Retirement Series, Vol. 8, ed. J. Jefferson Looney et al. (Princeton: Princeton University Press, 2011), 26–29. Copyright © 2011 by Princeton University Press.

Charles Willing Hare to Harrison Gray Otis, October 1, 1814. Samuel Eliot Morison, *The Life and Letters of Harrison Gray Otis, Federalist, 1765–1848*, Vol. 2 (Boston and New York: Houghton Mifflin, 1913), 176–78.

John C. Sherbrooke to Henry, Earl Bathurst, November 20, 1814. "A Side Light on Federalist Strategy during the War of 1812," ed. J. S. Martell, *The American Historical Review* 43:3 (April 1938), 559–63. Reprinted with permission of Oxford University Press on behalf of The American Historical Association.

The Duke of Wellington to the Earl of Liverpool, November 9, 1814. *Supplementary Despatches, Correspondence and Memoranda of Field Marshal Arthur Duke of Wellington, edited by His Son*, Vol. 9 (London: John Murray, 1862), 424–26.

Daniel Webster: "Speech on the Conscription Bill," December 9, 1814. *The Writings and Speeches of Daniel Webster: National Edition*, Vol. 14 (*Hitherto Uncollected Speeches in Congress and Diplomatic Papers*, Vol. 2), ed. Edward Everett (Boston: Little, Brown, 1903), 55–69.

Treaty of Peace and Amity between His Britannic Majesty and the United States of America, Concluded at Ghent, December 24, 1814. *American State Papers: Foreign Relations*, Vol. 1, ed. Walter Lowrie and Matthew St. Clair Clarke (Washington, D.C.: Gales & Seaton, 1833), 745–48.

Albert Gallatin to James Monroe, December 25, 1814. *The Writings of Albert Gallatin*, Vol. 1, ed. Henry Adams (Philadelphia: J. B. Lippincott, 1879), 645–47.

The Earl of Liverpool to George Canning, December 28, 1814. *Supplementary Despatches, Correspondence and Memoranda of Field Marshal Arthur Duke of Wellington, edited by His Son*, Vol. 9 (London: John Murray, 1862), 513–15.

George R. Gleig: from *The Campaigns of the British Army at Washington and New Orleans, in the Years 1814–1815*, Fourth Edition, Corrected and Revised (London: John Murray, 1836), 252–56, 260–62.

Thomas ap Catesby Jones to Daniel T. Patterson, March 12, 1815. Arsène LaCarrière Latour, *Historical Memoir of the War in West Florida and Louisiana in 1814–15*, translated from the French by H. P. Nugent (Philadelphia: John Conrad & Co., 1816), Appendix xxxiii–xxxvi.

Harrison Gray Otis et al.: Report and Resolutions of the Hartford Convention, January 6, 1815. Theodore Dwight, *History of the*

Hartford Convention, with a Review of the Policies of the United States Government, which Led to the War of 1812 (New York: N. & J. White/Boston: Russell, Odiorne & Co., 1833), 352–79.

Harry Smith: from *The Autobiography of Lieutenant-General Sir Harry Smith*, Vol. 1, ed. G. C. Moore Smith (London: John Murray, 1901), 234–38.

A Kentucky Soldier's Account of the Battle of New Orleans, January 8, 1815. "A Contemporary Account of the Battle of New Orleans by a Soldier in the Ranks," *Louisiana Historical Quarterly* 9:1 (January 1926), 11–15.

Harry Smith: from *The Autobiography of Lieutenant-General Sir Harry Smith*, Vol. 1, ed. G. C. Moore Smith (London: John Murray, 1901), 240–44.

Andrew Jackson to James Monroe, January 13, 1815. *Niles' Weekly Register* 7:24 (February 11, 1815), 373.

Thomas Jefferson to Marquis de Lafayette, February 14, 1815. *Thomas Jefferson: Writings*, ed. Merrill D. Peterson (New York: The Library of America, 1984), 1360–66.

James Madison: Special Message to Congress, February 18, 1815. *James Madison: Writings*, ed. Jack N. Rakove (New York: The Library of America, 1999), 707–9.

National Aegis: "The Peace," February 22, 1815. *National Aegis* (Worcester, Mass.) 14:685 (February 22, 1815), 2.

George Prevost: General Order, April 3, 1815. *The Letters of Veritas, Re-published from the Montreal Herald; Containing a Succinct Narrative of the Military Administration of Sir George Prevost, During His Command in the Candas* (Montreal: W. Gray, 1815), 78–80.

Lewis Peter Clover: from "Reminiscences of a Dartmoor Prisoner," by "L.P.C.," *Knickerbocker Magazine* 23:5 (November 1844), 456–63.

John Quincy Adams to William Eustis, August 31, 1815. http://www.gilderlehrman.org/collections/7aa53954-7786-4046-866f-575423551832. Courtesy of The Gilder Lehrman Institute of American History.

James Madison: Annual Message to Congress, December 5, 1815. *James Madison: Writings*, ed. Jack N. Rakove (New York: The Library of America, 1999), 710–18.

This volume presents the texts of the printings chosen as sources here but does not attempt to reproduce features of their typographic design. The texts are printed without alteration except for the changes previously discussed and for the correction of typographical errors. All ellipses in the texts appeared in the printings chosen as sources.

Spelling, punctuation, and capitalization are often expressive features, and they are not altered, even when inconsistent or irregular. The following is a list of typographical errors corrected, cited by page and line number: 4.9, on obligation; 8.20–21, Constituation; 18.32, remonstrances,; 49.7, restoratien; 82.13, tocall; 86.23–24, *Indepence*; 109.4, bat; 115.8, They They; 116.3, the the; 119.24, "Or; 120.2, "I; 120.4, "Our; 123.8, We; 125.34, roung; 136.34, Michillimackinack,; 153.3, forsincerity; 177.33, procession; 187.33, of even; 202.37, wo,; 236.15, or of; 237.38, pursued; 238.11, the; 247.8, impostible:; 272.21, though; 274.32, Mills,; 341.20, King.; 354.30, Britishers.'; 363.38, Exeelency; 396.23, *Essex.*; 403.1, "It; 407.1, when; 414.23, where he; 447.9, buck shot; 461.34, Convan; 469.22, to by; 481.39; sensens; 486.32, if off; 563.40, their; 570.20, in habitants,; 625.21, now the; 628.32, ere in; 629.20; possessions rights,; 687.16–17, endited.

Notes

In the notes below, the reference numbers denote page and line of this volume (the line count includes headings, but not rule lines). No note is made for material included in the eleventh edition of *Merriam-Webster's Collegiate Dictionary*. Biblical references are keyed to the King James Version. Quotations from Shakespeare are keyed to *The Riverside Shakespeare*, ed. G. Blackmore Evans (Boston: Houghton Mifflin, 1974). For further historical and biographical background, references to other studies, and more detailed maps, see Donald R. Hickey, *The War of 1812: A Forgotten Conflict, Bicentennial Edition* (Urbana: University of Illinois Press, 2012); Hickey, *Don't Give Up the Ship! Myths of the War of 1812* (Urbana: University of Illinois Press, 2006); Alan Taylor, *The Civil War of 1812: American Citizens, British Subjects, Irish Rebels, & Indian Allies* (New York: Alfred A. Knopf, 2010); J. MacKay Hitsman, *The Incredible War of 1812: A Military History* (originally published in 1965, updated edition prepared by Donald E. Graves et al., Montreal: Robin Brass Studio, Inc., 1999); *Encyclopedia of the War of 1812*, edited by David S. Heidler and Jeanne T. Heidler (Annapolis, Md.: Naval Institute Press, 1997); and *The Encyclopedia of the War of 1812: A Political, Social, and Military History* in three volumes, edited by Spencer Tucker et al. (Santa Barbara, Ca.: ABC-CLIO, 2012).

1.22–24   certain Documents . . . Affairs with Great Britain] Accompanying Madison's message was diplomatic correspondence between Secretary of State James Monroe and Augustus John Foster, British minister to the United States, dealing with the charge that Americans had encouraged and assisted British sailors to desert from Royal Navy vessels recently in U.S. ports. Also included were Monroe's exchanges with Jonathan Russell, American chargé d'affaires in Paris, detailing Russell's efforts to prove that France had indeed revoked the Berlin (1806) and Milan (1807) decrees with respect to the U.S., as Napoleon's foreign secretary had suggested it would effective November 1810 if the U.S. upheld its rights against Britain, presumably by re-imposing non-importation against her. (Desperate for leverage, the Madison administration had taken this démarche on faith and on November 2, 1810, issued a proclamation publicizing the alleged repeal and calling on Britain to rescind its Orders-in-Council; on February 2, 1811, to increase the pressure, it reimposed strict non-importation on Britain. But French restrictions on American neutral rights had continued unabated throughout, and the British government gave little credence to the claim that they had ever been lifted.) The *National*

Intelligencer, the Madison administration's organ, published these documents on June 4 and 6, 1812.

2.32   The communication]   Impressment reemerged as a grievance for the U.S. government after war between France and Great Britain resumed in 1803. Beginning in December of that year, Madison, as Thomas Jefferson's secretary of state, had sent a series of letters to James Monroe, then the U.S. minister in London, instructing him to pursue a convention with the British that would outlaw impressments in exchange for provisions prohibiting deserters from the Royal Navy from serving on American ships.

2.38–39   have wantonly . . . blood]   A reference to the *Chesapeake-Leopard* affair of June 22, 1807, when the USS *Chesapeake*, in international waters having just departed from Norfolk, Virginia, was fired upon and four of its crew seized by HMS *Leopard*.

3.20–22   "that particular ports . . . to enter."]   A paraphrase of instructions issued by the British Admiralty in January 1804 relative to the blockade of the French West Indian colonies of Martinique and Guadeloupe, which Madison felt the "paper blockade" of U.S. ports clearly contravened.

3.32   her Enemy]   France.

4.33–36   a correspondence . . . disclaimed.]   In a January 14, 1811, letter to Lord Richard Wellesley, the British foreign secretary, American minister William Pinkney had urged the British government to "take our views and principles from our own mouths; and that neither the Berlin decree, nor any other act of any foreign state, may be made to speak for us what we have not spoken for ourselves."

5.3–4   commerce with an enemy]   A reference to the extensive trade carried on by Britain and France in violation of restrictions imposed on one another, largely through special licenses carried by nominally neutral ships. As Madison suggests, there was a flourishing black market in forged licenses.

5.7–9   every experiment . . . modifications]   Measures designed and implemented by Presidents Jefferson and Madison and their secretary of the treasury, Albert Gallatin: the Non-Importation Act (passed by Congress April 18, 1806), restricting the import of certain British manufactured goods; the Embargo Act (December 22, 1807), barring American ships and goods from leaving port; the Second (January 11, 1808), Third (March 12, 1808), and Fourth (April 25, 1808) Embargo Acts, vastly increasing police powers to enforce the measure against widespread resistance; the Non-Intercourse Act (March 1, 1809), which prohibited all trade with Great Britain and France and their colonies; and the Non-Importation Act (February 2, 1811), which banned all imports from Great Britain.

5.24   this communication]   Madison had instructed Pinkney to convey this "encouragement" in instructions dated February 10, 1809, with the caveat that only Congress had the power to declare war.

6.23–24   There was . . . established.]   On April 19, 1809, a little more than a month after his inauguration, Madison issued a proclamation revoking non-intercourse against Britain after negotiations with British minister David Erskine had led him to believe the British government would reciprocate by revoking the Orders-in-Council. But the British foreign secretary disavowed the so-called Erskine Agreement, and on August 9, 1809, Madison rescinded his proclamation and reimposed non-intercourse against Britain.

6.39–7.2   a secret agent . . . happy union.]   A reference to John Henry, an Irishman who had emigrated to the United States in 1798 and had lived in the Northeast before moving to Montreal in 1805. In 1808–9, he was employed by Sir James Craig, the governor-general of British North America, to travel throughout New England and send reports back on the state of affairs there and on the prospects for Federalist opposition should war break out between the U.S. and Britain. Feeling he was inadequately compensated for this mission, Henry persuaded the Madison administration to buy his secret correspondence for $50,000, the government's entire secret service fund. The President sent the documents to Congress, believing they would expose the treasonous tendencies of the Federalists and increase support for war, but in the end the large sum paid and the lack of any evidence in the letters of actual disloyalty proved embarrassing to the administration and its Republican allies in Congress.

7.4–5   the warfare . . . Savages]   In the decades after the American Revolution, Indian tribes in the Old Northwest were subject to increasing pressure from American settlers moving into the lands beyond the Ohio River. In response to this pressure, beginning in 1805, Tenskwatawa, a Shawnee religious leader also called the Prophet, preached a revival of traditional Indian ways, after 1808 primarily at a village (Prophet's Town) located at the confluence of the Wabash and Tippecanoe Rivers. His brother Tecumseh meanwhile sought to organize various tribes into a kind of confederacy to resist further encroachment on native lands. By 1810, sporadic fighting broke out along the frontier and in November 1811, U.S. troops and militia under William Henry Harrison clashed with Indians near Prophet's Town (the Battle of Tippecanoe). British officials vehemently denied American accusations that they were encouraging Indian resistance from their commercial and military outposts in Canada.

11.27–29   the last War . . . the present one.]   Respectively, the War of the Second Coalition, which began in 1799 and ended with the Treaty of Amiens on March 25, 1802, and the long war between Britain and France that had been ongoing since May 18, 1803, when Britain broke the brief peace by declaring war on France.

11.39–12.1   an attack was made]   The British had long upheld the so-called Rule of 1756, which stipulated that if a belligerent nation's commerce had been closed to another country's trade in peace, that trade could not be opened in wartime. Thus prohibited from carrying trade directly between France and her Caribbean colonies, American traders had attempted to evade the restriction by interrupting the voyage with a layover in an American port, thereby nominally transforming an illegal direct trade into an indirect and legal triangular trade. In the *Essex* decision of May 1805, the British High Court of Admiralty modified the rules defining these "broken voyages," and in July 1805 the British navy began to seize American ships in the Caribbean, the attack to which the report here refers.

13.6–7   That difference . . . accommodated.] In the Treaty of Amity, Commerce, and Navigation, Between His Britannic Majesty and the United States of America, also known as the Jay Treaty, signed on November 19, 1794.

14.4   parts which suffered most] That is, the coastal states most involved in overseas trade.

15.7   the distinguished Statesman] Charles James Fox had been foreign secretary when on May 16, 1806, Great Britain proclaimed a partial blockade of the northern European coast, to be strictly enforced only between the Seine and Ostend Rivers. Beyond those limits, vessels would be intercepted and detained only if they held contraband or were carrying trade directly between enemy ports. James Monroe, American minister to Britain, welcomed this blockade as an attempt by the British government to alleviate the effect on American commerce of the *Essex* decision without specifically repudiating it, and as a measure of conciliation designed to forestall the imposition of the threatened partial nonimportation act (which Congress had already passed although suspending its operation). Fox died four months after his blockade was instituted.

18.17   by a secret mission] See note for 6.39–7.2.

19.22–25   a Minister of France . . . United States.] In 1806 Comte Denis Decrès, the French minister of the marine and the colonies, had given John Armstrong Jr., the American minister to France, reason to believe that U.S. shipping was exempt from the Berlin Decree under the terms of the September 30, 1800, trade compact between the U.S. and France. Though he had also suggested to Armstrong that the matter would ultimately need to be decided by Napoleon, the Jefferson administration eagerly took Decrès's assurance at face value, and on January 7, 1807, the president communicated it as an official declaration to Congress. In October, however, the French emperor announced that no such exemption had ever been contemplated.

20.34–35   the arrangement . . . in 1809] See note for 6.23–24.

23.22   Another *communication* is inclosed] The former president forwarded to the current a letter from Samuel B. Malcolm of Utica, New York, seeking assistance securing an appointment as a federal district judge.

23.28   quids] After the Republicans became ascendant in 1801, gaining control of both the presidency and Congress, fissures began to emerge within the party in the key states of Pennsylvania and New York; dissident factions were called Quids (after *tertium quid*: a "third something," neither Federalist nor regular Republican). John Randolph of Virginia led a somewhat unrelated faction of Quids in Congress in opposition to the dominant wing of the party, whom he accused of governing as crypto-Federalists. Self-styled defenders of the Constitution, the "Old Republicans," as Randolph's Quids were usually called, stood in opposition to any aggrandizement of federal, especially executive, power, and would join Federalists in opposition to the War of 1812.

25.27   Genl. Johnson] Brigadier General Thomas Johnson (1766–1826) of the Sixth Brigade of Tennessee Militia.

25.36   the *Prophet*] See note for 7.4–5.

26.7   the wretches upon the wabash] That is, Tecumseh, Tenskwatawa, and their people.

26.17   2nd Division] In 1811 the Tennessee militia was divided into two divisions. Jackson commanded the more westerly 2nd Division, drawn from frontier settlements near Nashville.

28.13   Post Vincennes] The U.S. Army maintained a small garrison at Fort Knox on the Wabash River at Vincennes, until 1813 the capital of the Territory of Indiana.

30.3   *John Taylor*] Virginian John Taylor (1753–1824), usually called John Taylor of Caroline, was an agriculturalist and sometime politician who wrote influential works articulating orthodox republican theory.

31.7   the President's message] Madison's Third Annual Message, delivered to Congress on November 5, 1811.

32.7   The old establishment] Amid the war scare of 1808, Congress appropriated $4 million for eight new army regiments, bringing the total authorized enlistment to 9,921 officers and men. By 1812 barely half of these ranks had been filled.

32.21   Mr Adams measure] John Adams was president when, in May 1798, escalating tensions between the U.S. and France led the Federalist-controlled Congress to create a "Provisional Army" of 10,000 men. To avoid the problems associated with short-term enlistments, the term of service was expressly linked to the duration of the "existing differences between the United States and the French Republic."

34.3–4   the treaty . . . was rejected] On December 31, 1806, Monroe, the American minister to Great Britain, and U.S. special envoy William Pinkney signed the Monroe-Pinkney Treaty with the British. To Monroe's great frustration, President Jefferson withheld the treaty from the Senate because it did not resolve the matter of impressment and came attached with a note appended by the British government claiming the right to retaliate against French trade restrictions, anything in the treaty notwithstanding.

34.11–12   My letter from Richmond] After returning to the United States in 1807, his pride wounded by the administration's disavowal of his treaty,

Monroe allowed a faction of Republicans to advance him as an alternative to Madison to succeed Jefferson in the presidential election of 1808. Monroe reconciled with Madison in 1810, and on September 10 of that year, in an effort to reestablish himself in the good graces of the party establishment, he wrote a lengthy letter defending his diplomatic record and explaining his challenge to Madison's nomination. While addressed to Taylor, the letter was intended for circulation among party leaders at the December session of the Virginia Assembly in Richmond.

35.11–12   Spain . . . provisions]   Despite French protests, American merchants carried on a lucrative trade supplying American grain to British forces fighting on the Iberian Peninsula under Arthur Wellesley (later the Duke of Wellington). This trade, which continued even after the U.S. declared war, was creatively rationalized by former president Jefferson: "[I]f we could, by starving the English armies, oblige them to withdraw from the peninsular, it would be to send them here; and I think we had better feed them there for pay, than feed and fight them here for nothing." (Letter to James Ronaldson, January 12, 1813.)

38.23   *ignus futuus*]   Ignis fatuus, a false or delusionary hope.

38.26–27   ideot monarch . . . in his name]   By the terms of the Regency Act of February 1811, George III, seventy-three years old and suffering once more from mental illness, was deemed incompetent and his eldest son, George, the Prince of Wales, was named as regent to serve in his stead.

41.30   "straight betwixt two"]   Cf. Philippians 1:23.

43.12–13   contending for the *breeches*]   That is, fighting to see who wears the pants in the family.

44.27   Govr. Wright]   Robert Wright (1752–1826), formerly governor of Maryland, 1806–9, was a member of the Twelfth Congress when he declared in a May 6, 1812, speech that "should the signs of treason and civil war discover themselves in any quarter of the American Empire . . . I have no doubt the evil would soon be radically cured, by hemp and confiscation."

45.24   Mr. Hamilton's]   Paul Hamilton (1762–1816) was secretary of the navy from May 15, 1809, to December 31, 1812.

45.27–28   Governor Barbour]   James Barbour (1775–1842) was governor of Virginia from January 3, 1812, to December 1, 1814.

45.32–33   General Kosciuzko . . . mr Barnes]   Tadeusz Andrzej Bonawentura Kościuszko (1746–1817) was a Polish officer who served in the Continental Army in the Revolutionary War. When he visited America in 1797 he was awarded a large sum from Congress as back pay for his wartime service. The next year, before returning to Europe, he gave Jefferson his power of attorney to manage the investment of this fund in the United States. John Barnes (c. 1728–1826) was Jefferson's financial agent and collector of customs at Georgetown.

47.5   the previous question]   In parliamentary procedure, a motion to end debate. It is better known today as cloture.

49.35–38   "Why quit . . . or caprice?"]   From Washington's Farewell Address, September 19, 1796.

50.32   an expedition]   A reference to William Henry Harrison's march to Prophet's Town. See note for 7.4–5.

56.9–10   Pamphelion's Hotel . . . Stewart's Gardens]   Watering holes in the Fell's Point section of Baltimore.

56.36–37   Edward Johnson . . . judge Scott]   Edward Johnson (1767–1829) was for six terms the mayor of Baltimore (1808–16, 1819–20, 1822–24). Though appalled by the riot, he was reluctant to call out the militia to suppress it. John Scott was a judge of the criminal court in Baltimore County.

58.27   Montgomery]   In the Federal Hill section of Baltimore.

59.24   Mr. Abell]   John S. Abel, a magistrate.

59.36   Brigadier-General Stricker's]   John Stricker (1758–1825) commanded the 3rd (or Baltimore) Brigade of the 3rd Division of the Maryland militia.

60.9   Major Barney]   William Bedford Barney (1781–1838) was a cavalry officer in the Maryland militia, and the son of Commodore Joshua Barney (see p. 502 in this volume). At the time of the riots he was a Republican candidate for the Maryland House of Delegates.

61.40   The Whig]   The *Baltimore Whig*, a daily newspaper published from July 2, 1810, to May 6, 1814.

62.13   col. Sterett]   Lieutenant Colonel Joseph Sterrett (1773–1821) led the 5th Baltimore Regiment of the Maryland militia.

62.15   colonel Harris]   Colonel David Harris (1770–1844) commanded the 1st Artillery Regiment of the Maryland militia.

63.11–12   General Lingan]   James McCubbin Lingan (1751–1812) was an officer in the Maryland line of the Continental Army during the Revolutionary War, much of which he spent on a British prison ship after being captured at Fort Washington on November 16, 1776. After the war he was a senior officer in the Maryland militia. Though he pleaded for mercy during the melee described here, citing his war service, his advanced age, and the needs of his large family, he was stabbed in the chest and died several hours later. Among the others seriously injured were Alexander Hanson (1786–1819), editor of the *Federal Republican*, and Henry "Light-Horse Harry" Lee (1756–1818), a hero of the Revolutionary War, former governor of Virginia and congressman, and the father of Robert E. Lee.

63.15   the immortal saviour of the nation]   General Washington, under whom Lingan served in the Continental Army.

64.3   Mr. Burral]   Charles Burrall (c. 1763–1836), a Federalist, was post-master of Baltimore from 1800 to 1816. During the riots he sent an express to Washington appealing to President Madison for federal protection of the post office. While Madison conceded that the post office was "under the sanction of the U.S.," he doubted that "any defensive measures, were within the Executive sphere." (Letter to John Montgomery, August 13, 1812.)

65.11   the attorney-general of Maryland]   John Montgomery (1764–1828), a Republican, served in the Maryland House of Delegates (1793–98) and in Congress (1807–11) before resigning to become Maryland's attorney general (1811–18).

71.9–10   "He that . . . against it."]   Pickens may be paraphrasing from the *National Intelligencer*, the administration's newspaper, which in its May 14 edition had declared that "he that is not for us must be considered as against us and treated accordingly." Or perhaps he had seen a pamphlet published in Boston in late June entitled *Report of the Committee of the Senate of Massachusetts*, which included a June 26 "Address of the Senate, to the People of the Commonwealth of Massachusetts," by Samuel Dana, president of the Massachusetts Senate, in which Dana asserted that "the rightful authority has decreed. Opposition must cease: He that is not for his country, is against it." Like Pickens's letter, Dana's address was appended to Madison's message and proclamation of war; it also included the report of the House Committee on Foreign Relations. The phrase in question evokes Matthew 12:30.

76.34–35   "*was both . . . to the United States*"]   Channing quotes from James Monroe's February 28, 1808, letter to James Madison, subsequently published with other documents related to the Monroe-Pinkney Treaty as a pamphlet in Washington.

77.28–29   a severe law]   On July 6 Congress voted to prohibit any sea-borne trade with the British Empire, depriving many American merchants of a way to bring home stockpiles then in British ports; an allowance was made for the use of British licenses to trade in non-British ports, like those on the Spanish peninsula.

79.40   the oppressor of mankind.]   Napoleon.

80.20–21   her insulting . . . our government]   A reference to the XYZ Affair of 1798, when agents of French foreign minister Talleyrand solicited a £50,000 (or $220,000) bribe from American envoys as a precondition for any negotiations; the agents also demanded that the Americans agree to loan France $12 million and repudiate critical remarks about French policy made by President Adams. The American commissioners refused to pay, and described their brusque reception in dispatches sent to Secretary of State Timothy Pickering on October 22 and November 8, 1797. Pickering received the coded dispatches from the envoys on March 4, 1798, along with an uncoded letter reporting that the Directory had closed French ports to neutral shipping and made all ships carrying British products subject to capture. After the dispatches were decoded, Adams consulted with his cabinet, which divided over whether to seek a declaration of war. Adams sent a message to Congress on March 19 announcing failure of the peace mission and requesting the adoption of defensive measures. In response to a request from the House of Representatives, Adams submitted the dispatches to Congress on April 3, and they were quickly published, with Talleyrand's agents referred to as X, Y, and Z. Revelation of the XYZ Affair caused popular furor against France in the U.S., helping to bring the two countries into a state of quasi-war, 1798–1801, during which American shipping suffered significantly.

81.9–10   the enemy's provinces.]   Canada.

83.18   civil war]   The Revolutionary War, during which a fifth of the American population remained loyal to the British Crown.

89.1–2   Settled . . . loyalty]   Upwards of 50,000 loyalists fled from the newly independent United States to Britain's Canadian colonies in the period from 1776 to 1785, including approximately 30,000 to the Maritimes and at least 10,000 to Quebec, which in 1791 would be divided into the colonies of Upper Canada and Lower Canada. These refugees were followed by a second wave of roughly 30,000 immigrants from the United States, mostly into Upper Canada, in the period from 1792 to 1812. Often dubbed the "Late Loyalists," these migrants came not for political reasons, but in search of free land and low taxes.

92.18–19   Petite Côte . . . Canard]   In present-day LaSalle, Ontario, located just north of the Canard River, approximately midway between Amherstburg to the south and Windsor to the north along the shorter "little coast" on the Canadian side of the Detroit River.

93.30–31   Major Muir . . . Brownstown]   Captain Adam Charles Muir (1770–1829), a Scotsman, served with the British 41st Regiment of Foot at Amherstburg. He led detachments from the regiment in several forays against American troops and supply lines in the summer and autumn of 1812, including this expedition to Brownstown (near present-day Gibraltar, Michigan), across the Detroit River from Petite Côte.

93.33   River Raisin]   A key position on the American supply line from Ohio, the River Raisin discharges into Lake Erie at present-day Monroe, Michigan, approximately twenty miles southwest of Amherstburg.

94.13   Richardson of Amherstburg]   Possibly a reference to Dr. Robert Richardson, surgeon of the garrison at Fort Amherstburg, but more likely to his fifteen-year-old son John, who was a volunteer with the 41st (see p. 220 in this volume).

94.37   Superintendent Elliott]   Matthew Elliott (c. 1739–1814) was born in Ireland and came to North America in 1761, settling first in Pennsylvania before becoming an Indian trader in the Ohio country. He served as a British Indian agent during the Revolutionary War and in 1796 he was first named superintendent of Indians and Indian affairs for the District of Detroit, only to be dismissed the following year. He was reinstated in 1808, and was instrumental in persuading Indians living in American territory to join the British in the event of war.

95.5   Monguagon]   Or Maguaga, near present-day Trenton, Michigan.

97.8   Colonel Procter]   Colonel Henry Procter (c. 1763–1822) was commander of the 41st Regiment, and the senior British officer at Fort Amherstburg.

97.33   General Procter]   A trick of memory on de Boucherville's part: Procter would become a general the following year.

98.36–37   Colonel Miller . . . strong]   Lieutenant Colonel James Miller (1776–1851) of New Hampshire commanded the 4th U.S. Infantry Regiment. At the Battle of Monguagon his regiment was augmented by Ohio militia, bringing the total strength of American forces engaged to approximately 600. The British and Indian force consisted of about 350 to 400 men.

100.7–8   a certain island]   One of several clustered in the Detroit River off the southern tip of Grosse Ile.

100.25   Sauteau]   Saulteaux Indians.

102.3   *Thomas H. Cushing*]   Massachusetts-born Thomas Humphrey Cushing (1755–1822) served in the Continental Army from 1776 to 1784, rising to the rank of captain. He spent part of the Revolutionary War as a British prisoner. Shortly after war was declared in 1812 he was appointed adjutant general of the U.S. Army.

102.23   Captain Wells]   Born in Pennsylvania and raised in Kentucky, William Wells (c. 1770–1812) had been captured by Miami Indians as a youth and taken to the area along the Eel River (in present-day Indiana), where he was adopted into an Indian family; he later married the daughter of the Miami chief Little Turtle. He fought with the Miamis against U.S. forces in the early 1790s, but by 1795 he had reconnected with his white family and been appointed a captain in the Legion of the United States. He eventually settled at Fort Wayne, acting as U.S. Indian agent and playing an instrumental role in persuading the Miamis not to join Tecumseh's confederacy. His niece, Rebecca, married Nathan Heald at Fort Wayne in 1811.

103.35   Lina T. Helm]   Linai Taliaferro Helm (d. 1838) of Virginia was a lieutenant in the 1st U.S. Infantry Regiment, which he had joined in 1807. His seventeen-year-old wife Margaret, stepdaughter of Indian trader John Kinzie (see note for 146.39), also survived the attack.

103.38   the mouth . . . St. Joseph]   Present-day St. Joseph, Michigan.

104.4   Captain Roberts]   On July 17, 1812, Captain Charles Roberts had led a mixed force of British regulars, French voyageurs, and Indians from Fort

St. Joseph on St. Joseph Island in Lake Huron to Mackinac (Michilimackinac) Island in the strait between Lakes Huron and Michigan, capturing the fort there without a fight.

105.3   *William Eustis*] A surgeon during the Revolutionary War, Massachusetts-born William Eustis (1753–1825) was a two-term congressman (1801–5) before being appointed secretary of war by President Madison in March 1809.

106.9   Governor of Nova Scotia] Lieutenant General John C. Sherbrooke (see p. 594 of this volume). On July 3, 1812, he issued a proclamation that commanded His Majesty's subjects in Nova Scotia and New Brunswick to respect the property and persons of U.S. citizens.

106.12–13   one of the exigencies . . . exists] Article 1, section 8, of the U.S. Constitution ascribes to Congress the power "to provide for calling forth the Militia to execute the Laws of the Union, suppress Insurrections, and repel invasions." Article 2, section 2, states that the "President shall be Commander in Chief of the Army and Navy of the United States, and of the Militia of the several States, when called into the actual Service of the United States."

106.14   the Council] The Massachusetts Governor's Council, an advisory body of nine members.

106.23   Supreme Judicial Court] Of Massachusetts.

106.40–107.1   Eastport . . . at Passamaquoddy] In the District of Maine, then part of Massachusetts.

107.21–22   manner proposed by General Dearborn] In a June 22 letter to Strong, Dearborn had written that the militia companies he requested "are intended for the following ports and harbors, viz: Passamaquoddy, one company of artillery, and four companies of infantry, with a full complement of officers, to be commanded by a major; Marblehead, Salem, Cape Ann, and Newburyport, two companies of artillery and two companies of infantry; Boston, four companies of artillery and eight companies of infantry, with one lieutenant colonel commandant and one major; and eight companies of infantry for the defence of Rhode Island."

110.17   Mr. Higginbotham] David Higginbotham (1775–1853) was a Virginia merchant and one of Jefferson's creditors. He had written to Madison on August 12 regarding a diplomatic appointment.

110.18   Col: Monroe] Secretary of State James Monroe had risen to the rank of lieutenant colonel in the Revolutionary War.

110.20   Mass. & Cont.] Massachusetts and Connecticut.

110.26–27   little attraction . . . volunteer act] Initially the administration planned to rely on short-term volunteers, but the incentives offered to U.S. volunteers in the enabling legislation were paltry: the government paid no bounty but simply allowed men who served at least a month to keep the weapons they had been issued. In addition, the legislation initially gave the states the authority to appoint the volunteer officers, and most were slow to act.

111.18   Tomkins at Niagara]   Daniel D. Tompkins (1774–1825) was governor of New York, 1807–17. He toured the state's fortifications after war was declared and, identifying the frontier along the Niagara River as particularly vulnerable, dispatched state militia there under the command of former New York lieutenant governor Major General Stephen Van Rensselaer.

111.22–23   Genl. D.]   On August 15 Major General Dearborn had written to inform Secretary of War Eustis that he was "pursuing measures with the view of being able to operate with effect against Niagara & Kingston" while simultaneously moving toward Montreal.

112.2–5   a proposal . . . for its object.]   Proposals for truces emanated from Lieutenant Governor Sherbrooke in Halifax and from George Prevost, Governor-General of British North America, in Montreal. The August 17 edition of the Baltimore *American and Commercial Daily Advertiser* picked up a report from the August 10 *Albany Gazette* to the effect that Colonel Edward Baynes, adjutant general of British forces in Lower Canada, had met with Dearborn and Tompkins to report the suspension of the Orders-in-Council, announce that Augustus Foster had been instructed to open negotiations with the U.S., and relay Prevost's suggestion that an armistice be established until further news could be received from London and Washington. An armistice was implemented on August 9, but (because the British made no concessions on impressment) it was repudiated by the Madison administration on August 15.

113.26   Lieut Hanks Doctor Reynolds]   Unaware that war had been declared, Lieutenant Porter Hanks, commander of the small U.S. garrison at Fort Mackinac, was surprised by a British force and forced to surrender the post on July 17. (See note for 104.4.) He was paroled back to the United States (that is, released with a pledge not to fight until "exchanged" for a British prisoner) and confined at Fort Detroit, awaiting a court-martial for his surrender at Mackinac. Dr. James Reynolds, of Zanesville, Ohio, was surgeon's mate in the 3rd Ohio Regiment.

113.27   Colo Cass]   When war was declared New Hampshire native Lewis Cass (1782–1866) was a prominent lawyer in Zanesville, Ohio, as well as the U.S. marshal for the state. He closed his office and resigned his position to accept appointment as colonel of the 3rd Ohio Regiment, one of three volunteer militia regiments from the state dispatched to join William Hull's Army of the Northwest. His regiment crossed from Detroit to Sandwich on July 12, and conducted successful raids on the approaches to Fort Amherstburg in the days following, but fell back for want of specific instructions from Hull.

114.2–4   Colo McArthurs . . . Major Denny]   Duncan McArthur (1772–1839) served in the Ohio legislature from 1804 to 1812 and was a major general in the Ohio militia. In the spring of 1812, his men elected him to command the 1st Ohio Volunteer Regiment as a colonel. Like Colonel Cass, with whom he clashed over seniority, McArthur was not present at Fort Detroit when it was surrendered. Colonel James Findlay (1770–1835), who commanded the 2nd Ohio Regiment, was present, and he was taken prisoner with Hull. Major James Denny of Circleville, Ohio, served in McArthur's regiment.

114.35   marke]   Marquee.

116.4   Mr Atwater]   Reuben Atwater (1768–1831) was secretary of the Michigan Territory and served as its acting governor during Hull's absence, 1811–12.

116.25–31   altho I had heard . . . betray me.]   The British had decided to repatriate the militia, intending to keep only their senior officers—including Lucas—and the regular U.S. Army troops as prisoners.

122.15   'NOT THE LITTLE BELT.']   On May 1, 1811, *Guerrière* had stopped the U.S. brig *Spitfire* off the coast of New Jersey and detained one of its crew. Incensed, Commodore John Rodgers (1772–1838) of the U.S. frigate *President* was keen to find the British ship. On the night of May 16, *President*, sailing off the coast of Virginia, exchanged fire with an unknown warship that turned out to be the British sloop-of-war *Little Belt*, no match for the American frigate; the sloop sustained heavy damage and casualties, with nine dead and twenty-three wounded. Accounts differed as to who hailed first or who fired first in the engagement, which the Americans cheered as retribution for the *Chesapeake-Leopard* Affair (see note for 2.38–39) and the British protested as a dishonorably unequal contest, one, as this slogan suggests, they would not soon forget.

132.34–35   he inherits . . . that hero]   De Witt Clinton was the nephew and protégé of the recently deceased George Clinton (1739–1812), who had been the first governor of the state of New York (1777–95) and vice president under both Jefferson and Madison (1805–12).

137.2   scheme of taxation]   In March 1812, Congress had approved a loan of $11 million to deal with the anticipated costs of war, but only $6.5 million was raised from leery creditors. To meet the shortfall Congress did not turn to internal or direct taxes, which were anathema to the Republican majority, but instead authorized the issue of $5 million in one-year interest-bearing treasury notes and passed significant increases in customs duties: taxes on imported goods were doubled, a 10 percent surcharge was imposed on goods imported in foreign ships, and those ships were subjected to tonnage duties four times greater than before. The customs duties were particularly unpopular in the North, where most of the nation's imports were consumed, and where opposition to the war was greatest.

139.31   the 18 fires]   Louisiana had become the eighteenth state in the Union on April 30, 1812.

140.2   the peace made at St. Louis.]   A treaty between the U.S. and the Great and Little Osage was concluded at St. Louis in August 1809.

143.31   Black Rock]   On the eastern (U.S.) shore of the Niagara River, two miles north of Buffalo and about a mile and a half across the river from the British garrison at Fort Erie.

143.32–33   Doctor Chapin]   Cyrenius Chapin (1769–1838); see p. 366 in this volume.

144.3   Captain Jennings]   Jennings, of the New York militia, had been placed under arrest by Lieutenant Colonel Philetus Swift for withholding pay from his company. He had earlier in the summer achieved some notoriety for producing a mock requisition for ordinance to the governor that went as follows:

> Great Daniel D., we send to thee
> For two great guns and trimmings:
> Send them to hand, or you'll be d____d.
> By order of   Capt. Jennings.

146.1   Mr. Stickney]   Benjamin Franklin Stickney (1775–1857) had become the U.S. Indian agent at Fort Wayne in March.

146.39   Mr. Kinzie]   John Kinzie (1763–1828) was an Indian trader (or factor) and interpreter. See also note for 103.35.

147.10   Mr. S. Johnston]   Stephen Johnston was Benjamin Stickney's clerk.

147.32   the 4th Instant]   The fourth of this month, in this case, September 4.

147.33–34   Winnemac . . . others]   This party of Indian leaders included at least two Potawatomi chiefs: Winamac (d. 1821), who had reportedly fought at the Battle of Tippecanoe, and Five Medals, whose village would be destroyed on September 16.

148.18   Lt. Ostrander]   Philip Ostrander (d. 1813) of the 1st Infantry had been stationed at Fort Wayne since 1807.

148.39   the next day]   September 6.

149.3   "that caution . . . safty"]   From *The Birds* by Aristophanes.

150.10   paries]   Prairies.

150.34   the Miami to Defyance]   Fort Defiance was built in 1794 at the confluence of the Auglaize and Maumee Rivers.

151.7   Lt: Whistler]   John Whistler (c. 1756–1829) was born in Ulster and served in the British army during the Revolutionary War. After the war he and his wife emigrated to the United States, and he joined the 1st Infantry Regiment of the U.S. Army. He had helped construct Fort Dearborn in 1803, and commanded there until 1810, when he was transferred to Fort Wayne. He and his wife were present at Detroit when it was surrendered to the British, and were taken prisoner to Montreal. (He was the grandfather of James Abbot McNeil Whistler, the artist.)

152.22–23   Falstaff's men]   Cf. *1 Henry IV* IV.ii.61–72 and *2 Henry IV* III.ii.

152.27   Mr Brenton]   Lieutenant Colonel Edward Brabazon Brenton (1763–1845), a native of Nova Scotia, was a deputy judge advocate and a member of the Nova Scotia Council before he became Prevost's civil secretary in 1811.

153.17   Mr. Mure]   John Mure (c. 1776–1823) was a Scottish merchant who spent most of his life in Quebec, where he was a civic leader. On January 6, 1812, Prevost made him an honorary member of Lower Canada's Executive Council. He was also an officer in the Quebec militia, in which Cochran was commissioned an ensign.

153.21   Colonel Baby]   François Bâby (1768–1852) was born to the leading family in the western district of Upper Canada. He held numerous political and administrative positions in the colony, and was lieutenant colonel of the 1st Regiment of Kent militia. His suit against the United States for £2450 in damages to his property during the American occupation of Windsor came to naught, but the British administration did offer him £444 in compensation.

154.29   House of Assembly]   Strachan was chaplain of the Upper Canada legislature, which met in York, the provincial capital, and which consisted of an elected Assembly and an appointed Legislative Council.

154.32   worm fever]   A common diagnosis in the early nineteenth century, used to indicate a fever or enteritis during which worms are passed in the feces. According to the findings of Dr. Leopold Anthony Golis of Vienna, as reported in *The Medico-Chirurgical Review and Journal of Medical Science* (New York, 1823), vol. II, p. 471, "worm fever attacks phlegmatic, over-fed, large-bellied, bad-complexioned children, and according to my experience, girls as often as boys."

155.9–10   your province]   John Richardson (c. 1754–1831) lived in Montreal and was a member of the Executive Council for Lower Canada.

155.25   Democrats]   Members of the faction that formed in opposition to the Federalist policies of the Washington administration were variously called Republicans and, especially after 1801, Democrats. The Democratic-Republican Party, as it came to be known, was the forerunner of the Democratic Party.

155.37   Ogdensburgh]   Ogdensburg, New York, on the St. Lawrence River, approximately fifty miles northeast (downriver) from Lake Ontario.

156.14   the American war]   The Revolutionary War.

158.13   the Loyal Sock]   Loyalsock Creek enters the West Branch Susquehanna River approximately eighty miles north of Carlisle, near Williamsport, Pennsylvania.

160.21–22   ultimo]   Last month.

162.1   Gen. Smyth's]   Brigadier General Alexander Smyth of the U.S. Army; see p. 169 of this volume.

162.24–25   Brock & Aid . . . slain]   Both Isaac Brock and his aide-de-camp Lieutenant Colonel John Macdonell (1785–1812) were killed leading charges to regain the American position on the heights at Queenston.

164.34   the Indians of St Regis]   Mohawk Indians living at Akwesasne, where the St. Regis River flows into the St. Lawrence River. The international boundary established by the Treaty of Paris (1783) bisected the tribe's land. Soon after war was declared in 1812, the British constructed a blockhouse on tribal land and stationed French Canadian voyageurs to guard the border. New York militia attacked this fortification on October 22, with the support of some of the tribe's members.

167.23–24   the United States . . . Florida]   In March of 1812, General George Mathews (1739–1812) of Georgia (formerly the state's governor) led an incursion into Spanish East Florida hoping to raise a rebellion among the many Americans ("Patriots") who had been moving into the colony since the 1790s. Resistance from Spanish troops and Seminole Indians soon forced the filibusters to withdraw and their so-called Patriot War was quickly disavowed by the Madison administration, though a small force remained in Spanish territory for a year before finally leaving. After war was declared against Great Britain in June, the president attempted to secure congressional authorization for a preemptive invasion of East Florida, lest Britain use it as a staging area for attack, and Tennessee militia were mustered for duty. Opponents in Congress blocked the action.

170.6   Burlington and Saratoga?]   A reference to Revolutionary War battles at Bennington, Vermont (which Smyth confuses with Burlington, Vermont), and Saratoga, New York. At Saratoga a combined American force of regulars and militia forced the surrender of British general John Burgoyne's army of 5,000 men on October 17, 1777.

170.9   Six Nations]   The Six Nations of the Iroquois: the Mohawk, Oneida, Onondaga, Cayuga, Seneca, and Tuscarora.

170.15   "conquer but to save."]   Quoting a line voiced by Vice Admiral Horatio Nelson in "The Battle of the Baltic," a patriotic poem written by Scottish poet Thomas Campbell (1777–1844) shortly after the British naval victory over a Danish-Norwegian fleet off Copenhagen in April 1801:

> Out spoke the victor then
> As he hail'd them o'er the wave:
> "Ye are brothers! ye are men!
> And we conquer but to save—
> So peace instead of death let us bring:
> But yield, proud foe, thy fleet,
> With the crews, at England's feet,
> And make submission meet
> To our King."

170.19   Montgomery]   On August 28, 1775, an American force of 1,200 men led by General Richard Montgomery (1738–1775) left Fort Ticonderoga and invaded Canada by way of Lake Champlain. Montgomery was killed on December 31 in an assault on the fortress city of Quebec. His body was found by the British and given a decent burial. It was removed to New York City in 1818.

171.24–25   Colonels Allen, Lewis and Scott] Colonel John Allen (1771–1813) led the 1st Regiment of Kentucky Riflemen; Colonels William Lewis (1767–1825) and John Mitchell Scott (1765–1812) commanded respectively the 5th and 1st Regiments of the Kentucky Volunteers.

172.3   Colonel Simrall] James Simrall III (1781–1824) led the 1st Regiment of Kentucky Light Dragoons.

172.4   Wayne's route] In the summer of 1794, Major General Anthony Wayne (1745–1796) led a U.S. force against a confederacy of Indian tribes in the Northwest Territory. The force traveled north from Fort Washington (Cincinnati, Ohio) to the Maumee River, near present-day Toledo, where it achieved victory at the Battle of Fallen Timbers (August 20).

172.21–22   Captain Bland Ballard] Bland Williams Ballard (1761–1853), a veteran of Wayne's army, was an officer in Allen's 1st Rifle Regiment.

172.23   Munday] Harrison Munday (1776–1865), lieutenant of the 2nd Company of the 1st Rifle Regiment.

173.15   Captain Simpson] Captain John Simpson (d. 1813) of the 1st Rifle Regiment was also a veteran of Wayne's army. He had been elected to Congress before this expedition got under way, but would not live to fill his seat.

173.27   General Winchester] A veteran of the Revolutionary War, James Winchester (1752–1826) had offered his services to the government at the start of the war and been commissioned a brigadier general, charged with raising an army of twelve hundred regulars and militia in Kentucky to reinforce Hull's force at Detroit. Hull surrendered before Winchester's army could be fully mustered, and thereafter a controversy ensued over whether he or Harrison would succeed Hull as ranking officer of the Northwestern Army. Kentucky in the meantime appointed Harrison a major general in the militia, forcing the administration's hand on the issue of seniority because it was so dependent on Kentucky troops. A presidential order of September 17 resolved the matter in Harrison's favor.

173.33   General Tupper] Brigadier General Edward W. Tupper (d. 1823) of the 1st Brigade of the Ohio militia was attached to Harrison's army.

174.12   Logan] Spenica Lawbe (c. 1774–1812) was a Shawnee Indian who had been raised in the family of U.S. Army general Benjamin Logan, who had led raids into the Northwest Territory in the 1780s. Lawbe served as a scout for Harrison's army, among whose ranks he was known simply as Captain Logan.

178.18   lynn bark] The bark of the linden tree, which can be peeled in long strips and was often used in the construction of Indian structures.

178.38   General Payne] John Payne (1764–1837), a native of Fairfax County, Virginia, was commissioned brigadier general of the 2nd Brigade of Kentucky militia in August 1812.

179.12   Governor Shelby] Isaac Shelby (1750–1826), who had led American militia to victory at the Battle of King's Mountain (October 7, 1780) during the Revolutionary War, was Kentucky's first governor, 1792–96, and was reelected to that office in August 1812.

181.28   fateauge] Fatigue.

182.20   Simmerals] See note for 172.3.

184.10   Roasting years] Ears of corn.

184.11   gum] A hollowed-out log.

185.17   Pierce] Captain Benoni Pearce led a company of Ohio Volunteer Light Dragoons.

186.2   Captain Butler's] James R. Butler (d. 1842) led a detachment of militia from Alleghany County, Pennsylvania, called the Pittsburg Blues.

189.5   Leutenant Hickman's] David M. Hickman was second lieutenant in Garrard's company, part of the 4th Kentucky Brigade.

189.11   Captain Hopkins] Samuel Goode Hopkins (1784–1834) led a company of the 2nd Regiment of Kentucky Light Dragoons.

189.17   Bourbon Blues] The nickname for Garrard's mounted unit, formed in Bourbon County, Kentucky.

190.3   Dr. E Bayse] Edmund Basye was second in command of Gerard's company.

191.16–17   Boosing] Foraging.

194.8–10   Col. Allen . . . Col. Lewis] See note for 171.24–25.

194.12   Colonel Elliot] See note for 94.37.

196.10–11   Col. Wells . . . Montgomery] Colonel Samuel Wells (1754–1830) commanded the 17th U.S. Infantry Regiment (his brother was William Wells—see note for 102.16); Major Elijah McClanahan (1770–1857) led the 2nd Battalion of John Mitchell Scott's 1st Regiment of Kentucky Volunteers; Captain Nathaniel Gray Smith Hart (1785–1813) had raised a company as part of the Lexington (Ky.) Light Infantry, which were attached to the Northwestern Army; Dr. John Irvine (d. 1813) was senior surgeon of the Northwestern Army, as he had been for Anthony Wayne's army in 1794; Dr. Alexander Montgomery (1750–1813) was surgeon to the 17th Infantry.

196.31   Ensign Harrow] Joseph Harrow, of Captain Samuel L. Williams's company of Colonel William Lewis's 5th Kentucky Volunteers.

197.38   Capt. Price] James C. Price (1779–1813) was captain of the Jessamine Blues, a company of the 5th Regiment raised in Jessamine County, Kentucky.

198.11   Major Madison] George Madison (1763–1816) was major of the 2nd Battalion of the 1st Kentucky Rifle Regiment.

199.8   Major Graves] Benjamin Franklin Graves (1771–1813) commanded the 2nd Battalion of the 5th Kentucky Volunteers.

199.19   Dr. Todd, Dr. Bowers]   John S. Todd (1787–1865) was surgeon to the 5th Kentucky Volunteers; Gustavus Miller Bower (1790–1864) was his surgeon's mate.

201.37   Col. Elliott]   See note for 94.37.

214.22   Captain M'Neile]   Outside the Ontario Government Buildings in Toronto is a plaque with the following inscription:

> Pro Patria. In memory of Captain Neal McNeal, Volunteer Donald Maclean, and the soldiers of the Royal Artillery, 8th Regiment, Royal Newfoundland Regiment, Glengarry Light Infantry, York and Durham Militia, and Indians, killed in action, and their comrades who fought here, facing fearful odds, in defence of the Capital of Upper Canada, 27th April, 1813.

215.10   governor's house]   Major General Sir Roger Hale Sheaffe (1763–1851) succeeded Isaac Brock as lieutenant governor and military commander of Upper Canada.

215.13   the fleet]   The U.S. Lake Ontario squadron under Commodore Isaac Chauncey had set sail from Sackets Harbor, New York, on April 25. It carried Major General Henry Dearborn and a landing party of seventeen hundred men commanded by Brigadier General Zebulon Pike. Chauncey's flagship was the 24-gun sloop *Madison*.

218.15   "meteor flag"]   A nickname for the British Red Ensign, which featured the Union Jack as a canton against a solid red field.

218.23   26 gun frigate]   Construction had begun on the *Sir Isaac Brock* in late 1812.

220.30   the Miami]   The Maumee River.

221.28   General Clay]   Green Clay (1757–1826) was a Kentucky legislator before he obtained a commission as a major general of the Kentucky militia in 1812.

221.39   flying artillerymen]   Soldiers manning horse-drawn guns.

222.14–15   their second in command]   Colonel William Dudley (1766–1813), who led some eight hundred men in the attack on the British battery. Approximately 80 percent of his men were killed or captured.

224.31–32   he had combated . . . with success]   Richardson is here misinformed: Tecumseh had not been present for the Battle of Tippecanoe.

225.9   Major Muir]   See note for 93.30–31.

226.1   Minoumini]   Menominee, a tribe of upper Michigan and Wisconsin.

229.10   Cartouche]   Louis Dominique Garthausen (1693–1721), alias Cartouche, a notorious French bandit.

230.13   William Pitt the little]   More commonly called William Pitt the Younger (1759–1806), prime minister of Great Britain, 1783–1801 and 1804–6.

231.15   France accepted . . . as to us.] See note for 1.22–24.

232.3–4   two nephews of General Washington] Sometime around 1800, John Robinson Grayson (1779–1822) and his twin brother Thomas were impressed from the brig *Polly*, which belonged to Lund Washington, George Washington's cousin. Though related to the Washington family by marriage, the Grayson brothers were not the General's nephews.

233.5   Alexander] Less than two months after war was declared, Count Nikolai Petrovich Rumiantzov, Tsar Alexander's chancellor, had proposed Russian mediation, an offer that when it reached Washington early in 1813 (along with news of Napoleon's Russian debacle) was eagerly seized upon by the Madison administration. Without consulting Congress it announced its acceptance in the *National Intelligencer* on March 9, 1813, and dispatched Albert Gallatin, the secretary of the treasury, and James A. Bayard, Federalist senator from Delaware, to St. Petersburg to join the American minister there, John Quincy Adams, for the negotiations. Only on May 25, after Congress had been called into special session to deal with pressing financial matters, did the president seek Senate confirmation for the commissioners, who were by then already in Europe. Their journey to Russia would be in vain, though, as the British cabinet unanimously rejected the Tsar's offer.

235.25   Two Mile creek] A small river that empties into Lake Ontario two miles west of the Niagara River.

235.34–35   Boyd's division . . . Chandler's.] Massachusetts native John Parker Boyd (1764–1830), who had commanded the 4th U.S. Infantry Regiment at the Battle of Tippecanoe, was promoted to brigadier general in 1812. Maryland attorney William H. Winder (1775–1824) was commissioned a lieutenant colonel in the U.S. Army in the months before war was declared; he was soon dispatched to the Niagara frontier, where in March 1813 he was promoted to brigadier general. Former congressman John Chandler (1762–1841) was a major in the Massachusetts militia in 1812 when he received a commission as a brigadier general in the U.S. Army.

237.36   Prevost Guard] Provost guard, or military police.

238.17   Hindman] Jacob Hindman (1789–1827) of Maryland was a captain of the 2nd U.S. Artillery Regiment.

239.15   Col. Miller] See note for 98.36–37.

240.24   a light bob] A light infantryman.

240.35   funky] According to Francis Grose's *A Classical Dictionary of the Vulgar Tongue* (London, 1785), to funk is "to smoke, figuratively to smoke or stink through fear."

241.14   Major Drummond] William Drummond (d. 1814), nephew of Lieutenant General Gordon Drummond (see note for 378.3), had served for fourteen years in the West Indies before exchanging into the New Brunswick Fencibles, as a major, in 1809. Fencibles were soldiers raised in the Canadian provinces and treated as regular soldiers, with the exception that they could not serve overseas. Shortly after Drummond transferred into the New Brunswick Fencibles, the unit was recommissioned as a regular army regiment, the 104th Foot.

241.16   an ADC]   Possibly Captain Henry Milnes (d. 1813), one of Prevost's aides-de-camp.

241.25–26   like the old French Guards]   At the Battle of Fontenoy (May 11, 1745), a regiment of French royal guards, when confronted on the battlefield by a regiment of English troops, were supposed to have politely declined an English challenge to fire first, and were then put to rout.

241.37–38   we little fellows]   As a rule, the British army recruited small and agile men to serve in the light infantry, and large and imposing men to serve as grenadiers.

242.1   Old Dick]   Captain Richard Leonard (1776–1833), commander of the 104th Foot's grenadiers, had served as an assistant engineer at the British siege of Alexandria, Egypt (1801).

242.5   Sir James Yeo]   James Lucas Yeo (1782–1818) joined the Royal Navy at the age of ten, and as a captain had been awarded a Portuguese knighthood for naval actions against French forces in Guiana, in South America, in 1809. On March 13, 1813, he was commissioned commodore and commander-in-chief on the Great Lakes, charged with "the defence of His Majesty's Provinces of North America."

242.12   Roderick Dhu]   A hard-charging Scottish chieftain from Walter Scott's 1810 epic poem *The Lady of the Lake*, which sold 25,000 copies in just eight months and secured the author's fame.

242.23   Sub.]   Subaltern, or junior officer.

242.25   *Pike*]   A key objective of the British raid was the seizure of a powerful new American warship, the 28-gun frigate *General Pike*, then nearing completion in the Sackets Harbor shipyard. A junior U.S. Navy officer ordered the ship burnt, but it was later repaired and launched.

242.35   my Servant Mills]   Officers in the British army often chose a private to function as a manservant.

243.7   brother Jonathan]   As England was often personified as John Bull, so America was frequently styled "brother Jonathan." Of uncertain origin, "Jonathan" embodied the conventional British stereotype of the Yankee, a figure distinguished by boorish provincialism and crass and cunning commercialism.

243.28   DQMG]   Captain Andrew Gray, of the Nova Scotia Fencibles, was deputy quarter master general under Prevost.

243.31   no *step*]   That is, there were no officers killed, allowing subalterns to "step up" in rank.

244.1 Wm and Miss Robison] William and Ann Ellice Robison were two of the seven children of Captain Thomas and Elizabeth Robison, at whose house in Kingston Le Couteur stayed.

245.21–22 St. John's river] As Americans called the Richelieu, which connected Lake Champlain with "the town of St. Johns," Saint-Jean-sur-Richelieu.

245.24–25 Old Jamaica] Rum.

249.40–250.1 Gen. Chandler . . . Col. Baerstler] Brigadier Generals John Chandler and William Winder stumbled into British lines and were taken prisoner amid the confusion of the Battle of Stoney Creek (June 6, 1813). Colonel Charles G. Boerstler (1778–1817), who had succeeded to command of the 14th U.S. Infantry Regiment when Winder was promoted to brigadier general, surrendered to Lieutenant James Fitzgibbon at the Battle of Beaver Dams (June 24, 1813).

250.21 "Sacra . . . begare."] A roughly phonetic rendering of the French, which might be translated: "In the name of God! In the name of God! Let's fight!"

252.19–20 Capt. Herrick's] When they were captured on the Richelieu, the U.S. ships *Growler* and *Eagle* had a combined complement of 112 men, including their regular navy crews and 34 infantry volunteers from New Hampshire and Maine under Captain Oliver Herrick (1782–1852) of Lewiston, Maine.

252.21 "cob"] To strike, especially on the buttocks, with something flat.

257.32 fought . . . the 12th April] At the Battle of the Saintes, April 9–12, 1782, fought in the Caribbean between the islands of Guadeloupe and Dominica, a British fleet under Admiral Sir George Rodney defeated a French fleet led by the Comte de Grasse. This was the last major naval engagement related to the War of American Independence.

258.33–34 Captain Littlejohn . . . *Berwick*] On March 7, 1795, HMS *Berwick*, fresh off a refitting at Corsica, sailed under Captain Adam Littlejohn to join the British fleet at Leghorn (Livorno, Italy). En route she encountered the French fleet and, after a brief action during which Littlejohn was killed, was forced to surrender.

260.22 St. Johns.] Physician and botanist James Macbride (1784–1817) resided in Pinesville, South Carolina, approximately fifty miles north of Charleston and near St. John's Parish, where Calhoun's wife Floride's family lived.

262.23 FitzGibbon] Irish-born James Fitzgibbon (1780–1863) became a soldier at fifteen and arrived in Quebec in 1802 as a sergeant major in the 49th Regiment of Foot. By 1812 he was a lieutenant, and after the Battle of Stoney Creek (June 6, 1813) he sought and was granted permission to lead "50 chosen men to be employed in advance of the Army, and with authority to act against the Enemy as he pleased and on his own responsibility solely."

263.14   Capt. FitzGibbon] For his actions at Beaver Dams, Fitzgibbon would be appointed captain in the Glengarry Light Infantry Fencibles in October 1813.

266.7–8   "Sago Nitchie."] A corruption of the Ojibway greeting "shaygo niigii," meaning "hello friend!"

267.25   bilious fever] Another common nineteenth-century diagnosis, referring to a severe gastrointestinal infection. Dr. William Buchan's widely consulted *Domestic Medicine, or, A Treatise on the Prevention and Cure of Diseases, by Regimen and Simple Medicines* (London, 1769, with more than a score of subsequent editions) suggests that "when a continual, remitting, or intermitting fever is accompanied with a frequent or copious evacuation of bile, either by vomit or stool, the fever is denominated bilious." Most common in the summer, the fever might be accompanied with "the bloody flux," or dysentery.

267.31   take the bark] Taken in powder form, the bark of the cinchona tree, known in the nineteenth century as Peruvian or Jesuit's bark, was thought effective for fevers. It does contain quinine, which is useful against malarial fevers.

268.5–7   King . . . Gilman] Monroe's roll call of opposition in the Senate includes one Federalist, Rufus King (1755–1827) of New York, and several Democratic Republicans: William Branch Giles (1762–1830) of Virginia, Samuel Smith (1752–1839) of Maryland, Michael Leib (1760–1822) of Pennsylvania, Obadiah German (1766–1842) of New York, and Nicholas Gilman (1755–1814) of New Hampshire.

268.8–9   The two members . . . Bledsoe] Louisiana was represented in the Senate by James Brown (1766–1835) and Eligius Fromentin (c. 1767–1822), both Democratic Republicans. Monroe also singles out four other Republicans opposing the administration's appointments: John Gaillard (1765–1826) of South Carolina, David Stone (1770–1818) of North Carolina, Joseph Anderson (1757–1837) of Tennessee, and Jesse Bledsoe (1776–1836) of Kentucky.

268.35–38   Genl. Dearborn . . . assign'd him.] After the many setbacks of the 1812 campaign, Henry Dearborn had tendered his resignation, but Madison had declined to accept it. In the 1813 campaign, with illness increasingly aggravating his inherent indecisiveness, Dearborn failed to forcefully press advantages gained at York and Fort George, and when news of the capture of the American force at Beaver Dams reached Washington shortly after this letter was written, Republican congressmen forced the administration to remove him from command and reassign him to New York City. Morgan Lewis (1754–1844), who had previously been New York's governor, began the war in the state Senate, before resigning to become quartermaster general of the U.S. Army. By 1813 he was a major general on the Niagara frontier, in temporary command at Fort George. Brigadier General Wade Hampton (1751–1835) of Virginia, a veteran of the Revolutionary War, was placed in charge of coastal fortifications at Norfolk, Virginia, in 1812 before being elevated to major general in 1813 and reassigned to command an army stationed near Plattsburgh, New York. He was later superseded by James Wilkinson (1757–1825), who in 1812 was a brigadier general in command of the Seventh Military District, headquartered in New Orleans, where he had in the spring of 1813 led an invasion of Spanish West Florida. In the early summer he was promoted to major general and placed in command of American forces in New York.

269.2–3   his (the Secys.)]   John Armstrong Jr. (1758–1843), a veteran of the Continental Army and U.S. minister to France from 1804 to 1810, had replaced William Eustis as secretary of war on January 13, 1813, despite opposition from Secretary of State Monroe and Treasury Secretary Gallatin.

270.32   Major Crutchfield's or Captain Cooper's]   Major Stapleton Crutchfield (1775–1818), who led some 450 militia in defense of Hampton, had described the British attack in a June 20 letter to Virginia governor John Barbour. "Captain Cooper of the Cavalry" had written his account in two letters to Lieutenant Governor Charles K. Mallory.

272.37   York]   Yorktown, Virginia, approximately twenty miles northwest of Hampton.

276.24–25   At the foot of the Rapids]   That is, at Fort Meigs.

282.14   captain Hunter's]   James Hunter (d. 1837) of the 17th U.S. Infantry Regiment.

290.7   Davy]   Davy Jones, an evil sea spirit who sought to draw sailors to his "locker," the ocean floor.

292.12   the commodore]   Master commandant Oliver Hazard Perry (1785–1819) was in charge of the U.S. squadron on Lake Erie.

294.26   Do]   Ditto.

295.2   Wm H Allen]   Commissioned a midshipman in the U.S. Navy in 1800, William Henry Allen (1784–1813) had been a member of the crew of the USS *Chesapeake* in 1807 when it was attacked by HMS *Leopard*.

295.6   Lieut Watson]   William H. Watson (d. 1823) had been commissioned a midshipman in 1808, a lieutenant on March 7, 1813.

295.16   ol olivar]   Olive oil.

297.38   cataplas]   Cataplasm, a poultice.

298.34   *San Salvadore*]   HMS *Salvador del Mundo*, formerly a 122-gun ship of the line, was recommissioned as a receiving ship at Plymouth in 1803. Nine members of the *Argus*'s crew, suspected of being British subjects, were being held on her.

299.17   Epigrastric region]   That is, the epigastric, or abdominal, region.

299.31   subsultus tendinum]   A twitching of the tendons, common in fevers.

300.28–29   in a different . . . to avoid him]   Jackson was staying at the Nashville Inn, diagonally across Court-House Square from the City Hotel.

301.5   Col. Coffee]   John Coffee (1772–1833) had raised the 2nd Regiment of Volunteer Mounted Riflemen at the beginning of the war, serving under Jackson's command. He was married to Mary Donelson, niece of Rachel Donelson, Jackson's wife.

301.7–8   Mr. Alexander Donelson]   Major Alexander Donelson was Coffee's aide and brother-in-law.

301.9   Capt. Hammond and Mr. Stokley Hays]   Eli Hammond (1764–1842) of Nashville led a company of Tennessee rangers under Jackson's command. Stockley Donelson Hays (1788–1831) was a nephew of Rachel Donelson Jackson.

301.31   Mr. Searcy]   Bennett Searcy (1765–1818) had been appointed circuit court judge on June 22. An old ally of Jackson's, he had moved with him to Tennessee from North Carolina in 1788.

308.5–6   "Can such things . . . wonder,"]   Cf. *Macbeth* III iv.110–11.

309.25–26   "troubled night" . . . "star of peace"]   Cf. the last stanza of Thomas Campbell's poem "Ye Mariners of England":

> The meteor flag of England
> Shall yet terrific burn;
> Till danger's troubled night depart
> And the star of peace return.
> Then, then, ye ocean-warriors!
> Our song and feast shall flow
> To the fame of your name,
> When the storm has ceased to blow!
> When the fiery fight is heard no more,
> And the storm has ceased to blow.

310.4   Tripolitan war]   Also known as the First Barbary War (1801–5), a conflict between the United States and Tripoli (now in Libya), begun when Americans refused to continue payment of tribute to the piratical rulers (deys) of the North African Barbary states of Algiers, Tunis, Morocco, and Tripoli.

310.21   Commodore Rodgers]   See note for 122.15.

310.24–25   Stoney Town]   Stonington, Connecticut.

311.1   Mr. Hamilton]   See note for 45.24.

311.4   Miss Mason]   Elizabeth Champlin Mason (1791–1858).

312.7   Captain Elliot]   Maryland native Jesse Duncan Elliott (1782–1845) was a career naval officer who had been a lieutenant on the USS *Chesapeake* in 1807 when it was attacked by HMS *Leopard*. Irving here refers to an action on October 9, 1812, when Elliott led an expedition that captured two British warships, HMS *Detroit* (the former USS *Adams* that had been captured when General Hull surrendered Detroit) and HMS *Caledonia*, from under the guns of Fort Erie (not, as Irving suggests, "Fort Malden"—that is, Fort Amherstburg in Malden—at the opposite end of the lake). *Detroit* had to be destroyed, but the USS *Caledonia* became the nucleus of the American squadron on Lake Erie.

313.3–9   Purser M'Grath . . . Lieutenant Smith] Humphrey Magrath was purser on *Niagara*, having been previously in temporary command of *Caledonia* (now under Captain Daniel Turner); he took his own life in 1814. Lieutenant John Packett (d. 1820) of Virginia commanded *Ariel*. Oliver Perry's cousin Samuel Champlin (1789–1870) of South Kingston, Rhode Island, commanded *Scorpion*. Thomas C. Almy (1787–1813), also from Rhode Island, commanded *Somers*. Lieutenant Augustus H. M. Conkling of Virginia commanded *Tigress*. George Senat was acting sailing master aboard *Porcupine*; he was killed in a duel in 1814. South Carolina native Lieutenant Thomas Holdup Stevens (1795–1841) commanded *Trippe*; Irving appears to have confused his name.

313.36   "and the boldest holds his breath;"] Cf. Campbell's poem "The Battle of the Baltic" (see note for 170.15):

> Like leviathans afloat
> Lay their bulwarks on the brine;
> While the sign of battle flew
> On the lofty British line:
> It was ten of April morn by the chime:
> As they drifted on their path
> There was silence deep as death;
> And the boldest held his breath
> For a time.

315.26   Lieutenant Yarnall] John J. Yarnell (b. 1786) of Pennsylvania. He died at sea in 1815, commanding the USS *Epervier*. (See biographical note for James Inderwick.)

316.40   Lieutenant Brooks] John Brooks of Massachusetts. His father, for whom he was named, would become the state's eleventh governor in 1816.

317.8   younger brother] James A. Perry (1801–1822).

317.29   another engagement] The Scottish-born Robert Heriot Barclay (1786–1837) lost his arm leading a boarding party during an attack on a French convoy in November 1809.

319.36–38   "the conduct . . . to immortalize him!"] The exclamation point appears to be Irving's.

320.37–38   "Grand . . . combattant,"] French: "Great talker, poor fighter."

324.13   our father with one arm.]   Barclay.

326.5–6   the Moravian village]   Moraviantown, on the Thames River, in present-day Chatham-Kent, Ontario. Procter expected Rottenburg to send reinforcements from Center Division command in the Niagara region toward the west to meet his retreat, but the cautious Rottenburg instead was looking eastward, toward Kingston, moving his headquarters there in early October.

326.24   the American general]   Harrison.

327.1–2   Lieut. Holmes]   Dublin-born Benjamin Holmes (1794–1865) had been commissioned a lieutenant in the Canadian Light Dragoons on January 30, 1813.

327.6   the Chatham river]   Today known as McGregor Creek, which flows into the Thames at Chatham-Kent.

327.30   Lieut. Bullock]   Richard Bullock (1760–1824) commanded the 41st Regiment's Grenadiers. He remained in Canada after retiring from the army in 1815.

328.38   Lieutenant Hailes]   Harris William Hailes had achieved the rank of lieutenant in the 41st in April 1810. He was later a lieutenant colonel in the Canadian Fencibles in New Brunswick.

330.22   Colonel Johnson]   Congressman Richard Mentor Johnson (1780–1850) raised and led a regiment of Kentucky mounted volunteers. He parlayed his role in Tecumseh's death into a political career that culminated in the vice presidency (1837–1841) under Martin Van Buren.

333.25–26   General McClure]   Irish-born George McClure (1770–1851) was a brigadier general of the New York militia. In September of 1813, he led a brigade of two thousand militiamen to Fort George.

336.28   the Naiad . . . Miss Willson]   Deborah Willson was the proprietor of a tavern near the Table Rock overlooking Niagara Falls.

337.17–18   Chauncey . . . last month]   U.S. commodore Isaac Chauncey had lost perhaps his best chance to confront and defeat Sir James Yeo's squadron on September 28, when he forced the British vessels, including HMS *Wolfe*, into Burlington Bay at the southwestern corner of Lake Ontario but failed to pursue them for fear that high winds would cause him to run aground.

337.34   Col. Touzel]   Lieutenant Colonel Helier Touzel was inspector of militia on Jersey.

338.1–2   DeCarteret]   Lieutenant John Daniel De Carteret of the 96th Regiment of Foot.

339.22   Cumberland-head]   A peninsula in Lake Champlain, opposite Plattsburgh.

339.33   Chazy]   A small village in New York, approximately fourteen miles north of Plattsburgh.

340.2   Odletown]   Present-day Odelltown, Quebec, roughly two miles north of the international boundary.

340.9   Champlain]   A village in New York, roughly a mile south of the border.

340.11   Chateaugay]   A village four miles south of the border and thirty-six miles more or less due west from Chazy. From it, the Châteauguay River flows northward into Canada.

341.20   Colonel King]   William King, of the 15th Infantry Regiment, was Hampton's adjutant.

342.4–5   Major Snelling]   Josiah Snelling (1782–1828), of the 4th Infantry Regiment, had been present at the surrender of Detroit and recently exchanged.

352.11–12   the Capes of Virginia.]   Capes Charles and Henry, which frame the entrance to Chesapeake Bay.

353.34   *avant courier*]   French: literally, a forerunner; in this case, a warning shot.

358.28   Mr. M]   Monroe.

359.20   *au fait*]   French: well informed.

359.32–35   the unprecedented . . . coast.]   At the same time Admiral Warren was placed in command of the unified North American and West Indian stations in August 1812 he was authorized to propose an armistice to Secretary of State Monroe.

360.32–33   Mr Rose . . . Mr. Liston]   George H. Rose (1771–1855) had been dispatched as a special envoy to Washington in November 1807 to deal with the *Chesapeake-Leopard* Affair; when President Jefferson and Secretary of State Madison refused to treat the affair separately from other grievances with Britain, Rose broke off negotiations and returned to England in February 1808. Robert Liston (1742–1836) was the British minister to the U.S. from 1796 to 1800. His position was compromised when two letters to Peter Russell, administrator of Upper Canada, which seemed to confirm Republican suspicions of collusion between the Adams administration and the British government, were made public.

363.30–31   In another . . . expectations]   Major General Wilkinson's expedition against Montreal.

364.27   confidential business]   On December 10, shortly after the second session of the Thirteenth Congress convened, the House went into secret session and after two days of debate passed a new Embargo Act, 85 to 57. The Senate approved the measure 20 to 14, and on December 17 the president signed it into law.

364.30   Judge Todd]   Thomas Todd (1765–1826) of Kentucky was an associate justice of the U.S. Supreme Court from 1807 until his death.

364.32–37   We shall . . . P. Master.]   John Jordan Jr., postmaster at Lexington, Kentucky, since 1802, had died on September 9, 1813. Connecticut Republican Gideon Granger (1767–1822) was U.S. postmaster general from 1802 to 1814. Clay's preferred nominee to succeed Jordan, former Kentucky congressman John Fowler (1755–1840), was appointed to the post on April 1, 1814.

364.38   Davis and Young]   Benjamin Davis and Thomas B. Young were appointed ensigns in the 17th Infantry Regiment (Kentucky), May 14, 1814, then transferred to the 24th Regiment (Tennessee) as third lieutenants.

365.1   Genl. Floyd]   John Floyd (1769–1839) commanded the 1st Brigade of the Georgia militia.

366.32   Four Mile Creek]   A small river that empties into Lake Ontario four miles west of the Niagara River.

366.34   J. C. Spencer]   Lawyer John Canfield Spencer (1788–1855) of Canandaigua, New York, was appointed brigade judge advocate on the Northern frontier in 1813.

367.20   Joseph Wilcox]   In 1800, Dublin-born Joseph Willcocks (1773–1814) had immigrated to Upper Canada, where his cousin, Peter Russell, the province's administrator, helped to establish him as a major landowner at York. Though a member of the provincial assembly and, at the start of the war, its liaison to the Six Nations, in July 1813 he betrayed his country and raised a company of Canadian volunteers (mostly recent immigrants from the United States) to fight on the American side.

368.36   Forty Mile Creek]   Forty miles west of the Niagara River, emptying into Lake Ontario in present-day Grimsby, Ontario.

369.3   Col. Hopkins]   Caleb Hopkins (1770–1818), U.S. collector of customs for the port of Genesee (Rochester), was a colonel in the New York militia.

369.10   the subjoined documents.]   A series of affidavits from New York militiamen substantiating Chapin's claims and testifying that McClure was overheard rejoicing about the burning of Newark, saying that he wished a similar fate upon his opponents in Buffalo, and threatening that he would withdraw troops from the town toward that end unless its citizens arrested "that damned rascal" Chapin.

370.18–19   Captain Leonard]   Nathaniel Leonard (1768–1844) was a veteran soldier in command of the 1st Artillery Company of the 24th Infantry Regiment. His fraternization with British officers prior to the war bred questions about his loyalty. After Fort Niagara was surrendered, George McClure wrote: "His uniform attachment to British men and measures, added to the circumstanc of his not effecting his escape, when in his power, strengthens me in a suspicion that there was a secret understanding with regard to this disgraceful transaction."

370.35   Lewiston]   About seven miles south of Fort Niagara, across the river from Queenston.

371.40   "anxious . . . look behind,"] Cf. "Elegy Written in a Country Churchyard" by the English poet Thomas Gray (1716–1771):

> For who, to dumb Forgetfulness a prey,
>   This pleasing anxious being e'er resigned,
> Left the warm precincts of the cheerful day,
>   Nor cast one longing lingering look behind?

372.39–40   "departed . . . coast,"] Writing as he was during the season of Epiphany, Howe may be making an ironic allusion to Matthew 2:12.

373.1   Grand river] In 1784, British officials set up a large reservation on the Grand River (approximately fifty miles west of the Niagara) for tribes of the Six Nations of the Iroquois that had fought against the Americans during the Revolution.

374.35–375.1   General Wadsworth] William Wadsworth (1765–1833) was a brigadier general in the New York militia, in command of the 7th Brigade, comprising the 18th, 19th, and 20th Regiments of the state's force, hailing from Seneca, Cayuga, and Ontario Counties respectively.

375.25   Manchester, Schlosser] That is Fort Schlossen in Manchester, present day Niagara Falls, New York, approximately fifteen miles north of Black Rock.

376.6–24   Lieut.-Colonel Boughton . . . McMahon's] Seymour Boughton (1772–1813) led New York's 12th Regiment of Calvary; Samuel Blakeslee (1759–1834) led the 20th Regiment of New York (Ontario County) militia; Benajah Mallory (c. 1764–1853) would assume command of the Canadian Volunteers after the death of Joseph Willcocks on September 4, 1814; Connecticut native Parmenio Adams (1776–1832) later represented Genesee County in Congress; Timothy S. Hopkins (1776–1853) of Williamsville (Amherst), New York, was appointed lieutenant colonel in the state militia by Governor Tompkins in 1811, and he served as brigadier general throughout the war; Erastus Granger (1765–1826) was postmaster at Buffalo and U.S. Indian agent to the Senecas; John McMahon (or McMahan) led four companies of self-styled "minutemen" from Chautauqua County.

377.27   General Porter's] Black Rock's leading citizen, Congressman Peter Buell Porter (1773–1844), had been a strong advocate for war in Washington before leaving Congress, where he chaired the House Foreign Relations Committee, to raise and command a brigade of Volunteer New York militia.

378.3   Lieut.-General Drummond] Born in Quebec and educated in England, Gordon Drummond (1772–1854) joined the British army in 1789 and served in the West Indies and Mediterranean before returning to Canada in 1808 as a major general. After a brief stint in Ireland, he was once more in Canada in 1813, as commander of British forces in Upper Canada. William Drummond (see note for 241.14) was his nephew.

378.4   Major General Riall] Phineas Riall (1775–1850) was born in Ireland

and was a career officer, having entered the army in 1794. He had led the forces that raided the American villages along the Niagara.

379.7–8   11 Mile Creek]   Present-day Ellicott Creek; the encampment was likely in what is today Williamsville, New York.

387.17   *Kingston . . . 1814*]   Henry Kent sent this account to his father, John, who was employed at the Royal Hospital in Plymouth. John Kent in turn submitted it to the editors of the *Naval Chronicle* of London, which published it, and the following cover, in the magazine's 33rd volume (January–June 1815):

MR. EDITOR,   *Royal Hospital, Plymouth, 22d October, 1814.*

I DO myself the honour of transmitting to you, an account of the march of my youngest son, Lieutenant Henry Kent, which if you think likely to prove interesting to the readers of the NAVAL CHRONICLE, the insertion of it will oblige, Sir, your humble servant, John Kent.

387.26   Captain Collier]   Commander Edward Collier (1783–1872) had volunteered in January 1813 for service on the Lakes. He was placed in charge of a detachment of 210 officers and men, including men from the sixty-man crew of the 14-gun HMS *Manly*, as well as from the 12-gun brig *Thistle*, and the sloops *Fantome* and *Arab*. Henry Kent and William Russell were his lieutenants.

388.8   as being the senior officer.]   Relative to Lieutenant Russell, that is.

388.24   Presque Isle]   In Maine today, then in territory disputed between the U.S. and Great Britain.

390.1–2   Lake Tamasquata]   Lake Temiscouata, approximately thirty miles east of the St. Lawrence and twenty miles northeast of the present international boundary.

390.15   carioles]   Toboggans, drawn by dogs or horses.

390.16   Riviere de Caps]   At or near present-day Rivière-du-Loup, Quebec.

390.17   Kamaraska]   Kamouraska, on the St. Lawrence, approximately one hundred miles downriver (northeast) from the city of Quebec.

390.18–19   Riviere Oneille]   Rivière Ouelle.

390.37   *Æolus* and *Indian*]   Both ships had been left at Quebec when their crews were dispatched to Kingston to man other vessels. HMS *Aeolus*, 32 guns, had been captained by Stephen Popham (see pp. 435–437 of this volume).

391.11   St. Augustine]   St-Augustin-de-Desmaures.

391.18   Masquinonge]   Maskinongé.

391.20   Pegerrigue]   Repentigny.

391.21   La Chiene]   Lachine.

391.23   Lord Nelson]   A statue to honor the naval hero was erected in Montreal in 1808.

391.30   Long Son]   Long Sault, now called the International Rapids, just south of Cornwall, Ontario.

391.31–32   Chrystian's Farm . . . Wilkin's army]   In October 1813, Major General James Wilkinson embarked from Sackets Harbor with a large army, some 7,300 strong, the western prong (to Wade Hampton's eastern force) in Secretary of War Armstrong's plan for a pincer attack on Montreal. His progress was ponderous, which allowed Lieutenant Colonel Joseph W. Morrison, in command of a force of 1,200 British regulars, Canadian fencibles, and Mohawks, to establish a strong defensive line at Crysler's Farm, where an American force of three thousand under Brigadier General John P. Boyd was defeated on November 11. By that date Wilkinson had learned that Hampton had turned back to Plattsburgh, and used this as an excuse to call off the campaign and establish winter quarters at French Mills (Fort Covington), New York.

391.37–38   Captain Owen]   Commander Charles Cunliffe-Owen (1786–1872).

392.29–30   The result . . . already know.]   For the British attack on Oswego, May 16, 1814, see p. 435 of this volume.

394.37–38   General Byng's . . . Sir John Hope's]   Wellington may be referring to reports he had sent to Bathurst concerning the Battles of Nivelle (November 10, 1813) and the Nive (December 9–13), where Brigadier General John Byng (1772–1860) and Lieutenant General Sir John Hope (1765–1823) figured prominently in the action.

396.33–34   Greenwich hospital]   Established in the 1690s to provide care and pensions for disabled Royal Navy seamen.

399.3   Lieut. Ingraham]   On March 16, 1814, William Ingram, first lieutenant of *Phoebe*, had come aboard *Essex* under a flag of truce. He was mortally wounded on March 28.

400.20   "Paddy in the cat-harpins,"]   Nautical slang for jack-of-all-trades. Often pronounced "cat-harping," a cathaprin is a short rope or iron cramp used to brace in the shrouds toward the masts so as to give a freer sweep to the yards.

404.11–12   Essex Junior . . . Captain Downes]   The British whaler *Atlantic* was captured by *Essex* off the Galapagos Islands on April 29, 1813. She was renamed *Essex Junior* and Lieutenant John Downes (1786–1854) served as her captain.

407.3–4   Brig Genl. Roberts]   Isaac Roberts (1754–1816) led a brigade of Tennessee militia.

410.38   Mrs. Caffery]   Mary Donelson Caffrey, sister of Rachel Jackson.

412.14   the regiment]   Young commanded a detachment of the 8th, or King's, Regiment of Foot, in which he had served since 1790.

414.30   Gen'l Smith's]   Career soldier Thomas Adams Smith (1781–1844) had participated in the Patriot War in Florida as the captain of a rifle company before being transferred north and made a brigadier general in 1813.

414.31–32   General Bissell's] Daniel Bissell (1768–1833) of Connecticut had begun the war as a colonel in the 5th Infantry Regiment but was promoted to brigadier general on March 4, 1814.

414.35   General Macomb's] Detroit-born Alexander Macomb (1782–1841) was an engineer who had served under Wilkinson in the Southwest before the war; in 1812 he transferred to artillery and rose rapidly through the ranks, becoming a brigadier general in January 1814.

417.31–32   Captain Shortland . . . massacre] Thomas George Shortland (1771–1827), Royal Navy, was commandant of Dartmoor when, on April 6, 1815, seven prisoners were killed and thirty-one wounded by prison guards. For an account of the event that became known as the Dartmoor Massacre, see pp. 699–705 of this volume.

418.16   cachot, (or black hole)] A dungeon, usually for solitary confinement.

419.13   the despot of former times] Louis XIV of France, who once declared "L'État, c'est moi": "the state, it is I."

420.13   an ignorant negro] See pp. 577–580 of this volume.

423.7   British oil] A popular elixir of the day, thought to be beneficial for myriad maladies.

423.21   'Peripneumonia notha.'] Compiled by a board of British and American scholars and published in London in 1813, *Pantologia. A New Cyclopædia*, includes the following entry:

> PERIPNEUMONIA NOTHA. Bastard or spurious peripneumony. Practitioners, it would appear, do not all affix this name to the same disease; some affirming it is a rheumatic affection of the respiratory muscles, while others consider it as a mild peripneumony. It is characterized by difficulty of breathing, great oppression at the chest, with obscure pains, cough, and occasionally an expectoration.

424.16   *Vice Admiral of the Red*] Squadron colors were inaugurated during the reign of Elizabeth I when the English fleet was subdivided into three squadrons: the admiral's squadron carried a red flag, the vice admiral's a white, and the rear admiral's a blue. As the Royal Navy grew in size during the seventeenth century and squadrons became too large for one admiral to control effectively, three admirals were assigned to each squadron: a full admiral in command, a vice admiral as his second, and a rear admiral as his third in command. The squadrons were ranked Red, White, and Blue in order of seniority and admirals took rank according to the color of their squadron. Thus Cochrane, as vice admiral of the Red, was more senior than a vice admiral of the White, who would in turn outrank a vice admiral of the Blue.

426.24–25   Mr. Rives] William Cabell Rives (1793–1868) graduated from Jefferson's alma mater, the College of William and Mary, in 1809, and by 1814 was a practicing attorney in Charlottesville. He later served in both the U.S. and Confederate Congresses.

427.11–15   'Leon . . . cacciator.'] Translation from the Italian in Lester J. Cappon, ed., *The Adams-Jefferson Letters: The Complete Correspondence Between Thomas Jefferson and Abigail and John Adams* (Chapel Hill: University of North Carolina Press, 1988), 431:

> The lion stricken to death
> realizes that he is dying,
> and looks at his wounds from which
> he grows ever weaker and weaker.
> Then with his final wrath
> He roars, threatens, and screams,
> which makes the hunter
> tremble at him dying.

427.21   des cinq . . . (an. 8.)] On November 9, 1799, or 18 Brumaire, Year VIII, in the calendar of the French Republic, Napoleon executed a coup d'état by overthrowing the legislative Council of 500 (the Directory) and replacing it with the three-member Consulate, with himself as first consul. Napoleon's famous entrance into the assembly at Saint-Cloud occurred on the following day.

428.2   our right in the fisheries] Off Newfoundland and the Canadian Maritimes. Jefferson here slyly provokes his correspondent, who had been indefatigable in securing British recognition of the traditional rights of New England fishermen during the negotiations of the Treaty of Paris in 1783.

428.21–22   'non tali . . . eget.'] "The time is past/For help like this, for this kind of defending." From the *Aeneid* (Bk. II, ll. 521–22), translation by Robert Fitzgerald.

433.6   Levett Harris] From 1803 to 1816, Levett Harris (c. 1784–c. 1839) of Philadelphia was U.S. chargé d'affaires in Russia. John Warren was in St. Petersburg as ambassador-extraordinary in the early months of Tsar Alexander's reign and Harris's tenure. On July 19, 1813, President Madison appointed Harris secretary to the peace mission dispatched to St. Petersburg.

436.6–9   Lieut. Cox . . . Lieut. McVeagh] Thomas S. Cox was a first lieutenant of the 2nd Battalion of Royal Marines. James Brown (1792–1864) and Patrick M'Veagh were second lieutenants. A co'horn, or coe'horn, is a small bronze mortar mounted on a wooden block with handles, light enough to be carried short distances by two men.

436.24   Captain Spilsbury] Commander Francis Brockell Spilsbury (1784–1830) was captain of HMS *Montreal*. After the war he retired from the Royal Navy and settled in Canada.

436.30   Mr. Hoare] Charles Hoare, late of HMS *Manly*. He was likely among the men who travelled overland to Kingston with Henry Kent.

436.39–437.1   Lieutenants Majoribanks . . . Loveday's]   Acting Lieutenants John Marjoribanks, James Rowe, and Edward Loveday.

437.4   Major Appling]   Georgian Daniel Appling (1787–1817) had participated as a captain in the Patriot War of 1812 before being promoted to major in April 1814 and transferred to Sackets Harbor, where he assumed command of a rifle battalion.

439.5   Lieut. Ridgely]   Charles Goodwin Ridgeley (1784–1848) of Baltimore had served in the First Barbary War. He would be promoted to captain in February 1815, and placed in command of the sloop *Eire*.

439.12   Capt. Harrington]   Brooks Harrington commanded a company of the 55th Regiment of the New York militia.

439.13   Col. Mitchell]   When Commodore Chauncey became aware that the British were targeting Oswego, he asked for support from Major General Brown, who dispatched a battalion of the 3rd U.S. Artillery Regiment, led by Lieutenant Colonel George Edward Mitchell, to secure the post. After mounting a staunch defense, Mitchell and his men retreated up the Oswego River to the falls, where the ordinance for *Superior* was safely sequestered. He then marched his men overland to Sackets Harbor, where he assumed temporary command. He represented Maryland in Congress after the war.

439.14   Captain Harris']   Samuel Devens Harris of Massachusetts raised and led a company of the 2nd Regiment of Light Dragoons.

439.15   Major McIntosh's]   John W. McIntosh of Georgia led a light artillery corps.

440.23–24   Roberts' Corners]   Today a hamlet in Henderson, New York, approximately fifteen miles north of Sandy Creek, more than halfway to Sackets Harbor.

441.7   M. W. Gilbert]   Marianus W. Gilbert of Watertown, New York, sponsored various privateering schemes during the war. He later served as Jefferson County's treasurer.

443.19   This young soldier]   Private William Fairfield.

443.20   Captain Bliss's]   New Hampshire native John Bliss, of the 11th U.S. Infantry Regiment.

444.27   General Scott]   Winfield Scott had been made a brigadier general in March of 1814.

445.21   vastus internus]   Also known as the vastus medialis, the segment of the quadriceps muscle that covers the inner femur.

445.38   saturnine poultice]   A large bandage or wrap treated with "saturnine lotion," a concoction of lead acetate ("salt of Saturn") and water or vinegar. It was commonly used in veterinary medicine as well.

447.11 os parietale] The parietal bone, one of a pair of bones forming the sides of the cranium.

447.12 dura mater] A membrane of the brain.

447.15 tentorium] A tent-like section of dura mater supporting the occipital lobes and covering the cerebellum.

448.23–27 Major T. S. Jesup . . . Thomas Biddle] Thomas Sydney Jesup (1788–1860) had been an adjutant to William Hull and been taken prisoner at Detroit and later exchanged; Henry Leavenworth (1783–1834) of Connecticut and New Hampshire native John McNeil Jr. (1784–1850) had become majors in August 1813; for Samuel Devens Harris see note for 439.14; for Jacob Hindman see note for 238.17; Marylander Nathaniel Towson (1784–1854) led the crew that captured HMS *Caledonia* in October 1812 (see note for 312.7); Philadelphia-born Thomas Biddle (1790–1831) had transferred to the 2nd Artillery in July 1812 and had been wounded during the capture of Fort Erie.

448.31 Marquess of Tweedale] George Hay (1787–1876), formerly an aide-de-camp of Wellington's in Spain, was lieutenant colonel of the 100th Regiment of Foot in 1814. He was also the eighth Marquis of Tweeddale, of the Scottish peerage.

449.1 "Be in their . . . remembered."] Cf. *Henry V* IV.iii.55.

449.17 *tête de pont*] A bridgehead.

450.1 Street's Creek] Also known as Ussher's Creek, approximately a mile and a half south of Chippawa.

450.7 *ponton*] Pontoon.

450.8 McRee and Wood] Major William McRee (1788–1833) was chief engineer of the Northern Army. Eleazer Derby Wood (1783–1814) was his assistant, having previously been chief engineer of the Northwestern Army. Both were among the first graduates of the U.S. Military Academy at West Point (founded March 16, 1802).

450.30 Ripley's brigade] Eleazar Wheelock Ripley (1782–1839), who began the war as lieutenant colonel of the 21st Infantry Regiment, was made a brigadier general in April 1814.

451.20 Bastia and Calvi] Key French forts on the island of Corsica, which Horatio Nelson reduced in the spring and summer of 1794.

452.36 General Moreau] French general Jean Victor Marie Moreau (1763–1813), whose successes as a battlefield commander had made him Napoleon's only military rival, was banished by Bonaparte to the United States in 1804. He lived on an estate in New Jersey until 1813, when he returned to Europe to join the allied campaign against Napoleon and was mortally wounded at the Battle of Dresden (August 27, 1813).

453.18–19   New England States . . . at Hartford] For the Hartford Convention, see pp. 648–665 in this volume.

453.32   Mansfield's life] *The Life and Military Services of Lieut.-General Winfield Scott* by Edward D. Mansfield (New York, 1862).

454.30   General Gaines] Virginian Edmund Pendleton Gaines (1777–1849) had the distinction earlier in his career of having arrested Aaron Burr and served as a witness at his treason trial. He had served in the Northwestern Army as Harrison's adjutant general before transferring to command of Sackets Harbor, as a brigadier general, early in 1814.

455.13–14   thrown out . . . Secretary of War] The following letter appeared in the *National Intelligencer* on August 5, 1814, and was reprinted in the August 13 edition of *Niles' Weekly Register*:

Hon. John Armstrong, secretary of war

Head-quarters, Chippewa, July 25, 1814

DEAR SIR—On the 23d inst. I received a letter by express from general Gaines, advising me, that on the 20th the heavy guns that I had ordered from the harbor, to enable me to operate against forts George and Niagara, were blockaded in that port [Sackets Harbor], together with the rifle regiment that I had ordered up with them [see note for 439.13]. I had ordered these guns and troops in boats, provided the commodore should not deem it prudent or proper to convey them in his fleet, not doubting but that he would have been upon the lake for their protection, and that the enemy would have been driven into port or captured. As gen. Gaines informed me that the commodore was confined to his bed with a fever, and as he did not know when the fleet would sail, or when the guns and forces that I had been expecting would even leave Sackett's Harbor, I have thought it proper to change my position, with a view to other objects. You know how greatly I am disappointed, and therefore I will not dwell upon the painful subject. And you can best perceive, how much has been lost by the delay,—and the command of lake Ontario being with the enemy—reliances being placed upon a different state of things. The Indians all left me some time since.—It is said that they will return, but this you will perceive depends upon circumstances. The reinforcements ordered on from the west have not arrived.

Yours, respectfully and truly,

JACOB BROWN

An anonymous letter to Armstrong dated July 20, 1814, and presumably from army officers at Sackets Harbor, was similarly critical of Chauncey: "There was a fine opportunity of fighting and winning the long wished for battle, but lost because the only man in the fleet who was not ready was the commanding officer." Chauncey's letter to Brown was published in the September 8 edition of the *National Intelligencer*.

457.24   Twelve-Mile Creek]   In the vicinity of Beaver Dams, five miles west of Lundy's Lane.

458.22   Captain Glew]   Joseph Barry Glew (1783–1838), a veteran of the Peninsular War.

458.23   Jonathan]   See note for 243.7.

458.28   Bannaret]   Baronet.

459.13–14   Lt. Colonel Battersby]   Born in Ireland, Francis Battersby (1775–1845) was second in command of the Glengarry Light Fencibles, an infantry regiment.

460.8–9   the son . . . Hull]   Captain Abraham Fuller Hull (b. 1786), of the 9th U.S. Infantry Regiment.

460.28   Poor Moorsom]   Lieutenant Henry Nathaniel Moorsom, of the 104th, was the deputy assistant adjutant general.

460.31   Street's Mills]   More commonly known as Bridgewater Mills, a hamlet on the Niagara River between Chippawa and Lundy's Lane.

461.15   Toronto]   European settlement at Toronto (*Tkaronto*—"where there are trees standing in the water"—in the aboriginal language) dates to the 1720s, when the French built the first fort there. It was called York from 1793 until 1834, when the name reverted and Toronto was incorporated as a city.

461.33–34   Major General Conran]   Henry Conran (c. 1767–1829), who had served in India and Ceylon early in his career, had become a major general on January 1, 1812.

466.20   blind]   That is, blindfold.

469.18   Col. Drummond . . . Coates]   Lieutenant General Drummond gave command of the night attack to his nephew William (see note for 241.14), now in command of the 104th; Le Couter and James Coates (b. 1793) were among his lieutenants.

469.20   Col. Scott]   Colonel Hercules Scott of the 103rd Regiment of Foot.

470.4   Badajoz or St. Sebastian]   Fortresses in Spain that had been reduced, in 1812 and 1813 respectively, by British forces under Wellington. See note for 518.36.

471.14   Captain Shore's]   George Shore (1787–1851) had served in the New Brunswick Fencibles, which was later recommissioned as the 104th Regiment of Foot.

471.39   Belle Vue]   Le Couteur's parents' home in St. Brelade, on the island of Jersey.

472.9–10   a charge of No. 4]   A fine buckshot used to hunt fowl.

472.18–20   Col. M . . . Col. P]   Lieutenant Colonel Christopher Myers (c. 1774–1817) of the 100th Foot and Lieutenant Colonel Thomas Pearson (1781–1847) of the 23rd Foot.

472.28–29   Major Leonard & Maclauchlan]   Possibly Richard Leonard (see note for 242.1); Lieutenant James A. McLauchlan (1796–1865) of the 104th.

479.28–30   There was a . . . Folks son]   As an example of the steadfastness of his people to the principles of the Treaty of New York, Big Warrior points to a May 1803 council at Otciapofa, when representatives of the Creek, Cherokee, Chickasaw, and Choctaw peoples met in order to deal with British filibuster William Augustus Bowles (1763–1805), who was attempting to establish an independent Creek nation under British protection. Folch y Juan (1754–1829), Spanish military commander at Pensacola since 1796, and later governor of West Florida, 1796–1811, had sent his son Estevan to the council to arrest Bowles.

481.11   Washingtons Treaty]   The Treaty of Washington, concluded at the nation's capital on November 14, 1805, completed the cession of Creek lands east of the Ocmulgee River in Georgia begun in the Treaty of New York.

481.28   the little warrior]   In April 1813, Little Warrior, a Weoka chief who had killed Americans along the Ohio River, was arrested and put to death by Creek leaders.

484.34–35   Cockburn . . . Percy]   Rear Admirals George Cockburn (see biographical note), David Milne (1763–1845), Edward Griffith (1767–1832), and Henry Hotham (1777–1833) and Captains Samuel Jackson, Alexander Skene, Samuel Pym, James Nash, Sir Thomas Cochrane (the admiral's nephew), and William Percy.

485.23   Jasseurs]   HMS *Jaseur* (18 guns).

485.28–32   On the 17th. . . . Squadron.]   Cockburn divided his squadron, leaving the smaller draft vessels to guard the Patuxent River, where the American flotilla was bottled up, and mounting a diversionary expedition up the Potomac with his heavier ships. The vessels remaining at the Patuxent included the heavy frigate *Severn*, 40 guns, commanded by Joseph Nourse; HMS *Aetna*, under Richard Kenah, a bomb ship carrying eight 24-pound carronades and two mortars; and HMS *Manly*, which, after her commander and crew left her at Halifax (see note for 387.26), was placed under the command of Vincent Newton and sailed to join the Chesapeake squadron. Cockburn led the Potomac expedition from his flagship HMS *Albion*, a 74-gun ship of the line. With him were HMS *Loire* (44 guns), commanded by Thomas Brown, and HMS *Regulus* (44 guns), Robert Ramsay, captain.

486.3   Hhds.]   Hogsheads, large barrels. Fully packed with tobacco, a typical hogshead could weigh one thousand pounds.

487.29–31   Since which . . . immediately.]   For Sir Peter Parker (1785–1814), see page 539 in this volume. HMS *Hebrus*, a 36-gun frigate, was commanded by Edmund Palmer. The commander-in-chief was Major General Robert Ross (1766–1814), recipient of the Peninsula Gold Cross for his service with Wellington in Spain.

488.7   Col. Malcolm] Lieutenant Colonel James Malcolm (1767–1849) commanded a battalion of Royal Marines assigned to the Chesapeake fleet. His brother Pulteney was a rear admiral on the North American station.

488.23   Nomini] Nomini Hall, the plantation estate of the late Robert Carter III (1728–1804) and family, on an estuary of the Potomac in Westmoreland County, Virginia.

488.26   the Island of St. Georges] Now connected to the northern (Maryland) bank of the Potomac by a causeway.

488.28   Rosinante] The celebrated steed of Don Quixote, in the novel by Cervantes.

490.27   Lower Marlborough] Lower Marlboro, Maryland, on the Patuxent, approximately thirty miles southeast of Washington.

491.2   Nottingham] In present-day Upper Marlboro, approximately six miles upriver from Lower Marlboro.

491.10   Pig Point] Now called Bristol Landing, in Lothian, Maryland.

491.11   Captain Robyns] Cornishman John Robyns (1780–1857) commanded the detachment of Royal Marines aboard Cockburn's flagship. He led a 400-man battalion put ashore at Pig Point.

491.26   General Winder] After being captured at the Battle of Stoney Creek, June 6, 1813, Brigadier General William Winder was held prisoner for several months in Canada before being paroled and returned to duty late in the spring of 1814. Increasingly concerned about British activity in the Chesapeake, President Madison in July ordered Winder south to assume command of the newly created Tenth Military District, established to better coordinate the defense of the presumptive targets of Baltimore and Washington. A native Marylander and nephew of the state's Federalist governor, Winder was chosen less for his military ability than for his potential to enlist his uncle's support in mobilizing the militia.

491.39   1813.] Either a printer's error, or Scott miscopied. This should be 1814, as it appears in the Saturday, August 27, 1814, edition of *Niles' Weekly Register*.

492.2   Scorpion] USS *Scorpion* was a floating battery rigged as a sloop, carrying four guns and a crew of twenty-five men.

492.35   "R. G. Hite"] Major Robert G. Hite of the 12th Infantry Regiment was assistant adjutant general for the Tenth Military District.

492.37–39   "To the Citizens . . . &c.] Scott here quotes the opening line of a public notice from Washington mayor James H. Blake, urging those men exempt from militia duty to organize patrols to guard the city.

493.29   Extract . . . Mr. Pleasants] More accurately a pair of extracts, as the two sentences presented here were not continuous in the original letter addressed to Congressman James Pleasants (1769–1836) of Virginia and reprinted in *Niles' Weekly Register* on November 5, 1814. According to the *Register*, Pleasants had read the letter on the House floor as the body considered a measure to compensate Barney and his men for personal property lost when the flotilla was destroyed.

494.17   Commander-in-chief]   Vice Admiral Cochrane.

494.27   The captain of the fleet]   Rear Admiral Edward Codrington (1770–1851).

496.36   Lieutenant Evans]   Irishman George De Lacey Evans (1787–1870), Ross's quartermaster general, was, like his commander, a veteran of the Peninsula Campaign. He would be a member of Parliament for Westminster from 1833–41 and 1846–65.

497.39   Colonel Thornton]   William Thornton (c. 1779–1840) had been decorated for service leading the 85th Regiment of Foot in the Peninsular campaign. At Bladensburg he commanded a light brigade consisting of the 85th and elements of other regiments. His life ended in suicide.

498.21   Lieutenant-colonel Wood]   William Wood (d. 1870). Like William Thornton, he survived his wounds but was left behind at Bladensburg, committed to the custody of Commodore Barney, who, though himself injured and a prisoner on parole, took personal charge of the British officers' care.

498.36   rockets]   Congreve rockets, still relatively novel weapons that were difficult to target effectively but whose "red glare" could be highly intimidating to green troops.

498.37   Wilkinson's Memoirs]   *Memoirs of My Own Times* by General James Wilkinson, in three volumes (Philadephia, 1816), I, 770–71. Wilkinson had faced a court of inquiry after the failure of his campaign in late 1813, accused of drunkenness and neglect of duty among other infractions but acquitted on all the charges. He never again had a command, however, and was therefore not involved with the planning or implementation of the defense of Washington, which he criticized with relish in his memoir.

498.38   Colonel Brookes's brigade]   In his August 30 report to Lord Bathurst about the Battle of Bladensburg, Ross described the role played by Arthur Brooke (1772–1843): "In support of the Light Brigade I ordered up a Brigade under the Command of Colonel Brooke who with the 44th. Regiment attacked the Enemy's Left, the 4th. Regiment pressing his Right with such effect as to cause him to abandon his Guns:—His First Line giving way was driven on the Second which yielding to the irresistible attack of the Bayonet and the well directed Discharge of Rockets got into confusion and fled leaving the British Masters of the Field."

499.15   Mr. J. McDaniel . . . Tonnant.]   Jeremiah McDaniel, master's mate of HMS *Tonnant*, an 80-gun ship of the line that served as Vice Admiral

Cochrane's flagship during much of the Chesapeake campaign. Once a main-stay of the French fleet, *Tonnant* ("Thundering" in French) had been captured by Horatio Nelson at the Battle of the Nile in 1798.

500.37–38   Dragon . . . Captain Barrie] HMS *Dragon* (74 guns) was commanded by Robert Barrie (1774–1841), who had for much of 1813 served as commodore of the Chesapeake squadron in Cockburn's absence.

501.26   Brannan's Official Letters] *Official Letters of the Military and Naval Officers of the United States, During the War with Great Britain*, collected and arranged by John Brannan (Washington City, 1823).

501.28   An American writer] Scott here tries to make a chorus out of James Wilkinson, from whose memoir he again quotes (I, 783).

502.19   ELK RIDGE] Elkridge, Maryland, is eight miles southwest of Baltimore.

502.23–24   "Old Fields."] Roughly five miles south of Bladensburg, in present-day Forestville.

502.33   Eastern Branch] The Anacostia River.

502.35   Commodore Tingey's] British-born Thomas Tingey (1750–1829) began his career in the Royal Navy but married an American woman during the Revolution and by 1798 was commissioned a captain in the U.S. Navy. In 1800 he was charged with establishing the naval yard at Washington, which he commanded until his death.

503.21   Captain Miller] One hundred twenty U.S. Marines under Samuel Miller of Massachusetts, later the Marine Corps's first adjutant, were attached to Barney's command.

504.35   Captain Wainwright] John Wainwright was captain of Vice Admiral Cochrane's flagship *Tonnant*.

507.4   Col. C] Possibly Colonel Henry Carbery or Carberry (1757–1822) of the 36th U.S. Infantry, to whom Armstrong had given the task of dispensing arms for the defense of the city of Washington.

507.27   Mr. Carroll] Charles Carroll (1767–1823) of Bellevue, a large estate in Georgetown whose mansion, now known as the Dumbarton House, is today the Headquarters of the National Society of The Colonial Dames of America. Jean Pierre Sioussat (1781–1864), doorman at the Executive Mansion, recalled Carroll as "a gentleman intimate in the President's family."

507.33–34   two gentlemen of New York] Robert Gilbert Livingston De Peyster (1795–1873) and financier Jacob Barker (1779–1871), the latter of whom had been instrumental in securing crucial loans to support the government's war effort. Many years after the war controversy developed surrounding the rescue of the Stuart portrait, with Charles Carroll's son publicly claiming the honors for his father. Barker later substantiated the notion that "Several persons assisted in taking down the portrait, and the most active was the venerable Mr. Carroll." On February 11, 1848, Dolley Madison wrote to De Peyster to refute the claim, citing her letter to her sister:

> On the contrary, Mr. Carroll had left me to join Mr. Madison, when I directed my servants in what manner to remove it from the wall, remaining with them until it was done. I saw Mr. Barker and yourself (the two gentlemen alluded to) passing, and accepted your offer to assist me, in any way, by inviting you to help me to preserve this portrait, which you kindly carried, between you, to the humble but safe roof which sheltered it awhile. I acted thus because of my respect for General Washington—not that I felt a desire to gain laurels; but, should there be a merit in remaining an hour in danger of life and liberty to save the likeness of anything, the merit in this case belongs to me.

508.34–35 Richard Rush . . . Mr. Duvall] Richard Rush (1780–1859), son of physician and patriot Benjamin Rush, was Madison's attorney general; either John T. Graham (1774–1820), chief clerk at the state department, or his brother George (1772–1830), who served in the same capacity in the war department; Tench Ringgold (1776–1844) would later serve as U.S. marshal in Washington; Gabriel Duvall (1752–1844) of Maryland was an associate justice of the Supreme Court, having been appointed by Madison in 1811.

509.14 Daniel Carroll] Jennings appears to have confused Charles Carroll with his brother, also a friend of the Madisons. Daniel Carroll's estate, Duddington Place, occupied much of the land that is now the National Mall.

509.16 Mr. Cutts] Former Massachusetts congressman Richard Cutts (1771–1845) was the husband of Anna Payne Cutts (1779–1832), Dolley Madison's sister.

510.7–8 a house] Jennings here suggests that Dolley Madison had been turned away from Wiley's Tavern, in Fairfax County, which she and her husband had selected as their rendezvous site.

510.17–18 the house . . . Taylor] John Tayloe III (1770–1828) of Virginia offered his Washington mansion to the President and First Lady after the destruction of the Executive Mansion. Known as the Octagon House because of its unusual design—by William Thornton, architect of the U.S. Capitol Building—Tayloe's mansion still stands in Washington's Foggy Bottom section, and is the headquarters of the American Architectural Foundation.

510.27 John Susé] See note for 507.27.

511.28 Isis] As the Thames River is called where it flows through Oxford.

518.36 St. Sebastian's] The large French garrison in the northern Spanish port city of San Sebastián was subjected to a lengthy siege by Wellington's army from July 7 to September 8, 1813, when it finally surrendered. In the final stage of the siege, from August 31, British and Portuguese soldiers were within the city itself, which they ransacked, pillaged, and burnt, leaving only a few buildings standing.

523.16   grum]   Surly.

524.35   Jo. Gales]   English-born Joseph Gales Jr. (1786–1860) was the owner and editor of the Washington *National Intelligencer*, the Madison administration's organ. Cockburn made a point of targeting the paper's office.

535.3   *Benjamin Chambers*]   A veteran of the Revolutionary War, Benjamin Chambers (1749–1816) was in charge of all militia forces on Maryland's Eastern Shore.

535.20   Belle Air]   In present-day Fairlee, Maryland, approximately seven miles west of Chestertown.

536.3   capt. Wickes . . . Beck]   Simon Wickes and John Beck.

536.7   major Wickes . . . Chambers]   Joseph Wickes was Reed's second in command, and the brother-in-law of Captain Ezekiel Forman Chambers (1788–1867), who was Brigadier General Benjamin Chambers's son, and later a U.S. senator.

537.6–14   lieutenant Eunick . . . captain Wilson]   Lieutenant Thomas Ennick, Ensign William Skirven, Captain Thomas B. Hynson, Lieutenant Richard Grant, Captain Aquila M. Usselton, Lieutenants John Reed and Morgan Brown, Lieutenant Henry Tilghman, Ensign Richard S. Thomas, Captain Frederick Wilson.

541.3   *a Friend in Boston*]   David Everett, who edited the Boston *Yankee* for publishers Thomas Rowe and Joshua Hooper Jr., had previously been Munroe's partner at the *Boston Patriot*. (See biographical note for Munroe.)

541.31   Chief Justice Nicholson]   Former congressman Joseph H. Nicholson (1770–1817) was chief justice of the sixth judicial district of Maryland (Baltimore) and captain of the company of "gentleman volunteers" that assisted in the defense of Fort McHenry. Francis Scott Key's wife Mary was his sister-in-law.

543.26   Capt. Evans]   Captain Frederick Evans of the U.S Army's 2nd Artillery Regiment was second in command at the fort.

543.28   Fort Covington]   A V-shaped fortification named for Brigadier General Leonard Covington (1768–1813), a Maryland native who was killed at the Battle of Crysler's Farm.

547.3   *Charles Howard*]   Charles Howard (1802–1869) married Elizabeth Key (1803–1897) on November 9, 1825. They had eleven children, including Francis, their first, and McHenry, their eighth.

548.16   Major Peter]   Former U.S. Army officer George Peter (1779–1861), who would later represent Maryland in Congress, filling a vacancy caused by the resignation of Alexander Contee Hanson, the Federalist newspaper publisher who had been attacked in the Baltimore riots of June and July 1812.

549.5   Richard West]   Richard W. West was also Mary Key's brother-in-law, and Francis Scott Key was the West family's attorney.

550.19   his father's on Pipe Creek]   John Ross Key (1754–1821) lived at "Terra Rubra," the family's estate on Big Pipe Creek in Carroll County, Maryland.

555.21   rencontre of videttes]   Encounter of mounted sentries.

556.19   Sir David Dundas]   Major General Sir David Dundas (1735–1820), a veteran of the Seven Years' War and the wars against Revolutionary France, was the author of *Principles of Military Movements, Chiefly Applied to Infantry, Illustrated by Manoeuvres of the Prussian Troops* (London, 1788).

557.18–19   American U. E. Loyalists]   American colonists who fled to Canada during the Revolution were called United Empire Loyalists.

558.1–2   Billy R.]   At the end of February 1814, Lieutenant General Drummond decided to combine the various detached companies of the Incorporated Militia of Upper Canada into a single battalion force, which came under the command of Captain William Robinson of the King's 8th Regiment, who was given the militia rank of lieutenant colonel.

558.39–40   Col. P.]   Lieutenant Colonel Thomas Pearson (cf. note for 472.18–20). At Lundy's Lane, Pearson had commanded the mixed brigade of regulars and militia, which held the right flank of the British position.

561.9   Capt. Hale]   Captain Horace Hale of the 11th U.S. Infantry Regiment.

564.32   letters from . . . Cassin.]   Macdonough's purser on *Saratoga*, George Beale, Jr., appended the following letters to the commodore's report:

> United States Brig Eagle,
> Plattsburgh, Sept. 12, 1814.
>
> SIR,
>
> I am happy to inform you that all my officers and men acted bravely, and did their duty in the battle of yesterday, with the enemy.
>
> I shall have the pleasure of making a more particular representation of the respective merits of my gallant officers, to the Honorable the Secretary of the Navy.
>
> I have the honor to be, Respectfully sir,
>
> Your most obedient servant,
>
> ROBERT HENLEY.

> United States Schooner Ticonderoga,
> Plattsburgh Bay, Sept. 12, 1814.
>
> SIR,
>
> It is with pleasure I state that every officer and man under my command, did their duty yesterday.
>
> Yours respectfully,
>
> STEPHEN CASSIN,
> *Lieutenant-Commandant*

565.3   *Samuel H. Smith*]   In 1800 Samuel Harrison Smith (1772–1845) founded the *National Intelligencer*, a triweekly paper strongly supportive of the Jefferson administration. When he left the paper in 1810—he would later become the president of the Bank of Washington—Joseph Gales Jr. (see note for 524.35) took over.

565.26   Copenhagen]   For three days beginning on September 2, 1807, the Royal Navy had attacked Copenhagen in a preemptive strike to capture or destroy the Danish fleet before it could fall into French hands. The bombardment, which included the use of Congreve rockets, killed more than two thousand civilians and destroyed almost a third of the city.

565.31–33   Van Ghent . . . Thames]   From June 9 to 14, 1667, in the penultimate month of the Second Anglo-Dutch War (1665–67), Vice Admiral Michiel de Ruyter (1607–1676) and Lieutenant Admiral Willem Joseph van Ghent (1626–1672) led a successful naval operation against British defenses at the mouth of the Thames River, and against the Royal Navy Dockyard at Chatham, destroying or capturing many ships but in the end electing not to put the yard itself to the torch.

568.33–35   On the 11th . . . guns.]   Having eluded her British pursuers, *General Armstrong* chased an unknown vessel for nine hours, ultimately discovering it to be another American privateer, *Perry*, John Colman captain, which had thrown its guns overboard in an attempt to gain speed.

572.11   Captain Lloyd]   After the American privateer was scuttled and its crew transferred to shore, Robert Lloyd, captain of HMS *Plantagenet*, wrote a forceful letter to the governor of Fayal insisting that he facilitate the return of two members of the crew Lloyd believed to be British deserters.

573.13   Mr. Dabney]   A merchant and wine importer drawn to the Azores for business, John Bass Dabney (1766–1826) was the first U.S. consul to the Azores, serving from 1806 until his death.

574.13   viva voce]   Latin: with the living voice; orally.

574.29–30   "he has a . . . multitude."]   Cf. *2 Henry IV* I.iii.89–90.

576.1   "potent . . . seignors,"]   Cf. *Othello* I.iii.76.

579.7–8   "taking an enemy . . . their brains,"]   Cf. *Othello* II.iii.290–91.

579.9   cent. per cent.]   One hundred percent.

580.19–20   'What in the captain's . . . rank blasphemy.']   Cf. *Measure for Measure* II.ii.130–31.

582.19   now the President . . . point]   In cabinet meetings of June 23, 24, and 27, 1814, the Madison administration decided to drop impressment as a point of contention in the peace talks. The news reached the American commissioners in Ghent—who were already contemplating abandoning the issue on their own initiative—just as the talks were getting under way.

582.28–30   the just and humane . . . of Washington]   Policies Pickering had played a prominent role in implementing. See his biographical note in this volume.

585.30   her territories]   Until 1820, Maine was a part of Massachusetts.

587.35–588.1   meridian . . . Northwardly]   Jefferson sarcastically proposes the Richelieu River, which forms a more or less straight north-south line from Lake Champlain to Sorel-Tracy, Quebec, where it flows into the St. Lawrence. Such a boundary would require the British to forfeit all the Great Lakes and Montreal.

588.11–12   or you have misapprehended.]   In his October 10 letter to Jefferson, Madison had written as follows:

> It seems clear, according to your reasoning . . . that a circulating medium, to take the place of a bank or metallic medium, may be created by law and made to answer the purpose of a loan, or rather anticipation of a tax; but as the resource can not be extended beyond the amount of a *sufficient* medium, and of course can not be *continued* but by successive re-emissions & redemption by taxes, resort must eventually be had to loans, of the usual sort, or an augmentation of taxes, according to the public exigencies: I say augmentation of taxes, because these absorbing a larger sum into circulation, will admit an enlargement of the medium employed for the purpose.

589.7   p.c.]   Percent.

589.30–31   which is perfectly sound]   On November 9, less than a month after Jefferson wrote this letter, the Treasury defaulted on quarterly interest payments due to bondholders in Boston.

592.7   Campbells Reports]   Formerly a War Hawk in the Senate, George Washington Campbell (1769–1848) became the secretary of the treasury in February 1814. On September 30, 1814, he issued a report providing an audit of the U.S. government's finances for the nine months ending June 30, 1814. It was published as a pamphlet in Washington soon thereafter.

592.20   resignation]   Of Madison, that is.

593.36   Harry]   Harrison Gray Otis Jr. (1792–1827).

594.31   A Gentleman]   This appears to have been Castine merchant Thomas Adams, who represented the Penobscot region in the Massachusetts legislature. His claim to have been sent on his mission by Governor Strong cannot be verified.

594.35–595.1   M Genl. Gosselin]   Gerald Gosselin (1769–1859), who had become a major general in June 1813, was in command of British operations at Castine after Sherbrooke's return to Halifax.

595.5   Admiral Griffith]   Edward Griffith (1767–1832) had risen to the rank of rear admiral in August 1812 as commander of the Royal Navy's North Sea fleet. In 1813 he was transferred to Halifax to oversee the construction and repair of the fleet there, and in the fall of 1814 he was in command of British naval forces in Maine.

595.10–11   Executive of Massachusetts]   Governor Caleb Strong.

598.11–12   resolve . . . of Massachusetts]   On October 16, 1814, the Massachusetts legislature promulgated the following:

> Resolved, that twelve persons be appointed as delegates from this Commonwealth, to meet and confer with delegates from the other New-England states, or any other, upon the subject of their public grievances and concerns; and upon the best means of preserving our resources; and of defence against the enemy; and to devise and suggest for adoption by those respective states such measures as they may deem expedient; and also to take measures, if they shall think it proper, for procuring a convention of delegates from all the United States, in order to revise the Constitution thereof, and more effectually to secure the support and attachment of all the people, by placing all upon the basis of fair representation.

600.5   those Colonies on the Continent]   That is, the provinces of British North America.

600.29   the order of the Admiral]   The May 14, 1814, edition of *Niles' Weekly Register* included the text of an April 25, 1814, proclamation by Admiral Cochrane that announced the extension of a "strict and rigorous" British blockade to the New England coast.

602.25   Duc d'Orléans . . . Blacas]   Louis Philippe III, the Duke of Orléans (1773–1850), was the head of a cadet branch of the Bourbon family. He would later reign as the King of the French from 1830 to 1848. Pierre Louis Jean Casimir de Blacas (1771–1839) was minister de la Maison du Roi (minister in charge of the royal household) under Louis XVIII, functioning as the restored king's prime minister.

603.14–15   you persist . . . from hence]   Both Liverpool and Bathurst had written to Wellington on November 4 expressing concern for his safety and urging him to find a pretext for removing himself from Paris.

603.27–28   the troops . . . last summer]   By September some 13,000 veterans of Wellington's army and other British forces on the Continent had been redeployed to America, including a large force under Major General Robert Ross that sailed in June from Bordeaux to the Chesapeake by way of Bermuda.

603.39–40   what the Americans . . . to be]   During the War of 1812, officials in London often received their first intelligence of battles and movements from American newspapers.

604.1   Fort Moreau]   The central and largest of three forts built on a line just south of Plattsburgh, between the Saranac River and Lake Champlain.

607.5   Mr. Ingersoll]   Charles Jared Ingersoll (1782–1862) was chairman of the House Judiciary Committee.

607.20–21   in the particular . . . provides]   See note for 106.12–13.

611.5   says a profound writer]   Edmund Burke, in his *Reflections on the Revolution in France*, published in 1790.

611.33   Mr. Gaston]   Federalist William Gaston (1778–1844) was formerly speaker of the North Carolina legislature.

611.34   Assignats of France.]   Inflationary paper currency issued by the French Revolutionary government (1789–96), largely on the security of appropriated church lands.

613.36   his last letter of instructions]   In his April 15, 1813, instructions to Albert Gallatin, John Quincy Adams, and James A. Bayard, Secretary of State Monroe had offered a lengthy dissertation on impressment. To the notion, advanced by the Prince Regent, that in seizing British seamen from American vessels Great Britain was acting on a principle that applied to the United States as well—that, in other words, if U.S. vessels stopped and searched British ships for American citizens, the Crown would respect their right to do so—Monroe responded pointedly:

> The semblance of equality, however, in this proposition, which strikes at first view, disappears on a fair examination. It is unfair, first, because it is impossible for the United States to take advantage of it. Impressment is not an American practice, but utterly repugnant to our constitution and laws. In offering to reciprocate it, nothing was offered, as the British government well knew.

618.38–40   "the doctrine . . . of mankind."]   Article 10 of the New Hampshire Bill of Rights, adopted on June 2, 1784.

619.19   the fabled serpents' teeth]   From the Greek legends of Cadmus and Jason.

623.40   Nova Scotia]   At the time of the signing of the Treaty of Paris in 1783, the Canadian territory bordering the province of Maine was part of Nova Scotia. The province of New Brunswick was created out of western Nova Scotia the following year, an administrative response to the influx of American Loyalists who settled along the western shore of the Bay of Fundy.

624.22   St. Andrew's]   A fishing village at the tip of a peninsula where the St. Croix River discharges into Passamaquoddy Bay.

625.32   river . . . Cataraguy]   The Châteauguay River.

629.7   restore to such . . . nations]   Article 9 might have been interpreted as invalidating the treaty that Andrew Jackson had imposed on the Creeks on August 9, 1814, but Jackson and his supporters argued that as the Creeks had been pacified at Fort Jackson and were therefore not at war with the United States at the time of ratification, they were not subject to the article's terms. This became the official U.S. position, and the British did not contest it.

632.17 the Algerines] The United States continued at loggerheads with the Dey of Algiers, who sought tribute for safe passage along the North African coast of the Mediterranean Sea. The U.S. would declare war on Algiers on March 3, 1815, initiating the Second Barbary War. (See note for 310.4.)

632.23 the article . . . Utrecht] Article 15 of the Peace and Friendship Treaty of Utrecht between France and Great Britain, signed on April 11, 1713, reads as follows:

> The subjects of France inhabiting Canada, and others, shall hereafter give no hinderance or molestation to the five nations or cantons of Indians, subject to the dominion of Great Britain, nor to the other natives of America, who are friends to the same. In like manner, the subjects of Great Britain shall behave themselves peaceably towards the Americans who are subjects or friends to France; and on both sides they shall enjoy full liberty of going and coming on account of trade. As also the natives of those countries shall, with the same liberty, resort, as they please, to the British and French colonies, for promoting trade on one side and the other, without any molestation or hinderance, either on the part of the British subjects or of the French. But it is to be exactly and distinctly settled by commissaries, who are, and who ought to be accounted the subjects and friends of Britain or of France.

632.24 our treaty with Spain] Signed on October 27, 1795, the Treaty of Friendship, Limits, and Navigation Between Spain and the United States—also known as the Treaty of San Lorenzo or, in America, as Pinckney's Treaty—established the border between the United States and the Spanish colonies and guaranteed U.S. navigation rights on the Mississippi. In the first section of Article 5, which deals with the Indian nations along the southern borderlands, each of the "two High contracting Parties" pledges not to allow Indians within their territory to attack the citizens or subjects of the other. The second part, to which Gallatin here refers, reads as follows:

> And whereas several treaties of Friendship exist between the two contracting Parties and the said Nations of Indians, it is hereby agreed that in future no treaty of alliance or other whatever (except treaties of Peace) shall be made by either Party with the Indians living within the boundary of the other; but both Parties will endeavour to make the advantages of the Indian trade common and mutualy beneficial to their respective Subjects and Citizens observing in all things the most complete reciprocity: so that both Parties may obtain the advantages arising from a good understanding with the said Nations, without being subject to the expence which they have hitherto occasioned.

632.28 Moose Island] In Passamaquoddy Bay, site of the town of Eastport.

633.2 construction of . . . 1783] It was customary for belligerent nations in Europe to regard past treaties as nullified by present conflicts, and the British negotiators argued that the U.S. declaration of war in 1812 nullified the Treaty of 1783. But the Americans countered that because the Treaty of

Paris constituted British recognition of the independent sovereignty of the United States, it was qualitatively different from other international accords, and therefore could not be abrogated.

636.22   excluded . . . six months]   That is, when winter made transatlantic voyages difficult and passage of the St. Lawrence frequently impossible.

637.8   Bristol and Liverpool]   Much of the domestic opposition to the ministry's policies with regard to America—first the Orders-in-Council, and then the war itself—had come from commercial lobbies in Bristol and Liverpool, coastal cities that were centers of the lucrative transatlantic trade and disproportionately underrepresented in Parliament.

637.11   your friend Gladstone]   John Gladstone (1764–1851) had made a fortune as a partner in a Liverpool mercantile firm that traded in both the East and West Indies and by 1812 established himself as a regional power broker. He was a great admirer of Canning and managed the campaign to elect him to Parliament for Liverpool. (He was the father of William Gladstone, the prime minister.)

637.12   The negotiations at Vienna . . .]   For details on matters raised on this and the next page, see Harold Nicholson, *The Congress of Vienna: A Study in Allied Unity, 1812–1822* (1946, reprint 2001).

641.1   the St. Pierre]   Known today as the Minnesota River.

641.2   the Moingona]   The Des Moines River.

641.26–31   Yazous . . . Rouge . . . Noir]   The Yazoo, Red, and Black Rivers.

645.1   Malhereux islands]   At the eastern end, or "mouth," of Lake Borgne.

645.4   Petite Coquilles]   A U.S. fort on the narrow strip of land separating Lake Borgne and Lake Pontchartrain.

645.15   Nos. 156, 162, and 163]   The Navy's unglamorous gunboats were not afforded names. The two schooners under Jones's direction were *Sea Horse* and *Alligator*, one gun apiece.

645.30   Mr. Johnson]   Sailing Master William Johnson, U.S. Navy, commanded *Seahorse*'s fourteen-man crew.

657.18–19   the apportionment . . . states]   A reference to Article I, section 2, clause 3 of the U.S. Constitution, the so-called three-fifths clause:

Representatives and direct Taxes shall be apportioned among the several States which may be included within this Union, according to their respective Numbers, which shall be determined by adding to the whole Number of free Persons, including those bound to Service for a Term of Years, and excluding Indians not taxed, three fifths of all other Persons.

667.12   Colonel Thornton]   The 85th Regiment of Foot, led by William Thornton (see note for 497.39), was charged with mounting the assault on the American position on the western bank of the Mississippi.

667.20   Colonel Renny]   Robert Renny, of the 21st Regiment of Royal Fusiliers, was brevetted a lieutenant colonel just before the assault on Jackson's defenses commenced.

667.24   General Gibbs's]   Major General Samuel Gibbs (1771–1815) was Pakenham's second in command.

668.18   Toulouse]   On April 10, 1814, Wellington's forces engaged in a costly battle for the city of Toulouse that marked the end of his long campaign in the Iberian Peninsula and southern France. He entered the city on the morning of April 12, and that afternoon was greeted with the news of Napoleon's abdication.

668.24   Tylden]   Lieutenant Colonel Sir John Maxwell Tylden (1787–1866) of the 43rd Regiment was an acting assistant adjutant general on January 8.

669.7   Buenos Ayres]   In 1806 and 1807, Great Britain attempted to seize the Spanish colonies on the Río de la Plata. British forces twice targeted Buenos Aires: occupying it for a little more than a month in 1806 before being expelled, then mounting a second failed assault in July 1807 that resulted in 311 killed, 679 wounded, and 1808 captured or missing.

670.13   Col Smiley]   Thirty-five-year-old James S. Smiley was later promoted to major of the militia in Nelson County, Kentucky.

670.15–16   brass pieces]   Light artillery.

670.20   Capt. Patterson]   Robert Patterson had assumed command of a company of Kentucky militia on November 20, 1814.

671.2   Henry Spillman]   Henry Spillman was a private in Captain John Farmer's company of Kentucky militia.

671.6   Lieut. Ashby]   Willoughby Ashby, also of Farmer's company.

671.16   Ambrose Odd]   Private Ambrose Audd, of Captain Leonard P. Higdon's company.

671.20–21   Col. Slaughter]   Former Kentucky lieutenant governor Gabriel Slaughter (1767–1830) had raised a company in Mercer County in response to Governor Shelby's call for volunteers to serve in Jackson's army in New Orleans. He was later Kentucky's seventh governor, 1816–20.

671.34   Ensign Weller]   First Sergeant David Weller, of Farmer's company.

676.29   Colonel Butler]   Robert Butler (1786–1860) was married to Rachel Hays, a niece of Rachel Jackson.

677.36   D'Este]   Identified by Smith in a footnote earlier in the autobiography:

    * Augustus Frederick (b. 1794), only son of Augustus Frederick, Duke of Sussex (son of George III.), by his marriage with Lady Augusta Murray. The two children of this marriage, when disinherited by the Royal Marriage Act, took the name D'Este.

677.38   Blakeney] Decorated Peninsular veteran Lieutenant Colonel Sir Edward Blakeney (1778–1868) led the 7th Regiment of Royal Fusiliers. He would later become a field marshal.

678.24   Secretary Wylly] Lieutenant Colonel Alexander Campbell Wylly of the 7th Regiment of Foot, who had been Pakenham's aide-de-camp.

680.1   facines] Fascines.

683.7–8   the date of the *jeu de paume*] On June 20, 1789, at Versailles, the deputies of the Third Estate, having been locked out of their regular meeting place after breaking with the Estates General and pronouncing themselves the National Assembly, convened on the *Jeu de Paume,* an indoor tennis court, in defiance of King Louis XVI's order to disperse. There they took what became known as the Tennis Court Oath (*Serment du jeu de paume*), pledging not to disband until a new French constitution had been adopted.

684.13–15   The gazettes say . . . constitution] In this case the gazettes were mistaken: Ferdinand VII of Spain was not replaced by his father, the former king Charles IV, and would reign until his death in 1833.

684.29   the late capitulation of the king] As a precondition of his restoration, the allies at Vienna had demanded that Louis XVIII issue a constitution—what became known as the Charter of 1814—which established a bicameral legislature, provided for limited male suffrage, and codified a bill of rights to preserve freedom of religion, speech, and the press.

685.39–40   Endymion . . . President] The USS *President* was captured on January 15, 1815, by a British squadron that included HMS *Endymion.*

686.14   *douceurs*] French: sweets; in this case emolument.

687.15   favors of Philip] Bribes. Philip of Macedon was accused, most famously by Demosthenes, of exercising influence through corruption.

687.27–28   An author of real ability] Louis Hue Girardin, who held the chair of Modern Languages, History and Geography at the College of William and Mary.

687.37–38   Count Rochambeau . . . York] The Comte de Rochambeau (1725–1807) had led the French army that joined American forces under George Washington in the capture of a British army at Yorktown, Virginia, in October 1781.

688.9   Mr. Ticknor] George Ticknor (1791–1871) had graduated from Dartmouth in 1807 and been admitted to the Massachusetts bar in 1813. With letters of introduction from John Adams, he undertook a tour of the middle and southern states, 1814–15, which included visits with the President and with Jefferson, who in turn, as here, provided Ticknor with letters of introduction for his planned European tour.

695.20   federal aid . . . federal opposition.] That is, with the aid and in spite of the opposition of the Federalists.

699.23   the former occasion]   The prisoners had previously celebrated the news of the treaty signing at Ghent.

700.18   'Hunger will break . . . walls;']   A proverb. Cf. *Coriolanus* I.i.205–6.

704.2   Mr. CHARLES KING]   Son of Senator Rufus King, the former (and future) American minister to Great Britain, Charles King (1789–1867) had been educated in England. After the inquiry was concluded and Shortland was acquitted of ordering his men to fire, King admitted that "I yet confess myself unable to form any satisfactory conclusion, though, perhaps, the bias of my mind is that he did give such an order."

706.24   Mr Langdon]   The Eustis and Langdon families were multiply conjoined by marriage: William Eustis was married to Caroline Langdon, daughter of Woodbury Langdon, who had served in the Continental Congress and who was the only brother of New Hampshire governor John Langdon. Caroline's brother, Henry Sherburne Langdon, who may be the individual referred to here, was married to Eustis's sister Ann.

707.5   "gratuitous compliment,"]   On July 3, 1815, Stephen Decatur signed a peace treaty with the Dey of Algiers, and agreed to return two Algerian vessels that the American squadron had captured.

707.13   Mr Changuion]   In May 1814, Francois D. Changuion had been dispatched to the United States as a minister plenipotentiary of the Dutch government, with instructions to negotiate a new commercial treaty with the United States that would replace the 1782 agreement that Adams's father had negotiated.

707.21   their great Ally]   Great Britain.

708.13   Mr Everett]   Alexander Hill Everett (1790–1847) had studied law in John Quincy Adams's office and accompanied him to Russia in 1809 as an attaché. In 1815, he was posted to the Netherlands as Eustis's secretary. (He was the older brother of Edward Everett, who three decades later would assume Adams's post at the Court of St. James.)

708.18   Mr Pederson]   Peder Pederson (d. 1851) negotiated a commercial treaty with Secretary of State Henry Clay in 1826.

710.15–16   Commodore Bainbridge]   William Bainbridge (1774–1833), a veteran of the First Barbary War, had succeeded William Hull as captain of the USS *Constitution* in September 1812.

710.22–23   a convention . . . commerce]   Signed on July 3, 1815, at London. The U.S. negotiators were Adams, Clay, and Gallatin. The British delegation included Henry Goulburn and William Adams. All five had been commissioners at Ghent.

711.1   Detroit]   Where, on September 8, 1815, the United States concluded a treaty with representatives of the Wyandot, Delaware, Seneca, Shawnee, Miami, Chippewa, Ottawa, and Potawatomi Indians.

711.3   a station on the Mississippi] Portage des Sioux (present-day St. Charles, Missouri), where on July 18 and September 16, 1815, representatives of several western tribes signed treaties with the United States.

711.14   the act] An Act fixing the Military Peace Establishment of the United States, approved March 3, 1815. Section 5 called for the president to complete the discharge of all "officers, non-commissioned officers, musicians, and privates" not otherwise designated for retention by May 1.

Index

Abel, John S., 59
Ackley, Gad, 441
Adams, Abigail, 631
Adams, John, 23, 32, 688, 709;
    Jefferson's letter to, 426–28
Adams, John Quincy, 432, 622, 630–
    31, 706–8
Adams, Louisa Catherine, 631
Adams, Parmenio, 376–77
Adams, Thomas, 594
Adams, William, 622, 630
Adams (U.S. naval officer), 122
Aeolus, HMS, 390
Agriculture, 3, 7, 24, 33, 44–45, 70,
    110, 131–32, 658–59
Alabama, 406, 409, 476, 479
Albany, N.Y., 136, 143, 627
Albion, HMS, 485, 500
Aldham (purser), 257
Alexander I, Tsar of Russia, 233, 427,
    432, 434, 635, 637–38
Alexandria, Va., 548
Alexandria Gazette, 272
Alfred (privateer), 417
Algiers, 39, 632, 707, 709–10
Allen, Clark, 439–40
Allen, John, 171, 173, 194
Allen, William Henry, 294–95, 297–
    99
Almy, Thomas C., 313
Alvord, Dr., 371
Amherstburg (a.k.a. Malden), Upper
    Canada, 92–94, 98–101, 203–6,
    227, 323, 326
Amsterdam, Netherlands, 707
Anacostia River, 502–3, 506, 511–14
Analectic Magazine, 306
Anderson, Joseph, 268
Anglicans, 154
Annapolis, Md., 267
Anne Arundel County, Md., 491
Anti-war sentiments, 46–68, 72–84,
    110, 453
Apalachicola River, 644
Appling, Daniel, 437–39
Argentina, 669
Argus, USS, 294–99, 522

Ariel, USS, 313
Arkansas River, 641
Armistead, George, 541–42
Armstrong, John, 220, 339, 374, 456,
    477, 503, 507, 509–10, 607, 686
Army, British, 7, 18, 104, 111–12, 136,
    152–53, 155–56, 166, 173, 209, 211–13,
    247, 250, 253, 284, 320, 335–38,
    394–95, 424, 429–32, 483–84, 594,
    600, 603–4, 623, 636, 639, 642,
    684–85, 706; attack on Black Rock
    and Buffalo, 374–80; attack on
    Washington, 506–26, 565, 609;
    Battle of Beaver Dams, 262–66;
    Battle of Bladensburg, 490–505;
    Battle of Caulk's Field, 535–38; Battle
    of Châteauguay, 339–44; Battle
    of Chippawa, 448–53; Battle of Fort
    Erie, 465–75; Battle of Fort
    Stephenson, 281–83; Battle of
    Lacolle Mill, 413–16; Battle of Lake
    Champlain, 562; Battle of Lundy's
    Lane, 457–64; Battle of New
    Orleans, 666–81; Battle of
    Queenston Heights, 160–62, 262;
    Battle of Sackets Harbor, 240–44;
    Battle of Sandy Creek, 435–41;
    Battle of the Thames, 325–32; Battle
    of York, 214–19; bombardment of
    Fort McHenry, 541–44, 548–53;
    defense of Fort Amherstburg, 85,
    88–91, 323–24; fighting in Michigan
    Territory, 92–101, 113–17, 193–206;
    general orders after peace, 696–98;
    on Niagara frontier, 143–44, 169–
    70, 366–86, 412, 560–61; retreat
    from Washington, 526–32; siege of
    Fort Erie, 555–59; siege of Fort
    George, 235–39, 276; siege of Fort
    Meigs, 220–27; siege of Fort
    Wayne, 145; skirmish on the
    Sandusky, 278–80. *See also* Militia;
    Volunteers
Army, U.S., 32–33, 47, 52, 69, 105–8,
    110–12, 134–35, 155–56, 158–59, 211,
    268, 272, 284, 300, 312, 335–38, 352,
    363–65, 454–56, 483, 603, 623, 652–

53, 662, 684–85; attack on Fort Amherstburg, 85–88, 90; Battle of Beaver Dams, 262–66; Battle of Bladensburg, 490–505; Battle of Caulk's Field, 535–38; Battle of Châteauguay, 339–41; Battle of Chippawa, 448–53; Battle of Fort Erie, 444–47, 469–75; Battle of Fort Stephenson, 281–83; Battle of Horseshoe Bend, 409–11; Battle of Lacolle Mill, 413–16; Battle of Lake Champlain, 562; Battle of Lundy's Lane, 457–61; Battle of the Mississinewa, 181–92; Battle of New Orleans, 666–81; Battle of Queenston Heights, 160–62; Battle of Sackets Harbor, 240–44; Battle of Sandy Creek, 435–41; Battle of the Thames, 326–32; Battle of Tippecanoe, 27–28, 582; Battle of York, 217–18; conscription, 606–20; defense of Fort Erie, 555–59; defense of Fort McHenry, 541–44, 548–53; defense of Fort Meigs, 220–27; defense of Fort Wayne, 145–51; defense of Washington, 506–7, 511–16; deserters, 442–43; executions, 406–8; fighting at Black Rock and Buffalo, 374–80; fighting in Michigan Territory, 92–100, 113–17, 193–206; following attack on Washington, 526–32; at "Fort Starvation," 171–80; Indian policy, 27–28, 333, 477–78; in Madison's 1815 message to Congress, 711–14; massacre at Fort Dearborn, 102–4; on Niagara frontier, 143–44, 169–70, 366–86, 442–43, 560–61; as prisoners, 152–53, 245–55, 276; siege of Fort George, 235–39; skirmish on the Sandusky, 278–80. *See also* Militia; Volunteers
Ashby, Willoughby, 671
Askow, Captain, 253–54
Atchinson, John, 375
Atherton, William, 171–80
Atwater, Reuben, 116
Audd, Ambrose, 671
Auglaize River, 173
Austria, 433
Azores, 568–73

Bâby, François, 94, 97, 153
Bainbridge, William, 710
Baird, Ensign, 116
Baker, Anthony, 639, 689
Baker, John, 53
Baldwin, Midshipman, 564
Balhetchet, William, 425, 484
Ball, Charles, 345–52
Ball, James V., 181, 183
Ballard, Bland W., 172
Baltimore, Md., 38, 352, 433, 490–91, 496, 502, 535, 555, 568, 621, 682, 708; defense of, 541–46, 550–53; riots in, 54–68
Baltimore County, Md., 491
Baltimore Patriot, 541
Barbados, 417
Barbary pirates, 39, 310, 632, 707, 709–10
Barbour, James, 45
Barclay, Robert H., 303–5, 312, 316–17, 319, 323, 393
Barker, Jacob, 507
Barlow, Joel, 9, 19, 51–52
Barnes, John, 45
Barney, Joshua, 345, 485, 491–93, 499–505, 508–9, 515, 528
Barney, William B., 60, 62, 66
Barnwell (ship's master), 403
Barrie, Robert, 500
Barthe, Jean Baptiste, 94
Bascom, Mr., 144
Batavia, N.Y., 368, 372, 374–75
Bathurst, Henry, 211–13, 393, 429–31, 594, 603
Battersby, Francis, 459
Baxter, Charles, 296–97
Bayard, James A., 46, 432, 622, 630–31
Bay of Fundy, 624
Baylies, Hodijah, 664
Baynes, Edward, 696–98
Basye, Edmund, 190
Beale, George, 564
Beanes, William, 544, 549–53
Beasly, Mr., 422
Beauport, Lower Canada, 250
Beaver Dams, Upper Canada, 262–66, 367
Beck, John, 536–37

Beckwith, Thomas Sidney, 211, 270, 272–73, 698
Belgium, 637
Bender, Lieutenant, 94, 98
Benedict, Md., 490, 495, 502, 531
Benton, Jesse, 300–1
Benton, Thomas Hart, 300–2
Berlin Decree, 4–6, 8–9, 19–20, 76, 231
Bermuda, 270, 360, 387, 424, 483–85, 511, 539
Berthe (British soldier), 98–100
Berthelet (trader), 93
Berwick, HMS, 258
Biddle, Thomas, 448
Bigelow, Abijah, 53
Bigelow, Timothy, 664
Big Warrior, 479–82
Bissell, Daniel, 413
Bissley (U.S. sailor), 403
Blackbird, 103, 276–77
Black Hawk, 284
Black Rock, N.Y., 366, 374–79, 381, 384, 448, 465, 469, 483, 561
Bladensburg, Md., 491, 497–505, 507–9, 511–16, 518, 522–23, 528, 530, 550
Blake, Dr., 537
Blakeney Edward, 677
Blakeslee, Samuel, 376–79
Blanchard (U.S. soldier), 252
Bland, Francis, 403
Bledsoe, Jesse, 268
Bleecker, Harmanus, 53
Bliss, George, 664
Bliss, John, 443
Blockades, 3, 5–6, 12, 14–17, 30, 76, 211, 230, 434, 533–34
Blount, Willie, 25–26
Blue Jacket, 95–96
Bodley, Thomas, 363
Boerstler, Charles, 250, 264–65, 684
Bogardus (U.S. naval officer), 290
Boilvin, Nicholas, 139
Bolin, Joseph, 509
Boston, Mass., 72, 105–6, 108, 121, 152, 256, 358, 363, 541, 595, 648, 664
Boucherville, Thomas Verchères de, 92–101
Boughton, Seymour, 376, 379
Bouthilier, Alexis, 94
Bouton, Philip, 335, 338
Bower, Gustavus M., 199

Boyd, John Parker, 235–36
Boyle, Thomas, 533–34
Brandywine River, 433
Brazil, 533
Breckenridge, James, 53
Brenton, Edward B., 386
Brenton, Mr., 152
Briggs, Mrs., 274
Brigham, Elijah, 53
Briscoe (free man of color), 57
Britain, 42–43, 54, 72, 120, 134, 307–8, 321, 358–59, 394, 421, 467–68, 477, 532, 656, 694; American bonds with, 79–80; U.S. declaration of war against, 36–37, 43, 47, 69, 88, 228–29, 231–32, 489, 597; defense of Canada, 85–91; diplomatic attempts to resolve crisis, 30–31, 33–35, 111–12; hostile acts by, 1–23, 38–41, 50–53, 69–70, 75–77, 136, 360–61, 427–28; Indian allies of, 7, 17–18, 26–29, 41, 50–51, 69, 76, 85–87, 90, 92–101, 111, 113, 140–41, 156–57, 161–62, 164–68, 209, 276–77, 284, 393, 450, 481–82, 581–84, 587, 637; in Napoleonic wars, 426–27, 602, 706; Orders-in-Council, 1, 3–4, 6, 15–19, 21–22, 30, 75, 231–32, 427, 587, 693, 695; Parliament, 30, 63, 136, 164, 231, 622, 636, 638; and peace talks, 426–27, 429, 432–34, 562, 581–86; Treaty of Ghent, 621–30; U.S. "blockade" of, 533–34; as wartime enemy, 229–33
Brock, Isaac, 88–91, 113, 118–19, 143, 153, 156, 160, 162, 167, 262
Broke, Philip B. V., 256–59
Brooke, Arthur, 498, 541, 555
Brooks, John, 316–17
Brown, Captain, 153
Brown, Dr., 143
Brown, Jacob, 240, 445, 448, 450–52, 454, 457, 459, 560, 685
Brown, James, 436
Brown, Lieutenant (Maryland soldier), 537
Brown, Lieutenant (New York soldier), 436
Brown, Major, 515
Brown, Tom, 292–93
Browne, Benjamin F., 416–22, 574–80
Browne, Captain, 485–86

Brownstown, Michigan Territory, 92–95, 97–99
Brum (sailing master), 564
Bryant, Lemuel, 289
Buenos Aires, Argentina, 669
Buffalo, N.Y., 104, 170, 366–68, 373–77, 379, 381, 442, 444–45, 448, 451, 454, 469, 483
Buffalo Creek, 333
Buffalo Gazette, 366
Bullard, Captain, 97
Bullock, Richard, 327
Buncombe County, N.C., 69
Burke, Edmund, 611
Burke County, N.C., 69
Burlington, Upper Canada, 239, 323, 454–55
Burlington, Vt., 343
Burnet (trader), 103
Burrall, Charles, 64
Bush, Lieutenant, 125
Butler, James R., 186, 190
Butler, Robert, 676–77
Butler's Barracks, 461–64
Byfield, Shadrach, 465–68
Byng, John, 394
Byron, Lord (George Gordon), 539–40

Cabinet, American, 48, 55, 111, 502–3, 506, 509, 522, 606, 709
Cabinet (Ministry), British, 3, 6–7, 13, 21, 31, 33, 35, 70, 111, 587, 631, 686, 708
Cabot, George, 664
Cadotte brothers, 94
Caffrey, Mary Donelson, 410–11
Caledonia, USS, 313
Calhoun, John C., 10, 260–61, 709
Calvert County, Md., 345, 348
Calypso, HMS, 572
Camp, Captain, 379
Campbell, George W., 592, 606
Campbell, John B., 181–82, 188–89, 483
Canada, 51, 53, 81, 118, 322, 424–25, 483–84; American invasion of, 31, 44–45, 47, 85, 90, 110–11, 135–36, 141, 152, 170, 361–64, 606–7, 609, 612, 619, 696; British defense of, 381, 393–94, 429–32, 591, 603, 636, 639, 708; and Treaty of Ghent, 584, 623–28, 636. *See also* Lower Canada;

New Brunswick; Nova Scotia; Upper Canada
Canandaigua, N.Y., 160, 367, 375
Canning, George, 635, 687
Cape Cod, 107
Capel, Thomas Bladen, 256
Capitol, U.S., burning of, 517, 521, 523–24, 526, 565, 606
Carberry, Henry, 508
Carlisle, Pa., 158
Carnation, HMS, 568–72
Carroll, Charles, 507
Carroll, Daniel, 509
Carroll, William, 300–1, 406, 685
Cass, Lewis, 113–14, 117
Cassin, Stephen, 563–64
Castine, Mass. (now Me.), 108, 594–96
Castlereagh, Viscount (Robert Stewart), 4, 6, 20, 30, 229, 231, 432–33, 621, 635, 687, 706
Caughnawagas, 264, 336
Caulk's Farm, Battle of, 535–39
Chaine, Esidore, 27
Chambers, Benjamin, 535, 538
Chambers, Ezekiel F., 536–37
Chambers, Major, 222, 281
Chambly, Lower Canada, 245–46
Champion, Epaphroditus, 53
Champlin, Samuel, 313
Chandler, John, 235, 249
Changuion, François D., 707
Channing, William Ellery, 72–84
Chapin, Cyrenius, 143, 366–69
Chappune, 147
Charleston, S.C., 211
Charwell, HMS, 392
Chasseur, USS, 533–34
Châteauguay River, 339–44, 625–26, 697
Chatham River, 327
Chauncey, Isaac, 311–12, 337, 440, 454–57
Chautauqua County, N.Y., 376
Chazy, N.Y., 339–40
Chelsea Naval Hospital, 467–68
Cherokees, 139, 476–78, 480, 482
Cherub, HMS, 396, 400
Chesapeake, USS, 2, 256–59
Chesapeake Bay, 211, 270, 345, 349, 353, 357, 360, 387, 432, 485–90, 500, 502, 508, 511, 539, 550, 552, 555, 639

Cheshire County, N.H., 648
Chestertown, Md., 535
Chicago, Illinois Territory, 102–3, 146–47, 150, 276
Chicago River, 102–3
Chickasaws, 480, 482
Chile, 396–405
Chippawa, Upper Canada, 448–54, 457, 561, 685
Chippewas, 146, 332
Chippeway, HMS, 313
Chittenden, Martin, 53
Choctaws, 139, 480, 482
Christianity, 79, 84, 277, 331, 384
Chub, HMS, 562
Churchill, Sylvester, 376–77
Churchill (U.S. soldier), 254
Cincinnati, Ohio, 171
Clagett, Lieutenant, 543
Clark, Jim, 190
Clark, William, 139, 142
Claus, William, 276
Clavering, Lieutenant, 258
Clay, Green, 221–23, 225
Clay, Henry, 1, 260, 363–65, 432, 622, 630–31, 682
Clemm, Sergeant, 543
Clemow, Lieutenant, 94
Clinton, De Witt, 130–38, 207
Clover, Lewis Peter, 699–705
Coates, James, 469
Cochran, Andrew W., 152–53
Cochran, Rebecca, 152
Cochrane, Alexander, 424–25, 483–85, 490, 494–95, 504, 533, 535, 539, 541, 544, 550–52, 639, 642, 644, 666
Cochrane, Thomas, 551–52
Cockburn, George, 211, 270, 272–73, 484–87, 489–96, 498–501, 504, 522, 524, 526, 549–50, 552
Codrington, Edward, 494
Coffee, John, 301, 410, 685
Cohorn, HMS, 436
Cold Springs, N.Y., 368
Coles, Edward, 1
Collier, Edward, 387–88
Colton, Dr., 271–74
Columbia, USS, 522
Comet, USS, 533
Commerce, 1–5, 7–8, 12–13, 15–22, 30, 33–35, 39, 41, 45, 48, 52, 69, 77–78,
89, 110, 130–32, 136, 138, 230–31, 260, 426, 428, 432–33, 593–94, 611, 637, 641, 651, 656, 658–59, 663, 695, 707, 710, 715, 717
Confiance, HMS, 562–64
Congregationalists, 72
Congress, U.S., 72, 106, 111, 135, 165, 207, 260, 363–64, 432, 553, 565–67, 581, 584, 586–87, 591, 593, 648, 652–53, 657–58, 661–63; conscription bill, 606–20; and declaration of war, 36, 56; Federalist Party in, 260, 267–68, 565, 689; Madison's annual message to (1811), 1, 31; Madison's annual message to (1815), 709–17; Madison's peace treaty message to, 689–91; Madison's war message to, 1–10, 23, 47; Republican Party in 260, 689. *See also* House of Representatives, U.S.; Senate, U.S.
Congress of Vienna, 433, 621, 631–32, 635, 637–38, 706
Conjockaty Creek, 376–77
Conkling, Augustus, 313
Connecticut, 110, 591, 595, 598, 648, 662, 664, 682
Connecticut River, 625–26
Conran, Henry, 461–62
Conscription, 606–20, 662
Constitution, U.S., 8, 18, 48, 55, 106, 109, 131, 134–35, 453, 650, 654–55, 714, 716; call for constitutional convention, 591–93; and conscription, 606–7, 612–15, 618, 662; proposed amendments to, 649, 657–61, 663
Constitution, USS, 121–29
Cooper, Captain, 270, 273
Cooper, Edward, 465, 468
Cooper, James Fenimore, 285
Cornel (nurse), 254
Cosnahan, Midshipman, 258
Cotton, 428
Council (Massachusetts), 105–7
Cowell, J. G., 402–3
Cox, Thomas, 436
Crane, Philip, 538
Crawford, William H., 36, 294
Crawley, John, 25
Creeks, 25–26, 28, 365, 405, 408–9, 476–82, 644, 707
Croghan, George, 278–83, 302

Crutchfield, Major, 270, 274
Crysler's Farm, Battle of, 339, 391, 442, 697
Cuba, 44
Cumberland Head, N.Y., 339, 343
Cunliffe-Owen, Charles, 391
Curtis, Daniel, 145–51
Curtiss, Mr., 368
Cushing, Thomas H., 102, 104
Cuthbert, Susan Stockton, 522
Cuthbertson, Ensign, 158
Cutts, Richard, 509–10
Czartoryski, Adam, 637

Dabney, John B., 573
Dacres, James R., 121, 124, 127–29
Dane, Nathan, 664
Danton, Georges-Jacques, 686
Darnell, Allen, 199, 202
Darnell, Elias, 193–206
Dartmoor Prison, 245, 417–23, 574–80, 699–705
Davenport, John, Jr., 53
Davis, Benjamin, 364
Dayton, Ohio, 186, 188–89
Dearborn, Henry, 105–8, 111–12, 235, 239, 264, 268, 685
De Carteret, John Daniel, 338
Decatur, Stephen, 709
Decrès, Denis, 19
Deer, William, 286
Defiance, Ohio, 150, 172–73, 175–76
De Haven, P. W., 264–65
De La Montaigne, Jacob, 138
De Lancey, James, 243
Delaware, 46
Delawares, 328
Delphy, Richard, 294
Democracy, 600–1
Democratic-Republican Party. See Republican Party
Denison, Dr., 296, 299
Denmark, 708
Denny, James, 114, 116
De Peyster, Robert, 507
De Rottenburg, Francis, 384
Deserters, 442–43
D'Este, Augustus Frederick, 677–78
Detroit, HMS, 303, 313–14, 317
Detroit, Michigan Territory, 93–95, 102–4, 114–16, 118, 143, 145–47, 151,
172, 193, 206, 220, 320, 323, 326, 332, 431, 684, 697, 711
Detroit River, 85, 93, 98–100, 114, 117, 206
Devor (U.S. soldier), 236–37
De Witt, Benjamin, 138
Dexter (U.S. soldier), 415–16
Diplomacy, 30–35, 111–12
District of Columbia, 58. See also Washington, D.C.
Donelson, Alexander, 301
Downes, John, 404
Downie, George, 562
Dragon, HMS, 500
Drummond, Gordon, 241–43, 378, 457–59, 469–70, 472, 475, 560, 685, 698
Duck River, 25
Dudley, William, 225
Duffy, Ebenezer, 290
Dundas, David, 556
Dunlop, William, 461–65, 555–59
Dunn, Dick, 128
Dunn (ship's clerk), 257
Dusenberry, Midshipman, 403
Duvall, Gabriel, 508

Eagle, USS, 562–63
Eames (U.S. soldier), 255
Earl, Arnold, 440
East Indies, 695
Eastport, Mass. (now Me.), 106–7
Eberts, James, 94
Edinburgh Review, 358
Edwards, William M., 294
Eggert, Francis, 295, 297
Eldridge, Joseph C., 276
Election of 1812, 207, 260
Elkton, Md., 270
Elliot, Jesse D., 312–13, 316
Elliot, Major, 471
Elliott, Matthew, 94, 194, 201, 281
Ellis, Daniel, 440
Ely, William, 53
Elzey, Dr., 267
Embargo Act, 35, 167, 310
Embargoes, 31, 33–35, 658–59, 663
Emery (U.S. soldier), 252
Emmett, Thomas Addis, 138
Emott, James, 53
Endymion, HMS, 685–86

Ennick, Lieutenant, 537
Essex, USS, 396–405
Essex Junior, USS, 404–5
Etough (ship's master), 258
Eustis, William, 105, 109, 135, 169, 706
Evans, Frederick, 543
Evans, George D., 496
Evaton, Bill, 252
Everett, Alexander H., 708
Everett, David, 541

Fair American (cartel ship), 358
Fairfax County, Va., 506
Fairfield, William, 444
Falkiner, Lieutenant, 258
Fallon, Lieutenant, 472
Fanny (merchant ship), 568
Fantome, HMS, 387
Farmer, Captain, 673
Farnum, Lieutenant, 378–79
Farragut, David G., 399–404
Faulkner, Dr., 94, 101
Favorite (merchant ship), 682
Fayal, Azores, 568–73
Federalist Party, 31, 33, 41, 43, 169, 358, 362, 502, 547, 586, 631, 692, 709; and Baltimore riots, 54; British view of, 155, 432, 595–96; call for constitutional convention, 591–93; call for peace treaty, 426, 489, 581–82; in Congress, 260, 267–68, 565, 689; election of 1812, 130, 260; and Hartford Convention, 648; on invasion of Canada, 363; opposition to war, 23, 34, 44, 46, 606, 695; and Treaty of Ghent, 689
Federal Republican, 54–56, 58, 64, 66
Ferdinand VII, King of Spain, 684
Ferris, Benjamin, 138
Finan, Patrick, 214–19
Finch, HMS, 562
Finlay, John, 294
Fish, Preserved, 138
Fisheries, 428, 432, 581, 585, 587, 621, 632–34, 695, 707–8
Fitch, Asa, 53
Fitzgibbon, James, 262–65
Five Medals, 147
Florida, 44, 136, 167, 211, 479–81, 623, 640, 644, 707
Floyd, John, 365

Flummerfelt, Cornelius, 118–20
Folch y Juan, Estevan, 479
Fort Amherstburg (in Malden), Upper Canada, 85, 88, 111, 113, 136, 141, 193–94, 196, 198–99, 202–6, 220, 227, 303, 312, 323, 325–26
Fort Bowyer, Ala., 644, 696
Fort Covington, Md., 543
Fort Dearborn, Illinois Territory, 102–3, 145–47, 150
Fort Defiance, Ohio, 172
Fort Detroit, Michigan Territory, 85, 93–95, 102–4, 113–16, 118–20, 143, 145–47, 150, 152, 165, 167, 332, 382
Fort Erie, Upper Canada, 144, 155, 169, 239, 444–45, 448, 461–62, 465, 469–75, 555–61, 685
Fort George, Upper Canada, 120, 136, 143–44, 206, 214, 235–39, 264, 276, 333–34, 366, 370, 374, 381, 384–85, 454–55, 460–61, 465, 685
Fort Greene Ville, Ohio, 181, 188
Fort Jackson, Mississippi Territory, 476, 479
Fort Mackinac, Michigan Territory, 102, 104, 111–13, 147, 154, 382
Fort McHenry, Md., 541–46, 552–53, 555
Fort Meigs, Ohio, 220–27, 278, 281
Fort Moreau, N.Y., 604
Fort Niagara, N.Y., 111, 144, 155, 158, 169, 235, 366–68, 370, 374, 412, 431, 454–55
Fort Ontario, N.Y., 392, 435
Fort Schlosser, N.Y., 375, 384, 450
"Fort Starvation" (Camp No. 3), Ohio, 171, 174–77
Fort Stephenson, Ohio, 278, 281–84
Fort Strother, Mississippi Territory, 406
Fort Wayne, Indiana Territory, 27, 102–4, 145, 147–51, 171–73
Fort Williams, Mississippi Territory, 409
Forty Mile Creek, 368–69
Foster, Augustus John, 34, 122
Fowler, John, 364
Fox, Charles James, 15
Foxes, 139–40
France, 3, 36, 39, 43, 54, 74, 89, 294, 317; American bonds with, 80;

decrees of, 4–6, 8–9, 19–20, 76, 231, 232–33, 484, 656; hostile acts by, 4–6, 8–9, 19–21, 23, 41, 51–53, 70, 76–77, 80, 228–31; in Napoleonic Wars, 393, 426–27, 511, 602, 706; post-Napoleonic, 602–3, 682–84, 686, 706–8; trade with, 1, 4, 12, 15–19, 21

Frank (U.S. soldier), 415–16

Franklin, Tenn., 300

Frazer, Lieutenant, 380

Frederick, Md., 548, 550

Fredericktown, Md., 270

Fredericton, N.B., 240, 387–88

Freedom of the press, 55, 58

Freeman, John, 509

Free persons of color, 57, 345, 352, 509

French immigrants, 54, 56

French and Indian War, 89

French John (servant), 507

French Mills, N.Y., 413

French Revolution, 61, 63, 228, 611, 684, 686

Frenchtown, Md., 270

Frenchtown (now Monroe), Michigan Territory, 193–203, 220, 684

Freneau, Philip, "The Battle of Lake Erie," 303–5

Frolic, USS, 417

Frontier, 7, 17, 25–26, 76, 86, 88, 112, 132, 158, 166, 181, 194, 332, 385, 430–31, 710–11

Frost (U.S. soldier), 255

Fugitive slaves, 345–52, 424

Gaillard, John, 268

Gaines, Edmund P., 454, 469, 685

Gales, Joseph, 524

Gales (Baltimore rioter), 59

Gallatin, Albert, 52, 267–68, 432–34, 523, 622, 630–34

Gambier, James, 622, 630

Gamble, Peter, 564

Gardiner, George, 294

Garrard, James, 174–75

Garrard, William, 181, 189

Gassaway, Louis, 68

Gaston, William, 260, 611

General Armstrong (privateer), 568–72

General Greene, USS, 310

General Pike, USS, 242

Genesee County, N.Y., 374, 376

Genoa, Italy, 637

George, Prince of Wales (Prince Regent of Great Britain and Ireland), 38, 211, 229, 231, 639, 696, 698

George III, King of Great Britain and Ireland, 6, 88–91, 93, 101, 120, 140–41, 162, 165, 170, 211, 229, 245, 323–24, 373, 464, 557

Georgetown (in District of Columbia), 270, 509–10, 548–49

Georgetown, Ohio, 171

Georgia, 25, 365, 405, 476

German, Obadiah, 268

German (U.S. sailor), 121

German immigrants, 54

Gerry, Elbridge, 267–68

Ghent, Belgium, 432, 434, 562, 581, 591, 621, 630–31, 635

Gibbs, Samuel, 667, 669, 681, 685

Gilbert, Marianus W., 441

Gilbert, William W., 138

Giles, William Branch, 268

Gilman, Nicholas, 268

Girardin, Louis Hue, 687

Gladstone, John, 637

Glanville, John, 538

Glegg, J. B., 91

Gleig, George R., 511–21, 526–32, 639–43

Glew, Joseph B., 458

Goddard, Calvin, 664

Gold, Thomas R., 53

Goldsborough, Charles, 53

Goldsmith, Tom, 285, 289–91

Goodrich, Chauncey, 664

Gordon, Colonel, 377

Gordon, Dr., 537

Gosselin, Mr., 595

Goulburn, Henry, 622, 630

Grafton County, N.H., 648

Graham, John T., 508

Graham, Midshipman, 564

Grand Manan Island, 624

Grand River, 373

Granger, Erastus, 333, 376, 378

Granger, Gideon, 364

Grant, Richard, 537

Graves, Benjamin F., 199

Greene, Mass. (now Me.), 254–55

Greenville, Ohio, 181, 188
Griffiths, Edward, 595
Grosvenor, Thomas P., 260, 267
Growler, USS, 245–46, 562
Guerrière, HMS, 121–29
Gulf of Mexico, 632, 644

Hague, The, Netherlands, 707
Hailes, Harris W., 222, 328
Hale, Horace, 561
Halifax, Nova Scotia, 112, 121, 245, 256, 270, 349, 360, 387, 389, 431, 485, 585–87, 594
Hall, Amos, 374–80
Hall, James, 296, 298
Hall, William, Jr., 665
Hamilton, Paul, 45, 135, 311, 319–20
Hamilton, Upper Canada, 383
Hamilton, USS, 292–93
Hammond, Eli, 301
Hampton, Va., 270–75
Hampton, Wade, 268, 339, 341–44, 685
Hanks, Jarvis, 442–43, 474–75, 560–61
Hanks, Lieutenant, 113
Hanson, Alexander Contee, 54–55, 58–62
Hanway (U.S. soldier), 251
Hare, Charles Willing, 591–93
Harford County, Md., 491
Harrington, Brooks, 439–40
Harrington, William, 296–97
Harris, David, 62
Harris, Levett, 433
Harris, Samuel, 138
Harris, Samuel D., 439, 448
Harrison, William Henry, 27, 150, 171, 173, 175–78, 181, 193, 200, 220–24, 278–83, 303, 312, 330–32, 364, 582, 685
Harrow, Joseph, 196–97
Hart, Nathaniel G., 196
Hartford, Conn., 648
Hartford Convention, 453, 595, 598–99, 601, 619, 631, 648–65, 682, 686, 709
Havre de Grace, Md., 270
Hawkins, Benjamin, 476, 479, 481–82
Hawthorne, Nathaniel, 417
Haynes, Colonel, 680
Hays, Stockley, 301

Haywood (U.S. soldier), 251
Haywood County, N.C., 69
Hazard, Benjamin, 665
Heald, Nathan, 102–4, 146
Hebrus, HMS, 487
Helm, Linai T., 103
Henley, Robert, 563–64
Henry, John, 41
Herrick, Captain, 252, 254–55
Herrick, Corporal, 254
Herring, Elbert, 138
Hibbard, Nathaniel W., 438–41
Hickman, David M., 189
Higdon, Leonard P., 671
Higginbotham, David, 110
Hillhouse, James, 664
Hillyar, James, 398–400, 404–5
Hindman, Jacob, 238, 449, 454
Hite, Robert G., 492
Hoare, Charles, 436
Hodges, Ben, 124
Hoffman, Dr., 403
Hogan, Dan, 125
Hollister, Charles, 440
Holmes, Benjamin, 327
Holsen, Reverend, 272–73
Hope, John, 394
Hope, Mr., 274–75
Hopkins, Caleb, 369
Hopkins, Mrs., 274
Hopkins, Samuel G., 189
Hopkins, Timothy S., 376–77
Horner, William E., 444–47
Horseshoe Bend, Battle of, 409–11, 476
Hosmer, Major, 380
Hospitals, 444–47, 461–64, 467–68, 530
Hossington, Grout, 440
House of Delegates (Maryland), 54–68
House of Representatives, U.S., 1, 69, 260, 432, 581, 586, 593, 689, 709; Address of the Minority . . . on the Subject of War with Great Britain, 46–53; and declaration of war, 10, 33, 36; Report on Causes and Reasons for War, 10–22; Webster's speech on conscription, 606–20
House of Representatives (Massachusetts), 594, 597–600
Howard, Charles, 547

Howe, Eber D., 370–74
Hudson, Dr., 296, 298–99
Huffington, Mr., 505
Huffman, George, 674–75
Hull, Isaac, 121–23, 126–28
Hull, William, 85–88, 90, 94–95, 102, 111–16, 118–21, 134, 143–45, 152–53, 167, 214, 220, 245, 366, 382, 460, 684
Hull (U.S. soldier), 460
Humphreys County, Tenn., 25
Hunt, Alvin, 438
Hunter, Andrew, 522–23
Hunter, HMS, 313
Hunter, James, 282
Hunter, Mary Stockton, 522–25
Hunter, Thomas, 335
Hurons, 27–29, 100
Hutchens (Baltimore rioter), 57
Hutchinson (U.S. soldier), 250–51
Hynson, Thomas B., 537

Illinois River, 641
Illinois Territory, 27, 102–3, 139, 145–47, 284
Immigrants, 54, 57–58, 656, 660, 663
Impressment of sailors, 1–2, 8, 16–17, 22, 38–39, 41, 51, 69, 76–77, 208, 229, 231–32, 358, 361, 427, 434, 581–82, 587, 613, 621, 688, 693, 695, 699
Inderwick, James, 294–99
India, 708
Indian, HMS, 390
Indiana Territory, 102–4; Battle of the Mississinewa, 181–88; Battle of the Tippecanoe, 27–28, 582; siege of Fort Wayne, 145–51
Indians, 44, 110, 112, 263, 312, 317, 361–62, 365, 388, 429, 431, 663, 707; American allies, 139–42, 170, 333–34, 435–37, 448, 476, 479; British allies, 7, 17–18, 26–29, 41, 50–51, 69, 76, 85–87, 90, 92–101, 111, 113, 140–41, 156–57, 161–62, 164–68, 209, 276–77, 284, 393, 450, 481–82, 581–84, 587, 637; fighting in Indiana Territory, 145–50, 181–92; fighting in Lower Canada, 414; fighting in Michigan Territory, 92–104, 113–16, 193–206; fighting in Mississippi Territory, 406, 409–10, 476–82;

fighting in New York, 240, 370–73, 376–78, 435–37; fighting in Ohio, 171–75, 178–79, 220, 222–26, 279–82, 284; fighting in Upper Canada, 264–66, 323–26, 406, 448, 450, 460; Jackson's attitude toward, 25–26, 476–78, 644; Madison's address to, 139–42; and Treaty of Ghent, 581–84, 587, 621, 629, 632, 637, 710–11; U.S. Army policy toward, 27–28, 333, 477–78. *See also individual tribes*
Ingersoll, Charles J., 10, 607
Ingram, William, 399
Iowas, 139–40
Ireland, 214, 239, 533–34
Irish immigrants, 54, 57–58
Iroquois, 164, 170, 448
Irvine, John, 196
Irving, Washington, 267, 306–22
Isaacs, Midshipman, 401–3
Italy, 637

Jackson, Andrew, 300–1; attitude toward Indians, 25–26, 476–78, 644; at Battle of Horseshoe Bend, 409–11; at Battle of New Orleans, 666, 677, 679–82, 685; execution of soldier, 406–8
Jackson, Rachel, 409
Jackson, Richard, Jr., 53
Jamaica, 135, 568, 639, 644
Jefferson, Thomas, 130, 133, 167, 592, 696, 709; correspondence with Madison, 23–24, 44–45, 110–12, 587–90; letter to Adams, 426–28; letter to Madame de Staël, 228–34; letter to Marquis de Lafayette, 682–88; Monroe's letter to, 267–69; sale of library, 565–67
Jeffrey, Charlotte Wilkes, 358
Jeffrey, Francis, 358–62
Jennings, Captain, 144
Jennings, Paul, 508–10
Jesup, Thomas S., 448, 451–52
Jesus, 72–73
Jobling (British soldier), 242
Johns, Lieutenant, 258
Johnson, Edward, 56, 60, 62–64, 66
Johnson, Mr., 144
Johnson, Richard M., 330–31, 686
Johnson, Thomas, 25

Johnson, William, 645
Johnston, Stephen, 147
Jones, Joshua, 294
Jones, Thomas ap Catesby, 644–47
Jones, William, 319–20, 396, 456, 501–2, 522, 562, 606
Jordan, John, 364
Jordan, Joseph, 295, 297
Justin, Joshua, 564

Kamouraska, Lower Canada, 390
Keane, John, 639, 642, 667, 669, 681, 685
Kellam, James, 296–97
Kennebunk, Mass. (now Me.), 108
Kent, Henry, 387–92
Kentucky, 97, 99–100, 111, 167, 171–72, 175, 179, 181, 193–95, 279, 327, 329, 336, 363, 584, 670
Key, Francis Scott, 544–54
Key, Mary, 548, 550, 553
Key, Philip Barton, 53
Kickapoos, 27–28, 146
King, Charles, 704
King, Rufus, 268, 648
King, William, 341
Kingman, Ike, 123
Kingsbury, Jacob, 145, 151
Kingsbury (U.S. naval officer), 404
Kingston, Upper Canada, 111, 154, 214–15, 219, 240, 335–37, 387, 390, 455–56, 467
Kinsale, Md., 487
Kinzie, John, 146
Knaggs, Captain, 116
Knoxville, Tenn., 300
Kościuszko, Tadeusz, 45, 112

Lacolle Mill, Battle of, 413–16, 697
Lacolle River, 414–15
Lacroix (trader), 93
Lady Prevost, HMS, 313
Lafayette, Marquis de (Marie-Joseph du Motier), 682
Lais, HMS, 437
Lake Borgne, 640, 642–47, 666
Lake Champlain, 339–40, 431, 562–64, 685
Lake Erie, 111, 155–56, 206, 220, 235, 374, 393–94, 431, 483, 584–85, 587,

603–4, 626, 641, 708; Battle of, 303–5, 312–24, 685
Lake Huron, 320, 626–27
Lake Michigan, 140, 641
Lake Ontario, 111, 214–15, 235, 239–40, 285–93, 311, 323, 374, 393–94, 435, 438–40, 454–55, 584–85, 587, 603–4, 626, 708
Lake Pontchartrain, 640
Lake St. Clair, 326
Lake Superior, 587, 626–27
Lake Témiscouata, 390
Lake of the Woods, 627–28, 633
Lambert, John, 666–69, 676–78
Langdon, Henry S., 706
Latham, Lieutenant, 459
Laurence, Lieutenant, 499
Law, Lieutenant, 258
Law, Lyman, 53
Lawbe, Spenica (Logan), 174
Law of nations, 1–2, 12–14, 79, 361
Lawrence, Colonel, 375
Lawrence, James, 256, 258, 313
Lawrence, John, 387
Lawrence, Samuel A., 138
Lawrence, USS, 303, 313–19
Leake, Midshipman, 258
Leavenworth, Henry, 448, 452
Le Couteur, John, 240–44, 264–66, 335–38, 457–60, 469–73
Leib, Michael, 268
Leipzig, Battle of, 393, 427
Leonard, Nathaniel, 370
Leonard, Richard, 243, 472
Leonardstown, Md., 486
Leopard, HMS, 2
Lewis, Joseph, Jr., 53
Lewis, Leonard, 286, 289
Lewis, Morgan, 268
Lewis, William, 171, 194, 196–98
Lewiston, N.Y., 143, 160, 366, 370–71, 374–75, 381
Lexington, Ky., 188
Library of Congress, 565–67
Lincoln County, N.C., 69
Lingan, James M., 63
Linnet, HMS, 562
Lisbon, Portugal, 110, 635
Liston, Robert, 360
Little Belt, HMS, 313
Littlejohn, Adam, 258

Little Warrior, 481
Livermore, Mass. (now Me.), 255
Liverpool, Earl of (Robert Jenkinson), 602, 621, 635–38, 706
Lloyd, Burton, 572
Lloyd, Robert, 571–72
Logan (Spenica Lawbe), 174
Loire, HMS, 485–86
London, England, 4–5, 11, 211, 256, 422, 429, 432, 467–68, 565–66, 639, 696, 706–7
Long Days of June, 147
Longfellow, Stephen, Jr., 664
Long Island, 595
Longueuil, Lower Canada, 94
Louis XVIII, King of France, 602, 706
Louisiana, 139, 268, 639–41; Battle of Lake Borgne, 642–47; Battle of New Orleans, 666–82
Loveday, Edward, 438
Lovett, John, 267
Lower Canada, 90, 110–11, 115–16, 144, 152, 155–56, 168, 211, 361, 389–91, 429–31, 585–86; Battle of Châteauguay, 339–44; Battle of Lacolle Mill, 413–16; general orders after peace, 696–98; prison ship in, 245–55
Loyalists, 89–90, 165, 262, 557
Lucas, J., 115–16
Lucas, Robert, 113–17
Lundy's Lane, Battle of, 457–61, 560, 690
Lycoming Creek, 158
Lyman, Daniel, 665
Lyman, Joseph, 664
Lyman, Midshipman, 403

Macbride, James, 260
Macdonough, Thomas, 562–64, 685
Machekethie (Indian town), 27
MacIntyre, Lieutenant, 222
Macomb, Alexander, 414, 685
Madawaska, Lower Canada, 389
Madawaska River, 389–90
Madison, Dolley, 139, 506–10
Madison, George, 198
Madison, James, 30, 49, 69, 85, 130, 133, 152–53, 260, 267–68, 333–34, 363, 432, 464, 477, 481–82, 501,
503, 505, 519–20, 522, 544, 550, 581–82, 591–93, 606–7, 621–22, 685, 692; address to Indian nations, 139–42; annual message to Congress (1811), 1, 31; annual message to Congress (1815), 709–17; correspondence with Jefferson, 23–24, 44–45, 110–12, 587–90; flees Washington, 502, 506–10; interviewed by Francis Jeffrey, 358–62; order for militia preparation, 105–6; peace treaty message to Congress, 689–91; proclamation of war, 36–37, 44, 69, 72, 105, 112, 489; second inaugural address, 207–10; war message to Congress, 1–10, 23, 47, 69
Magnet, HMS, 392
Magnor, John, 538
Magrath, Dr., 299
Magrath, Humphrey, 313
Magraw (gardener), 510
Maguaga, Michigan Territory, 92, 328
Maine, District of (part of Massachusetts), 106–8, 245, 251, 254–55, 431, 585–87, 594–96, 604, 633, 648
Maisonville, Alexis, 94
Majoribanks, John, 436
Malabar, HMS (prison ship), 245, 247–55
Malcolm, James, 488
Malden, Upper Canada. *See* Amherstburg; Fort Amherstburg
Mallet, Jack, 291–92
Mallory, Benajah, 376, 378
Manchester, N.Y., 366, 375
Manley, Jesse, 25
Manly, HMS, 387
Manton, Edward, 665
Manufacturing, 7, 70, 432–33, 658, 715
Maple, John Fordyce, 294
Marat, Jean-Paul, 686
Marblehead, Mass., 108
Maria (sloop), 116
Marlboro, Md., 490, 494–95, 531, 544, 549
Martin (U.S. sailor), 504
Marvin, Captain, 375
Maryland, 270, 485–88, 511–14, 529–31, 545–47; Baltimore riots, 54–68;

Battle of Bladensburg, 490–505; Battle of Caulk's Farm, 535–38; bombardment of Fort McHenry, 541–44, 548–53; fugitive slaves in, 345–53

Mason, Elizabeth Champlin, 312

Massachusetts, 46, 72, 84, 428, 581, 585–86, 591, 601, 631, 634, 682, 692; British view of, 594–600; defiance of War Department, 105–10; and Hartford Convention, 648, 662, 664, 686–87; USS *Chesapeake* versus HMS *Shannon*, 256–59. *See also* Maine, District of

Maumee River. *See* Miami (Maumee) River

McArthur, Duncan, 114, 116–17

McBryde, Archibald, 53

McClanahan, Major, 196

McCloud, Colin, 295, 297

McClure, George, 276, 333, 366–69, 375, 381, 385

McDaniel, Jeremiah, 499

McFeely, George, 158–59, 235–39, 412–15

McIntosh, John W., 439

McKesson, John, 138

McKnight (U.S. naval officer), 403

McLauchlan, James A., 472

McMahon, John, 376, 378

McNeal, Neal, 214–16

McNeil, John, 448, 452

McPherson, R. H., 344

McRee, William, 450

McVeagh, Patrick, 436

Meigs, Return J., Jr., 220

Melpomene, HMS, 485

Menelaus, HMS, 487, 536, 539

Menominees, 226

Methodists, 510

Miami (Maumee) River, 145, 150, 171–79, 193–96, 220–21, 223, 225, 227, 276, 281, 324

Miamis, 102–3, 145, 147, 171–75, 178–79, 181, 190, 192, 332

Michigan Territory, 85, 276, 320, 364, 383, 431; Battle of River Raisin, 193–203; fighting at Brownstown and Maguaga, 92–100; surrender of Fort Detroit, 113–20, 152, 382

Michilimackinac (Mackinac) Island, 104, 111–12, 136, 382, 697, 707

Milan Decree, 4–6, 8–9, 19–20, 76, 231

Militia, 32, 44, 110, 162, 245, 260, 588, 591, 594, 607–8, 615, 648, 652–53, 662, 714; Georgia, 365; Kentucky, 193; Maryland, 59–67, 353, 491, 502, 514, 523, 535, 541; Massachusetts, 105–8; Michigan Territory, 114, 152; New York, 143, 155, 160–61, 169–70, 333, 366, 370, 374–79, 435–36, 438–40, 444, 448, 450–52, 560–62; Ohio, 85, 152, 220; Tennessee, 25–26, 406, 411; Upper Canada, 118, 153, 215, 262, 558; Virginia, 45, 270, 273–74

Miller, James, 98, 114, 239, 560

Miller, Samuel, 503–4

Miller, Sylvanus, 138

Milnor, James, 53

Mississinewa River, 181–82

Mississippi River, 29, 139–40, 166, 587, 621, 633–34, 639–42, 666–67, 673, 711

Mississippi Territory, 25, 406–8, 645; Battle of Horseshoe Bend, 409–11; Treaty of Fort Jackson, 476–82

Missouri River, 97, 641

Missouri Territory, 139

Mitchell, George E., 57, 439

Mobile, Ala., 696

Mobile Bay, 644

Mohawk River, 164

Mohawks, 264, 266, 336

Molesworth (British soldier), 93

Monguagon, Michigan Territory, 95, 97

Monroe, James, 11, 18, 37, 110, 432, 506, 508, 631, 679, 689; and Francis Jeffrey's interview of Madison, 358–62; letter to Jefferson, 267–69; letter to John Taylor, 30–35; new proposal for invasion of Canada, 606–7, 612–15

Monteath, Midshipman, 564

Montgomery, Alexander, 196

Montgomery, Dr., 403

Montgomery, John, 60, 65, 68

Montgomery, Major, 410

Montgomery, Midshipman, 564

Montgomery, Richard, 170

Montgomery County, Md., 58

Montreal, HMS, 392, 436

Montréal, Lower Canada, 110–11, 147, 214, 246–47, 323, 335, 337, 339, 366, 391, 413, 467, 562

Montreal–South West Fur Company, 154

Moodie, Major, 242–43

Moore, Lieutenant, 243–44

Moorsom, Henry N., 460

Moose Island, 632, 634

Moreau, Jean-Victor, 452

Morning Chronicle (London), 533, 539

Morris, Gouverneur, 591

Morris, Lieutenant, 125, 343

Morrison, Joseph Wanton, 391

Moseley, Jonathan O., 53

Moulton, William, 294

Muir, Adam C., 92–98, 225

Mulcaster, William Howe, 392

Mumford, Gurdon S., 138

Munday, Harrison, 172

Munroe, Isaac, 541–43

Mure, John, 153

Myers, Christopher, 238, 472

Myers, Ned, 285–93

Nanticoke River, 349

Napier, Charles, 270

Naples, Italy, 637

Napoléon I (Napoléon Bonaparte), 1, 53, 79, 228–30, 233, 393–94, 426–27, 602, 682, 684, 706

Nash, Captain, 299

Nashville, Tenn., 300–1

National Advocate (New York City), 692

National Aegis (Worcester, Mass.), 692–95

National debt, 591–92, 611, 659, 712–13

National Intelligencer (Washington, D.C.), 526, 565, 670, 692

Navy, British (Royal), 1–3, 17, 45, 79, 135–36, 146, 156, 211–12, 218, 337, 353, 382, 387–93, 424, 429, 467, 508, 531, 555, 581, 584–85, 587, 600, 603–4, 609, 623, 639, 642, 666, 685–86, 696, 699, 708; Battle in Azores, 568–73; Battle of Lake Borgne, 644–47; Battle of Lake Champlain, 562–64; Battle of Lake Erie, 303–5, 312–24; Battle of Sackets Harbor, 240–42; Battle of Sandy Creek, 435–41; bombardment of Fort McHenry, 541–42, 544, 548–53; in Chesapeake Bay, 270–75, 345–52, 485–501, 535–39; HMS *Guerrière* versus USS *Constitution*, 121–29; HMS *Pelican* versus USS *Argus*, 294–99; HMS *Phoebe* versus USS *Essex*, 396–405; HMS *Shannon* versus USS *Chesapeake*, 256–59; on Lake Ontario, 454–56; prison ship, 245–55. *See also* Impressment of sailors; Seizure of ships

Navy, U.S., 45, 47, 52, 69, 135–36, 138, 220, 235, 336–37, 339, 345, 353, 364, 417, 431–33, 457, 485, 508, 510, 517, 521–22, 524, 526, 550, 584–85, 587, 623, 632, 652, 666, 685–86, 696; Battle of Lake Borgne, 644–47; Battle of Lake Champlain, 562–64; Battle of Lake Erie, 303–5, 312–23, 685; Battle of Sackets Harbor, 240, 242; Battle of Sandy Creek, 435–41; Battle of York, 214–18; biographical profile of Perry, 306–22; in Chesapeake Bay, 491–93, 502–4; destruction of USS *Scourge*, 285–93; on Lake Ontario, 454–56; in Madison's 1815 message to Congress, 709–10, 713–15; USS *Argus* versus HMS *Pelican*, 294–99; USS *Chesapeake* versus HMS *Shannon*, 256–59; USS *Constitution* versus HMS *Guerrière*, 121–29; USS *Essex* versus HMS *Phoebe*, 396–405

Navy Department, U.S., 606

Nelson, Horatio, 320, 391, 451, 539

Netherlands, 637, 706–8

Netley, HMS, 392

Neutrality, 1–4, 8, 11–16, 19, 23, 34, 45, 77, 135, 164, 166, 231, 233, 361, 394, 568, 594

Newark (Niagara-on-the-Lake), Upper Canada, 88, 119, 143, 238, 366–68, 370, 381, 384–85

New Brunswick, 240, 387–88, 430, 585–86, 594, 624–25, 634

Newburyport, Mass., 108

Newfoundland, 429, 621, 695

New Hampshire, 595, 598, 606, 648, 662, 665

New Jersey, 121

New London, Conn., 310, 360

New Orleans, La., 53, 568, 604, 636, 639, 641–42, 648, 666–82, 685–86, 688, 696, 705, 709

Newport, R.I., 145, 310–11

New York, 53, 104, 111, 251, 339–40, 383, 431, 595; Battle of Lake Champlain, 562–64; Battle of Sackets Harbor, 240–44; Battle of Sandy Creek, 434–41; fighting on Niagara frontier, 143, 160, 169–70, 333, 366–81, 384, 412, 444, 560–61

New York City, 130, 154, 294, 311, 358, 405, 433, 435, 591, 639, 682, 692, 708; Committee of Correspondence for De Witt Clinton, 130–38

New-York Mercantile Advertiser, 568

Niagara, HMS, 392

Niagara, USS, 303, 313, 315–16

Niagara Falls, 336, 457, 697

Niagara River, 143, 235, 320, 333, 335, 366–67, 370, 374, 381, 444–45, 448–50, 452, 460–61, 469, 555, 685, 697

Nicholson, Joseph H., 541–43, 553

Nickerson (British soldier), 458–59

Nile, Battle of the, 320

Niles, Hezekiah, 38–43

Niles' Weekly Register (Baltimore), 479, 490–93, 533, 699. *See also Weekly Register*

Non-Importation Acts, 20, 30–31, 34, 111, 167

Non-Intercourse Acts, 31, 34, 167

Norfolk, Va., 270, 433

North Carolina, 69–71

Northcutt, William B., 181–92, 278–81

Norton, John, 264

Norton, Major, 380

Nottingham, Md., 491, 531

Nova Scotia, 106, 112, 136, 245, 429–31, 585–86, 594, 623–26

Nugent, John, 296–97

Ocheubofau (Indian town), 479

Odelltown, Lower Canada, 340, 412–15

Odenheimer, Lieutenant, 403

Ogden, Midshipman, 403

Ogdensburg, N.Y., 155–56, 383, 697

Ohio, 40, 85, 88, 111, 113, 150, 152, 336, 583–84, 593; following Battle of the Mississinewa, 188–92; siege of Fort Meigs, 220–27; skirmish on the Sandusky, 278–80; winter at "Fort Starvation," 171–80

Ohio River, 111, 166, 587, 641

Olcott, Mills, 665

Oneidas, 333, 435–37

Onondagas, 333

Ontario. *See* Upper Canada

Ontario, N.Y., 375–76

Ontario County, N.Y., 373

Orange, Va., 508

Orders-in-Council, 1, 3–4, 6, 15–19, 21–22, 30, 75, 111, 231–32, 363, 427, 587, 693, 695

Ormstown, Lower Canada, 339, 344

Osages, 139–40

Osgood (U.S. soldier), 287, 289, 293

Ostrander, Philip, 148

Oswego, N.Y., 435, 438, 697

Otis, Harrison Gray, 591, 648–65

Ottawas, 92, 94, 174, 276–77, 332, 336

Packett, Lieutenant, 313

Page, Captain, 538

Pakenham, Edward, 666–70, 673–74, 678, 681, 685

Paris, France, 9, 61, 63, 228, 426–27, 566, 602–3, 686

Parker, Edward, 255

Parker, George, 646

Parker, Margaret, 539

Parker, Peter, 487, 535–37, 539–40

Parker, Richard E., 270–75

Parliament, British, 30, 63, 136, 164, 231, 622, 636, 638

Parrish, Joel, 408

Passamaquoddy Bay, 107, 604, 622, 624, 634

Pass Christian, Mississippi Territory, 645

Patapsco River, 544, 552

Patent Office, 606

Patriotism, 8, 34, 49, 71–73, 75, 112, 124, 131, 137, 176, 179, 210, 214, 307, 353, 357, 544, 547, 682–84, 690, 693

Patterson, Daniel T., 644

Patterson, Robert, 670

Patuxent River, 345, 485, 490–91, 502, 544, 548

Payne, John, 178–79

Peace talks, 426–27, 429, 432–34, 562, 581–87, 591–92, 595, 604, 621, 661
Pearce, Benoni, 185
Pearson, Joseph, 53
Pearson, Thomas, 472
Pederson, Peder, 708
Pelican, HMS, 294
Penley, Joseph, Jr., 245–55
Pennsylvania, 10, 36, 104, 131, 150, 158–59, 207, 591, 709
Penobscot River, 594, 596, 604, 634
Pensacola, West Florida, 480–81, 644
Perry, Captain, 465
Perry, James A., 317
Perry, Oliver Hazard, 235, 292, 303–23, 685
Perry, Raymond, 564
Peter, George, 548
Peterson (U.S. soldier), 252
Philadelphia, Pa., 36, 206, 358, 591
Philips (U.S. sailor), 286–87
Phillips, Mr., 373
Phoebe, HMS, 396–405
Phoenix, HMS, 467
Pickens, Israel, 69–71
Pickering, Thomas, 581–86
Pike, Zebulon, 217, 685
Pinckney, Thomas, 476
Pinckney's Treaty, 632
Pinkney, William, 364
Piqua, Ohio, 147, 150, 171
Pitkin, Timothy, Jr., 53
Pitt, William (the Younger), 230
Pittsburgh, Pa., 102, 104, 190
Plantagenet, HMS, 568–72
Platt, Midshipman, 564
Plattsburgh, N.Y., 343, 383, 562, 621, 696
Pleasants, James, 493
Plymouth, Mass., 107
Pocomoke Sound, 354
Poland, 635, 637–38
Popham, Stephen, 435–37, 439
Population, 40
Porcupine, USS, 313
Porter, David, 396, 398, 400–5
Porter, Peter B., 333, 377–78, 448, 450–52, 560
Portland, Mass. (now Me.), 108
Portugal, 35, 74, 80, 110, 136, 393, 568–69, 635

Potawatomis, 28, 92, 95, 103, 145–46, 332
Potomac River, 352, 488, 502–3, 506, 510–14, 520, 548–50, 593
Potter, Elisha R., 53
Pratt, Sergeant, 237
Pratt (U.S. soldier), 254–55
Preble, USS, 562
Prescott, William, 664
Presidency, 660–61, 663
President, USS, 685
Presque Isle, N.B., 388
Presque Isle, Pa., 104, 116, 193, 303
Prevost, George, 112, 152–54, 240–41, 243, 304, 335, 381–86, 393, 429–31, 483–84, 562, 603–4, 621, 685, 696–98
Price, James C., 197
Prisoners of war, return of, 623
Prisons, 245, 417–23, 574–80, 699–705
Prison ships, 245, 247–55
Privateers, 23, 52–53, 79, 352, 417, 423, 485, 533–35, 568, 571–72, 699
Procter, Henry, 97–98, 104, 193, 198, 220, 227, 281, 284, 323, 325–27, 332, 685
Protestantism, 79
Purdy, Robert, 339–44
Put-in-Bay (Lake Erie), 303, 312

Quakers, 41
Québec. *See* Lower Canada
Québec City, Lower Canada, 115–16, 120, 152, 245, 247, 250, 253–55, 361, 386, 390–91, 429–31, 463, 467, 585–87, 594, 634, 686, 696
Queen Charlotte, HMS, 152, 303–5, 313, 392
Queenston, Upper Canada, 143–44, 160, 239, 262, 367, 454–55, 460–60
Queenston Heights, Battle of, 160–63, 169, 262, 684, 697
Queenstown, Md., 270
Quids, 23
Quincy, Josiah, 46, 53

Rainsford, Charles, 243
Ramsay, Captain, 485
Ransom, Captain, 376
Raymond, Lieutenant, 258
Red Jacket, 333–34, 448

Red Stick Creeks, 25–26, 406, 409–10, 476, 479–80
Reed, John, 537
Reed, Lieutenant, 127
Reed, Philip, 535–38
Reed, William, 53
Regent, HMS, 392
Regulus, HMS, 485
Reid, Samuel C., 568–73
Reilly, Jack, 292
Renny, Robert, 667, 669
Republican Party, 30, 33, 38, 41, 43, 133, 136, 153, 165, 362, 541, 593, 648, 692, 709; and Baltimore riots, 54; British view of, 155, 595; call for peace treaty, 426, 489; in Congress, 260, 689; election of 1812, 130, 260; on invasion of Canada, 363; opposition to war, 23; support for war, 1, 10, 36, 606, 695
Revenge, USS, 310
Revenue, 598, 611, 615, 715
Revolutionary War, 11, 16, 21–22, 42, 45, 83, 85–86, 156, 164, 170, 557, 583, 685, 687, 692
Reynolds, James, 113
Rhea, James, 145, 147–48, 150
Rhode Island, 145, 433, 591, 598, 648, 662, 665
Riall, Phineas, 378, 412, 448–49, 451, 457
Rice, 428
Richardson, John (British soldier), 94, 220–27, 325–31
Richardson, John (fur trader), 154
Richardson, Robert, 101
Richelieu River, 245–46
Richmond, Va., 34, 685
Richmond Enquirer, 270
Riddle, Major, 375
Ridgeley, Charles C., 439
Ridgely, Henry Moore, 53
Riker, R., 138
Ringgold, Tench, 508
Riots, 54–68
Ripley, Eleazar W., 450–52, 560
River Raisin, 93–94; Battle of, 193–203, 671, 697
Rives, William C., 426
Roach (U.S. sailor), 401
Roberts, Charles, 104

Roberts, Isaac, 407
Roberts, John, 36
Robertson, James, 689
Robespierre, Maximilien-François de, 228, 684, 686
Robinson, William Henry, 698
Robinston, Mass. (now Me.), 106–7
Robyns, John, 491
Rochambeau, Comte de (Jean de Vimeur), 687
Rochester, N.Y., 372
Rock River, 284
Rodgers, John, 136, 310
Rodney, George Brydges, 257
Ronan, George, 103
Rose, George H., 360
Ross, Robert, 490–91, 494–96, 498, 500–1, 504, 511, 513, 515–18, 522–23, 527, 532–33, 541, 550–51, 621, 639, 666
Rota, HMS, 568–77
Rowe, James, 436
Rowley, Owsley, 485
Rowley, Robert, 485–89
Royal George, HMS, 392
Rundels, Major, 200
Rush, Richard, 508
Russell, John, 267
Russell, Jonathan, 4–6, 18, 432, 622, 630
Russell, William, 387, 391
Russell (British soldier), 224
Russia, 233, 267–68, 393, 426–27, 432–34, 635, 637–38, 707
Russle, Captain, 410
Rutherford County, N.C., 69

Sackets Harbor, N.Y., 240–44, 311, 335, 337, 339, 431, 435, 438–41, 454–55, 561
St. Andrews, N.B., 624–25
St. Augustine, Fla., 230
St. Croix River, 594, 625–26, 633
St. George, Thomas B., 85
Saint John, N.B., 387
Saint John River, 388
St. John's River, 245–46
St. Joseph, Michigan Territory, 103, 145, 276
St. Lawrence, HMS, 467
St. Lawrence River, 245–46, 335, 339, 383, 390, 625, 633

St. Marys, Ga., 230
St. Marys City, Md., 488
St. Marys River, 145
St. Michaels, Md., 270
St. Petersburg, Russia, 432–33
Salem, Mass., 108, 252, 417
Samwell, Midshipman, 257
Sand Creek, 195
Sandusky Bay, 312
Sandusky River, 278–82
Sandwich (now Windsor), Upper Canada, 85, 88, 113, 119–20, 206, 382–83
Sandy Creek, Battle of, 435–41
San Salvador, USS, 298–99
Saratoga, USS, 562–64
Sardinia, 637
Saukenuk (Indian town), 284
Sauks, 139–40, 284
Saulteaux, 100
Scoffield, Lieutenant, 413
Scorpion, USS, 313, 492
Scot (U.S. soldier), 187
Scott, Hercules, 469–70, 472
Scott, James, 353–57, 490–501
Scott, John, 56, 59, 62
Scott, John Mitchell, 171
Scott, Oliver, 441
Scott, Winfield, 235, 238–39, 442, 444, 448–53, 457, 461, 682, 685
Scourge, USS, 285–93
Searcy, Bennett, 301
Secord, James B., 262
Secord, Laura Ingersoll, 262–64
Sedition, 110
Seeley, Lieutenant, 376, 378–79
Seizure of ships, 1–2, 13, 22, 77, 229, 358, 361, 433, 693
Seminoles, 479
Senat, George, 313
Senate, U.S., 1, 23, 294, 432, 593, 622, 709; conscription bill, 606, 608; and declaration of war, 10, 33, 36, 46; diplomatic confirmations, 267–68; ratification of Treaty of Ghent, 639, 689
Senecas, 333
Severn, HMS, 485
Shannon, HMS, 256–59
Shawnees, 25, 27–28, 92–96, 101, 140, 226, 330

Shed (U.S. soldier), 252
Shelburne, HMS, 417
Shelby, Isaac, 179, 329, 685
Sherbrooke, John C., 431, 594–601, 604, 697
Sherman, Roger Minot, 664
Shoaff, Dr., 267
Shoops (U.S. soldier), 236–37
Shore, George, 243, 458, 471–72
Shortland, Thomas G., 417–18, 700, 702, 704
Sibly, Ensign, 113
Sickles, John H., 138
Simpson, John, 173
Simrall, James, 172, 174, 182, 186
Sinclair, Jacob, 255
Sioussat, Jean-Pierre, 507
Sioux, 139, 640
Skinner, John S., 544, 550–53
Skirven, William, 537
Slaughter, Gabriel, 671
Slaves, 33, 40, 42, 83, 164, 212–13, 272–73, 345–52, 424–25, 508–10, 531, 629, 657, 663, 707
Smiley, James S., 670, 672
Smith, Harry, 666–69, 676–78
Smith, James, 509
Smith, John G., 272
Smith, Midshipman, 258
Smith, Moses, 121–29
Smith, Nathaniel, 664
Smith, Robert, 30
Smith, Samuel, 268
Smith, Samuel H., 565
Smith, Thomas, 414
Smith (U.S. soldier), 250–52
Smuggling, 31
Smyth, Alexander, 162, 169–70, 366
Snelling, Josiah, 342
Somers, USS, 313
Sorel, Lower Canada, 245
Sorel River, 414
South Carolina, 10, 131
Spain, 12, 35, 44, 74, 80, 136, 167, 211, 393–94, 426, 511, 594, 607, 632, 644, 684
Spencer, Isaac, 537
Spencer, John C., 366
Spillman, Henry, 671
Spilsbury, Francis B., 435–36

Spunner, Captain, 461
Staël, Madame de (Anne-Louise-
    Germaine Necker), 228
Stanbury, J. J., 534
Star, HMS, 392
"Star-Spangled Banner," 544–46, 547–
    48, 553–54
State Department, U.S., 606
Stephens (British sailor), 257
Sterrett, Joseph, 62, 67
Steuben County, N.Y., 368
Stevens, Thomas H., 313
Stewart, Alvan, 160
Stickney, Benjamin F., 146–47
Stirling (merchant ship), 285
Stockholm, Sweden, 228
Stone, David, 268
Stoney Creek, 697
Story, Joseph, 692
Strachan, John, 154–57, 164–68
Stricker, John, 59–60, 62, 64, 66–67
Strong, Caleb, 72, 105–9, 581, 594–95,
    599, 648
Stuart, Gilbert, 506–7, 509–10
Stuart, Philip, 53
Sturges, Lewis B., 53
Sukey (servant), 509–10
Sullivan, George, 53
Superior, USS, 435, 438, 454
Supreme Court (Massachusetts), 106
Surprise, HMS, 551–52
Susquehanna River, 158
Sutherland, Lieutenant, 94, 328
Sweden, 228, 267–68
Swift, Philetus, 143
Swift, Zephaniah, 664
Switzerland, 637

Taggart, Samuel, 53, 363
Tallan, Captain, 94
Tallapoosa River, 409–10, 479
Tallesachee (Indian town), 482
Tallmadge, Benjamin, 53
Tallmadge, Matthias B., 138
Taney, Roger B., 547–54
Tariffs, 715
Taxation, 32, 40–41, 52, 70, 78, 136–37,
    260, 588–90, 592, 595, 621, 636, 638,
    652, 656–57, 662–63
Tayloe, John, 510

Taylor, John, 30
Tecumseh, 25, 27–29, 85, 98, 101, 113,
    167, 220, 222, 224, 226, 323–27,
    329–32, 406, 429
Tennessee, 25, 406, 671, 673
Tenskwatawa (The Prophet), 25–27,
    429
Territorial acquisition, 602, 604, 621–
    22, 631–34
Thais, HMS, 572
Thames River, 326–32, 383, 406, 685
Thistle, HMS, 388
Thomas, Joshua, 664
Thomas, Moses, 306
Thomas, Richard S., 537
Thornton, Anna Maria, 139
Thornton, William, 497–98, 515, 667
Thwing, Midshipman, 564
Ticknor, George, 688
Ticonderoga, USS, 562–63
Tigress, USS, 313
Tilghman, Henry, 537
Times (London), 429
Tingey, Thomas, 502
Tippecanoe River, 27–28, 582
Tobacco, 428, 486–88, 494, 531, 548
Todd, John S., 199
Todd, Lucy Payne Washington, 506
Todd, Thomas, 364
Tohopeka (Indian town), 409–10
Tompkins, Daniel D., 111, 134, 143–44,
    292, 374, 560
Tonnant, HMS, 499, 544
Toronto. *See* York, Upper Canada
Touzel, Helier, 337
Towson, Nathaniel, 448, 450, 452
Trafalgar, Battle of, 317, 539
Trail of Tears, 479
Trant, James, 291–93
Treadwell, John, 664
Treasury, U.S., 611, 659, 712
Treasury Department, U.S., 32, 52, 136,
    592, 606
Treaty of Fort Jackson, 476–82
Treaty of Ghent, 621–39, 679, 682,
    688–91, 696, 706–10
Treaty of New York, 476, 479
Treaty of Paris, 583, 623–27, 633, 637
Treaty of San Lorenzo, 632
Treaty of Utrecht, 632

Trinidad, 348
Tripoli, 710
Tripolitan War, 310
Trippe, USS, 313
Trois-Rivières, Lower Canada, 247
Trotter (U.S. Army officer), 186, 188
Tucker, Dr., 267
Tukabatchee (Indian town), 479
Tunis, 710
Tupper, Edward W., 173–74, 194
Turks, 39
Tuscarora, N.Y., 366
Tuscaroras, 372
Tweeddale, Marquess of (George Hay), 448–49
Two Mile Creek, 235
Tylden, John M., 668

Union (merchant ship), 699
Unitarians, 72
Upper Canada, 104, 110–11, 153–56, 164–65, 168, 170, 211, 320, 323, 335–38, 391–92, 429–31, 454–55; Battle of Beaver Dams, 262–66; Battle of Chippawa, 448–53; Battle of Fort Erie, 444–45, 461–75, 555–61; Battle of Lundy's Lane, 457–60; Battle of Queenston Heights, 160–62, 262; Battle of the Thames, 326–31; Battle of York, 214–19; fighting on Niagara frontier, 143–44, 366–86, 444–45; offensives into U.S. territory from, 85–94, 98–101, 113, 118–20, 193–94, 196, 198–99, 202–6; siege of Fort George, 235–39, 276
Upper Creeks, 479
Usselton, Aquila M., 537

Vallette, Lieutenant, 564
Valparaiso, Chile, 396–405
Van Rensselaer, Solomon, 160, 162
Van Rensselaer, Stephen, 143–44, 160–62, 169, 684
Van Voorhis, Isaac, 103
Van Wyck, Pierre C., 138
Vermont, 595, 598, 648–49, 662, 665
Villeré, Jacques, 666
Vincennes, Indiana Territory, 28
Vincent, John, 235

Virginia, 30, 95, 130–31, 150, 169, 270–75, 352, 354, 489–90, 687
Volunteers, 32, 98, 101, 110, 113, 116, 155, 169, 171–72, 179, 181, 265, 374, 376, 378, 380, 442, 541

Wabash River, 27, 140, 166, 181, 224
Wadsworth, William, 375
Wagner, Jacob, 55–58
Wainwright, John, 504
Waldo, Daniel, 664
Wallis, Lieutenant, 258
Ward, Samuel, 665
War Department, U.S., 25, 105, 113, 268, 591, 606
Wardlaw, Dr., 272
Wardsworth, Lieutenant, 125
War Hawks, 1, 10
Warner (U.S. sailor), 504
War powers, 659–60, 663
Warren, Colonel, 376–77, 380
Warren, John B., 211, 270, 273, 359, 382, 424, 433, 533
Warsaw, Poland, 638
Washington, D.C., 1, 30, 37, 46, 64, 69, 110, 135, 139, 207, 260, 267, 300, 333–34, 339, 352, 358–60, 363, 433, 547–48, 550, 567, 629, 682, 685, 689, 709, 716; British advance on, 490–92, 494, 496, 501–4; British attack on, 506–10, 515–29, 532, 535, 544, 565–66, 606, 609
Washington, George, 49–50, 57, 83, 133, 150, 232, 481, 506–7, 509–10, 582, 651, 655, 709
Waterloo, Battle of, 532, 706–7
Watson, Lieutenant, 295
Watt, Lieutenant, 257
Wayne, Anthony, 172
Weas, 332
Webber (U.S. soldier), 251–53
Webster, Daniel, 606–20
Webster, Tom, 186
Weekly Register, 38. *See also Niles' Weekly Register*
Weller, David, 671–72
Wellington, Duke of (Arthur Wellesley), 393–95, 426, 430, 511, 594, 602–5, 621, 635–36, 666, 676, 706

Wells, Samuel, 196
Wells, William, 102–3, 145–46
Wesley, John, 204
West, Benjamin, 665
West, Richard W., 549
West Indies, 345, 347–49, 404, 417, 425, 533, 568, 572, 591, 639, 644
Wheaton, Laban, 53
Whistler, William, 151
White, James, 295, 297
White, Leonard, 53
White House, burning of, 506, 509–10, 517, 519–21, 526
Whitting, Captain, 415–16
Wickes, Joseph, 536–37
Wickes, Simon, 536–37
Wicomico River, 486
Wilberforce, William, 164
Wilde, Samuel Sumner, 664
Wilkinson, James, 268, 333, 337, 339, 381, 391, 413, 415, 498, 501, 685
Willcocks, Joseph, 367
Williams, Alexander O., 572
Williamson, Midshipman, 564
Williamsport, Pa., 158
Wills, Captain, 272–74
Willson, Deborah, 336
Willson, Jared, 160–63
Wilmer, Lieutenant, 403
Wilson, Frederick, 537
Wilson, Henry, 186
Wilson, Mrs., 346
Wilson, P., 138
Wilson, Thomas, 53
Wilson (U.S. soldier), 279–80
Winamac, 147–48

Winchester, James, 171, 173–74, 178, 193, 196, 198, 220, 684
Winder, William H., 235, 250, 491, 502–3, 506, 508, 685
Windham County, Vt., 648–49
Winnebagos, 27–28, 139–40, 146
Winter, Lieutenant, 293
Wiscasset, Mass. (now Me.), 108
Witherell, James, 116
Wolfe, HMS, 392
Wood, Eleazar W., 450
Wood, Jacob, 440
Wood, John, 405
Wood, William, 498, 515
Woolsey, Melancthon, 435, 438–39
Worcester, Mass., 692
Wright, Robert, 44
Wyandots, 332
Wylly, Alexander C., 678

Yankee (Boston), 541
Yarnall, John J., 315, 317
Yazoo River, 641
Yeo, James L., 240, 242, 337, 435, 696
York (Toronto), Upper Canada, 118–20, 154, 164, 214–19, 240–41, 289, 383, 454, 685
Yorktown, Va., 272
Young, Captain, 564
Young, John, 295, 297
Young, Robert, 412
Young, Thomas B., 364

Zachariah (Virginia farmer), 355–57
Zanesville, Ohio, 113

THE LIBRARY OF AMERICA SERIES

The Library of America fosters appreciation and pride in America's literary heritage by publishing, and keeping permanently in print, authoritative editions of America's best and most significant writing. An independent nonprofit organization, it was founded in 1979 with seed funding from the National Endowment for the Humanities and the Ford Foundation.

1. Herman Melville: *Typee, Omoo, Mardi*
2. Nathaniel Hawthorne: *Tales and Sketches*
3. Walt Whitman: *Poetry and Prose*
4. Harriet Beecher Stowe: *Three Novels*
5. Mark Twain: *Mississippi Writings*
6. Jack London: *Novels and Stories*
7. Jack London: *Novels and Social Writings*
8. William Dean Howells: *Novels 1875–1886*
9. Herman Melville: *Redburn, White-Jacket, Moby-Dick*
10. Nathaniel Hawthorne: *Collected Novels*
11. Francis Parkman: *France and England in North America*, vol. I
12. Francis Parkman: *France and England in North America*, vol. II
13. Henry James: *Novels 1871–1880*
14. Henry Adams: *Novels, Mont Saint Michel, The Education*
15. Ralph Waldo Emerson: *Essays and Lectures*
16. Washington Irving: *History, Tales and Sketches*
17. Thomas Jefferson: *Writings*
18. Stephen Crane: *Prose and Poetry*
19. Edgar Allan Poe: *Poetry and Tales*
20. Edgar Allan Poe: *Essays and Reviews*
21. Mark Twain: *The Innocents Abroad, Roughing It*
22. Henry James: *Literary Criticism: Essays, American & English Writers*
23. Henry James: *Literary Criticism: European Writers & The Prefaces*
24. Herman Melville: *Pierre, Israel Potter, The Confidence-Man, Tales & Billy Budd*
25. William Faulkner: *Novels 1930–1935*
26. James Fenimore Cooper: *The Leatherstocking Tales*, vol. I
27. James Fenimore Cooper: *The Leatherstocking Tales*, vol. II
28. Henry David Thoreau: *A Week, Walden, The Maine Woods, Cape Cod*
29. Henry James: *Novels 1881–1886*
30. Edith Wharton: *Novels*
31. Henry Adams: *History of the U.S. during the Administrations of Jefferson*
32. Henry Adams: *History of the U.S. during the Administrations of Madison*
33. Frank Norris: *Novels and Essays*
34. W.E.B. Du Bois: *Writings*
35. Willa Cather: *Early Novels and Stories*
36. Theodore Dreiser: *Sister Carrie, Jennie Gerhardt, Twelve Men*
37a. Benjamin Franklin: *Silence Dogood, The Busy-Body, & Early Writings*
37b. Benjamin Franklin: *Autobiography, Poor Richard, & Later Writings*
38. William James: *Writings 1902–1910*
39. Flannery O'Connor: *Collected Works*
40. Eugene O'Neill: *Complete Plays 1913–1920*
41. Eugene O'Neill: *Complete Plays 1920–1931*
42. Eugene O'Neill: *Complete Plays 1932–1943*
43. Henry James: *Novels 1886–1890*
44. William Dean Howells: *Novels 1886–1888*
45. Abraham Lincoln: *Speeches and Writings 1832–1858*
46. Abraham Lincoln: *Speeches and Writings 1859–1865*
47. Edith Wharton: *Novellas and Other Writings*
48. William Faulkner: *Novels 1936–1940*
49. Willa Cather: *Later Novels*
50. Ulysses S. Grant: *Memoirs and Selected Letters*
51. William Tecumseh Sherman: *Memoirs*
52. Washington Irving: *Bracebridge Hall, Tales of a Traveller, The Alhambra*
53. Francis Parkman: *The Oregon Trail, The Conspiracy of Pontiac*
54. James Fenimore Cooper: *Sea Tales: The Pilot, The Red Rover*
55. Richard Wright: *Early Works*
56. Richard Wright: *Later Works*
57. Willa Cather: *Stories, Poems, and Other Writings*
58. William James: *Writings 1878–1899*
59. Sinclair Lewis: *Main Street & Babbitt*
60. Mark Twain: *Collected Tales, Sketches, Speeches, & Essays 1852–1890*
61. Mark Twain: *Collected Tales, Sketches, Speeches, & Essays 1891–1910*
62. *The Debate on the Constitution: Part One*
63. *The Debate on the Constitution: Part Two*
64. Henry James: *Collected Travel Writings: Great Britain & America*
65. Henry James: *Collected Travel Writings: The Continent*

66. *American Poetry: The Nineteenth Century*, Vol. 1

67. *American Poetry: The Nineteenth Century*, Vol. 2

68. Frederick Douglass: *Autobiographies*

69. Sarah Orne Jewett: *Novels and Stories*

70. Ralph Waldo Emerson: *Collected Poems and Translations*

71. Mark Twain: *Historical Romances*

72. John Steinbeck: *Novels and Stories 1932–1937*

73. William Faulkner: *Novels 1942–1954*

74. Zora Neale Hurston: *Novels and Stories*

75. Zora Neale Hurston: *Folklore, Memoirs, and Other Writings*

76. Thomas Paine: *Collected Writings*

77. *Reporting World War II: American Journalism 1938–1944*

78. *Reporting World War II: American Journalism 1944–1946*

79. Raymond Chandler: *Stories and Early Novels*

80. Raymond Chandler: *Later Novels and Other Writings*

81. Robert Frost: *Collected Poems, Prose, & Plays*

82. Henry James: *Complete Stories 1892–1898*

83. Henry James: *Complete Stories 1898–1910*

84. William Bartram: *Travels and Other Writings*

85. John Dos Passos: *U.S.A.*

86. John Steinbeck: *The Grapes of Wrath and Other Writings 1936–1941*

87. Vladimir Nabokov: *Novels and Memoirs 1941–1951*

88. Vladimir Nabokov: *Novels 1955–1962*

89. Vladimir Nabokov: *Novels 1969–1974*

90. James Thurber: *Writings and Drawings*

91. George Washington: *Writings*

92. John Muir: *Nature Writings*

93. Nathanael West: *Novels and Other Writings*

94. *Crime Novels: American Noir of the 1930s and 40s*

95. *Crime Novels: American Noir of the 1950s*

96. Wallace Stevens: *Collected Poetry and Prose*

97. James Baldwin: *Early Novels and Stories*

98. James Baldwin: *Collected Essays*

99. Gertrude Stein: *Writings 1903–1932*

100. Gertrude Stein: *Writings 1932–1946*

101. Eudora Welty: *Complete Novels*

102. Eudora Welty: *Stories, Essays, & Memoir*

103. Charles Brockden Brown: *Three Gothic Novels*

104. *Reporting Vietnam: American Journalism 1959–1969*

105. *Reporting Vietnam: American Journalism 1969–1975*

106. Henry James: *Complete Stories 1874–1884*

107. Henry James: *Complete Stories 1884–1891*

108. *American Sermons: The Pilgrims to Martin Luther King Jr.*

109. James Madison: *Writings*

110. Dashiell Hammett: *Complete Novels*

111. Henry James: *Complete Stories 1864–1874*

112. William Faulkner: *Novels 1957–1962*

113. John James Audubon: *Writings & Drawings*

114. *Slave Narratives*

115. *American Poetry: The Twentieth Century*, Vol. 1

116. *American Poetry: The Twentieth Century*, Vol. 2

117. F. Scott Fitzgerald: *Novels and Stories 1920–1922*

118. Henry Wadsworth Longfellow: *Poems and Other Writings*

119. Tennessee Williams: *Plays 1937–1955*

120. Tennessee Williams: *Plays 1957–1980*

121. Edith Wharton: *Collected Stories 1891–1910*

122. Edith Wharton: *Collected Stories 1911–1937*

123. *The American Revolution: Writings from the War of Independence*

124. Henry David Thoreau: *Collected Essays and Poems*

125. Dashiell Hammett: *Crime Stories and Other Writings*

126. Dawn Powell: *Novels 1930–1942*

127. Dawn Powell: *Novels 1944–1962*

128. Carson McCullers: *Complete Novels*

129. Alexander Hamilton: *Writings*

130. Mark Twain: *The Gilded Age and Later Novels*

131. Charles W. Chesnutt: *Stories, Novels, and Essays*

132. John Steinbeck: *Novels 1942–1952*

133. Sinclair Lewis: *Arrowsmith, Elmer Gantry, Dodsworth*

134. Paul Bowles: *The Sheltering Sky, Let It Come Down, The Spider's House*

135. Paul Bowles: *Collected Stories & Later Writings*

136. Kate Chopin: *Complete Novels & Stories*

137. *Reporting Civil Rights: American Journalism 1941–1963*

138. *Reporting Civil Rights: American Journalism 1963–1973*

139. Henry James: *Novels 1896–1899*

140. Theodore Dreiser: *An American Tragedy*

141. Saul Bellow: *Novels 1944–1953*

142. John Dos Passos: *Novels 1920–1925*

143. John Dos Passos: *Travel Books and Other Writings*

144. Ezra Pound: *Poems and Translations*
145. James Weldon Johnson: *Writings*
146. Washington Irving: *Three Western Narratives*
147. Alexis de Tocqueville: *Democracy in America*
148. James T. Farrell: *Studs Lonigan: A Trilogy*
149. Isaac Bashevis Singer: *Collected Stories I*
150. Isaac Bashevis Singer: *Collected Stories II*
151. Isaac Bashevis Singer: *Collected Stories III*
152. Kaufman & Co.: *Broadway Comedies*
153. Theodore Roosevelt: *The Rough Riders, An Autobiography*
154. Theodore Roosevelt: *Letters and Speeches*
155. H. P. Lovecraft: *Tales*
156. Louisa May Alcott: *Little Women, Little Men, Jo's Boys*
157. Philip Roth: *Novels & Stories 1959–1962*
158. Philip Roth: *Novels 1967–1972*
159. James Agee: *Let Us Now Praise Famous Men, A Death in the Family*
160. James Agee: *Film Writing & Selected Journalism*
161. Richard Henry Dana, Jr.: *Two Years Before the Mast & Other Voyages*
162. Henry James: *Novels 1901–1902*
163. Arthur Miller: *Collected Plays 1944–1961*
164. William Faulkner: *Novels 1926–1929*
165. Philip Roth: *Novels 1973–1977*
166. *American Speeches: Part One*
167. *American Speeches: Part Two*
168. Hart Crane: *Complete Poems & Selected Letters*
169. Saul Bellow: *Novels 1956–1964*
170. John Steinbeck: *Travels with Charley and Later Novels*
171. Capt. John Smith: *Writings with Other Narratives*
172. Thornton Wilder: *Collected Plays & Writings on Theater*
173. Philip K. Dick: *Four Novels of the 1960s*
174. Jack Kerouac: *Road Novels 1957–1960*
175. Philip Roth: *Zuckerman Bound*
176. Edmund Wilson: *Literary Essays & Reviews of the 1920s & 30s*
177. Edmund Wilson: *Literary Essays & Reviews of the 1930s & 40s*
178. *American Poetry: The 17th & 18th Centuries*
179. William Maxwell: *Early Novels & Stories*
180. Elizabeth Bishop: *Poems, Prose, & Letters*
181. A. J. Liebling: *World War II Writings*
182s. *American Earth: Environmental Writing Since Thoreau*
183. Philip K. Dick: *Five Novels of the 1960s & 70s*
184. William Maxwell: *Later Novels & Stories*
185. Philip Roth: *Novels & Other Narratives 1986–1991*
186. Katherine Anne Porter: *Collected Stories & Other Writings*
187. John Ashbery: *Collected Poems 1956–1987*
188. John Cheever: *Collected Stories & Other Writings*
189. John Cheever: *Complete Novels*
190. Lafcadio Hearn: *American Writings*
191. A. J. Liebling: *The Sweet Science & Other Writings*
192s. *The Lincoln Anthology: Great Writers on His Life and Legacy from 1860 to Now*
193. Philip K. Dick: *VALIS & Later Novels*
194. Thornton Wilder: *The Bridge of San Luis Rey and Other Novels 1926–1948*
195. Raymond Carver: *Collected Stories*
196. *American Fantastic Tales: Terror and the Uncanny from Poe to the Pulps*
197. *American Fantastic Tales: Terror and the Uncanny from the 1940s to Now*
198. John Marshall: *Writings*
199s. *The Mark Twain Anthology: Great Writers on His Life and Works*
200. Mark Twain: *A Tramp Abroad, Following the Equator, Other Travels*
201. Ralph Waldo Emerson: *Selected Journals 1820–1842*
202. Ralph Waldo Emerson: *Selected Journals 1841–1877*
203. *The American Stage: Writing on Theater from Washington Irving to Tony Kushner*
204. Shirley Jackson: *Novels & Stories*
205. Philip Roth: *Novels 1993–1995*
206. H. L. Mencken: *Prejudices: First, Second, and Third Series*
207. H. L. Mencken: *Prejudices: Fourth, Fifth, and Sixth Series*
208. John Kenneth Galbraith: *The Affluent Society and Other Writings 1952–1967*
209. Saul Bellow: *Novels 1970–1982*
210. Lynd Ward: *Gods' Man, Madman's Drum, Wild Pilgrimage*
211. Lynd Ward: *Prelude to a Million Years, Song Without Words, Vertigo*
212. *The Civil War: The First Year Told by Those Who Lived It*
213. John Adams: *Revolutionary Writings 1755–1775*
214. John Adams: *Revolutionary Writings 1775–1783*
215. Henry James: *Novels 1903–1911*
216. Kurt Vonnegut: *Novels & Stories 1963–1973*
217. *Harlem Renaissance: Five Novels of the 1920s*

218. *Harlem Renaissance: Four Novels of the 1930s*

219. Ambrose Bierce: *The Devil's Dictionary, Tales, & Memoirs*

220. Philip Roth: *The American Trilogy 1997–2000*

221. *The Civil War: The Second Year Told by Those Who Lived It*

222. Barbara W. Tuchman: *The Guns of August & The Proud Tower*

223. Arthur Miller: *Collected Plays 1964–1982*

224. Thornton Wilder: *The Eighth Day, Theophilus North, Autobiographical Writings*

225. David Goodis: *Five Noir Novels of the 1940s & 50s*

226. Kurt Vonnegut: *Novels & Stories 1950–1962*

227. *American Science Fiction: Four Classic Novels 1953–1956*

228. *American Science Fiction: Five Classic Novels 1956–1958*

229. Laura Ingalls Wilder: *The Little House Books, Volume One*

230. Laura Ingalls Wilder: *The Little House Books, Volume Two*

231. Jack Kerouac: *Collected Poems*

232. *The War of 1812: Writings from America's Second War of Independence*

233. *American Antislavery Writings: Colonial Beginnings to Emancipation*

234. *The Civil War: The Third Year Told by Those Who Lived It*

235. Sherwood Anderson: *Collected Stories*

236. Philip Roth: *Novels 2001–2007*

237. Philip Roth: *Nemeses*

238. Aldo Leopold: *A Sand County Almanac & Other Writings on Ecology and Conservation*

239. May Swenson: *Collected Poems*

240. W. S. Merwin: *Collected Poems 1952–1993*

241. W. S. Merwin *Collected Poems 1996–2011*

To subscribe to the series or to order individual copies, please visit www.loa.org or call (800) 964.5778.

*This book is set in 10 point ITC Galliard Pro, a
face designed for digital composition by Matthew Carter
and based on the sixteenth-century face Granjon. The paper
is acid-free lightweight opaque and meets the requirements
for permanence of the American National Standards Institute.
The binding material is Brillianta, a woven rayon cloth made
by Van Heek–Scholco Textielfabrieken, Holland.
Composition by Dedicated Book Services. Printing and
binding by Edwards Brothers Malloy, Ann Arbor.
Designed by Bruce Campbell.*

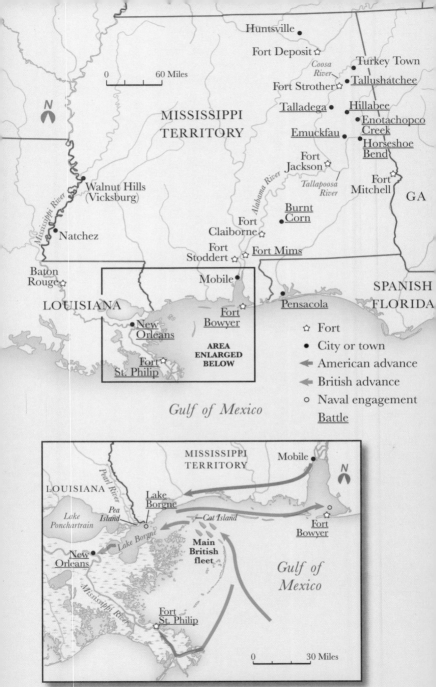

Lucidity Information Design, LLC